Lecture Notes in Computer Science 2342

Edited by G. Goos, J. Hartmanis, and J. van Leeuwen

W0246254

Lecture Notes in Computer Science 2347

Edited by G. Goos, J. Hartmanis, and J. van Leeuwen

Springer

Berlin
Heidelberg
New York
Barcelona
Hong Kong
London
Milan
Paris
Tokyo

Ian Horrocks   James Hendler (Eds.)

The Semantic Web – ISWC 2002

First International Semantic Web Conference
Sardinia, Italy, June 9-12, 2002
Proceedings

Springer

Series Editors

Gerhard Goos, Karlsruhe University, Germany
Juris Hartmanis, Cornell University, NY, USA
Jan van Leeuwen, Utrecht University, The Netherlands

Volume Editors

Ian Horrocks
University of Manchester, Department of Computer Science
Oxford Road, Manchester, M13 9PL, UK
E-mail: horrocks@cs.man.ac.uk

James Hendler
University of Maryland, Computer Science Department
College Park, MD 20742, USA
E-mail: hendler@cs.umd.edu

Cataloging-in-Publication Data applied for

Die Deutsche Bibliothek - CIP-Einheitsaufnahme

The semantic web : proceedings / ISWC 2002, First International Semantic Web
Conference, Sardinia, Italy, June 9 - 12, 2002. Ian Horrocks ; James Hendler
(ed.). - Berlin ; Heidelberg ; New York ; Barcelona ; Hong Kong ; London ;
Milan ; Paris ; Tokyo : Springer, 2002
    (Lecture notes in computer science ; Vol. 2342)
    ISBN 3-540-43760-6

CR Subject Classification (1998): C.2, I.2, H.4, H.5, H.3, K.4, F.3

ISSN 0302-9743
ISBN 3-540-43760-6 Springer-Verlag Berlin Heidelberg New York

Springer-Verlag Berlin Heidelberg New York
a member of BertelsmannSpringer Science+Business Media GmbH

http://www.springer.de

© Springer-Verlag Berlin Heidelberg 2002
Printed in Germany

Typesetting: Camera-ready by author, data conversion by Steingräber Satztechnik GmbH, Heidelberg
Printed on acid-free paper   SPIN: 10869943   06/3142   5 4 3 2 1 0

Preface

This volume contains the papers presented at the First International Semantic Web Conference (ISWC 2002) held in Sardinia, Italy, 9–12th June, 2002. The conference followed on from the highly successful Semantic Web Working Symposium held at Stanford University, USA in 2001.

A total of 133 papers were submitted to ISWC 2002, comprising 95 research papers, 22 position papers, and 16 system description papers. Each submission was evaluated by at least two referees, mainly members of the Program Committee. This resulted in the selection of 40 papers for presentation at the conference and publication in this volume. Of these, 27 are research papers, 6 are position papers, and 7 are system description papers.

We would like to thank the many people who made ISWC 2002 possible. In particular, we are grateful to the following groups and individuals: Jeff Pan for help with the conference management software and proceedings; the program committee for their reviewing efforts and advice on organizational details; Michele Missikoff and Nicoletta Dessí for conference organization and local coordination; Jérôme Euzenat for financial organization and the conference web site; Asunción Gómez-Pérez for organizing the tutorials; Raphael Malyankar for organizing the poster session; Steffen Staab, Siegfried Handschuh, and Marc Ehrig for organizing semantic markup; Deborah McGuinness and Ying Ding for arranging sponsorship; and the sponsors themselves for their moral and financial support.

April 2002

Ian Horrocks
James Hendler

Conference Organization

General Chair

James Hendler (University of Maryland, USA)

Program Chair

Ian Horrocks (University of Manchester, UK)

Organization Chair

Michele Missikoff (Istituto di Analisi dei Sistemi ed Informatica — CNR, Italy)

Program Committee

Michel Biezunski, Coolheads Consulting, USA
Harold Boley, DFKI, Kaiserslautern, Germany
Tiziana Catarci, University of Rome "La Sapienza", Italy
Peter Crowther, Network Inference, UK
Vassilis Christophides, ICS-FORTH and University of Crete, Greece
Isabel Cruz, University of Illinois at Chicago, USA
Stefan Decker, Stanford University, USA
Steven A. Demurjian, University of Connecticut, USA
Ying Ding, Free University of Amsterdam, The Netherlands
Max J. Egenhofer, University of Maine, USA
Peter Eklund, University of Queensland, Australia
Jérôme Euzenat, INRIA Rhône-Alpes, France
Dieter Fensel, Free University of Amsterdam, The Netherlands
Richard Fikes, Stanford University, USA
Tim Finin, University of Maryland-Baltimore County, USA
Jeremy Frumkin, University of Arizona, USA
Asunción Gómez-Pérez, Universidad Politecnica de Madrid, Spain
Nicola Guarino, LADSEB-CNR, Padova, Italy
Lynda Hardman, CWI, Amsterdam, The Netherlands
Frank van Harmelen, Free University of Amsterdam, The Netherlands
Pat Hayes, University of West Florida, USA
Jeff Heflin, Lehigh University, USA
Masahiro Hori, IBM Tokyo Research Laboratory, Japan
Nick Jennings, Southampton University, UK
Jana Koehler, IBM Research Laboratory, Rueschlikon, Switzerland

Additional Referees

ISWC 2002 Officials

Tutorial Chair:	Asunción Gómez-Pérez (Universidad Politecnica de Madrid)
Local Coordination:	Nicoletta Dessí (Università di Cagliari)
Sponsor Chairs:	Deborah McGuinness (Stanford University) Ying Ding (Vrije Universiteit Amsterdam)
Finances and Web:	Jérôme Euzenat (INRIA Rhône-Alpes)
Poster Chair:	Raphael Malyankar (Arizona State University)
Metadata Chair:	Steffen Staab (University of Karlsruhe)

Conferences Preceding ISWC 2002

Semantic Web Working Symposium (SWWS), Stanford University, USA, 2001

ISWC 2002 Patrons and Sponsors

Patrons

Platinum Sponsors

Gold Sponsors

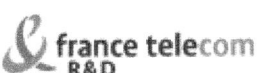 

Silver Sponsors

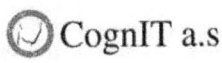 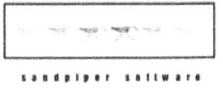 

ISWC 2002 Poster Session

The following posters were presented at the ISWC 2002 Poster Session.

Learning Organizational Memory
Marie-Hélène Abel, Dominique Lenne, Omar Cissé

Approximate Ontology Translation and its Application to Regional
Information Services
Jun-ichi Akahani, Kaoru Hiramatsu, Kiyoshi Kogure

Adding Semantics to Scientific Collaboration Documents
Muthukkaruppan Annamalai, Lito Cruz, Leon Sterling, Glenn Moloney

Semantic Web + Cooperative Web = Web Semantics
Daniel Gayo Avello, Dario Álvarez Gutièrrez

A Graph Visualization/Transformation Framework
Daniel Ayers

An Ontology-Based Aproach to model virtual learning environments
Francesco Maria Aymerich, Nicoletta Dessi

Active Document Enrichment using Adaptive Information Extraction from
Text
Fabio Ciravegna, Alexiei Dingli and Daniela Petrelli

Six Challenges for the Semantic Web
V. Richard Benjamins, Asunción Gómez-Pérez, Oscar Corcho, Jesús Contreras

QuizRDF: Search Technology for the Semantic Web
John Davies, Richard Weeks, Uwe Krohn

An Ontology for Intellectual Property Rights
Jaime Delgado, Isabel Gallego, Roberto García, Rosa Gil

SemTalk: Authoring the Semantic Web with MS Visio
Christian Fillies, Gay Wood-Albrecht, Frauke Weichhardt

Building an Integrated Formal Ontology for Semantic Interoperability in the
Fishery Domain
Aldo Gangemi, Frehiwot Fisseha, Ian Pettman, Johannes Keizer

Challenging DAML+OIL by a Commercial Technology — What can the
Semantic Web learn from it? (Preliminary Results)
Rolf Grütter, Joachim Peer, Beat F. Schmid

Information System Concepts based on semiotics: The FRISCO Approach
Wolfgang Hesse

Table of Contents

Position Papers

System Descriptions

Semantic Web Enabled Web Services

Dieter Fensel[1], Christoph Bussler[2], and Alexander Maedche[3]

[1] Vrije Universiteit Amsterdam (VU)
Faculty of Sciences, Division of Mathematics and Computer Science
De Boelelaan 1081a, 1081 HV Amsterdam, the Netherlands
Fax: +31-84-872 27 22, phone: +31-6-51850619
dieter@cs.vu.nl

[2] Oracle Corporation
500 Oracle Parkway, Redwood Shores, 94065, CA, U. S. A.
Phone: +1-650-607-5684
chris.bussler@oracle.com

[3] Forschungszentrum Informatik FZI
Forschungszentrum Informatik, Haid-und-Neu-Str. 10-14, 76131 Karlsruhe, Germany
Fax: (+49) 721 9654 803, phone: (+49) 721 9654 802
maedche@fzi.de

Abstract. Web Services will transform the web from a collection of information into a distributed device of computation. In order to employ their full potential, appropriate description means for web services need to be developed. For this purpose we define a full-fledged *Web Service Modeling Framework* (WSMF) that provides the appropriate conceptual model for developing and describing web services and their composition. Its philosophy is based on the following principle: *maximal de-coupling* complemented by *scalable mediation service*.

The current web is mainly a collection of information but does not yet provide support in processing this information, i.e., in using the computer as a computational device. Recent efforts around UDDI, WSDL, and SOAP try to lift the web to a new level of service. Software programs can be accessed and executed via the web based on the idea of web services. A service can provide information, e.g. a weather forecast service, or it may have an effect in the real world, e.g. an online flight booking service. Web services can significantly increase the Web architecture's potential, by providing a way of automated program communication, discovery of services, etc. Therefore, they are in the centre of interests of various software developing companies. In a business environment this translates into the automatic cooperation between enterprises. An enterprise requiring a business interaction with another enterprise can automatically discover and select the appropriate optimal web services relying on selection policies. They can be invoked automatically and payment processes can be initiated. Any necessary mediation is applied based on data and process ontologies and the automatic translation of their concepts into each other. An example are supply chain relationships where a manufacturing enterprise of short-lived goods has to frequently seek suppliers as well as buyers dynamically. Instead of constantly searching for suppliers and

I. Horrocks and J. Hendler (Eds.): ISWC 2002, LNCS 2342, pp. 1–2, 2002.
© Springer-Verlag Berlin Heidelberg 2002

buyers by employees the web service infrastructure does it automatically within the defined constraints.

Still, there need to be done more work before the web service infrastructure can make this vision true. Current technology around UDDI, WSDL, and SOAP provide limited support in mechanizing service recognition, service configuration and combination (i.e., realizing complex workflows and business logics with web services), service comparison and automated negotiation. Therefore, there are proposals such as WSFL that develops a language for describing complex web services or DAML-S that employees semantic web technology for service description. The Web Service Modeling Framework (WSMF) follows this line of research. It is a full-fledged modeling framework for describing the various aspects related to web services. Fully enabled E-commerce based on workable web services requires a modeling framework that is centered around two complementary principles:

– Strong de-coupling of the various components that realize an E-commerce application.
– Strong mediation service enabling anybody to speak with everybody in a scalable manner.

These principles are rolled out in a number of specification elements and an architecture describing their relationships.

WSMF is the methodological framework developed within SWWS,[1] a recent European project aiming on Semantic Web enabled Web Services. SWWS accounts for three main challenges:

– Provide a comprehensive Web Service description framework, including the definition of a Web Service Modeling Framework WSMF (establishing a tight connection to industrial like XML, RDF, WSDL, WSFL and research efforts like, DAML+OIL, OWL, etc.
– Define a Web Service discovery framework that goes beyond simple registration means (like UDDI) and provides full-fledged ontology-based and metadata driven service discovery.
– Provide a scalable Web Service mediation framework that is fundamentally based on the P2P approach in order to provide direct connectivity between service requesters and service providers. This framework also includes means for configuration, composition and negotiation.

SWWS has a large industrial advisory board with more than 60 members and is the nucleus of an initiative for a large integrated project within framework VI of the research funding schema of the European Commission.

Semantic Web enabled Web Services are a key-enabler for intelligent web services. Intelligent web services have a revolutionary potential for many applications areas such as eWork, eCommerce, eGoverment, eLearning, etc. We will sketch this potential during the talk.

---

[1] Project partners are the Vrije Universiteit Amsterdam (coordinator), NL; FZI, Germany; Isoco, Spain; Shinka Technologies, Germany; Ontotext, Bulgaria; and Hewlett-Packard (HP), UK.

The Grid, Grid Services and the Semantic Web: Technologies and Opportunities

Carl Kesselman

USC/Information Sciences Institute
4676 Admiralty Way, Suite 1001
Marina del Rey, CA 90292-6695, USA
carl@isi.edu

Abstract. Grids are an emerging computational infrastructure that enables resource sharing and coordinated problem solving across dynamic, distributed collaborations that have come to be known as virtual organizations. Unlike the web, which primarily focuses on the sharing of information, the Grid provides a range of fundamental mechanisms for sharing diverse types of resource, such as computers, storage, data, software, and scientific instruments. In this talk, I will introduce the Grid concept and illustrate it with application examples from a range of scientific disciplines. It is likely that technology that is being developed for the Semantic Web will have important roles to play in Grid Services; I will explore some of these potential areas of Semantic Web technologies, identifying those that I think offer the most potential.

Grids are an emerging computational infrastructure that enables resource sharing and coordinated problem solving across dynamic, distributed collaborations that have come to be known as virtual organizations. Unlike the web, which primarily focuses on the sharing of information, the Grid provides a range of fundamental mechanisms for sharing diverse types of resource, such as computers, storage, data, software, and scientific instruments. By enabling the on demand sharing and coordinated use of resources across collaborating organizations, Grids are enabling entirely new classes of applications to be developed across a range of application domains including climate modeling, particle physics, biology, and aeronautics to name a few. Furthermore, the application of Grid technology to problems in the commercial sector has been recognized, as evidenced by recent announcements by IBM, Sun, Platform Computing, and Entropia, among others.

A recent advance in Grid technologies has been the recognition of the relationship between Grids and Web technologies, specifically those developed to support Web Services (e.g. WSDL, SOAP, UDDI, and WSIL). While the Grid deals with the creation, discovery and management of transient services, Web services provides mechanisms for discovering services as well as describing service interfaces in terms of abstract operations, and mapping of these operations onto concrete data transport mechanisms. The relationship between the Grid and Web services is being codified in a new specification called the Open Grid Services Architecture (OGSA).

I. Horrocks and J. Hendler (Eds.): ISWC 2002, LNCS 2342, pp. 3–4, 2002.

In this talk, I will introduce the Grid concept and illustrate it with application examples from a range of scientific disciplines. I will give high level description of how Grid infrastructure is structured and the current state of practice with respect to existing Grid software and services. I will then describe the on going work in OGSA.

It is likely that technology that is being developed for the Semantic Web will have important roles to play in Grid Services. Many decision making processes that go into assembling services into an application can be empowered by providing richer, and deeper descriptions of service properties and semantics. In this talk, I will explore some of these potential areas of Semantic Web technologies, identifying those that I think offer the most potential.

Matching RDF Graphs

Jeremy J. Carroll

Hewlett-Packard Laboratories Bristol, UK
jjc@hpl.hp.com

Abstract. The Resource Description Framework (RDF) describes graphs of statements about resources. RDF is a fundamental lower layer of the semantic web. This paper explores the equality of two RDF graphs in light of the graph isomorphism literature. We consider anonymous resources as unlabelled vertices in a graph, and show that the standard graph isomorphism algorithms, developed in the 1970's, can be used effectively for comparing RDF graphs. The techniques presented are useful for testing RDF software.

1   Introduction[1]

The semantic web is being built on top of an RDF [1] layer. This paper concerns a technique useful for testing and debugging within that RDF layer.

The RDF specification [1] defines a data model and a syntax. The syntax is defined on top of the XML syntax [2]. The data model is defined in terms of resources, often identified with URIs [3], and literals. Some of the resources are "anonymous". The data model is a set of triples, often thought of as a graph. The anonymous resources correspond to blank nodes in the graph [4].

The processing of RDF graphs occurs in the lower layers of semantic web processing. In practice the correctness of implementations requires the ability to perform unit tests within the RDF layer. The ability to compare two RDF graphs for equality is a fundamental component of such unit tests. For example, the RDF Test Cases Working Draft [5] gives many examples of tests requiring that the graphs read in from two different files should be equal.

Fortunately, the problem of graph equality, usually referred to with the mathematical term "graph isomorphism" is a well-understood one, that is solved for practical use. Less fortunately, the literature is not very accessible. Mathematical texts on graph theory (e.g. [6]) define the concept of graph isomorphism, but do not address the algorithmics. There is an excellent study on the problem from the point of complexity theory [7], again not a practical guide. Graph isomorphism does appear in Skiena's book of algorithms [8] but space considerations only allows a sketch solution. Fortin's technical report [9] gives an in-depth account of algorithms for the graph isomorphism problem.

---

[1] Thanks to anonymous referees and others who have given valuable feedback on earlier versions of this paper.

I. Horrocks and J. Hendler (Eds.): ISWC 2002, LNCS 2342, pp. 5–15, 2002.

A further difficulty presented by RDF graphs is that they do not fit any of the standard graph theoretic categories. They are directed graphs with labelled edges and partially labelled nodes. The partial node labelling is not addressed in prior work.

So, the intended contribution of this paper is as a "how to" guide, for developers of RDF based systems who need to provide a graph equality function, typically for test and debugging purposes.

Graph equality is not usually required or useful for end users, for whom it is believed that inference and entailment are more useful concepts. The model theory of Hayes [4] shows that subgraph isomorphism is the important concept for simple entailment between RDF graphs. This is, of course, a different concept from graph isomorphism. In particular two RDF graphs are semantically equivalent, under Hayes' model theory if they entail one another. This is a weaker condition than that of being isomorphic, which is the condition explored in this paper.

The paper shows how the iterative vertex classification of Read and Corneil [10] (section 6, pp 346-347) is applicable to RDF graphs.

We describe the algorithm and its use within Jena 1-3-0 [11].

2   An Example

If the two data models consist of identical sets of triples then the two data models are equal. This is particular useful for graphs with no blank nodes. However, when there are blank nodes in the RDF graph it is a mistake to limit equality to only such cases.

We explore this with a simple RDF/XML file with anonymous resources:

```
<rdf:RDF
     xmlns:rdf="http://www.w3.org/1999/02/22-rdf-syntax-ns#"
     xmlns:t="http://example.org/brothers#"
     xml:base="http://example.org/brothers">
     <rdf:Description   t:name="John">
       <t:child   t:name="Robert"/>
       <t:child   t:name="Jeremy"/>
       <t:child   t:name="Terry"/>
     </rdf:Description>
</rdf:RDF>
```

An RDF processor may produce a corresponding set of triples such as:

```
_:a3 <http://example.org/brothers#name>  "Robert"  .
_:a1 <http://example.org/brothers#name>  "John"  .
_:a1 <http://example.org/brothers#child>  _:a9  .
_:a1 <http://example.org/brothers#child>  _:a3  .
_:a9 <http://example.org/brothers#name>  "Terry"  .
_:a6 <http://example.org/brothers#name>  "Jeremy"  .
_:a1 <http://example.org/brothers#child>  _:a6  .
```

The syntax[2] we use for such triples is the "N-triple" syntax being used by the RDF working group [5]. The gensyms such as "_:a9", are identifiers for the blank nodes in the corresponding graph.

With a different gensym algorithm, or by a semantic-free reordering of the XML input, the same processor may give a different set of triples:

```
_:a3 <http://example.org/brothers#name> "Jeremy" .
_:a6 <http://example.org/brothers#name> "Terry" .
_:a1 <http://example.org/brothers#name> "John" .
_:a1 <http://example.org/brothers#child> _:a9 .
_:a1 <http://example.org/brothers#child> _:a3 .
_:a9 <http://example.org/brothers#name> "Robert" .
_:a1 <http://example.org/brothers#child> _:a6 .
```

A naive notion of equality suggests these are unequal, because the anonymous nodes have been given different gensyms (for example that with name "Jeremy" is _:a6 in the first and _:a3 in the second).

This is not consistent with the intended reading of anonymous resources being like resources but without a name. Nor is it consistent with either the N-triple definition [5], and the newer RDF Model Theory [4]. Both are clear that the blank node identifiers have file scope, and such cross-file comparisons are inappropriate. Indeed, the abstract syntax for RDF is a graph from which the blank node identifiers have been erased, thus no identifier of a blank node is significant. So the graph isomorphism problem, in this example, amounts to finding the bijection between the blank node identifiers that makes the two sets of triples equivalent. The bijection being:

```
a1  ⟶  a1.
a6  ⟶  a3.
a9  ⟶  a6.
a3  ⟶  a9.
```

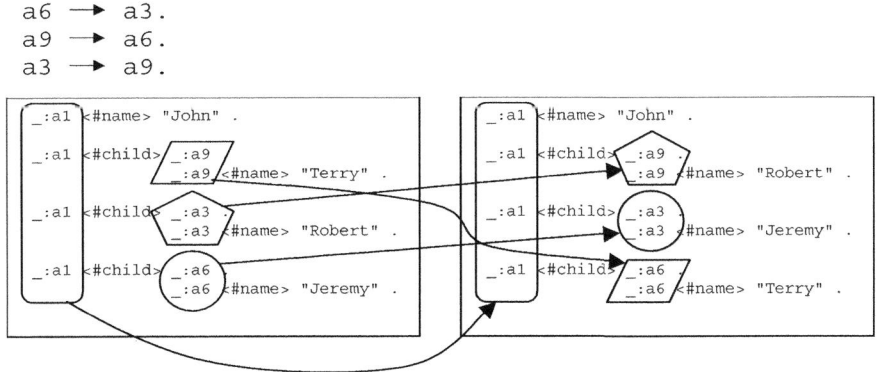

Fig. 1. An equivalence mapping between blank nodes

In very small examples, such as this one, it is plausible that a brute force search over all such permutations of anonymous resources will suffice. This has a factorial

---

[2] We use relative fragment URIs for compactness; these are not legal N-triple.

complexity and even with a dozen anonymous nodes ceases to provide the interactive feedback that is useful in debugging and testing.

The bijection between the two sets of blank nodes induces a labelled digraph isomorphism.

3   Graph Isomorphism Theory

In the graph isomorphism literature (e.g. [9], [10]) a graph typically consists of a set of unlabelled nodes or vertices, with a set of undirected unlabelled pairs of vertices called edges. The graph isomorphism problem is: "Given two graphs, are they the same?" and "If they are, which vertices from one correspond to which vertices in the other?"

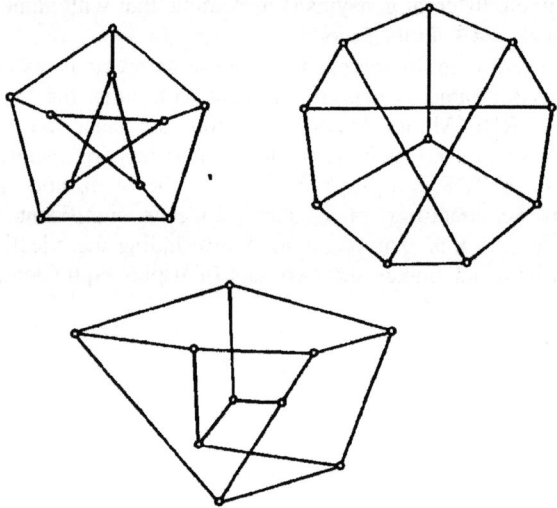

Fig. 2. Isomorphic graphs from [10].

Figure 2 shows three isomorphic graphs; note each has ten vertices shown by the small circles.

Most of the many variants of graphs have equivalent isomorphism problems. These included labelled digraphs: in which the edges have a label and a direction.

Within RDF data models it is possible to encode an unlabelled digraph by using a single property label (e.g. rdf:value) for the edges and anonymous resources for each vertex. Undirected graphs can be encoded by encoding each edge of the graph as two RDF triples, one in each direction.

In this way it can be seen that RDF data model equality and the graph isomorphism problem are equivalent from a theoretical point of view. However, in practice RDF data model equality is significantly easier because:

• most of the vertices are labelled with the URI of a resource.
• most of the edges have distinctive labels from the URI of the property of the triple.

- the XML syntax imposes significant (and unmotivated) restrictions on where anonymous resources can occur.

We view the third point as an error that should be corrected; and regard the other two points as important factors in the design of an effective algorithm.

4   Iterative Vertex Classification Algorithms

Standard graph isomorphism algorithms are non-deterministic, i.e. they involve guessing, e.g. (from [10], section 2).

1. Label the vertices V_1 of G_1.
2. Label the vertices V_2 of G_2.
3. If $|V_1|=|V_2|$ set n = $|V_1|$ else the graphs are not isomorphic.
4. Guess a mapping from V_1 to V_2 (note: n! choices)
5. Check all the edges are the same. (at most, n^2 checks).

This is a slow method: brute force search over all the permutations of the vertices. There are n! different guesses to make, and maybe only one of them is correct. An implementation of this algorithm needs to use backtracking or some similar technique to consider the other guesses in the usual case that step 5 finds that the edges are not the same.

It is possible to greatly reduce the amount of guessing by classifying the vertices. The underlying idea of this method is to look for distinctive characteristics of the vertices, and then to only guess a mapping (in step 4) which maps any vertex in a class with some given characteristics to a vertex in the other graph of the equivalent class with the same characteristics. For example if a vertex is adjacent to three other vertices (i.e. it is at the end of three edges), then it can only map to a vertex that is also adjacent to three further vertices (this is a classification by 'degree').

If the two graphs do not have equal numbers of vertices with each class of characteristics then the two graphs are not isomorphic.

Now we can make better guesses, we modify the algorithm above to be:

1. Label the vertices V_1 of G_1.
2. Label the vertices V_2 of G_2.
3. If $|V_1|=|V_2|$ set n = $|V_1|$ else the graphs are not isomorphic.
4. Classify the vertices of both graphs.
5. For each class c in the classification
   a.   Find the sets $V_{1,c}$ and $V_{2,c}$ of nodes which are in c
   b.   If $|V_{1,c}|=|V_{2,c}|$ set $n_c = |V_{1,c}|$ else the graphs are not isomorphic.
   c.   Guess a mapping from $V_{1,c}$ to $V_{2,c}$ (note: n_c! choices)
6. Check all the edges are the same. (at most, n^2 checks).

This is an improvement because the total number of different guesses has been (substantially) reduced. (We make a number of small guesses instead of one large one). We can improve performance again by evaluating each of the checks of step 6 as early as possible, during step 5, as soon as both vertices involved in an edge have had their mapping assigned.

Iterative vertex classification (also known as partition refinement, in e.g. [12]) is when we use the information from our current classifications to reclassify the vertices producing smaller sets of each classification. In this we don't see a vertex classification as only a function of the vertex and the graph, but also of the current classification of the vertices of the graph. So for example, iterating on the degree classification above, we can classify a vertex by e.g. "This is adjacent to four vertices which have degree three," (or in more words, "This is adjacent to four vertices which are, in turn, adjacent to three vertices"). The typical classification is formed by AND-ing lots of classifications like that together.

Once we have made one guess aligning two vertices, we can re-classify the other vertices as to whether they are adjacent to the aligned vertices or not.

This can also apply after we have guessed. The full algorithm looks like:

1. Label the vertices V_1 of G_1.
2. Label the vertices V_2 of G_2.
3. If $|V_1|=|V_2|$ set n = $|V_1|$ else the graphs are not isomorphic.
4. Classify all the vertices of both graphs into a single class.
5. Repeat:
   a. Repeat – generate a new classification from the current classification
       i.   Reclassify each vertex by the number of vertices of each class in the current classification it is adjacent to.
       ii. If the new classification is the same as the current classification go to 5(b)
       iii. If any of the new classes has different numbers of members from the two graphs then fail and backtrack to the last guess [step 5(c)].
       iv. If any of the new classes is small enough (e.g. size 2) go to 5(b)
       v.   Set the current classification as the new classification and go to 5(a)i
   b. If every class has one element from each graph then this defines an isomorphism and we are finished.
   c. Choose a smallest class with more than two vertices. Select an arbitrary vertex from V_1 in this class. (Non-deterministically) guess a vertex from V_2 in this class, hence picking a pair of vertices; when we run out of guesses, we backtrack to the last guess.
   d. Generate a new classification from the current classification by putting the pair of vertices, selected and guessed in 5(c), into its own class and otherwise leaving everything unchanged.
6. If we backtrack through all the guesses in 5 then we have failed and the graphs are not isomorphic.

This is substantially more complicated than the original algorithm but gives much, much better performance. Yet better solutions to the graph isomorphism problem can be found [12], [13]; typically they use more sophisticated invariants than the adjacency one described here, and they use the 'automorphism group' of one of the graphs to eliminate many redundant guesses. However, for RDF graphs the above algorithm will generally be sufficient.

5   Vertex Classification for RDF

The code found in Jena [14] is based on the iterative vertex classification algorithm above. It classifies each non-anonymous resource by its URI and each literal by its string. It classifies each anonymous resource on the basis of the statements in which it appears. The classification considers the role in which an anonymous resource appears in a statement, and the other items in the statement.

This allows substantial use to be made of the labelled vertices and edges. The non-deterministic parts will not be used except when the labels do not allow us to directly distinguish one anonymous node from another.

The graph isomorphism algorithm above is then used, with minor variation[3]. The principle variation is the use of hash codes in the reclassification process.

An anonymous resource can play three different roles in an RDF statement: it can be subject, object or both. The ModelMatcher code [14] goes further and will allow anonymous resources in the predicate position. This gives a further four possibilities of where the anonymous resource occurs in the triple.

The iterative vertex classification then amounts to the following:

- The reclassification of a statement depends on the current classification of the resources in the statement.
- The reclassification of an anonymous resource depends on the reclassifications of all the statements it appears in, and the role it plays in each appearance.
- The reclassification of a non-anonymous resource or a literal is its original classification.

6   Partition Refinement by Hashcode

The invariants discussed above seem to have quite complicated representations; which suggests that comparing them may be slow. A simple way to proceed is always use hash-codes for each invariant value, combining them in commutative and associative or non-commutative fashion depending on whether we are discussing a set or a sequence at that point.

Thus the code in Jena ModelMatcher proceeds in this fashion:

- The code of an anonymous resource is the sum of its relative codes with respect to each triple it participates in. Note this means that an anonymous resource that participates in two triples of a certain class is distinguished from one that participates in three triples of that class.
- The relative code of an anonymous resource with respect to a triple is the sum of a multiplier times the secondary code of the triple's subject, predicate and object excluding those positions filled by the anonymous resource. The multiplier is chosen to distinguish the subject, predicate and object.
- The secondary code of a non-anonymous resource or literal is its Java hashCode.
- The secondary code of an anonymous resource is its code from the previous iteration (which identifies the current classification).

---

[3] A minor variation is that an emphasis is placed on finding singleton classes.

The anonymous resources are classified on the basis of their codes. We may, of course, get a hash collision. This will have the consequence of combining two partitions. While this will decrease the efficiency of the algorithm it does not impact its correctness.

7   Other Equivalences

We may wish to ask if two RDF graphs are equivalent with a notion of vertex equivalence that allows non-anonymous resources with different URIs to be identified, or that allows non-anonymous resources to be identified with anonymous ones.

In these cases we need to use a similar approach, the underlying problem is still graph isomorphism, but we use a different classification procedure. For example if we wish to allow the identification of different reifications of a statement, we would initially classify all reifications in a single class, and otherwise use the above algorithm.

Another natural example comes from the use of rdf:Bag which is defined as an unordered container, yet the container membership statements are distinguished rdf:_1, rdf:_2 etc. This suggests that a statement equivalence that maps all of these to the same class would be natural for many applications.

A further natural equivalence between RDF graphs is given by the model theory [4]. Here the relevant notion of equivalence is, "do the two graphs entail one another?" This is a weaker condition than graph isomorphism, and the techniques described here are not suitable for this problem.

8   Use of Graph Isomorphism within Jena

As indicated in the introduction, the primary motivation for graph equality testing is for unit testing and debugging of underlying RDF infrastructure. Thus the major use of this code in Jena is in testing code:

- It is used by the RDF Core WG to apply the test cases to a suite of RDF/XML parsers [15]. This involves using a parser to convert RDF/XML into N-triple and then comparing this N-triple document with a reference N-triple document using graph isomorphism.
  It is used within the unit test code for ARP to check its conformance with the RDF Test Cases. This involves loading an RDF/XML file with the parser as one graph and loading a second graph from the reference N-triple document, and comparing the two graphs for isomorphism.
- It is used for additional parser tests within Jena.
- It is used for RDF writer tests of the form:
  - take an RDF graph
  - write it out
  - read it in as a new graph
  - compare new with old, if they are not the same then there is an error.

Further use can be made whenever operations within an RDF platform are meant to leave a graph unchanged.

The implementation within Jena is itself tested using some pathological cases based on slightly distorted unlabelled hypercubes (both directed and undirected). Unlabelled graphs are represented within RDF by:

- always using a label `rdf:value` for every edge
- always using blank nodes

Undirected edges are represented by using two directed edges (one in each direction).

As an example consider the 3-dimensional directed hypercube below (the vertex labels are only part of the diagram, not part of the graph):

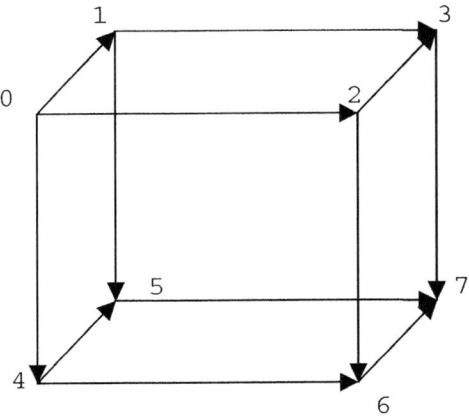

Fig. 3. A directed hypercube

We can distort this by duplicating a vertex:

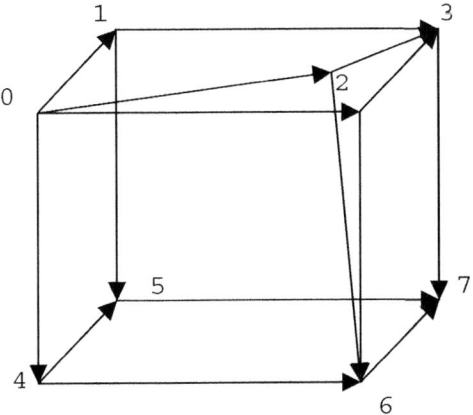

Fig. 4. A distorted directed hypercube

Before this distortion vertices 1, 2, and 4 were in the same class. After this distortion, the new vertex is indistinguishable from vertex 2, and the distinction between vertex 2 and vertex 4 is quite subtle.

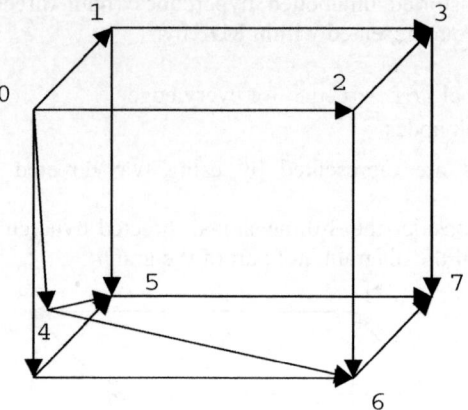

Fig. 5. An isomorphic distorted directed hypercube

Moreover, given two graphs differently distorted in this fashion, we know that they are isomorphic if and only if the number of bits in the (informal) node label of the duplicated nodes is the same. Compare figure 4 with figure 5 and figure 6.

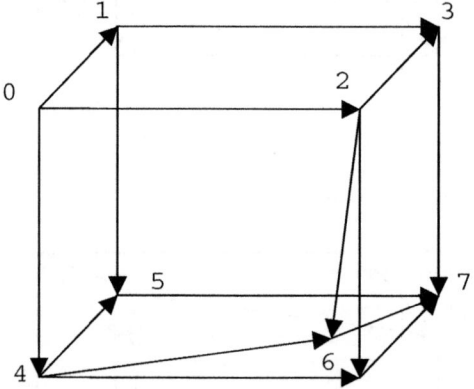

Fig. 6. A non-isomorphic distorted directed hypercube.

Thus we can produce a number of different, moderately difficult test cases for graph isomorphism, for which the correct result (isomorphic or not) is known.

Working on 8 dimensional hypercubes with 256 vertices each test takes less than a second on an off-the-shelf PC and Java 1.3. (The measured results are between 75 and 670 milliseconds, depending on the exact details of the deformity).

Since realistic uses of this functionality involve RDF graphs for which the variation in edge and node labels is much greater, resulting in a much better first vertex classification, the algorithm performs adequately for its intended purpose.

9   Conclusions

It is possible to use techniques from the graph isomorphism literature to compare RDF graphs while equating anonymous resources.

It is not necessary to use some of the more sophisticated techniques suggested, due to the large amount of labelling found in RDF graphs. Performance problems may be experienced if graph theorists use RDF tools to store and communicate pathological examples; but standard usages of RDF are not pathological.

These techniques could be extended to cope with a richer notion of equivalence between resources.

References

1. Ora Lassila, Ralph R. Swick: Resource Description Framework (RDF) Model and Syntax Specification. World Wide Web Consortium (1999) http://www.w3.org/TR/1999/REC-rdf-syntax-19990222.
2. Tim Bray, Jean Paoli, C.M. Sperberg-McQueen, Eve Maler: Extensible Markup Language (XML) 1.0 (Second Edition). World Wide Web Consortium (2000) http://www.w3.org/TR/2000/REC-xml-20001006.
3. T. Berners-Lee, R. Fielding, U.C. Irvine, L. Masinter: Uniform Resource Identifiers (URI): Generic Syntax. RFC 2396. IETF (1998).
4. Patrick Hayes (ed): RDF Model Theory. W3C Working Draft (2001) http://www.w3.org/TR/rdf-mt/
5. Art Barstow, Dave Beckett (eds): RDF Test Cases. W3C Working Draft (2001) http://www.w3.org/TR/rdf-testcases/
6. Reinhard Diestel: Graph Theory. 2nd edition, Springer (2000).
7. J. Köbler, U Schöning, J. Torán: The Graph Isomorphism Problem, Its Structural Complexity. Birkhauser (1993).
8. Steve Skiena: The Algorithm Design Manual. Springer (1998).
9. Scott Fortin: The Graph Isomorphism Problem. Technical Report TR 96-20. Department of Computer Science, University of Alberta (1996). ftp://ftp.cs.ualberta.ca/pub/TechReports/1996/TR96-20/TR96-20.ps.gz
10. Ronald C. Read, Derek G.Corneil: Graph Isomorphism Disease. Journal of Graph Theory 1 (1977) 339-363.
11. Brian McBride, Jeremy Carroll, Ian Dickenson, Dave Reynolds, Andy Seaborne: Jena 1-3-0. Hewlett-Packard Labs (2002) http://www.hpl.hp.com/semweb/jena-top.html
12. Brendan D. McKay: Practical Graph Isomorphism. Congressus Numerantium 30 (1981) 45-87. http://cs.anu.edu.au/~bdm/papers/pgi.pdf
13. Brendan D. McKay: Nauty. (1994) http://cs.anu.edu.au/~bdm/nauty/
14. Jeremy Carroll: ModelMatcher.java found in [11] (2001)
15. Aaron Swarz: Test Case Results. http://lists.w3.org/Archives/Public/w3c-rdfcore-wg/2001Sep/0001.html

Layering the Semantic Web: Problems and Directions

Peter F. Patel-Schneider[1] and Dieter Fensel[2]

[1] Bell Labs Research
Murray Hill, NJ, U.S.A.
`pfps@research.bell-labs.com`
[2] Vrije Universiteit Amsterdam (VU)
Amsterdam, the Netherlands
`dieter@cs.vu.nl`

Abstract. The Resource Description Framework and the Resource Description Framework Schema Specification are supposed to be the foundations of the Semantic Web, in that all other Semantic Web languages are to be layered on top of them. It turns out that such a layering cannot be achieved in a straightforward way. This paper describes the problem with the straightforward layering and lays out several alternative layering possibilities. The benefits and drawbacks of each of these possibilities are presented and analyzed.

1 Introduction

The World Wide Web (WWW) has drastically changed the availability of electronically accessible information. The WWW currently contains some 3 billion static documents, which are accessed by over 300 million users internationally. At the same time, this enormous amount of data has made it increasingly difficult to find, access, present, and maintain the information required by a wide variety of users. This is because information content is presented primarily in natural language. Thus, a wide gap has emerged between the information available for tools aimed at addressing the problems above and the information maintained in human-readable form.

In response to this problem, many new research initiatives and commercial enterprises have been set up to enrich available information with machine-processable semantics. Such support is essential for "bringing the web to its full potential". The Semantic Web activity of the World Wide Web Consortium is chartered to design this future "semantic web"—an extended web of machine-readable information and automated services that extend far beyond current capabilities [3,9,10]. The explicit representation of the semantics underlying data, programs, pages, and other web resources, will enable a knowledge-based web that provides a qualitatively new level of service. Automated services will improve in their capacity to assist humans in achieving their goals by "understanding" more of the content on the web, and thus providing more accurate filtering, categorization, and searches of information sources. This process will ultimately lead to an extremely knowledgeable system that features various specialized reasoning services. These services will support us in nearly all aspects of our daily life—making access to information as pervasive, and necessary, as access to electricity is today.

I. Horrocks and J. Hendler (Eds.): ISWC 2002, LNCS 2342, pp. 16–29, 2002.

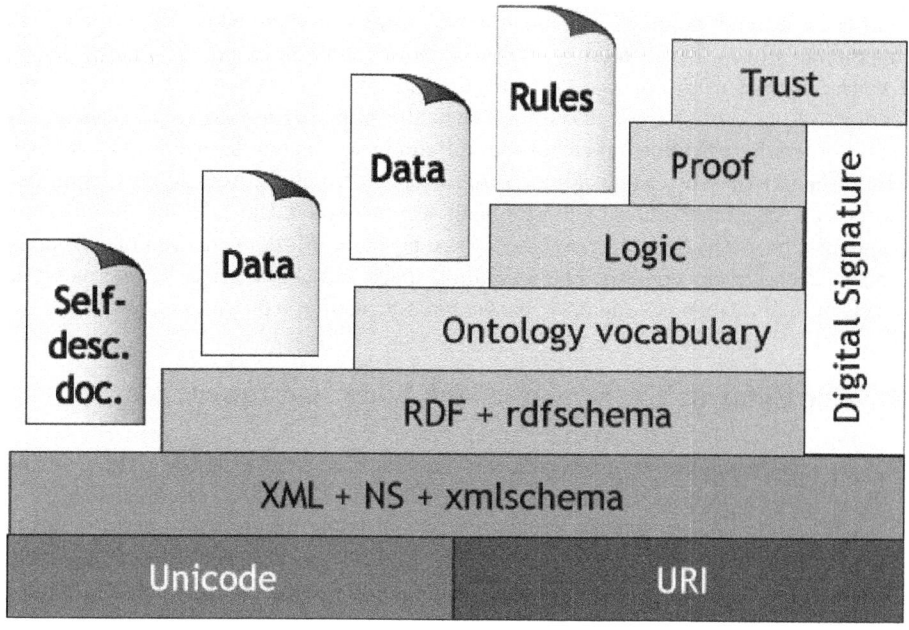

Fig. 1. The Semantic Web Tower

Realizing this vision of the semantic web requires a number of intermediate and related steps. Tim Berners-Lee envisioned a semantic web language tower [http://www.w3c.org/2000/Talks/1206-xml2k-tbl/slide10-0.html] (see Figure 1) that provides intermediate language standards. Based on XML as the universal syntax carrier, a tower of successively more powerful languages are defined. The Resource Description Framework (RDF) [15] and Resource Description Framework Schema Specification (RDFS) [7] define a standard for representing simple metadata—shallow machine-processable semantics of information. The next step is is currently under development by the W3C Web Ontology Working Group (http://www.w3.org/2001/sw/WebOnt/). which is producing a Web Ontology Language, tentatively called OWL. Further extensions will provide rule languages and finally a full-fledged machine processable semantic web.

We are currently working on a small piece of the overall puzzle. This paper reports lessons learned when trying to layer OWL on top of RDF and RDFS.[1] It turns out that OWL cannot be defined as semantic extension of RDF(S) while retaining the syntax of RDF. We will explain the problems we encountered when trying this and we also discuss several alternative workarounds. Each of these have their advantages and drawbacks. The main contribution of the paper is to provide deeper insights on how the language tower of the semantic web can be organized.

Although this paper concentrates on a particular problem, that of layering OWL on top of RDF(S), there are layering decisions to be made whenever a new representation formalism has to be compatible with an existing representation formalism. This

---

[1] We will use RDF(S) to refer to the combination of RDF and RDFS.

will occur at other points of the semantic web tower, has occured in the past, and will undoubtably occur in the future.

The content of the paper is organized as follows. In Section 2, we describe the context of our problem. We discuss the semantic web language tower as sketched by Tim Berners-Lee. Section 3 sketches four different ways on how to layer OWL on top of RDF. Section 4 discusses one of these solutions in more details. Actually this "solution" is rather a characterization of the problem we encountered in layering the different languages properly. Section 5 discusses three possible solutions. Instead of indicating one solution we elaborate the entire solution space and characterize the alternative in terms of their advantages and draw-backs. Finally, Section 6 provides conclusions.

2   The Context: The Semantic Web Language Tower

Giving a real semantics to the semantic web language tower as sketched by Tim Berners-Lee in Figure 1 requires serious work to clarify many of the present technical issues.

URIs and Unicode provide standard ways to define references to entities and to exchange symbols. XML provides a standard way to represent labeled trees and XML Schema provides a mechanism to define grammars for legal XML documents. Finally, the name space mechanism of XML (NS) allows the combination of documents with heterogeneous vocabulary. These concepts provide the syntactic underpinnings of the semantic web.

The first layer of the semantic web is provided by RDF.

The Resource Description Framework (RDF) "is a foundation for processing meta-data; it provides interoperability between applications that exchange machine-under-standable information on the Web." [15]. Basically, RDF defines a data model for describing machine processable semantics of data. As stated in the RDF Model and Syntax Specification [15], the basic data model for RDF consists of three object types:

- Resources: A resource may be an entire Web page; a part of a Web page; a whole collection of pages; or an object that is not directly accessible via the Web; e.g. a printed book. Resources are always named by URIs.
- Properties: A property is a specific aspect, characteristic, attribute, or relation used to describe a resource.
- Statements: A specific resource together with a named property plus the value of that property for that resource is an RDF statement.

In a nutshell, RDF defines object-property-value-triples as basic modeling primitives and introduces a standard syntax for them. An RDF document will define properties in terms of the resources to which they apply.

RDF Schema [7] defines a simple modeling language on top of RDF. RDF Schema introduces classes, is-a relationships between classes and properties, and domain and range restrictions for properties as modeling primitives.

RDF and RDF schema (RDF(S) hereafter) use XML as a carrier syntax but do not employ any semantics expressed by XML, instead using their own semantics for XML syntax.

The OIL definition:

```
<rdfs:Class rdf:ID="Herbivore">
  <rdfs:type rdf:resource="oil:DefinedClass">
  <rdfs:subClassOf rdf:resource="Animal" />
  <rdfs:subClassOf>
    <oil:NOT>
      <oil:hasOperand rdf:resource="Carnivore" />
    </oil:NOT>
  </rdfs:subClassOf>
</rdfs:Class>
```

What an RDF Schema system understands:

```
<rdfs:Class rdf:ID="Herbivore">
  <rdfs:type rdf:resource="unknown:DefinedClass">
  <rdfs:subClassOf rdf:resource="Animal" />
  <rdfs:subClassOf>
    <rdf:Description />
  </rdfs:subClassOf>
</rdfs:Class>
```

Fig. 2. OIL versus RDF Schema

The term Ontology vocabulary (and data based on top of it) in the semantic web tower may cause irritation. We guess that the author refers to an ontology language that is a restricted subset of logic to define terminology. Currently, a language called OWL is under development for this purpose. Most of this paper is about on how to define OWL on top of XML and RDF(S). Whereas the relationship between XML and RDF is a simple syntactic one, the relationship between RDF(S) and OWL necessarily has semantic components as well. The details of this relationship involve a rich decision space of proper syntactic and semantic layering.

The semantic web tower figure mentions Logic on top of Ontology layer. On the one hand, this may be misleading as any Ontology language should be properly grounded in logical notions. On the other hand, this may be taken as a hint that on top of an Ontology language a richer logical language should be provided. Again, we may expect complicated discussions on an appropriate layering. For example, proposals for web logic languages may employ a special semantics, such as minimal model semantics, to make inference more amenable to computer implementation.

Proof and trust seem to be rather applications than a new language level. Anyway they are far beyond current efforts.

Currently many layering ideas oriented to syntactical and semantical extensions compete which each other (http://lists.w3.org/Archives/Public/www-webont-wg/) [6,8]. Working out the proper relationship seems to be much more challenging than just developing one layer. So even before we design the ontology language, we need a vision of how the levels in the semantic web tower relate to each other.

OIL [11,12], a predecessor of OWL, was defined as a syntactic extension of RDF-Schema which means that every RDF-Schema ontology is a valid ontology in the new language (i.e., an OIL processor will also understand RDF Schema). However, the other direction is also available: defining an OIL extension as closely as possible to RDF Schema allows maximal reuse of existing RDF Schema-based applications and tools. However, since the ontology language usually contains new aspects (and therefore new vocabulary, which an RDF Schema processor does not know), 100% compatibility is not possible. Let us examine an example. The OIL expression in Figure 2 defines herbivore as a class, which is a sub-class of animal and disjunct to all carnivores. An application limited to pure RDF Schema is still able to capture some aspects of this definition. It sees that herbivore is a subclass of animal and a subclass of a second class, which it cannot understand properly. This seems to be a useful way to preserve complicated semantics for simpler applications.

Recently, a interesting feature of this approach become visible. In general one would assume that an OIL/OWL agent can draw more conclusions than an RDF Schema aware agent. This we will call the model theoretic interpretation of the semantic web language tower. However, based on the RDF model theory [13] this turned out to be not true. Because RDF "sees" the syntactical definition of an ontology it can draw conclusions that OWL, which is situated at a logical level, cannot. That is, not every model for an OWL ontology is also a model for the underlying RDF representation. (http://lists.w3.org/Archives/Public/www-webont-wg/2001Dec/0116.html) Therefore, defining the model theory of OWL as an extension of the model theory of RDF and representing OWL constructs syntactically in RDF leads to paradoxical situations, i.e., ill-defined model theories for OWL. We will explain these problems in more detail in the next Sections.

3   Layering in the Semantic Web

What is the relationship between the various layers in this Semantic Web tower? Well this does depend somewhat on which layers are being considered, but there are some principles and some basic kinds of relationships that can be considered.

First, the various layers are languages, so they have a syntax. The syntax of one layer can be an extension of the previous layer, the same as the previous layer, a subset of the previous layer, or just different from that of the previous layer. For example, the syntax of RDF is a subset of the syntax of XML, as RDF uses XML syntax, but not all XML documents are valid RDF documents.

Second, the various layers, or at least most of them, have a semantics or meaning. As the Semantic Web is based on meaning, we should expect that the meanings provided by one layer form the foundation for the next layer. Otherwise, how can this be called a semantic web? So we should expect that one layer semantically extends the previous layer, in that all meanings of the previous layer are maintained by the next layer, and that extra meanings are provided by that layer. For example, this is the relationship between RDF and RDF Schema, where RDF Schema maintains all the meanings of RDF, but adds new meanings of its own.

However, there is a point where the Semantic Web moves out of the semantic realm and into the syntactic realm. At this point we do not expect that the semantics of the layer, if any, are preserved. For example, the foundation of the Semantic Web is Unicode strings and URIs. However, not all of the Unicode strings in an RDF document are strings; instead these strings are given a different meaning in the Semantic Web.

In fact, the Semantic Web treats XML as part of the syntactic realm. The semantics of XML documents are not retained in RDF. Instead RDF provides its own meaning for XML documents; a meaning that is not compatible with the XML data model meaning of the document.

In fact, the only semantic layering currently in the W3C-approved semantic web is the layering between RDF and RDF Schema. RDF Schema uses precisely the syntax of RDF. That is, all RDF documents are syntactically-valid RDF Schema documents. RDF Schema is also a semantic extension of RDF. That is, the RDF Schema meaning of RDF constructs incorporates the RDF meaning of these constructs.

There are at least four proposed layerings of OWL on top of RDF(S).

1. Same-syntax semantic extension: In this proposed layering, which is the same layering relationship as that between RDF and RDF Schema, the syntax of OWL would be the same as the syntax of RDF and the semantics of OWL would be an extension of the semantics of RDF Schema. This looks like the most natural proposal. However, as we will show below, this approach leads to an ill-defined model theory of OWL. Therefore, we describe this solution rather as an enumeration of potential problems than as an actual solution. This "solution" is the point where our analysis departs.

2. Syntax and semantic extension: In this proposed layering the semantics of OWL is defined as an extension of the semantics of RDF Schema. The syntax of OWL is also an extension of the syntax of RDF. In this proposal many syntactical constructs of OWL would not be defined in RDF but instead would use non-RDF XML syntax. This proposal avoids the paradoxical situations of the previous layering proposal. However, new parsers would be required to process the OWL language and an RDF(S) aware agent has a very limited understanding of an OWL ontology.

3. Same-syntax, but diverging semantics: In this proposal layering, OWL syntax would again be RDF syntax, or a subset of RDF syntax, but the meaning of some constructs would be different from their meaning in RDF or RDF Schema. In essence, OWL would treat RDF as a syntax carrier, just as RDF treats XML as a syntax carrier. Actually, most reasonable versions of this approach would not completely discard the RDF and RDF Schema meanings, and considerable overlap is possible. Here an RDF(S) aware agent may understand many aspects of an OWL ontology (as far as they are not beyond his RDF(S) horizon), however, would give some of them a different meaning from his RDF(S) point of view.

4. Differing syntax and semantics: In this proposal layering, OWL differs from RDF and RDF Schema in both syntax and semantics. Again, although the formalisms would diverge, considerable overlap is possible and even desirable.

In the next section we will explain further the first "solution" which is actually not a solution but a way to describe the problem we encountered. In Section 5, we describe the other three solutions in more detail.

4   The Problem when Layering OWL on Top of RDF(S)

As stated above, the most attractive way to layer OWL on top of RDF(S), at least at first glance, is to use the same layering relationship as that between RDF and RDF Schema. That is, OWL would have the same syntax as RDF and the semantics of OWL would be an extension of the semantics of RDF(S). This layering relationship was the one expected to be used by the designers of RDF(S), at least we so believe based on various statements about RDF(S). However, as we explain in this section, it is just not possible to extend this layering relationship to the ontology level because it leads to semantic paradoxes.

Naïve users may argue that semantic paradoxes are not important in the semantic web. After all, should the semantic web not be able to represent contradictions, and maybe even reason effectively in the presence of contradictions, and semantic paradoxes are just like built-in contradictions? Yes, but the key point is precisely that semantic paradoxes are built-in—they are present in all situations and thus they cause all situations to be ill-defined, resulting in a complete collapse of the logical formalism.

4.1   The Problem in General Terms

The problem with the same-syntax extension of RDF(S) to OWL is roughly the same as the problems that destroyed the initial formalization of set theory. This paradox, discovered by Russell, results from an attempt to make sets too powerful.

In the formalization of set theory that contains Russell's paradox, there is a (very large) collection of built-in sets. All models for sets include these built-in sets, and usually many more. Unfortunately, these built-in sets include the set consisting of those sets that do not contain themselves. Is this set a member of itself? If it is then it cannot be, because it contains exactly those sets that do not contain themselves, and it does contain itself. If it is not then it must be, via similar reasoning.

This violates the very principles of set theory, i.e., that set membership should be a well-defined relationship. Because this set has to be in every model for sets, there are no models for sets, resulting in a complete collapse of this formalization of set theory.

OWL layered on top of RDF Schema as a same-syntax extension has the same problem. We believe that to make the logical foundations of classes in the extension work correctly, there has to be a large collection of built-in classes in any model. Unfortunately, this collection includes the class that is defined as those resources that do not belong to the class. Membership in this class is ill-defined, via reasoning similar to the reasoning for Russell's paradoxical set above. This violates the semantic underpinnings of classes, resulting in no models for OWL defined in this way.

RDF(S) does not fall into this paradox because it does not need a large collection of built-in classes, not having any way to define classes.

4.2   The Problem in Detail

To understand the details of the problem with a same-syntax and extended semantics layering of OWL on top of RDF(S) it is first necessary to understand a bit about the syntax and semantics of RDF(S).

The surface syntax, i.e., the XML syntax, of RDF(S) is being modified by the RDF Core Working Group, but the basic ideas are unchanged. Further, the RDF Core Working Group is developing a syntax of RDF(S) [2] in terms of N-triples [1], a cut-down version of N3. So, for the purposes of this discussion, it suffices to view RDF syntax as a collection of triples in the form of < subject property object >, where subject is a URI or an anonymous node ID, object is a URI or anonymous node ID or literal, and property is a URI.

Recently, a semantics for RDF(S) has been defined by the RDF Core WG [13] The model-theoretic semantics defines model-theoretic interpretations, how these interpretations provide meaning for RDF(S), and how one RDF(S) knowledge base can entail another. The details of interpretations cannot be given in a paper of this length, but the general ideas are fairly standard. Basically, interpretations are built on resources, i.e., referenceable objects, literal values, e.g., strings, and binary relationships between resources or from resources to literal values. Both URIs and anonymous node IDs denote resources, and literals denote literal values, e.g., strings. Triples denote relationships between resources or from resources to literal values that belong to a property. The only unusual part of this model theory is that properties are also resources. From interpretations the usual idea of models, i.e., interpretations that satisfy a KB, follow, as does entailment, i.e., all models of one KB are also models of another.

RDF itself has a simple built-in theory having to do with the types of resources. It provides a property between resources, rdf:type, that links a resource to the types that the resource belongs to. As all properties are resources in RDF, so rdf:type is a resource. The extra meaning of rdf:type accruing from its status as a relationship between resources and their types is formally defined in the model theory for RDF.

RDF Schema extends this theory by creating a theory of classes and properties. Classes in RDF Schema are those resources that can have members, i.e., RDF Schema classes are resources that can be the object of triples whose predicate is rdf:type. RDF Schema defines several built-in classes, including rdfs:Class, the class of all classes, and rdfs:Resource, the class of all resources. RDF Schema also defines several relationships between classes, including rdfs:subClassOf, the subclass relationship. All these resources are given meaning by the RDF(S) model theory.

However, the RDF Schema theory of classes and properties is very weak. For example, it is not possible in RDF Schema to provide defined classes—classes that give a formula that determines which resources belong to them. The intent of OWL is to provide an even richer theory of classes and properties, allowing for defined classes and more relationships between classes. Some of these defined classes are called restrictions in OWL. There are restrictions in OWL that provide local typing for properties and restrictions in OWL that ensure that there are several values (or at most several values) for a property that belong to a particular class. There is also a construct in OWL that creates a class from a set of resources.

It is this richer theory of classes that clashes with the underlying principles of RDF(S), resulting in paradoxes in a same-syntax and extended semantics layering of OWL on top of RDF(S). Let's now investigate how these semantic paradoxes arise.

As this layering of OWL on top of RDF(S) is a same-syntax layering, all OWL syntax is also RDF syntax, which is also the same as the RDF Schema syntax. Therefore every syntactic construct has to be either a URI, an anonymous node ID, a literal, or a triple. As the semantics of OWL in this layering is an extension of the semantics of RDF(S) the denotation of these constructs has to be the same as their denotation in RDF(S) and the semantic constraints on them have to include the semantic constraints on them in RDF Schema. Further, as OWL classes are an extension of RDF Schema classes, the OWL relationship from resources to their OWL classes must incorporate the RDF Schema relationship between resources and RDF Schema classes, namely rdf:type, and OWL classes must include RDF Schema classes. Let us call the property that is the OWL relationship from resources to their types, owl:type, which can either be rdf:type or some super-property of rdf:type.

Now consider entailment in this version of OWL. Suppose we have an OWL interpretation that contains an RDF Schema class, Person, a property child, and an object John that has no outgoing child relationships. OWL contains the notion of a restriction of a property to a type, i.e., given a property, say child, and a class, say Person, it is possible to create the restriction corresponding to those resources whose children all belong to Person. John belongs to this restriction in this interpretation because John has no children and thus all John's children belong to Person. Therefore we need that any interpretation like the one above is a model for John belonging to this restriction. However, restrictions are resources and thus this can only happen if there is a resource that corresponds to the restriction, and that includes John as a member. So, this simple interpretation will not be correct, in our view, unless it includes such a resource and the appropriate owl:type relationships to it.

Thus OWL interpretations must include resources for many restrictions, essentially all the restrictions that can be built out of the classes and properties that are in the interpretation. As well, OWL interpretations must have the correct owl:type relationships to these resources. In this way, each OWL interpretation must have a theory of restrictions, including self-referential restrictions, and also other OWL constructs. Some of these restrictions can refer to themselves, as there are self-referential loops in RDF Schema classes and thus this cannot be ruled out in restrictions.

We are now in the same situation that the original formalization of set theory was, as the following shows.

Consider the restriction that states it is precisely those resources that have at most zero values for the property owl:type that belong to the class that consists of the restriction itself. In the N-triples syntax for RDF, this is

```
_:1 a owl:Restriction .
_:1 owl:onProperty owl:type .
_:1 owl:maxCardinalityQ 0 .
_:1 owl:hasClassQ _:2 .
_:2 oneOf _:3 .
_:3 owl:first _:1 .
_:3 owl:rest owl:nil .
```

This restriction, read slightly differently, is the restriction that consists of those resources that do not belong to it. This is not the paradoxical Russell set, but is paradoxical. Consider any resource. If it belongs to the restriction then it does not, but if it does not then it does. Just as with the Russell set, if this restriction is in an interpretation then the class membership relationship is ill-defined. However, this restriction is in all OWL interpretations, because it is constructed only from resources that must be in all OWL interpretations. Therefore all OWL interpretations have an ill-defined class membership relationship and thus this layering of OWL is paradoxical.

5 Solutions for Layering OWL on Top of RDF(S)

Given that the most attractive layering solution leads to semantic paradoxes, what can be done? One approach would be to change RDF or RDF Schema in some way, perhaps by removing some of the parts of RDF Schema that participate in the paradoxes. However, if we want to keep all of RDF and RDF Schema, it is necessary to pick one of the other solutions. The intent of this paper, however, is not to actually do the picking. Instead, this paper is concerned with laying out the benefits and drawbacks of the various solutions so that an informed decision can be made between them.

5.1 Limiting Entailment

One way of keeping the same-syntax extension relationship between RDF Schema and OWL would be to simply give up on the entailments that require the presence of the problematic restrictions in all interpretations. This would, however, result in some rather strange consequences.

For example, if John belonged to Student and Employee it would not follow that John belonged to the intersection of Student and Employee, because this intersection would not necessarily exist in all the required interpretations.

5.2 Syntactic and Semantic Extension

In the syntactic and semantic extension layering proposal, OWL defines new syntactic constructs that do not exist in RDF or RDF Schema. However, the syntactic constructs of RDF are all valid syntactic constructs of OWL, and have the same meaning in OWL as they had in RDF and RDF Schema, or an extension of that meaning. (Even the RDF constructs that are not addressed by OWL, such as reification, remain as valid OWL syntax.) The new syntactic constructs of OWL are given meanings that are compatible with the RDF and RDF Schema meaning of related RDF constructs.

The natural way of defining OWL in this layering proposal is to make the restrictions of OWL be new syntax. These restrictions would have a separate meaning defined by the OWL model theory. For example, a possible syntax for a maximum cardinality restriction like the one above could be:

```
<owl:cardinality maximum=''0'' property=''friend''>
Person
</owl:cardinality>
```

This syntactic construct would be given its own meaning by the OWL model theory, which would not include its presence as a resource in interpretations. In this way the model theory of OWL would not be subject to the semantic paradox above.

This relationship between RDF(S) and OWL would be the same as the relationship between propositional and modal logics. There are many other examples of this sort of layering between logical and knowledge representation formalisms.

In this proposal for OWL there would still be considerable overlap between RDF and RDF Schema, on one hand, and OWL on the other. OWL would still have classes and properties, and would have all the RDF Schema classes, like rdfs:Class and rdfs:-Resource. It is just that restrictions would not be classes. An OWL system would be able to process RDF(S) documents, and would give them a meaning that was compatible with the meaning given to them by an RDF(S) system. An OWL document would generally include three portions: an RDF(S) portion that set up base facts and typing relationships, such as John's friend is Mary and John is a Person; an RDF(S) portion that creates classes and gives some relationships between them, such as Student and Person are classes and Student is an rdfs:subClassOf Person; and an OWL-only portion that gives meaning to some of the classes, such as Student is defined to be those Persons who are enrolled in a School.

An OWL document would thus not be completely parseable by RDF(S) parsers. However, many OWL documents would include significant RDF(S) content and an RDF(S) system that was prepared to ignore the OWL constructs could still extract considerable information from an OWL document. For example, an RDF(S) system would have access to all base-level facts, the classes, and their subclass relationships, which would all still be in RDF(S) form.

In this proposed layering, the Semantic Web tower would be considered as a tower of more-and-more powerful logical languages, all sharing a common semantic core. Higher languages would be have more syntactic constructs and would extend the meaning for constructs from lower languages, but would be compatible with the meanings that come from the lower languages. Systems built for the lower languages could be considered sound but incomplete reasoners for the higher languages, only on the syntax of the lower language if they did not allow for unknown constructs, but if they allowed for unknown constructs they would be incomplete reasoners for the higher languages.

Nevertheless, this layering view has some problems. RDF(S) is not just about base facts, but also includes a theory of classes and properties. These classes and properties are resources and thus can participate in base-level facts. This is not a problem in RDF(S) because of its limited expressive power, but can cause problems in more-expressive languages, like OWL. For example, OWL could end up having to deal with transitive properties that are transitive only because they are the value of a property in some resource. Even worse, this transitivity could be conditional because the property might or might not be the value, depending on some other information.

For example, if John is a Person whose friends are all transitive properties, and John has a friend that is either bar or baz, then either bar or baz is a transitive property. This conditional transitivity can give rise to extraordinarily-complex and difficult patterns of reasoning.

5.3 Same Syntax, But Diverging Semantics

In the same-syntax but diverging semantics layering proposal OWL has the same syntax (or maybe a subset of RDF syntax) but does not abide by (all of) the RDF(S) meaning.

This may seem rather strange at first glance. After all, shouldn't the Semantic Web retain meaning from lower languages. However, the Semantic Web does not do this at the lowest levels, as it ignores the meaning provided by XML in favor of a different RDF meaning for documents.

One way to rationalize this form is layering is to view RDF(S) as a means for reasoning about the syntax of an ontology. RDF would make distinctions based on the form of the ontology constructs, for example the order of conjuncts in a conjunction, or whether two classes are explicitly stated to be disjoint as opposed to having disjointness inferred from their properties. On the other hand, OWL would be solely interested with the logical consequences of ontology constructs and would not have any access to their form. In this view RDF would not be viewed as a basic ontology language but instead as a syntactic mechanism for defining ontology languages.

In support of this view, RDF(S) has many strange features considered as an ontology language, including reification, syntactic containers, and the heory of RDF Schema classes and properties. These features may only make sense if you use RDF(S) as a mechanism for defining ontology languages.

For example, it may make sense to distinguish at some level between the definition of

- a relation r as an attribute of a class c versus
- as a global property r with c as its domain.

Logically these two are the same but from a modeling point of view they are quite different. By having two types of entailments we can capture this without running into any problems. With syntactical RDF(S) reasoning we can ask for different syntactical styles of an ontology and with semantical OWL reasoning we infer logical consequences of an ontology.

This layering relationship allows us to deal with different modeling paradigms. We would define a frame syntax for OWL in RDF(S), making sure that it behaves the same as the non-frame version at the logical level but behaves different at the syntactical level, i.e., in the frame version you could ask whether something is explicitly defined as an attribute or as a property. This layer allows us to capture, infer, and query modeling information, as opposed to logical information.

So, although this layering proposal goes against the logical-extension view of the Semantic Web, it does have its own benefits.

5.4 Diverging Syntax and Diverging Semantics

One problem with the above approach is that RDF is a terrible syntax for complex constructs. As everything is RDF is a triple, if OWL has the same syntax as RDF, all OWL syntax has to be encoded as one or more triples.

This is not a severe problem if an OWL syntactical construct can indeed be encoded as one triple. However, most OWL syntactical constructs are more complicated. For example, the cardinality constructs used above have four components, and have to be encoded as four triples. Encoding a syntactical construct as more than one RDF(S) triple results in several severe problems.

First, the triples are not connected. An RDF(S) document could be missing some of the triples. If so, what syntactical construct is being encoded? For example, a cardinality restriction might be missing the property. Second, there is no way in RDF(S) to require that only the appropriate triples are present. For example, a cardinality restriction might have extra, random triples attached to it, such as saying that a cardinality restriction has a friend. Even worse, a cardinality restriction might have two properties or two numbers. What is being said here? So it might be useful to diverge from the RDF(S) semantics even when extended the syntax, because adhering to the semantics causes computational difficulties.

What then remains of the Semantic Web tower? Well, one could say that RDF(S) really should have been just about triples, and that the class and property theory embedded in RDF Schema is not useful. This would then result in an extension of this base-triple portion of RDF, and not a total breakdown of the Semantic Web tower.

In this layering view, OWL takes the useful portion of RDF syntax and semantics, and replaces the rest (both syntax and semantics) with a syntax and semantics that works for the ontology layer.

6   Conclusions

The biggest problem with the layering of OWL on top of RDF(S) comes not from any particular aspect of RDF(S) itself but instead from a vision of the developers and users of RDF(S). In this vision RDF encompasses the whole of the semantic web—all information in the semantic web is written in RDF syntax and the basic meaning of all this information is provided by RDF. The higher layers of the semantic web serve to provide extra meaning for the information that goes beyond the scope of RDF, but they are not free to either extend the syntax of RDF nor are they free to modify the basic meaning provided by RDF.

RDFS is an example of such an extension. RDFS uses the same syntax as RDF and extends the meaning of some constructs but retains their RDF meaning. However, RDFS is a very small extension of RDF. More significant extensions to RDF(S) require either an extension to the syntax of RDF or some deviation from the semantics of RDF(S). Perhaps the main lesson to be learned here is that a representation formalism should not claim the entire universe, always leaving open the possibility that extensions to it will need their own ways of stating information or their own ways of providing meaning for the information they state.

Figuring out the proper principles for building up the semantic web language tower will require more work and recalls earlier approaches in knowledge representation [5,4] and knowledge modeling [14]. This work should prevent the language tower of the semantic web from ending up like the famous tower of Babel.

In this paper we took the first steps into the direction of a blue print for the semantic web language tower. We were focusing on how to build the fundament for OWL, which is the first floor of the ontology-enabled web. We explained some problems that occur when naïvely building OWL on top of RDF and we described three possible strategies to overcome the problem. Instead of prefering one solution we describe the solution space with various choices and their pros and cons. It will be up to the Web Ontology (Web-

Ont) Working Group of the Semantic Web Activity of the W3C, the recommendation organization of the World Wide Web, to determine the actual strategy to use in OWL.

Acknowledgement

This work was done in the context of the Web Ontology (WebOnt) Working Group (http://www.w3c.org/2001/sw/WebOnt) of the W3C.

References

1. Art Barstow and Dave Beckett. RDF test cases. W3C Working Draft, 15 November 2001, http://www.w3.org/TR/rdf-testcases/.
2. Dave Beckett. RDF/XML syntax specification (revised). W3C Working Draft, 18 December 2001, http://www.w3.org/TR/rdf-syntax-grammar/.
3. Tim Berners-Lee, James Hendler, and Ora Lassila. The semantic web. *Scientific American*, May 2001.
4. R. J. Brachman. The myth of the one true logic. *Computer Intelligence*, 3(3), August 1987.
5. Ronald J. Brachman. What ISA is and isn't: An analysis of taxonomic links in semantic networks. *IEEE Computer*, 16(10):30–36, October 1983.
6. J. Broekstra, M. Klein, S. Decker, D. Fensel, F. van Harmelen, and I. Horrocks. Enabling knowledge representation on the web by extending RDF schema. *Electronic Transactions on Artificial Intelligence (ETAI)*, to appear.
7. Resource description framework (RDF) schema specification 1.0. W3C Candidate Recommendation, 27 March 2000, http://www.w3.org/TR/rdf-schema, March 2000.
8. Stefan Decker, Frank van Harmelen, J. Broekstra, M. Erdmann, Dieter Fensel, Ian Horrocks, M. Klein, and S. Melnik. The semantic web - on the respective roles of XML and RDF. *IEEE Internet Computing*, 2000.
9. D. Fensel and M. Musen. Special issue on semantic web technology. *IEEE Intelligent Systems (IEEE IS)*, 16(2), 2001.
10. Dieter Fensel, James Hendler, Henry Lieberman, and W. Wahlster, editors. *Semantic Web Technology*. MIT Press, Boston, 2002.
11. Dieter Fensel, Ian Horrocks, Frank van Harmelen, Stefan Decker, M. Erdmann, , and M. Klein. OIL in a nutshell. In R. Dieng et al., editor, *Knowledge Acquisition, Modeling, and Management, Proceedings of the European Knowledge Acquisition Conference (EKAW-2000)*, Lecture Notes in Artificial Intelligence, LNAI 1937. Springer-Verlag, October 2000.
12. Dieter Fensel, Ian Horrocks, Frank van Harmelen, Deborah L. McGuinness, and Peter F. Patel-Schneider. OIL: An ontology infrastructure for the semantic web. *IEEE Intelligent Systems*, 16(2), May 2001.
13. Patrick Hayes. RDF model theory. W3C Working Draft, http://www.w3.org/TR/rdf-mt/, 2001.
14. Allen Newell. The knowledge level. *AI Magazine*, 2(2):1–20, Summer 1981. The Presidential Address, AAAI-80, Stanford, California.
15. Resource description framework (RDF): Model and syntax specification. W3C Recommendation, 22 February 1999, http://www.w3.org/TR/1999/REC-rdf-syntax-19990222/, February 1999.

Notions of Indistinguishability
for Semantic Web Languages*

Jaap Kamps and Maarten Marx

Language and Inference Technology Group, ILLC, Universiteit van Amsterdam
{kamps,marx}@science.uva.nl

Abstract. The paper reviews the notions of expressiveness of description logics from (N. Kurtonina and M. de Rijke. Expressiveness of concept expressions in first-order description logics. *Artificial Intelligence*, 107:303–333, 1999) and exemplifies their use in the development in Semantic Web languages. The notion of bisimulation—which characterizes the description logic $\mathcal{ALC}$—provides a direct link to what's in the field of sociology called social network analysis. The perspective on data in this field—data are represented as labeled graphs—fits exactly the modeling intuitions of web languages like OIL and DAML+OIL. This is exemplified in the study of trophic networks. A further connection is established between web languages and hybrid logic, and an extension of OIL with a limited form of self reference is proposed.

1 Introduction

This paper describes foundational work which we hope benefits the further development of Semantic Web languages. The design of these languages is difficult because of the numerous imposed constraints and desires. In several cases, these pull in opposite directions. For instance, the desire to have great expressive power goes against the constraint of having reasonable inference support.

At present it looks like the eventual web language will be strongly based on description logic (as the languages[1] OIL and DAML+OIL are). Description logic provides a logical basis to the well known traditions of frame-based systems, semantic networks and KL-ONE like languages, semantic data models and type systems. Complexity issues for subsumption and consistency problems have been studied extensively (cf. the review article [7]). Relatively few papers study the expressiveness of description languages [3,4,6,12].

Here we review the results from [12] from a modeling perspective. These results can be summarized as follows. Given a domain of individuals and a set of relations and atomic concepts, a structural notion of indistinguishability between individuals is defined for a large number of languages[2] within the description logic family. This notion is such that on finite domains two individuals are

---

* This research was supported by the Netherlands Organization for Scientific Research (NWO, grants # 4000-20-036 and #612-000-106.)

[1] We refer to the version of OIL described in [8] and the DAML+OIL specification from www.daml.org/2001/03/daml+oil-index.

[2] To be precise, for all languages in the lattice between $\mathcal{FL}^-$ and $\mathcal{ALCNR}$.

I. Horrocks and J. Hendler (Eds.): ISWC 2002, LNCS 2342, pp. 30–38, 2002.
ⓒ Springer-Verlag Berlin Heidelberg 2002

structurally indistinguishable if and only if no concept defined in the corresponding description language can separate them. The structural notion thus provides a semantic definition of the maximum granularity of the concepts which can be defined in a certain description logic.

We exemplify the use of this semantic-syntactic interface from two different directions. First we link the languages proposed for the Semantic Web to the field within sociology called social network analysis. With the help of the semantic-syntactic interface we are able to discover some surprisingly strong connections and similarities. Then we find a simple extension of the description logic $\mathcal{ALC}$, known as "hybrid logic" which arguably has maximum first order expressive power for Semantic Web languages.

2   Semantic Web and Social Network Analysis

In this section, we link the languages proposed for the Semantic Web to the field within sociology called social network analysis.

In social network analysis, real world data are modeled as a (labeled) graph, called a *network*. The range of applications of this modeling technique is virtually unlimited. The nodes could be published papers with vertices from paper A to paper B if A cites B [13]. Or the nodes could be web pages and the vertices denoting links between pages [11]. Another example is WordNet, in which the nodes are synsets and the vertices denote overlap [10]. In more traditional sociological or anthropological examples, the nodes are often individuals (humans, animals, animal species, organizations) and the vertices —called *ties*—indicate certain interactions (parent-of, is-friend-of, eats, is-competitor-of, etc.), cf., [17], the *Social Networks* journal, the Proceedings of the Sunbelt conferences, or the page http://www.heinz.cmu.edu/project/INSNA/.

The key idea behind this way of modeling data—and now we come to the link with web-languages—is that structure in the data can be discovered by inspecting the structure of the network. The assumption is that a *position* in the network is structurally determined: that is, only by its links to other elements in the network. A position in a network is most naturally thought of as a subset of its nodes. For instance, in an organization chart (organigram) of an organization (where the nodes are individuals and the vertices denote the hierarchical structure) typical positions are the CEO, the managerial level, the support staff, the technical core and the workforce. In such a chart, two individuals occupy the same (e.g., managerial) position, not because they have ties to and from the same individuals, but because they have ties to and from individuals *in the same position*. Formally,

(∗)   two individuals occupy the same position in a network if they have similar ties to and from individuals in the same position.[3]

The view of a position as a subset of individuals in a network of relations is exactly the same as the semantic meaning of a concept in the web languages OIL

---

[1] In social network jargon, this means that they are regular equivalent.

and DAML+OIL. As the logicians and computer scientists might have remarked, (*) is nothing but the definition of bisimilarity (disregarding atomic properties in (*)):

> For $(N, R_1, \ldots, R_k)$ a labeled graph, we say that nodes $a, b \in N$ are bisimilar (notation: aBb) if
>
>   (1). aR_ic implies the existence of a $c' \in N$ such that bR_ic' and cBc';
>
> (**)   (2). cR_ia implies the existence of a $c' \in N$ such that $c'R_ib$ and cBc'.
>
> If the graph also contains a set of unary properties $P_1, \ldots, P_m$ it is also required that
>
>   (0). P_ia holds if and only if P_ib holds.

Now logic, in particular the work of Kurtonina and de Rijke [12], comes in to create the strong connection with the semantic web languages. They have extended the work of Hennesy–Milner and van Benthem on the connection between bisimilarity and modal logic to the hierarchy of description logics between $\mathcal{FL}^-$ and $\mathcal{ALCNR}$. These languages are the logical basis behind OIL and DAML+OIL and several weaker frame–based languages. The strength of these results lies in the fact that they relate the purely semantic notion of "the sameness" or "indistinguishability" to the purely syntactic notion of being definable in a certain language. The surprising and remarkable thing now is that the core language[4] behind OIL, the description logic $\mathcal{ALCI}$ ($\mathcal{ALC}$ with inverse roles), is *exactly* the right language to describe positions—as defined semantically in (*) and (**)—in a network. This strong claim is based on the following facts:[5]

(1)   If two elements occupy the same position in a network, they cannot be distinguished by an $\mathcal{ALCI}$ concept.

(2)   In finite networks, two elements which occupy different positions in a network, can be distinguished by an $\mathcal{ALCI}$ concept.

Moreover the language $\mathcal{ALCI}$ is, at least for first order definable concepts, complete:

(3)   Every position which is first order definable is definable by an $\mathcal{ALCI}$ concept.

---

[4] The description logic $\mathcal{ALCI}$ corresponds to the following OIL fragment:

- all OIL **class-expressions** are permitted except those which have **slot-constraints** with cardinality restrictions.
- all components of OIL **slot-def**'s are permitted except **subslot-of** and **properties** (this last component is used to specify transitivity or symmetry of a slot).

[5] These facts are just the translation to the terminology of the present paper of the well known characterization theorem of modal logic, cf., [12].

We view this as strong support for the claim that web languages like OIL and DAML+OIL are well designed. We find this support especially promising because the range of applications of the two fields shows such a clear and vast overlap.

Indistinguishability notions like bisimulation provide an upper bound on the grain-size of the definable concepts: bisimilar individuals are not distinguished. Results of the form (1) and (3) are then very useful: (1) says that individuals which are indistinguishable with a certain grain-size cannot but be classified in the same way if a certain language is used. This is a safety criterion: you cannot differentiate in the language what should be considered the same. (3) states the reassuring fact that all concepts with a certain grain-size can be defined in a certain language.

A recent study in the field of ecological network analysis [9] uses the notion of a position as defined in (*) to derive a foodweb from a data set.[6] A foodweb or trophic network describes the energy flow between species (in particular who eats who). Of interest for the Semantic Web community is the data-mining perspective. In [9] a foodweb is constructed from a set of noisy data using existing software.[7] A semantic network containing four distinct classes is found, here reproduced in Figure 1.

Each class consists of a (often huge) number of species. The arrows indicate who is eaten by who. Now obviously this ontology can be described in a web language. The description of it in OIL is given in the same Figure. To get an impression of the contents of the concepts, the top predators contain e.g., screech owls, boa snakes and parasitic insects, the intermediate consumers contain specialist herbivores and detritivores such as decomposers and various insects, the basals contain primarily generalist omnivores such as insects, spiders and birds, and the primary producers contain plants, algae, nectar, dead wood and detritus.

3   Delimiting the Design Space, a Case for Hybrid Logic

Within the literature of social network analysis one can also find (semantic) definitions of positions which differ from the one in (*). (Again these can be tightly linked to concept-definition languages, using the technique of [12].) They all agree on the following principle though:

(#)   a position is determined by the properties of its elements and their ties to other elements in the network. In particular, elements in the network which cannot be reached by a path of ties (in forward or backward direction) are irrelevant.

For instance, to describe positions in an organization *only* the organizational members occurring in the organizational chart are relevant. We note that this

---

[6] The data consisted of 156 compartments, each consisting of various levels of species aggregations (compartments could have from 1 up to 429 different species). The relations between the compartments were obtained by direct observation and from the literature.

[7] The REGE algorithm, incorporated in the package UCINET V, has been used [15].

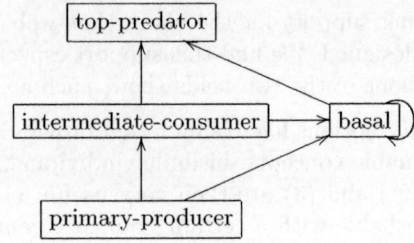

slot-def *eats*
    inverse *is-eaten-by*

class-def defined primary-producer
    subclass-of species
    slot-constraint *eats*
        value-type ⊥
    slot-constraint *is-eaten-by*
        value-type intermediate-consumer **OR** basal

class-def defined intermediate-consumer
    subclass-of species
    slot-constraint *eats*
        value-type primary-producer
    slot-constraint *is-eaten-by*
        value-type top-predator **OR** basal

class-def defined basal
    subclass-of species
    slot-constraint *eats*
        value-type primary-producer **OR** basal **OR** intermediate-consumer
    slot-constraint *is-eaten-by*
        value-type top-predator **OR** basal

class-def defined top-predator
    subclass-of species
    slot-constraint *eats*
        value-type basal **OR** intermediate-consumer
    slot-constraint *is-eaten-by*
        value-type ⊥

disjoint-with top-predator, basal, intermediate-consumer, primary-producer

Fig. 1. A foodweb from [9] and its description in OIL.

principle is also behind description logic[8] and OIL. Principle (#) implies that first order logic is too expressive as a position definition language. For, consider the two models (or networks) below. Here elements are indicated by points and the relation (named R) by the arrow. Element x is related to y (notation: Rxy) if there is an arrow from x to y. According to principle (#), the element a should occupy the same position in both networks. but the formula $\exists y(\neg Rxy \land x \neq y)$ distinguishes them.

There exists a sub language of first order logic which exactly captures this principle and which is very close to the description logic $\mathcal{ALC}$. It is called *hybrid logic*[9]. It extends $\mathcal{ALC}$ with a mechanism for naming and referring to individuals as follows: a new set of primitive concepts, called nominals[10], are introduced. These nominals can be bound by a binder $\downarrow$. So if C is a concept and w a nominal, then also $\downarrow w.C$ is a concept. The meaning of $\downarrow w.C$ consists of all elements d which form the interpretation of C under the assumption that all occurrences of w in C denote the set $\{d\}$. For instance, in a domain of web pages, the concept $\downarrow w.\exists\, \mathtt{has\_link}\, w$ denotes all pages with a link to themselves; the concept $\downarrow w.\forall\, \mathtt{has\_link}\, \exists\, \mathtt{has\_link}\, w$ denotes all pages d which only link to pages which have a link back to d.

The $\downarrow$ binder provides self-reference not available in OIL and DAML+OIL. This feature can be useful when the graph like nature of the network is important; e.g., in the network of papers with citation ties from [13] it is important to separate the self-citations (a citation to a paper with the same author). We give further examples in the next section.

The principle that non-reachable elements should not contribute to the meaning of concepts should in our opinion also be behind semantic web languages. We note again that this principle is already endorsed by description logic and OIL and DAML+OIL. A result from [2] then sets a frontier to these languages:

(##)   each first order semantic web language should be a fragment of hybrid logic.

This bold claim is based on a semantic characterization of hybrid logic similar to the ones described in the previous section ([2], Theorem 3.11). It says that a concept whose meaning is not affected by non–reachable elements is first order definable if and only if it is definable in the hybrid language.

---

[8] In technical terms: DL is preserved under generated submodels. This means that if in a DL model an individual d belongs to some DL concept C, it still belongs to C if all individuals which are not reachable by a path of (forward and backward) slot relations from d are removed from the model.

[9] Cf. the hybrid logic page: www.hylo.net.

[10] Nominals are closely related to the **ONE-OF** constructor: the interpretation in a model of **ONE-OF**$\{d\}$, for d a name of an element in the model, is the singleton set $\{d\}$. The interpretation of a nominal is always a singleton set.

The close connection between hybrid logic and description logic is described in [1]. The formal properties of hybrid logic are well investigated, cf. for instance [2]. The full language is undecidable but [14] contains a useful decidable fragment, called $\mathcal{ALCI}\text{self}^{\exists}$, which extends $\mathcal{ALCI}$ with a form of self-reference. The next section exemplifies this.

4   A Self Referential Web Language

In this section we discuss an extension of OIL which allows for self reference in concept definitions. This extension is based on the hybrid logic discussed in the previous section, but presented here in a limited decidable format. Instead of using variables, we decided to use the pronouns "I" and "me". This example is an indication that the discussed semantic constraints are very useful in guiding the search for and design of future web languages.

The example is discussed in the pseudo-XML syntax of OIL. The following constructions are added to the language:

- ME is a predefined class name;
- within each class-definition the component

I.slot-constraint *relation*

followed by any of the OIL fields **has-value, value-type** or any of the cardinality restrictions, may occur, for any slotname *relation*.

As an example consider the class of narcissist web pages: web pages which have a link to themselves:

class-def defined narcissist-webpage
    subclass-of webpage
    I. **slot-constraint** *has-link*
        has-value ME

The semantics of I and ME is exactly the same as that of $\downarrow x$ and x, respectively. So an element d is in the interpretation of slot constraint I.ϕ, if d is in the interpretation of ϕ assuming that every occurrence of ME in ϕ denotes $\{d\}$.

The second example comes from a paper describing the annotation of photographs using semantic web languages [16]. One of the concepts defined there is a "monkey scratching his head". This concept can be defined in the extension of OIL as

class-def defined head-scratching-monkey
    subclass-of monkey
    I. **slot-constraint** *scratch*
        has-value head **AND**
            slot-constraint *part-of*
                has-value ME

Such definitions are not possible[11] in OIL or DAML+OIL without the use of I and ME. One of the examples in [16] describes a user who wants to find a picture of a monkey doing something with its head. In OIL this query can be represented as

subclass-of monkey
I. **slot-constraint** *action*
      has-value head **AND**
        slot-constraint *part-of*
          has-value ME

With the slot-definition specifying that scratching is an action, this query subsumes the class head-scratching-monkey, which will cause that photographs thus annotated are given as an answer. Without the I, me apparatus, one can only specify that a monkey is scratching some head. The query then cannot be represented in the specific way as it is stated, leading to possibly wrong answers (pictures of monkeys scratching the head of their spouse, for instance).

In [14] this expansion is discussed in more detail, and a tractable version of the language is presented.

5 Wrap Up

We have emphasized the importance of semantic characterizations of Web languages. The characterization of $\mathcal{ALC}$ in terms of bisimulation showed a surprising connection with the field of social network analysis. Web research can learn a lot from this field because its datastructures—networks—are everywhere in Web applications. As an example, Google's successful Pagerank measure goes back to centrality measures in [5].

The second contribution of the paper consists of the connection between hybrid logic and web languages. There are two good reasons to consider hybrid logic as an upper expressivity bound for web languages and as a guide in the design process. Firstly, its extremely simple syntactic structure which is a very intuitive extension of the description logic $\mathcal{ALC}$. Secondly, its semantic characterization as the fragment of first order logic whose truth is unaffected by unreachable elements, a natural semantic invariance for web languages. We illustrated how easy hybrid ideas combine with the web language OIL in an example about photo annotation.

---

[11] Of course a concept own-head can be defined in OIL, which is subsumed by head. But not all of the meaning of own-head is captured in this way. Moreover, all concepts which can be used in self referential expressions then need to be duplicated, and logical relations which could be inferred in the I–me set up have to be explicitly stated as well (e.g., that own-mouth is *part-of* own-head).

References

1. C. Areces. *Logic Engineering*. ILLC–DS–00–8, Institute for Logic, Language and Computation, University of Amsterdam, 2000.
2. C. Areces, P. Blackburn, and M. Marx. Hybrid logics: Characterization, interpolation and complexity. *Journal of Symbolic Logic*, 66(3):977–1010, 2001.
3. F. Baader. A formal definition for the expressive power of terminological knowledge representation languages. *Journal of Logic and Computation*, 7:33–54, 1997.
4. A. Borgida. On the relative expressiveness of description logics and predicate logics. *Artificial Intelligence*, 82:353–367, 1996.
5. R. Burt. *Toward a Structural Theory of Action: Network Models of Social Structure, Perception and Action*. Academic Press, 1982.
6. M. Cadoli, L. Palopoli, and M. Lenzerini. Datalog and description logics: Expressive power. In *Proc. International workshop on Database Programming Languages*, number 1369 in LNCS. Springer, Berlin, 1998.
7. D. Calvanese, G. De Giacomo, D. Nardi, and M. Lenzerini. Reasoning in expressive description logics. In A. Robinson and A. Voronkov, editors, *Handbook of Automated Reasoning*. Elsevier Science Publishers, 1999.
8. S. Bechhofer et. al. An informal description of standard OIL and instance OIL (OIL whitepaper). Available at the OIL page www.ontoknowledge.org/oil/.
9. J. Johnson, S. Borgatti, J. Luczkovich, and M. Everett. Network role analysis in the study of food webs: An application of regular role coloration. *Journal of Social Structure*, 2(3), 2001.
10. J. Kamps and M. Marx. Words with attitude. In *Proceedings of the 1st International Conference on Global WordNet*, pages 332–341. CIIL, Mysore India, 2002.
11. J. Kleinberg and S. Lawrence. The structure of the web. *Science*, 294:1849–1850, 2001.
12. N. Kurtonina and M. de Rijke. Expresiveness of concept expressions in first-order description logics. *Artificial Intelligence*, 107:303–333, 1999.
13. S. Lawrence. Online or invisible. *Nature*, 411(6837):521, 2001.
14. M. Marx. Narcissists, stepmothers and spies. Proceedings of the 2002 International Workshop on Description Logic workshop, Toulouse, 2002.
15. L. Freeman S. Borgatti, M. Everett. *UCINET V. Software for Social Network Analysis*. Natick: Analytic Technologies, 1999.
16. A. Th. Schreiber, B. Dubbeldam, J. Wielemaker, and B. J. Wielinga. Ontology-based photo annotation. *IEEE Intelligent Systems*, pages 2–10, May/June 2001.
17. S. Wassermann and K. Faust. *Social Network Analysis*. Cambridge University Press, Cambridge, UK, 1994.

The Usable Ontology: An Environment for Building and Assessing a Domain Ontology

Michele Missikoff[1], Roberto Navigli[2], and Paola Velardi[2]

[1] IASI-CNR, Viale Manzoni 30, Roma, Italy
missikoff@iasi.rm.cnr.it
[2] Dipartmento di Scienze dell'Informazione,
via Salaria 113, 00198 Roma, Italy
{navigli,velardi}@dsi.uniroma1.it

Abstract. Experience shows that the quality of the stored knowledge determines the success (therefore the effective usage) of an ontology. In fact, an ontology where relevant concepts are absent, or are not conformant to a domain view of a given community, will be scarcely used, or even disregarded. In this paper we present a method and a set of software tools aimed at supporting domain experts in populating a domain ontology and obtaining a shared consensus on its content. "Consensus" is achieved in an implicit and explicit way: implicitly, since candidate concepts are selected among the terms that are frequently and consistently referred in the documents produced by the virtual community of users; explicitly, through the use of a web-based groupware aimed at consensus building.

1 Introduction

The development of the *Semantic Web* [25], aimed at improving the "semantic awareness" of computers connected via the Internet, requires a systematic, computer-oriented representation of the world. Such a world model is often referred to as an ontology. Though the role of ontologies in the Semantic Web solutions is widely recognized, several barriers must be overcome before they become practical and *usable* tools. Once the formal principles and the basic domain concepts have been assessed (a result eventually achieved in many projects), ontology engineers must face the time-consuming and expensive task of populating the ontology and making it accessible to the users of a given virtual community. The absence of powerful tools to support and speed-up this process is a major obstacle to a wide-spread usage of ontologies in web applications. In this paper we present the results of a project aiming at developing a set of integrated methods for semi-automatic learning, verification and maintenance of domain ontologies. Two European projects, *Fetish* [22] and *Harmonise* [23], both in the Tourism domain, provided an application test bed to verify the effectiveness and usability of the proposed methods.

I. Horrocks and J. Hendler (Eds.): ISWC 2002, LNCS 2342, pp. 39–53, 2002.

1.1 The Usable Ontology

Creating ontologies is a difficult process that involves specialists from several fields. Philosophical ontologists and Artificial Intelligence logicists are usually involved in the task of defining the basic kinds and structures of concepts (objects, properties, relations, and axioms) that are applicable in every possible domain. The issue of identifying these very few "basic" principles, referred to as the *top ontology* (TO), is not a purely philosophical one, since there is a clear practical need of a model which has as much generality as possible, to ensure reusability across different domains [13].

Domain modelers and knowledge engineers are involved in the task of identifying the key domain conceptualizations, and describing them according to the organizational *backbones* established by the Top ontology. The result of this effort is referred to as the *upper domain ontology* (UDO), which includes usually a few hundred application-domain concepts.

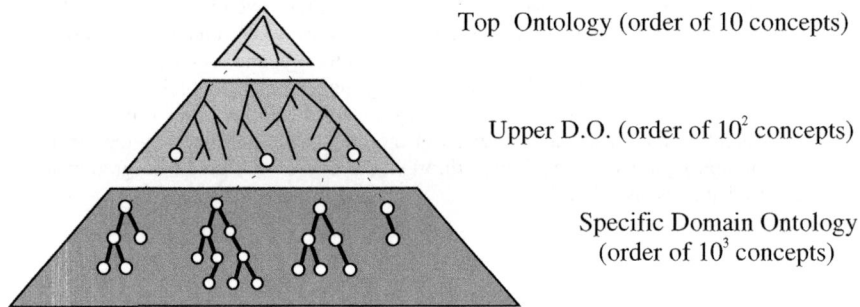

Top Ontology (order of 10 concepts)

Upper D.O. (order of 10^2 concepts)

Specific Domain Ontology
(order of 10^3 concepts)

Fig. 1. The three levels of generality of a Domain Ontology.

While many ontology projects eventually succeed in the task of defining an Upper Domain Ontology[1], populating the third level, that we call the *specific domain ontology* (SDO), is the actual barrier that very few projects could overcome (e.g. Wordnet [3], Cyc [6] and EDR [18]), at the price of inconsistencies and limitations.
It turns out that, although ontologies are recognized as crucial resources for the Semantic Web, in practice they are not available, and when available they are not used outside specific research environments[2].

Which features are mostly needed to build *usable* ontologies?

Coverage: the domain concepts must be there: the SDO must be sufficiently (for the application purposes) populated. Tools are needed to extensively supporting the task of identifying the relevant concepts and the relations among them.
Consensus: decision making is a difficult activity for one person and it gets even harder when there is a group of people that must reach the consensus on a given issue

- -

[1] In fact many ontologies are already available on the Internet including a few hundred more-or-less extensively defined concepts.
[2] For example Wordnet is widely used in the Computational Linguistics research community, but large scale IT applications based on WordNet are not available.

and, in addition, the group is geographically dispersed. When a group of enterprises decide to cooperate in a given domain, they have firstly to agree on many basic issues, i.e., they must reach a <u>consensus</u> of the business domain. Such a common view must be reflected by the domain ontology.

Accessibility: the ontology must be easily <u>accessible</u>: tools are needed to easily integrate the ontology within an application that may clearly demonstrate the advantage of the ontology, e.g., improving the ability to share and exchange information through the web.

In this paper we present a general architecture and a battery of systems to foster the creation of such "usable" ontologies. Consensus is achieved both in an *implicit* and *explicit* way. Implicit, since candidate concepts are selected among the terms that are frequently and consistently referred in the documents produced by the virtual community of users; explicit, through the use of a web-based groupware aimed at consensual construction and maintenance of an ontology. Within this frame, the proposed tools are: *OntoLearn*, for the automatic extraction of domain concepts from the thematic web sites, *ConSys*, for the validation of the extracted concepts, and *SymOntoX*, that is the ontology management system.

1.2 An Ontology Engineering Environment

Hereafter we shortly outline the proposed software environment. The above mentioned systems have been developed and are being tested in the context of two European projects, Fetish [15] and Harmonise [16], where they are used as the basis of a semantic interoperability platform for small and medium-sized enterprises, operating in the tourism domain.

Figure 2 sketchily reports the proposed ontology engineering method, i.e., the sequence of steps and the intermediate output that are produced in building a domain ontology.

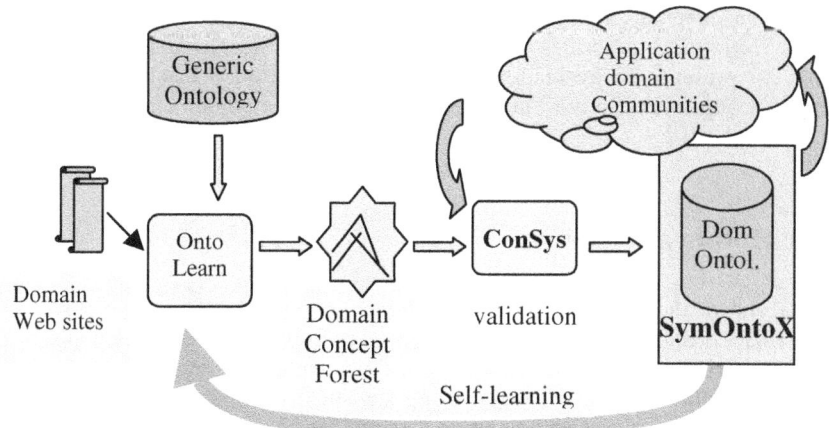

Fig. 2. The Ontology Engineering Chain.

As shown in Figure 2, *ontology engineering* is an iterative process involving machine concept <u>learning</u> (*OntoLearn*), machine-supported concept <u>validation</u> (*Consys*) and <u>ontology management</u> (*SymOntoX*).

OntoLearn explores available documents and related web sites to learn domain concepts, and to detect taxonomic relations among them (*Specific Domain Ontology*). Initially, a generic lexical database (WordNet) is used as a background knowledge.

The subsequent processing step in Figure 2 is *ontology validation*. This is a continuous process supported by a web-based *groupware* aimed at consensus building, called *ConSys* [9]. It is used to achieve a thorough ontology validation with experts and representatives of the communities that are active in the application domain.

ConSys operates in connection with *SymOntoX* [27], an *ontology management* system, used by the ontology engineers to define and maintain the concepts and their mutual connections, thus allowing a semantic net to be constructed. SymOntoX uses a knowledge representation method, referred to as *OPAL* (Object, Process, Actor modeling Language) [10], that is an extension of XML based methods, such as DAML+OIL [19]. The ontology engineers use the environment provided by SymOntoX to attach automatically learned concepts sub-trees under the appropriate nodes of the upper domain ontology, to enrich concepts with additional information, and to perform consistency checks.

Figure 2 shows that in the ontology engineering chain several cycles are necessary: the <u>learning cycle</u> highlights the progressively growing role of the domain ontology as a background knowledge for learning new concepts; the <u>validation cycle</u> highlights the many interactions that are necessary between knowledge engineers and domain experts in order to assess the information represented in the domain ontology.

The main focus of this paper is the description of a tool, *OntoLearn*, aimed at extracting knowledge from electronic documents to support the rapid construction of a domain ontology. A brief account of the *ConSys* system is also provided.

The rest of the presentation is organized as follows: in Section 2 we describe in more detail the OntoLearn system: Section 2.1 describes the method to extract terminology from web sites, Section 2.2 presents the knowledge-based semantic interpretation method, along with a summary of the knowledge representation scheme, Section 2.3 describes the creation of a Specific Domain Ontology, and Section 2.4 presents an evaluation of *OntoLearn*. Section 3 briefly describes the validation groupware, *Consys*. Further research and expected outcomes are discussed in the Conclusion.

2   The OntoLearn System

Figure 3 shows the architecture of the *OntoLearn* system. There are three main phases: First, a domain terminology is <u>extracted</u> from available documents in the application domain (specialized web sites or documents exchanged among members of a virtual community), and <u>filtered</u> using statistical techniques and documents in different domains for contrastive analysis. Second, terms are <u>semantically interpreted</u>, i.e., we associate unambiguous *concept* names to the extracted terms. *Automatic semantic interpretation is a novel aspect of our research, since in the literature the task of associating terms to concepts is a burden of the ontology engineers* [7, 16].

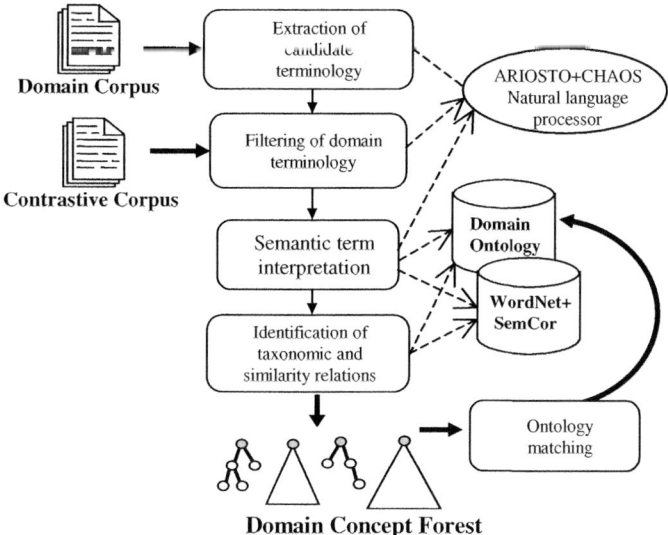

Fig. 3. Architecture of OntoLearn.

Third, taxonomic (i.e., generalization/specialization) and similarity relations among concepts are detected, and a *Specific Domain Ontology* (hereafter SDO) is generated. Ontology matching (i.e., the integration of SDO with the existing upper ontology) is performed in connection with *SymOntoX* and *ConSys*.

Initially, we assume that only a small *domain upper ontology* is available (a realistic assumption indeed), therefore a semantic interpretation is based on external (non domain-specific) knowledge sources, such as *WordNet* [3, 28] and the semantically tagged corpus *SemCor* [26]. WordNet is a large lexical knowledge base (described later in more detail), whose popularity is recently growing even outside the computational linguistic community. SemCor is a corpus of semantically annotated sentences, where every word is annotated with a sense tag, selected within the WordNet sense inventory for that word.

As soon as the ontology engineering and validation processes result in a sufficiently rich *domain ontology*, the role of the latter in automatic concept learning progressively overcomes that of WordNet. Eventually, new terms are semantically disambiguated and taxonomically organized using only the information already stored in the domain ontology.

2.1 Identification of Relevant Domain Terminology

Terminology is often considered as the surface appearance of relevant domain concepts. The objective of this phase is to extract from the available documents a domain terminology. The domain-related documents are retrieved browsing web sites with an initial set of domain terms[3], and then progressively specializing the search when new terms are learned.

---

[3] In our application domain, an initial upper ontology of about 300 terms was available.

We use a linguistic processor, ARIOSTO+CHAOS [1], to extract from the domain documents a list of *syntactically plausible* terminological patterns, e.g., compounds (*credit card*), prepositional phrases (*board of directors*), adjective-noun relations (*manorial house*). Then, two measures based on information theory are used to filter out non-terminological (e.g., *last week*) and non-domain specific terms (e.g., *net income* in a Tourism domain). The first measure, called *Domain Relevance*, computes the conditional probability of occurrence of a candidate term in the application domain (e.g., Tourism), relative to other corpora that we use for a contrastive analysis (e.g., Medicine, Economy, Novels, etc.). The second measure, called *Domain Consensus*, computes the *entropy* of the probability distribution of a term across the documents of the application domain. The underlying idea is that only terms that are *frequently* and *consistently* referred in the available domain documents reflect some <u>*implicit*</u> <u>*consensus*</u> on the use of that term. These two measures have been formally defined and extensively evaluated in [14] and [15].

Let *T* be the terminology extracted after the filtering phase. Using simple string inclusion, we generate a *forest* of *lexicalized trees*. Figure 4 is an example of lexicalized tree ℑ extracted from our Tourism corpus.

However, lexicalized trees do not capture many taxonomic relations between terms, for example between *public transport service* and *bus service* in Figure 4.

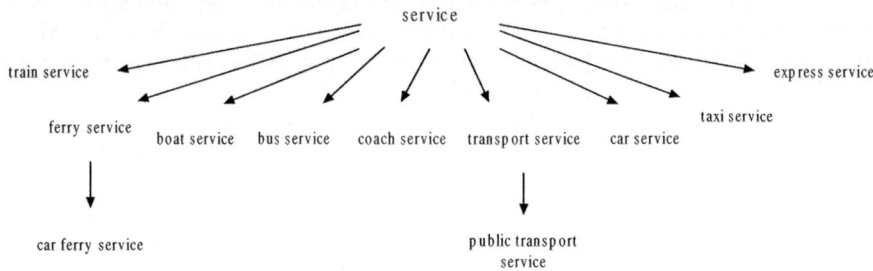

Fig. 4. A lexicalized tree.

2.2 Semantic Interpretation of Terms

The process of *semantic interpretation* is one that associates to each term $t = w_n \cdots w_2 w_1$ (where w_i is an atomic word) the appropriate *concept name*. The idea is that, though the string *t* is usually not included in the start-up ontology, we expect to find a conceptual entry for the various senses of w_i ($i=1, ..., n$): for example, though there are no concepts for "*room service*", we may find concept descriptions for "*room*" and "*service*" individually. Therefore, it should be possible to *compositionally create a definition* for *t*, selecting the *appropriate* (given the context *t*) concept definition for each w_i ($i=1, ..., n$).

As we said, we use WordNet as a start-up ontology, since the upper domain ontology is initially quite poor. In WordNet, a word sense is uniquely identified by a set of terms called *synset* (e.g., for the sense #3 of *transport*: { transportation#4, shipping#1, transport#3 }), and a textual definition called *gloss* (e.g. "*the commercial enterprise of transporting goods and materials*"). Synsets are taxonomically structured in a lattice, with a number of "root" concepts called *topmost* (e.g., { entity#1, something#1 }). WordNet includes over 120,000 words and over 170,000 synsets, with an average ambiguity of 1.4, but very few domain terms are present: for example, *transport* and *company* are individually included, but not "*transport company*" as a unique term.

Formally, a *semantic interpretation* is defined as follows: let $t = w_n \cdots w_2 w_1$ be a valid term belonging to a lexicalized tree $\mathfrak{T}$. The process of semantic interpretation is one that associates to each word w_k in t the appropriate WordNet synset S^k. The *sense* of t is hence defined as:

$$S(t) = \bigcup_k S^k, \; S^k \in Synsets(w_k) \text{ and } w_k \in t.$$

where $Synsets(w_k)$ is the set of synsets each representing a sense of the word w_k.

For instance:

$$S(\text{"transport company"}) = \{ \; \{ \text{ transportation#4, shipping#1, transport#3 } \}, \\ \{ \text{ company#1 } \} \; \}$$

corresponding to sense #1 of *company* ("*an institution created to conduct business*") and sense #3 of *transport*, previously reported.

Semantic interpretation is achieved by intersecting semantic information associated to each alternative sense of the words in t, and then selecting the "best" intersection. Semantic information is extracted from WordNet and represented in the form of a semantic net fragment, according to a representation scheme described in the next sub-section.

2.2.1 Semantic Representation of Concepts

For each sense of a word, several other types of semantic relations are supplied in WordNet, though these relations are not systematically and formally defined. As a first effort, we tried to establish a connection between semantic relations in WordNet and the concept representation method adopted in OPAL.

According to OPAL [10], an ontology is a *semantic net*, constructed by supplying a set of concepts and their semantic relationships. The list of relationships is briefly reported in what follows. In each description, a reference is made to the linguistic counterpart in WordNet, and a graphic symbol is reported. The latter will be used in constructing the diagrams (semantic nets) presented in the next sub-sections.

Generalization – This is an asymmetric relation, often indicated as *ISA* relation, that links a concept to its more general concepts (e.g. Hotel <u>ISA</u> Accomodation).
Its inverse is called *specialization*. In the linguistic realm this relation, defined between *synsets*, is called *hyperonymy* ($\xrightarrow{@}$) and its inverse *hyponymy* ($\xrightarrow{\sim}$).
Aggregation – This is an asymmetric relation that connects a concept representing a whole to another representing a component. It is often indicated as *PartOf* relation (e.g. Reception <u>PartOf</u> Hotel).

Its inverse is called *decomposition*. In the linguistic realm this relation, defined between *synsets*, is called *meronymy* ($\overset{\#}{\rightarrow}$), and *holonymy* ($\overset{\%}{\rightarrow}$) its inverse.

Similarity – This is a symmetric relation that links two concepts that are considered similar in the given domain. A similarity degree is often indicated (e.g. Hotel SimilarTo[0.8] Motel).

In the linguistic realm this relation, defined between *synsets*, is called *synonymy* when the similarity degree is 1^4, while *similarity* ($\overset{\&}{\rightarrow}$) and *correlation* ($\overset{\wedge}{\rightarrow}$) are used to indicate progressively weaker levels of similarity. In WordNet there is also a *dissimilarity* relation, *antonymy* ($\overset{!}{\rightarrow}$), for example *liberal* and *conservative*, indicating a degree of similarity =0. Furthermore, the relation *pertonymy* ($\overset{\backslash}{\rightarrow}$) relates the nominal and adjectival realization of a concept (e.g. *mother* and *maternal*).

Relatedness – This is a semantic relation that connects two concepts symmetrically related in the given domain. This relation assumes specific, domain dependent, interpretations. For example, in: Hotel RelatedTo Airport, the relation subsumes *physical proximity*. This weakly defined relation does not have a counterpart in WordNet, but it can be induced from concept definitions and from semantically annotated sentences in the SemCor corpus. Parsing the definitions (glosses) of a given concept, and the semantically annotated sentences including that concept, we generate a linguistic counterpart of "relatedness", represented by the *gloss* relation ($\overset{gloss}{\rightarrow}$) and the *topic* relation ($\overset{topic}{\rightarrow}$). The idea is that, if a concept c_2 appears in the definition of another concept c_1, or if c_2 appears in the near proximity of c_1 in an annotated sentence including c_1, then c_1 and c_2 are "related", i.e. $c_1 \overset{gloss}{\rightarrow} c_2$ or $c_1 \overset{topic}{\rightarrow} c_2$, respectively. For example, parsing the SemCor sentence: "*The rooms(#1) were very small but they had a nice view(#2)*" produces: *room*#1 $\overset{topic}{\rightarrow}$ *view*#2, while parsing the WordNet gloss for tourist#1 "someone who travels for pleasure" produces : tourist#1 $\overset{gloss}{\rightarrow}$ travel#2. Notice that the labels "gloss" and "topic" only refer to the *source* of the detected relation (SemCor, or WordNet glosses), not to its meaning. The semantic nature of the relation remains underspecified.

2.2.2 Concept Disambiguation

In order to provide a semantic interpretation for a complex term, all its atomic components must be disambiguated, i.e., the correct sense (given the context) for each word must be identified. To disambiguate the words in a term $t = w_n \cdot \ldots \cdot w_2 \cdot w_1$ we proceed as follows:

a) If t is the first analyzed element of $\mathfrak{I}$, manually disambiguate the root node (w_1 if t is a compound) of $\mathfrak{I}$.

---

[4] Strict synonyms are those belonging to the same synset.

b) For any $w_k \in t$ and any synset S_i^k of w_k (the i-th synset that WordNet defines for w_k) create a *semantic net SN*. Semantic nets are automatically created using the semantic relations described in the previous sub-section, extracted from WordNet and SemCor (and possibly from the Upper Domain Ontology).
To reduce the size of a SN, concepts at a distance greater than 3 arcs from the SN center, S_i^k, are not considered. Figure 5a is an example of SN generated for sense #1 of *airplane*.

Let then $SN(S_i^k)$ be the semantic network for sense i of word w_k.

c) Starting from the "head" w_1 of t, and for any pair of words w_{k+1} and w_k ($k=1,\ldots,n-1$) belonging to t, intersect alternative pairs of SNs. Let $I = SN(S_i^{k+1}) \cap SN(S_j^k)$ be one such intersection for sense i of word $k+1$ and sense j of word k. Note that in each step k, the word w_k is already disambiguated, either manually (for $k=1$) or as a result of step k-1.
d) For each alternative intersection, identify common *semantic patterns* in I, and select the sense for w_{k+1} producing the "strongest" intersection[5].
To identify common semantic patterns several heuristic rules are used, e.g.:

$$(1)\ \exists\, G,M \in Synset_{WN} : S_1 \overset{gloss}{\longrightarrow} G \overset{@ \leq 3}{\longrightarrow} M \overset{\leq 3\ @}{\longleftarrow} S_2$$

where $Synset_{WN}$ is the whole set of synsets in WordNet and the heuristic (named "gloss+parallelism") reads: "*given two central concepts S_1 and S_2, there exist two concepts G and M in $SN(S_1) \cap SN(S_2)$ such that G appears in the gloss of S_1 and both G and S_2 reach the concept M through a hyperonymy path of length ≤ 3* ".

Figure 5b is an example of one such intersection for *transport#3* and *company#1*. The bold arrows identify a pattern matching the "gloss+parallelism" heuristics (rule 1 above):

$$transport\#3 \overset{gloss}{\longrightarrow} enterprise\#2 \overset{@\ 1}{\longrightarrow} organization\#1 \overset{2\ @}{\longleftarrow} company\#1.$$

2.3 Creating a Specific Domain Ontology

Initially, all the terms in a tree $\mathfrak{I}$ are independently disambiguated. Subsequently, taxonomic information in WordNet (or in the upper domain ontology) is used to detect *is-a* relations between *concepts*, e.g., $ferry\ service \overset{@}{\longrightarrow} boat\ service.$

---

[5] The algorithm is here oversimplified for sake of space. 11 heuristics are used to identify different semantic paths between SNs, and some amount of backtracking occurs between steps c) and d). Each SN intersection is evaluated by a score vector where each heuristic contributes to one of its component. The "strongest intersection" is given by the maximum score vector.

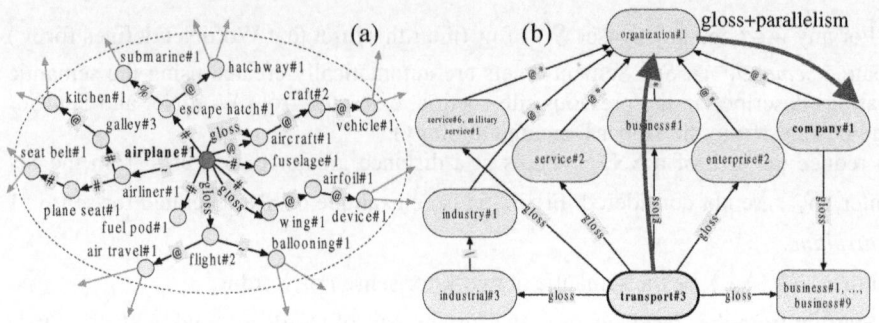

Fig. 5. a) example of semantic net for *airplane#1* b) example of intersecting semantic patterns for *transport#3* and *company#1*.

In this phase, since all the elements in $\mathfrak{S}$ are jointly considered, some interpretation error produced in the previous disambiguation step is corrected. In addition, certain concepts are *fused* in a unique concept on the basis of pertonymy, similarity and synonymy relations (e.g. respectively: *manor house* and *manorial house*, *expert guide* and *skilled guide*, *bus service* and *coach service*). Notice again that we detect semantic relations between *concepts*, not words. For example, *bus#1* and *coach#5* are synonyms, but this relation does not hold for other senses of these two words. Each lexicalized tree $\mathfrak{S}$ is finally transformed in a *domain concept* tree Υ. Figure 6 shows the concept tree obtained from the lexicalized tree of Figure 4.

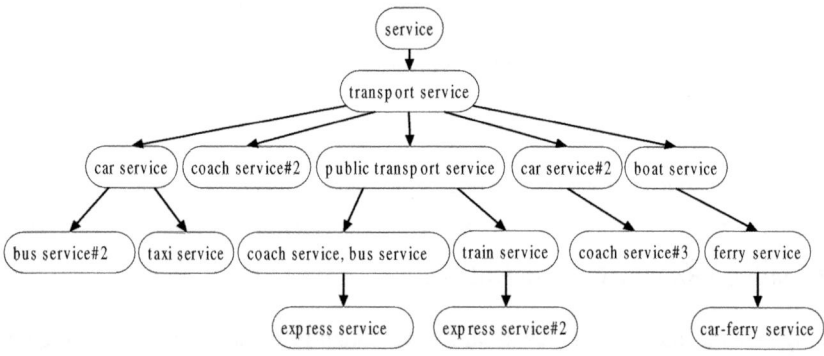

Fig. 6. A Domain Concept Tree.

For clarity, in Figure 6 concepts are labeled with the associated terms (rather than with synsets), and numbers are shown only when more than one semantic interpretation holds for a term, as for *coach service* and *bus service* (e.g., sense #3 of "bus" refers to "old cars" in WordNet).

2.4 Evaluation of the OntoLearn System

OntoLearn is a knowledge extraction system aimed at improving human productivity in the time-consuming task of building a domain ontology. Though a complete field evaluation is still in progress within the Harmonise project using the Consys groupware (see next Section), some crude fact indicates the validity of our method. Our experience in building a tourism ontology for the European project Harmonise reveals that, after one year of ontology engineering activities, the tourism experts were able to release the most general layer of the tourism ontology, comprising about 300 concepts. Then, we decided to speed up the process developing the *OntoLearn* system, aimed at supporting the ontology engineering tasks. This produced a significant acceleration in ontology building, since in the next 6 months[6] the tourism ontology reached 3,000 concepts.

The OntoLearn system has been also evaluated independently from the ontology engineering process. We extracted from a 1 million-word corpus of travel descriptions (downloaded from Tourism web sites) a terminology of 3840 terms, manually evaluated[7] by domain experts participating in the Harmonise project. We obtained a precision ranging from 72.9% to about 80% and a recall of 52.74%. The precision shift is motivated by the well-known fact that the intuition of experts may significantly differ[8]. The recall has been estimated by submitting a list of 6000 syntactic candidates (first step of Section 2.1) to the experts, requiring them to mark truly terminological entries, and then comparing this list with that obtained by our statistical filtering method described in Section 2.1.

The authors personally evaluated the semantic disambiguation algorithm described in Section 2 using a test bed of about 650 extracted terms, which have been manually assigned to the appropriate WordNet concepts. These terms contributed to the creation of 90 syntactic trees. The entire process of semantic disambiguation and creation of domain trees has been evaluated, leading to an overall 84.5% precision. The precision grows to about 89% for highly structured sub-trees, as those in Figure 6. In fact, the phase described in Section 2.3 significantly contributes at eliminating disambiguation errors (in the average, 5% improvement). We also analyzed the individual contribution of each of the heuristics mentioned in Section 2.2.2 to the performance of the method, but a detailed performance report is omitted here for sake of space. The results of this performance analysis led to a refinement of the algorithm and the elimination of one heuristic.

3. Creating a "Consensus": The ConSys System

As we mentioned in the previous sub-section, a full evaluation of the Tourism ontology, called *OntoTour*, is still in progress. A specific groupware has been conceived to facilitate decision-making and the creation of consensus about the

---

[6] The time span includes also the effort needed to test and tune OntoLearn. Manual verification of automatically acquired domain concepts actually required few days.

[7] Here manual evaluation is simply deciding whether an extracted term is relevant, or not, for the tourism domain.

[8] This very fact stresses the need of a consensus building groupware, as Consys.

content of the ontology. The system, called *ConSys*, is briefly described in this section. More details are given in [9].

Group decision-making is a very difficult activity. Difficulties even increase if the participants do not meet face-to-face, but are geographically dispersed and work mainly asynchronously, communicating via the Internet.

ConSys aims at supporting the group of domain experts in the discussion and decision-making process required by ontology building. Essentially, *ConSys* creates a virtual space where the members of the decision group can meet and interact. The main characteristics of *ConSys* are:

- Distributed, open environment, accessible via the Internet, by using a web browser;
- Facilitated organizational communication, by means of predefined interaction templates;
- Decision-making support, provided by specific functions and roles;
- Enhanced document management, for consultation during decision-making;
- Group dynamics carefully conceived, drawn from approaches like: MDM (Multi-participant Decision-Making), GDSS (Group Decision Support System), Formal Consensus techniques [2], speech act theory [12];
- Discussion rules enforcement, e.g., message length or frequency.

The group operates in a virtual space organized into four different virtual rooms (See Figure 7), specialized in terms of activities performed therein.

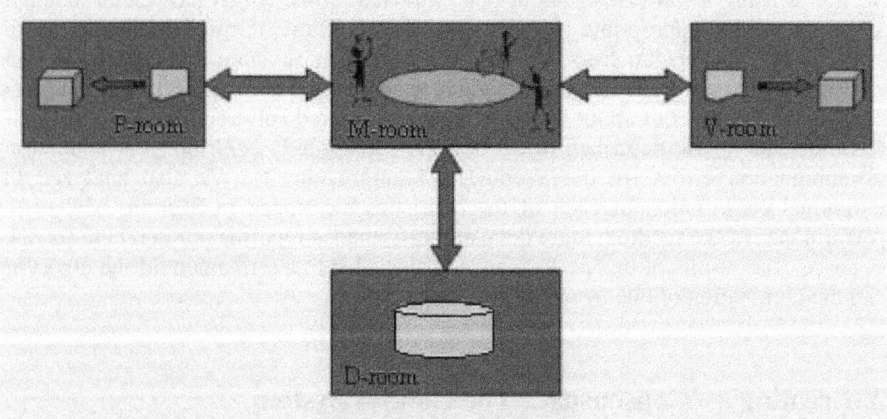

Fig. 7. The rooms of ConSys.

Meeting Room - This is the main room (*M-room*), where the participants meet to debate the issue at hand, express their opinion, make proposals and ask the group to agree. There are precise rules that must be followed by the participants in the M-room. Primarily, they must interact according to a number of predefined *speech acts*, as detailed in [9].

Documentation Room – This is a space (*D-room*) where all the relevant documents are stored and made available to all the group members. To support their positions, members may include documents, referred to as *supporting evidence*[9]. In the *D-room* there are also complete accounts of previous decisions, with records of discussions and related supporting evidence.

Polling Room – This room (*P-room*) is opened when polling is necessary. The result of a poll has an orientation value, therefore its outcome is not mandatory nor binding for the group.

Voting Room – The primary goal of *ConSys* is to facilitate the reaching of a large consensus on the ontology entries. However, if the group gets stalled with two (or more) opposing positions, a voting is required. Then, the participants are asked to enter the *voting room* (*V-room*) to cast their ballot. The result of voting will decide which proposals will be actually included in the ontology.

The construction of an ontology typically starts from a first set of concepts (the Upper Domain Ontology *kernel*) that is generally less controversial and therefore can be approved by the group in a short time. At the same time, it represents a sort of training set for the group, allowing members to progressively know each other, and to get acquainted with the fundamental mechanisms that regulate the group activities. Starting with a least controversial matter is very useful, since initially problems mainly emerge from misunderstandings, unclear statements, involuntary violation of the rules. Therefore, in the first phase, the controversy will be more formal than substantial.

Once the group has accepted the ontology kernel, the actual ontology validation activity starts. The interactions among participants take place according to a predefined set of *speech acts* [17]. Each member of the decision group must check in at the M-room, then he/she can send memos to the group. A memo is classified according to the speech act that represents the intent of the sender.

Conclusions

In this paper we presented an ontology engineering architecture aimed at facilitating the task of populating domain ontologies and building a shared consensus about their actual content.

The work presented in this paper is novel in several aspects:

- Many methods have been proposed to extract domain terminology or word associations from texts and use this information to build or enrich an ontology. *Terms* however are put in a one-to-one correspondence with domain *concept names*, while we perform a *semantic interpretation*. By doing so, we can automatically determine that, for example, *swimming pool* is a kind of *hotel*

---

[9] For example, the supporting evidence of a concept proposed by OntoLearn is the set of automatically retrieved sentences including its lexical realization (terminology), and its related definition (Section 2.2).

facility, and *bus service* is a kind of *public transportation service*. This has clear implications, for example, in automatic document indexing[10].

- Thanks to semantic interpretation, we are able to detect not only taxonomic, but also other types of relations (e.g., similarity, pertonymy). The amount of extracted semantic relations is being extended in our on-going work, exploiting the information obtained from the intersections of semantic nets SNs (see Figure 5b).
- Though WordNet is not an ontological standard for the Semantic Web, it is *de facto* one of the most widely used general purpose lexical database, as also witnessed by the considerable funding, devoted by the European Community to its extension (for example, the EuroWordNet project [21]). An explicit relation between a domain ontology and WordNet may favour interoperability and harmonization between different ontologies.
- Ontology learning issues have been considered in strict connection with ontology engineering and validation issues. We put a special emphasis on the notion of *consensus*, since an ontology, where the relevant concepts are absent or are not conformant with a domain view of a given community, will be scarcely used, or even disregarded. In our system consensus is achieved both in an implicit and explicit way. Implicit, since the relevant concepts are captured based on their systematic appearance in the documents shared by a virtual community of users. Explicit, since we developed a groupware aimed at the ontology building process.

References

1. Basili R., Pazienza M.T. and Velardi P. *An Empirical Symbolic Approach to Natural Language Processing*, Artificial Intelligence, n. 85, pp.59-99, (1996).
2. Buttler C.T. and Rothstein, A. *A guide to Formal Consensus*. Food not Bombs Publishing, (1987).
3. Fellbaum, C. *WordNet: an electronic lexical database*, Cambridge, MIT press, (1995).
4. Hirst M., St-Onge D. *Lexical chains as representations of context for the detection and correction of malapropisms.* In C. Fellbaum, editor, WordNet: An electronic lexical database and some of its applications. The MIT Press, Cambridge, MA, (1997).
5. Harabagiu S. and Moldovan D. *Enriching the WordNet Taxonomy with Contextual Knowledge Acquired from Text*. AAAI/MIT Press, (1999).
6. Lenat, D.B. *CYC: a large scale investment in knowledge infrastructure*, in Communication of the ACM, vol. 3, N. 11.
7. Maedche A. and Staab S. *Semi-automatic Engineering of Ontologies from Text* Proceedings of the Twelfth International Conference on Software Engineering and Knowledge Engineering (SEKE'2000) (2000).
8. Milhalcea, R. and Moldovan. D. *eXtended WordNet: progress report*. NAACL 2001 Workshop on WordNet and Other Lexical Resources, Pittsbourgh, June (2001).
9. Missikoff M., Wang X.F., *Consys - A Group Decision-Making Support System For Collaborative Ontology Building*, in Proc. of Group Decision & Negotiation 2001 Conference, La Rochelle, France, (2001).

---

[10] Automatic document indexing is an application we are currently looking at, in order to measure the effectiveness of our term extraction and interpretation method.

10. Missikoff M., *OPAL - A Knolwedge-Based Approach for the Analysis of Complex Business Systems*, LEKS, IASI-CNR, Rome, (2000),
11. Morin E., *Automatic Acquisition of semantic relations between terms from technical corpora*, Proc. of 5th International Congress on Terminology and Knowledge extraction, TKE-99, (1999).
12. Searle, J.R and Vanderveken, D. *Foundations of Illocutionary Logics*, Cambridge University Press, (1985).
13. Smith, B. and Welty, C. *Ontology: towards a new synthesis*, Formal Ontology in Information Systems, ACM Press, (2001).
14. Velardi P., Missikoff M. and Basili R. *Identification of relevant terms to support the construction of Domain Ontologies*. ACL-EACL Workshop on Human Language Technologies, Toulouse, France, July (2001).
15. Velardi P., Missikoff and P. Fabriani *Using Text Processing Techniques to Automatically enrich a Domain Ontology*. Proc. of ACM Conf. On Formal Ontologies and Information Systems, ACM_FOIS, Ogunquit, Maine, October (2002).
16. Vossen P. *Extending, Trimming and Fusing WordNet for technical Documents*, NAACL 2001 workshop on WordNet and Other Lexical Resources, Pittsbourgh, July (2001).
17. Winograd, T. *A Language/Action Perspective on the Design of Cooperative Work*, in Computer Supported Cooperative Work: A Book of Readings, I. Greif (ed) Morgan Kauffmann, (1988).
18. Yokoi T. *The EDR electronic dictionary*, Communications of the ACM, vol. 38, N. 11.

Web Sites Citations

19. DAML+OIL http://www.daml.org/2001/03/daml+oil-index
20. ECAI-2000 1st Workshop on *Ontology Learning* http://ol2000.aifb.uni-karlsruhe.de/
21. EuroWordNet http://www.hum.uva.nl/~ewn/
22. Fetish EC project ITS-13015 http://fetish.singladura.com/index.php
23. Harmonise EC project IST-2000-29329 http://dbs.cordis.lu
24. IJCAI-2001 2nd Workshop on *Ontology Learning* http://ol2001.aifb.uni-karlsruhe.de/
25. Semantic Web Community Portal http://www.semanticweb.org/index.html
26. SemCor *The semantic concordance corpus* http://mind.princeton.edu/wordnet/doc/man/semcor.htm
27. SymOntos, a symbolic ontology management system http://www.symontos.org
28. WordNet 1.6 http://www.cogsci.princeton.edu/~wn/w3wn.html

Sesame: A Generic Architecture for Storing and Querying RDF and RDF Schema

Jeen Broekstra[1], Arjohn Kampman[1], and Frank van Harmelen[2]

[1] Aidministrator Nederland b.v., Amersfoort, The Netherlands
{jeen.broekstra, arjohn.kampman}@aidministrator.nl
[2] Faculty of Sciences, Vrije Universiteit, Amsterdam, The Netherlands
frank.van.harmelen@cs.vu.nl

Abstract. RDF and RDF Schema are two W3C standards aimed at enriching the Web with machine-processable semantic data.
We have developed Sesame, an architecture for efficient storage and expressive querying of large quantities of metadata in RDF and RDF Schema. Sesame's design and implementation are independent from any specific storage device. Thus, Sesame can be deployed on top of a variety of storage devices, such as relational databases, triple stores, or object-oriented databases, without having to change the query engine or other functional modules. Sesame offers support for concurrency control, independent export of RDF and RDFS information and a query engine for RQL, a query language for RDF that offers native support for RDF Schema semantics. We present an overview of Sesame as a generic architecture, as well as its implementation and our first experiences with this implementation.

1 Introduction

The Resource Description Framework (RDF) [13] is a W3C Recommendation for the formulation of metadata on the World Wide Web. RDF Schema [4] (RDFS) extends this standard with the means to specify domain vocabulary and object structures. These techniques will enable the enrichment of the Web with machine-processable semantics, thus giving rise to what has been dubbed the Semantic Web.

We have developed Sesame, an architecture for storage and quering of RDF and RDFS information. Sesame is being developed by Aidministrator Nederland b.v.[1] as part of the European IST project On-To-Knowledge[2]. Sesame allows persistent storage of RDF data and schema information, and provides access methods to that information through export and querying modules. It features ways of caching information and offers support for concurrency control.

This paper is organized as follows. In section 2 we give an introduction to RDF and RDFS. Readers who are already familiar with these languages can skip

---

[1] See http://www.aidministrator.nl/

[2] On-To-Knowledge (IST-1999-10132). See http://www.ontoknowledge.org/

I. Horrocks and J. Hendler (Eds.): ISWC 2002, LNCS 2342, pp. 54–68, 2002.

this section. In section 3 we discuss why a query language specifically tailored to RDF and RDFS is needed. In section 4 we look at Sesame's modular architecture in some detail. In section 5 we give an overview of the SAIL API and a brief comparison to other RDF API approaches. Section 6 discusses our experiences with Sesame until now, and section 7 looks into possible future developments. Finally we provide our conclusions in section 8.

2   RDF and RDFS

RDF is a W3C recommendation that was originally designed to standardize the definition and use of metadata-descriptions of Web-based resources. However, RDF is equally well suited for representing arbitrary data, be they metadata or not.

The basic building block in RDF is an subject-predicate-object triple, commonly written as $P(S, O)$. That is, a subject S has an predicate (or property) P with value O. Another way to think of this relationship is as a labeled edge between two nodes: $[S] - P \rightarrow [O]$.

This notation is useful because RDF allows subjects and objects to be interchanged. Thus, any subject from one triple can play the role of a object in another triple, which amounts to chaining two labeled edges in a graphic representation. The graph in figure 1 for example, expresses three statements.

RDF also allows a form of reification in which any RDF statement itself can be the subject or object of a triple. This means graphs can be nested as well as chained. On the Web this allows us, for example, to express doubt or support for statements created by other people.

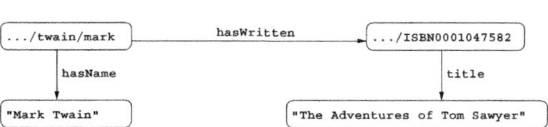

Fig. 1. An example RDF graph.

The RDF Model and Syntax specification also proposes an XML syntax for RDF data models. One possible serialization of the above relations in this syntax looks like this:

```
<rdf:Description rdf:about="http://www.famouswriters.org/twain/mark">
    <s:hasName>Mark Twain</s:hasName>
    <s:hasWritten rdf:resource="http://www.books.org/ISBN0001047582"/>
</rdf:Description>

<rdf:Description rdf:about="http://www.books.org/ISBN0001047582">
    <s:title>The Adventures of Tom Sawyer</s:title>
</rdf:Description>
```

Since the proposed XML syntax allows many alternative ways of writing down information, the above XML syntax is just one of many possibilities of writing down an RDF model in XML.

It is important to note that RDF is designed to provide a basic subject-predicate-object model for Web-data. Other than this intended semantics – described only informally in the standard – RDF makes no data modeling commitments. In particular, no reserved terms are defined for further data modeling.

RDF Schema is a mechanism that lets developers define a particular vocabulary for RDF data (such as the predicate hasWritten) and specify the kinds of objects to which predicates can be applied (such as the class Writer). RDFS does this by pre-specifying some terminology, such as Class, subClassOf and Property, which can then be used in application-specific schemata. RDFS expressions are also valid RDF expressions – in fact, the only difference with 'normal' RDF expressions is that in RDFS an agreement is made on the *semantics* of certain terms and thus on the *interpretation* of certain statements. For example, the subClassOf property allows the developer to specify the hierarchical organization of classes. Objects can be declared to be instances of these classes using the type property. Constraints on the use of properties can be specified using domain and range constructs.

Above the dotted line in figure 2, we see an example RDF schema that defines vocabulary for the RDF example we saw earlier: Book, Writer and FamousWriter are introduced as classes, and hasWritten is introduced as a property. A

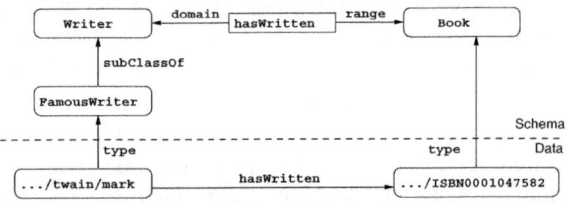

Fig. 2. An example RDF Schema.

specific instance is described below the dotted line, in terms of this vocabulary.

3   The Need for an RDFS Query Language

RDF documents and RDF schemata can be considered at three different levels of abstraction:

1. at the *syntactic level* they are XML documents.[3]
2. at the *structure level* they consist of a set of triples.
3. at the *semantic level* they constitute one or more graphs with partially predefined semantics.

We can query these documents at each of these three levels. We will briefly consider the pros and cons of doing so for each level in the next sections. This will lead us to conclude that RDF(S) documents should really be queried at the semantic level. We will also briefly discuss RQL, a language for querying RDF(S) documents at the semantic level, which has been implemented in the Sesame architecture.

---

[3] Actually, this is not necessarily true; non-XML syntaxes for RDF exist, but XML is the most widely used syntax for RDF.

3.1   Querying at the Syntactic Level

As we have seen in section 2, any RDF model (and therefore any RDF schema) can be written down in XML notation. It would therefore seem reasonable to assume that we can query RDF using an XML query language (for example, XQuery [8]).

However, this approach disregards the fact that RDF is not just an XML notation, but has its own data model that is very different from the XML tree structure. Relationships in the RDF data model that are not apparent from the XML tree structure become very hard to query.

As an example, consider again the XML description of the RDF model in figure 1. In an XML query language such as XQuery [8], expressions to traverse the data structure are tailored towards traversing a node-labeled tree. However, the RDF data model is a graph, not a tree, and moreover, both its edges (properties) and its nodes (subjects/objects) are labeled. In querying at the syntax level, this is literally left as an excercise for the query builder: one cannot query the relation between the resource signifying 'Mark Twain' and the resource signifying 'The Adventures of Tom Sawyer' without knowledge of the syntax that was used to encode the RDF data in XML.

Ideally, we would want to formulate a query like "Give me all the relationships that exist between Mark Twain and The Adventures of Tom Sawyer". However, using only the XML syntax, we are stuck with formulating an awkward query like "Give me all the elements nested in a Description element with an about attribute with value 'http://www.famouswriters.org/twain/mark', of which the value of its resource attribute occurs elsewhere as the about attribute value of a Description element that has a nested element title with the value 'The Adventures of Tom Sawyer'."

Not only is this approach inconvenient, it also disregards the fact that the XML syntax for RDF is not unique: the same RDF graph can be serialized in XML in a variety of ways. This means that one query will never be guaranteed to retrieve all the answers from an RDF model.

3.2   Querying at the Structure Level

When we abstract from the syntax, any RDF document represents a set of triples, each triple representing a statement of the form Subject-Predicate-Object. A number of query languages have been proposed and implemented that regard RDF documents as such a set of triples, and that allow to query such a triple set in various ways.

Look again at the example from figure 2. An RDF query language such as, for example, Squish [14] would allow us to query which resources are known to be of type FamousWriter:

```
SELECT ?x
FROM    somesource
WHERE   (rdf::type ?x FamousWriter)
```

The clear advantage of such a query is that it directly addresses the RDF data model, and that it is therefore independent of the specific syntax that has been chosen to represent the data.

However, a disadvantage of any query language at this level is that it interprets *any* RDF model only as a set of triples, including those elements which have been given a special semantics in RDFS. For example, since .../twain/mark is of type FamousWriter, and since FamousWriter is a subclass of Writer, .../twain/mark is also of type Writer, by virtue of the intended RDFS semantics of type and subClassOf. However, there is no triple that explicitly asserts this fact. As a result, the query

```
SELECT ?x
FROM    somesource
WHERE   (rdf::type ?x Writer)
```

will fail because the query only looks for explicit triples in the store, whereas the triple (/twain/mark, type, Writer) is not explicitly present in the store, but is implied by the semantics of RDFS.

3.3   Querying at the Semantic Level

What is clearly required is the means to query at the *semantic level*, that is, querying the full knowledge that a RDFS description entails and not just the explicitly asserted statements.

There are at least two options to achieve this goal:

1. Compute and store the closure of the given graph as a basis for querying.
2. Let a query processor infer new statements as needed per query.

While the choice of an RDF query language is in principle independent of the choice made in this respect, the fact remains that most RDF query languages have been designed to query a simple triple base, and have no specific functionality or semantics to discriminate between schema and data information.

RQL [12,1] is a proposal for a declarative query language that does explicitly capture these semantics in the language design itself. The language has been initially developed by the Institute of Computer Science at FORTH[4], in Heraklion, Greece, in the context of the European IST project MESMUSES[5]. We will briefly describe the language here; for a detailed description of the language see [12,5].

RQL adopts the syntax of OQL [7], and like OQL, the language is defined by means of a set of core queries, a set of basic filters, and a way to build new queries through functional composition and iterators.

The core queries are the basic building blocks of RQL, which give access to the RDFS specific contents of an RDF triple store. RQL allows queries such as Class (retrieving all classes), Property (retrieving all properties) or Writer (returning all instances of the class with name Writer). This last query returns of course also all

---

[4] See http://www.ics.forth.gr
[5] See http://cweb.inria.fr/Projects/Mesmuses/

instances of subclasses of Writer, since these are also instances of the class Writer, by virtue of the semantics of RDFS. Notice that in RQL, these semantics are defined in the query language itself: the formal query language definition makes a commitment to interpret the semantics of RDFS. This is notably different from an approach like Squish, where the designer/implementer is at liberty to interpret the RDFS entailment using one of the options mentioned earlier, or not at all.

For composing more complex queries, RQL has a select-from-where construction. In the from-clause of such a query, we can specify a *path expression*. These allow us to match patterns along entire paths in RDF/RDFS graphs. For example, the query

```
select Y, $Y
from FamousWriter{X}.hasWritten{Y : $Y}
```

returns all things written by famous writers, and the type of that thing, effectively doing pattern-matching along a path in the graph of figure 2. Notice that RQL path expressions explicitly enable free mixing of data and schema information.

4   Sesame's Architecture

Sesame is an architecture that allows persistent storage of RDF data and schema information and subsequent querying of that information. In section 4.1, we present an overview of Sesame's architecture. In the sections following that, we look in more detail at several components.

4.1   Overview

An overview of Sesame's architecture is shown in Figure 3. In this section we will give a brief overview of the main components.

For persistent storage of RDF data, Sesame needs a scalable repository. A DBMS is an obvious choice here. However, numerous DBMSs exist, each having their own strengths and weaknesses, targeted platforms, and APIs. Also, for each of these DBMSs, the RDF data can be stored in numerous ways.

As we would like to keep Sesame DBMS-independent and it is impossible to know which way of storing the data is best fitted for which DBMS or which application domain, all DBMS-specific code is concentrated in a single architectural layer of Sesame: the *Storage And Inference Layer* (SAIL).

This SAIL is an application programming interface (API) that offers RDF-specific methods to its clients and translates these methods to calls to its specific DBMS. An important advantage of the introduction of a separate layer is that it makes it possible to implement Sesame on top of a wide variety of repositories without changing any of Sesame's other components. Section 5 looks at the API in more detail.

Sesame's functional modules are clients of the SAIL API. Currently, there are three such modules: The *RQL query engine*, the *RDF admin module* and the *RDF export module*. Each of these modules is described in more detail in section 4.2.

Depending on the environment in which it is deployed, different ways to communicate with the Sesame modules may be desirable. For example, communication over HTTP may be preferable in a Web context, but in other contexts protocols such as Remote Method Invocation (RMI) or the Simple Object Access Protocol (SOAP) [3] may be more suited.

In order to allow maximal flexibility, the actual handling of these protocols has been placed outside the scope of the functional modules. Instead, protocol handlers are provided as intermediaries between the modules and their clients, each handling a specific protocol.

The introduction of the SAIL and the protocol handlers makes Sesame into a generic architecture for RDFS storage and querying, rather than just a particular implementation of such a system.

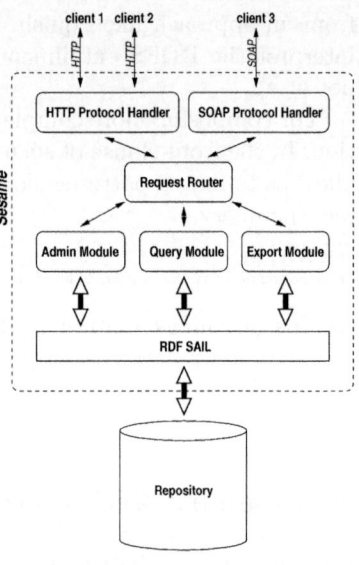

Fig. 3. Sesame's architecture.

Adding additional protocol handlers makes it easy to connect Sesame to different operating environments. The construction of concrete SAIL implementations will be discussed in section 5.

4.2   Sesame's Functional Modules

The RQL Query Module. In Sesame, a version of RQL was implemented that is slightly different from the language proposed by [12]. The Sesame version of RQL features better compliance to W3C specifications, including support for optional domain- and range restrictions as well as multiple domain- and range restrictions. It does, however, not feature support for datatyping as proposed in the original language proposal. See [5] for details.

The Query Module follows the path depicted in figure 4 when handling a query. After parsing the query and building a query tree model for it, this model is fed to the query optimizer which transforms the query model into an equivalent model that will evaluate more efficiently. These optimizations mainly consist of a set of heuristics for query subclause move-around. Notice that these pre-evaluation optimizations are not dependent on either domain or storage method.

The optimized model of the query is subsequently evaluated in a streaming fashion, following the tree structure into which the query has been broken down. Each object represents a basic unit in the original query and evaluates itself, fetching data from the SAIL where needed. The main advantage of this approach is that results can be returned in a streaming fashion, instead of having to build up the entire result set in memory first.

In Sesame, RQL queries are translated (via the object model) into a set of calls to the SAIL. This approach means that the main bulk of the actual evaluation of the RQL query is done in the RQL querying engine itself.

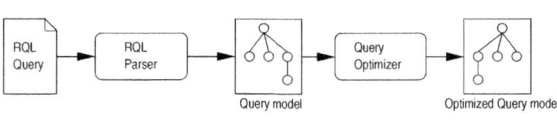

Fig. 4. The RQL parsing and optimization model.

Another approach would be to directly translate as much of the RQL query as possible to a query specific for the underlying repository. An advantage of this approach is that, when using a DBMS, we would get all its sophisticated query evaluation and optimization mechanisms for free. However, a large disadvantage is that the implementation of the query engine is directly dependent on the repository being used, and the architecture would lose the ability to easily switch between repositories.

This design decision is one of the major differences between Sesame and the RDFSuite implementation of RQL by ICS-FORTH (see [1]). The RDF Suite implementation relies on the underlying DBMS for query optimization. However, this dependency means that RDF Suite cannot as easily be transported to run on top of another storage engine.

A natural consequence of our choice to evaluate queries in the SAIL is that we need to devise several optimization techniques in the engine and the SAIL API implementation, since we cannot rely on any given DBMS to do this for us.

The Admin Module. In order to be able to insert RDF data and schema information into a repository, Sesame provides an admin module. The current implementation is rather simple and offers two main functions:

1. incrementally adding RDF data/schema information;
2. clearing a repository.

Partial delete (on a per-statement basis) functionality is not yet available in the current admin module, but support for this feature is under development.

The admin module retrieves its information from an RDF(S) source (usually an online RDF(S) document in XML-serialized form) and parses it using a streaming RDF parser (currently, we use the ARP RDF parser that is part of the Jena toolkit [6]). The parser delivers the information to the admin module on a per-statement basis: (Subject, Predicate, Object). The admin subsequently tries to assert this statement into the repository by communicating with the SAIL and reports back any errors or warnings that might have occurred.

The current implementation makes no explicit use of the transaction-functionality of SAIL yet, but we expect to implement this in the near future.

The RDF Export Module. The RDF Export Module is a very simple module. This module is able to export the contents of a repository formatted in XML-serialized RDF. The idea behind this module is that it supplies a basis for using

Sesame in combination with other RDF tools, as all RDF tools will at least be able to read this format.

Some tools, like ontology editors, only need the schema part of the data. On the other hand, tools that don't support RDFS semantics will probably only need the non-schema part of the data. For these reasons, the RDF Export Module is able to selectively export the schema, the data, or both.

5   The SAIL API

The SAIL API is a set of Java interfaces that has been specifically designed for storage and retrieval of RDFS-based information. The main design principles of SAIL are that the API should:

- define a basic interface for storing RDF and RDFS in, and retrieving and deleting RDF and RDFS from (persistent) repositories.
- abstract from the actual storage mechanism; it should be applicable to RDBMSs, file systems, or in-memory storage, for example.
- be usable on low end hardware like PDAs, but also offer enough freedom for optimizations to handle huge amounts of data efficiently on e.g. enterprise level database clusters.
- be extendable to other RDF-based languages like DAML+OIL [10].

Other proposals for RDF APIs are currently under development. The most prominent of these are the Jena toolkit [6] and the Redland Application Framework [2]. SAIL shares many characteristics with both approaches.

An important difference between these two proposals and SAIL, is that the SAIL API specifically deals with RDFS on the retrieval side: it offers methods for querying class and property subsumption, and domain and range restrictions. In contrast, both Jena and Redland focus exclusively on the RDF triple set, leaving interpretation of these triples as an excercise to the user. In SAIL, these RDFS inferencing tasks are handled internally. The main reason for this is that there is a strong relationship between the efficiency of the inferencing and the actual storage model being used. Since any particulary SAIL implementation has a complete understanding of the storage model (e.g. the database schema in the case of an RDBMS), this knowledge can be exploited to infer, for example, class subsumption more efficiently.

Another difference between SAIL and other RDF APIs is that SAIL is considerably more lightweight: only four basic interfaces are pre-defined, offering basic storage and retrieval functionality and transaction support, but not much beyond that. We feel that in some applications such minimality may be preferable to an API that has more features, but is also more complex to understand and implement.

The current Sesame system offers several implementations of the SAIL API. The most important of these is the SQL92SAIL, which is a generic implementation for SQL92 [11]. The aim is to be able to connect to any RDBMS while having to re-implement as little as possible. In the SQL92SAIL, only the definitions of the datatypes (which are not part of the SQL92 standard) have to be changed when switching to a different database platform. The SQL92SAIL features an inferencing module for RDFS, based on the RDFS entailment rules as specified in the RDF Model Theory [9]. This inferencing module computes the schema closure of the RDFS being uploaded, and asserts these implicates of the schema as derived statements. For example, whenever a statement of the form (foo, rdfs:domain, bar) is encountered, the inferencing module asserts that (foo, rdf:type, property) is an implied statement.

The SQL92SAIL has been tested in use with several DBMSs, including Post-greSQL[6] and MySQL[7] (see also section 6).

An important feature of the SAIL (or indeed of any API) is that it is possible to put one on top of the other. The SAIL at the top can perform some action when the modules make calls to it, and then forward these calls to the SAIL beneath it. This process continues until one of the SAILs finally handles the actual retrieval request, propagating the result back up again.

We implemented a SAIL that caches all schema data in a dedicated data structure in main memory. This schema data is often very limited in size and is requested very frequently. At the same time, the schema data is the most difficult to query from a DBMS because of the transitivity of the subClassOf and subPropertyOf properties. This schema-caching SAIL can be placed on top of arbitrary other SAILs, handling all calls concerning schema data. The rest of the calls are forwarded to the underlying SAIL.

Another important task that can be handled by a SAIL is concurrency handling. Since any given RQL query is broken down into several operations on the SAIL level, it is important to preserve repository consistency over multiple operations. We implemented a SAIL that selectively blocks and releases read and write access to repositories, on a first come first serve basis. This setup allows us to support concurrency control for any type of repository.

6 Experiences

A running demo of Sesame can be found at http://sesame.aidministrator.nl/, and the source code is available for download. The implementation follows the generic architecture described in this paper, using the following concrete implementation choices for the modules:

- We use both PostgreSQL and MySQL as database platforms. The reason we are running two platforms simultaneously is mainly a development choice: we wish to compare real-life performance.
- platforms. We have various repository setups running, combining different stacks of SAILs (including the SQL92SAIL, the PostgreSQL SAIL, the MySQL SAIL, and a schema cache and a concurrency handler) on top of each repository.
- A protocol handler is realised using HTTP.

---

[6] See http://www.postgresql.org/
[7] See http://www.mysql.com/

– The admin module uses the ARP RDF parser.

In this section, we briefly report on our experiences with various aspects of this implementation.

6.1   RDFS in Practice

While developing Sesame, many unclarities in the RDFS specification were uncovered. One of the reasons for this is that RDFS is defined in natural language: no formal description of its semantics is given. As a result of this, the RDFS specification even contains some inconsistencies.

In an attempt to solve these unclarities, the RDF Core Working Group has been chartered to revise the RDF and RDFS specifications. One of the results is a formal Model Theory for RDF [9], which specifies model and schema semantics more precisely and includes a formal procedure for computing the closure of a schema.

As mentioned in section 5, the SQL92SAIL features an inferencing module that follows the procedure described in the model theory. Our experiences are that a naive implementation of this formal procedure is painfully slow, but with relative ease it can be optimized to perform quite satisfactory. Improving this performance even further is currently work in progress.

6.2   PostgreSQL and SAIL

In our first test setup for Sesame we used PostgreSQL. PostgreSQL is a freely available (open source) object-relational DBMS that supports many features that normally can only be found in commercial DBMS implementations (see http://www.postgresql.org).

One of the main reasons for choosing PostgreSQL is that it is an object-relational DBMS, meaning that it supports subtable relations between its tables. As these subtable relations are also transitive, we used these to model the class and property subsumption relations of RDFS.

The SAIL that is used in this setup therefore is specifically tailored towards PostgreSQL's support for subtables (which is not a standard SQL feature). It uses a dynamic database schema that was inspired by the schema shown in [12]. New tables are added to the database whenever a new class or property is added to the repository. If a class is a subclass of other classes, the table created for it will also be a subtable of the tables for the superclasses. Likewise for properties being subproperties of other properties. Instances of classes and properties are inserted as values into the appropriate tables. Figure 5 gives an impression of the contents of a database containing the data from figure 2.

The actual schema involves one more table called resources. This table contains all resources and literal values, mapped to a unique ID. These IDs are used in the tables shown in the figure to refer to the resources and literal values. The resources table is used to minimize the size of the database. It ensures that resources and literal values, which can be quite long, only occur once in the database, saving potentially large amounts of memory.

In the test setup, several optimizations in the SAIL implementation were made, such as selective caching of namespaces and frequently requested resources to avoid repetitive table lookups.

Our experiences with this database schema on PostgreSQL were not completely satisfactory. Data insertion is not as fast as we would like. Especially incremental uploads of schema data can be very slow, since table creation is very expensive in PostgreSQL. Even worse, when adding a new subClassOf relation between two existing classes, the complete class hierarchy starting from the subclass needs to broken down and rebuilt again because subtable relations can not be added to an existing table; the subtable relations have to be specified when a table is created. Once created, the subtable rela-

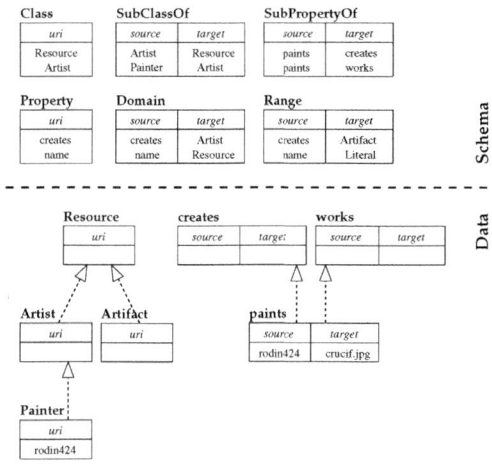

Fig. 5. Impression of the object-relational schema used with PostgreSQL

tions are fixed. Another disadvantage of the subtable-approach is that cycles in the class hierarchy can not be modeled properly in this fashion.

In a new setup, we used the SQL92SAIL to connect to PostgreSQL. The current version of this SAIL implementation takes a radically different approach: all RDF statements are inserted into a single table with three columns: Subject, Predicate, Object. While we have yet to perform structured testing and analysis with this approach, it seems to perform significantly better, especially in scenarios where the RDFS changes often.

For querying purposes, the original PostgreSQL SAIL performed quite satisfactory, especially when combined with a Schema-caching SAIL stacked on top (see section 5). We have yet to perform structured testing on querying with the new SQL92SAIL, but initial results show that it performs somewhat slower than the earlier PostgreSQL SAIL, which is to be expected.

6.3 MySQL

In initial tests with MySQL, we implemented a SAIL with a strictly relational database schema (see figure 6).

As can be seen, a number of dependencies arise due to the storage of Schema information in separate tables. In order to keep overhead to a minimum, every resource and literal is encoding using an integer value (the id field), to enable faster lookups. To encode whether a particular statement was explicitly asserted or derived from the schema information, an extra column is_derived is added where appropriate.

The main difference between this schema and the schema used in the PosgreSQL setup (see figure 5) is that in this setup, the database schema does not change when the RDFS changes. In application scenarios where the RDFS (the ontology) is unstable, this is an advantage because typically adding new tables to a database requires more time and resources than simply inserting a row in an existing table.

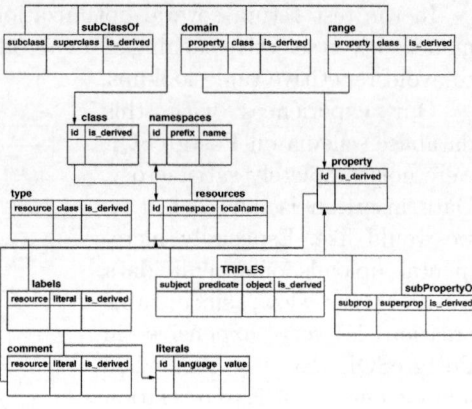

Fig. 6. Impression of the relational schema used with MySQL.

Like in the PostgreSQL SAIL, selective caching of namespaces and other optimization techniques were implemented in this setup. Overall, this approach performed significantly better in our test scenarios, especially on uploading.

7   Future Work

7.1   Transaction Rollback Support

While the SAIL API has support for transactions, it currently has no transaction rollback feature. Transaction rollbacks, especially in the case of uploading information, are crucial if we wish to guarantee database consistency. In the case of RDF uploads, transaction rollbacks can be supported at two levels:

– a single upload of a set of RDF statements can be seen as a single transaction, or alternatively, a single upload can be "chunked" into smaller sets to support partial rollback when an error occurs during the upload session.
– a single RDFS statement assertion can been seen as a transaction in which several tables in the database need to be updated. From the user point of view, the schema assertion is atomic ("A is a class"), but from the repository point of view, it may consist of several table updates, for instance, in the schema presented in figure 5, a new table would have to be created, and new rows would have to be inserted into the "Resources" and the "Classes" table.

Both levels of transaction rollback support may help ensure database consistency. Together with the concurrency support already present in the Sesame system, this will help move Sesame towards becoming an ACID[8] compliant storage system (note that this can only be guaranteed if the platform used for storage supports it).

---

[8] *Atomicity, Concurrency, Isolation, Durability.* These four properties of a transaction ensure database robustness over aborted or (partially) failed transactions.

7.2   Adding and Extending Functional Modules

Sesame currently features three functional modules. We plan to extend the functionality of these modules, as well as add new modules.

In the current admin module implementation, only incremental upload of RDF statements is supported. We plan to implement more advanced update support, most importantly support for deleting individual triples from the repository. A prototype implementation of this new feature already exists but has to be tested and extended further.

Plans for new modules include a graphical visualization component and query engines for different query languages (for example, Squish).

7.3   DAML+OIL Support

As mentioned in section 5, the RDF SAIL API has been designed to allow extension of the functionality, for example to include support for DAML+OIL. In the current implementation, this support is not present however. We plan to implement at least partial support for DAML+OIL storage and inferencing.

8   Conclusions

In this paper we have presented Sesame, an architecture for storing and querying RDF and RDF Schema. Sesame is an important step beyond the currently available storage and query devices for RDF, since it is the first publicly available implementation of a query language that is aware of the RDFS semantics.

An important feature of the Sesame architecture is its abstraction from the details of any particular repository used for the actual storage. This makes it possible to port Sesame to a large variety of different repositories, including relational databases, RDF triple stores, and even remote storage services on the Web.

Sesame itself is a server-based application, and can therefore be used as a remote service for manipulating RDF data on the Semantic Web. As with the storage layer, Sesame abstracts from any particular communication protocol, so that Sesame can easily be connected to different clients by writing different protocol handlers.

Important next steps to expand Sesame towards a full fledged storage and querying service for the Semantic Web include implementing transaction rollback support, versioning, extension from RDFS to DAML+OIL and implementations for different repositories. This last feature especially will be greatly facilitated by the fact that the current SAIL implementation is a generic SQL92 implementation, rather than specific for a particular DBMS.

References

1. Sofia Alexaki, Vassilis Christophides, Greg Karvounarakis, Dimitris Plexousakis, and Karsten Tolle. The RDFSuite: Managing Voluminous RDF Description Bases. Technical report, Institute of Computer Science, FORTH, Heraklion, Greece, 2000. See http://www.ics.forth.gr/proj/isst/RDF/RSSDB/rdfsuite.pdf.
2. David Beckett. The Design and Implementation of the Redland RDF Application Framework. In *Proceedings of Semantic Web Workshop of the 10th International World Wide Web Conference*, Hong-Kong, China, May 2001.
3. Don Box, David Ehnebuske, Gopal Kakivaya, Andrew Layman, Noah Mendelsohn, Henrik Frystyk Nielsen, Satish Thatte, and Dave Winer. Simple Object Access Protocol (SOAP) 1.1. W3c note, World Wide Web Consortium, May 2000. See http://www.w3.org/TR/SOAP/.
4. D. Brickley and R.V. Guha. Resource Description Framework (RDF) Schema Specification 1.0. Candidate recommendation, World Wide Web Consortium, March 2000. See http://www.w3.org/TR/2000/CR-rdf-schema-20000327.
5. Jeen Broekstra and Arjohn Kampman. Query Language Definition. On-To-Knowledge (IST-1999-10132) Deliverable 9, Aidministrator Nederland b.v., April 2001. See http://www.ontoknowledge.org/.
6. Jeremy Carrol and Brian McBride. The Jena Semantic Web Toolkit. Public api, HP-Labs, Bristol, 2001. See http://www.hpl.hp.com/semweb/jena-top.html.
7. R.G.G. Cattel, Douglas Barry, Mark Berler, Jeff Eastman, David Jordan, Craig Russell, Olaf Schadow, Torsten Stanienda, and Fernando Velez. *The Object Database Standard: ODMG 3.0*. Morgan Kaufmann, 2000.
8. Don Chamberlin, Daniela Florescu, Jonathan Robie, Jerome Simeon, and Mugur Stefanescu. XQuery: A Query Language for XML. Working draft, World Wide Web Consortium, February 2001. See http://www.w3.org/TR/xquery/.
9. Patrick Hayes. RDF Model Theory. Working draft, World Wide Web Consortium, September 2001. See http://www.w3.org/TR/rdf-mt/.
10. Ian Horrocks, Frank van Harmelen, Peter Patel-Schneider, Tim Berners-Lee, Dan Brickley, Dan Connoly, Mike Dean, Stefan Decker, Dieter Fensel, Pat Hayes, Jeff Heflin, Jim Hendler, Ora Lassila, Deborah McGuinness, and Lynn Andrea Stein. DAML+OIL. http://www.daml.org/2001/03/daml+oil-index.html, March 2001.
11. ISO. Information Technology-Database Language SQL. Standard No. ISO/IEC 9075:1999, International Organization for Standardization (ISO), 1999. (Available from American National Standards Institute, New York, NY 10036, (212) 642-4900.).
12. Gregory Karvounarakis, Vassilis Christophides, Dimitris Plexousakis, and Sofia Alexaki. Querying community web portals. Technical report, Institute of Computer Science, FORTH, Heraklion, Greece, 2000. See http://www.ics.forth.gr/proj/isst/RDF/RQL/rql.pdf.
13. O. Lassila and R. R. Swick. Resource Description Framework (RDF): Model and Syntax Specification. Recommendation, World Wide Web Consortium, February 1999. See http://www.w3.org/TR/REC-rdf-syntax/.
14. Libby Miller. RDF Squish query language and Java implementation. Public draft, Institute for Learning and Research Technology, 2001. See http://ilrt.org/discovery/2001/02/squish/.

A Formal Model for Topic Maps

Pascal Auillans[1], Patrice Ossona de Mendez[2],
Pierre Rosenstiehl[3], and Bernard Vatant[4]

[1] LaBRI - Université Bordeaux 1, 351 cours de la Libération, Talence, France
`auillans@labri.fr`
[2] CNRS UMR 8557, 54 Bd Raspail, Paris, France
`pom@ehess.fr`
[3] CNRS UMR 8557, 54 Bd Raspail, Paris, France
`pr@ehess.fr`
[4] Mondeca, 3 cité Nollez, Paris, France
`bernard.vatant@mondeca.com`

Abstract. Topic maps have been developed in order to represent the structures of relationships between subjects, independently of resources documenting them, and to allow standard representation and interoperability of such structures. The ISO 13250 XTM specification [2] have provided a robust syntactic XML representation allowing processing and interchange of topic maps. But topic maps have so far suffered from a lack of formal description, or conceptual model. We propose here such a model, based on the mathematical notions of hypergraph and connexity. This model addresses the critical issue of topic map organization in semantic layers, and provides ways to check semantic consistency of topic maps. Moreover, it seems generic enough to be used as a foundation for other semantic standards, like RDF [3].

1 Foreword: So Many Ways of *Going Meta*

Meta data, meta level, meta-structure, meta-model, meta-language... *going meta* has been a popular game lately when it comes to create buzz words. Unfortunately the *meta* prefix has been used and abused in quite different meanings, in different contexts, application fields and communities. Those various applications now have to inter-operate in order to achieve Semantic Web consistent development.

Linguists, mathematicians and logicians all use the notion of *meta-language*, with maybe slight differences, but all pointing at the more abstract and generic level necessary to describe the structure and rules for a given language. Inside a language itself, every other assertion represents somehow a *meta-level* which organizes and structures the objects it makes assertions about. Naming and classifying make a meta-level for real world objects, while assertions make one for concepts, and more assertions and logical coordination for assertions.... The linguistic use of meta therefore implies a hierarchical semantic stratification.

In the Web universe, the proliferation of standards and specifications has led to the notion of *meta-structure* or *meta-model*. In XML, DTDs and Schemas

I. Horrocks and J. Hendler (Eds.): ISWC 2002, LNCS 2342, pp. 69–83, 2002.
© Springer-Verlag Berlin Heidelberg 2002

have made familiar this notion in the form of standard document structure description.

But *going meta* does not mean necessarily going to an upper and more abstract structural level, it may mean going outside, after, before, besides or beyond, that is: in another semantic layer, to provide a description that is impossible to achieve from inside the reference layer. Illustration or annotation of a text document, and the other way round, caption of a figure, are basic examples. Generalizing annotation and caption, *meta-data*, providing standard description of resources, are considered a fundamental tool for Semantic web achievement.

2   Are Topic Maps Meta-language or Meta-data?

In this versatile meta-universe, where do topic maps stand? Some consider them as yet another meta-data format, based on the argument that the paradigm has explicitly split the world into two layers. The first layer contains *subjects*. Following topic maps terminology, a subject is whatever can be asserted about, be it abstract concept or real-world object, and is able to be represented by a topic in topic maps. The second layer contains *addressable resources*, which are whatever can be retrieved by computers in a network, singularly through URI addressing. The resources layer is the ground territory that subjects (topics) are mapping. Subjects, through their representation as topics, can be therefore considered as meta-data for resources. But topic maps represent also the structure of relationships between subjects, and therefore may be considered as a meta-language for structuring meta-data. In the "more meta than you" game, topic maps definitely rank well!

Considering that topic maps do not need any more organization in semantic layers,and that they could include their own meta-language, is therefore a tempting trap. The catchy slogan *In topic maps, everything is a topic*, has done nothing to prevent from this illusion of semantic homogeneity. And the implicit model under ISO 13250 XTM does not forbid whatever mismatch of semantic layers, leaving to human authors the entire responsibility of building in a consistent and meaningful way their structures of topics and associations. A formal model should make for this lack of rules, and provide means for checking consistency, through a formal definition of semantic layers. That is one of the main issues the present model will try to address.

3   Introducing Hypergraphs

The formal model we present here relies on the mathematical concept of hypergraph introduced by Berge in the Tihany colloquium in 1966 [7] (see also [6,8,10,11,18,24]). Properties of hypergraphs and topological aspects (through hypermaps) have been extensively studied (see, for instance [9,12,14,19,23]).

This work extends the presentation done in the *XML Europe 2001* conference [20].

Definition 1. *A hypergraph is a 5-tuple* $\mathcal{H} = (V, \lambda_V, E, \lambda_E, I)$, *where:*

- V, E, I *are disjoint finite sets, which we call as follows:*
  - V *is the* vertex set *of* $\mathcal{H}$,
  - E *is the* edge set *of* $\mathcal{H}$,
  - I *is the* incidence set *of* $\mathcal{H}$.
- $\lambda_V : V \to \mathcal{P}(I)$ *is a mapping from V to the set $\mathcal{P}(I)$ of all the subsets of I (the image of a vertex is a subset of I), which we call the* vertex-connector *of* $\mathcal{H}$, *satisfying the following conditions:*

$$\forall v \neq v' \in V, \quad \lambda_V(v) \cap \lambda_V(v') = \emptyset \tag{1}$$

$$\bigcup_{v \in V} \lambda_V(v) = I \tag{2}$$

(notice that, for any incidence $\alpha \in I$, there exists thus a unique vertex $v \in V$, such that $\alpha \in \lambda_V(v)$, that we shall call the vertex-endpoint *of α)*

- $\lambda_E : E \to \mathcal{P}(I)$ *is a mapping from V to $\mathcal{P}(I)$, that similarly satisfies the following conditions:*

$$\forall e, e' \in E, \quad \lambda_E(e) \cap \lambda_E(e') = \emptyset \tag{3}$$

$$\bigcup_{e \in E} \lambda_E(e) = I \tag{4}$$

(as previously, for any incidence $\alpha \in I$, there exists a unique edge $e \in E$, such that $\alpha \in \lambda_E(e)$, that we shall call the edge-endpoint *of α)*

A vertex $x \in V$ and an edge $e \in E$ are *incident* if $\lambda_V(x)$ and $\lambda_E(e)$ have a non-empty intersection. By transitivity, we define the *connected component* $\mathcal{H}[x]$ of $x \in V \cup E$: an element $y \in V \cup E$ belongs to $\mathcal{H}[x]$ if, and only if, either $y = x$ or there exists a (finite) sequence $z_1 = x, z_2, \ldots, z_{k-1}, z_k = y$, such that z_i is incident to z_{i+1} ($\forall 1 \leq i < k$). Such a sequence is called a *path* from x to y. We extend this definition to $V \cup E \cup I$ by setting $\mathcal{H}[\alpha]$ ($\alpha \in I$) to be equal to $\mathcal{H}[x]$, where x is the vertex-endpoint of α.

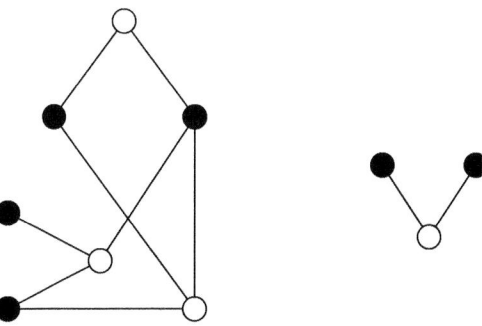

Fig. 1. A hypergraph (without multiple incidences), with two connected components

In a first coarse interpretation, the hypergraph model seems to match only the main topic maps objects, called topic nodes and association nodes in the terminology of PMTM4 model [1]. Hypergraph vertices map to topic nodes, edges map to association nodes, and incidences map to links between topic nodes and association nodes. Every other topic map property, including role specification, scope, topic type, association template, topic occurrence, topic name, topic subject, implies in fact crossing boarders of semantic layers - represented by connected components. The topic map model has therefore to include a mechanism to jump between connected components. That mechanism is introduced in the following section.

4   A General Model for Topic Maps

Definition 2. *A topic map is a triple* $\mathcal{T} = (\mathcal{H}, \mathcal{H}', \phi)$, *where:*

- $\mathcal{H} = (T, \lambda_T, A, \lambda_A, I)$ *is a hypergraph, the* homogeneous hypergraph *of* $\mathcal{T}$, *and we call*
  - topic set *of* $\mathcal{T}$, *the vertex set* T *of* $\mathcal{H}$,
  - association set *of* $\mathcal{T}$, *the edge set* A *of* $\mathcal{H}$,
  - incidence set *of* $\mathcal{T}$, *the incidence set* I *of* $\mathcal{H}$.
- $\mathcal{H}' = (X, \lambda_X, M, \lambda_M, I')$ *is a hypergraph, the* shift hypergraph *of* $\mathcal{T}$, *and we call*
  - element set *of* $\mathcal{T}$, *the vertex set* X *of* $\mathcal{H}'$,
  - meta-association set *of* $\mathcal{T}$, *the edge set* M *of* $\mathcal{H}'$,
  - meta-incidence set *of* $\mathcal{T}$, *the incidence set* I' *of* $\mathcal{H}'$.
- T, A, I, M *and* I' *are disjoint sets.*
- *The element set of* $\mathcal{T}$ *is the union of the topic set, the edge set and the incidence set of* $\mathcal{T}$:

$$X = T \cup A \cup I \qquad (5)$$

- *multiple incidences between a vertex and an edge of the shift hypergraph are not allowed:*

$$\forall (x, m) \in X \times M, \quad |\lambda_X(x) \cap \lambda_M(m)| \leq 1 \qquad (6)$$

- $\phi : M \to T$ *is an injective mapping (this means that two different elements are mapped to two different elements) from the meta-association set* M *to the topic set* T, *that we call the* lift *of* $\mathcal{T}$.
- *For any meta-association* $m \in M$ *and any element* $x \in X$, *if* x *is incident to* m *in* $\mathcal{H}'$, *then the lift* $\phi(m)$ *of* m *does not belong to* $\mathcal{H}[x]$:

$$\forall m \in M, \forall x \in X, \quad (\lambda_X(x) \cap \lambda_M(m) \neq \emptyset) \implies (\phi(m) \notin \mathcal{H}[x]) \qquad (7)$$

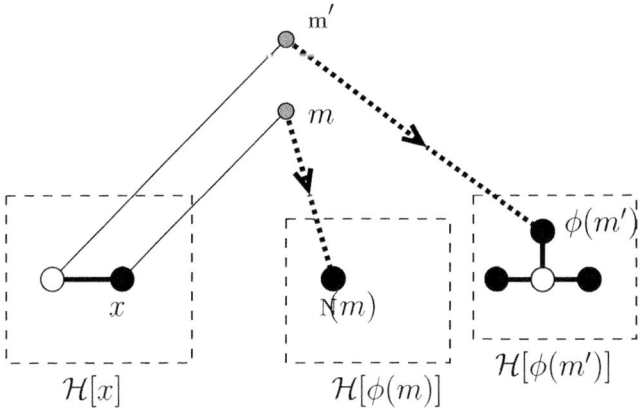

Fig. 2. A simple representation of the $(\mathcal{H}, \mathcal{H}', \phi)$ model

Property 7 justifies the terms of "homogeneous" and "shift" hypergraphs: intuitively, within a connected component of $\mathcal{H}$, all the topics, associations and incidences belong to the same semantic layer. Shifting of semantic layer is performed through a jump in the shift hypergraph.

Example 1. (See Fig 3)

The Solar System Topic Map [22] contains a certain number of semantic layers. In the connected component of $\mathcal{H}$ containing the "astronomical objects", a topic j represents the planet Jupiter, of which vertex connector $\lambda_T(j)$ includes an incidence α representing the "satellite of the Sun" role, which in turn belongs to the edge connector $\lambda_A(a)$, where a represents the "Sun Gravitational System" association. Those three elements belong to the same connected component of the homeogeneous hypergraph.

The topic j (as an element of X) is incident, in $\mathcal{H}'$, to a meta-association m, which corresponds (lifts) to "Solar System object" in a connected component of $\mathcal{H}$, representing another semantic layer (distinct from the one of j). The topics in this layer will represent classes of individual objects, and associations in this layer will be for instance class-subclass associations. The meta-incidence linking j to m thus represents the belonging of Jupiter to the topic type "Solar System object". Following the same principle, the association a is incident in $\mathcal{H}'$ to a meta-association (representing its relation to an association type) that lifts to "gravitational system". An identical mechanism lifts the incidences in the "objects" component of $\mathcal{H}$, into role types.

Example 2. It is possible to interpret (for part of the whole structure) the lift operation as a dual for the usual instantiation/derivation/representation of object oriented approaches. Such an interpretation may help to decompose a structure into semantic layers and give a strategy for building meta-associations and lifts, when the studied structure is somehow a "typing structure". We present figure 4 a possible structure for names and scopes.

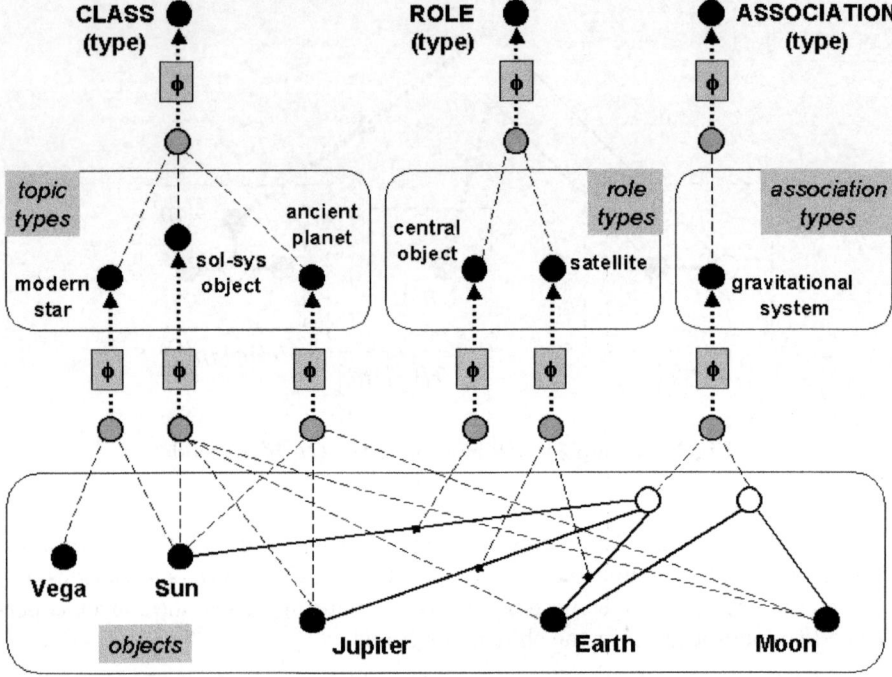

Fig. 3. Sample structure of a description of the solar system

5   Lift and Fixed Point Properties

In our model, Property (7) explicits that no connected component of the homogeneous graph may include a lift, which is consistent with the semantic of a lift, the change of semantic layer.

In practice, it is not always obvious to discover whether some *topic characteristic* should be coded through a lift, or if it should be coded using an association. In our model, a characteristic coded through a lift cannot have a fixed point. A consequence is that any characteristic having a fixed point has to be coded using an association.

Example 3. Consider, for instance, the data typing in a programming language like the C programming language. In such a language, types are only handled at compile time and there is a fundamental gap between types and data. Thus, it is possible to consider that the data and the types belong to two different semantic layers, and that the typing may be coded through a lift.

To the opposite, in a programming language like Pliant [21], types are objects, which in turn have a type. Obviously, the type Type is a fixed point for this relation. As the topic Type cannot belong to the same component as a topic obtained from it using exactly one lift, typing has to be coded by an association. Hence, all the types are connected to Type and, as all the data have to

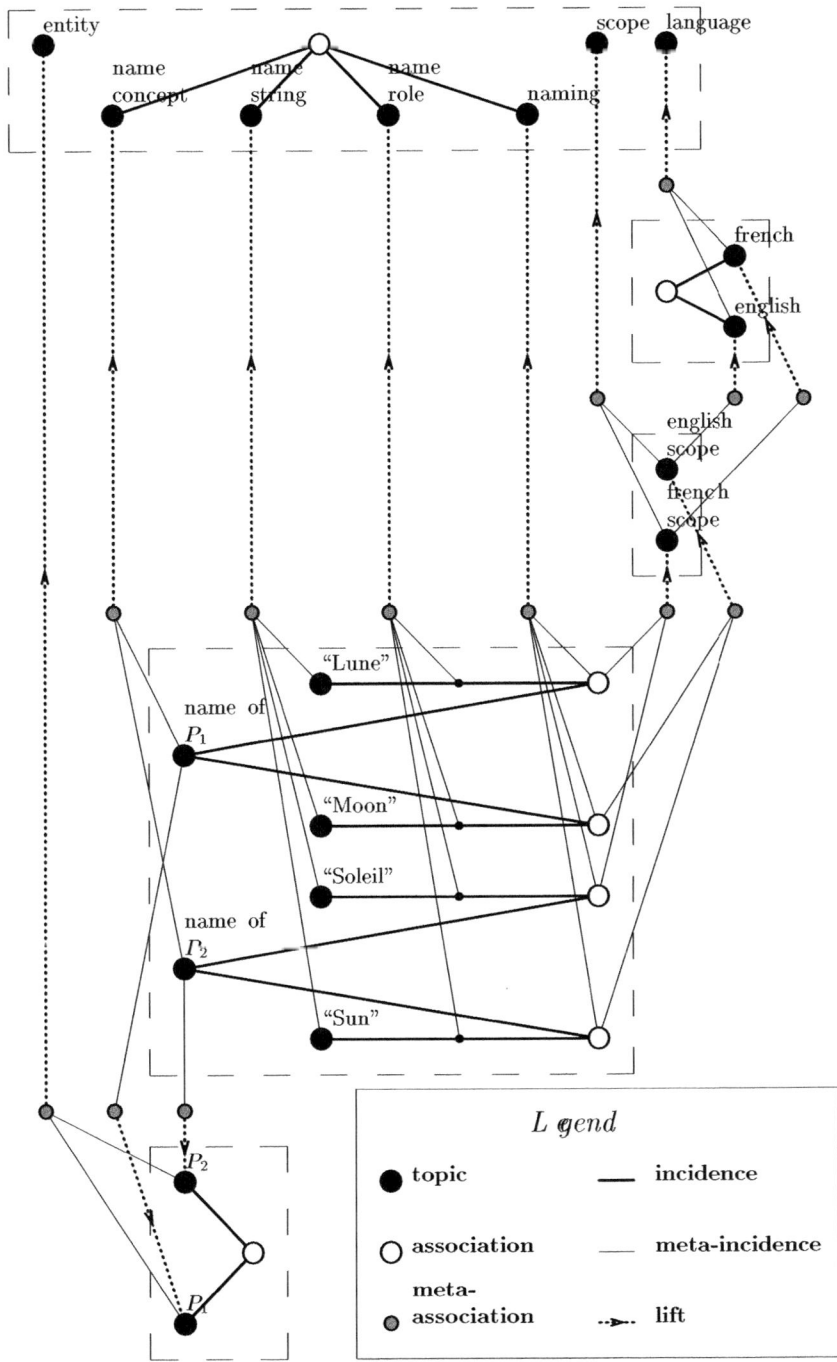

Fig. 4. Sample structure of names/scopes based on an interpretation of the lift dual to the instantiation/derivation/representation scheme .

be connected to one type, all the data and types belong to a same connected component.

In topic maps used for knowledge representation, in order to keep semantic layers clearly distinct, it therefore seems relevant to avoid fixed points for fundamental characteristics such as topic type, association template, and role specification.

6   Alternate $(\mathcal{H}, \theta)$ Description

The previous considerations on semantic layers lead to an alternate description of the model, using only one hypergraph, and introducing another way to deal with connected components.

A topic map $\mathcal{T}$ may be defined as a couple $(\mathcal{H}, \theta)$, where:

- $\mathcal{H} = (T, \lambda_T, A, \lambda_A, I)$ is the homogeneous hypergraph of $\mathcal{T}$,
- $\theta : T \to \mathcal{P}(T \cup A \cup I)$ is a mapping from the topic set of $\mathcal{T}$ to the set of the subsets of elements of $\mathcal{T}$, that we call the *covering* of the topic map, with the constraint that

$$\forall t \in T, \quad \mathcal{H}[t] \cap \theta(t) = \emptyset \tag{8}$$

The equivalence of both descriptions is explicited now.

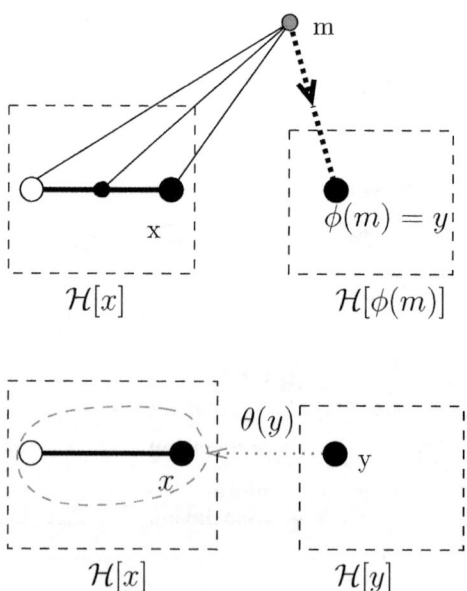

Fig. 5. Transformation of the $(\mathcal{H}, \mathcal{H}', \phi)$ model into the $(\mathcal{H}, \theta)$ one

Consider a topic map. Let $\theta : T \rightarrow \mathcal{P}(T \cup A \cup I)$ be defined by:

$$\forall t \in T, \quad \theta(t) = \begin{cases} \{x \in X, \lambda_M(m) \cap \lambda_X(x) \neq \emptyset\}, & \text{if } \exists m \in M, \phi(m) = t \\ \emptyset, & \text{otherwise} \end{cases} \quad (9)$$

Then, (8) is a directed consequence of (7). Notice that θ is well defined by (9) as ϕ is injective.

Conversely, assume we are given a couple $(\mathcal{H}, \theta)$ satisfying (8). Let M be a set of cardinality $|T \setminus \theta^{-1}(\emptyset)|$ and ϕ a bijection from M to $T \setminus \theta^{-1}(\emptyset)$ (thus defining an injection from M to T). Then, define:

$$X = T \cup A \cup I \quad (10)$$
$$I' = \{(\alpha, t) \in X \times T, \quad \alpha \in \theta(t)\} \quad (11)$$
$$\lambda_X : x \in X \mapsto \{(\alpha, t) \in I', \quad \alpha = x\} \subseteq I' \quad (12)$$
$$\lambda_M : y \in M \mapsto \{(\alpha, t) \in I', \quad \phi(m) = t\} \subseteq I' \quad (13)$$

then, denoting $\mathcal{H}' = (X, \lambda_X, M, \lambda_M, I')$, $\mathcal{H}'$ is clearly a hypergraph and the triple $(\mathcal{H}, \mathcal{H}', \phi)$ is a topic map, as (7) is a direct consequence of (8).

Last, both transformations are obviously inverse from each other.

For example, in SolSysTM, the covering of "Solar System object" will contain the topics "sun", "moon", "earth", "Jupiter". The covering of "astrology" will contain the association "astrological interpretation of Moon-Jupiter occultation".

7 Stratified Topic Maps

We now introduce a subclass of topic maps, where the covering application induce a partial order over the set of connected components, and that we call *stratified topic maps*. This subclass seems fit to represent most practical use cases, and their model provide tools for checking semantic consistency of such topic maps, looking for loops and other semantic mismatches.

Given two connected components $\mathcal{H}[x]$ and $\mathcal{H}[y]$ of the homogeneous hypergraph of a topic map, we say that $\mathcal{H}[y]$ is θ-*reachable* from $\mathcal{H}[x]$ and note $\mathcal{H}[x] \overset{\theta}{\rightarrow} \mathcal{H}[y]$ if there exists a sequence $(a_1, b_1, a_2, b_2, \ldots, a_p, b_p)$ (with $p \geq 1$), such that

$$b_i \in \theta(a_i) \qquad (1 \leq i \leq p) \qquad (14)$$
$$a_{i+1} \in \mathcal{H}[b_i] \qquad (1 \leq i < p) \qquad (15)$$
$$a_1 \in \mathcal{H}[x] \qquad (16)$$
$$b_p \in \mathcal{H}[y] \qquad (17)$$

A topic map is *stratified* if there exists no connected component $\mathcal{H}[x]$ of its homogeneous hypergraph, such that $\mathcal{H}[x] \overset{\theta}{\rightarrow} \mathcal{H}[x]$, which means that there are no "circuits" using lifts.

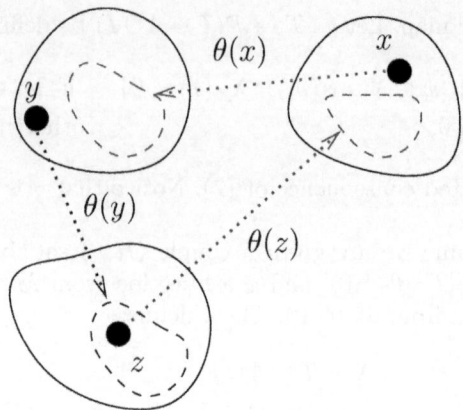

Fig. 6. A exemple of a non-startified topic map, since $\mathcal{H}[x] \xrightarrow{\theta} \mathcal{H}[x]$

In such a case, the set of all the connected components of the homogeneous hypergraph is partially ordered by

$$\forall x, y \in X, \quad (\mathcal{H}[x] < \mathcal{H}[y]) \iff (\mathcal{H}[y] \xrightarrow{\theta} \mathcal{H}[x]) \tag{18}$$

Considering a total order compatible with this partial order, the topic map may be unfolded and presented as a sequence $(\mathcal{H}_1, \ldots, \mathcal{H}_p)$ of disjoint (connected) hypergraphs with vertex set, edge set and incidence set T_i, A_i and I_i, together with a set of mappings $\theta_{i,j} : T_i \rightarrow \mathcal{P}(T_j \cup A_j \cup I_j)$ (with $p \geq i > j \geq 1$). Condition (8) is thus replaced by the stronger assertion that $\theta_{i,j}$ mappings go from higher hypergraphs to a lower ones. The topic map may be conversely defined from the $(\mathcal{H}_i)$ sequence and the $\{\theta_{i,j}\}$ family, by:

$$\mathcal{H} = \bigcup_{i=1}^{p} \mathcal{H}_i \tag{19}$$

$$\theta : t \in T \mapsto \bigcup_{j=1}^{i-1} \theta_{i,j}(t) \subseteq T \cup A \cup I, \qquad \text{where } i \text{ is such that } t \in T_i \tag{20}$$

8   Structural Properties

The practical study of the properties of a topic map will usually reduce to the study of the properties of components of its homogeneous hypergraph corresponding to a single semantic layer. Thus, we will be led to study structural properties of an hypergraph and will gain help from the extensive work already performed in this area. Notice that the power of hypergraph modeling for structure analysis is at the core of the use of such a model in domains like biochemistry to ease the study of probabilistic and topological systems with discrete interactions [15,16].

A fundamental type of relation between hypergraphs is the *minor relation*:

Definition 3 (from [10]). *A hypergraph is a* minor *of another hypergraph $\mathcal{H}$, if it arises from $\mathcal{H}$ as the result of successive elementary operations, performed in any order. Elementary operations include the deletion of a vertex, of an edge, of an incidence ("shrinking"), and the identification of two vertices incident to a common edge ("collapsing").*

This relation is the core of characterization theorems for classes of hypergraph, based on the following difficult theorem:

Theorem 1 (Robertson and Seymour 1987). *Let $\mathcal{F}$ be a family of hypergraphs such that no hypergraph in $\mathcal{F}$ is isomorphic to a minor of another hypergraph in $\mathcal{F}$. Then $\mathcal{F}$ is finite.*

As a consequence, if a class $\mathcal{C}$ of hypergraphs is stable by taking minors, there exists a finite set $\mathbb{F}\mathrm{orb}(\mathcal{C})$, such that, for any hypergraph $\mathcal{H}$, the hypergraph $\mathcal{H}$ belongs to $\mathcal{C}$ if and only if none of the hypergraphs in $\mathbb{F}\mathrm{orb}(\mathcal{C})$ is isomorphic to a minor of $\mathcal{H}$ (what may theoretically be tested in polynomial time for any fixed class $\mathcal{C}$).

9   Organization Levels and Minors

An important issue for our model stands in its ability to model a structure and a decomposition of it into organization levels.

In order to encode an organization level, we should keep in mind that any organization level has some "interface" with the underlying one:

> "Whatever organization level we apprehend it, from the molecule level to the whole organization level, one now understands that an organic unit is an open system from the informational point of view, since each organization level receives its informations from the susjacent level." [17]

Let us now show that organization levels may be coded within our topic map model.

In such a context, organization levels are stratified, and each structure level is related to a layer hosting its messages and a layer hosting its functionalities. Considering a structure level $\mathcal{H}_j$, together with its message topics MT_j and its functionality topics FT_j, it is natural to impose some semantic relations:

$$\forall t_F \in \mathrm{FT}_j, \quad \theta(t_F) \subseteq A \tag{21}$$

$$\forall t_M \in \mathrm{MT}_j, \quad \theta(t_M) \subseteq I \tag{22}$$

$$\forall t_F, t'_F \in \mathrm{FT}_j, \quad (t_F \neq t'_F) \Rightarrow (\theta(t_F) \cap \theta(t'_F) = \emptyset) \tag{23}$$

$$\forall t_M, t'_M \in \mathrm{MT}_j, \quad (t_M \neq t'_M) \Rightarrow (\theta(t_M) \cap \theta(t'_M) = \emptyset) \tag{24}$$

$$A_j = \bigcup_{t_F \in \mathrm{FT}_j} \theta(t_F) \tag{25}$$

$$I_j = \bigcup_{t_M \in MT_j} \theta(t_M) \tag{26}$$

and an additional univocity relation:

$$\forall t_M \in MT_j, \forall a \in A, \forall t \in T, \quad |\theta(t_M) \cap \lambda_A(a) \cap \lambda_T(t)| \leq 1 \tag{27}$$

Then, if $j > i$, the structure level $\mathcal{H}_j$ will be a presentation of $\mathcal{H}_i$ at an highest organization level if the topics of the structure level $\mathcal{H}_j$ correspond to vertex-disjoint connected sub-hypergraphs of $\mathcal{H}_i$ and if the inter class incidences and associations of $\mathcal{H}_i$ correspond to the incidences and associations of $\mathcal{H}_j$, with a further correspondence with messages and functionalities in MT_j and FT_j:

Any element of $\mathcal{H}_i$ is either related to some topic in T_j are to a message or to a functionality:

$$\forall x \in T_i \cup A_i \cup I_i, \quad \exists! y \in MT_j \cup FT_j \cup T_j, \quad x \in \theta(y) \tag{28}$$

The associations and incidences of $\mathcal{H}_i$ belonging to the image by θ of $FT_j \cup MT_j$ are called *inter-class* associations and incidences

The image of a topic $t \in T_j$ in $\mathcal{H}_i$ has to be induced by the topic images:

$$\forall a \in A_i, \quad (a \in \theta(t)) \iff (\lambda_A(a) \subseteq \bigcup_{y \in \theta(t) \cap T_i} \lambda_T(y)) \tag{29}$$

$$\forall \alpha \in I_i, \quad (\alpha \in \theta(t)) \iff (\alpha \in \bigcup_{a \in \theta(t) \cap A_i} \lambda_A(a)) \tag{30}$$

The functionality of any association of $\mathcal{H}_j$ is also the functionality of some corresponding inter-class association in $\mathcal{H}_i$:

$$\forall t_F \in FT_j, \quad |\theta(t_F) \cap A_i| = 1 \tag{31}$$

Incidences in $\mathcal{H}_j$ correspond to inter-class incidences in $\mathcal{H}_j$ related to a same message, that is: for any $t_M \in MT_j$, for any $t_F \in FT_j$, for any $t \in T_j$ and for any $a \in \theta(t_F) \cap A_j$, denoting a' the unique element of $\theta(t_F) \cap A_i$,

$$(\lambda_A(a) \cap \lambda_T(t) \cap \theta(t_M) \neq \emptyset) \iff (\exists t' \in \theta(t), \lambda_A(a') \cap \lambda_T(t) \cap \theta(t_M) \neq \emptyset) \tag{32}$$

Moreover, the image of a topic in T_j has to induce a connected sub-hypergraph of $\mathcal{H}_i$, that is, denoting $N(X)$ (for any subset $X \subseteq T$) the union of X, of the set of the incidences with an endpoint in X and of the set of the edges adjacent to a vertex in X:

$$\forall t \in T_i, \quad N(\theta(t) \cap T_j) \text{ is connected} \tag{33}$$

Actually, these relations implies that $\mathcal{H}_j$ is a minor of $\mathcal{H}_i$, what stresses the importance of the minor relation in the study of structural properties. One should also notice that our model naturally implies the existence of message and functionality topics, since any semantic shift correspond to a lift and thus to a topic. These topics are fundamentals: a message needs some material support to exist, some association needs some meaning to be pertinent.

10   Conclusion

Looking further on to applications, semantic consistency appears as a necessary condition for true interoperability. The founders of topic maps paradigm have constantly claimed their ambition to build a tool both allowing global and non-ambiguous knowledge interoperability, and respecting semantic diversity. It is generally claimed that topic maps interoperability is ensured by non-ambiguous definition of subjects, their one-to-one representation by topics, and clear definition of core relationships through standard syntax. Diversity is ensured by the intelligent use of scope, allowing the coexistence of different or even contradictory assertions over the same set of topics.

The constraints introduced by the proposed model both set reasonable limits and conditions to such a program, and provide tools for its effective achievement, providing those conditions are respected. Through internal consistency checking, the model allows topic map builders and users to become aware of the actual semantic layers structure in their topic maps, clarify or modify their choices if necessary, fine-tune the structure and track semantic mismatches. On the other hand, by its very generic nature, the model does not impose any specific layering or semantics, and for that matter is consistent with the general topic maps principle of diversity.

The consequences of the model for merging and interoperability are stronger than they first could appear, and have to be stressed in this conclusion. As a matter of fact, the model allows distinction between syntactic merging and semantic merging. The syntactic merging seems the only one to have been addressed so far, in a view of topic maps where merging can always been achieved, whatever the origin of topic maps, provided correct syntax and process are used. But a very interesting consequence of our model is that internal semantic consistency of two separate topic maps does not guarantee the consistency of their merging. If two topic maps have different choices for organization of semantic layers, a relationship implemented here as an association might be implemented through a lift there. In such a case, the merging would either induce a semantic inconsistency, or need a correction to ensure consistency, in the merged map.

This new constraint on merging may appear at first sight as a serious drawback for the model, and a major obstacle to its interoperability. But in fact, it provides a way to check if any intended merging makes sense at all, therefore avoiding syntactically correct but meaningless merging. This leads to the notion of classes of topic maps supporting a common and consistent semantic layering. Such perspectives do not weaken the original paradigm, but on the contrary provide it with further accuracy and efficiency, and effective conditions of true interoperability.

References

1. *PMTM4, a processing model for XML Topic Maps,* http://www.topicmaps.net/pmtm4.htm, S. Newcomb and M. Biezunski (eds).
2. *ISO/IEC 13250 topic maps,* http://www.y12.doe.gov/sgml/sc34/document/0129.pdf, 1999, (since decembre 2001, the DTD of XTM 1.0 is included within the ISO 13250 specification).
3. *Resource Description Framework (RDF) model and syntax specification,* http://www.w3.org/TR/REC-rdf-syntax/, 1999, O. Lassila and R.R. Swick (eds).
4. *Topic map foundational model requirements,* http://www.y12.doe.gov/sgml/sc34/document/0266.htm, 2001, G. Moore and L.M. Garshol (eds).
5. *XML Topic Maps (XTM) 1.0,* http://www.topicmaps.org/xtm/1.0/, 2001, S. Pepper and G. Moore (eds).
6. C. Berge, *Sur certains hypergraphes généralisant les graphes bipartis,* Combinatorial Theory and its Applications (A. Rényi P. Erdös and V.T. Sös, eds.), North-Holland, 1970, pp. 119–133.
7. _____, *Graphes et hypergraphes,* second ed., Dunod, Paris, 1973.
8. _____, *Hypergraphs, combinatorics of finite sets,* North-Holland, 1989, (translation of *Hypergraphes, Combinatoire des Ensembles Finis* (Gauthier-Villars, Paris, 1987).
9. R. Cori and A. Machì, *Maps, hypermaps and their automorphisms,* Expo. Math. **10** (1992), 403–467.
10. P. Duchet, *Hypergraphs,* Handbook of Combinatorics (R.L. Graham, M. Grötschel, and L. Lovász, eds.), vol. 1, Elsevier, 1995, pp. 381–432.
11. P. Erdös and A. Hajnal, *On chromatic number of graphs and set-systems,* Acta Math. Acad. Sci. Hungar. **17** (1966), 61–99.
12. Z. Füredi, *Matching and covers in hypergraphs,* Graphs and Combinatorics **4** (1988), 115–206.
13. P. Hayes, *RDF model theory,* http://www.w3.org/TR/rdf-mt/, 2001.
14. D.S. Johnson and H.O. Pollak, *Hypergraph planarity and the complexity of drawing Venn diagrams,* Journal of Graph Theory **11** (1987), 309–325.
15. W. Klonowski, *Probabilistic-topological theory of systems with discrete intercations. I. system representation by a hypergraph,* Can. J. Phys. **66** (1989), 1051–1060.
16. _____, *Probabilistic-topological theory of systems with discrete intercations. II. calculation of the hypergraph probabilistic representation; the* difference a posteriori *algorithm,* Can. J. Phys. **66** (1989), 1061–1067.
17. H. Laborit, *La nouvelle grille,* Laffont, 1974.
18. L. Lovász, *Combinatorial problems and exercises,* Akadémiai Kiadó/North-Holland, 1979.
19. P. Ossona de Mendez, *Representation of hypergraphs by contact of segments,* Conférence Internationale "Graphe et Combinatoire", 1995.
20. _____, *Combinatorial hypermaps vs topic maps,* XML Europe 2001, 2001, http://www.gca.org/papers/xmleurope2001/papers/html/s23-1.html.
21. H. Tonneau, *The Pliant project,* http://pliant.cx.

22. B. Vatant, *SolSysTM, a solar system topic map*,
    `http://www.universimmedia.com/topicmaps/solsystm.xml`.
23. T.R.S. Walsh, *Hypermaps versus bipartite maps*, J. Combinatorial Theory **18(B)**
    (1975), 155–163.
24. A.A. Zykov, *Hypergraphs*, Uspeki Mat. Nauk **6** (1974), 89–154.

Towards High-Precision Service Retrieval

Abraham Bernstein[1], Mark Klein[2]

[1]New York University, 44 West 4th Street, Suite 9-76, New York, NY 10012, U. S. A.
avi@acm.org
[2]MIT – CCS, 77 Massachusetts Ave, Room NE20-336, Cambridge, MA 02139, U. S. A.
m_klein@mit.edu

Abstract. The ability to rapidly locate useful on-line services (e.g. software applications, software components, process models, or service organizations), as opposed to simply useful documents, is becoming increasingly critical in many domains. Current service retrieval technology is, however, notoriously prone to low precision. This paper describes a novel service retrieval approached based on the sophisticated use of process ontologies. Our preliminary evaluations suggest that this approach offers qualitatively higher retrieval precision than existing (keyword and table-based) approaches without sacrificing recall and computational tractability/scalability.

1   The Challenge: High Precision Service Retrieval

Increasingly, on-line repositories such as the World Wide Web are being called upon to provide access not just to documents that collect useful *information*, but also to *services* that describe or even provide useful *behavior*. Potential examples of such services abound:

- *Software applications* such as web services (e.g. for engineering, finance, meeting planning, or word processing) that can be invoked remotely by people or software. See, for example, www.salcentral.com.
- *Software components* that can be downloaded for use when creating a new application. See, for example, www.mibsoftware.com and www.compoze.com.
- *Best practice repositories* that describe how to achieve some goal. See, for example, process.mit.edu/eph/ and www.bmpcoe.com.
- *Individuals* or *organizations* who can perform particular functions, e.g. as currently brokered using such web sites as guru.com, elance.com and freeagent.com.

As the sheer number of such services increase it will become increasingly important to provide tools to quickly find the services they need, while minimizing the burden for those who wish to list their services with these search engines [1]. Current service retrieval approaches have, however, serious limitations with respect to meeting these challenges. They either perform relatively poorly or make unrealistic demands of those who wish to index or retrieve services. This paper first reviews these approaches and then presents as well as evaluates a novel service retrieval approached based on the sophisticated use of process ontologies. It closes with a discussion if related work and open challenges for future work.

I. Horrocks and J. Hendler (Eds.): ISWC 2002, LNCS 2342, pp. 84–101, 2002.

2.   The State of the Art

Current service retrieval technology has emerged from several communities. The information retrieval community has focused on the retrieval of natural language documents, not services per se, and has as a result emphasized keyword-based approaches. The software agents and distributed computing communities have developed simple 'table-based' approaches for 'matchmaking' between tasks and on-line services. The software engineering community has developed by far the richest set of techniques for service retrieval [2]. We can get a good idea of the relative merits of these approaches by placing them in a *precision/recall* space (Figure 1):

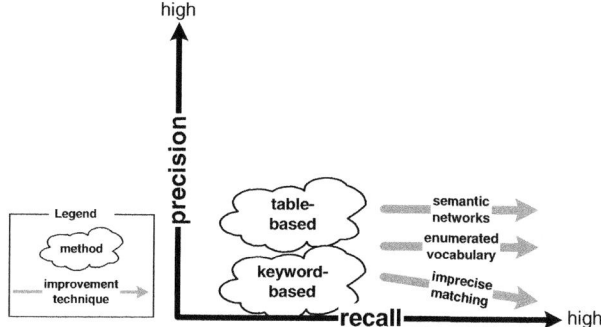

Fig. 1. The state of the art in service retrieval

Recall is the extent to which a search engine retrieves *all* of the items that one is interested in (i.e. avoiding false negatives) while *precision* is the extent to which the tool retrieves *only* the items that one is interested in (i.e. avoiding false positives) [3].

Most search engines, including service repositories such as www.uddi.org, look for items that contain the *keywords* in the query, which are sometimes prioritized using techniques such as TFIDF to increase effective precision [4]. Keyword-based approaches are, however, prone to both low precision, as irrelevant items may, e. g., contain the keyword, and imperfect recall due issues such as the use of synonyms (sometimes addressed with pre-enumerated vocabularies [5], semantic nets [6] and partial matching). The key underlying problem is that keywords are a poor way to capture the semantics of a query or item.

Table-based approaches [7] [8] [9] [10] [11] [12] are a second, increasingly popular, class of service model. A table-based service model consists of a typically fixed number of attribute value pairs describing the properties of an item. Figure 2, for example, shows a table-based model for an integer averaging service:

Description	a service to find the average of a list of integers
Input	Integers
Output	Real
Duration	number of inputs * 0.1 msec

Fig. 2. A table-based description of an integer sorting service

Both items and queries are described as tables: matches represent items whose property values match those in the query. All the commercial service search technologies we are aware of (e.g. Jini™, eSpeak, Salutation, UDDI/WSDL, [13]) use the table-based approach. The more sophisticated search tools emerging from the research community [14] [15] use ontologies and semantic nets to increase recall, e.g. returning a match if the input type of a service is equal to *or* a generalization of the input type specified in the query. Table-based models, however, do little to increase precision because of the impoverished range of information they capture, as they typically include a detailed description of how to *invoke* the service (i.e., parameter types, return types, calling protocols, etc.), but don't describe what the service actually *does*. The invocation-related information is of limited value for search purposes because services with different goals (e.g. services that compute averages, medians, quartiles, etc.) can share similar call signatures.

Other approaches (such as deductive retrieval [16] [17] [18] or execution-based retrieval [19] [20] [21]) are usually only suitable for limited application domains, as they are, typically, to complex (both from a computational and a usability perspective).

3   Our Approach: Exploiting Process Ontologies

Our challenge can thus be framed as being able to capture enough service and query semantics to substantively increase precision without reducing recall or making it unrealistically difficult for people to express these semantics. *Our central claim is that these goals can be achieved through the sophisticated use of process ontologies* [22]. In our approach, the salient behavior of a service is captured using process models, and these process models, as well as their components (subtasks, resources, and so on), are placed in the appropriate locations in the process ontology. Queries can then be defined (using a *process query language* we call PQL) to find all the services whose process models include a given set of entities and relationships. The greater expressiveness of process models, as compared to keywords or tables, offers the potential for substantively increased retrieval precision, at the cost of requiring that services be modeled in this more formal way. As we will see below, our preliminary evaluations suggest that the process-based approach offers qualitatively increased retrieval precision, and we will argue that this can be achieved with a reasonable expenditure of service modeling effort. Our approach can be viewed as having the functional architecture shown in (Figure 3), which we will consider below.

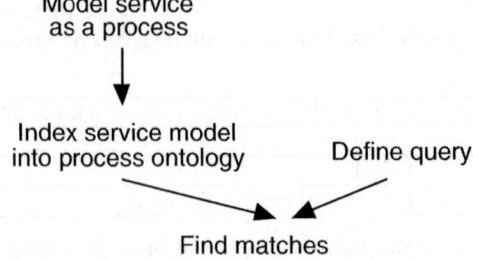

Fig. 3. Functional architecture of process-based service retrieval

3.1   Modeling Services as Process Models

The first step in our approach is to capture service behavior as process models. Why process models? To understand this choice, we need to understand more precisely the causes of imperfect precision (i.e. of false positives). One cause is that a component of the service model is taken to have an unintended *role*. For example, a keyword-based query to find mortgage services that deal with "payment defaults" (a kind of exception) would also match descriptions like "the payment defaults to $100/month" (an attribute value). The other cause for false positives occurs when a service model is taken to include an unintended *relationship* between components. For example, we may be looking for a mortgage service where insurance is provided for payment defaults, but a keyword search would not distinguish this from a service that provides insurance for the home itself. The trick to increasing retrieval precision, therefore, comes down to ensuring that the roles and relationships that are meaningful to the user are made explicit in both the query and the service model, so unintended meanings (and therefore false positives) can be avoided. We believe that process-modeling languages are well suited for this. Process modeling languages have been designed to capture the essence of different behaviors in a compact intuitive way, and have become ubiquitous for a very wide range of uses.

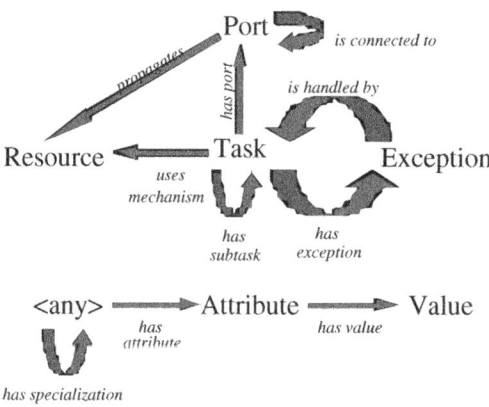

Fig. 4. Process model formalism

We use for our purposes a process modeling formalism (see Figure 4) that, similar to other processes modeling languages, includes the following components:

- *Attributes:* capture such information as a textual description, typical performance values (e.g. how long a process takes to execute), and so on.
- *Decomposition:* A process can be modeled as a collection of processes that can in turn be broken down ("decomposed") into sub-processes.
- *Resource Flows:* All process steps can have input and output *ports* through which *resources* flow allowing us to model consumed, used, and produced resources.
- *Mechanisms:* Processes can be annotated with the resources they *use* (as opposed to consume or produce). For example, the Internet can serve as a mechanism for a process.

- *Exceptions:* Processes typically have characteristic ways they can fail and, in at least some cases, associated schemes for anticipating and avoiding or detecting and resolving them. This is captured in our approach by annotating processes with their characteristic 'exceptions', and mapping these exceptions to processes describing how these exceptions can be handled [24].

Let us consider a simple example to help make this more concrete (Figure 5):

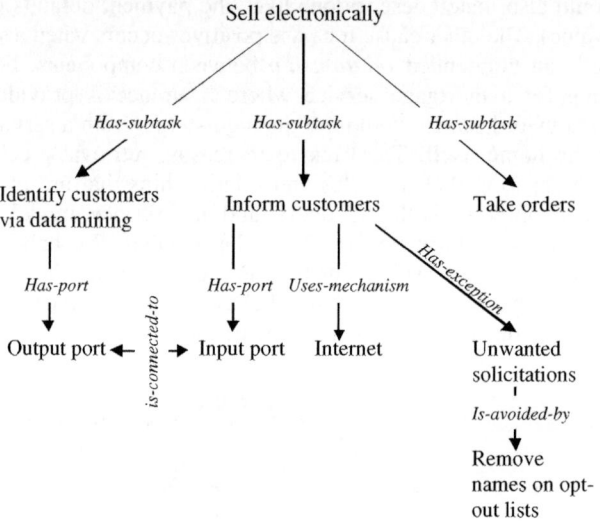

Fig. 5. An example of a process-based service model

This represents the process model for a service for selling items electronically. The plain text items represent entities (such as exceptions, ports and tasks), while the italicized items represent relationships between these entities. The substeps in this service model include 'identify potential customers via data mining', 'inform customers' (which uses the Internet as a mechanism), and 'take orders'. The potential exception of sending out unwanted solicitations is avoided by filtering out the names of individuals who have placed their names on 'opt-out' lists. Each of the entities can have attributes (not shown) that include their name, description, and so on.

Formally, any database of process descriptions (using the formalism above) can be defined as a typed graph:

$$Ont \ (Entities, \ Relationships) \tag{1}$$

where *entities* are the nodes in the graph and *relationships* are the graph edges. Furthermore, the following specifications apply:

- A node can only have one type ($\oplus$ denotes the logical exclusive-or operator):

$$x \in Entities \equiv (x \in Task) \oplus (x \in Resource) \oplus (x \in Port) \oplus (x \in Exception) \tag{2}$$
$$\oplus \ (x \in Attribute) \oplus (x \in Value)$$

- A relationship can only have one type and it connects nodes of certain types:

$$r(x, y) \in Relationships \equiv$$
$$[(r = Has\_specialiation) \wedge (x \in Entities) \wedge (y \in Entities) \wedge ((x, y) \in Has\_specialization)] \uplus$$
$$[(r = Has\_subtask) \wedge (x \in Task) \wedge (y \in Task) \wedge ((x, y) \in Has\_subtask)] \oplus$$
$$[(r = Has\_port) \wedge (x \in Task) \wedge (y \in Port) \wedge ((x, y) \in Has\_port)] \oplus$$
$$[(r = Uses\_mechanism) \wedge (x \in Task) \wedge (y \in Resource) \wedge ((x, y) \in Uses\_mechanism)] \oplus$$
$$[(r = Propagates) \wedge (x \in Port) \wedge (y \in Resource) \wedge ((x, y) \in Propagates)] \oplus \qquad (3)$$
$$[(r = Is\_handled\_by) \wedge (x \in Exception) \wedge (y \in Task) \wedge ((x, y) \in Is\_handled\_by)] \oplus$$
$$[(r = Has\_exception) \wedge (x \in Task) \wedge (y \in Exception) \wedge ((x, y) \in Has\_exception)] \oplus$$
$$[(r = Has\_subtask) \wedge (x \in Task) \wedge (y \in Task) \wedge ((x, y) \in Has\_subtask)] \oplus$$
$$[(r = Has\_attribute) \wedge (x \in Entities) \wedge (y \in Atribute) \wedge ((x, y) \in Has\_attribute)] \oplus$$
$$[(r = Has\_value) \wedge (x \in Attribute) \wedge (y \in Value) \wedge ((x, y) \in Has\_value)]$$

This representation is similar, and equivalent in expressiveness, to other full-fledged process modeling languages (e.g. IDEF [25], PIF [26], PSL [27] and CIMOSA [28]) and substantially more expressive than the keyword and table-based languages used in previous service retrieval efforts, by virtue of adding the important concepts of resource flows, task decompositions, and exceptions. It does not however, include primitives oriented at expressing control semantics, i.e. that describe *when* each subtask gets enacted. Such primitives were excluded for two reasons. First, most of the variation between process modeling languages occurs when representing control semantics, and we wanted a formalism to which a wide range of existing process models could easily be translated. Second, our experience to date that most service queries are concerned with *what* a process does, rather than *when* the parts of the process gets enacted.

Modeling service behaviors as process models of course involves manual effort, but we argue this need not be a major barrier. Because process formalisms are so widely used, many services already have process models defined for them, e.g., as part of their specification. The expertise needed to create such models is widely available. Process ontologies (see below) can reduce the modeling effort involved. Also, service providers will likely be motivated to create such process models, since they often differentiate themselves in the marketplace by how they provide their services, and process models make this explicit. Process models, finally, enable important uses other than search, such as automatic service composition.

3.2   Indexing Service Models into the Process Ontology

The second step of our approach is to index service models into a process ontology in order to facilitate later retrieval. An ontology consists, in general, of a hierarchy of entity descriptions ranging from the abstract at one end to the specific at the other. Items with similar semantics (e.g. processes with similar functions) appear close to each other, the way books with similar subjects appear close to each other in a library. Indexing a service comes down to placing the associated process model, as well as all of its components (attributes, ports, dependencies, subtasks and exceptions) on the appropriate branch in the ontology. Using an ontology is valuable for several reasons. It can reduce the burden of modeling a service, since one need only find the most similar process model in the ontology and then modify it to model a new service. Ontologies can increase recall, since similar services are co-located, one is apt to find relevant services simply by browsing the ontology near the matches one has already found. In addition, an ontology helps us find matches that are described using different, but semantically equivalent, terminology.

We build for this purpose on the MIT Process Handbook project. The Handbook is a process ontology, which has been under development at the Center for Coordination Science (CCS) for the past ten years [23] [29]. The growing Handbook database currently includes roughly 5000 process descriptions ranging over such areas as supply chain logistics, hiring, etc. The Handbook project has developed sophisticated tools that allow a knowledgeable user to index a process model in a matter of minutes. We believe that the Handbook ontology represents an excellent starting point for indexing many services because it is focused on business processes, which is what a high proportion of such services are likely to address.

3.3   Defining Queries

It is of course imaginable that we could do without queries entirely once services have been indexed into an ontology. One could simply browse the ontology to find the services that one is interested in, as in [30]. Our experience suggests however that browsing can be slow and difficult for all except the most experienced users. This problem is likely to be exacerbated when, as with online services, the space of services is large and dynamic. To address this challenge we have defined a query language called PQL (the Process Query Language) designed for retrieving process models indexed in an ontology. Process models can be straightforwardly viewed as entity-relationship diagrams made up of entities like tasks characterized by attributes and connected by relationships like 'has-subtask'. PQL queries are built up as combinations of three primitive clause types that check for these elements:

- Entity <entity> isa <entity type>
- Relation <source entity> <relationship type> <target entity> [*]
- Attribute <attribute> of <entity> {includes | equals} <value>

The 'entity' clause matches any entity of a given type (the entity types include task, resource, port and so on). The 'relation' clause matches any relationship of a given type between two entities (the relationship types include has-subtask, has-specialization, has-port, and so on). The optional asterisk finds the transitive closure of this relationship. The 'attribute' clause looks for entities with attributes that have given values. Any bracketed item <> can be replaced by a variable (with the format ?<string>) that is bound to the matching entity and passed to subsequent query clauses.

The 'When'-clause allows to group clauses into sub-queries:

- When {exists | does-not-exist} <query>

Let us consider a simple example to help make this more concrete. The query below searches for a sales service that uses the internet to inform customers:

```
attribute "Name" of ?sell includes "sell"
relation ?sell has-specialization ?process *
when exists (relation ?process has-subtask ?subtask *
            attribute "Name" of ?subtask includes "inform"
            attribute "Description" of ?subtask includes "internet")
```

The first clause searches for a processes in the ontology whose name includes "sell", the second finds all specializations of this, and the third checks if any subtasks of these services are "inform" processes with "internet" in their description. A PQL query is thus equivalent to a typed sub-graph pattern, and any search for a process model can then be treated as finding the nodes of type *task*, which match the graph pattern that represents the query.

The three clause types of PQL, and their variants, can be formalized as follows:

Relation x rel-type y
is defined as: $(x,y) \in$ rel-type, where rel-type $\in$ {has-specialization, has-subtask, ...}

Relation x rel-type y *
is formalized using a fixpoint/recursive definition, as:
$((x, y) \in rel\_type) \vee (\exists z : ((x,z) \in rel\_type) \wedge rel\_type(z,y)^*)$

Entity entity isa entity-type
is defined as:
entity $\in$ entity-type, where entity-type $\in$ {Task, Port, Resource, Exception, Attribute, ...}

Attribute attribute of entity equals value
is shorthand for two relationships, as follows:
has_attribute(entity, attribute) $\wedge$ has_value(attribute, value)

Attribute attribute of entity includes value
is defined as:
has_attribute(entity, attribute) $\wedge$ has_value(attribute, v1) $\wedge$ IsSubString(value, v1)

Note that PQL includes built-in functions, such as IsSubString, comparable to those in other query languages such as SQL. If any of the parameters to a predicate are preceded by a question mark (e.g., ?y), then it denotes a variable that needs to be bound to a value from the database/model that can fulfill its place.

The 'when' construct serves two roles. If used with the "exists" operator then it simply groups sub-queries in an intuitive way, and does not add any expressive power to PQL. For example:

Relation ?x Has_subtask ?y
When exists ((Relation ?y Has_subtask a))
is formalized equivalently with or without the "when" operator, as:
Has_subtask(?x,?y) $\wedge$ Has_subtask(?y, a)

If the when-statement is used with the "does-not-exist" option then it will only return a result if <query> does not. This introduces a form of *negation* into PQL, so:

When does-not-exist query
is defined as $\neg \exists x_{i=1..k}: x_{i=1..k} \in Entities :$ <query>
where: $x_{i=1..k}$ are the unbound variables in query.

The question of how to add negation to a query language is a non-trivial issue, as it may have major implications on its computational tractability. As will become obvious in section 5 below, the type of negation introduced here is consistent with an inflationary fixpoint approach, ensuring that the resulting language is bounded by polynomial time.

As a final example, let us consider how our original example PQL query is formalized:

Has_attribute(?sell, "Name") ∧ Has_value("Name", ?v1) ∧ IsSubString("sell", ?v1) ∧
Has_Specialization(?sell, ?process) ∧
Has_attribute(?process, "service?") ∧ Has_value("service?", "yes") ∧
(Has_subtask(?process, ?subtask) ∧
 Has_attribute(?subtask, "Name")∧Has_value("Name", ?v2)∧IsSubString("inform", ?v2) ∧
 Has_attribute(?subtask, "Description") ∧ Has_value("Description", ?v3) ∧
IsSubString("inform", ?v3))

PQL has been used successfully to represent a wide range of queries drawn from many different domains. Some other examples include "find a loan process that uses the internet, takes real estate as collateral, and has loan default insurance", "find all processes that take oil as an input and are prone to cause environmental damage", and so on. Our preliminary assessment is that PQL is sufficiently expressive to capture all queries describable in process-oriented terms.

3.4   Finding Matches

The algorithm for retrieving matches given a PQL query is straightforward. The clauses in the PQL query are tried in order, each clause executed in the variable binding environment accumulated from the previous clauses. The bindings that survive to the end represent the matching services. While we have not yet evaluated PQL's performance in detail yet, we do show (see below) that queries are within polynomial time complexity.

4   Empirical Evaluation

An initial version of the PQL interpreter has been implemented, and we have performed some preliminary evaluations of its precision and recall compared to existing (keyword and table-based) approaches. The following scheme was used for all of the evaluations described below. The roughly 5000 processes in the Process Handbook process ontology were treated as service models, which is reasonable since they all represent functions used in business contexts and many could imaginable be performed remotely. We then defined keyword and process-based queries that use the same keywords, operate over the same database of service models, and differ only in whether they use the role and relationship information encoded in the service models. We did not define a separate set of table-based service models and queries for this evaluation because, from the standpoint of retrieval precision, the keyword and table-based approaches are equivalent. The fact that table-based models differentiate name and description attributes does not help since descriptions almost invariably reprise the keywords included in the service name, and none of the queries we used made use of I/O specifications. In any case, if we had used queries that refer to such I/O specs, it would not change the relative precision of table- and process-based queries since both can use I/O information. We tested simple keyword search as well as TFIDF, the latter because its potentially greater effective precision makes it a dominant scheme for keyword-based search. All the queries in our evaluation had perfect recall, because of the consistency in the use of keywords in the process descriptions. While we do not anticipate that process-based search will differ significantly in recall from keyword and table-based, this remains a subject for future evaluation. The queries below, clearly, are only illustrative, since a complete evaluation would require executing a representative range of many queries.

Since our goal was to determine whether process-based retrieval improves on existing approaches, our evaluation focused on the value of the additional information captured by process-based service models as compared to keyword- and table-based models. This additional information falls into five categories: task decompositions, port connectivity, exception handling, task mechanisms, and specializations. We examine each category in the sections below.

4.1   Task Decomposition

Our process-based service model allows us to explicitly describe the subtasks that make up a service's behavior. This can help avoid confounding information that refers to different subtasks. Imagine, for example, that we are searching for a sales service that informs customers using the internet. We can frame this query as follows:

Table 1. Query types and actual Queries

Type	Query
Keyword-based	"Sell" "inform "internet"
Process-based	attribute "Name" of ?service includes "sell"
	when exists (relation ?service has-subtask ?subtask *
	attribute "Name" of ?subtask includes "inform"
	attribute ?attr of ?subtask includes "internet")

The keyword and table-based service models are not able to distinguish cases where "inform" and "internet" (or their synonyms) belong to the same subtask from cases where these keywords belong to different subtasks (and thus are probably not relevant). We would thus predict false positives and therefore lower precision for these approaches, and this is in fact what happens. There were 13 correct matches for this query, including such processes as "Sell travel services via electronic auction", "Sell books via electronic store" and so on. The PQL query had 13 correct matches out of the 18 it returned, for a precision of 72%. A simple keyword-based search had 280 returns, for a precision of roughly 5%. TFIDF did not improve much upon simple keyword search in this case: its precision reached a maximum of 6% (at match 163), and its' overall precision was lower because it allowed partial matches and therefore generated more total returns,

4.2   Task Mechanisms

Our process-based service model allows us to describe the mechanisms used by a task, thereby avoiding false positives due to the appearance of the same keyword with a different role. We can, for example, refine the PQL query given above so that it only matches services where the keyword "internet" appears as a mechanism (the added clauses are bold type):

> attribute "Name" of ?service includes "sell"
> when exists (relation ?service has-subtask ?subtask *
> attribute "Name" of ?subtask includes "inform"
> **relation ?subtask uses-mechanism ?mechanism**
> **attribute "Name" of ?mechanism includes "Internet")**

This query had 13 correct matches, as above, but this time out of 16 responses, for an improved precision of 81%.

4.3   Specialization

The has-specialization relationship enabled by our inclusion of a process ontology can be used to avoid false positives by ensuring that the service, and its components, have the semantics that we desire. For example, we can use this to refine the query presented above to only accept services whose subtask is a specialization of the generic "Inform" task, thereby pruning out services with subtasks that include the string "inform' in their name for unrelated reasons (e.g. the subtask named "Collect configuration information using Internet"):

> attribute "Name" of ?service includes "sell"
> when exists (relation ?service has-subtask ?subtask *
> attribute "Name" of ?subtask includes "inform"
> relation ?subtask uses-mechanism ?mechanism
> attribute "Name" of ?mechanism includes "Internet"
> **attribute "Name" of ?class equals "Inform"**
> **relation ?class has-specialization ?subtask)**

With this refinement, the query returns 13 correct matches out of 13 total, for an accuracy of 100%.

Similar ontologies have of course been made available for table-based service retrieval engines. UDDI, for example, provides the UNSPSC taxonomy of product and service categories and the NAICS taxonomy of industry codes, among others. The particular value of the ontology we utilize is that it captures functions that a business might require at a much finer grain than the taxonomies mentioned above. We believe this will be helpful for service retrieval since many queries will, no doubt, be looking for services to support business functions. At the time of writing our database did not categorize services using these other taxonomies, so we were unable to evaluate their relative merits.

4.4   Exception Handling

Our process-based service model allows us to explicitly delineate the exceptions faced by a service, as well as the handlers available for dealing with each exception. Imagine, for example, that we wish to find a sales service that informs customers via the internet but avoids the exception of sending unwanted solicitations (e.g. by filtering out the names that appear on "opt-out" lists). We can, for this purpose, refine the query described above as follows shown in Table 2.

Table 2. Query types and Query for exception handling Query

Type	Query
Keyword-based	"Sell" "inform" "internet" "avoid" "unwanted" "opt-out"

Process-based	attribute "Name" of ?service includes "sell"
	when exists (relation ?service has-subtask ?subtask *
	    attribute "Name" of ?subtask includes "inform"
	    relation ?subtask uses-mechanism ?mechanism
	    attribute "Name" of ?mechanism includes "Internet"
	    attribute "Name" of ?class equals "Inform"
	    relation ?class has-specialization ?subtask
	    relation ?subtask has-exception ?exception
	    attribute "Name" of ?exception includes "unwanted"
	    relation ?exception is-avoided-by ?handler
	    relation ?attr of ?handler includes "opt-out")

We would expect the keyword- and table-based models to incur false positives by finding services that have the same keywords in different roles, that have that exception but do not have a handler for it, or that use a different handler (e.g. allowing recipients to remove their name from subsequent solicitations) for the same exception. In this case, there was one correct match. PQL returned only that item, for a precision of 100%. Keyword-based search returned 188 matches (0.53% precision), and TFIDF did not do any better, returning 248 documents, with a maximum precision at 0.4%.

4.5   Port Connectivity

The final category of information uniquely provided by process-based service models is port connectivity, which captures the resource flow relationships between tasks. We may, for example, want a service that generates the lists of potential customers to inform by applying data-mining techniques, which implies that the output of a data mining subtask is an input to the inform customers subtask. This would imply a PQL query like the following:

```
attribute "Name" of ?sell includes "sell"
when exists (relation ?process has-subtask ?sub1
        attribute "Name" of ?sub1 includes "inform"
        relation ?sub1 has-port ?port1
        entity ?port1 isa input-port
        relation ?process has-subtask ?sub2
        attribute "Name" of ?sub includes "mining"
        relation ?sub2 has-port ?port2
        entity ?port2 isa output-port
        relation ?port1 is-connected-to ?port2)
```

A query like this can avoid false positives wherein a data-mining subtask exists in the service model, but it does not provide information to the inform customers step. The data-mining subtask may be applied instead, for example, to the database of sales generated by this service. We would therefore expect the keyword- and slot-based retrieval queries to demonstrate lower precision than PQL. At the time of writing we were unable to evaluate this because the Process Handbook ontology did not include sufficient port connectivity information; this will be addressed in future work.

4.6   Conclusions

While a wider range of queries and services needs to be evaluated, these test cases strongly suggest that the greater expressiveness of process-based service models can in fact result in qualitatively higher retrieval precision. Even a PQL query that only took advantage of the subtask relationships in the process-based models produced retrieval precision more than 10 times greater than keyword-based approaches. The relative advantage of PQL, moreover, increased radically as the number of relationships specified in the query increased.

5   Complexity Analysis

One of the major considerations for any retrieval capability is that it must return answers in a timely way. The speed at which queries get returned should be comparable to that of existing document retrieval mechanisms, which manage to search millions of documents in seconds. Even though our experience with the prototype implementation has been favorable (i.e., queries generally take several seconds at most, even though our implementation does not exploit well-known performance-enhancing techniques such as reverse indices or query optimization) there is still the question of how the performance will scale with the size of the database. The computational complexity of PQL can be most easily assessed by mapping it to formal query languages with known computational complexity. We will start by showing that PQL without the *-modifier can be mapped to first-order query languages like CALC whose complexity is in QLOGSPACE. We then extend the analysis by mapping PQL with the *-modifier to a DATALOG-type language whose computational complexity is polynomial. These are good results: polynomial complexity implies that the computation needed to enact a PQL query is bounded by a polynomial function in the size of the service model database. We can, thus, expect performance comparable to most database query languages.

5.2   The Complexity of PQL without the *-Modifier Is in QLOGSPACE

CALC can be loosely defined as all the queries that can be defined using first-order calculus (i.e., any query that can be defined using $\neg$, $\wedge$, $\vee$, $\forall$, $\exists$, without recursion/fixpoints) and has been shown to be in QLOGSPACE [31].

Theorem #1: Any PQL query (without the *-modifier) can be mapped to CALC
Proof: The Proof basically follows from the formal definition of the PQL clauses. All the relationships of the PQL-model are basically relations. For example, *Has_type* is basically a binary relation where both parameters are from the domain *Entities* (also defined in the data-model). Also, any PQL (without the *-modifier) clause can be written as a conjunction of Relationship assertions, basically limiting the scope of the relationship. Expressed formally:
1. PQL as a conjunction of relational assertions:
    A basic PQL query is defined as
    $r_1(p1_1, p2_1) \wedge r_2(p1_2, p2_2) \wedge \ldots \wedge r_k(p1_k, p2_k),$
            where 1) all $r_{i, i=1..k} \in$ Relationships

2) $pX_{i,i=1..k}$ are elements of the respective domains

3) some of the pX_i are bound to values

4) there might be some X, Y and i, j where $pX_i = pY_j$

Which can be rewritten as a CALC query

$$\{(pX_i, ...) \mid \exists\, pX_i, ... : r_1(p1_1, p2_1) \wedge r_2(p1_2, p2_2) \wedge ... \wedge r_k(p1_k, p2_k)\}$$

where the X and i denote the indices to unbound parameters.

2. Grouping does not any expressive power to PQL. Hence, it does not need to be mapped to CALC.

3. Grouping with negation adds the element of the negation of an existential quantifier to PQL, which is contained in the CALC language specification

□

Given Theorem #1 and the fact that CALC is in QLOGSPACE it follows that PQL (without the *-modifier) is in QLOGSPACE. As we are mainly interested in the time properties and QLOGSPACE is contained in polynomial time we can deduce that the time complexity of PQL (without *-modifier) is at worst polynomial.

5.2   The Complexity of PQL Is in Polynomial Time

The question remains what to do about the *-modifier. One option is to pre-compute the typed transitive hull for each of the relationships used in the data model, so that every relation would have a respective starred relation that would be its' transitive closure. Given this, any starred query would be in QLOGSPACE. There remains the question of the complexity of updating the starred relations when adding a new element.

Theorem #2: Updating the starred relationship on inserting a new element into the relationship is at worst linear in the size of the starred relationship.

Proof (sketch): When a new element **x** gets added to as being related to element **a** to relation R (i.e., as (a, x)) then all that would need to be done is to, first, add (a,x) to R and, second, query R* for all elements where some element y is related to a as follows (y, a) and then update R* for each of these y's with (y,x). Spelled out as an algorithm:

FOR EACH (y,z) in R*
  IF z = a THEN ADD (y, x) to R*
NEXT
  Which is at worst linear in the size of R*

□

Alternatively, we could evaluate the starred relationship at run-time, which is equivalent to computing the reachability of one node on a graph from another node, which is computable in DATALOG as follows:

Reachable(x, y) ← R(x,y)
Reachable(x, y) ← Reachable(x, u), R(u, y)

This is basically a different notation for the definition of the *-modifier above. Consequently, as reachabilty can be mapped to DATALOG and DATALOG has been shown to be in polynomial time ([31] pp. 437, 343-355), the evaluation of any PQL-query (including the *-modifier) can be computed in polynomial time.

As mentioned above one problem remains. Standard DATALOG does not contain negation. If we add negation the semantic interpretation of DATALOG becomes unclear. One has to decide whether one uses strictly inflationary fixpoint semantics, leading to a query language bounded in polynomial *time*, or whether one uses non-inflationary fixpoint semantics, leading to a language bounded by polynomial *space*. For computational tractability the former would be preferred. In our particular case we are lucky. First, the only part of PQL that uses fixpoint semantics is the computation of the starred relationships. These can be seen as pure DATALOG queries (i.e, without negation) embedded in a CALC query. Second, our language adheres to the inflationary semantics as it does not remove previously added result bindings when calculating the fixpoint. Hence it is contained in DATALOG¬, which is bounded by polynomial time.

6   Contributions of This Work

High retrieval service precision is widely recognised as a critical enabler for important uses that range from finding useful software components or applications, to finding best practice models, to tracking down people or organisations with the skills you need. Our work can be viewed as representing a new class of service retrieval technique that helps achieve these goals (Figure 6).

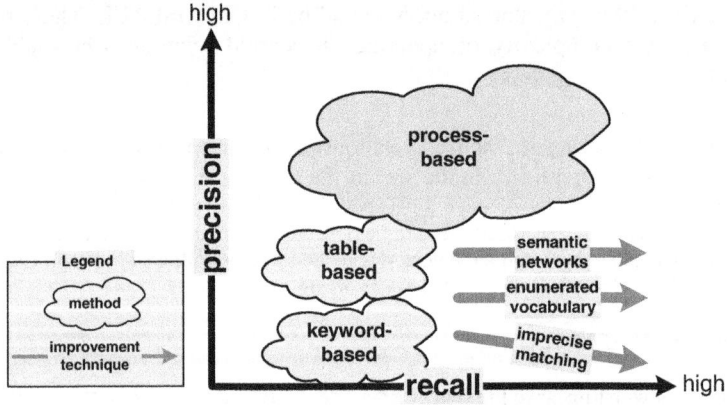

Fig. 6. The contribution of process-based service retrieval technology

Our evaluations to date suggest that process-based queries produce retrieval precision qualitatively greater than that of existing service retrieval approaches, while retaining polynomial complexity for query enactment. This work represents a significant contribution to work on pattern matching over generic graph-like representations, such as graph grammars [32], object-oriented query languages [33], and XQuery (a query language for XML; see http://www.w3.org/TR/xquery/). The unique value of our work comes from exploiting the more constrained semantics of process models to enable higher-precision service retrieval.

7   Next Steps

While our preliminary results are promising, many important challenges remain:

- *Evaluation:* PQL needs to be evaluated for a wide range of queries in order to assess its precision and recall performance as compared to existing approaches, and to suggest refinements in the language and associated interpreter. An important issue will be examining the tradeoff between the expressiveness of the service models, the accuracy/completeness of service model indexing, and the resulting precision/recall performance.

- *Increased recall:* PQL currently makes no use of standard recall-enhancing techniques such as synonym databases or inexact/partial matches. One immediate step will involve enhancing the PQL interpreter with a semantic net such as WordNet [34] that represents synonym and other useful relationships. This promises to be a powerful combination because a process-oriented query gives us crucial additional information about the role of the keywords in the query (e.g. a keyword in a task name is probably a verb, and a keyword in a mechanism name is probably a noun). Another key issue involves *modeling differences*. It is likely that in at least some cases a service may be modeled in a way that is semantically equivalent to but nevertheless does not syntactically match a given PQL query. We plan to explore for this purpose the use of query mutation operators that can modify a given PQL query in a way that (largely) preserves its semantics (e.g. by generalizing a type specification) while allowing a wider range of service matches.

- *Automated indexing.* A key criterion for a successful service retrieval approach is minimizing the manual effort involved in listing new services with the search engine. Ideally services can be classified automatically. Previous efforts for automatic service classification have used similarity metrics based mainly on word frequency statistics [35] [36] [37]. We plan to augment such approaches using the taxonomic reasoning and graph-theoretic similarity measures made possible by our approach to service modeling.

- *User interface.* PQL, like most query languages, is fairly verbose and requires that users be familiar with its syntax. An important part of our work will be to develop more intuitive interfaces suitable for human users, for example based on flowcharts or natural language.

References

1. Bakos, J.Y., *Reducing Buyer Search Costs: Implications for Electronic Marketplaces.* Management Science, 1997. **43**.
2. Mili, H., F. Mili, and A. Mili, *Reusing software: issues and research directions.* IEEE Transactions on Software Engineering, 1995. **21**(6): p. 528-62.
3. Salton, G., G. Salton, and M.J. McGill, *Introduction to Modern Information Retrieval.* 1983, New York: McGraw-Hill.
4. Salton, G. and M.J. McGill, *Introduction to modern information retrieval.* McGraw-Hill computer science series. 1983, New York: McGraw-Hill. xv, 448.
5. Prieto-Diaz, R., *Implementing faceted classification for software reuse.* 12th International Conference on Software Engineering, 1990. **9**: p. 300-4.

6.   Magnini, B., *Use of a lexical knowledge base for information access systems.* International Journal of Theoretical & Applied Issues in Specialized Communication, 1999. **5**(2): p. 203-228.
7.   Henninger, S., *Information access tools for software reuse.* Journal of Systems & Software, 1995. **30**(3): p. 231-47.
8.   Fernandez-Chamizo, C., et al., *Case-based retrieval of software components.* Expert Systems with Applications, 1995. **9**(3): p. 397-421.
9.   Fugini, M.G. and S. Faustle. *Retrieval of reusable components in a development information system.* in *Second International Workshop on Software Reusability.* 1993: IEEE Press.
10. Devanbu, P., et al., *LaSSIE: a knowledge-based software information system.* Communications of the ACM, 1991. **34**(5): p. 34-49.
11. ESPEAK, *Hewlett Packard's Service Framework Specification.* 2000, HP Inc.
12. Raman, R., M. Livny, and M. Solomon, *Matchmaking: an extensible framework for distributed resource management.* Cluster Computing, 1999. **2**(2): p. 129-38.
13. Richard, G.G., *Service advertisement and discovery: enabling universal device cooperation.* IEEE Internet Computing, 2000. **4**(5): p. 18-26.
14. Sycara, K., et al. *Matchmaking Among Heterogeneous Agents on the Internet.* in *AAAI Symposium on Intelligent Agents in Cyberspace.* 1999: AAAI Press.
15. Fensel, D. *An Ontology-based Broker: Making Problem-Solving Method Reuse Work.* in *Workshop on Problem-Solving Methods for Knowledge-based Systems at the 15th International Joint Conference on AI (IJCAI-97).* 1997. Nagoya, Japan.
16. Meggendorfer, S. and P. Manhart. *A Knowledge And Deduction Based Software Retrieval Tool.* in *6th Annual Knowledge-Based Software Engineering Conference.* 1991: IEEE Press.
17. Chen, P., R. Hennicker, and M. Jarke. *On the retrieval of reusable software components.* in *Proceedings Advances in Software Reuse. Selected Papers from the Second International Workshop on Software Reusability.* 1993.
18. Kuokka, D.R. and L.T. Harada, *Issues and extensions for information matchmaking protocols.* International Journal of Cooperative Information Systems, 1996. **5**: p. 2-3.
19. Podgurski, A. and L. Pierce, *Retrieving reusable software by sampling behavior.* ACM Transactions on Software Engineering & Methodology, 1993. **2**(3): p. 286-303.
20. Hall, R.j. *Generalized behavior-based retrieval (from a software reuse library).* in *15th International Conference on Software Engineering.* 1993.
21. Park, Y., *Software retrieval by samples using concept analysis.* Journal of Systems & Software, 2000. **54**(3): p. 179-83.
22. Klein, M. and A. Bernstein. *Searching for Services on the Semantic Web using Process Ontologies.* in *The First Semantic Web Working Symposium (SWWS-1).* 2001. Stanford, CA USA.
23. Malone, T.W. and K. Crowston, *The interdisciplinary study of coordination.* ACM Computing Surveys, 1994. **26**(1): p. 87-119.
24. Klein, M. and C. Dellarocas, *A Knowledge-Based Approach to Handling Exceptions in Workflow Systems.* Journal of Computer-Supported Collaborative Work. Special Issue on Adaptive Workflow Systems., 2000. **9**(3/4).

25. NIST, *Integrated Definition for Function Modeling (IDEF0)*. 1993, National Institute of Standards and Technology.
26. Lee, J. and M. Gruninger, *The Process Interchange Format "The Process Interchange Format and Framework v.1.2*. Knowledge Engineering Review, 1998(March).
27. Schlenoff, C., et al., *The essence of the process specification language*. Transactions of the Society for Computer Simulation, 1999. **16**(4): p. 204-16.
28. Kosanke, K., *CIMOSA: Open System Architecture for CIM*. 1993: Springer Verlag.
29. Malone, T.W., et al., *Tools for inventing organizations: Toward a handbook of organizational processes*. Management Science, 1999. **45**(3): p. 425-443.
30. Latour, L. and E. Johnson. *Seer: a graphical retrieval system for reusable Ada software modules*. in *Third International IEEE Conference on Ada Applications and Environments*. 1988: IEEE Comput. Soc. Press.
31. Abiteboul, S., R. Hull, and V. Vianu, *Foundations of Databases*. 1995, Reading, MA: Addison-Wesley Publishing.
32. Rozenberg, G., ed. *Handbook of Graph Grammars and Computing by Graph Transformation*. Vol. 3. 1999, World Scientific.
33. Kim, W., *Introduction to Object-Oriented Databases*. 1990, Cambridge, MA: MIT Press.
34. Fellbaum, C., ed. *WordNet: An Electronic Lexical Database*. 1998, MIT Press: Cambridge MA USA.
35. Frakes, W.b. and B.a. Nejmeh, *Software reuse through information retrieval*. Proceedings of the Twentieth Hawaii International Conference on System Sciences, 1987. **2**: p. 6-9.
36. Maarek, Y.s., D.M. Berry, and G.e. Kaiser, *An information retrieval approach for automatically constructing software libraries*. IEEE Transactions on Software Engineering, 1991. **17**(8): p. 800-13.
37. Girardi, M.R. and B. Ibrahim, *Using English to retrieve software*. Journal of Systems & Software, 1995. **30**(3): p. 249-70.

Automatic Generation
of Java/SQL Based Inference Engines
from RDF Schema and RuleML

Andreas Eberhart

International University in Germany
Campus 2, 76646 Bruchsal, Germany
eberhart@i-u.de
http://www.i-u.de/schools/eberhart/

Abstract. This paper describes two approaches for automatically converting RDF Schema and RuleML sources into an inference engine and storage repository. Rather than using traditional inference systems, our solution bases on mainstream technologies like Java and relational database systems. While this necessarily imposes some restrictions, the ease of integration into an existing IT landscape is a major advantage. We present the conversion tools and their limitations. Furthermore, an extension to RuleML is proposed, that allows Java-enabled reaction rules, where calls to Java libraries can be performed upon a rule firing. This requires hosts to be Java-enabled when rules and code are moved across the web. However, the solution allows for great engineering flexibility.

1 Introduction

The Semantic Web is about to open up exciting new possibilities and enable a wide array of new applications on the web, that are able to process large amounts of machine readable data. Starting with the basic RDF and RDF Schema markup languages, more powerful and higher level languages like DAML+OIL and RuleML are being specified and tools supporting them being developed. Nevertheless, we feel that the adoption of these new technologies with a wide user community is still lagging behind. In a recent study [5] we found that it is extremely hard to find RDF data on the web today, unless considerable effort is invested in the search process. One can only speculate about the reasons for this, but we believe that it is crucial for the success of the Semantic Web to provide tools that integrate with proven and widely used technologies, namely object oriented languages like Java or C#, database management systems (DBMSs), and Web Services. It is clear that such systems cannot offer the full range of features provided by an XSB-based solution for instance. However, the example of the CiteSeer research index [2] shows that it is at least as important to scale as it is to provide complex reasoning and inference functionality.

In this paper we present the OntoJava [4] and OntoSQL cross compilers. OntoJava automatically converts RDF Schema and RuleML

I. Horrocks and J. Hendler (Eds.): ISWC 2002, LNCS 2342, pp. 102–116, 2002.

sources into a set of Java classes that comprise a main memory object database with a built in forward chaining rule engine. OntoSQL maps both recursive and non-recursive rules onto SQL-99 running on an IBM DB2 database server. Both software packages are open source and can be obtained from http://www.i-u.de/schools/eberhart/ontojava/ and http://www.i-u.de/schools/eberhart/ontosql/.

The rest of the paper is organized as follows. The next section provides some background on RDF Schema, RuleML, and RDF query languages. Sections 3 and 4 then present the OntoJava and OntoSQL cross-compilers along with restrictions imposed by the respective mapping approach used. The remaining sections 5 and 6 describe future work, evaluate the approach, and summarize the paper.

2   Background

One of the main goals of the Semantic Web initiative is to promote sharing and reuse of semi-structured, machine-readable information on the web. A key to this strategy is the stack of mark-up languages consisting of RDF, RDF Schema,[1] and DAML+OIL.[2]. The recently started RuleML [1] initiative builds on this work, allowing rules to be encoded in a standard way. In the future it might even be possible to obtain the latest set of tax rules directly from the government.

Crucial pieces are engines that are able to store, handle, and process data encoded using these mark-up languages. A lot of work has been done in the area of storing and querying RDF data. The first RDF query languages like RDFDB mainly base on graph matching algorithms. This approach is augmented by features to also query the schema, as in RQL, and support for non-recursive rules in RDFQL. SquishQL is another variant being used in the RDQL and Inkling projects. Its syntax bases on SQL. The XSB deductive database is often used by Semantic Web related projects [3]. Apart from its query capabilities, XSB is also able to load facts from a relational database via an ODBC interface, allowing to easily access large amounts of data stored in commercial enterprise information systems.

Engines supporting RuleML are also available. A frequently used approach is to use stylesheets to transform the XML-based rules into the language of an inference system such as JESS. The TRIPLE language provides great flexibility by allowing the language semantics of RDF Schema, DAML+OIL, or others to be modeled in horn logic. Together with the query, these logic statements are then run against XSB [12]. A mapping of RuleML to the TRIPLE language is also possible. The RuleML initiative also joined forces with the Java Specification Request JSR-000094 to develop a Java rule engine API.[3]

---

[1] http://www.w3.org/RDF

[2] http://www.daml.org

[3] http://jcp.org/jsr/detail/94.jsp

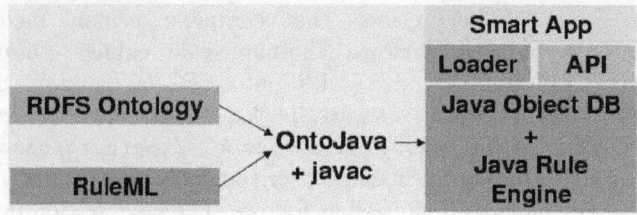

Fig. 1. The object database/inference engine generated by OntoJava can be loaded with RDF data and accessed by an application

3   OntoJava

The core idea behind OntoJava is that a directed, labeled RDF graph lends itself to being modeled using objects and object references of an object oriented programming language like Java. An object located in a main memory database represents every resource with its URI. We will examine to what extent the restrictions on the graph's arcs imposed by RDF Schema can be enforced by the language's type system and which restrictions are necessary. Apart form this discussion, we introduce the OntoJava cross compiler, that automatically converts RDF Schema, and RuleML into a set of Java Classes that act as a combined main memory object database with a built in forward chaining rule engine. Figure 1 illustrates this process and how a smart application can interface with the object database. An object-oriented language like Java offers many advantages and therefore the section concludes by proposing Java-enabled reaction rules and ways to customize the generated classes.

3.1   Mapping the Class Taxonomy

A class taxonomy, which can be expressed in RDF Schema, is the backbone of an ontology. Domain concepts are represented as classes with a hierarchy being imposed by the `subClassOf` property. Recent advances in the area of ontology mark-up languages resulted in the popular DAML+OIL approach [9], which bases on RDF Schema but is way more expressive. OntoJava works with RDF Schema, due to the availability of powerful editing tools such as Protégé [11]. Section 3.5 briefly covers how certain aspects beyond RDF Schema could be implemented by OntoJava. Consider the following example:

```
<rdfs:Class rdf:about="&pre;Person">
    <rdfs:subClassOf rdf:resource="&pre;Animal"/>
</rdfs:Class>
```

OntoJava maps every RDFS class into a Java class. The `subClassOf` property is similar to inheritance in object oriented systems with respect to both being transitive relationships defining the class hierarchy. However, the RDF Schema version is more flexible than its Java or C# counterpart since it allows multiple inheritance. OntoJava is therefore not able to handle multiple inheritance in the RDFS source at the moment. Section 3.6 outlines a simple solution for this limitation where RDF Schema classes are converted to interfaces which are then implemented. The RDF Schema example above is mapped to a class `Person` that inherits from `Animal`.

```
public class Person extends Animal
```

3.2   Mapping Properties

RDF Schema properties are defined with a domain and a range. Using the directed labeled graph metaphor, an arc's label identifies which property it refers to. The types of the resources connected by the arc must be the same class that's listed as the property's range or domain, or a subclass of it. The range is decisive for the type of the arc's source, the domain for its destination's type. Besides a class, the range of a property can also be a literal. Properties of classes can be defined as follows:

```
<rdf:Property rdf:about="&pre;isParentOf"
    <rdfs:domain rdf:resource="&pre;Person"/>
    <rdfs:range rdf:resource="&pre;Person"/>
</rdf:Property>

<rdf:Property rdf:about="&pre;name"
    <rdfs:domain rdf:resource="&pre;Person"/>
    <rdfs:range rdf:resource="&rdfs;Literal"/>
</rdf:Property>
```

Properties with a literal as the range are mapped directly into instance variables, which is quite straightforward. Note that it is easy to change this to get/set access methods. This becomes necessary if changes need to be tracked to support an undo operation or if multiple inheritance basing on interfaces is implemented. Relations to other instances are represented by a collection of references to other Java objects. This is the natural representation of a directed labeled graph in Java. The RDF Schema example above causes to following methods and variables to be defined in the class `Person`:

```
public class Person extends Animal {
    public String name;

    private HashSet isParentOf = new HashSet();
    public void putIsParentOf(Person p) {
        has.add(p);
    }
    public boolean getIsParentOf(Person p) {
        return has.contains(p);
    }
```

```
public HashSet getAllIsParentOf() {
    return isParentOf;
}
}
```

As sections 3.3 and 3.5 will explain further, the get/put access methods play an important role for the rule mechanism or when restrictions on the variables are to be checked. The corresponding get and put methods ensure that the appropriate data types, as defined in the RDF Schema property definition, are used. Note that the Java compiler enforces this. RDF Schema allows a property to have multiple domains, but only a single range. Multiple domains would result in several Java classes having variables and methods with the same name, which is no problem.

In terms of logic, the assertion $isParentOf(a, b)$ corresponds to the invocation of a.putIsParentOf(b). The query $isParentOf(a, b)$ can be answered by calling a.getIsParentOf(b) whereas a.getAllIsParentOf() yields the answer to $isParentOf(a, X)$. Finally, $isParentOf(X, Y)$ is answered by iterating over all person instances and calling getAllIsParentOf again.

Ternary relations are not part of RDF and are handled by a workaround of using an intermediate pseudo resource. A similar scheme can be applied to OntoJava by promoting a relation from a simple object reference to having its own object, which can then point to more than two constituents.

3.3   Mapping Rules

The two basic rule evaluation strategies are forward and backward chaining. Obviously a imperative language environment lends itself to forward chaining, where the rules are executed in an if-then fashion. Rule implications are simply asserted into the fact base as new facts. The popular Java Expert System Shell (JESS)[4] is another representative for this evaluation style, implementing the RETE [7] algorithm to ensure efficient rule execution.

Restrictions on the rules' expressiveness, namely disallowing negation, make sure, that exactly one minimal model exists for the set of rules [6]. A minimal model describes the smallest possible fact base, where for any variable assignment on any rule body yielding true, the rule's head is also true. Therefore, if the minimal model is contained in the current fact base, no more rules will fire and assert new facts. The order in which the rules are evaluated does not matter, since the fact base cannot shrink. If stratified negation is allowed, rules containing the not operator must be executed last. This feature is not yet implemented in OntoJava.

In OntoJava, each rule from the RuleML base is converted into a static method. The brute force approach would be to check the right side for all possible bindings of the free variables for each rule until no new assertion occurs, which would be quite inefficient. OntoJava implements the following optimizations. Every time an update takes place on a specific property of an

---

[4] http://herzberg.ca.sandia.gov/jess/

object, all rules are evaluated, that contain that property in their right side, i.e. the rules that are potentially affected by the change. This means that the rules are checked incrementally. Consider the rule $isUncleOf(A, C) \leftarrow isBrotherOf(A, B) \wedge isParentOf(B, C)$ which has some label, say rule5. Further assume that this is the only rule, which has the isBrotherOf predicate on the right side. This causes the following call to be placed in the putIsBrotherOf access method in the person class:

```
public void putIsBrotherOf(Person p) {
    if (!(isBrotherOf.add(p)))
        return;
    Rule.rule5(this, p, null);
}
```

First, the new relationship is stored by inserting it into the set datastructure. If the object was already in there, the add method returns false and the call returns. Otherwise, the rule is activated. Since the rule has three variables, three parameters are passed. We also know that the added relation is the only change to the database. Therefore, A and B, the first and second variable, must be bound to this, the current object, and p, the object inserted into the datastructure. Only C must be bound to all persons. Here, we can use the free variables' type information. A free variable appearing with a isParentOf predicate can only be bound to persons. Thus, instead of iterating over all objects, we only need to iterate over persons. The following shows the rule's code:

```
public static void rule5(Person a, Person b, Person c) {
    if a==null, iterate a over all persons
    if b==null, iterate b over all persons
    if c==null, iterate c over all persons
    with combinations of (a, b, c) {
        if (a.getIsBrotherOf(b) && b.getIsParentOf(c))
            a.putIsUncleOf(c);
    }
}
```

Note that the call to putIsUncleOf can again trigger other rules that are activated in the respective put method.

Obviously this approach will not perform efficiently for rules with many free variables, since all but two of the combinations of free variables need to be tested by nested loops. We are planning another optimization here by performing short circuit evaluation of parts of the condition at the outer loops. This should drastically reduce the number of combinations that need to be checked.

Rules with large amounts of free variables being checked in nested loops resemble a relational join very much. This leads to section 4 where we examine how rules can be evaluated top-down by an SQL engine.

3.4   Property Inheritance

RDF Schema defines the core property `subPropertyOf` with the following semantics:

$$parent(a, b) \leftarrow subPropertyOf(father, parent) \wedge father(a, b) \qquad (1)$$

This rule can be rewritten into a set of rules:

$$\{p(a, b) \leftarrow c(a, b) \mid subPropertyOf(c, p))\} \qquad (2)$$

Rather than implementing special handling for subproperties in the generated code of the access methods, we decided to reuse the built-in rule mechanism and include a rule for each subproperty relation defined in the RDF Schema source according to equation 2.

The transitivity of `subPropertyOf` is handled by the fact that asserting the parent property through the rule will in turn trigger another rule asserting the grandparent property, and so on.

3.5   Constraints

RDF Schema currently has no mechanism for defining further constraints. However, it is clear that this would be a valuable addition. DAML+OIL, for instance, offers a construct like `daml:maxCardinality` to restrict the number of outgoing arcs from an object. Dealing with a constraint violation includes detecting the violation, notifying the user, and finally reversing changes made to the data repository. Constraints cannot be checked incrementally, since partially inserted data might reflect an inconsistent state. Once the user issues some sort of commit, the conditions must be checked. It is definitely possible to generate constraint checks into each class. Violations could be flagged using Java exception mechanism. To make sure the operations of a transaction can be reversed, each object might clone the internal datastructures and retain a copy of the old values until a successful commit is issued.

3.6   Multiple Inheritance

Unlike C++, Java does not allow a class to have more than one superclass. The reason lies in ambiguities in which implementation of an inherited method m is to be called, if both super classes implement m. Java solves this ambiguity by disallowing multiple inheritance for classes and offering multiple inheritance for interfaces only. Since an interface only contains the method signatures and not the implementations, it is always clear which method a caller refers to. Consequently, an Java interface instead of a class will be generated for each RDF Schema class. A class `StudentWorker` that is derived from both `Student` and `Worker`, results in the following Java interfaces:

```
public interface Student extends Person { ... }
public interface Worker extends Person { ... }
public interface StudentWorker extends Student, Worker { ... }
```

An implementation class is generated for each interface. Note that the complete implementations of StudentImpl and WorkerImpl need to be repeated in StudentWorkerImpl. This is not really a problem since the implementation is generated automatically anyway.

```
public class StudentWorkerImpl extends PersonImpl
                        implements StudentWorker {
    ... implement Student, Worker, and StudentWorker methods
}
```

Finally, the following code then creates an instance of the class:

```
StudentWorker sw = new StudentWorkerImpl();
```

3.7 Defining Instances

RDF Schema defines the type property. A resource can be declared to be an instance of a class via a (ResourceURI, type, ClassName) triple. Unlike regular triples that are represented by storing a reference to the object in the respective data structure of the subject, the OntoJava framework handles this triple by instantiating an object of type ClassName:

```
ClassName obj = DB.createClassName(ResourceURI);
```

Thus, the triple is represented by the Java expression obj instanceof ClassName being true. Using a factory method offers further flexibility when custom behavior is to be added to the generated classes. Section 3.8 describes this mechanism in more detail. OntoJava also maintains global data structures allowing convenient access to the objects stored in the main memory database. Every object that is created by a factory method is immediately inserted in a global hash set using the resource's URI as the key allowing for efficient retrieval. Furthermore, a set data structure is maintained for each RDF Schema class to be able to quickly answer a query asking for all Person instances in the database.

Since the type predicate is treated in a special way, consequently, checking if a resource is of a specific type is not preformed by searching a type-predicate data structure but via the Java instanceof operator. The respective special handling for type predicates is built into the OntoJava software.

This behavior reveals a restriction of the OntoJava system. While in RDF, a class can be defined to be an instance of several classes, this is not possible in an object oriented programming environment. An instance can be viewed or cast to the interfaces and super classes related to the instance's class, but never to a completely unrelated class.

A solution for this limitation would be to implement the typing mechanism with own code instead of having it (partly) handled by the programming language environment. However, this would greatly complicate the code and make the application programming interfaces less descriptive, reversing major advantages of the solution. Furthermore, the Java compiler would no longer be able to catch RDF Schema violations at compile time. Since these points are important advantages of OntoJava, it seems reasonable to not opt for such a workaround and accept this limitation.

A workaround suggested for handling multi-class membership in classes $C_1, ..., C_n$ with Protégé is to create a new class C which inherits from $C_1, ..., C_n$.[5] An instance of this new class has the multi-class property, however, this would require creating, compiling, and loading new classes into the virtual machine at runtime.

3.8   Extending the Generated Classes

Extending the generated classes with own functionality can customize the system. As was mentioned in section 3.7, we use factory methods to create new objects in the database. Using the abstract factory design pattern [8], the user can replace the object factory with an own version that creates the customized classes instead of the original ones. The inference functionality remains since the new classes only extend the existing ones.

3.9   Namespaces

OntoJava's handling of namespaces is fairly rudimentary at the moment. One option, which was used in the examples shown so far, is to omit a certain namespace prefix from the RDF Schema source. Alternatively, the entire URI is used in class an method names. Here, we replace characters that cannot appear in variable names with an underscore. This results in very lengthy class and method names and makes the API quite unreadable. Nevertheless, this allows different RDF Schema sources to be combined into a single application.

3.10   Reaction Rules

Rather than asserting new facts, reaction rules perform an operation like sending mail or printing a message to the console. Usually the inference system defines a set of commands like print that can be used in reaction rules. Since we are dealing with a Java environment, it seems quite natural to allow Java statements to be embedded in reaction rule heads. The following example calls a web application, using a free variable as a parameter:

```
<_head><java>
    runtime.Loader.load("http://host/servlet/SearchGate?flight="
                        + <var>F</var>.name);
</java></_head>
```

The web application's RDF output is then loaded into the database using a runtime library. The implementation is quite simple. Instead of generating the call to the assertion method as shown in section 3.3, the code from the rule is printed. Only the variable references need to be replaced.

---

[5] http://smi-web.stanford.edu/projects/protege/protege-rdf/protege-rdf.html

This solution is flexible, but it also seems fairly proprietary. After all, rules are supposed to be exchanged across any platform and system. However, any kind of reaction rule command is proprietary. It seems natural to reuse an existing platform. Furthermore, applets apply the same concept. With Java being a cross-platform language and a virtual machine being installed on a large fraction of hosts, it seems fairly reasonable to load not just RuleML, but also some accompanying Java libraries for sending email etc.

3.11   A Sample Application

As shown in figure 1, any application can interface with the generated code. After an initialization call, the runtime data loader can be used to insert RDF triples from any URI into the database. The data loader is part of the runtime libraries that are provided. It is independent of the generated classes since it uses the Java reflection API. OntoJava does not implement any RDF query facility at the moment. Data can be obtained via global datastructures that can return all instances of a certain class. A reference to a stored object can also be obtained from its URI. The object graph can then be traversed using the get methods described in section 3.2. The put methods allow to application to assert further facts.

Figure 2 outlines a big advantage of OntoJava. The application as well as the generated engine is deployed as an applet guiding the user through the Frankfurt airport. In this example, the engine queries the flight information service via an HTTP request from a Java reaction rule. The data, which is returned in RDF format, is then loaded into the database triggering web pages being recommended. In our case, a map of terminal one is being displayed, because the user's flight is boarding there.

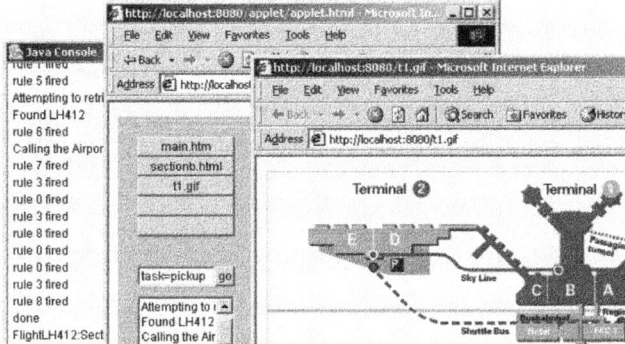

Fig. 2. An OntoJava enabled application. Rules trigger calls to the airport information system and suggest web pages to the user based on collected information.

The benefit of this application is quite clear. The development effort is minimal since a standard ontology about airports and the OntoJava generator can be used. The application is available at http://www.i-u.de/schools/eberhart/smartguide/.

4   OntoSQL

This section first compares the similarities and differences between the datalog-oriented RuleML version 0.8 and SQL. We pick up and elaborate ideas presented in [6] and the Edutella white paper [10], where a mapping of the RDF-QEL query language to SQL is discussed briefly.

The second part introduces the OntoSQL system, which is able to automatically generate the necessary tables and views in a relational database system, enabling it to act as a RuleML engine.

4.1   Mapping Datalog Queries to SQL

For this discussion we assume that the information is stored in a single table containing fact triples. We have three string columns, subject, predicate, and object, which are all part of the composite primary key, preventing the application to insert the same triple twice.

This storage schema is obviously very simplistic, yet sufficient for our analysis. Possible alternatives deal with models and optimize space requirements by introducing namespaces and URIs as entities in the schema.[6]

We distinguish between implication rules and queries. A rule $A \leftarrow B$ states that A_{var} is true if B_{var} is found to be true for a certain variable assignment. A query finds all variable assignments for which the search condition is true. We can generalize a query to be an implication rule with an empty left side: $\leftarrow B$.

We examine the mapping of queries first. Handling rules is complicated by the fact that the right side can depend on other rules. Section 4.2 explains how this is handled using SQL views.

Queries on a single predicate are mapped as follows:

```
isFatherOf(X, Y)
```

```
select * from fact where predicate = 'isFatherOf'
```

Conjunctions are translated to self-joins on the fact table. The join condition is determined by the occurrences of the variables in the query. Here, the object of the isParentOf triple must be the same resource as the subject of the isBrotherOf triple.

```
isParentOf(X, Y) and isBrotherOf(Y, Z)
```

---

[6] Sergey Melnik collected a list of proposals about ways of storing RDF data in relational databases at http://www-db.stanford.edu/~melnik/rdf/db.html

```
select * from fact a, fact b where
    a.object = b.subject and
    a.predicate = 'isParentOf' and
    b.predicate = 'isBrotherOf'
```

The SQL union operator can handle disjunctions. Note that generally, a disjunction like $A \leftarrow B \; or \; C$ can be written as two rules or queries $A \leftarrow B$ and $A \leftarrow C$, and vice versa.

```
isBrotherOf(X, Y) or isSisterOf(X, Y)
```

```
select * from fact where predicate = 'isBrotherOf'
union
select * from fact where predicate = 'isSisterOf'
```

4.2   Mapping Datalog Rules to SQL

As mentioned before, rules are similar to queries, except for the fact that implication results can influence other rules. Consider the following simple example consisting of two rules:

```
isSiblingOf(X, Y) <- isSisterOf(X, Y)
isRelatedTo(X, Y) <- isSiblingOf(X, Y)
```

The second rule depends on the first rule via the isSiblingOf property. To answer a query asking for all siblings, we could use the following SQL query that is embedded in a view:

```
create view isSiblingOf as
    select * from fact where predicate = 'isSiblingOf'
    union
    select subject, 'isSiblingOf', object from fact
        where predicate = 'isSisterOf'
```

The first subquery gets all isSiblingOf facts from the database. This is necessary since the user might assert a sibling relationship, if the gender of the sibling is not known. The second subquery processes the first rule. Except for the select clause, that explicitly states the predicate used on the rule's left side, the query corresponds directly to the datalog query isSisterOf(Y, Z). Wrapping the query in a view allows us to treat the view's name isSiblingOf as a table. The DBMS internally resolves the underlying SQL statement.

If a query for all related resources is posed, the same mechanism can be applied. Note that the SQL query references the view defined above:

```
create view isRelatedTo as
    select * from fact where predicate = 'isRelatedTo'
    union
    select subject, 'isRelatedTo', object from isSiblingOf
```

Since even this simple example results in quite elaborate queries, it makes a lot of sense to encapsulate the queries retrieving every triple with a given predicate in a separate SQL view. These views can then be reused in other views or queries, as demonstrated in the last example.

Now the user can run the SQL query `select * from isRelatedTo`. The SQL engine of the DBMS handles all rules. While this is very convenient, we must rely on the DBMS's optimizer to efficiently handle the range of joins and union operations triggered by a simple query like the one above.

4.3   Recursive Rules

Recursive rules, i.e. rules where the predicate on the left side also appears on the right side, cannot be handled with the methodology presented above. In order to make sure that the rule set can be converted, a predicate dependency graph is established. It contains a node for each predicate. Whenever a predicate A appears in the body of a rule which has the predicate B in its head, we define B to be dependent on A and we draw an arc from A to B. The rule set can be converted if the dependency graph is free of cycles, with the exception of a cycle caused by a linear recursion of a predicate with itself. These cases can be handled by recursive queries, which are defined in the SQL-99 standard:

```
create view isAncestorOf as
    with rec(subject, 'isAncestorOf', object, level) AS (
        select * from fact where predicate = 'isAncestorOf'
        union all
        select subject, 'isAncestorOf', object from Parent
        union all
        select a.subject, 'isAncestorOf', b.object, level+1
            from rec a, Parent b
            where a.object = b.subject and level < 9
    )
    select * from ancestor;
```

This view corresponds to $isAncestorOf(A, C) \leftarrow isAncestorOf(A, B) \land isParentOf(B, C)$. The first and the second subquery get all existing ancestor information and combine it with the parent information. This forms the basis for the recursive third subquery. DB2 does not terminate the query, if the data contains a cycle. The `level` parameter registers the depth of the recursion and prevents an endless loop by restricting the search to a certain depth.

We model every predicate as an SQL view. From the dependency graph we can conclude, that, with the exception of the case above, no view definition will be recursive. This allows us to run SQL queries similar to the ones shown in section 4.1 from arbitrary database clients. The rules will then be executed transparently by the system.

Note that even the fact table might actually be a view of a regular ER schema. This way, up to date information can be used without any need to upload data from an enterprise information system.

4.4 Building Applications with OntoSQL

The OntoSQL system bases on the parsers used in OntoJava. Rather than generating Java classes, SQL scripts are created according to the methodology presented in the previous sections. An application program can then simply query the views using the generic DBMS SQL interfaces.

Since we found DB2[7] to be the only DBMS currently supporting SQL 99 recursive queries, OntoSQL contains the following workaround in order to support other DBMSs as well. Rather than a recursive query, a sequence of self-joins on the fact table is preformed and the results combined by the union operator. This yields the correct results if the longest transitive closure sequence is smaller than the maximum number of self joins performed on the fact table.

5 Future Work

In this paper we illustrated certain features such as multiple inheritance and constraints. We are currently working on their implementation. An interesting issue would be to exploit object relational features such as SQL 99 types and inheritance and replace the simple fact table. This would allow more efficient data access and checking of RDF Schema types within the database engine. The next step from there would be a closer integration of OntoJava and OntoSQL. Security and portability aspects of Java reaction rules are other important topics. Finally, we are planning on running performance tests with the solutions to test their scalability. We expect to hit a maximum rulebase complexity with OntoSQL, which is imposed by the DBMS's limitation on the maximum query complexity.

6 Summary

OntoJava focuses on the ease of use and integration. This brings some inherent shortcomings such as an object not being able to have several types or the type information being absolutely necessary to store an object at all. Compared to logic-based approaches, OntoJava is restricted to simple forward reasoning with all derived facts having to be stored. Finally, it is not possible to ask ad-hoc queries.

We get many benefits from using a mainstream technology like Java. There is an abundance of tools like IDEs and debuggers available. The javadoc tools for instance can automatically create a browsable documentation of the ontology. Java's reflection interface also enables us to easily inspect the ontology from an application or browse the state of the object database. Many applications today are written in Java. OntoJava allows for easy extension and integration of the ontology into the existing IT landscape. Finally, it is possible to customize the inference mechanism. We are experimenting with probabilistic reasoning for document retrieval.

---

[7] The personal developer edition of DB2 version 7.2 is available at the IBM website.

OntoSQL addresses the forward chaining limitation of the Java approach. It is also not limited to main memory and provides persistence. We currently do not support updating data through a convenient API. The facts must be inserted manually since the views are not updateable due to the frequent use of the union operator.

We feel that OntoJava and OntoSQL are useful tools when developing applications using Semantic Web technology. Their strengths are the ease of use and the great tools support by basing it on mainstream technology.

References

1. H. Boley, S. Tabet, and G. Wagner. Design rationale of RuleML: A markup language for Semantic Web rules. In *Semantic Web Working Symposium*, 2001.
2. K. Bollacker, S. Lawrence, and C. L. Giles. CiteSeer: An autonomous web agent for automatic retrieval and identification of interesting publications. In K. P. Sycara and M. Wooldridge, editors, *Proceedings of the Second International Conference on Autonomous Agents*, pages 116–123, New York, 1998. ACM Press.
3. D. Brickley and L. Miller. RDF, SQL and the Semantic Web - a case study. http://ilrt.org/discovery/2000/10/swsql/, November 2000.
4. A. Eberhart. OntoJava - applying mainstream technology to the Semantic Web. International Conference on Electronic Commerce, Vienna, Austria, Workshop on Semantic Web-based E-Commerce and Rules Markup Languages, 2001.
5. A. Eberhart. Survey of RDF data on the web. Technical report, International University in Germany, 2001. http://www.i-u.de/schools/eberhart/rdf/.
6. R. A. Elmasri and S. B. Navathe. *Fundamentals of Database Systems*, chapter 24, pages 729–760. Addison-Wesley, second edition, 1992.
7. C. L. Forgy. Rete: A fast algorithm for the many pattern/many object pattern matching problem. *Artificial Intelligence*, 19:17–37, 1982.
8. E. Gamma, R. Helm, R. Johnson, and J. Vlissides. *Design Patterns*. Addison-Wesley, 1995.
9. J. Hendler and D. McGuinness. The DARPA Agent Markup Language. *IEEE Intelligent Systems*, 15(6):72–73, Nov./Dec. 2000.
10. W. Nejdl, B. Wolf, C. Qu, S. Decker, M. Sintek, A. Naeve, M. Nilsson, M. Palmer, and T. Risch. EDUTELLA: A P2P networking infrastructure based on RDF, November 2001. http://edutella.jxta.org/reports/edutella-whitepaper.pdf.
11. N. F. Noy, M. Sintek, S. Decker, M. Crubezy, R. W. Fergerson, and M. A. Musen. Creating Semantic Web contents with Protege-2000. *IEEE Intelligent Systems*, 16(2):60–71, 2001.
12. M. Sintek and S. Decker. TRIPLE - an RDF query, inference, and transformation language. In *Proceedings of the International Conference on Applications of Prolog*, Tokyo, Japan, October 2001.

Ontology-Based Integration of XML Web Resources*

Bernd Amann[1], Catriel Beeri[2], Irini Fundulaki[1], and Michel Scholl[1]

[1] Cedric-CNAM and INRIA-Rocquencourt
{amann|fundulak|scholl}@cnam.fr
[2] The Hebrew University, Israel
beeri@cs.huji.ac.il

Abstract. This paper deals with some modeling aspects that have to be addressed in the context of the integration of heterogeneous and autonomous XML resources. We propose an integration system, but the emphasis of this paper is neither on its algorithmic aspects nor on its technical details. Instead, we focus on the significance of offering appropriate high-level primitives and mechanisms for representing the *semantics* of XML data. We posit that support for such primitives and mechanisms is a pre-requisite for realizing the goals of the *semantic Web*.

1 Introduction

The last decade has seen the emergence of the Web as the central forum for data storage and exchange, and as the infrastructure for a large part of human communications and information-based activities in many domains, from art and medicine to business. The utility of the Web depends, however, on the development of models and paradigms for the representation and the manipulation of data, that enable the development of flexible and expressive applications.

Towards this end, XML [1] has been proposed as a standard for data exchange, possibly also for storage. Compared to the relational model, the defacto standard for database systems, its structural primitives for building trees of elements with attributes offer much more flexibility in data organization and format.

Clearly, such standardization efforts must be accompanied by formal and experimental studies of XML and its associated mechanisms: formal studies, to understand their expressive power and the computational complexity of the algorithms they require, and experimental studies, to better understand the requirement of potential application domains, and the support they require for conceptual modeling and manipulation of data. For example, the shortcomings of DTD's as the mechanism for specifying schematic properties of XML have been identified, and an effort to overcome those limitations has lead to the definition of XML Schema [16].

---

* This work was partly supported by the EC project C-Web (IST 1999-13479).

I. Horrocks and J. Hendler (Eds.): ISWC 2002, LNCS 2342, pp. 117–131, 2002.

In this paper we report on *XML data integration* issues, encountered during the C-Web project [13]. One of our goals was to design and implement a portal architecture or *mediator* [27] which can be considered as an experimental study on the use of XML for data integration. The resulting prototype [17], follows the *local as view approach* (LAV) [18] and offers to its users a virtual data repository in a given domain. The repository is virtual in that the actual data resides in some external sources. However, the users of the repository are not concerned with source location and source data organization which are taken care of by the integration portal. We posit XML-enabled data sources, with some support for XML querying, either by using XPath [10], or possibly (in the near future) by using XQuery [7].

Our emphasis in this paper is neither on the algorithmic details nor on the technical details of the system, which are thoroughly presented in [5,3,17]. Rather, we concentrate on the *data model* of the mediator and the mechanism for *describing* XML sources at the mediator. We also discuss at length *conceptual modeling* issues that need to be addressed in the context of a data integration project, and our approach to tackling them. Our study emphasizes the significance of offering appropriate high-level primitives and mechanisms for representing semantics of XML data. We posit that support for such primitives and mechanisms is a pre-requisite for realizing the goals of the *semantic Web*.

The outline of the paper is as follows. Section 2 is an overview of the approach to data integration using cultural XML resources. In Section 3 we present the integration model and discuss the studied problems and justify the decisions we have made. We conclude in Section 4 and present the future work.

2   System Overview

We present in this section a general overview of our system architecture, its main ideas, and main components. Detailed discussion of technical concepts and algorithms can be found in [3]. Our goal here is to provide sufficient understanding of the system and its underlying ideas, as a basis for the discussion of issues in subsequent sections.

2.1   XML Resources

We illustrate our approach using an example concerning the integration of two Web-accessible XML-based cultural information sources. The first source, located at URL *http://www.paintings.com*, contains information about painters and their paintings. The DTD of this source defines two element types (Painter and Painting) where each of them contains one XML attribute:

```
<!ELEMENT Painter  (Painting+)>
<!ATTLIST Painter  name  CDATA #REQUIRED>
<!ELEMENT Painting EMPTY>
<!ATTLIST Painting title ID #REQUIRED>
```

The second source, located at URL *http://www.all-about-art.com*, is more complete than the first source and describes paintings, artists and museums. Its DTD is the following:

```
<!ELEMENT Art      (Painting|Artist|Museum)*>
<!ELEMENT Painting Title>
<!ATTLIST Painting painter #IDREF #REQUIRED
                   museum  #IDREF #IMPLIED>
<!ELEMENT Artist   EMPTY>
<!ATTLIST Artist   name    #CDATA #REQUIRED
                   id      #ID    #REQUIRED>
<!ELEMENT Title    (#PCDATA)>
<!ELEMENT Museum   (Name,City)>
<!ATTLIST Museum   id      #ID    #REQUIRED>
<!ELEMENT Name     (#PCDATA)>
<!ELEMENT City     (#PCDATA)>
```

Although the two sources deal with the same subject, they differ in terms of both contents and terminology. The first source contains information about painters and their paintings and the data is organized by painter. The locations of the paintings in museums are deemed irrelevant and are not described. In the second source, painters, artists and museums are described. It organizes its data differently from the first source in that paintings and artists are described independently. To designate the painter and the museum of a painting the XML ID/IDREF mechanism is used.

As is common in integration scenarios, each of the sources may supply only *part* of the information sought by a user. For the information about painters, the sources use different terminologies (the first one uses the term Painter, the second Artist to designate a painter). Observe that information concerning the same entity types might be structured differently in different sources. For example, while in the first, paintings are arranged "below" the painters, the second source prefers to organize the same data by painting, with painters below their respective paintings.

2.2   The Global Schema

We base our integration project on the *local as view* approach [18]. That is, we assume a hypothetical global repository that contains all the information of interest to the user in a given subject area described by a global schema.

Each of the sources is a local view of this global repository. Being a view means that it contains only part of the relevant data. It may contain only information about some entity types, but not about others. Even concerning entity types that it contains, it may not contain information about all the entities of that type that are present in the global repository; or, it may not contain all information about an entity. And, its structure may differ from that of the global repository.

In our case, the local views (sources) are represented in XML. However, the data model used for the global schema is not XML, but rather an *ontology*. For us, an ontology is essentially a simple object-oriented schema describing concepts with typed multi-valued attributes and connected by binary, symmetric, many-to-many roles. Attributes and roles can be inherited through inheritance (*isa*) links between classes [4].

An example of an ontology for cultural artifacts, inspired by the ICOM/CIDOC Reference Model [14] is shown in Figure 1 as a labeled directed graph.

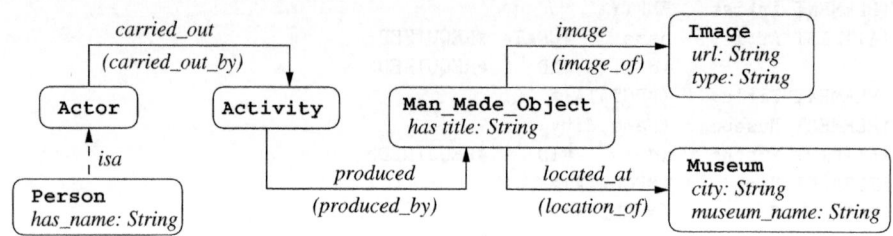

Fig. 1. An Ontology for Cultural Artifacts

Nodes of the graph represent the *concepts* of the ontology and their attributes. Each concept has a unique name represented in bold-face followed by a possibly empty list of attributes (name and type). The ontology describes six concepts for the representation of cultural data: Actor, Person, Activity, Man_Made_Object, Image and Museum. An example of an attribute is *has_name* of type String in concept Person.

Concepts are related to each other by *binary roles* depicted by solid arcs. *Inheritance* (isa) links between concepts are depicted by dashed arcs. The fact that an actor performs an activity (instance of concept Activity) to produce a man made object is represented by roles *carried_out* and *produced*. We postulate that each role has an *inverse* which is depicted in the figure in parentheses (e.g. for role *carried_out* its inverse is *carried_out_by*).

The high level of detail in this ontology is due to the desire to enable the modeling of as many sources as possible in the art domain. We defer to Section 3 the detailed discussion of why we use ontologies, rather than XML, for the global data model. Additional assumptions about ontologies and their components, as well as additional explanations are presented in Section 3.

2.3   Derived Ontologies

Each role has a *source* and a *target*. Roles r_1, r_2 can be concatenated, provided the target of r_1 and the source of r_2 are compatible, taking into account the *isa* relationships. For example, the *source* of role *carried_out* is concept Actor and its *target* is concept Activity. A role r can also be concatenated with an attribute a, under similar conditions. Concatenations of role/attribute sequences are referred to as *role paths*, and can be viewed as *derived roles* (or *derived attributes*, if the last member is an attribute). For example, role path *carried_out.produced* defines a derived role from concept Actor to concept Man_Made_Object. Each derived role has a *source* and *target*, and an inverse. For example, the inverse role path of *carried_out.produced* is *produced_by.carried_out_by*.

A *concept path* p is either of the form c, or of the form $c.r$, where c is a concept and r is a role path, where the *source* of r is c or a subconcept of c. A concept path $c.r$ defines a *derived concept*, standing for *"the instances of the target of r that can be reached from instances of its source by following r"*. For example, Person.*carried_out.produced* defines a subconcept of Man_Made_Object and stands for all the instances of concept Man_Made_Object that are reached from an instance of concept Person, following the role path *carried_out.produced*. Adding the derived concepts and derived roles to an ontology defines a *derived ontology* that properly contains the given one.

Reasoning about subset relationships between derived concepts, one can also derive *isa* relationships between them. For example, the derived concept Person.*carried_out.produced* is a subconcept of Activity.*produced* (in general, *suffixes* of derived concepts define more general derived concepts). Given a repository that conforms to a given ontology, extents of derived roles/attributes/concepts are uniquely defined, so a repository for the derived ontology is well-defined.

Our interest in the derived ontology is motivated by the fact that some sources may provide data only for derived concepts. The *isa* relationships in the derived ontology enable us to use these sources to provide answers in terms of the original concepts. For example, even if a source provides only information about Person.*carried_out.produced*, this allows us to obtain some instances of Man_Made_Object, although not necessarily all. Note that answers obtained from sources in the LAV approach are partial answers in any case.

2.4   Source Descriptions

To evaluate a user query expressed in terms of the ontology, we have to translate it into one or more queries on the XML sources. For this, we need to establish a correspondence between each source and the global ontology. This correspondence is described by a *mapping*, which is a collection of *mapping rules*. Mapping rules for XML are considered in [11], where several options of granularity for mapping rules between trees are mentioned (node-to-node, path-to-path, tree-to-tree, etc.). We have chosen the path-to-path approach. Specifically, the rules we use map a restricted sublanguage of XPath [10] (XPath *patterns* without predicates) to *schema paths* in the ontology. For example, the following rules map XML fragments of source *http://www.paintings.com* to the ontology of Figure 1:

R_1: http://www.paintings.com/Painter as u_1 ← Person
R_2: u_1/@name as u_2 ← has_name
R_3: u_1/Painting as u_3 ← carried_out.produced
R_4: u_3/@title as u_4 ← has_title

A rule has the form $r : u/q$ *as* v ← p, where r is the rule's label, u is either a URL or a variable, v is a variable, q is an XPath pattern and p is an ontology schema path. The variable v is *bound* (or defined) in the rule; if u is a variable, then it is a *use* of the variable, and we assume it is bound in some rule. The path q is called the *source path* of the rule and is an XPath pattern using only the *child* and *descendant* axis. The path p is a concept or role path in the ontology, called the *schema path* of the rule.

Rules define instances of derived concepts : XML fragments obtained by the rules are viewed as object instances of concepts. For example, mapping rule R_1 states that the elements of type `Painter` (bound in variable u_1), root elements of the XML documents in *http://www.paintings.com*, are instances of concept Person. Rules also define instances of (possibly derived) attributes and roles. For example rule R_2 specifies that the XML attribute `name` corresponds to the concept attribute *has_name*. More precisely, it tells that for any instance x of concept Person, we can obtain a value for concept attribute *has_name* by following path `@name` from the root of x (remind that x is an XML fragment). In the same way, rule R_3 defines instances of the derived role *carried_out.produced* connecting each instance of concept Person obtained by rule R_1 to all fragments, instances of concept Man_Made_Object, obtained by R_3 when evaluating location path `Painting` (which is an abbreviation of `child::Painting`).

Rule concatenation: Variables serve as a glue, that allows us to concatenate mapping rules. They are also convenient in the formulation and implementation of query processing. Finally, they can be used to express a *semantic relationship* between different XML elements. For example, the following mapping contains four rules from the source *http://www.all-about-art.com* to our ontology :

S_1: `http://www.all-about-art.com/Painting` as v_1 $\leftarrow$ Man_Made_Object
S_2: v_1/`id(@painter)` as v_2 $\leftarrow$ produced_by.carried_out_by
S_3: `http://www.all-about-art.com/Painter` as v_2 $\leftarrow$ Person
S_4: v_2/`@name` as v_3 $\leftarrow$ has_name
S_5: `http://www.all-about-art.com/Sculpture` as v_1 $\leftarrow$ Man_Made_Object

We see that one can reach v_2 (that binds instances of concept Person) by two different routes, and then continue one step down `@name` to obtain the value for attribute *has_name* for a person. In this example, the two routes, namely the *rule concatenation* $S_1 \circ S_2$ and the rule S_3 lead to the same element type. Observe also that S_1, and S_5 bind the same variable v_1, allowing us to relate different element types (`Painting` and `Sculpture`) that are semantically related, and have a similar structure.

2.5   Query Rewriting and Evaluation

The description of the global schema in terms of the ontology allows users to formulate structured queries, without being aware of the source specific structure. We illustrate querying with a simple sub-language of OQL defining *tree queries*. These queries allow no explicit joins and aggregate operators, but are sufficiently powerful to illustrate the issues of answering queries from source data, using the mapping rules. Given a user query q and a set of sources S, we need to get *all* possible answers that satisfy q. Since each source s may provide a subset of the possible answers for q, we need to evaluate query q over all (applicable) sources $s \in S$. Consider the query Q_1 below that requests *"the title of the objects created by Van Gogh"*:

Q_1: **select** c
      from   Person a,
            a.name b,
            a.carried_out.produced.has_title c,
    where $b =$ "Van Gogh"

In query Q_1, the variables and the paths that connect them form a tree. To evaluate this query over a source we need to rewrite it into a query that the source can answer. For that, we consider the binding paths of the query variables, and compare them to the schema paths of the mapping rules for a given source. For example, if we consider the mapping for source *http://www.paintings.com*, we can bind the variable a (associated with Person) with rule R_1, the variable b with rule R_2 , and the variable c with the path obtained by the *concatenation* of rule R_3 with rule R_4; we obtain a *variable to rule binding* (in this example there is exactly one; in the general case there may exist a set of such bindings, even for one source.)

The variable to rule binding is now used to replace the variable binding paths in the query **from** clause by the location paths of the mapping rules to which they have been associated. For the example query Q_1, this replacement produces the query $Q_1(a)$ illustrated below.

$Q_1(a)$: **select** c
       from `http://www.paintings.com/Painter` a,
             a.`/@name` b,
             a.`/Painting/@title` c,
     where $b =$ "Van Gogh"

If the source supports some general XML query language such as XQuery [7], then this query can be rewritten to the XQuery expression $Q_1(b)$ illustrated below, and sent to the source for evaluation.

$Q_1(b)$: **FOR** $a **IN** document("http://www.paintings.com")/Painter,
                $b **IN** $a/@name,
                $c **IN** $a/Painting/@title
     WHERE $b = "Van Gogh"
     RETURN $c

If the source supports only restricted query facilities such as XPath 1.0 [10], then the query needs to be rewritten into XPath. This is rather easy for this example, since we are requesting only the value of title elements, with some conditions on the paths leading to them. In the general case, an XQuery expression may need to be decomposed into several XPath queries, or the XPath query may return a larger tree that needs to be further filtered at the integration site to obtain the answer XML fragments (see [5] for more details).

Of course, such a rewriting of a user query to a source query should be attempted for each source. Some problems that arise when attempting to discover such rewritings are described later. However, assuming we have performed several rewritings, and obtained several answer sets, these have to be *merged* and presented to the user. The merge may be just a simple union, but often we can and should do better. If we obtain (possibly partial) information about the same entity from two sources, a *join* rather than union is called for.

To decide on, and to perform join, one needs to ensure that the entities represented by two elements, from different sources, are identical. This requires the use of *keys*, both in the global schema and in the sources. We will discuss keys in more detail in Section 3.

In some cases we cannot obtain a full answer from one source. Then, our rewriting algorithm [3] tries to find the *largest subquery*, the main subquery, of the user query that can be answered by the source. *Remainder subqueries* that cannot be answered by the source are identified, and processed against other sources. Results of the main and remainder subqueries are then joined at the integration site. Assume the following query Q_2 that requests *"the title of the objects created by Van Gogh, as well as the name and the city of the museum where they are exposed"*:

Q_2: **select** d, f, g
    from   Person a, a.name b,
           a.carried_out.produced c, c.has_title d,
           c.located_at e, e.museum_name f, e.city g
    where $b =$ "Van Gogh"

The source *http://www.paintings.com* does not contain any mapping rule whose schema path matches variable's e binding path (*located_at*). Consequently we can only obtain incomplete answers from this source: for an object created by Van Gogh, we do not get the museum where it is located, nor its name and city. To get this information, we identify the remainder subquery asking for *"the name and city of the museum of man made objects"*, that is, the subquery that involves the variables c, e, f, g, and process it against the other sources. The variable c is included in the remainder subquery since it is the *join variable* between the two queries. We will glue the results of the main and the remainder subqueries by joining on c. The two queries are:

$Q_2(a)$: **select** d, **c** $Q_2(b)$: **select** f, g, **c**
    from   Person a, a.name b **from**   Man_Made_Object c,
           a.carried_out.produced c, c.located_at e,
           c.has_title d e.museum_name f,
    where $b =$ "Van Gogh" e.city g

There is one issue that needs to be considered here. The values bound to c are elements which might be of different type. How do we know which elements represent the same man made object? Here also the answer is the use of *keys*. If a key for man made objects is available in the source *http://www.paintings.com*, on which the first subquery was evaluated, and the same key is available in whatever source against which the remainder subquery was evaluated, then a join can be performed. Otherwise, the best we can do is to present to the user only the partial results from the first source. Note that if such keys are available, then we can optimize the remainder subquery by first evaluating the first subquery, then using the values bound to c, and the corresponding keys to generate the remainder subquery for the other source. Obviously, this specific query may return a very large set of answers, so optimization is called for. The issue of optimization is described with other algorithmic issues in [3].

3   The Integration Model

In this section two issues are addressed: (i) we discuss the choice of *ontology* as the *integration data model*: a user is presented with and poses queries on an ontology that represents a certain domain of interest; (ii) we introduce the notion of *keys* as an essential feature for the querying and integration of data from heterogeneous XML sources.

3.1   XML Integration

Most previous data integration projects and the relevant theory were presented in the framework of the relational model [26,19,22]. When the sources are relational, using the relational model for integration has some advantages; in particular the same query language can be used to define the *source-global schema* mappings. However, we are concerned with sources that use XML.

Which model to use for the global data model in such a context is not an easy decision to make. An obvious question is *"Why not XML?"* Indeed, Xyleme [11], MIX [20], Nimble [25] and Agora [21] use XML. Nimble and MIX employ the *global as view approach* (GAV) and are not directly comparable to our approach. The major advantage of this approach is that the mediator is defined as a traditional view (query) on different sources and user queries can be rewritten to source specific queries by unfolding the view definitions.

However, as in Xyleme and Agora, we use the *local as view* (LAV) approach [18] where this advantage does not exist and query rewriting becomes necessary.

In the Agora system [21] an XML global schema is used for the integration of relational and XML resources. This schema is represented by a *generic relational* schema that faithfully captures the XML document structure. Then resources are represented as relational views over this generic schema. User queries are XQuery expressions over the XML global schema, which are then translated to SQL queries in terms of the generic relational schema; these SQL queries that are evaluated by the sources. Although XML is used as the global data model, an extended use of the relational model is made for source-global schema mappings as well as for query rewriting.

Xyleme [11] defines a global schema as a simple XML DTD (called *abstract DTD*). As in our approach, XML resources are described using path-to-path mappings where absolute source paths (starting from the document root) are mapped to absolute paths in the abstract DTD. Source paths *and* abstract paths can only follow descendant relationships. In addition, by using XML DTDs for the global user's data model, it is not possible to distinguish entities from relationships, which leads to less precise mappings.

Another usage of ontologies to access sets of distributed XML documents on a conceptual level is presented in [15]. The integration is achieved by the assumption that all documents respect a canonical DTD derived from the ontology. The expressive power of XML and DTD grammars is compared to more powerful ontology models.

3.2   Conceptual Integration Model for XML

In the choice of an integration model, several problems have to be dealt with when the sources are XML : two entities of the same type can be represented by two elements with different structure even in a single source; different sources with the same structure may use different tags; the structure of the same elements may differ between sources; as aforementioned, a piece of data can be represented by an element in one source, an attribute in another.

We use *concepts* to represent entity types. Each has a unique name; XML elements from sources, with different tags, may be mapped to the same concept. Thus, a user sees one concept name, and does not need to worry about the diversity of tags used in different sources. These are taken care by the mapping rules used by source authors to describe their source in the mediator. Each entity type in the global schema has a well defined structure. Sources may contain, for a corresponding entity type, only a subset of the entities of that type and also only a part of the entity's structure. This is commensurate with the LAV approach.

One might argue that a global data model based on XML could as well correctly take into account the above features [11]. In the following we briefly discuss the shortcomings of XML as a user-oriented, conceptual, data model. For simplicity, the discussion assumes DTD's are used to describe XML. Although in the XML Schema proposal [16], some of these shortcomings are partially solved, we believe that the following arguments merit attention and also help for a better understanding of XML Schema.

Let us first state some nice properties expected from a conceptual model. Such models distinguish between *entities* (or objects) and *values*, that may be simple or complex. Entities are related to each other by *relationships*, that may be constrained by various cardinality constraints. Often, the relationships are symmetric. Entities also have *attributes* that relate them to values. Entities are identified by *keys*. Finally, entity types may be related by *isa* relationships, that emphasize commonality of structure. All of these provide a user with a simple yet expressive model of a domain, with support for visual presentation of schemas, and both declarative and visual query languages.

In contrast, XML is a hierarchical data model, in which most relationships are directed from parent to child. There is no notion of a symmetric relationship, and unlike the case in the ODMG standard, there is no notion of inverse relationship to represent symmetry. Not all relationships in XML are hierarchical. The ID/IDREF mechanism allows for horizontal relationships, and these may be one-to-one or one-to-many. Still, these relationships are untyped and there is no mechanism that allows one to declare a symmetric relationship, that is represented by a pair of directional links.

Attributes and relationships. Conceptual models usually distinguish between attributes and relationships. In XML there is a distinction between attributes, for which only a single occurrence is allowed (but an attribute may be multi-valued!), and elements, for which either one or any number of occurrences are allowed. However, there are no clear guidelines when data should be represented in one of these forms and not the other. As a matter of fact, it is well-known that XML serves two masters: the *document community* and the *database community*. The distinction between attributes and elements is straightforward for documents: The sectional units of a book are represented as elements. Extra information about the book, such as publication data, is represented as attributes. This distinction, however, is quite meaningless for data. It is not clear at all that the notions of attributes and elements in XML correspond to attributes and relationships in conceptual models.

Isa **relationships.** Type inheritance described by *isa* relationships - not supported by DTD's but introduced in the XML Schema proposal-, conveniently summarizes similarity of structures. In a database context, these relationships also represent containments of sets of entities. If Person *isa* Actor, then if a query asks for actors with certain properties, and a source offers information about Person, it makes sense, in the LAV approach, to generate a query on this source to retrieve the persons that have these properties. These form a subset of the answer to the query.

In addition to its simplicity for representing common structure and its querying power (a query can request information about a concept or a subconcept there of) this feature also helps to overcome terminological differences between sources.

Symmetric relationships. With XML, a symmetric binary relationship is modeled by an asymmetric parent-child relationship between two elements. A source can choose either of the two element types as being the parent of the other. For example, Painting is a child of Painter in the source *http://www.paintings.com*. Another source might as well choose to invert this relationship, so Painting becomes a parent of Painter. Of course, binary relationships may as well be represented by the XML ID/IDREF mechanism. However, as of today, there is no established methodology that directs XML authors to generate XML documents in some *normal form*, in which entities are represented as top-level elements, and relationships between them as horizontal references. A first step in such a direction has recently been made in [6]. However, currently, in an integration scenario, we have to accept all possibilities.

If XML was chosen as the global data model, and element nesting as the representation of relationships, this problem of inverse hierarchies between a global schema and a source would force the use of the ancestor axis of XPath in mapping rules. This would not only render the source description complex but also significantly complicate query processing. Our symmetric representation of relationships, where each relationship has an inverse, and either direction can be used, is much more intuitive. It also allows us to view sources as simple hierarchies, whose description requires only the child and descendant axis of XPath.

In summary, the use of a simple conceptual model for the global data model has the advantages of simplicity and expressive power. While it can possibly be viewed as some veneer for an XML-based data model, we believe that these advantages are significant, and should not be given up.

3.3   Semantic Keys for XML

Keys are essential for data integration. In fact they are the only way to decide whether two XML fragments of two different sources are identical or not when considered as concept instances.

The XML resources we are dealing with are heterogeneous and autonomous. Consider for example our two sources *http://www.paintings.com* and *http://www.all-about-art.com*. The first source uses the ID attribute `title` to identify a painting (there might not exist two paintings of the same title). In the second source, ID attributes are used to identify museums and painters. Paintings are *not* identified by their title (there might exist two paintings with the same title in the second source). So, two distinct sources might provide us with different local key definitions and, for integration, we have to define keys at the global schema.

Key paths and identity. We define a *key on concept c* as a set of role paths with source c, called *key paths*. While, in general, a concept may have zero, one or more keys, we assume for simplicity that each concept has exactly one key, denoted $key(c)$. Observe that the key of a concept might be empty, which means that instances of this concept cannot be identified. We also assume for simplicity that isa-related concepts all share the same key.

For example, persons and actors are identified by their names: $key(\text{Actor}) = key(\text{Person}) = \{has\_name\}$. The key of concept Man_Made_Object is $\{has\_title,$ $produced\_by.carried\_out\_by\}$, which means that man made objects are identified by their title and the artist who produced them. Instances of concept Activity are not identifiable: $key(\text{Activity})=\emptyset$.

Calculating key values. In order to decide whether two instances α and β of some concept c are identical, we have to calculate and compare their *key values*. These values can be obtained by considering $key(c)$ as a *key query* evaluated on α and β. If all key paths $key(c)$ are attribute paths, this query simply follows all key paths starting from the corresponding instance. In the case of key paths ending in some concept, the query is obtained by replacing all target concepts by their key queries. For example, the following key query returns the key value for some instance of concept Man_Made_Object represented by the variable α :

> **select** t, n
> **from** α.has_title t,
> α.produced_by.carried_out_by p,
> p.has_name n

A concept c is a *joinable concept* if and only if it has a non-empty key and all concepts c' which are the target of a key path in $key(c)$ are joinable concepts. It is easy to see that key values can only be calculated for instances of joinable concepts (our notion of joinable concept is very similar to the notion of *value-representable* concept in [23]).

As in [2] and other semi-structured query languages, we assume that all attributes and roles in the global data model may be multi-valued and optional. This means that the result of a key query (the key value of an instance) is a *set of tuples* and we have the choice of defining the identity of an object by the whole set of tuples or just one tuple. As in most semi-structured query languages, we have chosen the second solution and define two fragments to be identical, if their key values are not disjoint.

Like user queries, key queries have to be rewritten w.r.t. the corresponding source mapping. This rewriting consists essentially in replacing schema paths by the rules' location paths that can be applied to some XML fragment of the source (similar to XML keys as defined in [9]). There might exist zero, one or several such rewritings which only return a *subset* of the "complete" key value (it is for example possible that our two sources identify the same artist by two different names). In other words, by the LAV approach, we might miss some tuples of the *real* key value of α in order to conclude that α is equal to some other instance β.

Observe that, unlike user queries, a key query is issued against a *single* source. If we do not obtain a complete binding for a source (i.e. some variables are not bound), key queries are not decomposed. We will end our discussion about keys with one other issue concerning the rewriting of key queries.

An existing mapping might not allow the system to find the instances of some concept c but be sufficient to find the key values of these instances. For example there might be no rule for binding path α.*produced_by.carried_out_by* p of the previous key query, but some other rule returning the name of the artist who has produced the artifact.

In this case, the key query might be *unfolded* by replacing all key paths p with target concept c' by the set of paths $p.q$ where q is a key path in $key(c')$. The previous key query would then be rewritten into the following query :

> **select** t, n
> **from** α.has_title t,
> α.produced_by.carried_out_by.has_name n

Observe that this rewriting is correct since the key of the replaced concept contains only one key path. If an artist would have been defined by a first name x and a last name y, unfolding would have relaxed the condition that x and y correspond to the same person.

4   Conclusions

This paper addressed the problems encountered, and the design choices made in the context of the integration of heterogeneous XML sources in the C-Web project. In particular we justified our choice of an ontology instead of XML as the mediator data model, and discussed the benefits we draw out of it.

In the context of the semantic Web, an applicable data model that could be used to represent our ontologies is RDF Schema [8] or DAML+OIL [12] which define all (DAML+OIL) or almost all (RDF Schema lacks the notion of inverse roles) the properties that we have identified to be necessary in the context of XML data integration. Authors in [24] advocate the need to develop a unified model for XML and RDF in order to bridge the gap between the syntax (XML) and the semantics (RDF) for Web applications. Our approach fits well into their context.

Another important problem raised by our cultural application example, is the exploitation of *semantic metadata*. By this, we denote information concerning the contents of a source, that is not present in the actual data, and thus cannot be represented by the *source-global schema* mappings. As far as we are aware of, all data integration projects, assume that all the information necessary for query processing is available in those mappings. The presence of other semantic metadata can be taken into account in our system in two different ways : first, to process queries that request information that is not present in the actual data and, secondly, to filter the sources which do not satisfy the query conditions before starting the rewriting process. We are working towards the choice of a language to define such semantic metadata, as well as an algorithm that exploits the metadata as well as the source-global schema mappings for query rewriting.

References

1. S. Abiteboul, P. Buneman, and D. Suciu. *Data On the Web: From Relations to Semistructured Data and XML*. Morgan Kaufmann, October 1999.
2. S. Abiteboul, D. Quass, J. McHugh, J. Widom, and J.L. Wiener. The Lorel query language for semistructured data. *International Journal on Digital Libraries*, 1(1):68–88, 1997.
3. B. Amann, C. Beeri, I. Fundulaki, and M. Scholl. XML Data Integration. Technical report, CEDRIC/CNAM, Paris, France, January 2002.
4. B. Amann, C. Beeri, I. Fundulaki, M. Scholl, and A-M. Vercoustre. Mapping XML Fragments to Community Web Ontologies. presented at WebDB, May 2001. http://cedric.cnam.fr/PUBLIS/RC255.pdf.
5. B. Amann, C. Beeri, I. Fundulaki, M. Scholl, and A-M. Vercoustre. Rewriting and Evaluating Tree Queries with XPath. Technical report, CEDRIC/CNAM, Paris, France, November 2001.

6. M. Arocenas and L. Libkin. A Normal Form for XML Documents. To appear, PODS 2002.
7. S. Boag, D. Chamberlin, M.F. Fernandez, D. Florescu, J. Robie, J. Siméon, and M. Stefanescu (eds.). XQuery 1.0: An XML Query Language. W3C Working Draft, December 2001. URL: http://www.w3.org/TR/xquery.
8. D. Brickley and R.V. Gupta (eds.). Resource description framework (RDF) schema specification 1.0. W3C Candidate Recommendation, March 2000.
9. P. Buneman, S.B. Davidson, W. Fan, C.S. Hara, and W. Chiew Tan. Keys for XML. In *Proc. WWW10*, pages 201–210, 2001.
10. J. Clark and S. DeRose (eds.). XML Path Language (XPath) Version 1.0. W3C Recommendation, November 1999. http://www.w3c.org/TR/xpath.
11. S. Cluet, P. Veltri, and D. Vodislav. Views in a Large Scale XML Repository. In *Proceedings VLBD*, Rome, Italy, September 2001.
12. D. Connoly, F. van Harmelen, I. Horrocks, D.L. McGuinness, P.F. Patel-Schneider, and L.A. Stein. Daml+oil (march 2001) reference description. W3C Note 18 December 2001, mar 2001.
13. CWeb. The CWeb (Community Webs) Project. http://cweb.inria.fr/.
14. M. Doerr and N. Crofts. Electronic organization on diverse data - the role of an object oriented reference model. In *Proceedings of 1998 CIDOC Conference*, Melbourne Australia, October 1998.
15. M. Erdmann and R. Studer. How to structure and access XML documents with ontologies. *Data Knowledge Engineering*, 36(3):317–335, 2001.
16. D. Fallside. XML Schema Part 0: Primer. W3C Recommendation, May 2001. http://www.w3.org/TR/XML-schema-0.
17. I. Fundulaki, B. Amann, C. Beeri, and M. Scholl. STYX : Connecting the XML World to the World of Semantics. Demonstration at EDBT'2002.
18. A.Y. Levy. Answering queries using views: a survey. *VLDB Journal*, 2001.
19. A.Y. Levy, A. Rajaraman, and J. Ordille. Querying Heterogeneous Information Sources Using Source Descriptions. In *Proc. of VLDB*, Bombay, India, September 1996.
20. B. Ludäscher, Y. Papakonstantinou, and P. Velikhov. A Framework for Navigation-Driven Lazy Mediators. In *Proc. of WebDB*. Philadelphia, USA, 1999.
21. I. Manolescu, D. Florescu, and D. Kossmann. Answering XML Queries over Heterogeneous Data Sources. In *Proceedings of VLDB*, Rome, Italy, September 2001.
22. R. Pottinger and A. Levy. A Scalable Algorithm for Answering Queries using Views. In *Proc. VLDB*, Cairo, Egypt, September 2000.
23. K.-D. Schewe, J. W. Schmidt, and I. Wetzel. Identification, genericity and consistency in object-oriented databases. In *Database Theory–ICDT '92*, pages 341–356, 1992.
24. J. Simeon and P. Patel-Schneider. The Ying/Yang Web : XML Syntax and RDF Semantics. To appear in Proc. of WWW Conference, 2002.
25. Nimble Technology. URL: http://www.nimble.com/.
26. J.D. Ullman. Information integration using logical views. In *Proc. ICDT*, pages 19–40, Delphi, Greece, 1997.
27. G. Wiederhold. Mediators in the Architecture of Future Information Systems. *IEEE Computer*, pages 38–49, March 1992.

Benchmarking RDF Schemas for the Semantic Web *

Aimilia Magkanaraki, Sofia Alexaki, Vassilis Christophides,
and Dimitris Plexousakis

Institute of Computer Science, FORTH
Vassilika Vouton, P.O Box 1385, GR 711 10, Heraklion, Greece
{aimilia, alexaki, christop, dp}@ics.forth.gr

Abstract. Describing web resources using formal knowledge (i.e., creating metadata according to a formal representation of a domain of discourse) is the essence of the next evolution step of the Web, termed the Semantic Web. The W3C's RDF/S (Resource Description Framework/Schema Language) enables the creation and exchange of resource metadata as normal web data. In this paper, we investigate the use of RDFS schemas as a means of knowledge representation and exchange in diverse application domains. In order to reason about the quality of existing RDF schemas, a benchmark serves as the basis of a statistical analysis performed with the aid of VRP, the Validating RDF Parser. The statistical data extracted lead to corollaries about the size and the morphology of RDF/S schemas. Furthermore, the study of the collected schemas draws useful conclusions about the actual use of RDF modeling constructs and frequent misuses of RDF/S syntax and/or semantics.

1. Introduction

In the next evolution step of the Web, termed the Semantic Web [2], vast amounts of information resources (data, documents, programs) will be made available along with various kinds of descriptive information, i.e., metadata. Better knowledge about the meaning, usage, accessibility, validity or quality of web resources will considerably facilitate automated processing of available Web content/services. The Resource Description Framework (RDF) [31] enables the creation and exchange of resource metadata as normal Web data. To interpret these metadata within or across user communities, RDF allows the definition of appropriate schema vocabularies (RDFS) [6]. However, the fact that several communities, even with similar needs, have developed their own metadata vocabularies independently indicates the need for schema repositories facilitating knowledge sharing. In this way, already defined concepts or properties for a domain can be either reused as such or simply refined to meet the resource description needs of a particular user community, while preserving a well-defined semantic interoperability infrastructure (i.e., through the RDF/S data model primitives such as *SubClassOf* and *SubPropertyOf*).

* This work has been partially supported by the EU Projects OntoWeb (IST-2000-29243) and Question-How (IST-2000-28767).

I. Horrocks and J. Hendler (Eds.): ISWC 2002, LNCS 2342, pp. 132–146, 2002.

There exist several ongoing efforts to build registries of available metadata vocabularies. Among those efforts we note the SCHEMAS Project [48], the DESIRE Registry [17], the SWAG Dictionary [50] and the Xmlns.com [61]. The SCHEMAS Project provides "a forum for metadata schema designers involved in projects under the IST Programme and national initiatives in Europe". Part of the work undertaken in this project was the construction of a registry for metadata schemas in RDF/S. The DESIRE Registry adopts the same approach as the SCHEMAS Project, while the Semantic Web Agreement Group Dictionary also highlights the need for interconnected vocabularies of terms, in order to form "a third party index, where parties can register the semantic connections between schemas". Finally, the experimental Xmlns.com intends to provide an Internet domain suitable for simple Web namespace management.

Although we share similar motivations with the above initiatives, the focus of our work is different. More precisely, we are interested in the structural analysis of the available RDF/S schemas from various applications. Our contribution is twofold: (a) we have collected (28 schemas from 9 different application contexts) and classified across two dimensions (i.e., domain of discourse, semantic depth of resource descriptions) available RDF/S schemas on the web, and (b) we provide complete statistics about the size and morphology of these schemas (e.g., number of classes/properties, breadth and depth of hierarchies). We believe that benchmarking existing RDF/S schemas, apart from being an added-value service of the above registries, is quite useful for testing the functionality and performance of existing RDF validation, storage, inference and query tools [30]. Furthermore, the conclusions presented in this paper about the actual use of RDF/S modeling constructs in real scale applications, provide a helpful feedback to the Semantic Web community regarding future versions or extensions of RDF/S. To the best of our knowledge, there has not been a previous attempt in this direction. The recent study of RDF data on the Web [21] does not comprise the harvested RDF/S schemas and mainly addresses Portal applications (e.g., Netscape Open Directory, as we have studied in [1]). The set of the schemas we collected are available on the "The ICS-FORTH RDF/S Schema Registry" Web page [44].

2. RDF/S in a Nutshell

The Resource Description Framework and Schema Language (RDF/S) ([31], [6]) aim to facilitate the encoding, exchange, processing and reuse of resource metadata while each user community is free to specify its own description semantics in a standardized, interoperable, human-readable manner via an XML-based infrastructure [59].

The RDF data model is based on the notion of "resource". Everything, concept or object, available on the web or not, can be modeled as a resource identified by a unique URI ([3]). With the constructs of the RDF data model we can describe interrelationships among resources in terms of named properties and values. Properties capture either attributes of a resource or binary relationships between resources. The definition of these attributes/relationships and their semantical attribution is accomplished through the RDF Schema Language (RDFS) [6].

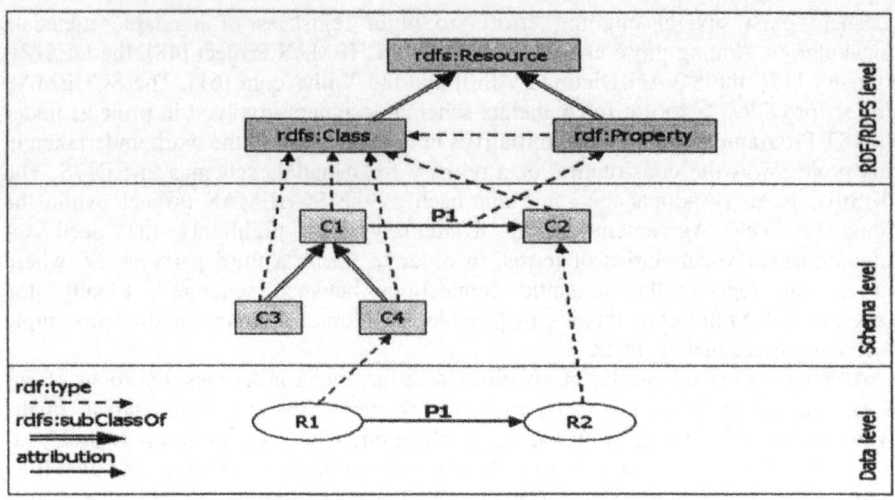

Fig. 1. Abstraction levels in a typical RDF/S schema

An RDF Schema declaration is expressed in the basic RDF Model and Syntax Specification [31] and consists of classes and properties. In other words, the RDF Schema mechanism provides a type system for RDF models i.e., a vocabulary of the valid terms that can be used to describe resources. We briefly summarize the basic RDF/S features, which are available for representing domain knowledge:

- **Core Classes**: The basic constructs of the RDF/S meta-language are *Class*, *Property* and *Container*, which correspond to entities, relations or attributes and complex or structured values, respectively.
- **Abstraction mechanisms**: RDF/S features the following abstraction mechanisms: (multiple) class or property inheritance and (multiple) classification of resources. The former is declared using the *rdfs:subClassOf* or *rdfs:subPropertyOf* core properties while the latter using the *rdf:type* core property. Typically, we identify three core abstraction levels, which are depicted in **Figure 1**.
- **Restriction mechanisms**: Although RDF/S does not provide elaborate mechanisms for defining property restrictions (as in the case of Description Logic or frame languages), we can declare simple domain and range restrictions through the *rdfs:domain* and *rdfs:range* core properties.
- **Documentation facilities**: The properties *label*, *comment*, *isDefinedBy* and *seeAlso* are used to document the development of a schema.
- **Reification mechanisms**: Although not expressible at schema level, RDF provides mechanisms for representing statements. This mechanism - formally known as *reification* - is applicable at the data level and the constructs used for this process are *statement*, *subject*, *predicate*, *object* and *type*.

The XML namespace facility [5] plays a crucial role in the development of RDF schemas, since it enables the reuse of terms from other schemas. With the use of an XML namespace, descriptive terms (i.e., class or property names) are uniquely identified by a URI (i.e., playing the role of a name prefix) as normal web resources.

To parse and validate RDF/S schemas, we have used the ICS-FORTH Validating RDF Parser (VRP) [55]. The parser analyzes syntactically RDF/XML statements according to the RDF Model and Syntax Specification [31] and the validator checks whether both the RDF schemas and related instances satisfy the semantic constraints implied by the RDF Schema Specification [6]. Additionally, VRP can extract statistics about the structure of schemas, as well as, quantitative data from related instances.

3. A Classification of Existing RDF/S Schemas

The set of the RDF/S schemas collected were classified under the following two dimensions: (a) the *application domain* they refer to and (b) the *semantic depth* in which they have been developed. **Table 1** presents the collected schemas classified according to these dimensions. The latter term refers to the degree in which the various relationships expressible in RDF/S (e.g., *subClassOf*, *subPropertyOf*, user-defined properties) are exploited in schema design.

Regarding the former dimension, we have identified the basic application domains presented below, which by no means restrict the range of possible knowledge domains that RDF/S can represent:

- **Cultural Heritage/Archives/Libraries**: The schemas of this sector serve two different functionalities: they either provide standardized definitions of concepts and processes referring to libraries, archives, museums and cultural heritage applications in general, or they provide guidelines for the encoding, structure and exchange of information.
- **Educational/Academic**: The schemas of this kind serve either as a vocabulary for facilitating the worldwide exchange of learning resources like exercises, diagrams, slides and videos or provide means to describe and formalize aspects of research activities and scientific publications.
- **Publishing/News**: The schemas of this sector provide vocabularies for the encoding and interchange of news information among individuals and mass media organizations (news agencies, newspapers etc.). They refer to any source of publication and electronic material in whichever format (CDROM, DVD, slide etc.), linkable or citable, in print or on-line and to its properties, such as its creator, period of validation, edition or subject-encoding scheme.
- **Audio-Visual**: Schemas under this category are essentially ontologies of the basic concepts used to represent information about people in the film industry, multimedia production and distribution. They also describe information about processes and events related to every aspect of film/multimedia production and selling, such as advertising, casting, acting etc. Up to now we have classified only one schema in this category but similar efforts are under development, e.g., MusicBrainz Metadata Initiative[1] [37].
- **Geospatial/Environmental**: The schemas of this sector encompass a terminology of concepts and guidelines for the representation and sharing of

---

[1] Although the related schema is still under development, the MusicBrainz RDF Data Dump can be downloaded from http://www.musicbrainz.org/download.html.

geospatial/geographical and environmental information. Although we have classified two schemas under this sector, this domain is currently less exploited than the others from a knowledge representation perspective.

- **Biology/Medicine**: The schemas classified under this category are mainly thesauri of terms and controlled vocabularies that provide definitions and semantic relations between the terms. The main functionality of such schemas is to facilitate interoperability among systems storing, processing and querying biological or medical data and to facilitate communication between people by providing registered definitions of the terms.

- **E-Commerce**: Such schemas are mainly dictionaries or taxonomies that clarify the terms used in e-commerce applications, e.g., real estate investment management, advertisement or web-based sales. They provide a central reference of registered definitions about accounts, actors, services, economic transactions etc. that are used to facilitate the communication between clients, vendors, enterprises, providers or any other entity that participates in economic transactions.

- **Ubiquitous/Mobile/Grid Computing**: As in the case of the Audio-visual domain, more efforts of this context are under way, e.g., efforts from the WAP Forum [56]. The schemas of this sector are mainly vocabularies of concepts enabling the exchange of data (e.g., technical characteristics of the client or the network) between devices, as well as data related to resource allocation by a Grid scheduler.

- **Cross-Domain**: These schemas are usually vocabularies providing general-purpose descriptive terms from a more extensive domain and can be used in a variety of application-neutral contexts. Thus, some of the schemas presented can serve as exchange formats or as thesauri of general terms with the aim of better facilitating communication and interoperability.

The latter classification dimension refers to the structure of the RDF Schemas, and in particular the semantic depth of resource descriptions in which they have been developed, i.e., the kind of relations used for modeling a domain. In the broader sense of the term, we can characterize each schema as an ontology, since it can constitute an agreed vocabulary shared among people and organizations. For the purpose of our study, we have adopted the following semantic depth levels used in the implementation of an ontology [18]:

- **Dictionaries and Vocabularies**: the schemas developed at this level define simple lists of concepts and their definitions. Most of the times, they consist only of class definitions and their structure is almost flat.

- **Taxonomies**: the characteristic of taxonomies is that the main relation they define between concepts is that of specialization. The hierarchy depth of taxonomies depends on the detail in which a schema implementer decides to refine domain concepts.

- **Thesauri**: besides defining relations among broader/narrower terms through the definition of hierarchies, a thesaurus also declares relations of equivalence, association and synonymy. The nature of these semantic relations is what distinguishes thesauri from taxonomies.

- **Reference Models**: a conceptual reference model combines all the previously stated relations to capture the semantics of a domain. This body of knowledge, describing a domain or subject matter, comprises a representation vocabulary for referring to the concepts in the subject area and the logical statements that describe the nature of the terms, the relations among the terms and the way the terms can or cannot be related to each other.

Table 1. Classification of RDF Schemas according to application domain and semantic depth

Application Domain	Dictionary/ Vocabulary	Taxonomy	Thesaurus	Reference Model
Cultural Heritage/ Archives/Libraries	•Euler [22] •RSLP-CLD [46]			•CIDOC [13]
Educational/ Academic	•IMS [29] •Universal [52]	•Mathem. International [34]		•CERIF [12]
Publishing/News	•BibLink [4] •DOI [19] •SlinkS [49] •RSS [47]			
Audio-Visual				•IMDB [28]
Geospatial/ Environmental	•CZM [14]			•GML [23]
Biology/Medicine			•Gene Ontology [24]	
E-Commerce		•BSR [7] •UNSPSC [53]		•RED [16]
Ubiquitous/ Mobile/Grid Computing	•CC/PP [10]			•P3P [42] •RDF Calendar [43] •Scheduler's Allocation Schema [26]
Cross-Domain	•CERES/NBII [11] •Dublin Core [20] •Lexical WordNet [58]		•MetaNet [35]	•Limber Thesaurus [32] •Top Level Ontology [51]

The set of schemas presented in **Table 1** indicates that RDF/S, due to its domain-neutral nature, is gaining acceptance for simple ontology construction (i.e., no logical axioms) in various sectors. Hence, we can argue that useful lessons can be learned from performing a detailed analysis of the defined schemas. Such an analysis reveals the degree to which RDF/S has been understood and adopted, as well as, common misunderstandings or mistakes. Its results can be used as feedback to schema designers. They also substantiate the need for tools for schema validation. The proliferation of schemas defined in RDF/S also calls for scalable tools for their storage and querying, such as the tools provided by the ICS-FORTH RDFSuite [45]. The analysis of the schemas is the topic of the next section.

4. Analyzing the Structure of RDF/S Schemas

Before presenting the statistics we extracted for the RDF/S schemas of our testbed, we consider useful to give some general comments regarding our overall experiment. First of all, harvesting schemas on the web was a time-consuming task due to inexistence of complete (RDF/S) schema repositories. This fact stresses the need for rich RDF/S schema registries. A second observation made was that a considerable number of schemas were developed with errors ranging from missing or wrong declarations of classes and properties, to misuse of the RDF/S modeling constructs and to confusion between the rdf and rdfs namespaces. This fact indicates the need for generally accepted RDF authoring, parsing and validation tools. We furthermore observed that schema designers utilize mostly the core RDF/S constructs (i.e., simple definitions of classes or properties). A last observation is related to the use of the Dublin Core Element Set [20] as a widely accepted top-level ontology that is either reused as such or refined by the schemas of our testbed (i.e., direct relationships between the schemas was not encountered). As suggested in [18] and [25], richer, cross-domain (top-level) ontologies (schemas) are needed to provide more elaborate forms of semantic interoperability between various application domains.

Table 2 illustrates the statistics extracted by our testbed. The columns of this table correspond to various structural characteristics of a schema. In particular, the sub-columns *"Total"* under the *"Classes"* and *"Properties"* columns refer respectively to the total number of classes and properties either locally defined in a specific schema or reused from an external namespace. The sub-columns *"Hierarchies"* are used to present respectively the number of class and property hierarchies declared and refer to hierarchies whose depth is greater than 0. Note that class hierarchies' roots are the direct subclasses of *rdfs:Resource,* while as a property hierarchy root we consider any property without superproperties. We can consider each hierarchy as a different "facet" of the schema implemented, that is orthogonal information assets under which resources can be classified. These statistics can be used to measure the "size" of a schema. Column *"subClassOf"* refers to detailed statistics about the class hierarchies defined and column *"subPropertyOf"* refers to statistics about the property hierarchies. *"Depth"* records the depth of class and property hierarchies, while *"Subnodes"* and *"Supernodes"* refer respectively to the in- and out-degrees of theses hierarchies (or schema DAGs in case of multiple inheritance). These statistics can be used to measure the "morphology" of a schema. In the case of class hierarchies, *"Depth"* is the length of the *subClassOf*-path from a node to the root. Depth is defined similarly for the case of property hierarchies, as the length of the *subPropertyOf*-path from a given property to the hierarchy root. *"Subnodes"* and *"Supernodes"* characterize, respectively, the number of subnodes and supernodes attached to a node when multiple *rdfs:SubClassOf* and *subPropertyOf* RDF/S properties are used. For each of the above 3 cases, we provide the maximum and average occurrence. The gathered statistics are reported for all schema hierarchies.

One general observation we can make from the data of **Table 2** is that most of the schemas define few classes and properties, with the exception of Real Estate Data Consortium [16], Basic Semantic Registry [7], UNSPSC [53] and Gene Ontology [24]. We can consider these schemas as rich domain models of the application to which they refer. Via the extensibility mechanisms of RDF/S, a designer can extend them by defining application-specific concepts. We can additionally observe that, when many classes are defined, the number of properties declared is relatively low and vice versa. It could be claimed that schema implementation is *property-centric* or *class-centric*, depending on whether the designer decides to model concepts as classes or properties. This choice is a design decision that has to be made in order to better capture the semantics of the modeled domain.

Table 2. Statistical data about the structure of schemas

Schema	Classes		Properties		SubClassOf						SubPropertyOf					
	Total	Hierar-chies	Total	Hierar-chies	Depth		Sub Nodes		Super Nodes		Depth		Sub Nodes		Super Nodes	
					Max	Avg	Max	Avg	Max	Avg	Max	Avg	Max	Avg	Max	Avg
CIDOC	77	3	205	20	8	4.4	7	1.1	2	1.1	2	1.2	10	0.4	2	0.4
Euler	20	2	22	4	1	1	14	0.8	1	0.8	1	1	1	0.2	1	0.2
RSLP-CLD	11	2	43	7	1	1	3	0.4	1	0.4	1	1	7	0.5	1	0.5
CERIF	42	2	142	3	1	1	13	0.3	1	0.3	1	1	18	0.3	1	0.3
IMS	17	1	8	1	2	2	5	0.7	1	0.7	1	1	2	0.3	1	0.3
Math. Internat.	211	1	0	0	11	7.9	43	1.6	9	1.6	-	-	-	-	-	-
Univers.	5	0	13	0	-	-	-	-	-	-	-	-	-	-	-	-
BibLink	14	2	20	2	1	1	5	0.6	1	0.6	1	1	1	0.1	1	0.1
DOI	13	1	13	0	1	1	7	0.6	1	0.6	-	-	-	-	-	-
SLinkS	20	1	56	4	2	1.6	2	0.2	1	0.2	1	1	1	0.1	1	0.1
RSS	6	0	9	3	-	-	-	-	-	-	1	1	2	0.4	1	0.4
IMDB	65	2	182	0	2	1.8	37	0.9	1	0.9	-	-	-	-	-	-
GML	20	3	33	1	3	1.9	5	0.8	2	0.8	2	2	6	0.6	1	0.6
CZM	77	1	66	0	6	4.3	4	0.9	1	0.9	-	-	-	-	-	-
Gene Ontology	6993	175	9	0	12	5	106	1.2	6	1.2	-	-	-	-	-	-
BSR	2714	230	1754	0	4	1.7	62	0.6	1	1	-	-	-	-	-	-
RED	5073	5	285	1	5	2.4	763	1.9	5	1.9	3	1.5	233	1.6	2	1.6
UNSPSC	16506	57	2	0	3	3	63	1	1	1	-	-	-	-	-	-
CC/PP	18	3	3	1	2	1.2	4	0.7	1	0.8	1	1	1	0.3	1	0.3
P3P	414	14	365	4	3	2.1	245	1.6	4	1.7	1	1	312	0.9	1	0.9
RDF Calendar	57	17	92	2	3	1.3	4	0.6	3	0.6	1	1	3	0.1	1	0.1
Schedul. Allocat.	16	1	23	2	1	1	3	0.2	1	0.3	1	1	2	0.2	1	0.2
Dublin Core	2	0	22	0	-	-	-	-	-	-	-	-	-	-	-	-
CERES/NBII	8	1	14	0	1	1	3	0.4	1	0.6	-	-	-	-	-	-
Lexical WordNet	9	1	5	0	2	1.3	4	0.6	1	0.6	-	-	-	-	-	-
Limber Thesaur.	11	1	17	3	2	1.3	3	0.4	1	0.5	1	1	4	0.6	1	0.6
MetaNet	66	3	11	2	2	1.6	17	0.9	2	1	1	1	2	0.3	1	0.3
TopLevel Ontology	189	1	141	1	11	6.3	11	1	3	1.1	6	3	18	1	2	1

Table 3. Percentage of Multiple Inheritance

Schema	% Multiple Inheritance of classes	% Multiple Inheritance of Properties
Real Estate Data Consort.	0.840	0.757
P3P	0.644	-
RDF Calendar	0.100	-
CIDOC	0.168	0.068
Mathematics International	0.333	-
GML	0.050	-
Gene Ontology	0.184	-
MetaNet	0.030	-
Top Level Ontology	0.068	0.035

In general, the schemas examined are shallow and they tend to be developed in breadth rather than depth. The maximum depth observed was 12 (Gene Ontology), while the maximum breadth (i.e., number of subnodes) was 763 (Real Estate Data Consortium). The fact that an ontology exhibits a sizable number of subnodes for a given node might indicate that there is a modeling deficiency and that the schema implementer should consider the addition of intermediate nodes [40]. Similarly, the sizable number of supernodes might signify that there are repeated declarations of subsumption relationships or that the modeling of the domain knowledge is not clear. The average number of subnodes, however, tends to be less than 1.0, a fact that indicates the existence of nodes not attached to a hierarchy. The number of hierarchies (whose depth is greater than 0) defined is also low, regardless of the number of classes or properties declared. This fact indicates the centralization of concepts around some top-level terms and the formulation of few large hierarchies instead of many small hierarchies of terms.

In particular, the number of schemas using the *subPropertyOf* construct is relatively small. The majority of schemas do not use this construct or they use it to a limited extent. Our study has shown that, when this construct is used, the top-level property is most of the times unconstrained (i.e., there are no imposed domain and range restrictions). Furthermore, *subPropertyOf* is used mainly for relationships between classes rather than attributes of a class. The phenomenon of properties with undefined range or domain was also encountered frequently for a set of non top-level properties. However, when domain restrictions were defined, it was noticed that several properties were declared with multiple domain definitions.

Additionally, from **Table 3**, we can see that *multiple inheritance* for classes, although not widely used (only in 9 out of 28 schemas), was more frequent than *multiple inheritance* for properties (only in 3 out of 28 schemas). The percentage of classes with multiple inheritance ranges from 33.3% (in Mathematics International) to 3% (in MetaNet) while for properties ranges from 6.8% (in CIDOC) to 3.5% (in Top-level Ontology), with the exception of the Real Estate Ontology, which is 84% for classes and 75.7% for properties and P3P, which is 64.4% for classes. Unfortunately, in the Real Estate Ontology the large number of multiple inheritance occurrences, is due to the repeated declaration of *SubClassOf/SubPropertyOf* of a class/property to all its ancestors in the corresponding hierarchy (no cycles in class/property hierarchies were detected). The same phenomenon is partially observed in P3P.

The examination of instance files reveals that *multiple classification* of resources was rarely used, apart from the case of the CIDOC ontology instance files. However, we must state that we have not found a substantial number of instance files for the examined RDF schemas (with the exception of the RSS schema widely used by Portals like CNET.com and xmlTree[2]). At schema level, multiple classification was observed only in the P3P ontology. Furthermore, we have not encountered at all the *reification* mechanism. Reification is not expressible at schema level in RDF/S and it is also highly likely that the mechanism is not widely understood. Furthermore, we can credit its absence to the fact that a schema/ontology designer wishes to represent domain knowledge and not statements about information resources. Finally, one construct that was not used was that of containers (Sequences, Bags, Alternatives). On the contrary, the domain and range restriction mechanisms for properties as well as the documentation facilities (*comment, label* etc) were extensively used.

One last corollary refers to the correlation between the richness of modeling techniques used and the semantic depth. As we can observe from **Table 2**, the majority of schemas classified as "Reference Models" in **Table 1** exhibit a rather complete use of RDF/S modeling constructs (e.g., Real Estate Data Consortium [16], CIDOC [13], CERIF [12], GML [23], P3P [42] and Top Level Ontology [51]). In contrast to other schemas, they define deep and/or broad hierarchies of both classes and properties. Furthermore, they utilize multiple inheritance for classes and/or properties to a greater extent than other schemas. Although it is rather premature to draw general conclusions about the morphological construction of RDF/S schemas, the evidence collected by our experiments points to a tight correlation of the notion of semantic depth to the variety of modeling constructs used by schema designers.

5. Towards Richer RDF/S Modeling Constructs

Besides commenting on the morphology of the examined schemas, the whole process of this survey gave us the stimulus to also study the modeling techniques actually used by schema designers. In this section, we will present the most common semantic errors made and will discuss the involved RDF/S modeling constructs. These errors are mainly due to modeling deficiencies that future RDF/S versions should cover. These deficiencies are partially addressed by current RDF/S extensions, such as DAML+OIL ([15]), and real-scale Semantic Web applications seems to demand the incorporation of credible solutions in the core RDF/S standard.

5.1 Meta-schemas

An important number of the RDF schemas of our testbed extend the core RDF/S meta-model. This is mainly performed by refining the classes *rdfs:Class* and *rdf:Property* using the *rdfs:subClassOf* relation (see **Figure 2**). We should note that the separation of meta-schemas, schemas and resource data is not clear in either RDF/S [6] or in the recent RDF M &T [27]. In fact, as eloquently commented in [39], RDF/S does not distinguish between the data and schema levels and all information is represented uniformly in the form of a graph. As a consequence, a number of

---

[2] http://home.cnet.com, http://www.xmltree.com

redundancies or semantic inconsistencies in class or property declarations arise, as explained in the sequel. We believe that a clear separation is useful for application designers as previous experience in semantic-networks suggests (e.g., Telos [38]).

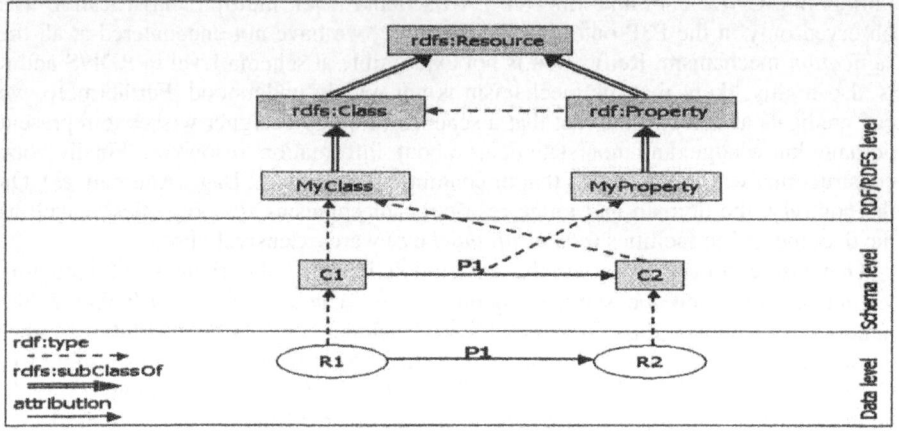

Fig. 2. Modeling Meta-schemas

The resources which extend the classes *rdfs:Class* and *rdf:Property* (e.g., *MyClass* and *MyProperty*) are of type *rdfs:Class* (see RDF M&T rule 9b). Although this kind of information should be inferred by the RDF processors, it has been explicitly stated in a number of RDF/S schemas of our testbed. Furthermore, since *MyClass* is subclass of *rdfs:Class* and *MyProperty* is subclass of *rdf:Property*, the resources that are declared instances of the class *MyClass* (e.g., C1) are classes, whereas the resources that are declared instances of the class *MyProperty* (e.g., P1) are properties (see RDF M&T rule 11). Hence, it is redundant to declare that a class (property) is both instance of a subclass of the *rdfs:Class* (*rdf:Property*) and instance of the *rdfs:Class* (*rdf:Property*).

We should also point out that in RDF/S a class can have as instances other classes without being declared as a subclass of *rdfs:Class* (i.e., as meta-class). However, it is advisable to declare explicitly such a class as a metaclass (as shown above) so that this knowledge can be exploited at the application level. In this manner, the separation between the different levels becomes clear.

Finally, although the RDF/S specification claims that properties are first-class citizens, properties are not treated as equally as classes. In RDF/S both a meta-class of classes and a meta-class of properties is a class, in contrast to the knowledge representation language Telos [38] where a meta-class of individuals is a class but a meta-class of properties (meta-property) is a property. Hence, while in Telos a meta-property can have domain and range, in the RDF/S model it cannot. Furthermore, notice that, at the data level, *P1* cannot be "of type" *P1*, as is the case for classes, where we say that a resource *R1* is of "type" *C1*. This is attributed to the fact that the *rdf:type* property is applicable only for classes and RDF/S does not provide us with an instantiation mechanism for properties at the data level.

5.2 Non-binary Relations

The RDF data model is based on binary relations, i.e., relations between two classes. However, there are modeling circumstances where the use of ternary or higher arity relations is needed. At the data level, we can implicitly represent ternary relations by using the *rdf:value* property and an intermediate resource [31]. The *rdf:value* property is used to denote the principal value of the main relation. To illustrate the representation of ternary relations, we use the following example in RDF/XML serialization.

```
<rdf:RDF
   xmlns:rdf="http://www.w3.org/1999/02/22-rdf-syntax-ns#"
   xmlns:a="http://www.ics.forth.gr/schemas/testschema#">
   <rdf:Description
         rdf:about="http://www.monitors.com/Trademark1">
         <a:size rdf:value="17"
          a:measure="inches"/>
   </rdf:Description>
</rdf:RDF>
```

This example illustrates the case where we need to represent, apart from the size of a monitor, the measuring system used (e.g., centimeters or inches). We would like to model such a relation in the schema as presented in the left part of **Figure 3**. The RDF/XML serialization of this ternary relation is given at the right part of **Figure 3**. The inability to model ternary or higher arity relations at the schema level stems from the fact that the domain of a property should always be a class. Thus, the syntax in the above format is not valid. In our testbed, the definition of a property as the domain of another property was encountered in several schemas.

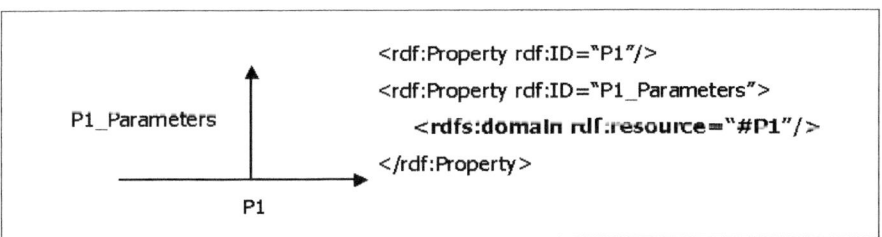

Fig. 3. Ternary relations at schema level

5.3 Enumerated Types and Specialization of rdfs:Literal

In our study, we observed the need for enumerated types, e.g., to define the possible values that a property can have (e.g., *Value1, Value2, Value3*). Although not explicitly supported by RDF/S, schema designers treated enumerated types by representing them as shown in **Figure 4**. The possible values the property can have are defined to be instances of its range class. Unfortunately, the same mechanism is not applicable in the case of the *rdfs:Literal*, i.e., we cannot define *Value1* or *Value2* as instances of *rdfs:Literal*.

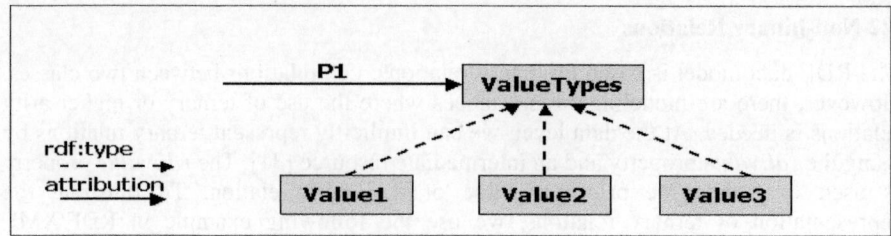

Fig. 4. Representing enumerated types

Additionally, a frequently encountered situation was the specialization of the *rdfs:Literal* class in order to support a richer set of data types. XML data types [60] can be used for this purpose while ensuring interoperability with other XML-based applications.

6. Related Work and Summary

During the last decade several studies have been conducted on the formal aspects of knowledge representation languages and ontologies ([33], [36], [54], [57]). In [9] a structured bibliography of studies related to ontologies is provided, while [8] and [25] list a set of B2B standards and content standardization efforts respectively, as well as classification criteria for them. In [41], a framework for comparing ontologies is developed and 10 representative ontologies are examined (e.g., CYC, Generalized Upper Model, UMLS, WordNet). From the set of qualitative comparison criteria proposed for ontologies, we can distinguish criteria referring to their general characteristics (e.g., purpose, coverage, size, formalism used, accessibility, design process, evaluation methods) and criteria about the content of the ontology (e.g., taxonomic organization, top-level divisions, internal structure of concepts, granularity). Our work is complementary, in the sense that it proposes *quantitative* criteria about the structure of RDF/S schemas representing various kinds of ontologies. The relationship between qualitative and quantitative ontology comparison is a subject, which deserves further study and experimentation. Intuitively, a qualitative criterion can be interpreted into a set of quantitative criteria. For example, the taxonomic organization of an ontology could possibly be determined by making a reduction to the number of property and class hierarchies and the in- and out-degrees of theses hierarchies. These statistics indicate whether an ontology is organized in large or a number of smaller taxonomies, as well as, the degree to which an ontology is well-structured and complete. We believe that the set of the schemas presented in this paper form a suitable testbed for the application of such qualitative/quantitative comparison of domain ontologies.

References

[1] S. Alexaki, V. Christophides, G. Karvounarakis, D. Plexousakis, K. Tolle. *"The ICS-FORTH RDFSuite: Managing Voluminous RDF Description Bases"*. In Proceedings of the 2nd International Workshop on the Semantic Web (SemWeb'01), in conjunction with WWW10, pp. 1-13, Hong Kong. May 1, 2001.

[2] Tim Berners-Lee, James Hendler, Ora Lassila. *"The Semantic Web"*. Scientific American. May 2001. <http://www.sciam.com/2001/0501issue/0501berners-lee.html>

[3] T. Berners-Lee, R. Fielding, L. Masinter. *"Uniform Resource Identifiers (URI): Generic Syntax"*. RFC 2396. August 1998. <http://www.ietf.org/rfc/rfc2396.txt>

[4] BIBLINK <http://hosted.ukoln.ac.uk/biblink>

[5] Tim Bray, Dave Hollander, Andrew Layman. *"Namespaces in XML"*. W3C Recommendation. January 14, 1999.

[6] D. Brickley, R.V. Guha. *"Resource Description Framework Schema (RDF/S) Specification 1.0"*. W3C Candidate Recommendation. March 27, 2000.

[7] Basic Semantic Registry < http://www.ubsr.org/ >

[8] Christoph Bussler. *"B2B Protocol Standards and their Role in Semantic B2B Integration Engines"*. In Bulletin of the Technical Committee on Data Engineering. Vol. 24, No. 1, pp. 3-11. IEEE Computer Society. March 2001.

[9] Massimiliano Carrara, Nicola Guarino. *"Formal Ontology and Conceptual Analysis: A Structured Bibliography"*. Version 2.5. March 22, 1999.
<http://www.ladseb.pd.cnr.it/infor/ontology/Papers/Ontobiblio/TOC.html>

[10] Composite Capability/Preference Profiles <http://www.w3.org/TR/CCPP-struct-vocab/>

[11] CERES/NBII Thesaurus Partnership Project <http://ceres.ca.gov/thesaurus/RDF.html>

[12] Common European Research Information Format <http://www.cordis.lu/cerif>

[13] CIDOC Reference Model <http://www.cidoc.icom.org/guide/guideint.htm>

[14] Costal Zone Management Ontology <http://dlforum.external.forth.gr:8080/>

[15] DAML+ OIL (March 2001) <http://www.daml.org/2001/03/daml+oil-index>

[16] Real Estate Data Consortium <http://www.dataconsortium.org/>

[17] DESIRE Metadata Registry <http://desire.ukoln.ac.uk/registry/>

[18] Martin Doerr, Nicola Guarino, Mariano Fernandez Lopez, Ellen Schulten, Milena Stefanova, Austin Tate. *"State of the Art in Content Standards"*. OntoWeb. Deliverable 3.1. Version 1.0. November 2001.

[19] Digital Object Infrastructure <http://www.doi.org/index.html>

[20] DUBLIN CORE Metadata Initiative <http://dublincore.org/>

[21] Andreas Eberhart. *"Survey of RDF data on the Web"*. Technical Report. International University in Germany. 2001 <http://www.i-u.de/schools/eberhart/rdf/rdf-survey.htm>

[22] European Libraries and Electronic Resources in Mathematical Sciences
<http://www.emis.de/projects/EULER/>

[23] Geography Markup Language <http://www.opengis.net/gml/00-029/GML.html>

[24] GENE ONTOLOGY <http://www.geneontology.org/GO.doc.html>

[25] Guarino, N., Welty, C., and Partridge, C. *"Towards Ontology-based harmonization of Web content standards"*. In S. Liddle, H. Mayr and B. Thalheim (eds.), Conceptual Modeling for E-Business and the Web: Proceedings of the ER-2000 Workshops. Springer Verlag, pp. 1-6. 2000.

[26] Dan Gunter, Keith Jackson. *"The Applicability of RDF-Schema as a Syntax for Describing Grid Resource Metadata"*. Document: GWD-GIS-020-1. June 2001.

[27] Patrick Hayes. *"RDF Model Theory"*, Working Draft, W3C. September 25, 2001

[28] Internet Movie Database <http://www.csee.umbc.edu/~skallu1/>

[29] IMS Global Learning Consortium <http://www.imsproject.org/rdf/index.html>

[30] Ora Lassila. *"Taking the RDF Model Theory Out For a Spin"*. To appear in Proceedings of the 1st International Semantic Web Conference, Sardinia, 2002.

[31] O. Lassila, R. Swick. *"Resource Description Framework (RDF) Model and Syntax Specification"*. W3C Recommendation. February 1999.

[32] Language Independent Metadata Browsing of European Resources <http://www.limber.rl.ac.uk/>

[33] Alexander Maedhe, Steffen Staab. *"Comparing Ontologies- Similarity Measures and a Comparison Study"*. Internal Report No. 408, Institute AIFB, University of Karlsruhe, Germany. March 2001.

[34] MATHEMATICS INTERNATIONAL <http://www.mathematik.uni-kl.de/~ontology/>

[35] METANET <http://archive.dstc.edu.au/RDU/staff/jane-hunter/harmony/jodi_article.html>

[36] Rajatish Mukherjee, Partha Sarathi Dutta, Sandip Sen. *"Analysis of domain specific ontologies for agent-oriented information retrieval"*. In the Working Notes of the AAAI-2000 Workshop on Agent-Oriented Information Systems (AOIS). 2000.

[37] MUSIC BRAINZ <http://www.musicbrainz.org>

[38] J. Mylopoulos, A. Borgida, M. Jarke, M. Koubarakis. *"Telos - a language for representing knowledge about information systems"*. ACM Transactions on Information Systems, 8(4):325-362. 1990.

[39] W. Nejdl, H. Dhraief, and M. Wolpers, *"O-telos-rdf: a Resource Description Format with Enhanced Meta-Modeling Functionalities Based on O-telos"*. In Workshop on Knowledge Markup and Semantic Annotation at the 1st Inrternational Conference on Knowledge Capture (K-CAP 2001), Victoria, BC., Canada. 2001.

[40] Natalya Fridman Noy, Deborah L. McGuinness. *"Ontology Development 101: A Guide to Creating Your First Ontology"*. Stanford Knowledge Systems Laboratory Technical Report KSL-01-05. March 2001.

[41] Noy, N. F. and Hafner, C. D. *"The state of art in ontology design"*. IA Magazine, 18 (3), pp. 53-74. Fall 1997.

[42] The Platform for Privacy Preferences Project <http://www.w3.org/P3P/>

[43] RDF CALENDAR <http://ilrt.org/discovery/2001/04/calendar/>

[44] RDF SUITE REGISTRY <http://139.91.183.30:9090/RDF/Examples.html>

[45] RDF SUITE <http://139.91.183.30:9090/RDF/>

[46] RSLP Collection Level Description <http://www.ukoln.ac.uk/metadata/rslp/>

[47] RDF Site Summary 1.0 <http://groups.yahoo.com/group/rss-dev/files/specification.html>

[48] SCHEMAS PROJECT <http://www.schemas-forum.org/>

[49] Scholarly Link Specification <http://www.openly.com/slinks/>

[50] SWAGD: WebNS.net - The SWAG Dictionary <http://webns.net/>

[51] TOP LEVEL ONTOLOGY <http://www-sop.inria.fr/acacia/personnel/phmartin/RDF/phOntology.html>

[52] UNIVERSAL <http://www.ist-universal.org/>

[53] Universal Standard Products and Services Classification <http://eccma.org/unspsc/>

[54] Pepijn R.S Visser, Dean M. Jones, T.J.M Bench-Capon, M.J.R Shave. *"An Analysis of Ontology Mismatches; Heterogenity versus Interoperability"*. AAAI 1997 Spring Symposium on Ontological Engineering, Stanford University, Canada.

[55] The Validating RDF Parser <http://139.91.183.30:9090/RDF/VRP/index.html>

[56] WAP: The WAP Forum Specifications <http://www.wapforum.org/what/review.htm>

[57] Peter C. Weinstein, William P. Birmingham. *"Comparing Concepts in Differentiated Ontologies"*. In Proceedings of the Twelfth Workshop on Knowledge Acquisition, Modeling and Management (KAW' 99). Banff, Alberta, Canada. October 1999.

[58] Princeton WordNet <http://www.cogsci.princeton.edu/~wn>

[59] XML <http://www.w3.org/XML/>

[60] The XML Schema Data types <http://www.w3.org/1999/XMLSchema-datatypes>

[61] XMLNS.com <http://www.xmlns.com>

Building the Semantic Web on XML

Peter F. Patel-Schneider and Jérôme Siméon

Bell Labs Research, Murray Hill, NJ, U.S.A.
{pfps,simeon}@research.bell-labs.com

Abstract. The semantic discontinuity between World-Wide Web languages, e.g., XML, XML Schema, and XPath, and Semantic Web languages, e.g., RDF, RDFS, and DAML+OIL, forms a serious barrier for the stated goals of the Semantic Web. This discontinuity results from a difference in modeling foundations between XML and logics. We propose to eliminate that discontinuity by creating a common semantic foundation for both the World-Wide Web and the Semantic Web, taking ideas from both. The common foundation results in essentially no change to XML, and only minor changes to RDF. But it allows the Semantic Web to get closer to its goal of describing the semantics of the World Wide Web. Other Semantic Web languages (including RDFS and DAML+OIL) are considerably changed because of this common foundation.

1 Introduction

The Semantic Web [3,4] is supposed to be an extension of the World-Wide Web where the meaning of data is available to and processable by computers. However, the current recommended Semantic Web languages (RDF [13] and RDFS [9]), as well as other Semantic Web languages such as DAML+OIL [8], are not built on top of the current World-Wide Web. We argue that, in order to describe the semantics of the World-Wide Web, the Semantic Web must be based on XML, the data format of the World-Wide Web.

RDF (the Resource Description Framework) and RDFS (the RDF Schema Specification), as well as other Semantic Web languages, do use the syntax of XML [16,6]. However, they do not give this syntax the same meaning that it is given in XML. Thus there is a semantic discontinuity at the very bottom of the Semantic Web, interfering with the stated goal of the Semantic Web: If Semantic Web languages do not respect World-Wide Web data, then how can the Semantic Web be an extension of the World-Wide Web at all?

The reason that RDF and RDFS, as well as other Semantic Web languages, do not give the same meaning to XML syntax that XML does is that RDF and XML have different modeling foundations. XML, as evidenced in the XML Information Set [17] and the XQuery Data Model [19] is based on a tree model where edges have no labels and outgoing edges from a node have a total order. This kind of model has its roots in semi-structured data [1] and databases. RDF and RDFS are based on a directed graph model where edges do have labels, but are unordered. This kind of model has its roots in the model theory for standard logics, such as first-order logic, and in models for knowledge representation languages, including frames [12] and description logics [2].

I. Horrocks and J. Hendler (Eds.): ISWC 2002, LNCS 2342, pp. 147–161, 2002.

Achieving the stated goals of the Semantic Web as an extension of the World-Wide Web requires the elimination of this discontinuity. This cannot simply be done by just using the XML foundation, as the Semantic Web needs more than just trees. Instead a new foundation must be created, augmenting the XML foundation with the capabilities needed by the Semantic Web. From this merged foundation a new Semantic Web can be created as a true extension of the World-Wide Web, able to employ any data from the World-Wide Web and give it computer-accessible and -manipulable meaning.

This document proposes a foundation for this new Semantic Web. Many aspects of this new Semantic Web are left for future elaboration, especially where they do not affect the broad outlines described herein.

2   Foundations for the World-Wide Web and the Semantic Web

The foundations of the World-Wide Web and the Semantic Web are the meanings of their major languages, XML (taken in the large) and RDF (including RDFS). The meanings of both XML and RDF are currently given in terms of data models, several for XML— including the XML Information Set [17] and the XQuery Data Model [19]—and the model specification for RDF [13].

2.1   The Current XML and RDF Foundations

It is, unfortunately, not so easy to pin down exactly what the information contained in XML documents is. The relevant XML recommendations, the XML Infoset and the XQuery Data Model, retain almost all of the bits of the document itself, including whitespace, comments, etc. This is *not* what is wanted for describing the information contained in a document. Therefore some abstraction of the information retained in these recommendations is needed to get to the real meaning of XML documents.

The basic espoused idea here is to ignore the information in an XML document that is specific to its status as a document and retain only the "data" in it. So, from the XQuery Data Model, one should ignore all processing instructions and comments, whitespaces, as well as the lexical form of typed data. Other aspects of the XQuery Data Model are also handled somewhat differently. For instance, an IDREF would be interpreted in a different way, more like a pointer than an actual child node, resulting in a directed acyclic node rather than a tree.

This results in a simplified, semantics driven, tree based, data model for XML. Some nodes in the tree correspond to XML elements. These nodes have labels that are the element names. Other nodes of the tree correspond to XML attributes. These nodes have labels that are the attribute names. Type information, derived from XML Schema documents, can also be present on these element nodes. Yet other nodes of the tree correspond to XML text nodes or XML attribute values (that are not typed by XML Schema or other means). These nodes have labels that are the text of the node or string-value of the attribute value. Yet other nodes of the tree correspond to typed text nodes or typed XML attribute values. These nodes have labels that are the typed value of the node or the typed value of the attribute. The outgoing edges from a node are equipped with a total order.

The RDF data model on the other hand is specified quite well in the RDF Model and Syntax Specification (RDF [13]), at least for the non-controversial aspects of RDF.

The data model underlying RDF is a directed graph. Nodes of the graph are labeled with identifiers, or literals (i.e., text), or are unlabeled. Edges of the graph are also labeled with identifiers. Some edges of the graph, those labeled with rdf:type, are have a built-in meaning. These edges link nodes to their types (a combination of element and attribute names and XML Schema types in XML parlance).

2.2   A New Foundation

Can these two data models be somehow merged together to form a common foundation for both XML and RDF? Several attempts in this direction have already been made. Melnik [11] created a version of RDF that can handle arbitrary XML, but uses extra information on how to handle the XML constructs that don't fit well into the RDF model. Boley [5] has a data model that can be used for both XML and RDF. However, his approach requires changes to XML to unify it with RDF. In [14], we propose our first attempt at a model theory for XML and RDF that allows to describe the semantics of both in a unified way.

Our approach is to create a data model that requires the minimal amount of change to both XML and RDF, and essentially no change to XML.

The difference between trees and directed graphs is easily reconciled. As directed graphs are a generalization of trees, we allow arbitrary directed graphs.

There are several ways to deal with the labels on edges in RDF graphs. One way would be to allow edges to optionally have labels, which would be very close to the RDF data model. However this would severely change the meaning of RDF documents viewed as XML document. Another way would be to move the XML Data Model node labels to the edges of the graph. This is an attractive alternative, but requries considerable change to both XML and RDF. Instead we use the XML data model directly, not allowing labels on edges. The result is that labeled edges in RDF graphs correspond to two unlabeled edges, with the label ending up on the node in the middle.

XML and RDF take different views of node labels as well. In XML some node labels are element names, which correspond to RDF types, not RDF labels. Other node labels are attribute names, which correspond to RDF edge labels. Yet other node labels are text or typed values, which correspond to RDF literals. RDF identifier labels have no corresponding label in the XML data model.

In our merge, nodes are of one of two kinds. One kind of node corresponds to text or value nodes from XML or literal nodes from RDF. These nodes are given labels that are their text or their typed value, as appropriate. The other kind of node corresponds to element or attribute nodes from XML or non-literal nodes or edge labels from RDF. These nodes are given two optional labels, one of which is the RDF identifier and the other of which contains the element or attribute names from XML or the rdf:type(s) or edge label from RDF. Two of these nodes in a graph cannot have the same RDF identifier.

To handle the edge ordering of XML, our data models partially order the outgoing edges from each node.

A final reconciliation that is needed is the difference in naming conventions between XML and RDF. XML uses qualified names, which are two-part names having a local part, whereas RDF uses URIs plus fragments. We propose to go with qualified names, abandoning direct use of URIs, although we generally treat qualified names as abbreviations for URIs plus fragments.

So we end up with a directed graph data model where edges have no label, text or value nodes have their text or value as their label, other nodes have two optional labels, both of which use Qnames, and there is a partial order on edges.

The data model for a document (XML or RDF) can now easily be determined. XML documents are treated just as before. The graph for an XML document in this data model is an ordered tree. The only change is in the node labels for non-text and non-value nodes, but this is only a cosmetic change. RDF documents are treated differently. In particular, they are treated as if they were XML documents, with two exceptions. First, if an RDF identifier occurs multiple times in a document, only one node is generated. Second, the outgoing edges resulting from an RDF document are unordered. This treatment of RDF documents does ignore some of the esoteric features of RDF, such as reification, and also does not handle some of the shorthand versions of RDF.

3   A New Semantic Web (Data Portion)

So what would data in this new Semantic Web look like?

At first glance, it would not be much different from the current Semantic Web. The content of most RDF data documents would not change,

```
<Organization rdf:ID="BUU">
  <purchase>
    <Item rdf:ID="po7" />
  </friend>
</Organization>
```

would still be a way to say that BUU is an organization that has made a purchase identified as "po7".

However, the role of the various languages would change to some extent.

The role of XML in this new Semantic Web would be quite different, and much stronger. Instead of just being a syntax-carrier, XML would be a major means of providing both syntax and semantics for the Semantic Web.

The meaning of XML documents in this new Semantic Web would be (very close to) their current XML meaning, instead of the different RDF meaning. So, as a Semantic Web document fragment,

```
<Organization>
  <purchase>
    <item />
  </purchase>
</Organization>
```

would have its current XML meaning of a tree fragment with three nodes.

The role of RDF in this new Semantic Web would also be quite different, and much weaker. RDF would no longer be the carrier of all information—that role would be at least partly taken over by XML. The existing RDF data model would not be a part of this new Semantic Web, being replaced by a data model much closer to the XML data model. So the RDF example above would not result in a two node graph fragment with a labeled edge, plus extra edges for the type information, but instead would result in the XML-style three-node graph fragment. This implies a much more consistent treatment of the semantics XML and RDF. Nonethless, most RDF constructs would have equivalent meanings.

4   Going Beyond Data

So far we have concentrated on the data portion of the Semantic Web. However, the goal of the Semantic Web is to provide machine-accessible and -processable meaning for this data. There are several ways of providing this meaning employed in the World-Wide Web and the Semantic Web, one used by RDF and RDFS and another used by XML Schema.

In the RDF and RDFS method, the meaning for data is provided by adding more nodes to the data model. These extra nodes represent classes, or categories, and connections are made from the data nodes to these class nodes, just like connections are made between data nodes. Some portion of the data model (rdf:type edges in RDF) is given special meaning to account for the special status of these nodes.

In the XML Schema method, the meaning for data is provided by separate means. XML Schema uses schema documents for this purpose. These separate documents are given special meaning and are processed differently from documents that carry data. XML Schema schema documents use XML syntax internally, but the meaning of schema documents is *not* the data model that would result from processing them as XML documents.

The RDF and RDFS method looks promising, and works well for limited formalisms like RDF and RDFS, but ends up causing problems for more-powerful formalisms. For example, a formalism that wants to express disjunctions would have to end up bypassing RDF and RDFS meaning, because that RDF and RDFS treat a collection of data as the conjunction of its parts. There is no mechanism to turn off this treatment the component parts of, for example, a disjunction, as it is only possible to *add* to meanings.

If the Semantic Web is to grow in power it will need to have constructs that do not fit into the RDF and RDFS approach. Therefore we will avoid the RDF and RDFS approach in favour of an approach more like the one used by XML Schema. Our approach will be to make a separation between data and meaning for the data, although we will not solely use the XML Schema separation method.

There are several kinds of meaning that can be supplied for data, and RDF and RDFS differ from XML Schema in this area also.

XML Schema is (only) concerned with providing typing and structuring information for isolated chunks of data. This is perfectly fine for XML which, because of its tree-like data model has only isolated chunks of data, but is not completely adequate in the graph-like world of the Semantic Web. XML Schema also is generally used to restrict the kinds of information that can be specified, which again goes against open-ended nature of the Semantic Web. Note that in addition, XML Schema also provides limited additions to the data model, most notably: typed values and type annotations.

So we propose that XML Schema retain its current role of restricting the form of XML documents and providing typing and structuring information for them. We propose that the meaning portions of RDF and RDFS be taken over by a Semantic Web Ontology language, which we will call SWOL. SWOL would roughly fill the same role as currently filled by DAML+OIL, but would have a much closer relationship to XML and XML Schema. Finally, for the parts that is handled by both XML Schema and RDFS (notably type annotations and containment relationship), we believe there is some need for coordination between XML Schema and the Web Ontology language.

5   A New Semantic Web

So what will this new Semantic Web look like? Again, there would not be much difference from the current World-Wide Web, at least as far as XML and XML Schema are concerned. Documents would still be parsed and validated, much as they are now. The only change here would be that the meaning provided by XML and XML Schema would end up being the Semantic Web meaning of XML documents, instead of being supplanted by the RDF meaning.

The situation is somewhat different from the RDF and RDFS side. RDF is reduced from the main language of the Semantic Web to an extension of XML that really only provides the identifiers (rdf:ID) that tie the XML data model nodes together to make a graph. RDFS is completely gone, being replaced by our as-yet-unspecified Semantic Web Ontology Language, SWOL.

5.1   Semantic Foundations for the New Semantic Web

Unfortunately, the machinery we have introduced so far is not sufficient to provide a semantic foundation for this new Semantic Web. Data models, as above, only work well for providing meaning for simple, inexpressive languages. The main point of data models—that a single data model can be used to capture the meaning of a document—breaks down for more-expressive languages, such as a Semantic Web Ontology Language. Data models even have problems when applied to RDF and RDFS, resulting in the W3C RDF Core producing a different formal foundation for RDF and RDFS [15].

The meaning of documents that contain disjunctive or vague information, such as saying that either John or Jim is the author or a web page, where the exact state of affairs of the world is not known, cannot be captured in a single data model, where everything is fixed and certain. The usual solution to this problem is to have a document correspond to any one of several interpretations, each of which correspond to one of the ways the vague information can be resolved. So the above disjunction would give rise to two classes of interpretations, one class where John is the author of the web page and one where Jim is.

This way of giving meaning to documents (usually referred to as collections of statements) is called model theory. Model theories have been developed for most of the well-known representation formalisms, including propositional logics, first-order logics, and description logics. In data models the meaning of a document is a single data model, which corresponds to the portion of the world being considered. In model theory the

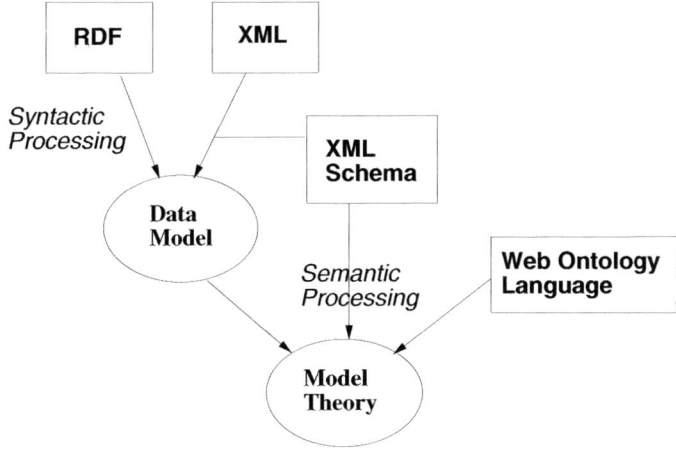

Fig. 1. From Documents to Model Theory

meaning of a document is a collection of interpretations. Each of these interpretations corresponds to one of possible ways the world could be, given the information under consideration.

The formal definition of our models are given below.

Resources, Names, Data Values, and Datatypes. This model theory assumes a universe of resources and data values. QNames are used as identifiers for resources.

Definition 1. *We call L the lexical space of strings, and U the value space of QNames, i.e., pairs of URIs and local parts. We call DT the subset of U corresponding to XML Schema primitive datatypes, and DV the union of the value spaces of the XML Schema primitive datatypes. In RDF elements of DV are generally called literals. The function $DTC : DT \to \mathcal{P}(DV)$, (where $\mathcal{P}$ is the powerset operator) maps XML Schema primitive datatypes to their value spaces and $DTS : DT \to (L \to DV)$, maps XML Schema primitive datatypes to their lexical to value maps. We define the union of the datatype mappings $XTS : L \to \mathcal{P}(DV)$, where $v \in XTS(l)$ iff $v = DTS(dt)(l)$ for some XML Schema datatype dt.*

Interpretations. Interpretations are the essential component of our model theory. An interpretation corresponds to one possible way the world can be, hence encoding a certain meaning for the information manipulated by an application. Interpretations give information about resources and related resources through relationships and semantic constraints. We define a notion of interpretation that is suitable for both XML and RDF documents, through the XQuery data model.

Definition 2. *An interpretation I is a six-tuple, $\langle R, E, EXT, CEXT, O, S \rangle$, where:*

R is a set of resources,
E is a set of relationships,

$EXT : E \to R \times (R \cup DV)$ *maps relationships to the resources they relate,*
$CEXT : U \to \mathcal{P}(R \cup DV)$ *maps classes to their extensions,*
$O : R \to \mathcal{P}(E \times E)$ *provides a local order on the relationships, and*
$S : U \to R$ *is a partial map from QNames to resources.*

An interpretation must also satisfy the following conditions:

1. $O(r)$ *is a strict partial order.*
2. *If* $\langle x, y \rangle \in O(r)$ *then* $EXT(x)$ *and* $EXT(y)$ *have* r *as their first element.*
3. *If* $d \in DT$ *then* $CEXT(S(d)) = DTC(d)$, *provided that* S *is defined on* d.

An interpretation can be thought of as a multigraph with an ordering on the edges. Resources (R) form the nodes of the graph. Edges of the graph are formed from relationships (E) and EXT. For instance, a relationship $e1 \in E$ with $EXT(e1) = \langle John, p \rangle$ indicates that the resource $John$ is related to the resource p, and a relationship $e2 \in E$ with $EXT(e2) = \langle p, po7 \rangle$ indicates that the resource p is related to the resource $po7$. We remark that there is no distinction at this point between $John$, usually thought of as an instance of a class, and p, which is usually thought of a property.

S provides a mapping between syntax (QNames) and their denotation (resources). S gives a means to identify these entities using QNames. There is no requirement that all resources have corresponding QNames, nor is there a requirement that QNames are all mapped to different resources.

$CEXT$ provides typing information for resources. For instance, if BUU is in $CEXT(Organization)$ then the resource BUU is of type $Organization$. Similarly, if p is in $CEXT(purchase)$ then the resource p is of type $purchase$. Loosely speaking, in RDF terms $CEXT$ serves for both property and class extensions. Or, considered another way, a property is presented as a type whose values and related tuples identify arcs in the traditional RDF graph structure.

Finally, O provides ordering information between the relationships that are related to a common resource. This information is not usually part of RDF model theories [15], but it is important to capture document order in XML documents.

5.2 SWOL

We now, finally, give some details on SWOL, our proposed web ontology language. SWOL is actually very close to a description logic [2], the only difference being a few minor changes to move away from edge-labelling.

The syntax of SWOL is unimportant, at least for now. We will introduce SWOL by means of an example that shows most of the relevant features of SWOL.

```
<swol:class name="Organization" defined="no">
  <swol:exists>
    <swol:class name="name"/>
    <swol:class name="xsd:String"/>
  </swol:exists>
  <swol:all>
    <swol:class name="purchase"/>
    <swol:class name="PurchaseOrderType"/>
```

```
    </swol:all>
  </swol:class>
```

This SWOL document fragment contains the definition of a class, named Organi-zation. Elements of this class, organizations, have a name, in the form of a string. Elements of the class also can have purchases, each of which must belong to the Pur-chaseOrderType.

For now, we can think of a SWOL document as a collection of several definitions of this sort, each with a name. There are actually many possibilities for SWOL, just as there are many description logics, varying in expressive power from frame-like formalisms up to very powerful ontology-definition formalisms. The particular expressive power of the W3C-recommended SWOL is under consideration by the W3C Web Ontology Working Group (although they are still working from an RDF base).

5.3   Models of XML and SWOL Documents

Now that we have defined our notion of interpretation, we need to explain how documents correspond to sets of interpretations. Intuitively, each node in the data model graph resulting from document (either validated or unvalidated) is mapped to a resource in the interpretation, and EXT relationships are built according to the edges of the data model graph.

Definition 3. *An interpretation $I = \langle R, E, EXT, CEXT, O, S \rangle$ is a model for a data model graph G if S is defined on all names in G, and there is a mapping $M : N \rightarrow R \cup DV$ that maps the nodes of G into either resources or data values. Further, the interpretation and mapping have to satisfy the following conditions.*

1. *If $n \in N$ is the top-level element of an XML document with URL u, then $M(n) = S(u)$.*
2. *For each $n \in N$ a untyped text node, $M(n) \in DV$ and $M(n) \in XTS(string - value(n))$.*
3. *For each $n \in N$ a typed value node with typed value v, $M(n) = v$.*
4. *For each other $n \in N$*
   (a) $M(n) \in R$.
   (b) If n has an identifier label id, then $M(n) = S(id)$.
   (c) For each name label of n, c, $\langle M(n), S(c) \rangle \in CEXT$.

Definition 4. *An interpretation $I = \langle R, E, EXT, CEXT, O, S \rangle$ is a model for a SWOL ontology document O if S is defined on all names in O. Further, the interpretation has to satisfy the following conditions for each definition in O.*

1. *For each definition in O of the form*
   ```
   <swol:class name="n" defined="yes"> d1 ... dn </swol:class>
   ```
   $CEXT(S(n)) = I(d1) \sqcap \ldots \sqcap I(dn)$.
2. *For each definition in O of the form*
   ```
   <swol:class name="n" defined="no"> d1 ... dn </swol:class>
   ```
   $CEXT(S(n)) \leq I(d1) \sqcap \ldots \sqcap I(dn)$.

where $I(d)$ (d is called a description) is defined as

1. *If d is* `<swol:class name="n"/>`
   then $I(d) = CEXT(S(n))$.
2. *If d is* `<swol:intersect> d1 ... dn </swol:intersect>`
   then $I(d) = I(d1) \cap \ldots \cap I(dn)$.
3. *If d is* `<swol:union> d1 ... dn </swol:union>`
   then $I(d) = I(d1) \cup \ldots \cup I(dn)$.
4. *If d is* `<swol:complement> d1 </swol:complement>`
   then $I(d) = R - I(d1)$.
5. *If d is* `<swol:all> d1 d2 </swol:all>`
   then $I(d) = \{r \in R : \forall \langle r, s \rangle \in EXT, s \in I(d1) \rightarrow s \in I(d2)\}$.
6. *If d is* `<swol:exists> d1 ... dn </swol:exists>`
   then $I(d) = \{r \in R : \exists \langle r, s \rangle \in EXT, s \in I(di), 1 \leq i \leq n\}$.

More-powerful versions of SWOL would have more possibilities for definitions and descriptions, but would have still have their meaning defined in this way.

5.4   Dealing with Models

Documents no longer correspond to single data models, but instead correspond to a set of interprepretations, the models of the document. Thus it is no longer possible to just get the information contained in a document by performing operations on the data model. Instead, we have to find out this information indirectly.

The usual method for finding out this information in model theory is via an entailment relationship. Basically, information (in the form of a query document) is present in a document if all the models of the document are also models of the query document. What we are saying here is that all the possible ways the world can be and still be compatible with the document (the models of the document) are also compatible with the query. Another way of saying this is that entailment captures what information is implicit in a document.

Definition 5. *Given a document, D, or collection of documents, see below, and another document, E, D entails E if all models of D are also models of E.*

Entailment is the simplest semantic relationship. It is also possible to define more-powerful semantic relationships, including variants of querying.

5.5   Multiple Sources of Information

Our notions of models and entailment above are not restricted to single documents, or even documents all of one kind. In fact, most of the interesting information sources will consist of several documents

- one or more XML (or RDF) documents containing base facts,
- zero or more XML Schema documents, brought in by the XML documents, and
- zero or more SWOL Ontology documents, brought in by explicit directives.

The first two kinds of documents are processed into data models, which are then given meaning in the semantics, whereas the third is given meaning directly.

So, an interpretation is a model of a set of data model graphs and a set of SWOL Ontology documents if is a model of each each of the data model graphs and each of the ontology documents separately.

5.6   Giving Direct Meaning to XML Schema Documents

So far the only meaning we have given to XML Schema Documents is their effect on the creation of XQuery data models. However, it is possible (but not necessary) to also have XML Schema Documents have a direct relationship to the model theory.

Whether one wants to do this depends on one's view of the status of XML Schema. If XML Schema definitions only constrain the form of XML documents then there should not be a direct connection between XML Schema documents and the model theory. In this view the definitions in an XML Schema document are *local*, that is, their import should only be felt by XML documents that directly reference the XML Schema document. Here two different XML documents could use the same element names but give them different meaning, by using different XML Schema documents. So, for example, one XML document could use one XML Schema document for purchases and another XML document could use a different XML Schema document, with a different definition of purchases, even though they both used the same (qualified) element names.

On the other hand, one might want to require that all purchases have similar meaning, although maybe not similar form. In this view the XML Schema document that defines purchase would not just affect one (or more) XML documents, but would have a direct and global impact on the model theory.

XML Schema is a (very) large specification, so the details of interpretations can model XML Schema documents are beyond the scope of this paper but the general outline is clear.

Definition 6. *An interpretation* $I = \langle R, E, EXT, CEXT, O, S \rangle$ *is a* model *for a XML Schema ontology document O if S is defined on all names in O. Further, the interpretation has to satisfy the following conditions for each "definition" in O.*

1. *For each global complex type, element, or attribute definition in O with name n,* $CEXT(S(n))$ *contains only those resources that have the pieces in the definition, in the correct order, and with the correct characteristics, but also, possibily, other pieces.*
2. ...

Not all the components of an XML Schema document have direct model-theoretic implications. In particular, default information does not give rise to any conditions, although, of course it *does* have model-theoretic effects through its effects on the data model.

In this way XML Schema documents can be added to the inputs of SWOL and end up with very similar status to SWOL ontology documents. XML Schema documents and SWOL ontology documents can even refer to definitions from the other kind of document and everything still works well.

6   Example

A simple example that shows how all this fits together, and gives some hint as to the power of the scheme, can be constructed on top of the purchase order example in the XML Schema primer [18] (http://www.w3.org/TR/xmlschema-0/#po.xml).

XML Schema is designed to constrain and give typing information for single XML documents, but if we want to describe collections of XML documents, particularly if these documents have differing formats, then something more than XML Schema is needed.

We assume the existence of a collection of different purchaseOrders and PurchaseOrderTypes each defined in a different XML Schema document, with different URLs. We will assume that each of these documents have a namespace, pos-i. Without loss of generality, we will assume that the different XML Schema documents use the same internal name for their top-level components.

We can use SWOL to define the Organization class, containing resources that have purchases that belong to the PurchaseOrderType.

```
<swol:class name="Organization" defined="no">
  <swol:all>
    <swol:class name="purchase">
    <swol:class name="PurchaseOrderType">
  </swol:all>
  ...
</swol:class>
```

This PurchaseOrderType is then defined as a generalization of the various PurchaseOrderTypes via

```
<swol:class name="pos-i:PurchaseOrderType" defined="no">
  <swol:class name="PurchaseOrderType" />
</swol:class>
```

We can then create a document that ties together various purchase orders, again, each in its own document with its own name, here given as po-i.

```
<Organization rdf:ID="foo">
  <purchase rdf:ID="po-1:">
  <purchase rdf:ID="po-2:">
  ...
</Organization>
```

However, all we have so far is a collection of purchase orders with no combined way of accessing the information in them, because they each have different elements names (because of their differing namespaces). To unify these elements, we have to provide a generalization of the different element names, as in

```
<swol:class name="pos-i:shipTo" defined="no">
  <swol:class name="shipTo" />
</swol:class>
<swol:class name="pos-i:items" defined="no">
  <swol:class name="items" />
</swol:class>
...
```

Now the various fields of the different PurchaseOrderTypes are considered to be sub-categories of the combined PurchaseOrderType we have created.

So far, we have not done much more than could have been done with RDF Schema, if RDF Schema was modified to deal with XML data and XML Schema types. However, we *can* go further. For example, we can say that our PurchaseOrderType can only be one of the other PurchaseOrderTypes, and nothing else, via:

```
<swol:class name="PurchaseOrderType" defined="yes">
  <swol:union>
    <swol:class name="pos-1:PurchaseOrderType" />
    ...
    <swol:class name="pos-n:PurchaseOrderType" />
  </swol:union>
</swol:class>
```

Using this, and other, facilities from SWOL, we can take information from disparate XML documents, using disparate XML Schema types, and access it in a uniform manner, resulting in a Semantic Web version of the World-Wide Web.

There are, of course, some things that we cannot do with SWOL, as SWOL is only a limited ontology language. Organizations of XML documents that require arbitrary inference will have to wait for the next level of this vision of the Semantic Web.

7   Conclusion

So what have we achieved?

We have created a semantic foundation for the Semantic Web that unifies it with the semantic foundation for the World-Wide Web. This semantic foundation takes the semantic foundation of XML, node-labelled ordered trees, and adds in semantic notions from RDF, including node identifiers and graphs. We then moved from data models, where a document corresponds to a single data structure, to model theory, where a document singles out a collection of interpretations, so as to allow for disjuntive or vague information, as needed in ontologies. In the process we eliminated some of the semantic notions from RDF, like edge labels, to achieve a better relationship between the XML expression of RDF and XML itself.

This model theory accepts several information sources:

1. XML documents, either validated or unvalidated;
2. XML Schema documents, either just as validations on XML documents or as input sources in their own right;
3. RDF documents containing RDF base facts; and
4. SWOL documents containing ontology definitions.

The details of SWOL and the details of how models are defined for XML Schema are not complete here. There are also several issues that remain to be finalized, in particular how to reconcile the URI view of names espoused by RDF against the QName view espoused by XML.

There are also several other ways to build the model theory. For example, it would be possible to go with the RDF view of models as having labels on edges. This would

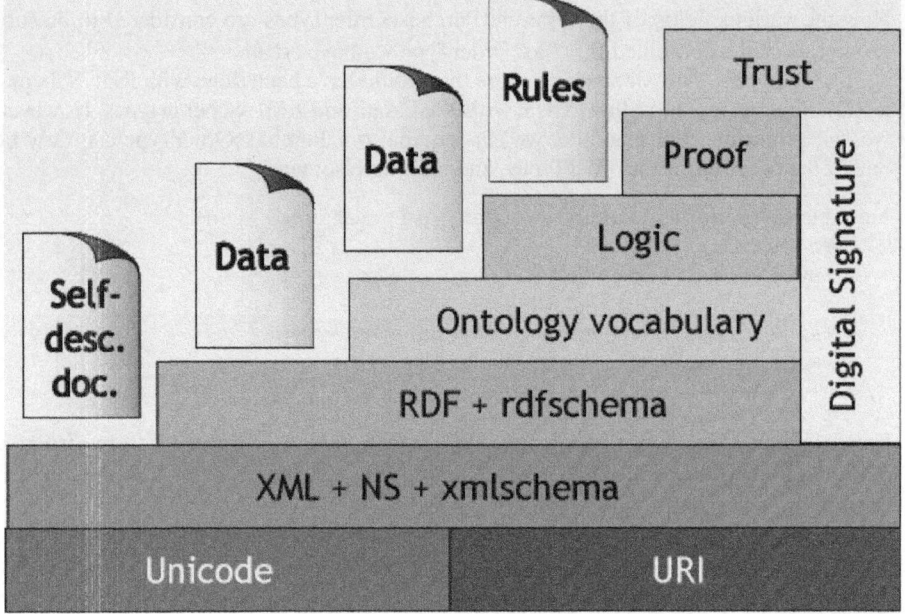

Fig. 2. Semantic Web Layers (figure by Tim Berners-Lee, http://www.w3c.org/2000/Talks/ 1206-xml2k-tbl/slide10-0.html)

require changes to XML, but XML documents are generally compatible with this way of viewing the world.

The result of the new semantic foundation is a new vision of the Semantic Web as a natural extension of the World-Wide Web. In this new Semantic Web, XML is no longer just "the universal format for structured documents and data on the Web" (http://www.w3.org/XML/), but instead is the major source of semantic information for the Semantic Web. XML Schema documents still play their current role of constraining and typing XML documents, but, since XML plays a larger role in this vision of the Semantic Web, even this use of XML Schema has more utility. XML Schema documents can also be used as global definitions of types, a new role for XML Schema. Ontology information, that cannot be represented by XML Schema, is carried by a new ontology language SWOL.

With this view of the Semantic Web, the bottom levels of the Semantic Web tower (Figure 2) finally fit together, with no inappropriate semantic disconnects. Further, with the division of documents into different categories (XML, XML Schema, SWOL), no one level claims the entire possible syntax, as was true for RDF, and extensions can be easily given their own syntax and their own place in the Semantic Web.

References

1. Serge Abiteboul, Peter Buneman, and Dan Suciu. *Data on the Web: From Relations to Semistructured Data and XML.* Morgan Kaufmann, 1999.
2. Franz Baader, Deborah L. McGuinness, Daniele Nardi, and Peter F. Patel-Schneider, editors. *The Description Logic Handbook: Theory, implementation, and applications.* Kluwer, to appear.
3. Tim Berners-Lee. *Weaving the Web.* Harper, San Francisco, 1999.
4. Tim Berners-Lee, James Hendler, and Ora Lassila. The semantic web. *Scientific American*, May 2001.
5. Harold Boley. A web data model unifying XML and RDF.
   `http://www.dfki.uni-kl.de/{$\sim$}boley/xmlrdf.html`,   September 2001.
6. Jon Bosak and Tim Bray. XML and the second-generation web. *Scientific American*, May 1999.
7. Ronald J. Brachman and Hector J. Levesque, editors. *Readings in Knowledge Representation.* Morgan Kaufmann Publishers, San Francisco, California, 1985.
8. DAML+OIL language. http://www.daml.org/language/, 2001.
9. Resource description framework (RDF) schema specification 1.0. W3C Candidate Recommendation, 27 March 2000, http://www.w3.org/TR/rdf-schema, March 2000.
10. John Haugeland, editor. *Mind Design.* Bradford Books, Montgomery, Vermont, 1981.
11. Sergey Melnik. Bridging the gap between RDF and XML, December 1999.
    `http://www-db.stanford.edu/{$\sim$}melnik/rdf/fusion.html`.
12. Marvin Minsky. A framework for representing knowledge. In Patrick Henry Winston, editor, *The Psychology of Computer Vision*, pages 211–277. McGraw-Hill, New York, 1975. An abridged version published in [10] and also published in [7].
13. Resource description framework (RDF): Model and syntax specification. W3C Recommendation, 22 February 1999, http://www.w3.org/TR/1999/REC-rdf-syntax-19990222/, February 1999.
14. Peter F. Patel-Schneider and Jérôme Siméon. The yin/yang web: Xml syntax and rdf semantics. In *Eleventh International World Wide Web Conference*, May 2002.
15. RDF model theory. http://www.w3.org/TR/rdf-mt/, 2002.
16. Extensible markup language (XML) 1.0 (second edition).   W3C Recommendation, http://www.w3.org/TR/REC-xml.
17. XML information set. http://www.w3.org/TR/xml-infoset/, October 2001.
18. XML Schema part 0: Primer. W3C Recommendation, 2 May 2001, http://www.w3.org/TR/xmlschema-0/.
19. XQuery 1.0 and XPath 2.0 data model. http://www.w3.org/TR/query-datamodel/, December 2001.

Trusting Information Sources One Citizen at a Time

Yolanda Gil and Varun Ratnakar

USC Information Sciences Institute
4676 Admiralty Way
Marina del Rey, CA 90292
{gil, varunr}@isi.edu

Abstract. This paper describes an approach to derive assessments about information sources based on individual feedback about the sources. We describe TRELLIS, a system that helps users annotate their analysis of alternative information sources that can be contradictory and incomplete. As the user makes a decision on which sources to dismiss and which to believe in making a final decision, TRELLIS captures the derivation of the decision in a semantic markup. TRELLIS then uses these annotations to derive an assessment of the source based on the annotations of many individuals. Our work builds on the Semantic Web and presents a tool that helps users create annotations that are in a mix of formal and human language, and exploits the formal representations to derive measures of trust in the content of Web resources and their original source.

1 Introduction

The Semantic Web can be described as a substrate to support advanced functions for collaboration (human-human, computer-human, computer-computer), sharing of Web resources, and reasoning about their content [3]. The markup languages that are being proposed for the Semantic Web will be the basis to develop reasoners, proof checking and derivation tools, and many other functions such as Web services. The Semantic Web will also be the basis for the Web of Trust, which will provide mechanisms to handle authentication, permission, and validation of attribution in a Web where, by design, anyone can contribute content, links, and services.

A lot of current emphasis on the Web of Trust is in accessing resources, specifically authentication and permission issues. Digital signatures and public keys support authentication. Proofs are another important technology in the Web of Trust, since permission schemes are often described with rules and statements (e.g., anyone working for company C should be allowed to access D) and will need to rely on proofs that can reason about the rules and conclude whether access should be granted. An important issue with respect to both authentication and permission is checking that a document can be attributed to the source specified. For example, if Joe Doe writes an article and publishes it claiming Henry Kissinger as the author, it should be possible to check the truth about the document's authorship.

I. Horrocks and J. Hendler (Eds.): ISWC 2002, LNCS 2342, pp 162–176, 2002.

Our work addresses a different issue on the Web of Trust regarding whether to trust the *content* of a Web resource depending on its source. It seems that people reach some times informal consensus on how and when to trust what a source says. Many qualifiers about sources seem to be common knowledge only to those familiar with the topic. Some sources are generally considered more trustworthy or reliable than others (e.g., [19]). Some sources are considered authoritative in specific topics (e.g., [14,22]). Some sources are preferred to others depending on the specific context of use of the information (e.g., student travelers may prefer [17], families may find [12] more preferable, and business people may go with [6]). Some sources are considered pretty accurate but it is understood they are not necessarily up to date (e.g., [5]). Finally, specific statements by traditionally authoritative sources can be proven wrong in light of other information, while the source's reputation will still hold. In this sense, there is a finer grain of detail in attributing trust to a source with respect to specific statements made by it.

These kinds of observations about sources are the result of informal consensus and should be captured by the Web of Trust. Individual users should be provided with tools to annotate their views and opinions on resources available on the Web, as well as to qualify and justify these views if they choose to. The Semantic Web will provide the markup languages and reasoners to derive consensus on how to assess a source based on these individual annotations about sources.

This paper describes our initial work on TRELLIS to enable users to express their trust on a source and the statements made by it, and to combine individual views into an overall assessment of each source of information. TRELLIS enables users to annotate how they analyze and use information for some decision making purpose. As the user considers information from different sources relevant to their purpose, they annotate their views as they find contradictory or complementary statements, make an opinion on what to believe in the absence of complete information. TRELLIS includes a vocabulary and markup language for semantic annotations of decisions and tradeoffs, and allows users to extend this vocabulary with domain specific terms or constructs that are useful to their particular task. We have used TRELLIS with a variety of scenarios to annotate tradeoffs and decisions (e.g., military planning), organize materials (e.g., search results), analyze disagreements and controversies on a topic (e.g., intelligence analysis), and handle incomplete and conflicting information (e.g., genealogy research).

The paper begins with an overview of TRELLIS as an information analysis tool. Then we describe how users can specify source descriptions and qualifications in TRELLIS. We show how TRELLIS derives ratings for each source, averaged over many users and many analyses. We discuss how these ratings can be presented in useful ways to users to help them assess sources in subsequent analysis with TRELLIS. We conclude with related work and a discussion of future directions.

2 Information Analysis in TRELLIS

TRELLIS is an interactive tool that helps users annotate the rationale for their decisions, hypotheses, and opinions as they analyze information from various sources. This section gives a brief overview of TRELLIS, more details can be found in [13]. TRELLIS is available on-line at trellis.semanticweb.org.

Our work is inspired by military intelligence analysts, but we believe that this kind of information analysis is a common task for many users in the information age. Intelligence analysis carries over to political, strategic, and competitive (business) areas. Someone doing genealogy research looks at various sources of information that may be incomplete and contradictory, make plausible hypotheses in the light of what is known, and create a consistent story about what happened in the family. Someone planning a vacation makes a lot of decisions after consulting many airlines and hotel possibilities, their friends traveling to the same destination may want to consult the same sources though perhaps making different choices.

Our goal is to enable users to create annotations of their analysis of alternative sources of information as they make a decision or reach a conclusion based on their analysis. Once this rationale is recorded, it can be used to help users justify, update, and share the results of their analysis. Users need support after they have made a decision, reached a conclusion, or made a recommendation, since they are often required to: 1) explain and justify their views to others, 2) update the decision in light of additional information or new data, 3) expose the intermediate products of the final recommendation to others that may be analyzing related information to make similar decisions.

TRELLIS includes a language for annotating information analysis, which can be extended by users to suit their needs. The language uses the following basic components. A *statement* is a piece of information or data relevant to an analysis, such as "Cuban pilots were trained in Czechoslovakia", "Prince Larry did not inhale". A statement may have been extracted, summarized, or concluded from a document. Documents are often an existing Web resource (text, imagery, or any other format) indicated by a URI, but can also be a user-provided document such as an email message or a note relating a conversation in which case TRELLIS helps users turn them into Web resources as well. The user can also create a statement to introduce a hypothesis, a conclusion, or an observation that will be used in the analysis, which may or may not be backed up by (associated with) a document. Every document has a source description, describing its creator, publisher, date, format, etc. Each statement and its source can have a source qualification specified as a degree of reliability and credibility. The next section explains in detail how sources are described in TRELLIS.

A *compound statement* is composed of several statements related by a construct. *Constructs* reflect how individual statements are related in the analysis. For example, a causal construct is used to form the compound statement: "Cuban pilots were trained in Czechoslovakia" and "Arrival of latest Soviet warplanes in Cuba" **results in** "A major upgrade of the Cuban Air Forces". Statements can have a *likelihood qualification*, which is a subjective informal indication of the analyst's reaction to a statement (or compound statement). This can indicate surprise, dismissal, saliency, accuracy, etc. A *reason* can be used to justify a compound statement, a source qualification, and a likelihood qualification.

These basic components are used to create *units*. The basic structure of a unit is:

> *statement* {and *statement*}* *construct* {and *statement*}*
> is {not} *likelihood-qualifier* because
> according to *source-description* which is
> *reliability-qualifier* because *statement* and
> *credibility-qualifier* because *statement*

An example of a unit, taken from a Special Operations planning analysis, is:

> water temperature unsustainable for SDV divers
> **is elaborated in**
> average March water temperature is 55-60 degrees
> **and**
> platoon requires minimum water temperature of 65 degrees
> **according to source**
> Cmdr Smith **which is**
> **completely reliable (A)**
> **because** Cmdr Smith has 15 years experience with JSOC
> **and**
> **probably true**
> **because** Cmdr Smith has been platoon cmdr for 3 years

The user may or may not provide all the components of a unit, only a statement is required to form a unit.

An analysis can be done with an overarching *purpose* (or topic), which is often a question or request that the information analyst starts with. An analysis is composed of many such units. They can be linked as subunits of one another. Units or statements can be left with no links to the overall analysis, and in that case they can be specified as attachments to the analysis. This is useful to indicate that they have been considered by the user but do not appear in the derivation of the final analysis (for lack of time, or because the analyst found better options to justify their conclusions). An analysis is represented as a tree, but can be a set of trees (especially if the user has not reached a final conclusion yet).

Our default set of constructs used in units is drawn from argumentation and discourse relations, logic connectives, action representations, causality, and object representations (see [13] for details). Some examples are {P}* contradicts {Q}*, {P}* is supported by {Q}*, {P}* before {Q}*, {P}* is summarized by {Q}*. Our emphasis is not on the completeness or semantics of these constructs, but rather on offering users a sensible set of constructs that they can draw from in forming an argument. Our experience has been that users often cannot pin down the logic behind their argument but would still like to reflect their conclusion and some sort of (informal) justification of it. Users can add additional constructs to suit their specific needs using the TRELLIS interface.

A very important feature of TRELLIS is that users can include in the analysis references to sources and indicate that they were dismissed and why, typically because
they contradict other information used in the analysis or simply because other sources
provided more precise or detailed data.

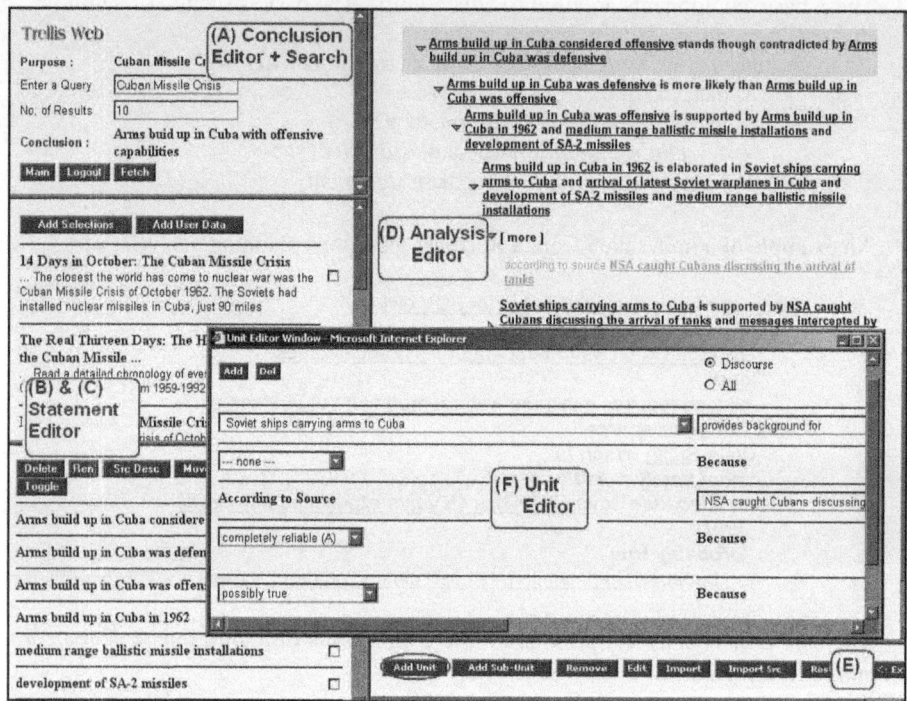

Fig. 1. A Snapshot of the TRELLIS user interface. From top-left counter clock wise the system shows the purpose and conclusions of the analysis (A), the original documents and associated statements (B&C), the units of the analysis (E,F), and the overall analysis (D).

Figure 1 shows the current TRELLIS user interface. The example is inspired on the
Cuban missile crisis, one of the most thoroughly studied cases of intelligence analy-
sis. The purpose of the analysis and the final conclusion are shown in Frame (A).
Analysis and opinions revolve around facts, statements, and hypotheses. With Frame
(B), users can search the Web and mark documents to be indexed by TRELLIS, or
can add their own documents which are then converted to a Web resource and given a
URI. Each resource is then associated with a short statement entered by the user in
Frame (C). Users can specify several statements per resource, each summarizing a
salient piece of information described within the resource in terms that are suitable to
the user. The 'Src Desc' button in Frame (C) allows users to enter meta-data about
the resource. Frame (E) invokes the Unit Editor (F). The overall analysis is composed using the Analysis Editor, shown in Frame (D).

TRELLIS generates annotations of the user's analysis in several markup languages
(XML, RDF, and DAML+OIL). The constructs used in units as well as the source
descriptions are represented in the corresponding schema languages and ontologies.

Each analysis is turned into an annotated Web document and contains links to all the resources referenced within. When users add new constructs to the language, the corresponding schemas and ontologies are updated.

```
<element rdf:ID="elem29">
  <title>Unstability of Cuban and Soviet governments</title>
  <link>/trellis_web/cached/demo_dir7_1011051896.html</link>
</element>
<statement rdf:ID="st1">
  <left_elem rdf:resource="#elem1" />
  <relation rdf:resource="http://excalibur.isi.edu:8888/trellis_web/library#stands_though_contradicted_by" />
  <right_elem rdf:resource="#elem2" />
  <qualifier />
  <sub_st rdf:resource="#st2" />
  <sub_st rdf:resource="#st15" />
</statement>
<statement rdf:ID="st2">
  <left_elem rdf:resource="#elem2" />
  <relation rdf:resource="http://excalibur.isi.edu:8888/trellis_web/guest/library#is_more_likely_than" />
  <right_elem rdf:resource="#elem3" />
  <qualifier />
  <sub_st rdf:resource="#st3" />
  <sub_st rdf:resource="#st11" />
  <sub_st rdf:resource="#st14" />
</statement>
<statement rdf:ID="st3">
  <left_elem rdf:resource="#elem3" />
  <relation rdf:resource="http://excalibur.isi.edu:8888/trellis_web/library#is_supported_by" />
  <right_elem rdf:resource="#elem4" />
```

Fig. 2. A part of semantic RDF markup of the analysis in Fig. 1. TRELLIS provides an RDF schema as well as a DAML ontology for the terms used in the markup.

TRELLIS allows users to view the markup of the annotations, as well as the schemas and ontologies for the underlying constructs. Figure 2 shows part of the semantic RDF markup annotations of the analysis shown in Figure 1. These annotations are posted as a Web document as we mentioned above, and are available to other tools for search, reference, and reasoning.

TRELLIS also supports sharing and collaboration. The user can search and view the analyses entered by other users, import relevant portions into their own analysis, and change the imported portions as they see fit (this is done through the "Import" button on the bottom right of the screen).

3   Source Attribution and Description

TRELLIS allows users to annotate the source attribution for each statement used in the analysis, to describe the source, and to make qualifications about it. Figure 3 shows an example, discussed in detail throughout this section.

For each document indexed in TRELLIS, the user can annotate meta-data regarding its attribution using the Dublin Core [8]. The Dublin Core (*dc:*) was developed as a standard to describe resources (e.g., documents). A document is described with 15 main attributes: dc:title, dc:creator, dc:subject, dc:description, dc:publisher, dc:contributor, dc:date, dc:type, dc:format, dc:identifier, dc:source, dc:language, dc:relation, dc:coverage, and dc:rights. Five of them are concerned with attribution of information. The *dc:creator* is an entity primarily responsible for making the content of the resource. The *dc:publisher* is an entity responsible for making the resource available. The *dc:contributor* is an entity responsible for making contributions to the content of the resource. The *dc:source* is a reference to a resource from which the present resource is derived. The *dc:relation* is a reference to a related resource.

Consider a pseudo-fictitious example of a document in an FA Times article from the CREUTERS agency that reports on drug problems in the Monarchy and that contains the statement "At a press conference last Monday, Duckingham Palace was adamant that Prince Larry did not inhale". In this case, the CREUTERS journalist would be the creator, FA Times the publisher, the Duckingham Palace spokesperson would be a contributor, the original CREUTERS article would be the source, and the tapes of the press conference could be specified as a relation.

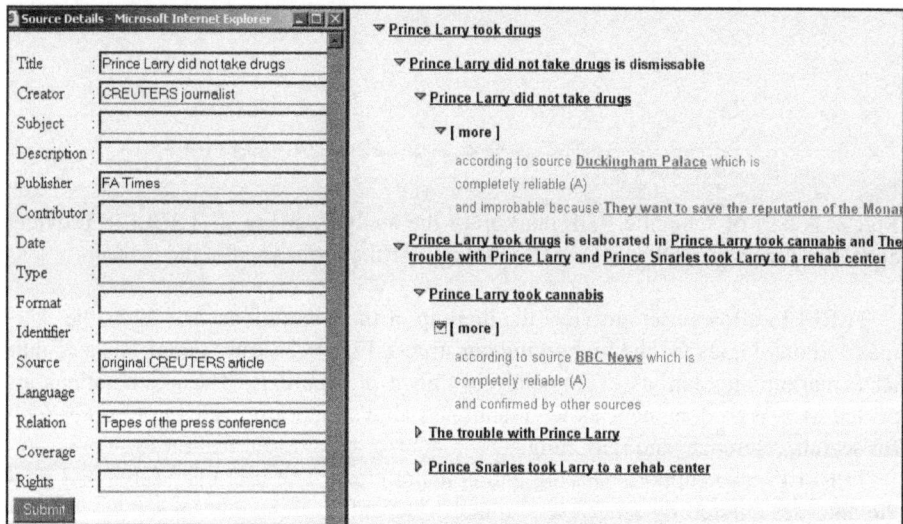

Fig. 3. An Example of attribution of a statement in TRELLIS, where the source stated in the analysis (shown on the right) may or may not be one of the entities mentioned in the DC metadata description (shown on the left).

In TRELLIS, document used in an analysis is first indexed with a short statement, as a way to summarize the particular aspect of the document used in the analysis. The statement points to the document, and must become part of an analysis unit. In the unit, the user can specify a *source* for that statement. This TRELLIS source can be any of the five fields in the Dublin Core metadata that are related to attribution and that we mentioned above, but can also be any other entity that is not indicated in it. TRELLIS gives the user this flexibility because the user may trust (or distrust) any of these sources enough to take some stand about the statement. In the rest of the discussion, we will refer to sources as those chosen by a TRELLIS user to be associated with a statement within a unit.

In our example, the user could use the statement "Prince Larry did not take drugs" to index the news article, but specify as its source one of: the FA Times, the publisher of the newspaper, CREUTERS, Duckingham Palace, or perhaps Prince Larry himself depending on the nature and the context of the analysis. In Figure 3, the source chosen by the user for that statement chosen by the user in their analysis (shown on the right) is Duckingham Palace, which is the dc:contributor (the DC metadata are shown on the left).

In TRELLIS, the user can also qualify the source of a statement by its *reliability* and *credibility*. Reliability is typically based on credentials and past performance of the source. Credibility specifies the analyst's view of probable truth of a statement, given all the other information available to the analyst. Reliability and credibility are not the same, for example a completely reliable source may provide some information that may be judged to be not very credible given other known information. In our example, Duckingham Palace may be judged to be a pretty reliable source based on its reputation, yet the user may decide the source to be not very credible in making this particular statement. In TRELLIS, we use the default ratings of reliability and credibility that are typically found in military intelligence manuals. Reliability is specified by a six-valued scale ranked A to F (completely reliable, usually reliable, fairly reliable, not usually reliable, unreliable, and not possible to judge). Credibility can have one of six values on a scale (confirmed by other sources, probably true, possibly true, doubtfully true, improbable, and not possible to judge).

When users introduce hypotheses in an analysis, they are designated as the source and are not allowed to give themselves any ratings.

Because an important goal is to give users maximum flexibility, TRELLIS does not require users to specify or qualify the sources for any of the statements.

In summary, the user can specify the source of a statement used in the analysis, which may or may not be one of the fields used in the Dublin Core meta-data for the document that supports the statement. Users can also qualify the source attribution according to its reliability and credibility.

4   Deriving an Assessment about a Source

As many users create multiple analyses that refer to common sources, TRELLIS creates an overall consensus assessment about each source as we explain in this section. We describe here our initial approach to get a rough approximation of the relative ratings of each source. In future work we plan to formalize, evaluate, and extend this approach to consider additional factors.

For each purpose or topic analyzed by the user, we derive a rating for each of the sources referenced in that analysis. First, we derive a rating for each statement associated to each source.

The first criterion for rating the sources is provided by the user in terms of R (reliability) and C (credibility) on a 1 to 6 scale. If the statement is unqualified in the unit, then an average value is taken (the fact that the user did not specify R and C is taken into account by one of the other rating variables described below).

For those sources where C and R are not specified in the unit (i.e., the unit just says "A according to source S", we track the use of the statement along the analysis tree as an indicator of the user's view on the source in the current analysis context. We describe the source to be one of the following depending on the status of 'A'.

- Used: This means that the user has found the statement relevant to the analysis and is using it to make the final conclusion. So if the user makes another upper level statement "'B' is supported by 'A'", then we track both 'B' and 'A' up the tree, since in some sense 'S' now transitively vouches for both 'A' and 'B'. In this way, when the final top-level conclusion is reached, we assume that the source 'S' was considered by the user to be a contributor to reaching a conclusion and thus the user had some level of trust on the source.
- Tainted: The system marks a statement by a source as *tainted* or *dismissed* if somewhere along the analysis tree the user refers to it with a pejorative construct (such as dismiss, or contradicts). Therefore, if any upper level statement uses such construct then the source 'S' is marked as tainted.
- Not used: The statement is not used in reaching the conclusion. This happens, as we mentioned, when users leave statements as part of the analysis in case they are useful in future updates of the analysis. Therefore, if the upper level statements do not transitively use 'A' such that the top level conclusion is never reached, then the source is marked as 'Unused'.

Therefore, each source-statement pair (s,a) has the following rating attributes:
1. $C(s,a)$ - Credibility - based on credibility qualifications over all the units that specify this qualifier for the source. On a scale of 1 to 6.
2. $R(s,a)$ - Reliability - based on reliability qualifications over all the units that specify this qualifier for the source. On a scale of 1 to 6.
3. $U(s,a)$ - Used - a count of the number of times it was used to reach a conclusion.
4. $T(s,a)$ - Tainted - a count of the number of times it was found to be *tainted*.
5. $N(s,a,)$ - Not Used - a count of the number of times it was unused in reaching the final conclusion.

The system's overall rating $O(s,a)$ of the source-statement pair is derived from the normalized averages of the above ratings:

$$O(s,a) = k1 * (C + R) + k2 * U - k3 * T - k4N$$

The coefficients k1, k2, k3, and k4 reflect the relative weight given to each individual factor. Here U, T and N are normalized with respect to the total number of times that the (s,a) pair is used. There might be some cases, as previously mentioned, where the user does not provide a credibility or a reliability and where TRELLIS assigns 3 (the average value) for C and R, then the formula for $O(s,a)$ allows other factors (if it is used in reaching a conclusion or not, if it is dismissed or not, if it is not considered in reaching a conclusion) to influence the final value for the rating of the source by adding to its rating with U and taking from its rating T and to a lesser extent N.

In the future, we would like advanced users to be able to change the coefficients k1, k2, k3, k4 so that they can control how much they would like to weigh different uses of the source by other users. The current values of the coefficients are set to 2/3, 2, 2, and 1 respectively.

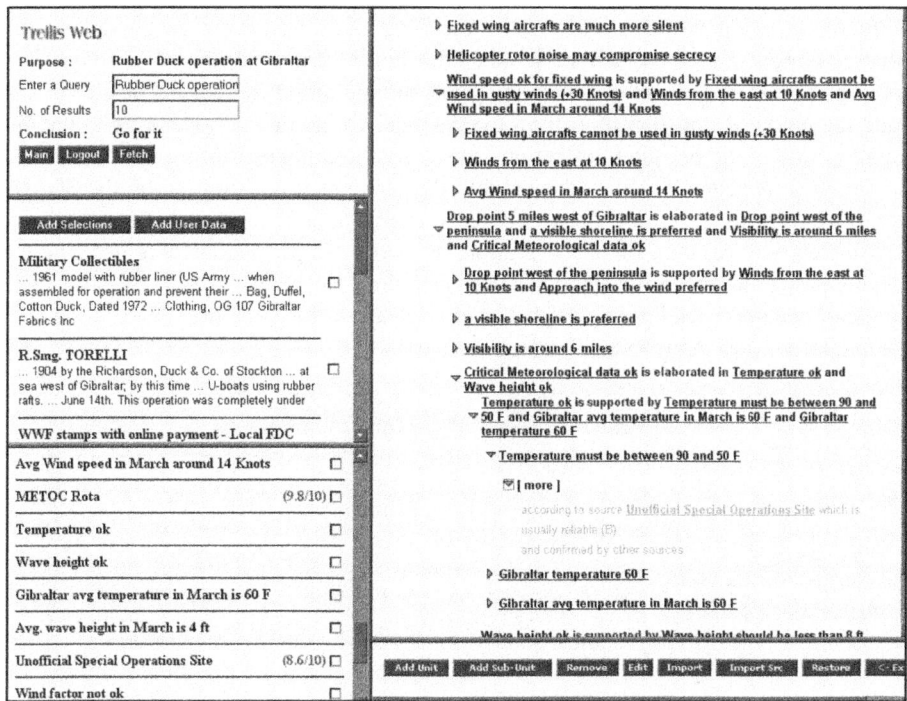

Fig. 4. An intelligence analyst is using TRELLIS to annotate the reasons why he chose a certain drop site and a certain mode of transport in a hypothetical operation

The overall rating O(s) for a single source is the average of all the ratings of its associated statements:

$$O(s) = 1 / N \quad \sum_{(i=1 \text{ to } N)} O(s, a_i)$$

TRELLIS derives and updates these ratings automatically as users enter different analyses that rely on those sources. The next section shows how these ratings are used and shown to the users to help them make decisions about what sources to trust.

5 Helping Users Select Sources

As a user is considering a topic for an analysis, he or she may wonder what sources were considered by other users on topics relevant to their analysis, as well as how those sources were rated by users in light of what they were considering and in light of their expertise on the topic. TRELLIS allows users to search for sources on specific topics, see how they rank based on their overall ratings, and view the details of a source's ratings based on the individual factors considered in deriving the ratings.

Figure 4 shows an intelligence analyst reasoning about the choice of a drop site and the mode of transportation for a hypothetical "rubber duck" operation in the Gibraltar area. A rubber duck operation is used by the military to insert SEALS into a target area. A rubber craft is dropped into the sea, which is then used by the SEALS to move towards the target. The intelligence analyst knows sources that provide critical meteorological data for the operation, as well as some manuals that describe the techniques preferred in carrying out the operation. He points to weather sources to indicate whether conditions match the critical meteorological data, and if the preferred techniques in the manual can be carried out.

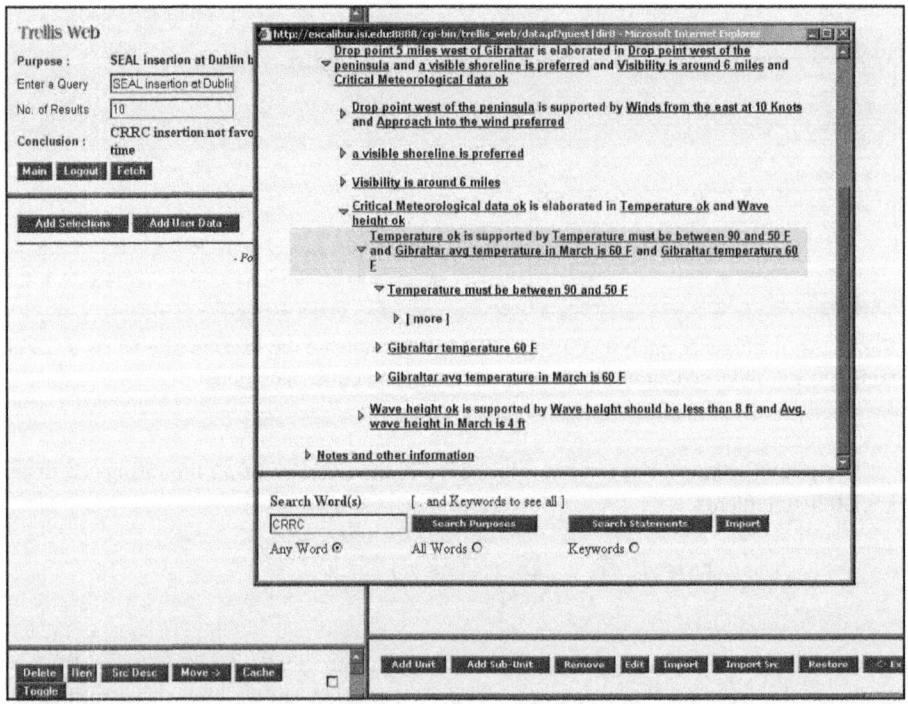

Fig. 5. An intelligence analyst considering whether a hypothetical mission is feasible is browsing the analysis done by another intelligence analyst for a mission that was shown in Figure 4.

Figure 5 shows a relatively inexperienced intelligence analyst trying to analyze the feasibility of a hypothetical "rubber duck" mission to Dublin. The analyst uses the

"Import" button to bring up the Analysis Browser window. He searches for "CRRC" (which is the craft used in a "rubber duck" operation) and finds the analysis of the previous intelligence analyst for a "rubber duck" operation to Gibraltar. He can now select a portion of this analysis and "import" it into his own analysis, or he can simply browse it and figure out what kind of sources will be needed. For example, the analyst finds out that according to a reasonably accurate source, the water temperature should be between 50 F and 90 F for the CRRC to be safe.

Now the analyst needs to find out the average water temperature in the Dublin area. He now invokes the "source query tool" by pressing the 'Import Src' button in the bottom right frame of the main window. Figure 6 shows the user query for "temperature" and the results that are returned. TRELLIS shows the rating of all sources that are related to the topic (here "temperature"). The analyst then selects the sources that he considers appropriate and imports them to his selection of statements and sources in the 'Statement Editor' (bottom-left frame of the main TRELLIS window).

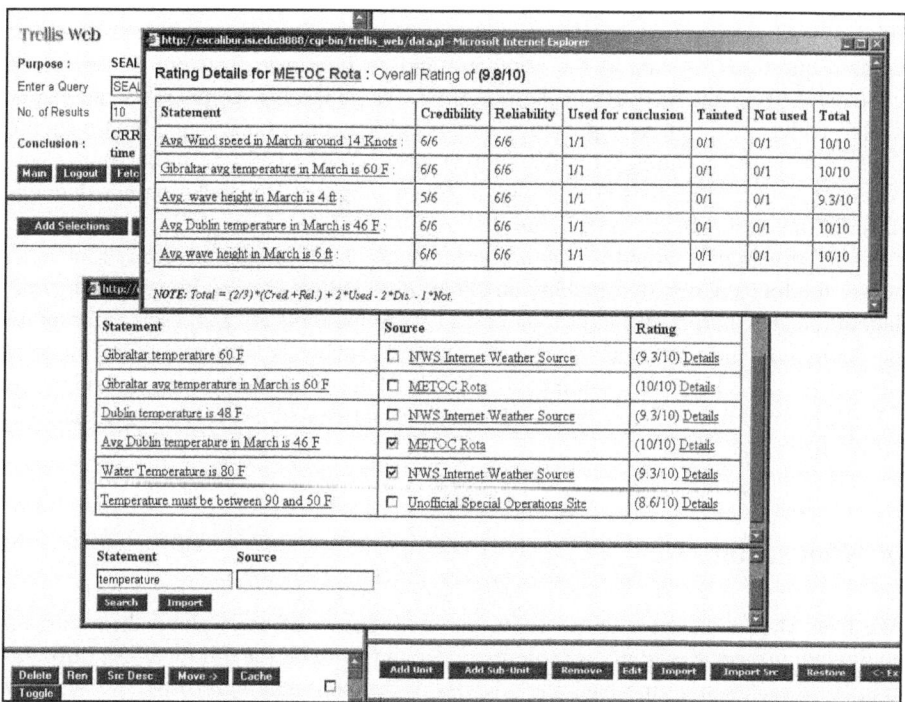

Fig. 6. TRELLIS shows users its assessment of a source based on previous analysis by other users, showing both an overall rating and the details about how the rating was derived.

The user can also see further details about the ratings of a source, shown at the top of Figure 6. This shows the detailed factors and ratings of the source for all statements that it has been used with.

6   Related Work

Annotea [15] is a general metadata annotation infrastructure that enables users to comment on resources (also using the Dublin Core as well as domain-specific markup in RDF), share and summarize these comments, and manage reply threads. Annotea's goals and emphasis are complementary to the work on TRELLIS, which has a more specific focus on information analysis for decision making.

Web users are often allowed to offer ratings that can be used by other users in deciding what or who to trust or perhaps prefer [20]. This kind of feedback schemas can be used to rate other users (e.g., [9]), products (e.g., [1]), or any other item of entertainment or informative value (e.g., [11,18]). These ratings capture a user's opinion about an item, but not about its source or producer. They also only have very limited ways for users to articulate their justification. TRELLIS also captures the context of an opinion based on the use of the source.

SEAS [16] uses an alternative approach to support similar kinds of analysis in the military and competitive intelligence arena. Users define argument templates that contain questions to support the argument and an inference structure to derive the conclusion from the answers to the questions. The approach emphasizes the use of shared patterns as well as support for automated inference on demand, and does not capture or generate ratings for the sources used. TRELLIS has more support for assessing sources but does not provide as much support for automation nor domain-specific standard patterns to facilitate sharing.

Other research is aimed to capture argumentation in collaborative environments, where the focus is decision making and consensus within a group by supporting collaboration and sharing of decision rationale [7]. Some tools are also geared to capture decisions and their rationale in specific contexts, such as software or engineering design [21]. They are customized to their domain and are not as general as TRELLIS, but they provide expressive representations to express design tradeoffs adequately.

7   Conclusions

We have shown an approach to capturing assessments of users about their trust on individual information sources as they are deciding whether and how to use information from each source in a specific analysis or decision making process. Users may express a range of opinions, such as dismissing the information in light of other sources, or express the credibility and reliability of the source explicitly or implicitly in their analysis. Our approach captures the trust of individual users based on an actual context of use of the source as well as their expertise on the topic as they go through the analysis. Other users benefit of these indications of trust as they decide which sources to use in new analyses and decisions.

In future work, we would like to use the approach presented as a basis to extend service descriptions with meta-data about whether other customers have found services trustworthy or reliable. Current languages for Web services as well as e-commerce applications [4,2,10] support the advertisement of services, but should be extended to allow qualifications of what is advertised with the customer's view on the actual performance of the provider. Our approach could be used to ensure truth in advertising by collecting feedback from individuals together with justifications for their opinions.

Many of the mechanisms necessary in the Web of Trust will be imposed by strict protocols of authentication, accessibility, and attribution. Our work opens the way for individuals to provide their assessment of truth in more subjective way that contributes to create a collective consensus of trust on information sources.

Acknowledgements

This work was funded by the US Air Force Office of Scientific Research (AFOSR) under grant F49620-00-1-0337. We would like to acknowledge Jim Blythe, Jihie Kim, Larry Kite, and Fred Bobbitt for their comments and suggestions about this work.

References

1.   Amazon Web Site, http://www.amazon.com.
2.   Ankolekar, A., Burstein, M., Hobbs, J.R., Lassila, O., Martin, D.L., McIlraith, S.A., Narayanan, S., Paolucci, M., Payne, T.R., Sycara, K., Zeng, H.: DAML-S: Semantic Markup for Web Services. In: International Semantic Web Workshop (2001).
3.   Berners-Lee, T., Hendler, J., Fensel, D.: The Semantic Web. In: Scientific American 78(3) (2001): 20-88.
4.   Christensen, E., Curbera, F., Meredith, G., Weerawarana, S.: Web Services Description Language (WSDL) 1.1. http://www.w3.org/TR/2001/NOTE-wsdl-20010315 (2001).
5.   CIA Factbook Web Site, http://www.cia.gov/cia/publications/factbook (2001).
6.   Concierge Web Site, http://www.concierge.com (2002).
7.   Conklin, J. and Begeman, M., gIBIS: A Hypertext Tool for Exploratory Policy Discussion, ACM Transactions on Office Information Systems, Vol. 6, pp. 303-331 (1988).
8.   DCES : The Dublin Core Element Set. http://dublincore.org/documents/dces/ (1999).
9.   eBay Web Site, http://www.ebay.com.
10. ebXML Web Site. http://ww.ebxml.org/.
11. Epinions Web Site. http://www.epinions.com.
12. Fodors Web Site. http://www.fodors.com.
13. Gil, Y. and Ratnakar, V. : TRELLIS: An Interactive Tool for Capturing Information Analysis and Decision Making. Internal Project Report (2001).
14. Janes Web Site. http://www.janes.com.
15. Koivunen, M.R. and Swick, R.: Metadata Based Annotation Infrastructure offers Flexibility and Extensibility for Collaborative Applications and Beyond. In: Proceedings of the K-CAP 2001 Workshop on Knowledge Markup and Semantic Annotation, Victoria, British Columbia (2001).

16. Lawrence, J. D., Harrison, I.W., Rodriguez, A. C.: Capturing Analytic Thought. In: Proceedings of the First International Conference on Knowledge Capture (K-CAP)
17. Lets Go Web Site. http://www.letsgo.com.
18. Movielens Web Site. http://www.movielens.umn.edu.
19. The New York Times Web Site. http://www.nyt.com.
20. Sarwar, B M., Karypis, G., Konstan, J.A., Riedl J.: Item-based collaborative filtering recommendation algorithms. In: To appear in Proceedings of the 10th International World Wide Web Conference (WWW10), Hong Kong (2001).
21. Shum, S.B.: Design Argumentation as Design Rationale. In: Encyclopedia of Computer Science and Technology (M.Dekker Inc: NY) (1996).
22. World Wide Web Consortium Web Site. http://www.w3c.org.

Querying the Semantic Web:
A Formal Approach

Ian Horrocks and Sergio Tessaris

Department of Computer Science
University of Manchester
Manchester, UK
{horrocks|tessaris}@cs.man.ac.uk

Abstract. Ontologies are set to play a key role in the Semantic Web, and several web ontology languages, like DAML+OIL, are based on DLs. These not only provide a clear semantics to the ontology languages, but allows them to exploit DL systems in order to provide correct and complete reasoning services.

Recent results shown that DL systems can be enriched by a conjunctive query language, providing a solution to one of the weakness of traditional DL systems. These results can be transfered to the Semantic Web community, where the need for expressive query languages is witnessed by different proposals (like DQL for DAML+OIL).

In this paper we present a logical framework for conjunctive query answering in DAML+OIL. Moreover, we provide a sound and complete algorithm based on recent Description Logic research.

1 Introduction

Description Logics (DLs) are a well-known family of knowledge representation formalisms based on the notion of concepts (classes) and roles (properties). DLs have proved useful in wide range of applications including configuration [18], databases [5,7] and ontological engineering (i.e., the design, maintenance and deployment of ontologies).

The use of DLs in ontological engineering has been highlighted by the recent explosion of interest in the Semantic Web [2]. Ontologies are set to play a key role in the Semantic Web, where they will provide a source of shared and precisely defined terms that can be used to describe web resources and improve their accessibility to automated processes [9]. Several prominent web ontology languages, in particular OIL and DAML+OIL [11], are based on DLs; this allows them to exploit formal results (e.g., w.r.t. the decidability and complexity of key inference problems [8]) and algorithm designs from DL research, as well as to use DL based knowledge representation systems to provide reasoning support for web applications [14].

In order to maximise the utility of Web ontologies, it will be necessary not only to reason with ontology classes, but also with individuals (web resources) that instantiate them, and in particular to answer queries over sets of such

I. Horrocks and J. Hendler (Eds.): ISWC 2002, LNCS 2342, pp. 177–191, 2002.

individuals (e.g., see [4]). This highlights a serious shortcoming of many DL based knowledge representation systems: the inadequacy of their query languages. In this paper we show how the query answering technique presented in [17] can be used to provide query answering services for conjunctive query languages such as the one recently proposed for DAML+OIL (see http://www.daml.org/listarchive/joint-committee/1052.html).

Recent years have witnessed the transfer of algorithmic techniques used for terminological reasoning (Tbox reasoning) to the development of both algorithms and optimised implementations that also support reasoning about individuals (Abox reasoning), e.g., see [10,12,22]. Although these systems provide sound and complete Abox reasoning for very expressive logics, they often have rather weak Abox query languages. Typically, these only support instantiation (is an individual a an instance of a class C?), realisation (what are the most specific classes a is an instance of?) and retrieval (which individuals are instances of C?). The reason for this weakness is that, in these expressive logics, all reasoning tasks are reduced to that of determining knowledge base (KB) satisfiability. In particular, instantiation is reduced to KB un-satisfiability by transforming the query into a negated assertion; however, this technique cannot be used directly for queries involving roles and variables.

In [6] and [17] it is shown that a more sophisticated reduction to KB unsatisfiability can be used for answering conjunctive queries similar to those supported by relational databases.[1] However, with DLs query answering cannot simply be reduced to model checking as in the database framework. This is because KBs may contain nondeterminism and/or incompleteness.

In this paper we show how, by placing certain restrictions on the use of variables in the query (in particular, their use in query cycles), we can adapt this technique to DAML+OIL. We will also show how some simple extensions can be supported. Completely removing these restrictions causes problems, in particular when variables are used to force cycles in the query. Due to lack of space, these problems are not discussed here; for full technical details the reader is referred to [21].

We will focus on the problem of answering boolean queries, i.e., determining if a query without free variables is true with respect to a KB. Retrieval, i.e., returning the set of all tuples (of individuals) that answer a query, can be turned into a set of boolean queries for all candidate tuples as described in [17]. Clearly this would be extremely inefficient if naively implemented, and we discuss some basic techniques that can be used to improve performance.

2   Preliminaries

2.1   DAML+OIL

DAML+OIL is an ontology language, and as such is designed to describe the *structure* of a domain. DAML+OIL takes an object oriented approach, with the

---

[1] This is inspired by the use of Abox reasoning to decide conjunctive query containment (see [15,5]).

structure of the domain being described in terms of *classes* and *properties*. An
ontology consists of a set of *axioms* that assert, e.g., subsumption relationships
between classes or properties. RDF is used to add assertions that resources[2]
(pairs of resources) are instances of DAML+OIL classes (properties). When a
resource r is an instance of a class C we say that r has type C.

From a formal point of view, DAML+OIL can be seen to be equivalent to
the expressive description logic $\mathcal{SHIQ}$ [16] with the addition of existentially defined classes (i.e., the oneOf constructor) and *datatypes* (often called concrete
domains in DLs [1]). A DAML+OIL ontology corresponds to a DL terminology
(Tbox), and the set of RDF axioms asserting facts about resources corresponds
to a DL Abox. As in a DL, DAML+OIL classes can be names (URIs) or *expressions*, and a variety of *constructors* are provided for building class expressions.
The expressive power of the language is determined by the class (and property)
constructors supported, and by the kinds of axiom supported.

Constructor	DL Syntax	Example
intersectionOf	$C_1 \sqcap \ldots \sqcap C_n$	Human $\sqcap$ Male
unionOf	$C_1 \sqcup \ldots \sqcup C_n$	Doctor $\sqcup$ Lawyer
complementOf	$\neg C$	$\neg$Male
oneOf	$\{x_1 \ldots x_n\}$	$\{$john, mary$\}$
toClass	$\forall P.C$	$\forall$hasChild.Doctor
hasClass	$\exists P.C$	$\exists$hasChild.Lawyer
hasValue	$\exists P.\{x\}$	$\exists$citizenOf.$\{$USA$\}$
minCardinalityQ	$\geqslant nP.C$	$\geqslant$2hasChild.Lawyer
maxCardinalityQ	$\leqslant nP.C$	$\leqslant$1hasChild.Male
cardinalityQ	$=n\,P.C$	$=$1 hasParent.Female

Fig. 1. DAML+OIL class constructors

Figure 1 summarises the constructors supported by DAML+OIL. The standard DL syntax is used for compactness as the RDF syntax is rather verbose.
In the RDF syntax, for example, Human $\sqcap$ Male would be written as

```
<daml:Class>
  <daml:intersectionOf rdf:parseType="daml:collection">
    <daml:Class rdf:about="#Human"/>
    <daml:Class rdf:about="#Male"/>
  </daml:intersectionOf>
</daml:Class>
```

---

[2] Everything describable by RDF is called a resource. A resource could be Web accessible, e.g., a Web page or part of a Web page, but it could also be an object that is
not directly accessible via the Web, e.g., a person. Resources are named by URIs plus
optional anchor ids. See http://www.w3.org/TR/1999/REC-rdf-syntax-19990222/
for more details.

while $\geqslant$2hasChild.Lawyer would be written as

```
<daml:Restriction daml:minCardinalityQ="2">
  <daml:onProperty rdf:resource="#hasChild"/>
  <daml:hasClassQ rdf:resource="#Lawyer"/>
</daml:Restriction>
```

The meaning of the first three constructors (intersectionOf, unionOf and complementOf) is relatively self-explanatory: they are just the standard boolean operators that allow classes to be formed from the intersection, union and negation of other classes. The oneOf constructor allows classes to be defined existentially, i.e., by enumerating their members.

The toClass and hasClass constructors correspond to slot constraints in a frame-based language and to value and existential restrictions in a DL. The class $\forall P.C$ is the class all of whose instances are related via the property P only to resources of type C, while the class $\exists P.C$ is the class all of whose instances are related via the property P to at least one resource of type C. The hasValue constructor is just shorthand for a combination of hasValue and oneOf.

The minCardinalityQ, maxCardinalityQ and cardinalityQ constructors (known in DLs as qualified number restrictions) are generalisations of the has-Class and hasValue constructors. The class $\geqslant nP.C$ ($\leqslant nP.C$, $=n\,P.C$) is the class all of whose instances are related via the property P to at least (at most, exactly) n *different* resources of type C. The emphasis on different is because there is no unique name assumption with respect to resource names (URIs): it is possible that many URIs could name the same resource.

Note that arbitrarily complex nesting of constructors is possible. Moreover, XML Schema *datatypes* (e.g., so called primitive datatypes such as strings, decimal or float, as well as more complex derived datatypes such as integer subranges) can be used anywhere that a class name might appear.

The formal semantics of the class constructors is given by DAML+OIL's model-theoretic semantics[3] or can be derived from the specification of a suitably expressive DL (e.g., see [14]).

As already mentioned, besides the set of constructors supported, the other aspect of a language that determines its expressive power is the kinds of axiom supported. Figure 2 summarises the axioms supported by DAML+OIL. These axioms make it possible to assert subsumption or equivalence with respect to classes or properties, the disjointness of classes, the equivalence or non-equivalence of individuals (resources), and various properties of properties.

Note that all of the class and individual axioms, as well as the uniqueProperty and unambiguousProperty axioms, can be reduced to subClassOf and sameClassAs axioms (as can be seen from the DL syntax). In fact sameClassAs could also be reduced to subClassOf as a sameClassAs axiom $C \equiv D$ is equivalent to a pair of subClassOf axioms, $C \sqsubseteq D$ and $D \sqsubseteq C$.

As we have seen, DAML+OIL allows properties of properties to be asserted. It is possible to assert that a property is unique (i.e., functional) and unambigu-

---

[3] http://www.w3.org/TR/daml+oil-model

Axiom	DL Syntax	Example
subClassOf	$C_1 \sqsubseteq C_2$	Human $\sqsubseteq$ Animal $\sqcap$ Biped
sameClassAs	$C_1 \equiv C_2$	Man $\equiv$ Human $\sqcap$ Male
subPropertyOf	$P_1 \sqsubseteq P_2$	hasDaughter $\sqsubseteq$ hasChild
samePropertyAs	$P_1 \equiv P_2$	cost $\equiv$ price
disjointWith	$C_1 \sqsubseteq \neg C_2$	Male $\sqsubseteq \neg$Female
sameIndividualAs	$\{x_1\} \equiv \{x_2\}$	{President_Bush} $\equiv$ {G_W_Bush}
differentIndividualFrom	$\{x_1\} \sqsubseteq \neg\{x_2\}$	{john} $\sqsubseteq \neg$\{peter\}
inverseOf	$P_1 \equiv P_2^-$	hasChild $\equiv$ hasParent$^-$
transitiveProperty	$P^+ \sqsubseteq P$	ancestor$^+$ $\sqsubseteq$ ancestor
uniqueProperty	$\top \sqsubseteq \leqslant 1P$	$\top \sqsubseteq \leqslant$1hasMother
unambiguousProperty	$\top \sqsubseteq \leqslant 1P^-$	$\top \sqsubseteq \leqslant$1isMotherOf$^-$

Fig. 2. DAML+OIL axioms

ous (i.e., its inverse is functional). It is also possible to use inverse properties and to assert that a property is transitive.

2.2 Description Logic

In this paper we concentrate on a DL less expressive than DAML+OIL, since answering to conjunctive queries over the complete DAML+OIL is still an open problem.

$\mathcal{SHIQ}$ is built over a signature of distinct sets of concept ($\mathcal{CN}$), role ($\mathcal{RN}$) and individual ($\mathcal{O}$) names. In addition, we distinguish two non-overlapping subsets of $\mathcal{RN}$ ($\mathcal{TRN}$ and $\mathcal{FRN}$) which denote the transitive and the functional roles. The set of all $\mathcal{SHIQ}$ roles is equal to the set of role names $\mathcal{RN}$ union the set of the inverse roles $\{R^- \mid P \in \mathcal{RN}\}$. The set of all $\mathcal{SHIQ}$ concepts is the smallest set such that every concept name in $\mathcal{CN}$ and the symbols $\top$, $\bot$ are concepts, and if C,D are concepts, R is a role, and n an integer, then $\neg C$, $(C \sqcap D)$, $(C \sqcup D)$, $(\forall R.C)$, $(\exists R.C)$, $\geqslant nR.C$, and $\leqslant nR.C$ are concepts.

An *interpretation* $\mathcal{I} = (\Delta^{\mathcal{I}}, \cdot^{\mathcal{I}})$ consists of a nonempty domain $\Delta^{\mathcal{I}}$ and a interpretation function $\cdot^{\mathcal{I}}$. The interpretation function maps concepts into subsets of $\Delta^{\mathcal{I}}$, individual names into elements of $\Delta^{\mathcal{I}}$, and role names into subsets of the cartesian product of $\Delta^{\mathcal{I}}$ ($\Delta^{\mathcal{I}} \times \Delta^{\mathcal{I}}$). Concept names are interpreted as subsets of $\Delta^{\mathcal{I}}$, while complex expressions are interpreted according to the following equations (see [19])

$$\top^{\mathcal{I}} = \Delta^{\mathcal{I}} \quad (C \sqcap D)^{\mathcal{I}} = C^{\mathcal{I}} \cap D^{\mathcal{I}}$$
$$\bot^{\mathcal{I}} = \emptyset \quad (C \sqcup D)^{\mathcal{I}} = C^{\mathcal{I}} \cup D^{\mathcal{I}}$$
$$\neg C^{\mathcal{I}} = \Delta^{\mathcal{I}} \setminus C^{\mathcal{I}}$$
$$(\forall R.C)^{\mathcal{I}} = \{x \in \Delta^{\mathcal{I}} \mid \forall y(x,y) \in R^{\mathcal{I}} \Rightarrow y \in C^{\mathcal{I}}\}$$
$$(\exists R.C)^{\mathcal{I}} = \{x \in \Delta^{\mathcal{I}} \mid \exists y(x,y) \in R^{\mathcal{I}} \wedge y \in C^{\mathcal{I}}\}$$
$$(\geqslant nR.C)^{\mathcal{I}} = \{x \in \Delta^{\mathcal{I}} \mid \sharp\{y \mid (x,y) \in R^{\mathcal{I}} \wedge y \in C^{\mathcal{I}}\} \geq n\}$$
$$(\leqslant nR.C)^{\mathcal{I}} = \{x \in \Delta^{\mathcal{I}} \mid \sharp\{y \mid (x,y) \in R^{\mathcal{I}} \wedge y \in C^{\mathcal{I}}\} \leq n\}$$

A role and its inverse must be interpreted according to the equation

$$R^{-\mathcal{I}} = \left\{ (x, y) \in \Delta^{\mathcal{I}} \times \Delta^{\mathcal{I}} \mid (y, x) \in R^{\mathcal{I}} \right\}.$$

In addition, the interpretation function must satisfy the transitive and functional restrictions on role names; i.e. for any $R \in \mathcal{TRN}$ if $(x, y) \in R^{\mathcal{I}}$ and $(y, z) \in R^{\mathcal{I}}$, then $(x, z) \in R^{\mathcal{I}}$, and for any $F \in \mathcal{FRN}$ if $(x, y) \in F^{\mathcal{I}}$ and $(x, z) \in F^{\mathcal{I}}$, then $y = z$.

The semantics of DL often includes a so called *unique name assumption*: an assumption that the interpretation function maps different individual names to different elements of the domain (i.e., $a^{\mathcal{I}} \neq b^{\mathcal{I}}$ for all $a, b \in \mathcal{O}$ such that $a \neq b$). Our approach does not rely on such an assumption, and can be applied to DLs both with and without the unique name assumption.

2.3   Knowledge Bases

A $\mathcal{SHIQ}$ knowledge base $\mathbf{K}$ is a finite set of statements of the form:

$$C \sqsubseteq D, R \sqsubseteq S, a{:}C, \langle a, b \rangle{:}R$$

where C, D are $\mathcal{SHIQ}$ concepts, R, S roles, and a, b individual names. The first two kinds of statement are called *terminological*, while the two latter ones are called *assertional*. Intuitively, terminological statements describe intensional properties of all the elements of the domain, while assertional statements assign properties of some named elements.

We say that an interpretation $\mathcal{I} = (\Delta^{\mathcal{I}}, \cdot^{\mathcal{I}})$ satisfies the terminological statement $C \sqsubseteq D$ ($R \sqsubseteq S$) iff $C^{\mathcal{I}} \subseteq D^{\mathcal{I}}$ ($R^{\mathcal{I}} \subseteq S^{\mathcal{I}}$), and the assertional statement $a{:}C$ ($\langle a, b \rangle{:}R$) iff $a^{\mathcal{I}} \in C^{\mathcal{I}}$ ($(a^{\mathcal{I}}, b^{\mathcal{I}}) \in R^{\mathcal{I}}$). When an interpretation $\mathcal{I}$ satisfies a statement α, we use the notation $\mathcal{I} \models \alpha$. An interpretation $\mathcal{I}$ satisfies (or is a model for) a KB $\mathbf{K}$ iff it satisfies all the statements in $\mathbf{K}$ (written as $\mathcal{I} \models \mathbf{K}$).

2.4   Query Language

Query answering services provided by a DL system can be seen as the process of verifying whether a given statement (the query) is a logical consequence of the knowledge base (written as $\mathbf{K} \models \alpha$). The meaning of logical consequence is given in terms of interpretations; i.e. a statement is logical consequence of a KB $\mathbf{K}$ if it is satisfied in every interpretation satisfying $\mathbf{K}$ ($\mathbf{K} \models \alpha$ iff for any interpretation $\mathcal{I}, \mathcal{I} \models \mathbf{K}$ implies $\mathcal{I} \models \alpha$). For example, instantiation can be written as $\mathbf{K} \models a{:}C$ (i.e., a is an instance of C in every model of $\mathbf{K}$).

Using the same mechanism, we extend the kind of queries we can ask by introducing a conjunctive query language whose terms are assertional statements (see [17]). For this purpose we consider a set of variable names $\mathcal{V}$ distinct from the individual names ($\mathcal{O}$). Analogously to conjunctive queries in the database setting, variables can be used in place of individuals and are considered as existentially quantified.

A DL *boolean conjunctive query* is defined as a conjunction of terms of the form $x{:}C$ or $\langle x, y\rangle{:}R$, where C is a concept, R is a role, and x, y are variable or individual names taken from $\mathcal{V} \cup \mathcal{O}$. We call the first kind *concept terms* and the latter kind *role terms*.

The semantics of a boolean conjunctive query follows the schema shown above for the knowledge bases. The difference is that we need to consider the variable names, since the satisfiability of a term may be affected by the assignment of the variables. Given an interpretation $\mathcal{I} = (\Delta^{\mathcal{I}}, \cdot^{\mathcal{I}})$, we consider *evaluations* defined as mappings from names in $\mathcal{V} \cup \mathcal{O}$ to elements of the interpretation domain $\Delta^{\mathcal{I}}$ (with the constraint that evaluations must agree with the interpretation function on the mapping of individual names). We say that the interpretation $\mathcal{I} = (\Delta^{\mathcal{I}}, \cdot^{\mathcal{I}})$ satisfies the term $x{:}C$ ($\langle x, y\rangle{:}R$) w.r.t. an evaluation ν, written as $\mathcal{I} \models_{\nu} x{:}C$ ($\mathcal{I} \models_{\nu} \langle x, y\rangle{:}R$), iff $\nu(x) \in C^{\mathcal{I}}$ ($\langle \nu(x), \nu(y)\rangle \in R^{\mathcal{I}}$). This is extended to arbitrary conjunctive queries: an interpretation $\mathcal{I}$ satisfies the conjunctive query $q = t_1 \wedge \ldots \wedge t_n$ w.r.t. an evaluation ν iff $\mathcal{I} \models_{\nu} t_i$ for every $i = 1, \ldots, n$.

Note that we do not require that variables are interpreted as the individual names appearing in the KB; instead they can be mapped to arbitrary elements of the interpretation domain. For example, let us consider the KB containing only the assertion $\texttt{sam}{:}\exists\texttt{Has\_child.FEMALE}$, and the query $\langle \texttt{sam}, y\rangle{:}\texttt{Has\_child}$. If we restrict variables to individual names only, then the query is not a logical consequence of the KB, because there is no individual name asserted to be related to $\texttt{sam}$. If we allow variables to range over arbitrary elements of interpretation domains, then the query is a logical consequence of the KB. This can be seen by considering that the query is equivalent to the query $\texttt{sam}{:}\exists\texttt{Has\_child}.\top$, and that the concept $\exists\texttt{Has\_child}.\top$ is more general than $\exists\texttt{Has\_child.FEMALE}$.

In answering boolean queries, we are not really interested in the evaluation itself but only on the satisfiability of the given query; we say that $\mathcal{I}$ satisfies the query q (written $\mathcal{I} \models q$) iff there is an evaluation ν such that $\mathcal{I} \models_{\nu} q$.

Query graph To present the query answering algorithm we associate a *query graph* to each conjunctive query. The main idea is to consider a conjunctive query as a directed graph, where the nodes are variable and individual names. In addition, concept and role terms provide labels for nodes and edges respectively.

For example, the query

$$x{:}\texttt{Start} \wedge \langle x, y\rangle{:}\texttt{Path} \wedge \langle x, z\rangle{:}\texttt{Path}$$

corresponds to the graph

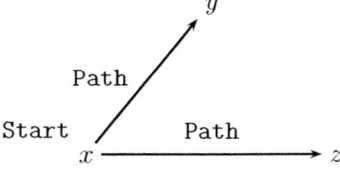

In this paper we restrict to queries whose graphs are acyclic (regardless the direction of the edges). For example, adding the term $\langle y, z\rangle{:}\texttt{Path}$ to the previous

query:
$$\{x\text{:Start}, \langle x, y\rangle\text{:Path}, \langle y, z\rangle\text{:Path}, \langle x, z\rangle\text{:Path}\}$$

makes the corresponding graph cyclical. This restriction leads to a much more efficient procedure, and the algorithm still works with very expressive DLs.

There is ongoing research to extend the algorithm to arbitrary shaped queries, and expressive DLs. Encouraging results have been published for DLs less expressive than DAML+OIL (see [6,17,20]).

Query retrieval Using the definition of boolean queries we can easily extend the formalism to retrieve arbitrary tuples of individual names. We use the notation $\langle x_1, \ldots, x_n\rangle \leftarrow q$ to indicate that variables $x_1, \ldots, x_n$ appearing in q must be bound to individual names, and constitute the answer to the query. We call these variables *distinguished*.

Formally, the *answer set* of a query $\langle x_1, \ldots, x_n\rangle \leftarrow q$ w.r.t. the KB **K** is the set n-ary tuples defined by

$$\{\langle a_1, \ldots, a_n\rangle \in \mathcal{O}^n \mid \mathbf{K} \models q[x_1/a_1, \ldots, x_n/a_n]\},$$

where $q[x/a]$ indicates the query q with all the occurrences of variable x substituted by the individual name a.

3   Answering Boolean Queries

In this section we show how to answer to boolean queries (see Section 2.4); i.e. queries not returning set of tuples but only a yes/no answer. In Section 4 we show that using this algorithm we can provide answers to non-boolean queries as well.

A boolean query can be partitioned in one or more connected components by considering its query graph. Unconnected components do not share variables, therefore they can be considered independently to each other.

For example, the query

$$\langle \text{Mary}, y\rangle\text{:children} \wedge y\text{:MALE} \wedge z\text{:STUDENT}$$

has two connected components: ($\langle\text{Mary}, y\rangle$:children $\wedge$ y:MALE) and (z:STUDENT). Since they not share any variable, the query is a logical consequence of a KB iff the two components $\langle\text{Mary}, y\rangle$:children $\wedge$ y:MALE and z:STUDENT are logical consequence of the KB.

Boolean query answering, i.e. logical consequence, can easily be reduced to a KB satisfiability problem if the query contains only a single concept term (this is the standard instantiation problem). For example,

$$\{\text{STUDENT} \sqsubseteq \text{PERSON}, \text{Tom:STUDENT}\} \models \text{Tom:PERSON}$$

iff the KB
$$\{\text{STUDENT} \sqsubseteq \text{PERSON}, \text{Tom:STUDENT}, \text{Tom:}\neg\text{PERSON}\}$$

is not satisfiable.

This is true not only for individual names, but for variables as well. The query x:PERSON is satisfied iff in every model of the KB the interpretation of PERSON is not the empty set. This can be verified by checking whether the KB plus the axiom PERSON $\sqsubseteq \bot$ is satisfiable. If this is the case, then there is at least a model of the KB in which the interpretation of PERSON is the empty set ($\bot$ is by definition the empty set).

This simple approach cannot be used in our case since a query may also contain role terms. However, the idea is to transform the initial query into an equivalent query containing only a single concept term (see [5,17]). In terms of query graphs this means collapsing the DAG into a single node, by eliminating all the edges.

Firstly, we consider queries containing only variable names; then we show that constants (i.e. individual names) can be handled in a similar fashion.

3.1   Queries without Constants

Let us consider the simple query $\langle y, z\rangle$:children $\wedge$ z:MALE. The query is satisfied if there is an element (y), related by role children to an element (z) of the class MALE.[4] Given the semantics of DL operators (see Section 2.2), the same query can be paraphrased as the single term y:$\exists$children.MALE.

The intuition from the example is substantiated by the fact that the query corresponds to the first order logic formula $\exists y \exists z(\text{children}(y, z) \wedge \text{MALE}(z))$, which is the first order logic translation of the term y:$\exists$children.MALE (see [3]). We indicate the transformation of query formulae suggested by this example, as the *rolling-up* of role terms.

Inverse role constructor (e.g. children$^-$) enables the rolling-up in both directions. In fact, the role term in the example can be rolled-up into the variable z obtaining the query z:$\exists$children$^-$.$\top$ $\wedge$ z:MALE.

Note that the transformation eliminates one of the variables (z in the example); therefore the equivalence is guaranteed iff the variable being eliminated does not appear anywhere else in the query.

Let us consider the query $\langle x, y\rangle$:children $\wedge$ $\langle y, z\rangle$:has_degree, and the KB containing the assertion Mary:($\exists$children.MALE $\sqcap$ $\exists$has_degree.PHD). This query is not a logical consequence of the given KB, because there is nothing in the KB forcing the role chain expressed by the query. A careless use of rolling-up, applied to the first role term, produces the query x:$\exists$children.$\top \wedge \langle y, z\rangle$:has_degree. The resulting query is a logical consequence of the KB; therefore this transformation does not guarantee correctness.

The problem highlighted by this example can be overcome by eliminating variables appearing in a single role term. Multiple concept terms (like x:MALE $\wedge$ x:PIG) are not a problem; since they can be collapsed into a single one by using the conjunction construct (e.g. x:(MALE $\sqcap$ PIG)). The assumption that the query graph is a DAG (see Section 2.4) ensures that there is always at least a variable appearing in one role term only.

---

[4] This must be true in every interpretation satisfying the KB being queried.

3.2   Queries with Constants

The rolling-up described in the last section cannot be used as it is when there are constants (i.e. individual names) in the query. The reason for this is that names are significant, so we cannot treat them as variables.

Let us consider the example of the previous section where we substitute variable z with an individual name:

$$\langle y, \text{Bill}\rangle\text{:children} \land \text{Bill:MALE}.$$

This query is not a logical consequence of a KB containing only the assertion Bill:MALE $\sqcap \exists$children.MALE; because the role term $\langle y, \text{Bill}\rangle$:children is not satisfied in every model of the KB. However, if we roll-up the role term, ignoring the fact that Bill is a constant, we obtain the query y:$\exists$children.MALE, which is a logical consequence of the assertion in the KB.

The problem can be solved by using the *one-of* DL construct, which enables to describe a concept by enumerating its members. For example, the interpretation of the concept { Sally, Bill } is the set containing the elements corresponding to Sally and Bill (see Section 2.2). It is not difficult to realise that a query term like Bill:MALE is equivalent to z:{ Bill } $\land$ z:MALE; where z is a newly introduced variable. In fact, the term z:{ Bill } guarantees that variable z is always interpreted as the constant Bill.

Generalising this idea, we can remove all the constants from the query by introducing appropriate concept terms involving the *one-of* DL construct. For example, the query example is transformed into

$$\langle y, z\rangle\text{:children} \land z\text{:MALE} \land z\text{:\{ Bill \}},$$

by replacing all the occurrences of Bill with the new variable z, and introducing the new term z:{ Bill }. Now the query can be rolled-up as described in Section 3.1, obtaining the concept term y:$\exists$children.(MALE $\sqcap$ { Bill }).

Note that it is not necessary to use same variable name for all the occurrences of a constant. The crucial point is that they all have to be constraint by a concept term involving the *one-of* construct. The query example can be transformed into the equivalent

$$\langle y, z'\rangle\text{:children} \land z'\text{:\{ Bill \}} \land z\text{:MALE} \land z\text{:\{ Bill \}},$$

since the terms z':{ Bill } and z:{ Bill } ensure that z' and z are always interpreted as the same element.

Unfortunately, the DL systems used to support reasoning in DAML+OIL do not provide the *one-of* construct. However, in our case we do not need the full expressivity of *one-of*, and it can be simulated by primitive concept names. The technique used is to substitute each occurrence of *one-of* with a new concept name not appearing in the knowledge base. These new concept names must be different for each individual in the query, and are called the *representative* concepts of the individuals (written P_a, where a is the individual name). In addition, assertions which ensure that each individual is an instance of its representative concept must be added to the knowledge base (e.g., $\text{Bill}:P_{\text{Bill}}$).

Representative concepts can be used instead of *one-of* to transform the queries. However, they cannot be used to eliminate *one-of* operators from KBs because a representative concept can have instances other than the individual which it represents (i.e., $P_a{}^{\mathcal{I}} \supseteq \{a^{\mathcal{I}}\}$).

4   Retrieving Answer Sets

Ideally, we would like to provide an efficient bottom up procedure for retrieving answer sets. However, in the context of expressive DLs this is not easily achievable, and we are not aware of any lead towards a solution.

It is important to stress the fact that, given the expressivity of DLs, query answering cannot simply be reduced to model checking as in the database framework. This is because KBs may contain nondeterminism and/or incompleteness, making the use of an approach based on minimal models infeasible. In fact, query answering in the DL setting requires the same reasoning machinery as logical derivation. To use model checking techniques for query answering we must be able to associate a "preferred" model to a given KBs, and this is quite difficult for arbitrary DL KBs.

Let us consider for example a simple KB containing the single axiom $\text{Elephant} \sqsubseteq \neg\text{Mouse}$, stating that elephants and mice are disjoint, and the Abox assertion $\text{hathi}:(\text{Elephant} \sqcup \text{Mouse})$. We can identify two minimal (w.r.t. inclusion) interpretations satisfying the KB: in the first the element mapped from the individual hathi is in the extension of the concept Elephant, while in the second it is in the extension of the concept Mouse. Which of the two interpretations can be considered the "preferred" one? The point is that there is not any general mechanism for choosing one, even with this trivial KB.

From the definition of answer set, given in Section 2.4, we can easily derive an algorithm for retrieving tuples of individuals answering a given query. In fact, using the boolean query answering algorithm applied to the query obtained by substituting the distinguished variables with constants, we can test the membership of a given tuple to the answer set. The idea is to iterate among all the possible assignment of the distinguished variables, and checking whether the corresponding tuples belong to the answer set.

Although this procedure is possibly not the most practical one,[5] it fits nicely with the recent proposal for the DQL DAML+OIL query language.[6] In fact, in the proposal a response to a query would consist of a single binding for the distinguished variables, and a "server continuation" which can be used to obtain the next answers (bindings).

---

[5] The naive evaluation of such a retrieval could be prohibitively expensive, but as we point out in Section 5 it is amenable to optimisation.

[6] The so called DQL query language, discussed in the joint-committee DAML mailing list (see http://www.daml.org/listarchive/joint-committee/1052.html).

Another feature of the above mentioned proposal is the possibility of returning partial bindings when the KB entails the existence of individuals, but those are not among the known names (i.e. not in the set of $\mathcal{O}$).

For example, a KB containing only the assertion Red:∃colour⁻.⊤ implies the existence of an element related to Red via the role colour. However, there is not any individual name which is asserted to correspond to this element. Any query like $\langle x, y \rangle \leftarrow \langle x, y \rangle$:colour, with x, y distinguished variables, would not return any answer (i.e. the empty set).

In the proposal is suggested that in such a case an answer would be a binding only for the variable y (the individual name Red), while x would be left unspecified (or a bind to a newly invented name representing an anonymous element).

This effect can be achieved in our framework by relaxing the conditions on the variables; i.e. making part of the distinguished variables no longer distinguished. For example, the query $\langle x, y \rangle \leftarrow \langle x, y \rangle$:colour can be relaxed into the query $\langle y \rangle \leftarrow \langle x, y \rangle$:colour, where x is no longer distinguished.

In our view, the task of relaxing the conditions should not be incorporated into the basic query answering mechanism, but left to an external layer. For example, this external layer would first tries to answer to the query as it is (leaving all the distinguished variables). If with these restrictions no answers can be retrieved, then different queries can be generated by making one or more variables non-distinguished. The process would continue until an answer is found, and returned to the user.

Several heuristics and ordering can be adopted for the selection of distinguished variables to be relaxed. We think that this mainly depends on the specifications of DQL, which is still an ongoing project. However, the main point is that our logical framework can be used to capture this feature.

5   Speeding Up the Answer

The rolling-up procedure is polynomial in the size of the query, and the KB satisfiability test is EXPTIME for the DL $\mathcal{SHIQ}$. Given the fact that boolean query answering is at least as expensive as KB satisfiability,[7] our algorithm is optimal w.r.t. the class of boolean acyclic conjunctive queries (assuming that the KB satisfiability test is optimal). However, we can use several heuristics to obtain a better behaviour in most of the cases (i.e. practical tractability).

We have empirical evidence that axioms in the KB are one of the major cause of practical intractability (see [13]). As seen in Section 3, the query need to be encoded as an axiom only if is rolled-up into a variable. When the query is rolled-up into an individual name, the query can be transformed into an Abox assertion. Therefore, the choice of node into which a query graph is rolled-up can be used to speed up the KB satisfiability test.

---

[7] A KB is unsatisfiable iff the query x:⊥ is a logical consequence of the KB.

Different optimizations can be directed to minimize the choice of individual name candidates for distinguished variables (see Section 4). In fact, in case of query retrieval of n-ary tuples we potentially have to test every possible element of $\mathcal{O}^n$. For reducing the number of candidate individuals for a variable name, we envisage two different techniques. The first one relies on the standard retrieval service provided by DL reasoners (i.e. retrieving all the individual names instances of a given concept), while the second on the structure induced by role terms in the query.

In our setting, the rolling-up is a cheap operation so we can use it to prune the number of candidates. The idea is to roll-up the query into a distinguished variable prior to substitute it with any individual name. The concept we obtain describes necessary conditions for the individuals that can be substituted to this distinguished variable. The concept is used to retrieve the list of individual names being instance of the concept, and the retrieved individuals are the candidates for the distinguished variable.

This technique is not an alternative to the boolean query answering, since tuples membership to the answer set still need to be verified by a boolean query answer. However, this may significantly reduce the number of boolean queries that need to be tested. Moreover, DL systems are usually optimised for retrieval, by means of internal indexes and specialised algorithms (see [10]).

The structure of role terms in the query (i.e. the "shape" of the query graph) can be used to reduce the number of candidates for distinguished variables. This idea is based on the observation that role assertions in the KB do not allow to express incomplete information as the concept assertions do. In fact, role assertions are usually limited to simple statements like $\langle a, b \rangle{:}R$. The crucial point is that two individual names can be related by a role only if there is a role assertion between them. Note that in expressive DLs, like $\mathcal{SHIQ}$, the names of the roles in the query and in the assertions do not need to match. This limited expressivity for roles is shared by most of the DLs studied and/or implemented. Note that this is no longer valid for languages including the *one of* operator, like DAML+OIL, or without the unique name assumption (see Section 2.2). Therefore, this kind of optimizations need to be used with extreme caution.

For example, if the underlying DL language allows the use of this optimization, and the query contains the role term $\langle x, y \rangle{:}\texttt{children}$ (with both x, y distinguished variables), then we can restrict their candidates to pair of individual names having an asserted role between them.

6   Conclusions

In this paper we have described a basic conjunctive query language for DAML+OIL (or any other description logic based ontology language), and presented a formal framework that precisely defines the meaning of such qeries. Moreover, we have shown how queries can be rewritten so that query answering is reduced to the problem of knowledge base satisfiability for the logic corresponding to the ontology language. This enables us to answer queries using standard reasoning techniques, and to guarantee that query answers will be sound and complete in the case that that our knowledge base satisfiability test is sound and complete. The idea is to use implemented description logic systems (or any other system capable of deciding knowledge base satisfiability) to provide sound and complete answers to queries.

There have been a number of proposals for query languages for RDF and DAML+OIL (a review of some of them can be found at http://139.91.183.30:9090/RDF/publications/state.html). However, the aproach we have described is, to the best of our knowledge, unique in formalising the problem and in describing a mechanism whereby sound and complete answers to non-trivial queries can be computed using an inference procedure.

The query rewriting relies on a restriction with respect to the use of variables and constants in query expressions, notably that no cyclical references are allowed. Relaxing this condition so that distinguished variables and constants can occur in query cycles is not too difficult, but dealing with non-distinguished variables ocurring in query cycles is still an open research problem (although the problem has been solved for less expressive description logics [17]).

It also remains to be seen how effective such techniques will be in practice. If implemented naively, it is clear that they would be extremely inefficient. However, as we have seen in Section 5, there are many possibilities for optimising implementations in order to speed up query answering. Moreover, this technique lends itself naturally to incremental query answering, where the system can return partial answers without having to wait until the complete answer has been computed.

References

1. Franz Baader and Philipp Hanschke. A schema for integrating concrete domains into concept languages. In *Proc. of IJCAI-91*, pages 452–457, 1991.
2. Tim Berners-Lee. *Weaving the Web*. Harpur, San Francisco, 1999.
3. Alexander Borgida. On the relative expressiveness of description logics and predicate logics. *Artificial Intelligence*, 82(1–2):353–367, 1996.
4. J. Broekstra, A. Kampman, and F. van Harmelen. Sesame: An architecture for storing and querying RDF data and schema information. In H. Lieberman D. Fensel, J. Hendler and W. Wahlster, editors, *Semantics for the WWW*. MIT Press, 2001.
5. Diego Calvanese, Giuseppe De Giacomo, and Maurizio Lenzerini. On the decidability of query containment under constraints. In *Proc. of PODS-98*, pages 149–158, 1998.
6. Diego Calvanese, Giuseppe De Giacomo, and Maurizio Lenzerini. Answering queries using views over description logics knowledge bases. In *Proc. of AAAI 2000*, pages 386–391, 2000.
7. Diego Calvanese, Maurizio Lenzerini, and Daniele Nardi. Description logics for conceptual data modeling. In Jan Chomicki and Günter Saake, editors, *Logics for Databases and Information Systems*, pages 229–264. Kluwer Academic Publisher, 1998.
8. Francesco M. Donini, Maurizio Lenzerini, Daniele Nardi, and Werner Nutt. The complexity of concept languages. *Information and Computation*, 134:1–58, 1997.

9. Dieter Fensel, Frank van Harmelen, Ian Horrocks, Deborah L. McGuinness, and Peter F. Patel-Schneider. OIL: An ontology infrastructure for the semantic web. *IEEE Intelligent Systems*, 16(2):38–45, 2001.
10. Volker Haarslev and Ralf Möller. RACER system description. In *Proc. of IJCAR-01*, 2001.
11. I. Horrocks and P. Patel-Schneider. The generation of DAML+OIL. In *Proc. of DL 2001*, pages 30–35, 2001.
12. I. Horrocks, U. Sattler, and S. Tobies. Reasoning with individuals for the description logic $\mathcal{SHIQ}$. In David MacAllester, editor, *Proc. of CADE-2000*, number 1831 in LNCS, pages 482–496. Springer-Verlag, 2000.
13. Ian Horrocks and Peter F. Patel-Schneider. Optimizing description logic subsumption. *J. of Logic and Computation*, 9(3):267–293, 1999.
14. Ian Horrocks and Ulrike Sattler. Ontology reasoning in the $\mathcal{SHOQ}$(D) description logic. In *Proc. of IJCAI-01*. Morgan Kaufmann, 2001.
15. Ian Horrocks, Ulrike Sattler, Sergio Tessaris, and Stephan Tobies. How to decide query containment under constraints using a description logic. In *Logic for Programming and Automated Reasoning (LPAR 2000)*, volume 1955 of *LNCS*, pages 326–343. Springer, 2000.
16. Ian Horrocks, Ulrike Sattler, and Stephan Tobies. Practical reasoning for expressive description logics. In Harald Ganzinger, David McAllester, and Andrei Voronkov, editors, *Proc. of LPAR'99*, number 1705 in LNAI, pages 161–180. Springer-Verlag, 1999.
17. Ian Horrocks and Sergio Tessaris. A conjunctive query language for description logic aboxes. In *Proc. of AAAI 2000*, pages 399–404, 2000.
18. Deborah L. McGuinness and Jon R. Wright. An industrial strength description logic-based configuration platform. *IEEE Intelligent Systems*, pages 69–77, 1998.
19. Manfred Schmidt-Schauß and Gert Smolka. Attributive concept descriptions with complements. *Artificial Intelligence*, 48(1):1–26, 1991.
20. Sergio Tessaris. Querying expressive dls. In *Proc. of DL 2001*, 2001.
21. Sergio Tessaris. *Questions and answers: reasoning and querying in Description Logic*. PhD thesis, University of Manchester, 2001.
22. Sergio Tessaris and Graham Gough. Abox reasoning with transitive roles and axioms. In *Proc. of DL'99*, 1999.

Semantic Configuration Web Services
in the CAWICOMS Project

Alexander Felfernig, Gerhard Friedrich, Dietmar Jannach, and Markus Zanker

Computer Science and Manufacturing, Universität Klagenfurt Universitätsstrasse 65-67,
9020 Klagenfurt, Austria
{felfernig, friedrich, jannach, zanker}@ifit.uni-klu.ac.at

Abstract. Product configuration is a key technology in today's highly specialized economy. Within the scope of state-of-the-art B2B frameworks and eProcurement solutions, various initiatives take into account the provision of configuration services. However, they all are based on the idea of defining quasi-standards for many-to-many relationships between customers and vendors. When moving towards networked markets, where suppliers dynamically form supply-side consortia, more flexible approaches to B2B integration become necessary. The emerging paradigm of Web services has therefore a huge potential in business application integration. This paper presents an application scenario for configuration Web services, that is currently under development in the research project CAWICOMS[1]. An ontology-based approach allows the advertisement of services and a configuration specific protocol defines the operational processes. However, the lack of standards for the semantic annotation of Web services is still a major shortcoming of current Web technology.

1 Introduction

The easy access to vast information resources offered by the World Wide Web (WWW) opens new perspectives for conducting business. State-of-the-art electronic marketplaces enable many-to-many relationships between customers and suppliers, thus replacing inflexible one-to-one relations dating to the pre-internet era of EDI (electronic data interchange). The problem of heterogeneity of product and catalogue descriptions as well as inter-company process definitions is resolved by imposing a common standard on all market participants. The non-existence of a single standard for conducting B2B electronic commerce constitutes a major obstacle towards innovation. Examples for competing and partly incompatible B2B frameworks are OBI, RosettaNet, cXML or BizTalk [25]. They all employ XML[2] as a flexible data format definition language, that allows to communicate tree structures with a linear syntax; however, content transformation between those catalog and document standards is far from being a trivial task [8]. The issue of marketplace integration mechanisms for *customizable* products is far more complex, because

---

[1] CAWICOMS is the acronym for "Customer-Adaptive Web Interface for the Configuration of Products and Services with Multiple Suppliers". This work was partly funded by the EC through the IST Programme under contract IST-1999-10688 (http://www.cawicoms.org).

[2] See http://www.w3.org/xml for reference.

I. Horrocks and J. Hendler (Eds.): ISWC 2002, LNCS 2342, pp. 192–205, 2002.

products have characterizing attributes that offer a range of different choices. Customers are enabled to configure goods and services according to their individual needs at no extra cost following the paradigm of *mass customization* [23]. Product configuration systems (configurators) support sales engineers and customers in coping with the large number of possible variants and product constellations.

The goal of the research project CAWICOMS is to enable configuration systems to deal simultaneously with configurators of multiple suppliers over the Web. This allows for end-to-end selection, ordering and provisioning of complex products and services supplied by an extended value chain. We employ an ontology-based approach that builds on the flexible integration of these configuration Web services. Furthermore, it can be shown how the capability of each configuration system can be described on the semantic level using an application scenario from the telecommunication domain. For representation of the semantic descriptions the evolving language standard of the 'Semantic Web' initiative [3], [12], OIL resp. DAML+OIL [9] is employed.

In Section 2 we start by giving an overview on the application domain. In Section 3 we describe the Web service architecture and in Section 4 a multi-layer ontology definition for our application domain is given. The interaction processes between the Web service providers and requestors are discussed in Section 5.

2   Application Scenario

Easy access to the corporate network and secure connections to business partners is crucial in today's economy. Virtual Private Networks (VPN) extend the intranet of a possibly multi-national company and are capable of meeting the access requirements at reduced cost using the worldwide IP network services and dedicated service provider IP backbones. VPN infrastructures are designed to be flexible and configurable in order to be able to cope with a rich variety of possible customer requirements. Therefore, the establishment of some concrete VPN involves different steps after determination of customer requirements like locations to be connected or specification of required bandwidth: selection of adequate access facilities from the customer site to some entry point to the VPN backbone, reservation of bandwidth within the backbone, as well as configuration of routing hardware and additional services like installation support.

Note, that it is very unlikely that all these products and services needed for the provision of such a VPN can be supplied by one single organization, but are in general made available by different specialized solution providers, e.g., Internet Service Providers, telecommunication companies or hardware manufacturers (see Figure 1). Therefore, VPNs are typically marketed by specialized resellers (or telecommunication companies like two of our application partners) that integrate the services of individual suppliers and offer complete VPN solutions to their customers.

The integrator/reseller company contracts with the customer and determines - according to the geographic location of the different sites and the qualitative requirements with regards to bandwidth, quality of service or cost limits - the layout of the network service. This configuration task includes the selection of adequate access facilities from the customer site to some entry point of a VPN backbone, reservation of bandwidth within the backbone, as well as parameter setting for routing hardware and configura-

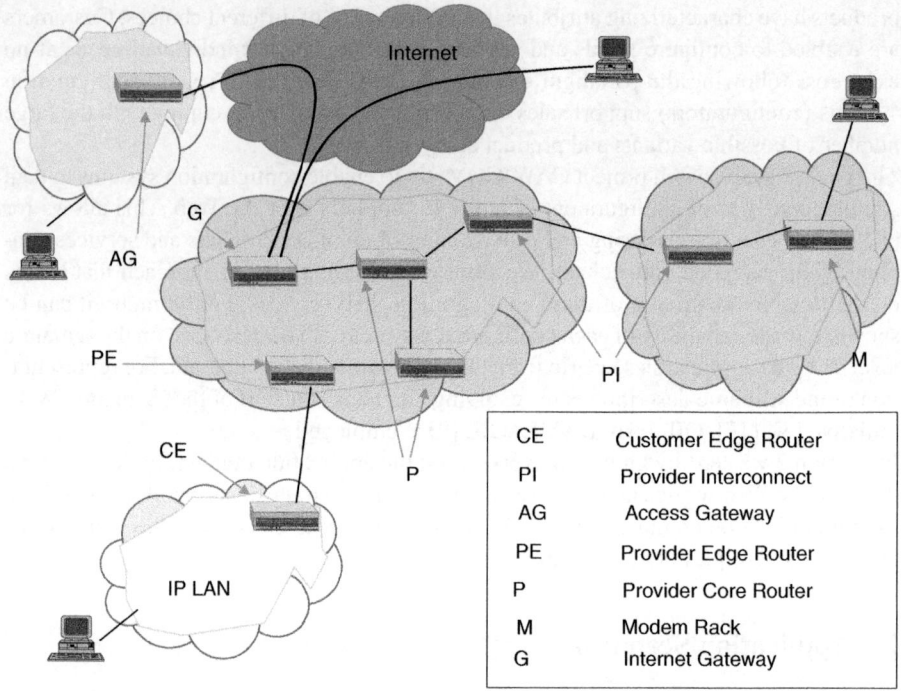

Fig. 1. IP-VPN sketch

tion of additional services like installation support. Considerable parts of this service package will then be sourced from the specialized solution providers [7].

3   CAWICOMS Environment

In the given application scenario, problem solving capabilities are distributed over several business entities that need to cooperate on a customer request for joint service provision. This Peer-to-Peer (P2P) interaction approach among a dynamic set of participants without a clear assignment of *client* and *server* roles asks for applying the paradigm of *Web services* [17]. It stands for encapsulated application logic that is open to accept requests from any peer over the Web.

3.1   Web Services

Basically, a Web Service can be defined as an interface that describes a collection of provided operations. In the following we interpret the application logic that configures a product as a standardized Web service. It can be utilized by interface agents interacting with human users in a Web shop as well as by agents that outsource configuration services as part of their problem solving capabilities. When implementing a Web Service the following issues need to be addressed [17]:

- *Service publishing* - the provider of a service publishes the description of the service to a service registry which in our case are configuration agents with mediating capabilities. Within this registry the basic properties of the offered configuration service have to be defined in such a way that automated identification of this service is possible.
- *Service identification* - the requestor of a service imposes a set of requirements which serve as the basis for identifying a suitable service. In our case, we have to identify those suppliers, that are capable of supplying goods or services that match the specific customer requirements.
- *Service execution* - once a suitable service has been identified the requirements need to be communicated to the service agent that can be correctly interpreted and executed. UDDI, WSDL, and SOAP are the evolving technological standards that allow the invocation of remote application logic based on XML syntax.

Following the vision behind the Semantic Web effort [3,12], the sharing of semantics is crucial to enable the WWW for applications. In order to have agents automatically searching, selecting and executing remote services, representation standards are needed that allow the annotation of meaning of a Web service which can then be interpreted by agents with the help of ontologies.

3.2   Ontologies

In order to define a common language for representing capabilities of configurable products and services we use a hierarchical approach of related ontologies [11,4]. Ontologies are employed to set a semantic framework that enables the semantic description of Web services in the domain of product configuration. Furthermore, we follow the proposal of [10] to structure the ontological commitments into three hierarchy levels (see Figure 2), namely the *generic ontology level*, the *intermediate level* and the *domain level*.

- *Generic ontology level* - Most modeling languages include some kind of meta-model for representing classes and their relationships (e.g. the frame ontology of Ontolingua [11], the UML meta-model [24] or the representation elements of ontology languages such as OIL or DAML+OIL). Such a meta-model can be interpreted as a generic level ontology. Example modeling concepts included in those ontologies are frame, class, relation, association, generalization, etc.
- *Intermediate ontology level* - the basic modeling concepts formulated on the generic ontology level can be refined and used in order to construct an intermediate ontology which includes wide-spread modeling concepts used in the domain. Such an ontology for the configuration domain is discussed in [26] who introduce component types, function types, port types and different kinds of constraints as basic configuration domain specific modeling concepts.
- *Domain ontology level* - finally, using the modeling concepts of the intermediate level, we are able to construct application domain specific ontologies (e.g. network services), which can also be denoted as a configuration models.

Note, that similar approaches to structure ontologies are already implemented in a set of ontology construction environments (e.g. [11]). Our contribution in this context is to illustrate their application for integrating configuration systems.

3.3   Interaction Scenario

In the following we sketch our Web service scenario that focuses on enabling automated procurement processes for customisable items (see Figure 2). Basically there exist two different types of agents, those that only offer configuration services (L) and those that act as suppliers as well as requestors for these services (I). The denotation of agent types derives from viewing the informational supply chain of product configuration as a tree[3], where a configuration system constitutes either an *inner node* (I) or a *leaf node* (L). Agents of type I have therefore the mediating functionality incorporated, that allows the offering agents to advertise their configuration services. Matchmaking for service identification is performed by the mediating capability that is internal to each configurator at an inner node. It is done on the semantic level that is eased by multi-layered ontological commitments (as discussed in the preceding subsection) among participants. It is assumed that suppliers share application domain ontologies that allow them to describe the capabilities of their offered products and services on the semantic level. An approach that abstracts from syntactical specifics and proposes a reasoning on the semantic level also exists for transforming standardized catalog representations in [8]. An abstract service description can be interpreted as a kind of standardized functional description of the product[4]. Furthermore, agents in the role of customers (service requestors) can impose requirements on a desired product; these requirements can be matched against the functional product description provided by the suppliers (service providers). If one or more supplier descriptions match with the imposed requirements, the corresponding configuration service providers can be contacted in order to finally check the feasibility of the requirements and generate a customized product/service solution.

4   Multi-layer Ontology Definition

As sketched in Figure 2 the semantic descriptions of the offered configuration services are based on the three layer approach of [10]. The creation of service profiles for each involved configuration system is supported by a set of knowledge acquisition tools, that allow the definition of the product structure with a graphical UML-based notation with precise semantics [5]. Using translators these implementation independent models are translated into proprietary knowledge bases of problem solving engines such as the Java-based *JConfigurator* from ILOG[5] [14].

However, in the following we will describe our approach employing DAML+OIL as a language for the Semantic Web with precise model theoretic semantics. The correspondence between representation concepts needed for modeling configuration knowledge bases and DAML+OIL is shown in [6]. The uppermost layer of our ontology is the *generic ontology level*. At this level the basic representation concepts and ontological modeling primitives are introduced. These are inherent to the concepts of the modeling language such as *class* and *slot* definitions in OIL. Therefore, it meets the expectations

---

[3] Note, that only the required configuration services are organized in a tree structure, which must not hold for the involved companies in the value chain of a product.

[4] In [18] this kind of description is denoted as a functional architecture of the configured product.

[5] See http://www.ilog.com for reference.

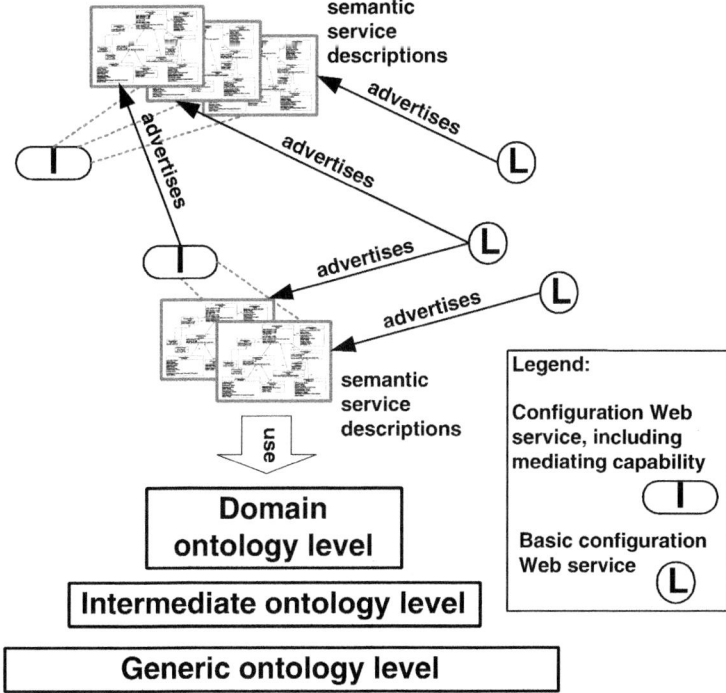

Fig. 2. Web service scenario

towards the uppermost layer and in the following subsection we move on to show which configuration domain specific modeling primitives are to be provided on the *intermediate ontology level*. For reasons of readability *OIL text* [1] is used for representation, i.e. no RDFS-based representation of DAML+OIL is used.

4.1 Basic Configuration Ontology

A general ontology for the configuration domain is important in order to allow easy configuration knowledge reuse and the integration of complex configurable products within marketplace environments. The ontologies proposed by [26] and [5] serve as a basis for the construction of application domain specific ontologies which allow the description of configuration services on a semantic level. Refined concepts of *classes* such as *component types*, *resource types*, *port types*, or *function types* are the basic modeling concepts useful for building the basic product structure. The ontology defined in [26] is based on the frame ontology of Ontolingua [11] and represents a synthesis of resource-based, function- based, connection-based, and structure-based approaches for representing configuration problems. A similar set of concepts is discussed in [5], where the configuration ontology is represented as a UML profile with additional first order formalizations guaranteeing a precise semantics for the provided modeling concepts.

4.2   Product Domain Ontology for Network Services

While the intermediate configuration ontology contains only the basic concepts for modeling product structures, it allows the construction of more specialized ontologies for specific application domains. Furthermore, axioms and slot constraints provided in OIL can be employed to formulate constraints on the configuration model. Exactly these concepts will be refined in the following for representing (application) domain specific ontologies that can be interpreted as a kind of functional product description [18], which is used as a basic framework for formulating capabilities of suppliers and requirements of customers. Figure 3 represents fragments of an ontology for defining configuration services for IP-based Virtual Private Networks (IP-VPN)[6]. For our example we will

```
begin-ontology
ontology-container
title Product Domain Ontology
description IP-based Virtual Private Networks

language "OIL"
ontology-definitions
slot-def protocol
subslot-of
  HasPart    //defined in Configuration Ontology
class-def AccessProtocol
subclass-of
  Function   //defined in Configuration Ontology

class-def RouterAccess
subclass-of
  AccessProtocol
class-def ModemAccess
subclass-of
  AccessProtocol
class-def InternetAccess
subclass-of
  AccessProtocol
class-def defined  Country

class-def defined  Town
  slot-constraint town_of cardinality 1 Country
class-def LineService
subclass-of
  Function   //defined in Configuration Ontology
  slot-constraint  bandwidth cardinality 1 integer
  slot-constraint  latency cardinality 1 integer
  slot-constraint  identifier has-value integer
class-def BackBoneSection
subclass-of
  LineService
  slot-constraint  access_from has-value AccessLine

class-def defined  AccessLine
subclass-of
  LineService
  slot-constraint  protocol cardinality 1 AccessProt ocol
  slot-constraint  access_to cardinality 1 BackBoneSection
  slot-constraint  pop cardinality 1 Town
instance-of UK Country

instance-of Manchester  Town
related town_of  Manchester UK
end-ontology
```

Fig. 3. Domain ontology for IP-VPN services

---

[6] The complete example ontology in DAML+OIL can be downloaded from http://www.cawicoms.org/ontology/ipvpn.rdfs.

concentrate on the provision of *AccessLines* that connect a customer location (slot *pop -* 'point of presence') to a *BackBoneSection*. The chosen *protocol* (a refinement of the *Has-Part* decomposition relationship in the configuration domain) can be either performed via a router, via a modem or via an internet connection to some access gateway (*Router-Access*, *ModemAccess* and *InternetAccess* are therefore specialized *AccessProtocols*). In addition, an *AccessLine* is characterized by a *bandwidth* and *latency* property that it inherits from its superclass *LineService*, which is in turn a refinement of the *Function* concept (abstract characteristic of a product or service) from the basic configuration ontology (*intermediate ontology level*). The instances contained in the ontology shown in Figure 3 can be interpreted as basic catalog entries representing common knowledge (e.g., British towns or zip codes), which are assigned to base classes of the application domain ontology (in this case *Manchester* is provided as basic instance of the class *Town*).

5   Web Service Scenario

The interaction between service providing agents can be differentiated into the three areas service publishing, identification and execution. As depicted in the scenario in Figure 2, only those agents can request a service that have the mediating capabilities to receive service advertisements and perform service identification.

5.1   Service Publishing

Now we will show how the ontologies defined in Section 4 are used to semantically describe the offered configuration services. Semantic description of the demanded services allows us to implement efficient matchmaking between supply and demand. Within these semantic annotations, restrictions on the domain and cardinality of slots, constraints on connections and structure, as well as the possible types of classes are possible. Furthermore, offered component instances can be represented as subconcepts (e.g. read from a catalog) of the classes of the service domain-specific configuration ontology. Additional supplier-specific constraints are introduced. Consequently, for the semantic description of the capability of a configuration service of a specific supplier the product domain ontology level provides the necessary base concepts that can be further refined. Figure 4 contains the semantic definition of the *AccessLine* services that are offered by the fictitious telecommunication service providers *BTT* and *Luton*. *BTT* serves customers located in the UK and Ireland (constraint on the slot pop) and can provide access to *BackBoneSections* 1 through 10 with a maximum *bandwidth* of 2000. In contrast *Luton* offers connections from towns in France and the UK. Only modem or internet are offered protocol choices, a lower *bandwidth* is supported and fewer *BackBoneSections* are accessible. For tailoring the application domain specific configuration ontology to supplier-specific circumstances tool support for acquisition and maintenance of configuration models is needed. Within the CAWICOMS project a *Knowledge Acquisition Workbench* is developed that provides the required tools for designing the service descriptions with a graphical UML-based notation. The generic and the intermediate ontology level as described in Section 4 are inherent to the modeling primitives offered by the tool suite and

```
class-def defined BTT_AccessLine
subclass-of
  AccessLine
  slot-constraint access_to value-type
    ((slot-constraint identifier value-type (min 1)) and
    (slot-constraint identifier value-type (max 10)))
  slot-constraint pop value-type ((slot-constraint town_of value-type (one-of UK))
    or (slot-constraint town_of value-type (one-of Ireland)))
  slot-constraint bandwidth value-type (max 2000)

class-def defined Luton_AccessLine
subclass-of
  AccessLine
  slot-constraint pop value-type ((slot-constraint town_of value-type (one-of France))
    or (slot-constraint town_of value-type (one-of UK)))
  slot-constraint access_to value-type
    ((slot-constraint identifier value-type (min 5)) and
    (slot-constraint identifier value-type (max 8)))
  slot-constraint bandwidth value-type (max 1200)
  slot-constraint protocol has-value (ModemAccess or InternetAccess )
```

Fig. 4. Semantic description of offered services

therefore static in our approach. The tool environment supports human experts in defining and maintaining the application domain specific ontological descriptions as well as in integrating them. The advertisement of the offered configuration services of different suppliers is therefore part of an offline setup process. The functional descriptions of the configurable products and services are communicated to all Web configurators that may act as customers for their configuration service and integrated into their domain ontologies by the human experts.

5.2   Service Identification

Having described service publication, we will now focus on the identification of relevant Web service providers for a concrete demand. This task has similarities with the *surgical* or *parametric search* problem [16], e.g. *"a laptop with at least 20GB hard-disk, 800MHz Pentium III processor or better, manufactured either by Dell or Compaq and costing less than 2000 USD"*. However, for the configuration domain we require even more enhanced search capabilities for identifying the appropriate supply. The reason is, that requirements cannot only be expressed as simple restrictions on product attributes, but also as constraints on the structure. The following example is based on the product domain ontology (Figure 3), requestors are enabled to semantically describe the requested service as can be seen in Figure 5. Let us assume that we search for an *AccessLine* provider that connects us from *Manchester* via *InternetAccess* protocol to *BackBoneSection* '3' with a *bandwidth* of 1200. Here the *bandwidth* slot-constraint is a simple attribute restriction, but the constraint on the slot *access_to* navigates to the related class *BackBoneSection* and restricts the structure. For this example we can intuitively determine that *BTT* is an appropriate supplier for the requested service, as the *Required_AccessLine* qualifies as a subclass to *BTT_AccessLine*. However, for the general case identification of subsumption relationships between offered and required concepts is too restrictive. Consider the case where we would need this *AccessLine* either from *Manchester* or from *Munich*. Assuming all other restrictions remain unchanged, the modified constraint on the slot

```
class-def defined  Required_AccessLine
subclass-of
  AccessLine
  slot-constraint  bandwidth value-type (equal 1200)
  slot-constraint  pop value-type (one-of Manchester)
  slot-constraint  protocol value-type InternetAccess
  slot-constraint  access_to has-value
    (slot-constraint  identifier has-value (equal 3))
```

Fig. 5. Semantic description of required service

pop is given in Figure 6[7]. Although *BTT* still provides an appropriate service, the constraint relaxation makes the subsumption of *Required_AccessLine* by *BTT_AccessLine* impossible. So formally the matchmaking task for identification of an appropriate con-

```
class-def defined Required_AccessLine_1
subclass-of
  AccessLine

  slot-constraint pop value-type ((one-of Manchester) or (one-of Munich))
```

Fig. 6. Modified service requirement

figuration service can be defined as follows.

Given: *A consistent description logic theory T that represents the three ontological layers of our marketplace, a set of concepts $S = \{S_1, \ldots, S_n\}$ that describe supply from n different suppliers, and a concept D representing the demanded service.*

Task: *Identify the set of concepts A, that contains all concepts S_a with $S_a \in A$, where S_a is an appropriate service for D and $A \subseteq S$.*

Definition (appropriate service): *A service S_a is an appropriate service for D, iff $S_a \cup D$ are consistent.*

Note, that this diverges from the approaches taken for matchmaking among heterogenous agents [27] or for Web service identification [17].

As already mentioned in the previous subsection, the configuration service models are defined within a knowledge acquisition environment and automatically translated into the proprietary knowledge representation formalism of a configuration agent. In our implementation this matchmaking task is therefore performed as part of the search process for a configuration solution of a constraint-based configurator engine. For the internal representation of the advertised service models as well as the service requests an object-oriented framework for constraint variables is employed [14]. Reasoning on service requirements as well as on service decomposition is performed by the underlying Java-based constraint solver. The formulation of service requests and their replies is enabled by a *WebConnector* component that owns an object model layer that accesses the internal constraint representation of the constraint engine. This object model layer represents the advertised configuration service descriptions. A service requestor agent

---

[7] Note, that the inherited cardinality constraint restricts slot *pop* to exactly one *Town*, which gives this constraint an *exclusive or* semantics.

imposes its service request via an *edit-query* onto the object-model layer and retrieves the configuration service result via a *publish-query*.

As will be also pointed out in the next subsection, the creation of standards for the definition of semantics of Web services will allow application independent mediating agents to accept service advertisements and to perform the service identification task, which is not the case in the current situation.

5.3   Service Execution

Requests for service execution must conform to an XML-based communication protocol (*WebConnector* protocol) developed for the configuration domain in accordance with the SOAP messaging standard. This protocol defines

- a fixed set of methods with defined semantics for the configuration domain, like creating components, setting values for parameters, initiation of the search process, or retrieving results,
- a mechanism to exchange complex data structures like configuration results and a language for expressing navigation expressions within these data structures (compare to XML-Schema and XPath), and
- extensibility mechanisms for special domains and support for a session concept in HTTP-based transactions.

This way the semantics of the process model of the configuration Web service is defined by a proprietary protocol. This assumption works for our specific requirement of realizing collaborative configuration systems, but is only half way towards the vision of Web services in the Semantic Web. Therefore, markup languages are required that enable a standardized representation of service profiles for advertisement of services as well as definitions of the process model. This way, the task of identifying appropriate services and the decomposition of a service request into several separate requests can be performed by domain independent mediators. Due to the lack of these standards, this mediating functionality is in our case performed by application logic integrated into the configuration systems. DAML-S[8] is an example for an effort underway that aims at providing such a standardized semantic markup for Web services that builds on top of DAML+OIL.

6   Related Work

Beside standards for representing product catalogs [8], there exists a number of approaches for standardizing electronic commerce communication (e.g. Commerce XML - cXML or Common Business Library - CBL) - these are XML-based communication standards for B2B applications[9], which also include basic mechanisms for product data interchange and can be interpreted as ontologies supporting standardized communication

---

[8] See http://www.daml.org/services for reference.

[9] An overview on existing e-Commerce frameworks for business to business communication can be found in [25].

between e-Business applications. However, these standards are restricted to the representation of standardized products, i.e. the basic properties of complex products, especially configurable products are not considered. Basic mechanisms for product data integration are already supported by a number of state-of-the-art B2B applications. However, the integration of configuration systems into electronic marketplace environments is still an open issue, i.e. not supported by today s systems. Problem Solving Methods (PSMs) [2] support the decomposition of reasoning tasks of knowledge-based systems into sets of subtasks and inference actions that are interconnected by knowledge roles. The goal of the IBROW project [20] is the semiautomatic reuse of available problem solving methods, where a software broker supports the knowledge engineer in configuring a reasoning system by combining different PSMs. A similarity to the work of [20] exists in the sense that the selection of suppliers (and corresponding configuration systems) is a basic configuration task, where configurators must be selected which are capable of cooperatively solving a distributed configuration task. The approach is different in the sense that the major focus is on providing an environment which generally supports a semi-automated reuse of problem solving methods, whereas our approach concentrates on the automated integration of configuration services in an e-business environment. The Infomaster system [15] provides basic mechanisms for integrating heterogeneous information sources in order to provide a unique entry point for the users of the system. Compared to our approach there is no support for the integration of configurable products and the underlying configuration systems. The design of large scale products requires the cooperation of a number of different experts. In the SHADE (Shared Dependency Engineering) project [22] a KIF-based representation [21] was used for representing engineering ontologies. This approach differs from the approach presented in this paper in the sense that the provided ontology is majorly employed as a basis for the communication between the different engaged agents, but is not used as a means for describing the capabilities of agents. The STEP standard [13] takes into account all aspects of a product including geometry and organisational data [19]. The idea of STEP is to provide means for defining application specific concepts for modeling products in a particular application domain. These application specific concepts are standardised into parts of STEP called *Application Protocols* which are defined using the EXPRESS data definition language (Application Protocols are EXPRESS schemas). EXPRESS itself includes a set of modeling concepts useful for representing configurable products, however the language can not be used to define an enterprise specific configuration model without leaving the STEP standard. Similarities to our approach can be seen in the role of application protocols in STEP which are very similar to the domain ontology level discussed in this paper.

7   Conclusions

The Semantic Web [3] is the vision of developing enabling technologies for the Web which supports access to its resources not only to humans but as well to applications often denoted as agent-based systems providing services such as information brokering, information filtering, intelligent search or synthesis of services [20]. This paper describes an application scenario for semantic Web services in the domain of configuring telecommunication services. It demonstrates how to apply Semantic Web technologies in order to support the integration of configurable products and services in an environment for distributed problem solving. DAML+OIL-based configuration service descriptions can be used in order to match them with given customer requirements and the matchmaking task to determine the adequacy of a service is defined. DAML+OIL formalisms are well suited for representing the component structure of configurable products, i.e. part-of associations and simple associations between component types and corresponding basic constraints. However, technologies supporting the vision of the Semantic Web are still under development. In order to support a full scenario of distributed configuration Web services, languages like DAML+OIL have to be extended with language elements supporting the formulation of service advertisements as well as process definitions for the interaction.

References

1. S. Bechhofer, I. Horrocks, C. Goble, and R. Stevens. OilEd: A Reason-able Ontology Editor for the Semantic Web. In *Proceedings of Joint Austrian/German Conference on Artificial Intelligence (KI)*, pages 396–408, Vienna, Austria, 2001.
2. R. Benjamins and D. Fensel. . *Special issue on problem-solving methods of the International Journal of Human-Computer Studies*, 49(4), 1998.
3. T. Berners-Lee. *Weaving the Web*. Harper Business, 2000.
4. B. Chandrasekaran, J. Josephson, and R. Benjamins. What Are Ontologies, and Why do we Need Them? *IEEE Intelligent Systems*, 14,1:20–26, 1999.
5. A. Felfernig, G. Friedrich, and D. Jannach. UML as domain specific language for the construction of knowledge-based configuration systems. *International Journal of Software Engineering and Knowledge Engineering (IJSEKE)*, 10(4):449–469, 2000.
6. A. Felfernig, G. Friedrich, D. Jannach, M. Stumptner, and M. Zanker. A Joint Foundation for Configuration in the Semantic Web. *Technical Report KLU-IFI-02-05*, 2001.
7. A. Felfernig, G. Friedrich, D. Jannach, and M. Zanker. Web-based configuration of Virtual Private Networks with Multiple Suppliers. In *Proceedings of the 7th International Conference on Artificial Intelligence in Design (AID)*, Cambridge, UK, 2002.
8. D. Fensel, Y. Ding, B. Omelayenko, E. Schulten, G. Botquin, M. Brown, and A. Flett. Product Data Integration in B2B E-Commerce. *IEEE Intelligent Systems*, 16(4):54–59, 2001.
9. D. Fensel, F. vanHarmelen, I. Horrocks, D. McGuinness, and P.F. Patel-Schneider. OIL: An Ontology Infrastructure for the Semantic Web. *IEEE Intelligent Systems*, 16(2):38–45, 2001.
10. A. Gangemi, D. M. Pisanelli, and G. Steve. An Overview of the ONIONS Project: Applying Ontologies to the Integration of Medical Terminologies. *Data and Knowledge Engineering*, 31(2):183–220, 1999.
11. T. Gruber. A translation approach to portable ontology specifications. *Knowledge Acquisition*, 5:199–220, 1993.
12. J. Hendler. Agents and the Semantic Web. *IEEE Intelligent Systems*, 16(2):30–37, 2001.
13. ISO. ISO Standard 10303-1: Industrial automation systems and integration - Product data representation and exchange - Part 1: Overview and fundamental principles. 1994.
14. U. Junker. Preference-programming for Configuration. In *Proceedings of IJCAI, Configuration Workshop*, Seattle, 2001.
15. A. M. Keller and M. R. Genesereth. Multivendor Catalogs: Smart Catalogs and Virtual Catalogs. *The Journal of Electronic Commerce*, 9(3), 1996.
16. D.L. McGuinness. Ontologies and Online Commerce. *IEEE Intelligent Systems*, 16(2):9–10, 2001.

17. Sh. McIlraith, T.C. Son, and H. Zeng. Mobilizing the Semantic Web with DAML-Enabled Web Services. In *Proceedings of the IICAI 2001 Workshop on E-Business and the Intelligent Web*, pages 29–39, Seattle, WA, 2001.
18. S. Mittal and F. Frayman. Towards a Generic Model of Configuration Tasks. In *Proceedings 11th International Joint Conf. on Artificial Intelligence*, pages 1395–1401, Detroit, MI, 1989.
19. T. Männistö, A. Martio, and R. Sulonen. Modelling generic product structures in STEP. *Computer-Aided Design*, 30,14:1111–1118, 1999.
20. E. Motta, D. Fensel, M. Gaspari, and V.R. Benjamins. Specifications of Knowledge Components for Reuse. In *Proceedings of 11th International Conference on Software Engineering and Knowledge Engineering*, pages 36–43, Kaiserslautern, Germany, 1999.
21. R. Neches, R. Fikes, T. Finin, T. Gruber, R. Patil, T. Senator, and W. Swartout. Enabling technology for knowledge sharing. *AI Magazine*, 12,3:36–56, 1991.
22. G.R. Olsen, M. Cutkosky, J.M. Tenenbaum, and T.R. Gruber. Collaborative Engineering based on Knowledge Sharing Agreements. In *Proceedings of the ACME Database Symposium*, pages 11–14, Minneapolis, MN, USA, 1994.
23. B.J. PineII, B. Victor, and A.C. Boynton. Making Mass Customization Work. *Harvard Business Review*, Sep./Oct. 1993:109–119, 1993.
24. J. Rumbaugh, I. Jacobson, and G. Booch. *The Unified Modeling Language Reference Manual*. Addison-Wesley, 1998.
25. S.S.Y. Shim, V.S. Pendyala, M. Sundaram, and J.Z. Gao. E-Commerce Frameworks. *IEEE Computer*, Oct. 2000:40–47, 2000.
26. T. Soininen, J. Tiihonen, T. Männistö, and R. Sulonen. Towards a General Ontology of Configuration. *AI Engineering Design Analysis and Manufacturing Journal, Special Issue: Configuration Design*, 12(4):357–372, 1998.
27. K. Sycara, M. Klusch, and S. Widoff. Dynamic Service Matchmaking among Agents in Open Information Environments. *ACM SIGMOD Record, Special Issue on Semantic Interoperability in Global Information Systems*, 1999.

Integrating Vocabularies:
Discovering and Representing Vocabulary Maps

Borys Omelayenko

Vrije Universiteit, Division of Mathematics and Computer Science
De Boelelaan 1081a,1081hv, Amsterdam, The Netherlands
www.cs.vu.nl/~borys
borys@cs.vu.nl

Abstract. The Semantic Web would enable new ways of doing business on the Web that require development of advanced business document integration technologies performing intelligent document transformation. The documents use different vocabularies that consist of large hierarchies of terms. Accordingly, vocabulary mapping and transformation becomes an important task in the whole business document transformation process. It includes several subtasks: map discovery, map representation, and map execution that must be seamlessly integrated into the document integration process. In this paper we discuss the process of discovering the maps between two vocabularies assuming availability of two sets of documents, each using one of the vocabularies. We take the vocabularies of product classification codes as a playground and propose a reusable map discovery technique based on Bayesian text classification approach. We show how the discovered maps can be integrated into the document transformation process.

1 Introduction

Historically business integration has been performed via costly Value-Added Networks (VANs) that use private exchange protocols and provide full range of network services for large companies. The structure of the messages and documents exchanged with VANs is specified according to the EDI X12 standard[1] that defines the structure for around 1000 plain text business documents. This architecture is a proven expensive but successful solution for large companies. However, each EDI implementation requires substantial labor effort to program and maintain, and this makes EDI solutions unacceptable for small and medium enterprises (SME) searching for cheap and easy integration solutions. SME tend to use Internet instead of costly VANs and are more flexible than the large companies in using XML-based standards for document exchange.

EDI suffers several generic document representation problems: unclear and complicated document syntax of plain text position-based formatting, unreadable semantics of document elements, weakly defined vocabularies of element

---

[1] www.disa.org

I. Horrocks and J. Hendler (Eds.): ISWC 2002, LNCS 2342, pp. 206–220, 2002.

values, and absence of any formal semantics of the documents. XML technologies provide a partial solution to these problems with unified syntax, implicit means for vocabulary representation, and explicit naming facilities for document elements. A number of XML-based document standards have recently been proposed trying to provide an explicit XML markup of documents and a number of tools have been developed to help in mediating between different EDI documents via XML, e.g. MS Biztalk[2]. They allow programming wrappers to translate EDI document structures to XML DTDs and then transform instance documents with XSLT [1]. However, XSLT stylesheets produced by these tools need to align different XML syntaxes, different data models, various vocabularies of XML tag names and their values, document places in a business process. An attempt to implement all these tasks with XSLT without making the semantics of document explicit leads to creation of very complicated, non-reusable and not maintainable stylesheets.

A more advanced approach [2] adopts the general idea of the Semantic Web to annotate the documents with machine-processable semantics and perform document processing based on this semantics. It assumes that first the documents are transformed from XML representation into their conceptual models in RDF [3]. Second, the models are mapped to a mediating ontology specifying shared formal semantics for each concept and containing a process ontology that specifies the order and dependency between the documents. Regular vocabularies used in the documents, e.g. product or country codes, are independently aligned to the vocabularies used in the mediating ontology. Furthermore, we need to separate between three different integration subtasks: document transformation, vocabulary mapping, and process aligning.

Vocabulary maps are large in size and homogeneous in structure, and their reuse seems to be a very efficient and relatively easy task. Automated map discovery techniques can be developed and successfully used because of the large size of vocabularies and availability of a great amount of documents using these vocabularies.

The products mentioned in product catalogues and other business documents are usually classified according to a certain product classification standard. Product codes need to be changed during the document transformation process if a pair of enterprises uses different product classification standards [4] but needs to exchange business documents. These standards form a kind of vocabularies and we use them as a playground and propose a reusable map discovery technique based on Bayesian text classification approach. In a certain sense this paper can be treated as a response to the product reclassification challenge [5] targeting a specific but very important and frequent task of product reclassification.

We define a vocabulary as a hierarchy of *terms* without multiple inheritances, constraints, properties, and other ontological primitives. Each term has an associated *term description* that specifies a free-text document associated with the term. In many cases lots of documents using a certain vocabulary are available at the companies, and each document can be treated as an extended description

---

[2] http://www.biztalk.org

of the term used in the document. In this paper we discuss the process of discovering the maps between two vocabularies assuming availability of two sets of documents, each using one of the vocabularies.

The paper is organized as follows: the product cataloguing task is described in Section 2 and the algorithm for map discovery is presented in Section 3. In Section 4 we present a roadmap for incorporating the maps into the document transformation process. The paper ends up with conclusions and discussion on related work in Section 5.

2   The Product Cataloguing Task

In the product cataloguing task [4] the documents represent free-text product descriptions classified according to a certain product encoding standard. The standards contain hierarchies of product categories used by the users to browse and search the collection of product descriptions.

The well-known product encoding standard UNSPSC[3] contains about 20.000 categories organized into four levels of taxonomy. Each of the UNSPSC category definitions contains only a category name with a short single-line description provided by the standardizing organization, e.g. category 43171903 'Central Processing units, motherboards, or daughterboards' (a subcategory of category 431719).

The descriptions of actual products as they appear in product catalogs are also short and specific. A pair of typical product descriptions with appropriate UNSPSC codes is presented in Figure 1.

UNSPSC code	Product description
43171903	PIII 800/133 S1 256
43172402	S170B 17" 60kHz Color Monitor

Fig. 1. A typical part of a product catalogue

Another product encoding standard Eclass[4] defines more than 12.000 categories organized in a four-level taxonomy and enriched with category attributes. UNSPSC classifies the products from the supplier's perspective while Eclass does it from the buyer's side[5]. Another product standard NAICS[6] is used by US companies and official structures for statistical and analytical purposes, that requires specific standards used by the companies to be mapped to NAICS. The difference between the product standards can be quite substantial, e.g. more than

---

[3] www.unspsc.org

[4] www.eclass.de

[5] This view is not stated explicitly, however, it is unofficially supported by the standard developers and users.

[6] http://www.census.gov/epcd/www/naics.html

100 UNSPSC categories from family 43 (codes 43xxxxxx) are mapped to around ten NAICS classes. The product reclassification task assumes a supplier using one encoding standard, a buyer using another one, and a mediator maintaining the maps between both standards to perform instance data reclassification with high speed.

```
<rdfs:Class rdf:about="unspsc:43171903"
  rdfs:label="Central Processing units, motherboards, or daughterboards">
  <rdfs:subClassOf rdf:resource="unspsc:431719"/>
</rdfs:Class>
<rdfs:Class rdf:about="unspsc:431719"
  rdfs:label ="Memory and Processor Units">
  <rdfs:subClassOf rdf:resource="unspsc:4317"/>
</rdfs:Class>
```

Fig. 2. Vocabulary definition in RDF Schema

Each category in a coding standard has a standard category description, e.g. '43171903 - Central Processing units, motherboards, or daughterboards', and a place in the hierarchy. The category codes form vocabulary terms, the category definitions form primary term descriptions, and the coding standards themselves are obvious vocabularies. The sets of product descriptions correctly classified to a certain category can be treated as a secondary description of the category, and we use them to discover the maps between the categories.

It is natural to expect that RDF Schema [6], an upcoming W3C standard for representing conceptual models on the Web will be widely used to represent vocabularies on the Semantic Web. RDF Schema allows representing hierarchies of classes and properties together with possible assignments of properties to classes. Vocabulary terms can be represented with RDF Schema classes as illustrated with a fragment of UNSPSC in Figure 2. Some of the standards are already public-available in RDF Schema, e.g. UNSPSC[7]. Document conceptual models using vocabularies can be also represented in RDF Schema, as illustrated in Figure 3 and discussed in [2]. The standard category description from Figure 2 together with the product descriptions belonging to the category (e.g. 'PIII 800/133 S1 256') forms the full description of the term '43171903', as far as it is seen from our examples.

```
<itemdescription rdf:about="ITEM_00005" code="unspsc:43171903"
description="PIII 800/133 S1 256"/>
<itemdescription rdf:about="ITEM_00007" code="unspsc:43172402"
description="S170B 17'' 60kHz Color Monitor"/>
```

Fig. 3. Two product catalog items in RDF

---

[7] http://protege.stanford.edu/ontologies.shtml

Machine learning techniques, namely Bayesian learning has been successfully applied to assist the user in classifying new products [4] using manually pre-classified examples. In the classification setting the terms are called classes and the task of assigning the right product code given a product description is called classification of the description[8]. Machine learning techniques generate product classification rules and we use them to discover explicit mappings between vocabulary terms.

3   Discovering Vocabulary Bridges

3.1   Naive-Bayes Classifier

Recent experiences in building product classification systems [7] show that Naive-Bayes classifier can be successfully applied to classify the products and it produces sound classification rules. These rules are represented in the form of conditional probabilities defined over full category descriptions, composed of all descriptions of the products classified to the category. The descriptions consist of natural-language words, e.g. English words. The Naive-Bayes classifier (see [8], Chapter 6 for an introduction) uses two kinds of probabilities: probability $P(w_k|c_j)$ that a certain word w_k will appear in a document belonging to category c_j, and probability $P(c_j)$ of each category c_j (probability that a new product description belongs to category c_j). These probabilities are estimated from the correspondent frequencies computed over full descriptions of each category, and the result is stored in a probability table for $P(w_k|c_j)$ illustrated in Table 1. Then, for each new product description to be classified, Naive-Bayes predicts its class with the following rule:

$$prediction = argmax_{c_j} P(c_j) \prod_k P(w_k|c_j)$$

where c_j denotes a class (a product category in our case), j iterates over all classes; w_k denotes a word that appeared in the full description of the category, k iterates over all words used in the descriptions, e.g. restricted English vocabulary.

Assume that we need to map the terms between two vocabularies used in two sets of documents, and these sets are disjoint, i.e. they do not contain a single product description explicitly classified to both product classification standards. Then we assume that we are able to train the Naive-Bayes classifier on each of these two sets of documents, and we have in our possession two probability tables similar to the one depicted in Table 1. These tables will be more coherent if the document sets are overlapping and contain some products that are present in both sets.

No mapping rules can be derived from these tables if the documents use different sets of words and terms. However, this is practically a rear case: the most

---

[8] Different communities look at similar tasks from different perspectives and have different names for them, e.g. in the knowledge engineering area the classification task would be rather called 'identification'.

informative words in product descriptions are model names and parameters, and some mapping information may be derived even if the rest of the product descriptions is specified in different languages.

Table 1. Probability table for Naïve-Bayes (a fragment), the cells represent $P(w_k|c_j)$ in %

| Classes c_j | Electric | Memory | Monitors | Notebooks |
Words w_k	component	modules		
256MB	0	20	0	0
Memory	0	40	0	0
M300	0	0	0	25
S710	0	0	11	0
17	0	0	11	0
Color	0	0	44	0
Monitor	0	0	56	0

3.2   Deriving the Maps

The probability tables computed by the Naive-Bayes classifier have several peculiarities inspired by the nature of the product classification task:

– The tables tend to be very sparse with a large fraction of cells containing zeroes, and only a relatively small fraction containing non-zero values. And even in the latter case the probabilities tend to belong to a fixed set of values (e.g. 1, 0.66, 0.33). This happens because the amount of distinct words that can be used in the full category descriptions is comparable to the number of classes (about 20.000 English words are used to describe the products classified to 20.000 classes) and to the number of available product descriptions. Hence, the number of word occurrences per class can be very low and this leads to generation of very sparse tables and rough probability estimates.
– The descriptions are very short and the words used there are very specific, and very often one word indicates only one class (e.g. product model name). This is quite unusual for the text classification task where the category of a description is derived from the combination of probabilities associated to several words, where each word can, in turn, point to several classes. As a result, Naive-Bayes cannot easily find the maximal probability estimation because all the probabilities $P(w_k|c_j)$ associated to a certain class c_j can be equal.
– The small number of available descriptions per class causes high noise in the probability estimates and one or two 'noisy' words, which occasionally occurred in a product description, may receive the same importance as the product name itself. This somehow contradicts with the nature of Bayesian

learning that assumes the probabilities to be 'trustable'. We need to weight the probability estimates to ensure that we will use only the probabilities calculated on the basis of sufficient number of examples. For this we weight each estimate with logarithm of the number of examples participated in computing this probability.

Let us look at the mapping discovery task from the probabilistic point of view. We denote the event that a random product description from the set D of all possible product descriptions is classified to the i-th class of the source standard with src_i and to the j-th class of the target standard with trg_j. The task of discovering a map between the source and the target classes is the task of discovering pairs of classes that maximize the probability that a random example from D will be classified to both classes, i.e. maximize the probability of co-occurrence of events src_i and trg_j: $argmax_{i,j}P(src_i \wedge trg_j|D)$.

It is easy to represent $P(src_i \wedge trg_j|D)$ via the Bayes rule and word occurrences w_k assuming that they are independent:

$$P(src_i \wedge trg_j|D) = \frac{P(D|src_i \wedge trg_j)P(src_j \wedge trg_j)}{P(D)} =$$

$$= \frac{\prod_k P(w_k|src_i \wedge trg_j)P(src_j \wedge trg_j)}{P(D)}.$$

We treat the events src_i and trg_j as independent (while, clearly, they are somehow correlated), and this allows deriving $P(w_k|src_i \wedge trg_j|D)$ via the probabilities that we have already estimated in the two Naive-Bayes classifiers trained for each of the vocabulary:

$$P(w_k|src_i \wedge trg_j|D) = P(w_k|src_i) \cdot P(w_k|trg_j)$$

We multiply the frequencies $P(w_k|c_j)$ from the probability tables by $ln(num_i)$, where num_i is the number of examples that participated in computing probability $P(w_k|c_j)$, to weight them due to the reasons mentioned above. Accordingly, we receive the final formula for discovering a one-to-one bridge between two terms from two vocabularies:

$$bridge = argmax_{i,j} \prod_k P(w_k|src_i)ln(num_i) \cdot P(w_k|trg_j)ln(num_j) \cdot P(src_i)P(trg_j)$$

where num_i and num_j denote the number of examples participated in computing probabilities $P(src_i)$ and $P(trg_j)$ respectively. $P(D)$ is omitted because it does not influence the $argmax$ result.

The amount of discovered bridges is quite high and it is difficult for the user to select the most important bridges. Accordingly, we rank each bridge t with the number of examples $num_i + num_j$ supporting the bridge:

$$Rank_t = num_i + num_j$$

where higher rank indicates a more important bridge. As a result the bridges that cover more examples get higher rank than those that cover fewer examples.

3.3   Experimental Investigation: English Dataset

For our current experiments we used two datasets of 100 examples each, the first dataset was classified according to Eclass, and the second – according to UNSPSC. Both datasets contained the products belonging to the same domain of computers and computer equipment, like the sample from Figure 1. The datasets were randomly drawn from a dataset of ten thousands products. They contained 32 UNSPSC and 20 Eclass categories that may be linked by 12 reasonable bridges, nine one-to-one and three two-to-one. 54% of the words (do not mix up with examples, i.e. product descriptions) have appeared in both document sets. The algorithm described above has derived 31 bridges, top seven of which are presented in Table 2.

Table 2. Experimental results

	UNSPSC	Eclass	Rank
1.	43171803 Desktop computers	240103 Hardware (workstation)	31
2.	43171801 Notebook computers	240109 Computer (portable)	18
3. ×	43172313 Hard drives	240103 Hardware (workstation)	13
4.	43172401 Monitors	240106 Screen	12
5. ×	43172402 Flat panel displays	240103 Hardware (workstation)	10
6.	43171802 Docking stations	240109 Computer (portable)	10
7.	43173002 Ethernet repeaters	240107 Periph. equip accessories (PC)	9

From the domain point of view most of the bridges are correct: 1,2,4,6, and 7, while 3 and 5 are wrong. These misclassifications can be easily caused by the small size of the training sets and general problems of the Naive-Bayes classifier discussed above. Interesting to mention that an attempt to remove all language-specific words (roughly one third of the words) from the datasets does not really change the results: the bridges have other order and rankings, but still the same bridges constitute the top (see Table 3).

Table 3. Experimental results: no-language dataset

	UNSPSC	Eclass	Rank
1.	43171803 Desktop computers	240103 Hardware (workstation)	31
2.	43171801 Notebook computers	240109 Computer (portable)	18
3. ×	43172401 Monitors	240103 Hardware (workstation)	10
4. ×	43172313 Hard drives	240103 Hardware (workstation)	10
5.	43171802 Docking stations	240109 Computer (portable)	10

3.4   Further Experiments

We tried the marginal case: to derive the maps between English document set and French document set (again, drawing the examples randomly, so the sets of products described in these two sets had quite a little overlap). In this experiment word overlap was equal to 18% (mostly made-up of numeric terms and model names) and as a result much less information was available to the mapping algorithm. The results are presented in Table 4. The first bridge seems to be reasonable, while the rest are not really (and also their rank is quite low). After examining the datasets we found that besides the products were belonging to the same domain (UNSPSC 4317xxxx) they were quite different in the English and French datasets.

Table 4. Experimental results: English to French bridges

UNSPSC	Eclass	Rank
1. 43171806 Servers	240103 Hardware (workstation)	18
2. × 43171801 Notebook computers	240107 Periph. equip accessories (PC)	14
3. × 43171803 Desktop computers	240107 Periph. equip accessories (PC)	7

In certain high-technical domains the descriptions are very-well identifying and the choice of the language does not influence the results a lot. However, we can expect the results to be worse in other domains that use free-text descriptions of products.

Besides the recall and accuracy for the generated bridges are numerically low they are still quite significant taking into account the complexity and novelty of the problem.

4   Incorporating the Bridges in the Document Transformation Process

The vocabulary integration task forms a part of the whole business document integration process and the vocabularies and mapping rules must be represented and processed in the same way as the rest of the documents.

4.1   Representing the Maps with the Mapping Meta-ontology

Mapping knowledge represented with the maps between the categories must be represented on the Web in the machine-processable manner. Providing a certain XML serialization for the maps is not sufficient, and the serialization must be augmented with a conceptual model and formal semantics of the maps. We developed an RDFT (RDF Transformation) mapping meta-ontology to specify different mappings that occur in the business integration task. In this section we briefly sketch the main concepts of RDFT used in the vocabulary integration task and refer the reader to more extensive documents and tools available from the RDFT project homepage[9].

The main concept of the RDFT meta-ontology is the bridge between two sets of rdf:Resources (two sets of concepts, either RDF classes or properties; only RDF classes are used in the vocabulary mapping tasks), one of which is regarded as the source set, and the other one as the target set. The bridges are grouped into maps, each of which is a collection of bridges serving a single purpose. The maps are identified by their URI's and form minimal reusable modules of RDFT bridges, e.g. the maps between country names in different languages, or between product categories as discussed in this paper.

An abstract class Bridge describes common properties of the bridges and restricts them to be either one-to-many or many-to-one. Each Bridge contains a ValueCorrespondence property linking to a map aligning the values of the concepts mapped in the bridge.

The bridges can represent several possible Relations, while only the EquivalentToSet relation is used in the vocabulary integration task. EquivalentToSet bridges specify that the source set of elements is equivalent to the target set of elements, e.g. a one-to-many EquivalentToSet bridge represents the fact that the source element (single-element set) is equivalent to the target *set* of several elements, while it is not equivalent to any of the target elements alone.

Several types of Bridges are defined in RDFT:

- Class2Class and Property2Property bridges between RDF Schema classes and properties. In RDF Schema classes are represented by their names, place in taxonomy, and properties that are attached to this class. Properties are defined as first-class objects together with classes, and they capture most of domain knowledge. Classes specify aggregation of properties, and we do not include class-to-property and property-to-class bridges in RDFT believing that they will introduce a conceptual mismatch and will not provide any added value from the application point of view.
- Tag2Class and Tag2Property bridges between XML tags from the source DTD and the target RDF Schema classes and properties. Tag2Class bridges are used to link vocabulary terms represented in XML documents to the appropriate classes created to represent these terms. An example of a Class2Class bridge between product categories encoded in RDF is presented in Figure 5.
- Class2Tag and Property2Tag bridges between RDF Schema classes and properties, and the elements of the target DTD. Class2Tag bridges are necessary to link back RDF classes representing vocabulary terms to XML term representation.

The values of RDF properties and XML tags mapped with the Property2Property and Tag bridges are transformed as specified in the ValueCorrespondence maps attached to the bridges that specify an XPath [9] value transformation procedure. It can be either a DeclarativeMap or a Procedu-

---

[9] http://www.cs.vu.nl/~borys/RDFT

ralMap. DeclarativeMaps are ordinary maps containing Class2Class bridges, where each class corresponds to a vocabulary term.

The XMLtag class corresponds to a DTD element or attribute, identifying them with the XMLtagName and XMLtagAttributeName. RDF Schema classes and properties are used to point to the classes and properties used in the bridges. However, RDF Schema does not provide any means to represent XML tags, and we define our own class to model them.

Important to mention that cyclic maps between two terms from different vocabularies are possible and occur quite often. The cyclic map consists of a super-term Src-A, mapped to term Trg-B in another vocabulary, whose super-term Trg-A is in turn mapped to the original term Src-B. This map is represented in Figure 4 with bold curved arrows.

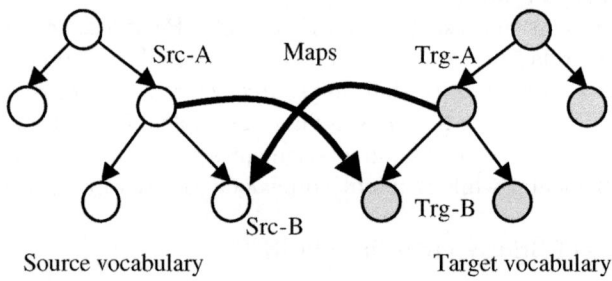

Fig. 4. Cyclic maps between the terms

In this case the map can be mistakenly interpreted as a subclass-of relationship between the terms Src-B and Trg-A, and Trg-B and Src-A. Modeling this map in such a way leads to declaring all four terms as equivalent. However, they are definitely not because two taxonomies are formed according to different classification principles. The bridges indicate that Trg-A is equivalent to Src-B and Src-A is equivalent to Trg-B but we may not derive any conclusions about Src-B and Trg-B from that.

Instance-driven semantics of the bridges leads to certain difficulties in specifying formal semantics of RDFT in terms of schema-oriented languages like DAML-OIL[10].

4.2   Vocabularies in XML Documents

Vocabularies may be encoded in XML with one of the following ways:

- An XML attribute may have a fixed list of values (so-called choice attributes) that are treated as vocabulary terms.
- An XML element may allow only EMPTY elements as its children, and the names of these tags are treated as vocabulary terms.

---

[10] http://www.ontoknowledge.org/oil/

```
<RDFT:Property2Property rdf:about="P2P">
        <RDFT:ValueCorrespondence rdf:resource="VC"/>
        <RDFT:SourceProperty rdf:resource="ProductCode"/>
        <RDFT:TargetProperty rdf:resource="Classification"/>
</RDFT:Property2Property>
<RDFT:DeclarativeMap rdf:about="VC">
    <RDFT:Brigdes rdf:resource="UNSPSC_ECLASS_00"/>
    <RDFT:Brigdes rdf:resource="UNSPSC_ECLASS_01"/>
</RDFT:DeclarativeMap>
<RDFT:Class2Class
rdf:about="UNSPSC_ECLASS_00">
    <RDFT:TargetClass rdf:resource="eclass:240109"/>
    <RDFT:SourceClass rdf:resource="unspsc:43171801"/>
    <RDFT:Relation rdf:resource="EquivalenceRelation"/>
</RDFT:Class2Class>
```

Fig. 5. A Property2Property bridge linking two different properties standing for the product classification code with the corresponding vocabulary map (DeclarativeMap) aligning different UNSPSC and Eclass terms via Class2Class bridges

– An XML element may have a #PCDATA type with additional knowledge that its free-text values represent the terms from a certain vocabulary (similarly, XML attributes may contain vocabulary terms as their #CDATA values).

The document integration architecture [2] envisages several transformation steps for each transformation transaction: XML-RDF transformation, several RDF-RDF steps, and the final RDF-XML transformation. Vocabulary terms can occur at two different levels: the level of document elements and the level of element values. In both cases they must be first translated to RDF representation with the Tag2Class bridges. Then the terms are aligned to the mediating vocabulary and then to the target vocabulary with the Class2Class bridges. Finally, the target XML encoding for the terms is restored with the Class2Tag bridges.

The terms remain the same while being translated from their XML serialization to RDF classes, and these steps do not require any vocabulary alignment. It is performed during the RDF-RDF transformations where different terms from different vocabularies are mapped with DeclarativeMaps.

5   Outlook and Discussion Issues

The vocabulary integration task discussed in this paper is quite specific with a number of restricting assumptions. However, this task occurs quite often in precisely the same setting that makes the solution widely reusable.

Besides the topic of vocabulary and namely catalog integration is relatively new, a certain work has been recently reported. The Naive-Bayes algorithm has been successfully applied to the task of text reclassification [10]. In this task some information about existing classification of short descriptions was used to reclassify them to another system of classes. It is similar to the task we discuss in the present paper but is not equivalent. It focuses at the issue of improving the results of product classification if the products have already been pre-classified. It assumes that the catalogs have precisely the same structure and existing classifications according to one standard can improve the classification results for another standard, while we make no assumptions on that. In addition, the approach [10] is limited to the search of one-to-one maps only. The focus was made on the artificial catalogs or news archives that have a limited number of classes and long descriptions. And the main feature of real-life product catalogs – short descriptions and huge amount of classes – is not addressed and not exploited.

In [11] different business standards are analyzed and a knowledge-engineering methodology for integrating them is sketched. From another perspective an attempt to look at the catalog integration problem from the graph-based point of view is made in [12], treating catalog structures as graphs to be aligned. We need to mention the work on automated schema integration [13], namely applied to matching XML documents [14]. Schema matching is an orthogonal task that must be solved for business integration in addition to the vocabulary mapping task.

Specifically in our work, RDFT modeling corresponds to generic OMG [15] recommendations for modeling data transformations. Conceptually an RDFT Map corresponds to TransformationMap in CWM, and the Bridge class is equivalent to the CWM's ClassifierMap (linking two concepts that are allowed to have instances). The Class2Class bridge corresponds to the source and target elements of the ClassifierMap class in CWM and our Property2Property bridge corresponds to the FeatureMap class in CWM. Due to pragmatical reasons we do not include class-to-property bridges in RDFT thus restricting CWM to a less expressive language.

We are also investigating the approaches to create tractable knowledge representation languages with limited expressiveness like CLASSIC [16] to make the mapping meta-ontology as expressive as possible without making the instance document transformation process too complex.

Let us sketch several possible future research directions in the product reclassification and vocabulary mapping area:

– The vocabularies contain the hierarchies of terms and these hierarchies must be taken into account while deriving maps between the terms. For examples, the classes assigned to product descriptions may not belong to the lowest level of the hierarchy, but to higher levels. Accordingly, a map discovery algorithm must be able to discover the maps between high-level categories, that is still not the case in our approach.

– In our approach one-to-many and many-to-one bridges are derived from one-to-one bridges by the following rule: if a pair of bridges connects several different source classes to a single target then it must be treated as a many-to-one bridge and vice versa. However, such an approach makes no difference between a many-to-one (one-to-many) bridge and an inconsistent bridge, and can be improved.

- Applicability of the Naive-Bayes classifier depends on the overlap between the words used in the documents and the overlap between product descriptions. In the marginal cases (e.g. very strong or very weak overlap) another algorithms may be needed, and an automated method selection procedure needs to be developed. We need to be able of selecting the subsets of product descriptions suitable for the bridge discovery task.

We are working now on a large-scale experimental investigation of the proposed techniques. However, it is difficult to make a good experimental setting to evaluate the results: no axiomatically correct maps are available between competing product encoding standards and their manual creation brings a certain degree of objectivism into the evaluation. However, the fact that the approach discovers valuable maps gives a hope for its stable behavior and usability. Practical usability remains a dominating quality criterion for the evaluation of our work as well as many other Semantic Web activities.

Acknowledgements

We would like to thank Dieter Fensel, Michel Klein, Maxym Korotky, Ellen Schulten, and Volodymyr Zykov for their helpful discussions and comments, and two anonymous reviewers for their comments.

References

1. Clark, J.: XSL Transformations (XSL-T). Technical report, W3C Recommendation, November 16 (1999)
2. Omelayenko, B., Fensel, D.: A Two-Layered Integration Approach for Product Information in B2B E-commerce. In Madria, K., Pernul, G., eds.: Proceedings of the Second International Conference on Electronic Commerce and Web Technologies (EC WEB-2001). Number 2115 in LNCS, Munich, Germany, September 4-6, Springer-Verlag (2001) 226–239
3. Lassila, O., Swick, R.: Resource Description Framework (RDF) Model and Syntax Specification. Technical report, W3C Recommendation, February 22 (1999)
4. Fensel, D., Ding, Y., Omelayenko, B., Schulten, E., Botquin, G., Brown, M., Flett, A.: Product Data Integration for B2B E-Commerce. IEEE Intelligent Systems **16** (2001) 54–59
5. Schulten, E., Akkermans, H., Botquin, G., Dorr, M., Guarino, N., Lopes, N., Sadeh, N.: The E-Commerce Product Classification Challenge. IEEE Intelligent Systems **16** (2001) 86–88
6. Brickley, D., Guha, R.: Resource Description Framework (RDF) Schema Specification 1.0. Technical report, W3C Candidate Recommendation, March 27 (2000)
7. Ding, Y., Korotkiy, M., Omelayenko, B., Kartseva, V., Zykov, V., Klein, M., Schulten, E., Fensel, D.: Goldenbullet in a nutschell. In: Proceedings of the 15-th International FLAIRS Conference, Pensacola, Florida, May 16-18, AAAI Press (2002)
8. Mitchell, T.: Machine Learning. McGraw Hill (1997)
9. Clark, J., DeRose, S.: XML Path Language (XPath), version 1.0. Technical report, W3C Recommendation, November 16 (1999)

10. Agrawal, R., Srikant, R.: On Integrating Catalogs. In: The 10-th International World Wide Web Conference, Hong Kong, May (2001)
11. Corcho, O., Gomez-Perez, A.: Solving Integration Problems of E-commerce Standards and Initiatives through Ontological Mappings. In: Proceedings of the Workshop on E-Business and Intelligent Web at the Seventeenth International Joint Conference on Artificial Intelligence (IJCAI-2001), Seattle, USA, August 5 (2001)
12. Navathe, S., Thomas, H., Amitpong, M.S., Datta, A.: A Model to Support E-Catalog Integration. In: Proceedings of the Ninth IFIP 2.6 Working Conference on Database Semantics, Hong-Kong, April 25-28 (2001) 247–261
13. Rahm, E., Bernstein, P.: A Survey of Approaches to Automatic Schema Matching. The VLDB Journal **10** (2001) 334–350
14. Anhai, D., Domingos, P., Halevy, A.: Reconciling Schemas of Disparate Data Sources: A Machine-Learning Approach. In: Proceedings of the ACM SIGMOD Conference, Santa Barbara, CA, May 21-24, ACM (2001)
15. CWM: Common Warehouse Model Specification. Technical report, Object Management Group (2001)
16. Borgida, A., Brachman, R., McGuinness, D., Resnik, L.: CLASSIC: A Structural Data Model for Objects. In: Proceedings of the 1989 ACM SIGMOD International Conference on Management of Data, Portland, OR, May 31 - June 2, ACM (1989) 59–67

OntoEdit: Collaborative Ontology Development for the Semantic Web

York Sure[1], Michael Erdmann[2], Juergen Angele[2],
Steffen Staab[1,2], Rudi Studer[1,2,3], and Dirk Wenke[2]

[1] Institute AIFB, University of Karlsruhe, 76128 Karlsruhe, Germany
{sure,staab,studer}@aifb.uni-karlsruhe.de
http://www.aifb.uni-karlsruhe.de/WBS/
[2] Ontoprise GmbH, Haid-und-Neu-Str. 7, 76131 Karlsruhe, Germany,
{angele,erdmann,wenke}@ontoprise.de
http://www.ontoprise.de/
[3] FZI Research Center for Information Technologies,
Haid-und-Neu-Str. 10-14, 76131 Karlsruhe, Germany
http://www.fzi.de/wim/

Abstract. Ontologies now play an important role for enabling the semantic web. They provide a source of precisely defined terms e.g. for knowledge-intensive applications. The terms are used for concise communication across people and applications. Typically the development of ontologies involves collaborative efforts of multiple persons. OntoEdit is an ontology editor that integrates numerous aspects of ontology engineering. This paper focuses on collaborative development of ontologies with OntoEdit which is guided by a comprehensive methodology.

1 Introduction

The vision of the Semantic Web introduces the next generation of the Web by establishing a layer of machine-understandable data e.g. for software agents, sophisticated search engines and web services. Ontologies play an important role for these knowledge-intensive applications as a source of formally defined terms for communication. They aim at capturing domain knowledge in a generic way and provide a commonly agreed understanding of a domain, which may be reused, shared, and operationalized across applications and groups. However, because of the size of ontologies, their complexity, their formal underpinnings and the necessity to come towards a shared understanding within a group of people, ontologies are still far from being a commodity.

In recent years, research aimed at paving the way for the construction of ontologies by ontology development environments [DSW+99,NFM00,ACFLGP01]. Thereby, we have seen different directions taken to support the engineering of ontologies.

1. Several seminal proposals for guiding the ontology development process by engineering methodology have been described [UK95,LGPSS99], which influenced the ontology development environments [ACFLGP01].
2. Inferencing mechanisms for large ontologies have been developed and implemented (e.g. [Hor98]) — also to support ontology engineering [BHGS01].

I. Horrocks and J. Hendler (Eds.): ISWC 2002, LNCS 2342, pp. 221–235, 2002.

3. Finally, the need to achieve consensus about an ontology was reflected by collaborative environments [TS98,Dom98,SPKR96,FFR96] for ontology engineering.

However, only few of these seminal approaches (e.g. [ACFLGP01]) have worked towards combining all of these urgent desiderata. This observation seems to reflect our own experience, viz. that it is far from trivial to offer a sound integration of these aspects. Therefore, OntoEdit is an ontology engineering environment that is rather unique in its kind as it combines methodology-based ontology development with capabilities for collaboration and inferencing. This paper is about how methodology and collaboration interact to support the ontology engineering process.[1]

Concerning the methodology, OntoEdit focuses on three main steps for ontology development (our methodology is based on [SAA+99], a detailed description can be found in [SSSS01]), viz. requirements specification, refinement, and evaluation. Firstly, all requirements of the envisaged ontology are collected. Typically for ontology engineering, ontology engineers and domain experts are joined in a team that works together on a description of domain and goal of the ontology, design guidelines, available knowledge sources (e.g. reusable ontologies and thesauri etc.), potential users and use cases and applications supported by the ontology. The output of this phase is a semi-formal description of the ontology. Secondly, during the refinement phase the team extends the semi-formal description in several iterations and formalizes it in an appropriate representation language. The output of this phase is a mature ontology (aka. "target ontology"). Thirdly, the target ontology needs to be evaluated according to the requirement specifications. Typically this phase serves as a proof for the usefulness of developed ontologies and may involve the engineering team as well as end users of the targeted application. The output of this phase is an evaluated ontology, ready for the roll-out into a productive environment.

Support for these collaborative development steps within the ontology development methodology is crucial in order to meet the conflicting needs for ease of use and construction of complex ontology structures. We will now introduce a case study, the development of an ontology for a semantic portal about our institute AIFB. Based on the process illustrated with this example, the remainder of the paper will be structured.

2   Case Study: SEmantic portAL (SEAL) at Institute AIFB

Based on our conceptual framework for "SEmantic portALs" (SEAL) we have developed an ontology based portal for our own institute AIFB[2]. The aim of the web application is the presentation of information to human and software agents taking advantage of semantic structures. The portal targets mainly students and researchers and presents typical information about persons, teaching-related topics and research-related topics. A detailed description of SEAL can be found in [MSS+02]. We briefly sketch the architectural idea of SEAL and then focus on describing aspects of the collaborative ontology development itself.

---

[1] In a recently submitted companion paper [SSA+02], we have described how methodology and inferencing interact to support the ontology engineering process.

[2] http://www.aifb.uni-karlsruhe.de

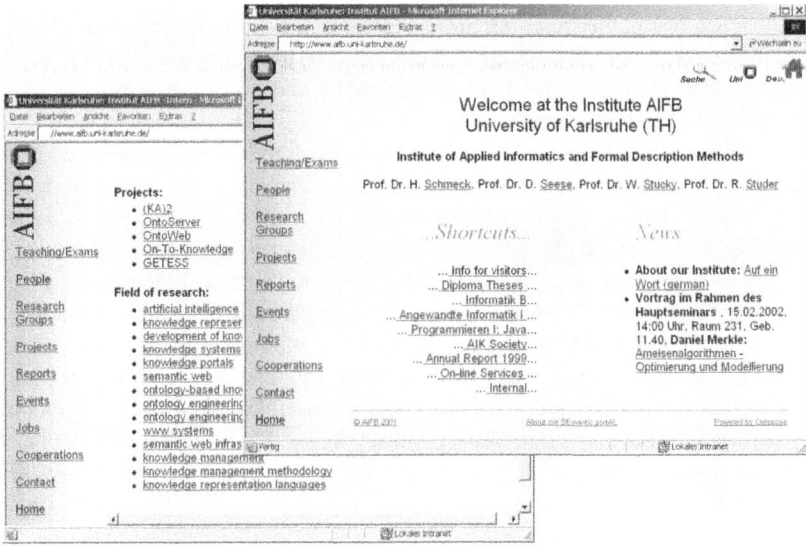

Fig. 1. The semantic portal at the institute AIFB

SEAL is a framework for managing community web sites and web portals based on ontologies. The ontology supports queries to multiple sources, but beyond that it also includes the intensive use of the schema information itself allowing for automatic generation of navigational views[3] and mixed ontology and content-based presentation. The core idea of SEAL is that Semantic Portals for a community of users that contribute *and* consume information require web site management *and* web information integration. In order to reduce engineering and maintenance efforts SEAL uses an ontology for semantic integration of existing data sources as well as for web site management and presentation to the outside world. SEAL exploits the ontology to offer mechanisms for acquiring, structuring and sharing information between human and/or machine agents.

For the AIFB ontology the ontology engineers had to deal mainly with (i) modeling navigational structures, (ii) the research topics investigated by different groups of the institute, (iii) topics related to teaching and last but not least (iv) personal information about members of the institute. Figure 1 shows two screenshots from our portal, viz. the entry point and parts of a researcher's homepage. On the left side of the screenshots the top-level navigational structure is shown. The right side of the researchers homepage shows projects this researcher is involved in and his personal research topics.

During the **requirements specification phase** (cf. Section 3) the ontology engineers set up the requirements specification for the ontology. To gather initial structures, they took themselves as an "input source" and collected a large set of research topics, topics related to teaching and personal information. Naturally, the ontology developers (viz. the knowledge management group) were not able to come up with all relevant structures by themselves and already in this phase they collaborated with domain experts, viz.

---

[3] Examples are navigation hierarchies that appear as `has-part` trees or `has-subtopic` trees in the ontology.

their colleagues from other research groups (information systems group, efficient algorithms group and complexity management group). In this section we show OntoEdit's support for capturing the requirements specification and his brainstorming support for the gathering of initial structures.

In the **refinement phase** (cf. Section 4) the "first draft" of the ontology was refined by structuring the concept hierarchy and addition of concepts, relationships and axioms. Like in the early stage, a tight collaboration of all groups was needed to refine the ontology, e.g. to formalize implicit knowledge like "someone who works in logic also works in theoretical computer science". In this section we present OntoEdit's advanced support for collaborative ontology engineering through transaction management.

Finally, in the **evaluation phase** (cf. Section 5) the ontology is evaluated according to the previously set up requirement specifications. In a first step, each group evaluated "their" requirements individually. In a second step the ontology as a whole was evaluated. In this section we illustrate OntoEdit's facilities for setting up test sets for evaluation, avoiding and locating errors in the ontology, using competency questions for evaluation and, last but not least, we describe how these components work together for support of collaborative evaluation.

3   Requirements Specification Phase

Like in software engineering and as proposed by [LGPSS99], we start ontology development with collecting requirements for the envisaged ontology. By nature this task is performed by a team of experts for the domain accompanied by experts for modeling. The outcome of this phase is (i) a document that contains all relevant requirement specifications (domain and goal of the ontology, design guidelines, available knowledge sources, potential users and use cases and applications supported by the ontology) (ii) a semi-formal ontology description, i.e. a graph of named nodes and (un-)named, (un-)directed edges, both of which may be linked with further descriptive text.

To operationalize a methodology it is desirable to have a tool that reflects and supports all steps of the methodology and guides users step by step through the ontology engineering process. Along with the development of the methodology we therefore extended the core functionalities of OntoEdit by two plug-ins to support first stages of the ontology development, viz. OntoKick and Mind2Onto[4].

OntoKick targets at (i) creation of the requirement specification document and (ii) extraction of relevant structures for the building of the semi-formal ontology description. Mind2Onto targets at integration of brainstorming processes to build relevant structures of the semi-formal ontology description. As computer science researchers we were familiar with software development and preferred to start with a requirement specification of the ontology, i.e. OntoKick. People who are not so familiar with software design principles often prefer to start with "doing something". Brain storming is a good method to quickly and intuitively start a project, therefore one also might begin the ontology development process with Mind2Onto.

---

[4] Describing the plug-in framework is beyond the scope of this paper, it is described in [Han01]. In a nutshell, one might easily expand OntoEdit's functionalities through plug-ins.

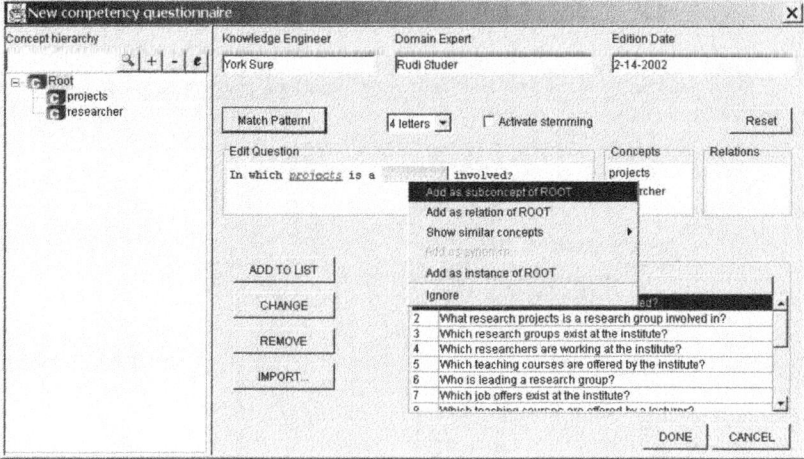

Fig. 2. OntoKick: Capturing of Competency Questions

OntoKick support for the collaborative generation of requirements specifications for ontologies. The collaborative aspect of OntoKick is not so much the support for distributed work of team members, but rather the support for personal interaction of ontology engineers and domain experts. This is a two step process. Firstly, OntoKick allows for describing important meta-aspects of the ontology, viz.: domain and the goal of the ontology, design guidelines, the available knowledge sources (e.g. domain experts, reusable ontologies etc.), potential users, use cases, and applications supported by the ontology. OntoKick guides the engineering team stepwise through all relevant aspects and stores these descriptions along with the ontology definitions.

Secondly, OntoKick supports the creation of a semi-formal ontology description. Naturally, domain experts are a valuable knowledge source for structuring a domain. A very common method for knowledge acquisition from domain experts are personal interviews. To structure the interviews with domain experts we use competency questions (CQ, cf. [UK95]). Each CQ defines a query that the envisaged ontology (respectively the ontology-based application) should be able to answer and therefore defines explicit requirements for the ontology. Typically, CQs are derived from interviews with domain experts and help to structure knowledge. We take further advantage by using them to create the initial version of the semi-formal description of an ontology and also for evaluation of the ontology in a later stage (cf. Section 5). Based on the assumption that each CQ contains valuable information about the domain of the ontology we extract relevant concepts, relations and instances (cf. Figure 2).

Figure 3 shows the main workbench of OntoEdit. It consists of several tabs, here the tab *Concepts & Relations* is selected. The left frame of the tab contains a concept hierarchy, the right frame contains relations[5] with their ranges that have the currently selected concept (here: Projekt) as domain. Further tabs include e.g. *Instances* for adding

---

[5] Please note that for exporting and importing of RDF/S one would prefer to talk about properties with domain and range restrictions instead of relations.

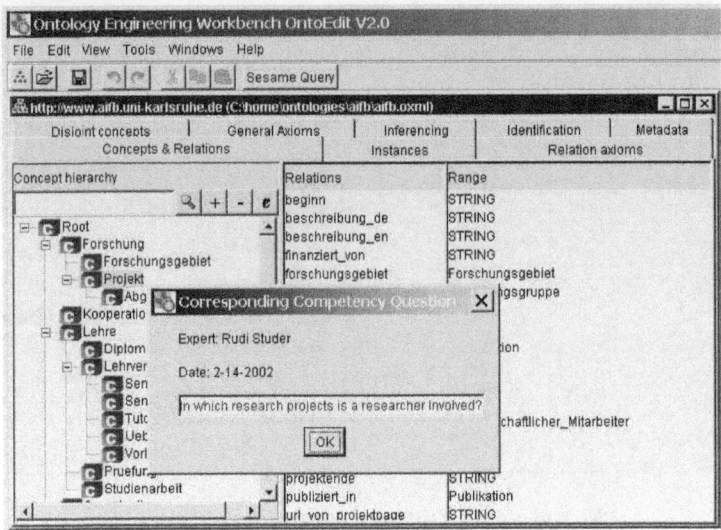

Fig. 3. OntoKick: Traceability of Competency Questions

and editing of instances or *Relation axioms* for adding and editing relational axioms like transitivity, symmetry and inverseness of relations (e.g.).

OntoKick establishes and maintains links between CQs and concepts derived from them. Figure 3 also includes the relevant CQ for the selected concept Projekt (provided by a right-click context menu). This allows for better traceability of the origins of concept definitions in later stages and improves quality assurance during the development process, i.e. by documenting the origins and the context of concepts, relations and instances. Therefore, a reached level of quality of the ontology can be reengineered by other ontology engineers.

"Real life" ontology modeling is supported by OntoKick as the following example illustrates with our SEAL scenario. First, the ontology engineer interviews an expert (i.e. his colleague). Thereby they identify CQs, e.g. "In which research projects is a researcher involved?" (cf. Figures 2 and 3). Based on these CQs the ontology engineer creates a first draft of the semi-formal description of the ontology and already graphically models it in OntoEdit. He identifies relevant concepts, relations and instances from of the above-mentioned CQ, e.g. the concept Projekte (German for projects). The instances might e.g. be prototypical instances that are used for evaluation purposes (cf. Section 5). After capturing CQs and modeling the ontology with OntoKick the ontology engineer is able to retrieve corresponding CQs for each concept, relation, and instance. This helps him and others to identify the context in which these elements were modeled.

Mind2Onto is a plug-in for supporting brainstorming and discussion about ontology structures. Especially during early stages of projects in general, brainstorming methods are commonly used to quickly capture pieces of relevant knowledge. A widely used method are mind maps[TM] [Buz74], they were originally developed to support more efficient learning and evolved to a management technique used by numerous companies. In general, a mind map[TM] provides information about a topic that is structured in a tree.

Each branch of the tree is typically named and associatively refined by it's subbranches. Icons and pictures as well as different colors and fonts might be used for illustration based on the assumption that our memory performance is improved by visual aspects. There already exist numerous tools for the electronically creation of mind maps™. Many people from academia and industry are familiar with mind maps™ and related tools – including potential ontology engineers and domain experts. Therefore the integration of electronic mind maps™ into the ontology development process is very attractive (cf. e.g. [LS02]).

We relied on a widely used commercial tool[6] for the creation of mind maps™. It supports collaborative engineering of mind maps™ through peer-to-peer communication and has advanced facilities for graphical presentations of hierarchical structures, e.g. easy to use copy&paste functionalities and different highlighting mechanisms. It's strength but also it's weakness lies in the intuitive user interface and the simple but effective usability, which allows for quick creation of mind maps™ but lacks of expressiveness for advanced ontology modeling. By nature, mind maps™ have (almost) no assumptions for it's semantics, i.e. branches are somehow "associatively related" to each other. This assumption fits perfectly well during early stages of ontology development for quick and effective capturing of relevant knowledge pieces and makes the mind map™ tool a valuable add-on.

Mind2Onto integrates the mind map™ tool into the ontology engineering methodology. Currently OntoEdit and the mind map™ tool interoperate through import and export facilities based on XML (cf. Figure 4). In our scenario we used the mind map™ tool to facilitate discussions about the research topic hierarchy. Most of the domain experts were already familiar with the tool, the other ones learned it's usage very quickly. Initially all workgroups of our institute created in joint sessions a mind map™ of relevant research topics. The peer-to-peer communication of the mind map™ tool provided the necessary workgroup functionalities for this effort.

4   Refinement Phase

The goal of this phase is to refine the semi-formal description of the ontology according to the captured requirements into a mature ontology, which is the output of this phase. Especially during the refinement phase, several teams were working simultaneously with OntoEdit on developing the ontology for our AIFB portal. Several sessions were necessary until e.g. the navigational structures were accepted by all members. In this phase also numerous relationships were added to refine the ontology (a task that e.g. the brainstorming tool is not capable of). After reaching a consensus, the created mind map™ (see previous section) was restructured in cooperation with the ontology engineers to facilitate the interoperability with OntoEdit, i.e. as a simple assumption we took the elements of a mind map™ as concepts and branches as SUBCONCEPTOF relationships between concepts (cf. Figure 4). After several discussions we decided to model research topics as subconcepts of the concept Forschungsgebiet (German for ResearchTopic) to form a hierarchy of research topics. The final version of the research topic hierarchy then was included into the ontology.

---

[6] MindManager™ 2002 Business Edition, cf. http://www.mindjet.com

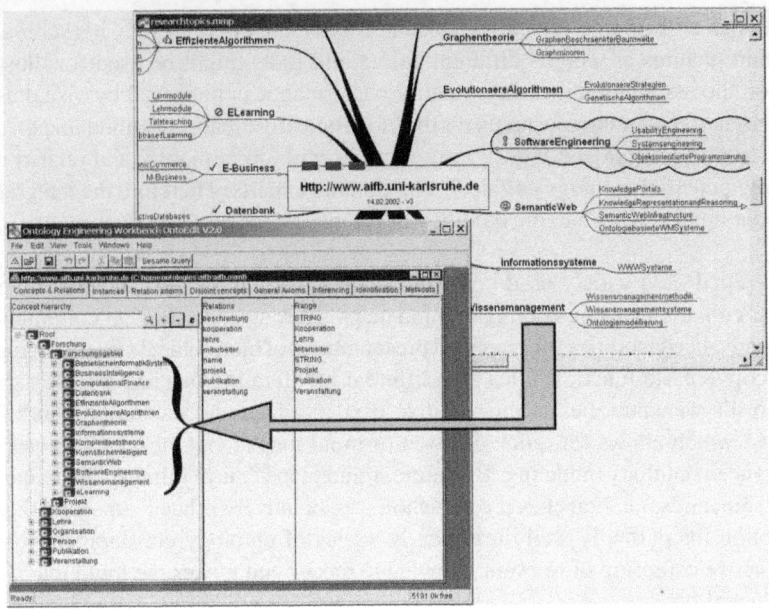

Fig. 4. Mind2Onto: Research topics as a mind map and in the ontology

In the current version of OntoEdit members of an engineering team can collaborate even though they are geographically distributed and still modify the ontology at the same time. We have developed a client/server architecture (cf. Figure 5) in which the clients connect to an ontology server and can change or extend the ontology. All clients are immediately informed of modifications the other ontologists do to the ontology. Engineers can store comments (e.g. explaining design decisions) in a documentation field for each concept and relation. By this way, one of the main features of ontologies, i.e. their consensual character, is supported. Collaborating ontologists must agree on the modeling decisions that are made. Therefore the possibility to monitor the development process of all collaborators is essential for reaching the goal of a shared ontology.

Transaction Management. In a distributed development environment certain mechanisms must be implemented to ensure safe development conditions, such as consistency of the models and the provision of a minimum degree of concurrency. To reach this goal we employed a locking and transaction protocol and implemented a distributed event model on the basis of Java-RMI (remote method invocation).

To guarantee consistent models the clients are forced to obtain locks for each resource (e.g. concept, instance, relation) that they want to modify (e.g. add a superconcept, add an attribute-value pair to an instance, or change the arity of a relation).[7] The server denies the (write-) access to a resource if the resource is not locked by the client that attempts

---

[7] The grounding datamodel of OntoEdit is OXML 2.0. This frame–based model offers a number of meta–classes, like *ontology*, *concept*, *relation*, but also *predicate* or *axiom*, with a rich set of properties and associations to facilitate ontology modeling: cf. http://www.ontoprise.de/download/oxml2.0.pdf for a reference manual.

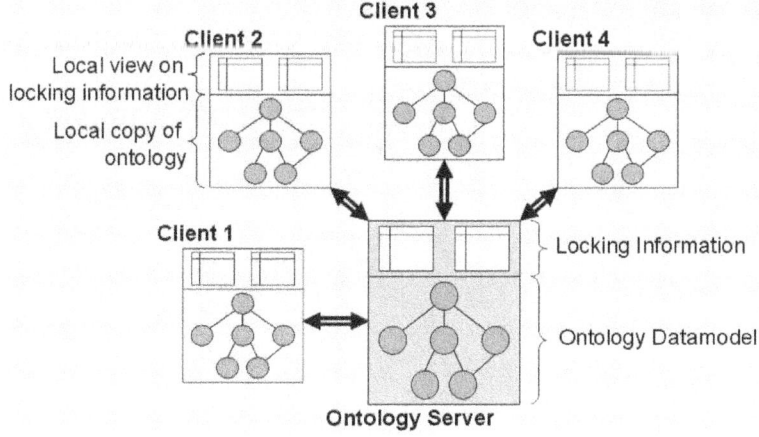

Fig. 5. Client/server architecture of OntoEdit

to modify it. Clients can obtain locks either by explicitly locking these resources, or more conveniently, by a begin of transaction (BOT) that is accompanied with a list of needed resources. If not all resources can be assigned to the calling client the BOT fails and the transaction is immediately aborted. Otherwise the server locks the needed resources for the client, so that no other client can manipulate them until the end of the transaction is reached. Now the client can manipulate the locked resources until it commits the transaction. After a commit all locked resources are freed again and the operations performed in the body of the transaction are actually applied to the datamodel. Afterwards, events are created to inform the other clients of the modifications performed. If the transaction needs to be aborted by the client all operations are undone, all locks are removed, and no events are fired.

Transactions may be nested to make complex operations possible without the need of rollback mechanisms. E.g. the datamodel procedure of moving a concept from one superconcept to another one consists of two subtransactions (remove a superconcept-relationship to the first superconcept and establish a new one for the second concept) that must be performed all together or none at all. Because of the necessity of nested transactions we implemented a strict two phase locking protocol (S2PL). In this protocol additional resources can be achieved (and locked) within the body of a transaction. Our implementation of the S2PL allows for arbitrarily nested transactions. The execution of inner transactions and the release of all locked resources is postponed until the outermost commit or abort is finally reached. Again, only after the final commit events are sent to the other clients. We employ the S2PL because (i) it allows for nested transactions and (ii) prevents cascading aborts. Thus, clients can be immediately informed if a planned operation will commit or is prohibited due to unavailable resources. (iii) S2PL prevents also deadlocks since resources are only locked in a BOT if all locks can be achieved. Other locking protocols are either too inflexible (like conservative locking (C2PL) that cannot lock resources in addition to the locks of the BOT and thus, is not suitable for nested transactions) or provide chances of deadlocks that must be appropriately handled.

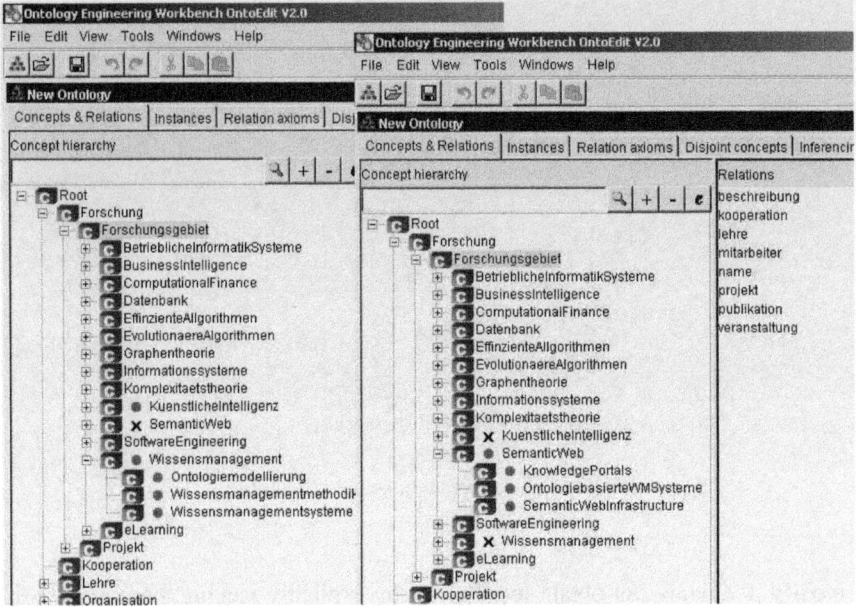

Fig. 6. Locked trees in OntoEdit

To reduce communication overhead, save bandwidth and because transactions are relatively short lived no information about transactions (esp. not about locked objects within a BOT) is communicated from the server to other clients, i.e. the local view on locking information within a client (cf. Figure 5) contains all resources that are locked by this client (by a BOT) but none that have been locked by a BOT of any other client. Nevertheless, another kind of locking information *is* distributed to all clients. An ontologist can lock a whole subtree of the concept hierarchy. The server informs all clients of this locking operation.

Locking Subtrees of the Concept Hierarchy. A common practice in ontology engineering is to start with a top level structure and to refine it later on. Different parts of an ontology can be refined by different ontologists or groups (cf. the research topics of the AIFB ontology). These collaborators should be able to work on their parts of the ontology with as few interference with other ontologists as possible. This is achieved in OntoEdit by the possibility of locking a complete subtree of the concept hierarchy. After the subtrees have been locked no conflicts can arise anymore, and what is equally important, the need to check for locking information *with the server* is reduced drastically. Since most modeling operations will occur within the scope of the subtrees, i.e. will mainly access already locked resources, the client can decide *locally* whether these operations are permitted or not.

This (tree-) locking information is distributed to all other clients and visually indicated in the GUI (cf. Figure 6). Crosses mark concepts that are locked by other clients and may not be edited. Bullets mark concepts that may be edited, altered and removed at will. Concepts without additional icons are currently not locked and therefore available for locking by any user.

Due to the distribution of this information clients can often check locally whether a transaction will be permitted or not. If all needed resources are marked as "locked by me" in the local view on the locking information (cf. Figure 5) a BOT can be safely accepted. If at least one resource is marked as being locked by another client the current client can definitively reject a BOT (or a lockSubTree request). Only if resources are requested in a BOT for which no information is locally available, the server has to be consulted.

What Does Locking a Concept Mean? Locking resources in relational databases means the DB administrators or application developers must decide whether to lock an attribute, a tuple, or a complete table (i.e. relation). Since the basic datamodel for ontologies is much richer (esp. due to hierarchical relationships between concepts, between relations, and between instances and concepts) the decision of what a lock entails is more complex.

The most simple answer would be to lock the complete ontology with all its components. But this solution is ruled out since it would disallow any kind of concurrency and distributed collaboration. Another simple answer would be to lock the resources that are to be modified within a transaction, e.g. the resource X in the transaction that states that concept X has a superconcept Y. Apparently, for this transaction concept Y should also be locked since a new subconcept for Y is defined. Thus, the second simple approach seems to lock too few resources.

Due to hierarchical relationships between concepts locking a concept X implies *read-locks* for all super-concepts of X and all their super-concepts, recursively. A read-lock marks a resource as being read-only, i.e. modifications to it are currently disallowed. If a read-lock for at least one superconcept cannot be achieved X will not be locked and the BOT fails. Thus, no operations may modify X. Read-locks can be yielded to multiple clients at the same time without conflict. If a client is the only one that read-locked a resource the client can achieve a stricter (write-)lock. Other clients cannot.

The reason why a lock propagates from one resource to another in the ontology can be seen in the following example scenario: Assume, X is a subconcept of Y and Y has a slot A with range Y. Assume, we want to restrict the value range of A for X from Y to X. Thus, in the BOT we just lock the concept X and call the appropriate operation on X. Before we send the commit another client (after locking Y) changes the name of A to B and commits. If we now commit our transaction the semantics of the combined operations is not defined. Does X now have two independent attributes A and B? Or is attribute A totally lost as well as our newly defined range restriction? Both situations are unsatisfactory. Thus, to prevent them superconcepts need to be read-locked.

The same holds for locking complete subtrees of the concept hierarchy. Here all subconcepts are locked in the same way as the root of the subtree and all superconcepts of the root. All superconcepts of the subconcepts of the root must be read-locked. This is necessary only if multiple-inheritance is allowed. Because the same rules for computing super- and subobjects of concepts etc. are available in the client and in the server some decisions whether a transaction is allowed or not may be made on the client side without connecting to the server. Thus the amount of queries sent over the network is reduced and processing times are enhanced.

5   Evaluation Phase

The last step in ontology development is about evaluating the formal ontology. The goal of the evaluation phase is to check whether the ontology fulfills the requirements specified during the first stage of the methodology (cf. Section 3). OntoEdit tackles several aspects for evaluation, i.e. (i) test sets of instances and axioms can be used for the analysis of typical queries, (ii) a graphical axiom editor in combination with an underlying inference engine[8] allows for error avoidance and location, (iii) competency questions might be formalized into queries and evaluated by using the facilities of (i) and (ii) and, last but not least, (iv) a namespace mechanism allows for using the facilities (i) – (iii) collaboratively.

Analysis of Typical Queries. The ontology engineer may interactively construct and save instances and axioms. OntoEdit contains a simple instance editor and an axiom editor that the ontology engineer can use to create test sets. A test set can be automatically processed and checked for consistency. Once the ontology evolves and needs changes to remain up-to-date, a test set may be re-used for checking validity of the ontology. This basic functionality is e.g. needed during the usage of Competency Questions.

Error Avoidance and Location. While the generation and validation of test cases allows for detection of errors, it does not really support the localization of errors. The set of all axioms, class and instance definitions express sometimes complex relationships and axioms often interact with other axioms when processed. Thus it is frequently very difficult to overview the correctness of a set of axioms and detect the faulty ones. In order to avoid problems, OntoEdit allows for defining several standardized properties of relationships by clicking on the GUI (viz. symmetry, transitivity and inverseness of relations) and a graphical rule editor for other types of axioms. In order to locate problems, OntoEdit takes advantage of the underlying inference engine, which allows for introspection and also comes with a debugger. A very simple but effective method to test axioms with test cases is e.g. to switch off and switch on axioms. A more sophisticated approach uses visualizations of proof trees by tracking back the drawn inferences to the test instances. Therefore semantic errors in rules may be discovered. A more detailed description of OntoEdit facilities for the "analysis of typical queries" and "error avoidance and location" can be found in [SSA+02].

Usage of Competency Questions. Competency Questions may help in two ways for evaluation. Firstly, they might provide prototypical instances for a test set (see above). Secondly, CQs itself define requirements for the ontology (–based application), therefore they provide a checklist of questions the ontology should be able to answer. E.g. from the CQ "Who is head of a research workgroup?" the concept Workgroup and the relation HEADOFGROUP (with domain Researcher and range Workgroup) are identified as relevant elements and therefore modeled in the ontology. A prototypical instance is e.g. an instance of Researcher, viz. "Rudi Studer", who is HEADOFGROUP of an instance of Workgroup, viz. the "Knowledge Management Group". Each CQ may now be formalized with the facilities described above into a query which is executed by the inference engine. The query result may be used to check whether the requirements expressed by the CQs are fulfilled by the current ontology.

---

[8] The underlying inference engine used for processing of axioms is Ontobroker (cf. [DEFS99])

Collaborative Evaluation. The three facilities above can be used collaboratively through support from the backbone inference engine for the handling of multiple test sets. A namespace mechanism allows for syntactically splitting up ontologies or ontology parts (i.e. concepts, relations, instances and axioms) into modules that can be processed by a single instance or separate instances of the inference engine. Members of the engineering team usually have different requirements and use case scenarios, e.g. expressed by their different CQs, therefore they typically need separate test sets for evaluation. In a two step approach we (i) evaluate locally each test set, i.e. each member (or e.g. each pair of ontology engineer and domain expert) evaluates his CQs, and (ii) evaluate globally the conjunction of test sets.

6 Related Work

A good overview, viz. a comparative study of existing tools up to 1999, is given in [DSW+99]. Typically the internal knowledge model of ontology engineering environments is capable of deriving is-a hierarchies of concepts and attached relations. On top of that we provide facilities for axiom modeling and debugging. Naturally, it could not fully consider the more recent developments, e.g. Protégé [NFM00], and WebODE [ACFLGP01].

WebODE has a well-known methodological backbone, viz. METHONTOLOGY, and is designed to integrate numerous aspects of an ontology lifecycle. [ACFLGP01] mentions that it offers inferencing services (developed in Prolog) and an axiom manager (providing functionalities such as an axiom library, axiom patterns and axiom parsing and verification), but the very brief mentioning of these functionalities is too short to assess precisely. About collaboration, it is said that this is supported at the knowledge level, but how this is achieved remains open.

Environments like **Protégé** [NFM00] or **Chimaera** [MFRW00] offer sophisticated support for ontology engineering and merging of ontologies. Protégé also has a modular plug-in design rational like OntoEdit, but lacks of sophisticated support for collaborative engineering. They provide limited methodological and collaborative support for ontology engineering. A system well-known for it's reasoning support is **OilEd** [BHGS01] in combination with the description logics (DL) reasoner **FaCT** [BHGS01]. Their collaborative and methodological support is rather weak.

Some tools explicitly support collaboration during ontology engineering. **APECKS** [TS98] is targeted mainly for use by domain experts, possibly in the absence of a knowledge engineer, and its aim is to foster and support debate about domain ontologies. It does not enforce consistency nor correctness, and instead allows different conceptualisations of a domain to coexist. **Tadzebao** [Dom98] supports argument between users on the ontology design, using text, GIF images and even hand drawn sketches. The strength of these approaches lies in the advanced support for communication. In contrast we provide a more sophisticated support for fine-granular locking of the ontology.

The web-based **Ontosaurus** [SPKR96] combines support for collaboration with reasoning and allow individuals to add to an ontology only when consistency is retained within the ontology as a whole. This approach takes advantage of the underlying representation language LOOM's reasoning abilities and consistency checking. Ontosaurus was inspired by the **Ontolingua** system [FFR96], which does not integrate an inferencing support as integral part of the ontology development environment. Due to the simple "state-less" HTML interaction, both systems have several limitations. E.g. does a server not maintain any state information about users, i.e. clients. Nor is it possible for a server to initiate an interaction on its own, e.g. alerting users to simultaneous changes by others. In general, no other approach is known to us that implemented fine-granular locking of ontologies like we do.

7   Conclusion

In this paper we presented (i) a motivational scenario, viz. the development of an ontology for the semantic portal of our institute, (ii) the methodology for ontology development that was applied in the scenario, (iii) the advanced collaborative tool support of OntoEdit for each step of the methodology. OntoEdit also has some features that could not be presented here, e.g. an extremely capable plug-in structure, a lexicon component, and an ontology mapping plug-in.

For the future, OntoEdit is planned to be developed in several directions: (i) The collaborative facilities will be further expanded, e.g. by adding a rights- and user-management layer on top of the locking mechanism and integrating communication and workgroup facilities (ii) new im- and exports will be developed, (ii) the integration of ontology construction with requirements specification documents will be generalized by means of semantic document annotation and (iv) the mind map™ tool will be integrated tighter into the ontology engineering process, e.g. through enabling direct communication between the tool and an ontology server, to name but a few.

Acknowledgements

Research for this paper was partially funded by EU in the project IST-1999-10132 "On-To-Knowledge".

References

ACFLGP01. J.C. Arprez, O. Corcho, M. Fernandez-Lopez, and A. Gomez-Perez. WebODE: a scalable workbench for ontological engineering. In *Proceedings of the First International Conference on Knowledge Capture (K-CAP) Oct. 21-23, 2001, Victoria, B.C., Canada*, 2001.

BHGS01. S. Bechhofer, I. Horrocks, C. Goble, and R. Stevens. OilEd: A reason-able ontology editor for the semantic web. In *KI-2001: Advances in Artificial Intelligence*, LNAI 2174, pages 396–408. Springer, 2001.

Buz74. T. Buzan. *Use your head*. BBC Books, 1974.

DEFS99. S. Decker, M. Erdmann, D. Fensel, and R. Studer. Ontobroker: Ontology based access to distributed and semi-structured information. In R. Meersman et al., editor, *Database Semantics: Semantic Issues in Multimedia Systems*. Kluwer Academic, 1999.

Dom98. J. Domingue. Tadzebao and WebOnto: Discussing, browsing, and editing ontologies on the web. In *Proceedings of the 11th Knowledge Acquisition for Knowledge-Based Systems Workshop, April 18th-23rd. Banff, Canada*, 1998.

DSW⁺99.   A. J. Duineveld, R. Stoter, M. R. Weiden, B. Kenepa, and V. R. Benjamins. Won-
             derTools? A comparative study of ontological engineering tools. In *Proc. of the
             Twelfth Workshop on Knowledge Acquisition, Modeling and Management. Banff,
             Alberta, Canada. October 16-21, 1999*, 1999.

FFR96.   A. Farquhar, R. Fickas, and J. Rice. The Ontolingua Server: A tool for collaborative
             ontology construction. In *Proceedings of the 10th Banff Knowledge Acquisition for
             KnowledgeBased System Workshop (KAW'95)*, Banff, Canada, November 1996.

Han01.   Siegfried Handschuh. Ontoplugins – a flexible component framework. Technical
             report, University of Karlsruhe, May 2001.

Hor98.   I. Horrocks. Using an expressive description logic: FaCT or fiction? In *Proceedings
             of KR 1998*, pages 636–649. Morgan Kaufmann, 1998.

LGPSS99.   M. F. Lopez, A. Gomez-Perez, J. P. Sierra, and A. P. Sierra. Building a chemical
             ontology using Methontology and the Ontology Design Environment. *Intelligent
             Systems*, 14(1), January/February 1999.

LS02.   T. Lau and Y. Sure. Introducing ontology-based skills management at a large insur-
             ance company. In *Proceedings of the Modellierung 2002*, Tutzing, Germany, March
             2002.

MFRW00.   D. McGuinness, R. Fikes, J. Rice, and S. Wilder. An environment for merging
             and testing large ontologies. In *Proceedings of KR 2000*, pages 483–493. Morgan
             Kaufmann, 2000.

MSS⁺02.   A. Maedche, S. Staab, R. Studer, Y. Sure, and R. Volz. SEAL – Tying up information
             integration and web site management by ontologies. *IEEE-CS Data Engineering
             Bulletin, Special Issue on Organizing and Discovering the Semantic Web*, March
             2002. To appear.

NFM00.   N. Fridman Noy, R. Fergerson, and M. Musen. The knowledge model of Protégé-
             2000: Combining interoperability and flexibility. In *Proceedings of EKAW 2000*,
             LNCS 1937, pages 17–32. Springer, 2000.

SAA⁺99.   G. Schreiber, H. Akkermans, A. Anjewierden, R. de Hoog, N. Shadbolt, W. Van de
             Velde, and B. Wielinga. *Knowledge Engineering and Management — The Com-
             monKADS Methodology*. The MIT Press, Cambridge, Massachusetts; London, Eng-
             land, 1999.

SPKR96.   B. Swartout, R. Patil, K. Knight, and T. Russ. Toward distributed use of large-scale
             ontologies. In *Proceedings of the 10th Knowledge Acquisition Workshop (KAW'96)*,
             Banff, Canada, November 1996.

SSA⁺02.   Y. Sure, S. Staab, J. Angele, D. Wenke, and A. Maedche. OntoEdit: Guiding on-
             tology development by methodology and inferencing. In *Submitted to: Prestigious
             Applications of Intelligent Systems (PAIS), in conjunction with ECAI 2002, July
             21-26 2002, Lyon, France*, 2002.

SSSS01.   S. Staab, H.-P. Schnurr, R. Studer, and Y. Sure. Knowledge processes and ontolo-
             gies. *IEEE Intelligent Systems, Special Issue on Knowledge Management*, 16(1),
             January/Febrary 2001.

TS98.   J. Tennison and N. Shadbolt. APECKS: A tool to support living ontologies. In *Pro-
             ceedings of the 11th Knowledge Acquisition Workshop (KAW'98)*, Banff, Canada,
             April 1998.

UK95.   M. Uschold and M. King. Towards a methodology for building ontologies. In
             *Workshop on Basic Ontological Issues in Knowledge Sharing, held in conjunction
             with IJCAI-95*, Montreal, Canada, 1995.

Towards a Modification Exchange Language
for Distributed RDF Repositories

Wolfgang Nejdl[1], Wolf Siberski[1], Bernd Simon[2], and Julien Tane[1, 3]

[1]Learning Lab Lower Saxony, Expo Plaza 1, 30539 Hannover, Germany
{nejdl, siberski, tane}@learninglab.de
[2]Abteilung für Wirtschaftsinformatik, Neue Medien, Wirtschaftsuniversität Wien,
Augasse 2-6, A-1090 Vienna, Austria
bernd.simon@wu-wien.ac.at
[3]Universität Karlsruhe, Institut AIFB, Karlsruhe, Englerstr. 11, 76131 Karlsruhe, Germany

Abstract. Many RDF repositories have already been implemented with various access languages and mechanisms. The aim of the EDUTELLA framework is to allow communication between different RDF repository implementations. Part of EDUTELLA is a Query Exchange Language (QEL) which can be used as lingua franca to retrieve information from RDF repositories. This work shows why we also need standardization of distributed modification capabilities. We describe use case scenarios for annotation and replication services and use them as guideline for our approach towards a Modification Exchange Language (MEL) for distributed RDF repositories.

1 Introduction

In order to realize the Semantic Web, repositories storing metadata on information and services need to become interoperable [0]. While a lot of query mechanisms and languages currently do exist, the realization of the Semantic Web still requires a lingua franca allowing interactions between repositories for the purpose of managing metadata in a distributed manner.

The EDUTELLA framework aims to provide an RDF-based infrastructure which allows services to exchange metadata via a peer-to-peer network [0]. A peer-to-peer architecture goes beyond the boundaries of a classical client-server architecture. Each node can act as a provider or consumer of information and services. The network as a whole provides a discovery mechanism for finding relevant information and service providers. This approach increases the flexibility of system design and contributes to a more effective infrastructure for discovery, delivery and processing of information and service [0]. We envision a peer-to-peer infrastructure as the primary infrastructure for the Semantic Web, due to the increased heterogeneity of interoperable, high-level services we expect on the Semantic Web.

Currently peer-to-peer networks are based on proprietary protocols. In order to make heterogeneous peer-to-peer networks interoperable, gateways have to be designed, which are based on open protocols with a well-defined semantic [0]. EDUTELLA already offers the possibility to refine and optimize information search via protocols for querying metadata from RDF repositories. Hence, a first step

I. Horrocks and J. Hendler (Eds.): ISWC 2002, LNCS 2342, pp. 236–249, 2002.

towards the interoperability of metadata repositories has been achieved by the definition of a Query Exchange Language. However, this is insufficient when it comes to annotation and replication within a network of distributed metadata repositories, where also a standardized mechanism to communicate metadata changes is needed.

In this paper we present a basic language designed for communicating metadata changes between distributed RDF repositories. The paper is organized as follows: In Section 2 use cases identifying our functional requirements are described. In Section 3 we discuss initial considerations, which are used as the basis for the design of our proposed language. This language, the Modification Exchange Language, is described in Section 4 as a possible means to standardize modification requests to RDF repositories. Section 5 addresses related work, and Section 6 presents concluding remarks.

2   Use Cases

To show why we need a standardized modification interface to RDF repositories we present two exemplifying use cases [0]. The first use case illustrates the need for replicating RDF repositories, a special instance of a general modification use case. The second use case describes the need for a Modification Exchange Language in the context of collaborative metadata authoring.

2.1 Integrated Systems for Teaching and Learning

In this use case two types of peers are involved: a learning management system (LMS), which supports instructors in the process of delivering learning, and a brokerage system (BS), which provides facilities for the exchange of learning resources.

A BS for learning resources supports instructors preparing their courses, by making educational content such as electronic textbooks, lecture notes, exercises, case studies, etc. stored at dispersed content repositories available at single virtual node. The idea behind brokerage systems is to support the re-use of learning resources and the collaborative development of it. Examples for brokerage systems for learning resources are: UNIVERSAL (http://www.ist-universal.org), Merlot (http://www.merlot.org), and GEM - The Gateway to Educational Materials (http://www.thegateway.org). Where as systems such as GEM and Merlot provide a loose integration of the various content sources via hyperlinks, UNIVERSAL aims at providing a tighter integration allowing the BS to grant and withdraw access rights at remote delivery systems based on learning resource metadata stored on a central node.

An LMS typically holds various learning resources in a repository. Instructors combine those resources to courses, which are then presented to their learners according to a course curriculum. Some learning management systems, for example Hyperwave's E-learning Suite, enables the sharing of individual learning resources among all instructors registered at a single system installation. Instructors can query the repository of a single system installation in order to search for an appropriate resource of one of their peers, which they would like to re-use in their own course.

However, up to now an open exchange of learning resources beyond the boundaries of single system installation is not available due to the lack of an appropriate infrastructure. One requirement for such an infrastructure would be the ability to replicate metadata describing learning resources of one LMS to a BS, so that it can be cached there and queried directly by all users of the BS. Metadata replication is a key element in such a usage scenario, which requires modification commands such as insert, update, and delete to be executed at remote copies of an RDF repository.

A survey [0] has shown that instructors have a clear preference towards opening already existing learning resource repositories selectively compared to redundantly uploading and managing their learning resources onto a central server. As a result, brokerage systems such as UNIVERSAL are aiming at making the metadata of dispersed learning resources available without requiring instructors to upload resources to a central server.

Integrating an LMS with a BS creates a peer-to-peer network, where the combination of both types of peers creates a new system with an added value. Whereas an LMS provides basic functionality for managing learning resources, a BS enhances this functionality by providing means for specifying usage conditions of the learning resources offered. In order to realize such a scenario of integrated services, brokerage systems are required to include the metadata describing learning resources stored at distributed LMS, so that it can provide customized offers of learning resources to remote instructors [0, 0].

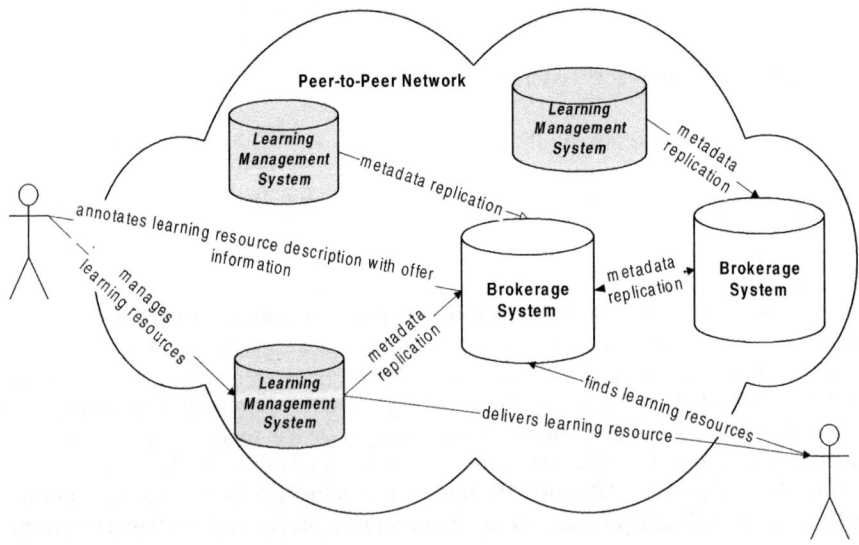

Fig. 1. Integrating LMS and BS by means of metadata replication

Figure 1 shows users interacting with an LMS and a BS using the LMS for providing general metadata on learning resources, for example title or educational objective, whereas the BS is used for specifying offer-related information such as price or usage restrictions. One can envision an extension scenario, where multiple brokerage systems use replication in order to enhance their repositories with content descriptions of allied systems. In a similar way replicating metadata from a BS to an LMS would be required, when an LMS aims to provide facilities for querying and presenting metadata of remote resources via its own user interface.

2.2 Collaborative Annotation

One of the core components of the Semantic Web is to have metadata available in a machine and human-understandable format. As part of the KAON Framework [0], the Ontomat annotizer [0] has been developed to tackle this need. It provides facilities for annotation and annotation-enhanced authoring KAON uses the same format for metadata and ontology, namely RDF, whose advantages have been agreed on by a large community of users [0].

On the one hand, realizing high quality markup is perceived to be a crucial aspect in the context of the Semantic Web [0]. On the other hand, annotation is a time consuming effort. As a result a collaborative approach for sharing, both, existing metadata and the annotation work has been proposed [0], which contributes to a reduction in costs.

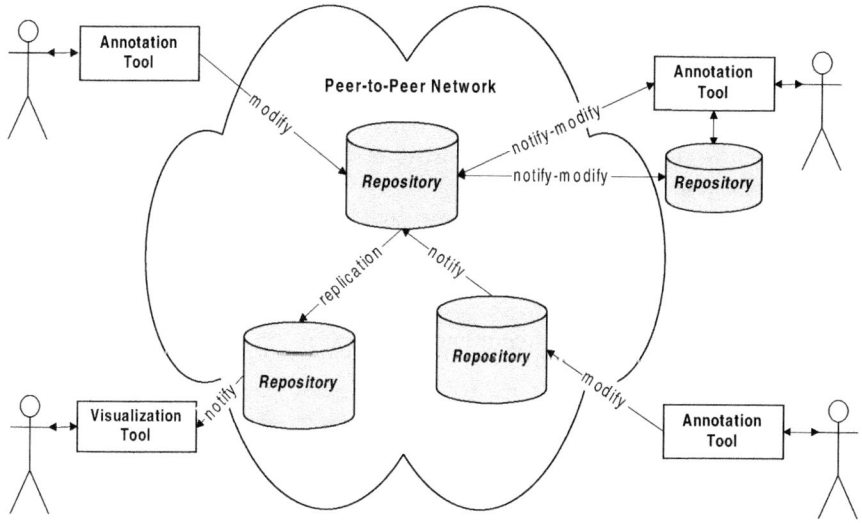

Fig. 2. Collaborative metadata authoring by means of notification and modification mechanisms

In order to preserve coherence between institutions, collaboration support for metadata authoring has to consider decentralization and a high level of heterogeneity. Indeed, each annotator may have different goals, use different tools and belong to diverse institutions. The important point is then to allow interaction between annotating applications and storage components without imposing the need for central control entities or a specific annotation framework.

Building on the query mechanism of the EDUTELLA project, the possibility to retrieve, both, metadata and ontologies has been added to the KAON framework in order to address collaborative aspects of metadata annotation. In addition, due to the distributed storage, performing collaborative work requires two important functionalities: notification and modification. First, other annotators might want to be notified of any recent change. Second, the metadata may be stored in a dispersed manner and accessed by annotators. This means that a modification protocol has to be designed to address the different needs imposed by collaborative annotation.

Collaborative metadata authoring tools can make great use of replication mechanisms. There are at least two reasons for this: First, performing queries for dispersed annotations may take too long. Hence, a caching mechanism relying on metadata replication can improve the overall system performance. Second, in a peer-to-peer network, peers are not expected to be constantly accessible. Replication would allow the annotator to have continuing access to previous states of annotation, which are updated as soon as the source repository becomes accessible again.

3 Design Considerations

Like the Query Exchange Language (QEL) the Modification Exchange Language (MEL) proposed in this paper is based on RDF. This has several advantages:
- In the spirit of the Semantic Web, messages are self-describing in a format suitable to be processed by all kinds of RDF tools;
- When stored persistently the messages build a journal of all modifications of a repository. As such a journal also consists of RDF statements, it can be queried using QEL queries;
- Existing approaches to describe statements and select RDF subgraphs can be used;
- By encoding the commands[1] in the message we avoid the need for a standardized repository API with operations for each command type.

The drawback of RDF-encoded messages is that the messages become quite bloated, as reification is needed with its circumstantial syntax.

3.1 Granularity Levels of Modification Commands

In an RDF-based environment several granularity levels of the minimum amount of metadata which can be addressed by a modification request can be distinguished: statement, resource with properties (either all properties or restricted by scope) or subgraphs. Each granularity has certain advantages and drawbacks:
- *Statement-centered*: Addressing RDF statements is the simplest solution. However, when updating statements (which will probably be the most frequent action compared to insert and delete) the lack of statement identifier in RDF causes

---

[1] In the context of RDBMS or other storage systems typically the terms 'insert/update/delete *statement*' are used. To avoid confusion with RDF statements, we use the term '*command*' instead.

difficulties. Essentially only insert and delete commands are available, and the complete triples have to be sent whenever a statement has to be deleted.

- **Resource-centered**: If change actions are grouped by resource, the set of all statements having the same resource as subject becomes the smallest modification unit. For inserts this leads to the same behavior as with the statement-centered approach. Delete operations can be performed by just submitting the URI of the resource. When updating a resource all statements regarding this resource have to be sent even when only some properties have changed. This is again unavoidable because of the missing statement identifier. Imagine a repository has stored (myCourse contributor A), (myCourse contributor B). Then an update statement arrives stating (myCourse contributor C). How should the resulting contributor set look like? AC, BC, ABC or C are possible choices, but to enable deletions the last choice is the only feasible. To avoid sending too much redundant information an update command could be scoped by a reference to a schema or schema element.

- **Subgraph-centered**: RDF query languages can deliver the query result as a subgraph of the repository. Therefore we can design modification commands as a combination of a query to specify the affected statements and a specification of the changes to these statements. For example, an update would consist of a query specifying the changed statement(s) and the description of the new statement(s). The repository can then change the selected statements accordingly.

For MEL we chose the subgraph-centered approach for the following reasons:

- This approach can handle variables in the modification specifications; while other approaches require explicit specification of all statements to be changed, this approach also supports change patterns.
- It enables replacing the object part of a statement without knowing its actual value.
- It integrates nicely with the existing query language QEL, which can be used to specify the subgraph selection.

In order to avoid the occurrence of inconsistent states of RDF repositories caused by remote modification commands, atomic modification commands have to be grouped into transactions. The handling of such transactions is often solved by sending the modification commands one by one, followed by a commit command. Such a design requires a stateful communication protocol, which is more complex and requires more resources than a stateless solution. We prefer the latter, and therefore allow modification messages to contain multiple commands which possibly form a logical unit. The repository can process such a message in one chunk, thereby avoiding the need to store a communication state.

3.2 Replication Design

Replication is a widely discussed topic in computer science and information systems research. Replication of data is required to increase the performance of a global information system [0] or enhance the reliability of a storage media [0]. Caching is a special form of data replication where the emphasize lies on improving the response time of systems for the most frequently accessed data [0]. It has been shown [0] that converting passive caches into replicated servers improves transmission times and results in a more evenly distributed bandwidth usage (because the replicas can be updated during low-traffic hours). In the context of the Semantic Web replication is an important mechanism for establishing value chains of integrated peers. Metadata needs to be forwarded from peer A to peer B, because peer B may be capable of providing a special service (e.g. brokerage of learning resources) peer A (e.g. a learning management system) is not able to provide.

The following list summarizes design considerations of replication mechanisms:

- Primary design objective: increased availability and reliability;
- Traceability of data providers: traceable vs. anonymous;
- Communication mode: synchronous vs. asynchronous, also called eager replication vs. lazy replication [0];
- Degree of initial modification distribution: update everywhere vs. primary copy, also called active vs. passive replication;
- Degree of consistency: strong consistency vs. weak consistency [0].

Our primary design objective of the replication protocol is to increase the availability of data in order to create value chains of integrated peers.

Currently we assume that the primary copies know their replicas and vice versa. Providers will be traceable by system; creating a (semi-) anonymous replication protocol is not a design goal here. Other, more complex, approaches would be:

- The primary copy publishes its changes to replication hubs which distribute them to the replicas.
- Replicas fetch changes from their primary copies on a scheduled basis.

Synchronous replication requires locking since an update transaction must update copies before it commits [0]. In a peer-to-peer environment synchronous replication is not feasible, because of temporary (un)availability of peers. This also supports the primary copy approach, where the metadata is updated at the repository holding the primary copy first, and is then distributed to the replicas. To avoid complex reconciliation procedures, modification commands must be sent to the primary copy first.

An RDF repository holding replicated metadata from more than one location will have to preserve the originating context with the metadata for the following reasons:

- Statements from different origins may be contradictory. Merging such statements into one statement would invalidate the complete repository content. When the context is preserved, one way to handle such cases would be to return separate results for each context. A more sophisticated solution could assign trust levels to replicated repositories and filter statements from less trusted repositories when contradictions occur.
- When merging repositories without considering their origin, delete and update actions may lead to undesired effects. One can imagine the following scenario: Professor X changes from university A to university B. Both universities are providing meta data about their staff, which are replicated by peer C. As X is now member of the staff of B, B inserts (among others) the statement (X teaches Economics) into its repository. This statement is replicated to C. Some time later, A deletes all statements about X from its repository, among them the statement (X teaches Economics). This must not result in the deletion of this statement at C because the statement is also asserted by B. C can handle this case correctly only if it stores the origins of all statements.

It is also advisable that the replicas know were the primary copy is stored when tight consistency is needed [0]. For example, a user at the BS intends to book a resource, the BS has to check back whether this resource is still available and provide the latest offer terms. In this case referring back to the primary copy is advisable.

3.3 Annotation Design

As described in the use case above, collaborative metadata authoring requires to be supported by an distributed environment and without a central control entity. Peer-to-peer networks address this need.

The heterogeneity problem of the annotation applications and storages can then be addressed by defining a set of application independent protocols for the exchange of metadata. However, we saw that exchanging metadata is not sufficient for a collaborative annotation scenario. A modification protocol should also be designed in order to allow:

Change notification: Annotators need to be informed of changes which could influence their annotation work. Basically, they need to know what has been inserted, updated or deleted. Moreover, the notifications should be as comprehensive and expressive as possible. Therefore, using the *subgraph-centered* approach should help to make modifications more easily visualizable.

Change request: Different annotators using a set of different repositories need a neutral way to request changes in the metadata that they store. If all use and support the same modification protocol, the actual task can be left to the implementation of the repository.

Some modifications might not require that you have specific information about which object you want to modify. For example, the set of all pages written by a given author might be marked as "regularly-updated".

4   The Modification Exchange Language (MEL)

4.1 Introduction

MEL is based on QEL, which is an RDF representation for Datalog queries. Datalog is a non-procedural query language based on Horn clauses. In this language a query consists of literals (predicates expressions describing relations between variables and constants) and a set of rules [0].

As in SQL we provide the commands *insert*, *delete* and *update*. All commands use a statement specification to describe the affected statements.

We describe the syntax in an informal notation similar to EBNF (Extended Backus-Naur Form)[2].

```
statementSpec = subjectSpec propertySpec objectSpec
subjectSpec = subject resourceSpec
propertySpec = property resourceSpec
objectSpec = object (resourceSpec | literalSpec)
resourceSpec = URI
```

---

[2] EBNF is not well suited for specifying RDF messages formally, because no order of the statements can and should be prescribed, but it allows a concise description.

literalSpec = STRING

A special type of resourceSpec is a variable, which must be declared in the command:
variableDeclaration = *hasVariable* resourceSpec

4.2 Format of Modification Commands

The *Delete* command consists of a statement specification and optionally a query constraint. All statements in the repository matching the specification are deleted. A constraintSpec can be any QEL query.

deleteCommand = *Delete* statementSpec {variableDeclaration} [constraintSpec]

The following example deletes all statements with property *dc:comment* and a subject of *rdf:type ...#Book* from the repository:

```
<edu:Delete rdf:about="#delete_cmd">
  <edu:oldStatement rdf:resource="#del_stmt"/>
  <edu:hasVariable rdf:resource="#U"/>
  <edu:hasVariable rdf:resource="#V"/>
  <edu:hasConstraint rdf:resource="#del_constraint"/>
</edu:Delete>

<edu:DeletedStatement rdf:about="#del_stmt">
  <rdf:subject rdf:resource="#U"/>
  <rdf:predicate rdf:resource="&dcq;comment"/>
  <rdf:object rdf:resource="#V"/>
</edu:QueryStatement>

<!-- QEL-1 query -->
<edu:Query rdf:about="#del_constraint">
  <edu:hasVariable rdf:resource="#U"/>
</edu:Query>

<edu:Variable rdf:about="#U">
  <rdf:type rdf:resource="http://www.lit.edu/types#Book"/>
</edu:Variable>
```

The *Insert* command syntax is similar to the delete syntax. Here the statement specification describes the new statements.

insertCommand = *Insert* statementSpec {variableDeclaration} [constraintSpec]

The simplest case is an insert of one RDF statement:

```
<edu:Insert rdf:about="#insert_cmd1">
  <edu:newStatement rdf:resource="#insert1_stmt"/>
</edu:Insert>

<edu:InsertedStatement rdf:about="#insert1_stmt">
  <rdf:subject
     rdf:resource="http://www.mylib.org/books#Book37"/>
  <rdf:predicate rdf:resource="&dc;title"/>
  <rdf:object rdf:resource="The Magic of RDF"/>
</edu:QueryStatement>
```

It is also possible to insert more than one statement with a single command. Suppose you want to add a book collection to a library. The following command inserts a new property lendingState for all resources of type Book, preparing all books for library business with one statement:

```
<edu:Insert rdf:about="insert_cmd2">
  <edu:newStatement rdf:resource="#insert2_stmt"/>
  <edu:hasConstraint rdf:resource="#insert2_constraint"/>
  <edu:hasVariable rdf:resource="#W"/>
</edu:Insert>

<edu:InsertedStatement rdf:about="#insert2_stmt">
  <rdf:subject rdf:resource="#W"/>
  <rdf:predicate rdf:resource="&lib;lendingState"/>
  <rdf:object rdf:resource="&lib;available"/>
</edu:QueryStatement>

<edu:Query rdf:about="#insert2_constraint">
  <edu:hasVariable rdf:resource="#W"/>
</edu:Query>

<edu:Variable rdf:about="#W">
  <rdf:type rdf:resource="http://www.lit.edu/types#Book"/>
</edu:Variable>
```

Update commands require two statement specifications, one for the replaced statements and one for the replacing statements:

updateCommand = *Update* 2*statementSpec {variableDeclaration} [constraintSpec]

The following example updates the modification date of the resource with the title 'Sample':

```
<edu:Update rdf:about="#update_cmd">
  <edu:newStatement rdf:resource="#new_stmt"/>
  <edu:oldStatement rdf:resource="#old_stmt"/>
  <edu:hasConstraint rdf:resource="#update_constraint"/>
  <edu:hasVariable rdf:resource="#X"/>
  <edu:hasVariable rdf:resource="#Y"/>
</edu:Update>

<edu:OriginalStatement rdf:about="#old_stmt">
  <rdf:subject rdf:resource="#X"/>
  <rdf:predicate rdf:resource="&dcq;modified"/>
  <rdf:object rdf:resource="#Y"/>
</edu:QueryStatement>

<edu:InsertedStatement rdf:about="#new_stmt">
  <rdf:subject rdf:resource="#X"/>
  <rdf:predicate rdf:resource="&dcq;modified"/>
  <rdf:object>
    <dcq:W3CDTF>
      <rdf:value>2002-02-03T:15:34:16+01:00</rdf:value>
    </dcq:W3CDTF>
  </rdf:object>
</edu:QueryStatement>
```

```
<edu:Query rdf:about="#update_constraint">
  <edu:hasVariable rdf:resource="#X"/>
</edu:Query>

<edu:Variable rdf:about="#X">
  <dc:title>Sample</dc:title>
</edu:Variable>
```

4.3 Format of Modification Messages

Each modification message is identified by a unique message identifier, which ensures the correct ordering of messages. This identifier is formed of at least two components (time, identifier of the modification originator) and an optional third one (request count). The originator identifier is a Universal Unique Identifier (UUID). A mechanism has to guarantee that UUIDs are unique, for example by combining hardware addresses, and random seeds. Time is coded using W3C's version of the date and time format (http://www.w3.org/TR/NOTE-datetime) with complete date plus hours, minutes, seconds and time zone designator. If multiple modification messages are created within a second, a request count can be used to uniquely identify the request.

messageID = originator timestamp [number]
originator = *messageOriginator* UUID
timestamp = *messageTimestamp* W3CDTF
number = *messageNumber* DIGIT

A modification message can hold multiple synchronization commands, which can be either an insert, delete or update command. All commands (and other necessary resources) are identified by a unique local fragment. The commands are contained in a sequence to preserve the order.

Additional message information can be added, for example when the message was created and modified for the last time, i.e. closed and prepared for sending it to the replicating peer. The name of the peer placing the request can also be attached.

message = messageID messageInformation commandList
messageInformation= {originator} {creationTime} {modificationTime}
commandList = {command}
command = insertCommand | updateCommand | deleteCommand
creationTime = W3CDTF
modificationTime = W3CDTF

An example is presented below:

```
<edu:ModificationMessage rdf:about="#msg1">
  <edu:messageOriginator>
    urn:jxta:uuid-BEFAF79B91504F2FA39FAEFE9C7A4602
  </edu:messageOriginator>

  <edu:messageTimestamp>
    <dcq:W3CDTF>
      <rdf:value>2002-02-03T:15:34:42+01:00</rdf:value>
    </dcq:W3CDTF>
```

```
   </edu:messageTimestamp>
   <edu:hasCommands>
     <rdf:Seq>
       <rdf:_1 rdf:resource="#cmd1"/>
       <rdf:_2 rdf:resource="#cmd2"/>
       <rdf:_3 rdf:resource="#cmd3"/>
     </rdf:Seq>
   </edu:hasCommands>
 </edu:ModificationMessage>
```

The receiving peer responds to the modification message by sending a response message which contains information about the update success.

5   Related Work

Several Web initiatives are currently extended with replication or modification protocols.

The Replication Architecture of the Lightweight Directory Access Protocol (LDAP) distinguishes between different replica types [0]. Each replica type has a certain set of operations assigned, which it is allowed to carry out. For example, the primary replica provides a full copy of the replica, to which all applications that require tight consistency direct their operations. On the contrary fractional replica accept only read-only LDAP operations. Introducing a hierarchy of replica peer types is worthwhile to consider in future versions of MEL.

The Universal Description, Discovery and Integration (UDDI) architecture [0] specifies the data replication process and interface required to achieve data replication between UDDI operators. The replication process makes use of XML. UDDI relies on SOAP, which provides the mechanism for using XML in simple message-based exchanges. UDDI operators sent controlled XML messages in order to communicate change records requests. The underlying message architecture is rather simple, as for example compared to LDAP, and does not support any semantically rich, self-containing messages.

The rdfDB Query Language [0] is a high level query language with a query syntax similar to SQLas far as selects are concerned. rdfDB provides modification commands according to the *statement-centered* approach: insert and delete commands which take lists of statements as an argument are available. Variables cannot be used within these commands.

Several other query languages are derived from rdfDB, e.g. RDQL [0] which is part of the Jena framework [0] and Inkling [0]. Interestingly, all of them have abandoned insert and delete and provide query capabilities only.

ANNOTEA is a client/server system for the creation of annotations [0]. All commands are sent to the server via HTTP. Commands to insert, update and delete annotations are provided, and a separate query language (Algae) is available. All messages are represented in RDF, enclosed in a HTTP PUT request. ANNOTEA uses the *resource-centered* approach. For insert as well as for update, the client sends all statements describing one resource in one chunk to the server. Update deletes all existing statements regarding the resource before inserting the sent statements. A delete message contains just the resource URI; the server deletes all statements where this resource is subject.

RQL [0] is a highly developed RDF query language used in RDFSuite [0] and Sesame [0]. It provides no modification commands, because in these systems repository modification is done through a special API.

TRIPLE [0] is an RDF query and transformation language based on frame logic, also without modification support.

6 Concluding Remarks

In this paper, we have discussed replication and annotation in a peer-to-peer network and extended QEL, the query language specified for EDUTELLA, with additional modification capabilities. We believe that standardizing a modification exchange language, such as the one proposed in this paper, will contribute to the evolution of the Semantic Web idea. Our work is a first step in this direction; we have not yet treated all necessary aspects for these services. For example, the question of how to authorize modification commands is an issue, which still has to be addressed. In addition a full validation of the use cases sketched still has to be carried out.

References

1. J. Helfin and J. Hendler. A Portrait of the Semantic Web in Action. IEEE Intelligent Systems, 16 (2), 54-59, 2001.
2. Wolfgang Nejdl, Boris Wolf, Changtao Qu, Stefan Decker, Michael Sintek, Ambjörn Naeve, Mikael Nilsson, Matthias Palmér and Tore Risch. EDUTELLA: A P2P Networking Infrastructure Based on RDF. Accepted for WWW2002, 2002.
3. L. Gong. Project JXTA: A Technology Overview. Sun Microsystems, Palo Alto, 2001.
4. B. Wiley. Interoperability Through Gateways. In: A. Oram (ed.), Peer-to-Peer - Harnessing the Power of Disruptive Technologies. O'Reilly, 2001.
5. I. Jacobsen and M. Christensen. Object-Oriented Software Engineering: A Use-Case Driven Approach. Addison-Wesley, Reading, 1992.
6. B. Simon. Faculty Members Meeting Electronic Education Markets - Determinants for Project Success. Working Paper, Department of Information Systems, Wirtschaftsuniversität Wien, Vienna, 2001.
7. S. Guth, G. Neumann and B. Simon. UNIVERSAL - Design Spaces for Learning Media. In: R. H. Sprague (ed.). Proceedings of the 34th Hawaii International Conference on System Sciences, 2001.
8. S. Brantner, T. Enzi, S. Guth, G. Neumann and B. Simon. UNIVERSAL - Design and Implementation of a Highly Flexible E-Market Place of Learning Resources. In: R. Hartley, Kinshuk, T. Okamoto and J. P. Klus (ed.). Proceedings of the IEEE International Conference on Advanced Learning Technologies, 2001.
9. The Karlsruhe Ontology and Semantic Web Tool Suite. http://kaon.aifb.uni-karlsruhe.de, 2001.
10. S. Handschuh, S. Staab and A. Mädche: CREAM - Creating relational metadata with a component-based, ontology-driven annotation framework. In: ACM K-CAP 2001. October, Vancouver, 2001.
11. S. Handschuh and S. Staab. Authoring and Annotation of Web Pages in CREAM. Accepted for WWW2002, 2002.

12. J. Hendler. Agents and the Semantic Web. IEEE Intelligent Systems, 16 (2), 30-37, 2001.
13. L. Qiu, V. N. Padmanabham, and G. M. Voelker. On the placement of web server replicas. In Proc. 20th IEEE INFOCOM, 2001.
14. B. Liskov, S. Ghemawat, R. Gruber, P. Johns, L. Shrira and M. Williams. Replication in the Harp file system. In: Proceedings of the 13th ACM Symposium on Operating Systems Principles, 1991.
15. R. Tewari, M. Dahlin, H. Vin, and J. Kay. Design Considerations for Distributed Caching on the Internet. In Proceedings of the Twentieth International Conference on Distributed Computing Systems, 1999.
16. M. Baentsch, L. Baum, G. Molter, S. Rothkugel and P. Sturm. Enhancing the Web's Infrastructure – From Caching to Replication. IEEE Internet Computing, 1(2):18--27, Mar. 1997.
17. J. Gray, P. Helland, P. O'Neil and D. Shasha. The dangers of replication and a solution. In: Proceedings of the 1996 ACM SIGMOD International Conference on Management of Data, 1996.
18. M. Wiesmann, F. Pedone, A. Schiper, B. Kemme and G. Alonso. Understanding replication in databases and distributed systems. In: Proceedings of 20th International Conference on Distributed Computing Systems (ICDCS'2000), Taipei, Taiwan, R.O.C. IEEE Computer Society Los Alamitos California, 2000.
19. B. Kemme and G. Alonso. A suite of database replication protocols based on group communication primitives. In: Proceedings of the 18th International Conference on Distributed Computing Systems (ICDCS), Amsterdam, The Netherlands, 1998.
20. J. Merrells, E, Reed, U. Srinivasan. LDAP Replication Architecture. IETF Internet Draft. http://www.ietf.org/internet-drafts/draft-ietf-ldup-model-06.txt, 2000.
21. R. Atkinson and J. Munter (eds.).UDDI Version 2.0 Replication Specification. uddi.org (2001). Available at http://www.uddi.org/pubs/Replication-V2.00-Open-20010608.pdf
22. R. V. Guha. RDFDB QL. http://web1.guha.com/rdfdb/query.html.
23. Andy Seaborne. RDQL - RDF Data Query Language. http://hpl.hp.com/semweb/rdql.html, 2001.
24. Brian McBride. Jena: Implementing the RDF Model and Syntax Specification. http://www-uk.hpl.hp.com/people/bwm/papers/20001221-paper/, 2000.
25. L. Miller. Inkling: RDF query using SquishQL. http://swordfish.rdfweb.org/rdfquery/ 2001.
26. J. Kahan, M. Koivunen, E. Prud'Hommeaux and R. Swick. Annotea: An Open RDF Infrastructure for Shared Web Annotations. In Proc. of the WWW10 International Conference. Hong Kong, 2001.
27. G. Karvounarakis, V. Christophides, D. Plexousakis and S. Alexaki. Querying CommunityWeb Portals. In: Proc. 17^{ièmes} Journees Bases de Donnees Avancees (BDA'01), Agadir, Maroc, 2001.
28. S. Alexaki, V. Christophides, G. Karvounarakis, D. Plexousakis and K. Tolle. The RDFSuite: Managing Voluminous RDF Description Bases. In: Proc. of the 2nd Int. Workshop on the Semantic Web, Hong-Kong, 2001.
29. J. Broekstra, A. Kampman and F. van Harmelen. Sesame: An Architecture for Storing and Querying RDF Data and Schema Information. In: D. Fensel, J. Hendler, H. Lieberman and W. Wahlster (eds.). Semantics for the WWW. MIT Press, 2001.
30. Michael Sintek and Stefan Decker. TRIPLE – An RDF Query, Inference, and Transformation Language. Deductive Databases and Knowledge Management Workshop (DDLP'2001), Japan, 2001.

Representing Disjunction and Quantifiers in RDF [*]

Drew McDermott and Dejing Dou

Yale Computer Science Department
New Haven, CT 06520, USA
{drew.mcdermott,dejing.dou}@yale.edu

Abstract. The advantage of the RDF/DAML+OIL family of languages over ordinary XML is that it is topic-neutral and composable. However, its expressivity is severely limited. This limitation is well known, and the usual remedy is *reification,* in which RDF is used to describe formulas in a richer language. We propose a method for encoding typed predicate calculus using reification, which handles bound variables cleanly and causes the size to increase by only a constant multiple. The method generalizes to virtually any system, a claim which we illustrate by describing our program, PDDAML, which encodes domain specifications in PDDL using our technique. We argue that reification, while logically suspect, is in practice benign because any algorithm capable of doing inferences using logical notations can be easily extended to "unreify" those notations as needed. We also argue that the ability to represent predicate calculus on the semantic web is crucial.

1   Introduction

The "semantic web" really ought to be called the "inferential web." Although people often talk as though RDF [7] and related tools such as DAML+OIL [12] specify the "meaning" of symbols, they really specify relations among symbols that allow inferences to be drawn. RDF can be thought of as a simple logical system in which assertions are made about objects denoted by URIs. By providing a uniform syntax, it allows for different RDF documents to be combined in a straightforward way. This contrasts with XML, in which the allowable contents of an element depend entirely on the meaning of its tag. In RDF, whether an element is a description or a property is easy to determine syntactically, and RDF puts no restrictions at all on what values a property can have. Hence an arbitrary RDF node can occur as the value of a property, and that node can itself have an indefinite amount of further descriptive material. A description in one document can be pointed to from another, without any restrictions on how the vocabularies of the two documents relate.

---

[*] This research was supported by the DARPA DAML program. The technical ideas in the paper were arrived in collaboration with Jonathan Borden, Mark Burstein, Doug Smith, and several other contributors to the www-rdf-logic mailing list.

I. Horrocks and J. Hendler (Eds.): ISWC 2002, LNCS 2342, pp. 250–263, 2002.

However, RDF does have limitations:

1. Its syntax is a graph structure, reminiscent of semantic networks. Such graph structures have well-known problems with scoping of quantifiers, negations, and disjunctions. RDF solves these problems by disallowing all these constructs. (Anonymous nodes can be considered to be existentially quantified, but the scope of the quantifier is the entire graph [5].)
2. It does not allow arbitrary terms, just bags and sequences.

There are two ways of fixing these bugs: by extending RDF, or by building on top of RDF using some sort of quotation device, such as reification. The former approach seems more natural, but runs into opposition from users and developers who believe that the simplicity of RDF is worth preserving. So in this paper we use the second approach.

Reification is the use of RDF to describe formulas in another language, which we call the *embedded language*. We use the word "another," but of course the language may look a lot like RDF itself. Describing a formula is a matter of providing an RDF graph whose properties correspond to the syntactic relations of the embedded language. For instance, consider a simple language whose grammar is

S → a | b | c
S → ⟨ S S S ⟩

The sentence ⟨ a ⟨ b b b ⟩ c ⟩ might be described by the RDF graph:

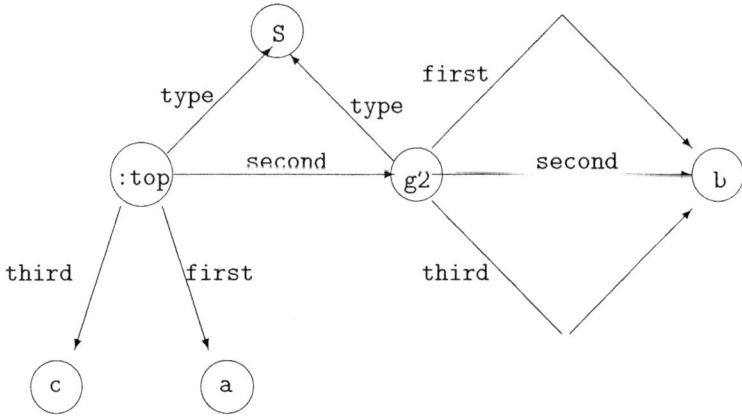

The graph is expressed in "triples" thus:

⟨top rdf:type S⟩
⟨top second g2⟩
⟨top third c⟩
⟨top first a⟩
⟨g2 rdf:type S⟩

```
⟨g2 first b⟩
⟨g2 second b⟩
⟨g2 third b⟩
```

Our goal in this paper is to explain how to embed logic in RDF using reification, and to argue that embedding logic this way is a good idea. We will use Lisp-like notation for logical formulas, specifically the typed logic of PDDL [8]. So the formula traditionally written as $\forall x(P(x) \supset Q(x))$ will be written as `(forall (x) (if (P x) (Q x)))`. If type declarations are involved, we declare the types of variables by writing "—*vars*— - *type*," as in

```
(forall (x y - animal)
    (if (and (predator x) (bigger x y))
        (fears y x)))
```

2   Our Approach

It is easy to do the wrong thing when embedding logic using reification. For instance, if one thinks of implication as a relationship between two reified formulas, then (if (if P Q) R) becomes a relationship between two objects, the first of which contains the reification of two reifications. As can be seen from the example above, reification blows up the size of anything it is applied to. We can tolerate one layer of this blowup, but any solution that requires reifications of reifications of . . . is ruled out.

Fortunately, this will not happen if we think of reifying entire expressions. Again appealing to our simple example, the fact that we have S's inside S's doesn't cause a blowup, because each S becomes a node of type S. Here we use *type* in the technical sense used in [7], and we view it as roughly synonymous with a DAML+OIL *class* [12]. To embed logic, we will simply take if, or, and other connectives to correspond to classes. So the formula (if (if P Q) R) will get transformed to

```
⟨top rdf:type drs:If⟩
⟨top drs:antecedent g3⟩
⟨top drs:consequent R⟩
⟨g3 rdf:type drs:If⟩
⟨g3 drs:antecedent P⟩
⟨g3 drs:consequent Q⟩
```

For conciseness we will use the N3 notation [1,2] for RDF instead of the XML serialization. The result is:

```
:top a drs:If;
    drs:antecedent [a drs:If;
                      drs:antecedent P;
                      drs:consequent Q];
    drs:consequent R.
```

Here we have pretended that P, Q, and R are atomic, but if they aren't we can just continue the process. We use the namespace prefix `drs:` to refer to symbols that are part of our system. For brevity, we will use `drs` as the default namespace, and drop it in what follows.

We extend N3 slightly, in the spirit of the type abbreviations used in [7]. When "a T" (N3's notation for `<rdf:type resource="`T`"/>`) occurs as the first element of a node (as it often, by convention, does), we use a little syntactic sugar to write it as $T/$. So the example above could be written:

```
:top If/
     antecedent [If/
                   antecedent P;
                   consequent Q];
     consequent R.
```

When we reach an atomic formula, of the form (*predicate* *—args—*), we use the basic trick of [7], describing it as having three parts, subject, predicate, and object. So (loves Fred Sally) would be represented as

```
[Atomic_formula/ rdf:subj Fred†;
                 rdf:pred loves†;
                 rdf:obj Sally†]
```

where we use daggers to remind you that in practice these terms will be resolved into URIs, or possibly something more complex.

The basic trick won't work unless there are exactly two *args*. In all other cases, we represent the arguments after the first by a *term sequence*, defined as a DAML+OIL list [12] whose elements are all terms.

Terms are defined in the usual way, as constants, variables, or *functional terms*, of the form (f *—args—*). We translate them into an instance of the class `Functional_term`, whose `function` property is $f^†$ and whose `term_args` property is a term sequence. So the logical formula

```
(child Bates (mother Bates) (father Bates))
```
"Bates is the child of Bates's mother and Bates's father."

would be translated into the RDF

```
[Atomic_formula/
 rdf:subj Bates†;
 rdf:pred child†;
 rdf:obj [Term_seq/
          rdf:_1 [Functional_term/
                  term_function mother†;
                  term_args[Term_seq/
                            rdf:_1 Bates†]];
          rdf:_2 [Functional_term/
                  term_function father†;
                  term_args [Term_seq/
                             rdf:_1 Bates†]]]]
```

Of course, we must also provide an XML serialization of the formula, which is what computers produce for consumption by other computers on the net:

```
<Atomic_formula>
    <rdf:subj> Bates† </rdf:subj>
    <rdf:pred> child† </rdf:pred>
    <rdf:obj>
        <Term_seq>
            <rdf:_1>
                    <Functional_term>
                        <term_function>mother†</term_function>
                        <term_args>
                            <Term_seq>
                                <rdf:_1>Bates†</rdf:_1>
                            </Term_seq>
                        </term_args>
                    </Functional_term>
            </rdf:_1>
            <rdf:_2>
                    <Functional_term>
                        <term_function>father†</term_function>
                        <term_args>
                            <Term_seq>
                                <rdf:_1>Bates†</rdf:_1>
                            </Term_seq>
                        </term_args>
                    </Functional_term>
            </rdf:_2>
        </Term_seq>
    </rdf:obj>
</Atomic_formula>
```

The only part of the translation framework left to explain is how variables are handled. The obvious variable binders (and declarers) are the standard quantifiers forall and exists, but there are other possibilities, such as the lambda expressions allowed by higher-order logic. Here we will focus on the standard quantifiers only, but the idea will work for all variable binders.

When a variable is declared, it is meaningful only within the scope of its quantifier. RDF provides no notion of scoping. A described entity may be given a name by the use of the ID attribute in a description of it. If you write <rdf:Description rdf:ID="x">, then anywhere else in the file you can refer to the object described by using the attribute resource="#x". Hence IDs behave like existential variables whose scope is the entire graph (or document) they occur in. There is no way to narrow the scope of an ID, thus avoiding name conflicts among variables that happen to have the same name. There is no way to declare an ID to correspond to a universally quantified variable.

The solution is to defer the issue to the quoted level. Name conflicts are avoided by making up a new name for each variable as it is encountered. Variables just become anonymous entities with features such as being universally quantified. So the formula (forall (x - Person) (moral_agent x)) would become

```
[Forall/
    quantifier_vars
        [variables_list/
            rdf:_1 :var_1];
    body
        [Atomic_formula/
            rdf:subj :var_1;
            rdf:pred moral_agent†]]
```

```
:var_1 a Var; name ''x"; type Person†.
```

Here we have made the rdf:type property ("a Var") of var_1 explicit, in order to contrast the rdf:type and the type (i.e., the drs:type) properties of a variable, which play two entirely different roles. The former identifies the the variable as a variable, syntactically; the second constrains the values of the variable to be objects of type Person.

The collection of classes Atomic_formula, Term_seq, etc. and their interrelations constitute an *ontology* in the formal sense. A DAML+OIL formalization of that ontology may be found at

http://www.cs.yale.edu/~dvm/daml/drsonto.daml.

Let us be perfectly clear about what we are doing here. When one uses reification, one commits to *describing* a formula rather than directly *expressing* it. The description of a formula does not by itself assert that formula. It may be taken as asserting that such a formula exists, but that assertion conveys no useful information, because every syntactically well-formed formula (and perhaps many others) already exist. Hence, reification is useful *only* when used in conjunction with tools that know to treat the description of a formula in a certain context as the assertion of that formula. We will come back to this issue in section 4.

3   Application: Web-PDDL

PDDL, the Planning Domain Definition Language [8], is used to define domains and problems for input to automated planners. It was originally developed as the input language for the semiannual AI Planning Systems (AIPS) Competition, but has gained acceptance as a standard for classical planners generally. PDDL continues to evolve under the guidance of the AIPS Competition Committee. In this paper, we have taken the liberty of evolving it in a slightly different direction, which we will discuss as we go. We will call the result Web-PDDL.[1]

---

[1] Some of the features we discuss are not yet fully operational, and we will point these out as we go.

Web-PDDL is not just a curiosity as far as the World-Wide Web is concerned. There is intense interest in development of notations for describing web services [3], and PDDL is ideal for that purpose. Its purpose is to describe sets of *actions* an agent can take, and what their *preconditions* and *effects* are. In the Web world, actions comprise the sending and receiving of messages; typical preconditions include knowing data to be included in a message, and typical effects include learning information, putting an order in a "shopping cart," or finalizing a purchase.

Web-PDDL uses the Lisp-like syntax described in section 2, with special extensions for describing actions and declaring the types of symbols. (The resulting enlarged ontology may be found at http://www.cs.yale.edu/~dvm/daml/pddlonto.daml) Type declarations, actions, and axioms are organized into *domains*. A domain can inherit the contents of other domains, so they can be mixed and matched [8]. Here is an example:

```
(define (domain www-agents)
  (:extends (uri ''http://www.yale.edu/domains/knowing")
            (uri ''http://www.yale.edu/domains/regression-planning")
            (uri ''http://www.yale.edu/domains/commerce"))
  (:requirements :existential-preconditions :conditional-effects)
  (:types Message - Obj Message-id - String)

  (:functions (price-quote ?m - Money)
              (query-in-stock ?pid - Product-id)
              (reply-in-stock ?b - Boolean)
              - Message)

  (:predicates (web-agent ?x - Agent)
               (reply-pending a - Agent  id - Message-id msg - Message)
               (message-exchange ?interlocutor - Agent
                                 ?sent ?received - Message
                                 ?eff - Prop)
               (expected-reply a - Agent sent expect-back - Message))

  (:axiom
      :vars (?agt - Agent ?msg-id - Message-id
             ?sent ?reply - Message)
      :implies (normal-step-value (receive ?agt ?msg-id)
                                  ?reply)
      :context (and (web-agent ?agt)
                    (reply-pending ?agt ?msg-id ?sent)
                    (expected-reply ?agt ?sent ?reply)))

  (:action send
      :parameters (?agt - Agent ?sent - Message)
      :value (?sid - Message-id)
```

```
:precondition (web-agent ?agt)
:effect (reply-pending ?agt ?sid ?sent))

(:action receive
    :parameters (?agt - Agent ?sid - Message-id)
    :vars (?sent - Message ?eff - Prop)
    :precondition (and (web-agent ?agt)
                       (reply-pending ?agt ?sid ?sent))
    :value (?received - Message)
    :effect (when (message-exchange ?agt ?sent ?received ?eff)
                  ?eff)))
```

This description, of domain www-agents, describes two actions, send and receive[2] The www-agents domain *extends* the domains knowing, regression-planning, and commerce, identified by URIs[3]

In turn, this domain can be used as a foundation for other, more specific domains about the content of particular messages. Symbols such as Agent (from the commerce domain, and know-val from the knowing domain, can be freely inherited here and in descendent domains. In other words, a domain closely resembles a DAML+OIL *ontology*, a resemblance we shall return to below.

The task at hand is to translate PDDL domain definitions into RDF. Many of the subexpressions of a domain definition are logical formulas of the sort we discussed in section 2, but the top level of a domain includes idiosyncratic constructs such as (:action *name* ...). But these new constructs present no particular problem, because we can use the same bag of tricks as in section 2, introducing rdf:types such as pddl:Action. For example, the embedding of the send action into RDF is

```
:send pddl:Action/
    pddl:parameters [Param_seq/ rdf:_1 :ag20; rdf:_2 :me21];
    pddl:value [Param_seq/ rdf:_1 :me22];
    pddl:precondition [Atomic_formula/
                            rdf:subj :ag20;
                            rdf:pred :web-agent;
                            rdf:obj drs:empty];
    pddl:effect [Atomic_formula/
                        rdf:subj :ag20;
                        rdf:pred :reply-pending;
                        rdf:obj [Term-seq/
```

---

[2] The :functions field of the domain definition is an extension of PDDL 1.0, but it will be incorporated into the PDDL2.1 the next official version. The :value field of :action definitions is our own extension, which we hope will eventually become an official part of PDDL.

[3] For testing purposes, we currently load all such domains in advance, and do not have the program actually visit remote sites for domains such as ''http://www.yale.edu/domains/commerce".

```
                                rdf:_1 :me22;
                                rdf:_1 :me11]].
  :ag20 Param/ name ''?agt"; type com:Agent .
  :me21 Param/ name ''?sent"; type com:Message .
  :me22 Param/ name ''?sid"; type com:Message-id .
```

(In this formula, the presence of `drs:empty` as the object ("`rdf:obj`") of the predicate `:web-agent` indicates that it is unary.)

The translation from PDDL to RDF is straightforward. We treat PDDL expressions as trees in the usual Lisp way. The first element of each expression gives its basic syntactic type. It is either a PDDL reserved word (such as `:precondition`), a connective (such as `and` or `when`), a predicate (such as `reply-pending`), or a function (such as `price-quote`). Connectives and functions are handled by a recursive walk through their arguments. A predicate is the beginning of an atomic formula, which is reified into four triples (for `rdf:type`, `rdf:subj`, `rdf:pred` and `rdf:obj`) as exemplified above, the only complexity being how the object is handled. In any case, because the subject and object may be arbitrary terms, the recursive walk must continue through them.

Each reserved word has its own special handler. For example, the word `:requirements` must be followed by a list of "requirement" names (we discuss the purpose of these in section 4). The handler for `:requirements` creates a `rdf:Bag` whose elements are strings corresponding to the requirement names, and makes it the value of the `requirements` property of the domain being constructed.

The output of this process is a set of triples, as described in [7], such as

```
  :www-agents requirements :bag309 .
```

which are equivalent to an RDF graph.

It is important to keep track of multiple pointers to a given node of that graph. For identifiers like `web-agent`, it is obvious that any occurrence of that identifier must be translated into the same internal node (which we give the name `:web-agent` in N3, or `resource="#web-agent"` in the XML version). For variables we have to use special internal names to avoid scope ambiguities, as explained in section 2. Every time we create a graph node, we enter it into a hash table to ensure that we can find it the next time we need a reference to it.

Having produced the set of triples, we print out its XML serialization, in as readable a format as we can. Space does not allow us to show that serialization here; we will continue to use N3 to show RDF encodings.

Wherever possible, the Web-PDDL translator outputs its content in a way compatible with DAML+OIL. As we said above, a domain resembles an ontology, so in fact we output the standard DAML+OIL ontology boilerplate as the top level of our domain representation:

```
<rdf:RDF
    xmlns:rdf = ''http://www.w3.org/1999/02/22-rdf-syntax-ns#"
    xmlns:rdfs ="http://www.w3.org/2000/01/rdf-schema#"
    xmlns:daml ="http://www.daml.org/2001/03/daml+oil.daml#"
    xmlns:xmls ="http://www.w3.org/2000/10/XMLSchema#"
    xmlns ="">

    <daml:Ontology rdf:about="">
        <rdfs:label>www-agents</rdfs:label>
        <daml:imports rdf:resource="http://www.daml.org/2001/03/daml+oil.daml"/>
        <daml:imports rdf:resource="http://www.yale.edu/domains/drsonto"/>
        <daml:imports rdf:resource="http://www.yale.edu/domains/pddlonto"/>
        <daml:imports rdf:resource="http://www.yale.edu/domains/knowing"/>
        <daml:imports rdf:resource="http://www.yale.edu/domains/regression-planning"/>
        <daml:imports rdf:resource="http://www.yale.edu/domains/commerce"/>
        Insert domain content here
    </daml:Ontology>
    </rdf:RDF>
```

Types in Web-PDDL resemble classes in DAML. In fact, types are simpler than classes. The relationships between types are declared once and for all, and two atomic-named types are disjoint unless one is a subtype of the other. Because they are simpler, PDDL types can simply *become* DAML classes. For the www-agents domain, we output[4]:

```
<daml:Class rdf:ID="Message"/>
<daml:Class rdf:ID="Message-id">
    <rdfs:subClassOf rdf:resource="#String"/>
    <daml:disjointWith rdf:resource="#Message"/>
</daml:Class>
```

Our translator can also translate back from a DAML+OIL ontology to Web-PDDL. It checks to see if the ontology imports the Web-PDDL ontology (''http://www.yale.edu/domains/pddlonto"), and if so it assumes that an occurrence of a description of a formula is to be taken as an occurrence of the formula itself. It also assumes that the classes declared in the ontology can be turned into Web-PDDL types.

Reconstructing the Lisp-like syntax of formula descriptions is straightforward. The translator parses XML into RDF triples. The triples are isomorphic to a Lisp list structure, with IDs playing the role of pointers, so it is easy to walk through the triples rebuilding the PDDL formulas. Of course, we have to undo the tricks we used for the arguments to functions and non-binary predicates.

We have made our program, called PDDAML, available on the web at ftp://ftp.cs.yale.edu/pub/mcdermott/daml_pddl_translation_doc.tar.gz,   and also from the daml.org tools library (http://www.daml.org/tools/pddl2daml). The program is written in Java. The internal object model for RDF graphs is based on that of Jena (an experimental RDF parser written by Brian McBride, and available at http://www.hpl.hp.co.uk/people/bwm/rdf), although we made several adjustments to it. We developed the algorithms for parsing, reifying, unreifying, and printing from scratch. Because PDDL looks like Lisp, and

---

[4] The current version of our algorithm does not actually map types to classes in this way, but treats types as ordinary PDDL symbols.

is conveniently represented as Lisp list structures internally, we used a simple implementation of Lisp's data types in Java. It may occasionally sound as if we are talking about a Lisp program, but Lisp-o-phobes may reassure themselves that the program is pure Java.

4 Objections and Replies

We have encountered several objections to the proposal we make here:[5]

1. "The fact that RDF can be used to encode the syntax of other, richer languages is already well known. DAML+OIL basically used the same trick to encode a description logic in RDF."
2. "DAML+OIL does 'layering' the right way, so that expressions in the new layer are also expressions in RDF, with the same meaning. The encoding of Web-PDDL lacks this property."
3. "Typed predicate calculus has little in common with RDF (e.g., object-oriented notions like class, subclass, range, and domain are not all directly applicable). There's a good reason why RDF has evolved toward description logics and not toward predicate calculus: theorem proving is a computational quagmire."
4. "A scheme of this sort is worthwhile only if everyone uses it. If another scheme gains popularity, no one will write programs that understand Web-PDDL, and so no one will represent anything in Web-PDDL."

To the first objection the reply is simple: We know of *no* previous system for representing disjunction and bound variables in RDF that does not suffer from exponential blowup. DAML+OIL does *not* use a "trick" similar to ours. In fact, it doesn't have to use any tricks, because RDF is essentially a subset of DAML+OIL. That's why DAML+OIL can *not* handle disjunction or implication, which are simply unrepresentable in RDF, due to the fact that asserting any RDF graph asserts all its subgraphs.

To objection 2 we reply that we have tried wherever possible to use DAML+OIL representations. For instance, we declare Web-PDDL types to be DAML+OIL classes instead of reifying their declarations. But there fewer opportunities for using DAML+OIL-style representations than one might think. A simple fact at the top level of a domain would qualify. For instance, if a domain asserted (sells wabash.com books), that could become a single triple :wabash.com :sells :books. instead of a description of an atomic formula. But domains usually assert type declarations and axioms, not atomic formulas.

As far as objection 3 is concerned, we agree that general-purpose theorem proving is unlikely to be a useful technique on the web, and that therefore various special-purpose techniques (such as Horn-clause theorem proving, or inference

---

[5] Some of these are quotes or paraphrases of comments from anonymous referees who rejected an earlier version of this paper submitted to the World-Wide Web 2002 conference.

using description logics) will play a key role. However, we disagree that the best way to control inference is by limiting the syntax of the representation langugage. A good illustration of this point comes from the field of automated planning. The planning problem is intractable, but that has not prevented the development of algorithms that can produce plans with hundreds of steps, in time measured in seconds, not hours.[6] These algorithms require domain specifications using notations of the complexity of Web-PDDL. One way this complexity is controlled is through a set of "requirement declarations" that allow domain definers to specify exactly which subset of PDDL the domain requires. In the www-agents domain we specified:

```
(:requirements :existential-preconditions :conditional-effects)
```

which allows a planner that can't cope with existential preconditions or conditional effects to recognize immediately that the domain is beyond its reach. But when all is said and done, any planner can potentially run forever on a problem that appears to be within its domain; the only way to prevent that is to ration the time it is allowed to take.

The obvious conclusion is that "notation-complexity control" is *not* the responsibility of the designers of RDF. On the other hand, RDF is not likely to evolve into a language with syntax so general that every notation in the world (PDDL, KIF [6], ...) is a subset of it. Hence there will probably always be a need for languages embedded in RDF by reification or some other "quoting" technique.

Achieving interoperability across the web requires managing several notational levels. At the lowest level we have XML, which is rapidly becoming a standard. Above that we have XML-based languages, which supply particular vocabulary items to allow domain-specific structures to be described. For many applications, this is all you need. However, to achieve the sort of self-description the semantic web would be based on, we need languages for describing resources in a way that is neutral and composable. RDF can play that role, but to achieve more expressive power we must go one step further and embed more complex languages in RDF.

All these levels may sound messy, but there are good reasons for each level, and the problem of translating them all into a uniform internal representation is tricky but tractable, as we have demonstrated. The difficult part arises when we run into differences in vocabulary — or "ontology" — among different information sources. That is a subject of ongoing research [11].

Finally, there is objection 4, that if our encoding does not become standard then no one will hear of it again. This does bother us, since it may keep us from becoming rich and famous. The real question, however, is whether something with essentially the same power is going to be necessary. We believe the answer

---

[6] We hasten to add that most of the domains these algorithms can handle are artificial; planners that can actually find plans in realistic domains such as web services are still in the "laboratory curiosity" stage.

is Yes. If the notation of the future improves on our proposal, or even if it's just inexplicably more popular, we will cheerfully switch to it.

5   Conclusion and Related Work

We have argued that it is possible and useful to embed general logic constructs in RDF and XML. We have demonstrated the possibility by providing a program, PDDAML, that translates between RDF/XML and PDDL, the Planning Domain Definition Language. We are incorporating this in a system for planning interactions with web services [9].

The key technical contribution is a method for representing arbitrary formulas with bound variables as elements of RDF classes. Logical symbols of the embedded language (such as or in predicate calculus) are translated into rdf:types, so that (or P Q) becomes a description of an entity of type Or whose arguments are $P*$ and $Q*$, the translations of P and Q. For a fuller technical description see [10]. Similar ideas were proposed in [4]. The N3 notation [2] was originally intended as a concise encoding of RDF graphs, and that is how we have used it here. Lately Berners-Lee has made extensions that go beyond the expressive power of RDF; if these should be incorporated into RDF it would make it easier for us to embed logic in RDF, and reduce the number of places where quotation devices would be necessary.

The ability to represent arbitrary formulas in RDF should free us from thinking of the semantic web as graph structures serialized as a nightmarish number of pointy brackets. The semantic web will surely exist as a marketplace of alternative notations, which will show up as alternative quotational ontologies at the notational level, just as alternative ontologies will coexist at the context level. Only a few of the competing notations will survive. We argue that the winners will be those notations that have the following properties:

- *Declarativeness:* Good notations will express truths. Any inference engine with access to their ontologies can make inferences from them.
- *Composability:* An expression from one source can be combined with an expression from another, regardless of whether their designers intended that.
- *Generality:* A notation should be able to express what people want to express.
- *Maintainability:* Information sources will evolve, and they must be comprehensible to their maintainers for this to be so.

If we are right, then notations such as WSDL [3] will wither away in favor of alternatives that *describe* services instead of dictating (to someone with a manual) how to write code to connect to them. Notations such as RDF will have to evolve to allow disjunctions and quantifiers, or quotational devices such as the one we have presented will have to become standard. And, finally, XML serializations should be hidden away from human view lest small children accidentally see them and become frightened. XML is a wonderful way of making data "self describing" to a computer; to a person, it's a way of concealing information. It is especially critical for the semantic web that better surface notations be found.

References

1. Tim Berners-Lee. Primer: Getting into rdf & semantic web using n3, 2000. http://www.w3.org/2000/10/swap/Primer.html.
2. Tim Berners-Lee. Notation 3, 2001. http://www.w3.org/DesignIssues/Notation3.html.
3. Erik Christensen, Francisco Curbera, Greg Meredith, and Sanjiva Weerawarana. Web Services Definition Language (Wsdl) 1.1. Technical report, W3C, 2001. , available at http://www.w3c.org/TR/wsdl.
4. Wolfram Conen, Reinhold Klapsing, and Eckhart Köppen. Rdf M&s revisited: from reification to nesting, from containers to lists, from dialect to pure Xml. In *Proc. Semantic Web Working Symposium*, pages 195–208, 2001.
5. Patrick Hayes. Rdf model theory, 2001. W3C Working Draft 25 September 2001. http://www.w3.org/TR/2001/WD-rdf-mt-20010925.
6. KIF. Knowledge Interchange Format: Draft proposed American National Standard (dpans). Technical Report 2/98-004, ANS, 1998. Also at http://logic.stanford.edu/kif/dpans.html.
7. Ora Lassila and Ralph R. Swick. Resource Description Framework (Rdf) Model and Syntax Specification. Technical report, W3C, 1999. , available at http://www.w3.org/TR/REC-rdf-syntax.
8. Drew McDermott. The Planning Domain Definition Language Manual. Technical Report 1165, Yale Computer Science, 1998. (CVC Report 98-003).
9. Drew McDermott. Estimated-regression planning for interactions with web services. In *Proc. AI Planning Systems Conference 2002*, 2002. To appear.
10. Drew McDermott, Jonathan Borden, Mark Burstein, Douglas Smith, and Richard Waldinger. A Proposal for Encoding Logic in Rdf/daml. Technical report, Yale CS, 2001. ftp://ftp.cs.yale.edu/pub/mcdermott/papers/noworry.ps.gz.
11. Drew McDermott, Mark Burstein, and Douglas Smith. Overcoming ontology mismatches in transactions with self-describing agents. In *Proc. Semantic Web Working Symposium*, pages 285–302, 2001.
12. Frank van Harmelen, Peter F. Patel-Schneider, and Ian Horrocks. Reference description of the daml+oil (march 2001) ontology markup language, 2001. Available at http://www.daml.org/2001/03/reference.html.

Towards Semantic Web Mining

Bettina Berendt[1], Andreas Hotho[2], and Gerd Stumme[2]

[1] Institute of Information Systems, Humboldt University Berlin
Spandauer Str. 1, D–10178 Berlin, Germany
http://www.wiwi.hu-berlin.de/~berendt
berendt@wiwi.hu-berlin.de
[2] Institute of Applied Informatics and Formal Description Methods AIFB,
University of Karlsruhe, D–76128 Karlsruhe, Germany
http://www.aifb.uni-karlsruhe.de/WBS
{hotho, stumme}@aifb.uni-karlsruhe.de

Abstract. Semantic Web Mining aims at combining the two fast-developing research areas Semantic Web and Web Mining. The idea is to improve, on the one hand, the results of Web Mining by exploiting the new semantic structures in the Web; and to make use of Web Mining, on the other hand, for building up the Semantic Web. This paper gives an overview of where the two areas meet today, and sketches ways of how a closer integration could be profitable.

1 Introduction

Semantic Web Mining aims at combining the two fast-developing research areas Semantic Web and Web Mining. The idea is to improve the results of Web Mining by exploiting the new semantic structures in the Web. Furthermore, Web Mining can help to build the Semantic Web.

The aim of this paper is to give an overview of where the two areas meet today, and to sketch how a closer integration could be profitable. We will provide references to typical approaches. Most of them have not been developed explicitly to close the gap between the Semantic Web and Web Mining, but they fit naturally into this scheme. We do not attempt to mention all the relevant work, as this would surpass the paper, but will rather provide one or two examples out of each category.

In the next section, we start with a brief overview of the areas Semantic Web and Web Mining. The two areas can co-operate in various ways: First, Web mining techniques can be applied to help create the Semantic Web. A backbone of the Semantic Web are ontologies, which at present are often handcrafted. This is not a scalable solution for a wide-range application of Semantic Web techologies. The challenge is to learn ontologies, and/or instances of their concepts, in a (semi-)automatic way. A survey of these approaches is contained in Section 3.

Conversely, background knowledge — in the form of ontologies, or in other forms — can be used to improve the process and results of Web Mining. Existing techniques are investigated in Section 4.

I. Horrocks and J. Hendler (Eds.): ISWC 2002, LNCS 2342, pp. 264–278, 2002.

Recent developments have included the mining of sites that become more and more Semantic Web sites, and the development of mining languages that can tap the expressive power of Semantic Web knowledge representation. Section 5 discusses them and shows how they make the Semantic Web and Web Mining grow closer to each other.

In Section 6, we then sketch how the loop can be closed: from Web Mining to the Semantic Web and back. We believe that a tight integration of these aspects will greatly increase the understandability of the Web for machines, and will thus become the basis for the development of further generations of intelligent Web tools.

2   The Semantic Web and Web Mining

In the first part of this section, we briefly recall our understanding of the Semantic Web. In the second part, we give an overview of Web Mining approaches by classifying them into three categories: Web content mining, Web structure mining, and Web usage mining. In the remainder of the paper, we will then discuss how to bring together these different domains.

2.1   Semantic Web

The Semantic Web is based on a vision of Tim Berners-Lee. The great success of the current WWW leads to a new challenge: a huge amount of data is interpretable by humans only; machine support is limited. Berners-Lee suggests to enrich the Web by machine-processable information which supports the user in his tasks. For instance, today's search engines are already quite powerful, but still return too often too large or inadequate lists of hits. Machine-processable information can point the search engine to the relevant pages and can thus improve both precision and recall. To reach this goal the Semantic Web will be built up in different levels: Unicode/Unified Resource Identifiers, XML, RDF, ontologies, logic, proof, trust.[3]

The main focus of our research is on RDF, ontologies, and logic. We consider the content of the Semantic Web as being represented by ontologies and metadata. This approach is reflected by the Karlsruhe Ontology framework KAON[4] which is based on a formal definition of our understanding of what an ontology is [46]. It is built in a modular way, so that different needs can be fulfilled by combining parts.

This definition constitutes a core structure that is quite straightforward, well-agreed upon, and that may easily be mapped onto existing ontology representation languages. Step by step the definition can be extended by taking into account axioms, lexicons, and knowledge bases [46].

The inference engine behind our implementation relies on F-Logic [26], but there are many other approaches. A complete overview would be a paper on

---

[3] see http://www.w3.org/DesignIssues/Semantic.html
[4] http://kaon.semanticweb.org

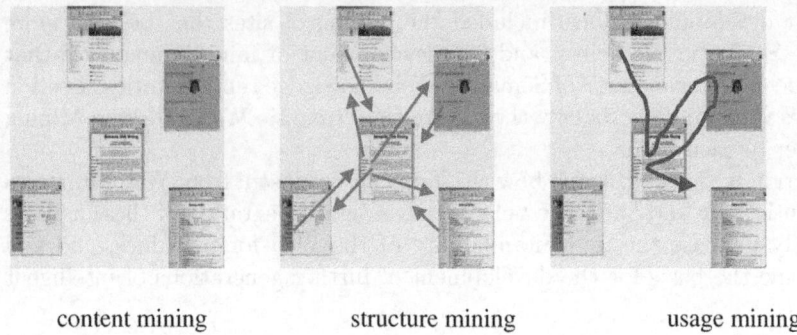

| content mining | structure mining | usage mining |

Fig. 1. The three areas of Web Mining.

its own. Hence we will only mention one, which is currently heavily discussed: DAML+OIL, a description logics formalism adapted to the Semantic Web.[5] We will not go into further detail here, but will rather discuss the topic of Web Mining and its relations to the Semantic Web in more depth.

2.2   Web Mining

Web mining is the application of data mining techniques to the content, structure, and usage of Web resources. This can help to discover global as well as local structure ("models" or "patterns" [19]) within and between Web pages. Like other data mining applications, Web mining can profit from given structure on data (as in database tables), but it can also be applied to semi-structured or unstructured data like free-form text. This means that Web mining is an invaluable help in the transformation from human understandable content to machine understandable semantics.

Three areas of Web mining are commonly distinguished: content mining, structure mining, and usage mining (see Fig. 1).

Content/text of Web pages. *Web content mining* is a form of text mining (for an overview, see [3]). The primary Web resource that is being mined is an individual page. Web content mining can take advantage of the semi-structured nature of Web page text. The HTML tags of today's Web pages, and even more so the XML markup of tomorrow's Web pages, bear information that concerns not only layout, but also logical structure.

Web content mining can be used to detect co-occurrences of terms in texts. For example, co-occurrences of terms in newswire articles may show that "gold" is frequently mentioned together with "copper" when articles concern Canada, but together with "silver" when articles concern the US. Trends over time may also be discovered, indicating a surge or decline in interest in certain topics such as the programming languages "Java". Another application area is event detection: the identification of stories in continuous news streams that correspond to

---

[5] http://www.daml.org

new or previously unidentified events (all examples from [7]). Further examples that allow the reconstruction of page content, and the discovery of relations in the domain under description, will be described in Section 6, where we will set them in relation to the Semantic Web.

Structure between Web pages. *Web structure mining* usually operates on the hyperlink structure of Web pages. The primary Web resource that is being mined is a set of pages, ranging from a single Web site to the Web as a whole. Web structure mining exploits the additional information that is (often implicitly) contained in the structure of *hyper*text. Therefore, an important application area is the identification of the relative relevance of different pages that appear equally pertinent when analyzed with respect to their content in isolation.

For example, hyperlink-induced topic search [27] analyzes hyperlink topology by discovering authoritative information sources for a broad search topic. This information is found in *authority* pages, which are defined in relation to hubs as their counterparts: *Hubs* are pages that link to many related authorities. The search engine Google, for instance, owes its success to the PageRank algorithm, which states that the relevance of a page increases with the number of hyperlinks to it from other pages, and in particular of other relevant pages [38].

Single pages too can be analyzed with respect to their structure, which gives information about their function, e. g., their function in the search for other pages. Cooley, Mobasher, and Srivastava [11] distinguish, based on [40], five types of Web pages: (i) "head" pages are entry points for a site, (ii) "navigation" pages contain many links and little information, (iii) "content" pages contain a small number of links and are visited for their content, (iv) "look-up" pages have many incoming links, few outgoing ones and no significant content, such as pages used to provide a definition or acronym expansion, and (v) "personal" pages have very diverse characteristics and no significant traffic.

Usage of Web pages. In *Web usage mining*, the primary Web resource that is being mined is a record of the requests made by visitors to a Web site, most often collected in a Web server log [43]. The content and structure of Web pages, and in particular those of one Web site, reflect the intentions of those who have authored and designed those pages, and their underlying information architecture. The actual behavior of those who use these resources may reveal additional structure.

First, relationships may be induced by usage where no particular structure was designed. For example, in an online catalog of products, there is usually either no inherent structure (different products viewed as a set), or one or several hierarchical structures given by product categories, manufacturers, etc. Mining the visits to that site, however, one may find that most (e. g., 80%) of those users who were interested in product A were also interested in product B. Here, "interest" may be measured by requests for product description pages, or the placement of that product into the shopping cart (indicated by the request for the respective pages). The identified association rules are at the center of cross-selling and up-selling strategies in E-commerce sites: When a new user shows interest in product A, she will receive a recommendation for product B (cf. [34, 28]).

Second, relationships may be induced by usage where a different relationship was intended. For example, sequence mining may show that most of those users who visited page C later went to page D, along paths that indicated a prolonged search (frequent visits to help and index pages, frequent backtracking, etc.) [10, 25]. This can be interpreted to mean that visitors wish to reach D from C, but that this was not foreseen in the information architecture, hence that there is at present no hyperlink from C to D. This insight can be used for static site improvement for all users (adding a link from C to D), or for dynamic recommendations personalized for the subset of users who go to C ("you may wish to also look at D").

It is useful to combine Web usage mining with content and structure analysis in order to "make sense" of observed frequent paths and the pages on these paths. This can be done using a variety of methods. Some methods classify pages in terms of a pre-defined ontology, while others rely on the extraction of keywords found in these pages, and subsequent human naming of the keyword clusters represented by frequent paths. The ontology itself can be hand-crafted or (semi-)automatically learned, and the classification of pages in terms of the ontology can also be (semi-)automated in various ways.

In the following section, we will first look at how ontologies and their instances can be learned. We will then go on to investigate how the use of ontologies, and other ways of identifying the meaning of pages, can help to make Web Mining go semantic.

3   Extracting Semantics from the Web

The effort behind the Semantic Web is to add semantic annotation to Web documents in order to access knowledge instead of unstructured material, allowing knowledge to be managed in an automatic way. Web Mining can help to learn definitions of structures for knowledge organization (e. g., ontologies) and to provide the population of such knowledge structures.

All approaches discussed here are semi-automatic. They assist the knowledge engineer in extracting the semantics, but cannot completely replace her. In order to obtain high-quality results, one cannot replace the human in the loop, as there is always a lot of tacit knowledge involved in the modeling process. A computer will never be able to fully consider background knowledge, experience, or social conventions. If this were the case, the Semantic Web would be superfluous, since then machines like search engines or agents could operate directly on conventional Web pages. The overall aim of our research is thus not to replace the human, but rather to provide him with more and more support.

3.1   Ontology Learning

Extracting an ontology from the Web is a challenging task. One way is to engineer the ontology by hand, but this is quite an expensive way. In [32], the expression

Ontology Learning was coined for the semi-automatic extraction of semantics from the Web in order to create an ontology. There, machine learning techniques were used to improve the ontology engineering process. An example is given in Section 6.

Ontology learning exploits a lot of existing resources, like text, thesauri, dictionaries, databases and so on. It combines techniques of several research areas, e. g., from machine learning, information retrieval (cf. [29]), or agents [47], and applies them to discover the 'semantics' in the data and to make them explicit. The techniques produce intermediate results which must finally be integrated in one machine-understandable format, e. g., an ontology.

3.2 Mapping and Merging Ontologies

With the growing usage of ontologies, the problem of overlapping knowledge in a common domain occurs more often and becomes critical. Domain-specific ontologies are modeled by multiple authors in multiple settings. These ontologies lay the foundation for building new domain-specific ontologies in similar domains by assembling and extending multiple ontologies from repositories.

The process of *ontology merging* takes as input two (or more) source ontologies and returns a merged ontology based on the given source ontologies. Manual ontology merging using conventional editing tools without support is difficult, labor intensive and error prone. Therefore, several systems and frameworks for supporting the knowledge engineer in the ontology merging task have recently been proposed [24, 6, 36, 33]. The approaches rely on syntactic and semantic matching heuristics which are derived from the behavior of ontology engineers when confronted with the task of merging ontologies, i. e., human behavior is simulated. Another method is FCA-MERGE which merges ontologies following a bottom-up approach, offering a global structural description of the process [44]. For the source ontologies, it extracts instances from a given set of domain-specific text documents by applying natural language processing techniques. Based on the extracted instances it uses the TITANIC algorithm [45] to derive a concept lattice. The concept lattice provides a conceptual clustering of the concepts of the source ontologies. It is explored and interactively transformed to the merged ontology by the ontology engineer.

3.3 Instance Learning

It is probably reasonable to expect users to manually annotate new documents to a certain degree, but this does not solve the problem of old documents containing unstructured material. In any case we cannot expect everyone to manually mark up every produced mail or document, as this would be impossible. Moreover some users may need to extract and use different or additional information from the one provided by the creator. For the reasons mentioned above it is vital for the Semantic Web to produce automatic or semi-automatic methods for extracting information from Web-related documents, either for helping in annotating new documents or to extract additional information from existing unstructured or partially structured documents.

In this context, Information Extraction from texts (IE) is one of the most promising areas of Human Language Technologies. IE is a set of automatic methods for locating important facts in electronic documents for subsequent use, e. g. for annotating documents or for information storing for further use (such as populating an ontology with instances). IE as defined above is the perfect support for knowledge identification and extraction from Web documents as it can — for example — provide support in documents analysis either in an automatic way (unsupervised extraction of information) or semi-automatic way (e. g. as support for human annotators in locating relevant facts in documents, via information highlighting). One such system for IE is FASTUS (cf. [21]). Another is the OntoMat Annotizer [20], which also supports authoring. The approach of [12] is discussed in Section 6.

4   Exploiting Semantics for Web Mining

Semantics can be exploited for Web Mining for different purposes. The first major application area is Web content mining, i. e., the explicit encoding of semantics for mining the Web content.

4.1   Web Content Mining

In [22], we propose an approach for applying background knowledge in the form of ontologies during preprocessing in order to improve clustering results and allow for selection between results. We preprocess the input data (e. g. text) and apply ontology-based heuristics for feature selection and feature aggregation. Based on these representations, we compute multiple clustering results using k-Means. The results can be characterized and explained by the corresponding selection of concepts in the ontology.

In another current project, we are working on facilitating the customized access to courseware material which is stored in a peer to peer network[6] by means of conceptual clustering. We will make use of techniques of Formal Concept Analysis, which have been applied successfully in the Conceptual Email Manager CEM [9]. Based on an ontology, it generates a search hierarchy of concepts (clusters) with multiple search paths.

4.2   Web Structure Mining

Web structure mining can also be improved by taking content into account. The PageRank algorithm mentioned in Section 2.2 co-operates with a keyword analysis algorithm, but the two are independent of one another. So PageRank will consider any much-cited page as 'relevant', regardless of whether that page's content reflects the query. To improve search results, however, it is desirable to consider this content. By also taking the hyperlink anchor text and its surroundings into account, CLEVER [4] can more specifically assess the relevance

---

[6] http://edutella.jxta.org/

for a given query. The Focused Crawler [5] improves on this by integrating top-ical content into the link graph model, and by a more flexible way of crawling Ontology-based focused crawling is proposed by [30].

4.3   Web Usage Mining

Exploiting the semantics of the pages visited along user paths can considerably improve the results of Web usage mining, since it helps the analyst understand what users were looking for, what content co-occurred, etc. The most basic form is again to use hand-crafted ontologies, in combination with automated schemes for classifying the large number of pages of a typical Web site according to an ontology of the site. For many current Web sites, this classification will be *ex post* and operate on pages that have been designed independently of an overall ontological schema (cf. [12]). However, a growing number of sites deliver pages that are generated dynamically in an interaction of an underlying database, information architecture, and query capabilities.

As an example, we have used an ontology to describe a Web site which operates on relational databases and also contains a number of static pages, together with an automated classification scheme that relies on mapping the query strings for dynamic page generation to concepts [2]. Pages are classified according to multiple concept hierarchies that reflect content (type of object that the page describes), structure (function of pages in object search), and service (type of search functionality chosen by the user). A path can then be regarded as a sequence of (more or less abstract) concepts in a concept hierarchy, allowing the analyst to identify strategies of search. This classification can make Web usage mining results more comprehensible and actionable for Web site redesign or personalization: The semantic analysis has helped to improve the design of search options in the site, and to identify behavioral patterns that indicate whether a user is likely to successfully complete a search process, or whether he is likely to abandon the site [12]. The latter insights could be used to dynamically generate help messages for new users.

In [1], we extend this approach by using the ontology to semi-automatically generate interesting queries for usage mining, and to create meaningful visual-izations of usage paths. The classification scheme can easily be generalized to a wide range of other sites, in particular if these also operate on one or several underlying relational databases.

The more structured the underlying model is, and the more pages in a site are generated exclusively based on it, the more closely pages correspond to well-defined ontological entities (e. g., [15]). And the smaller the gap between the model generating the pages and the model analysing requests for those pages, the better semantics can be exploited in Web usage mining. At this level, the distinction between the use of semantics of Web Mining (as described in this section) and the mining of the Semantic Web itself (as described in the next section) starts to blur. An outlook on semantic usage mining that also evaluates the query strings, but operates on pages generated from a full-blown ontology (a "knowledge portal" in the sense of [23]) will be given in the following section.

The approaches discussed so far associate pages with an ontology and thus make their semantics explicit. An alternative, recurring on the semantics of pages that are implicitly contained in their text, is the automatic extraction of content by keyword analysis using standard Information Retrieval techniques (e. g., TF.IDF). Usage paths can then be clustered according to common content. This may help the analyst understand what kind of information users were seeking along frequently travelled paths [8]. It may also be used to identify content that co-occurred frequently in user histories, and to generate recommendations on the basis of these co-occurrences. Using a common representation of feature vectors, [35] show how clustering can use and combine usage, content, and structure similarities.

Web usage mining that is semantic in this sense is not only helpful for an ex post understanding of the paths users took through a site, but can also be used to aid users on-line, e. g. to improve their queries in a search engine. [39] use a combination of IR techniques analyzing single pages, ontologies, and the mining of a user's previous search history to make recommendations for query improvement. The basic idea is to (a) offer terms that are shown in the hierarchy as related, and to (b) infer from terms that occurred frequently in previous search histories a relative weighting on the set of pages that are described only coarsely by the few terms of the initial current query.

5   Mining the Semantic Web

As the Semantic Web enhances the first generation of the WWW with formal semantics, it offers a good basis to enrich Web Mining: The types of (hyper)links are now described explicitly, allowing the knowledge engineer to gain deeper insights in Web structure mining; and the contents of the pages come along with a formal semantics, allowing her to apply mining techniques which require more structured input. In the previous section, we have already seen that the distinction between the exploitation of semantics for 'standard' Web Mining on one side and the mining of the Semantic Web on the other side is all but sharp. Anyway, in this section we study those approaches which belong more to the latter.

5.1   Semantic Web Content and Structure Mining

In the Semantic Web, content and structure are strongly intertwined. Therefore, the distinction between content and structure mining vanishes. However, the distribution of the semantic annotations may provide additional implicit knowledge. We discuss now first steps towards semantic Web content/structure mining.

An important group of techniques which can easily be adapted to semantic Web content/structure mining are the approaches discussed as *Relational Data Mining* (formerly called *Inductive Logic Programming* (*ILP*); see [14] for an introductory collection of articles). Relational Data Mining looks for patterns that involve multiple relations in a relational database. It comprises techniques for

classification, regression, clustering, and association analysis. It is quite straightforward to transform the algorithms so that they are able to deal with data
described in RDF or by ontologies. There are two big scientific challenges in this
attempt. The first is the size of the data to be processed (i. e., the scalability of
the algorithms), and the second is the fact that the data are distributed over the
Semantic Web, as there is no central database server. Scalability has always been
a major concern for ILP algorithms. With the expected growth of the Semantic
Web, this problem increases as well. Therefore, the performance of the mining
algorithms has to be improved, e. g. by sampling (see for instance [41]). As for
the problem of distributed data, it is a challenging research topic to develop
algorithms which can perform the mining in a distributed manner, so that only
(intermediate) results have to be transmitted, and not whole datasets.

5.2   Semantic Web Usage Mining

Usage mining can also be enhanced further if the semantics are contained explicitly in the pages by referring to concepts of an ontology. Semantic Web usage
mining can for instance be performed on log files which register the user behavior in terms of an ontology. A system for creating such semantic log files from a
knowledge portal [23] has been developed at the AIFB [37]. These log files can
then be mined, for instance to cluster users with similar interests in order to
provide personalized views on the ontology.

6   Closing the Loop

In the previous three sections, we have analyzed how to establish Semantic Web
data by data mining, how to exploit formal semantics for Web Mining, and how
to mine the Semantic Web. In this section, we sketch one out of many possible
combinations of these approaches. We will first *learn an ontology* using Web
Mining, then *fill the ontology* with instances by again using Web Mining, and
finally *mine the resulting data* in order to gain further insights. We will only give
a rough sketch in order to illustrate our ideas. The example is taken from the
Getess project[7] which provides ontology-based access to tourism Web pages in
Mecklenburg-Vorpommern[8], a region in north-eastern Germany.

One may split the first step, *ontology learning*, in two sub-steps. First a concept hierarchy is established using the knowledge acquisition method ONTEX
(Ontology Exploration, [17]). It relies on the knowledge acquisition technique
of Attribute Exploration [16] as developed in the mathematical framework of
Formal Concept Analysis [18]; and guarantees that the knowledge engineer considers all relevant combinations of concepts while establishing the subsumption
hierarchy. ONTEX takes as input a set of concepts, and provides as output a
hierarchy on them. This output is then the input to the second sub-step, together with a set of Web pages. [31] describes how association rules are mined

---

[7] http://www.getess.de/index_en.html
[8] http://www.all-in-all.de/

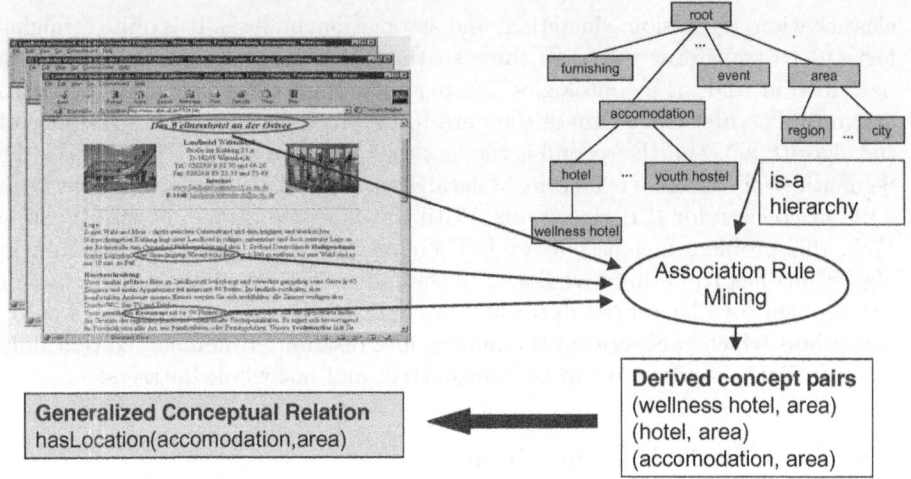

Fig. 2. Step 1: Mining the Web for learning ontologies.

from this input, which lead to the generation of relations between the ontology concepts (see Fig. 2). The association rules are used to discover combinations of concepts which frequently occur together. These combinations hint at the existence of conceptual relations. They are suggested to the user. As the system is not able to derive automatically names for the relations, the user is asked to provide them.

In the example shown in the figure, automatic analysis has shown that three concepts frequently co-occur with the concept "area". Since the ontology bears the information that the concept "wellness hotel" is a subconcept of the concept "hotel", which in turn is a subconcept of "accommodation", the inference engine can derive that only one conceptual relation needs to be inferred based on these co-occurrences: the one between "accommodation" and "area". Human input is then needed to identify that an accommodation "hasLocation" that is an area, i. e., to specify a name for the generalized conceptual relation.

In the second step, *the ontology is filled*. In this step, instances are extracted from the Web pages, and the relations from the ontology are established between them using techniques described in [12] (see Fig. 3), or any other technique described in Section 3.3. Beside the ontology, the approach needs tagged training data as input. Given this input, the system learns to extract instances and relations from other Web pages and from hyperlinks.

In the example shown in the figure, the relation "belongsTo" between the concepts "golf course" and "hotel" is instantiated by the pair (SeaView, Wellnesshotel), i. e., by the fact derived from the available Web pages that the golf course named "SeaView" belongs to the Wellness Hotel.

After the second step, we have an ontology and a knowledge base, i. e., instances of the ontology concepts and relations between them. These data are now input to the third step, in which *the knowledge base is mined*. Depending on the purpose, different techniques may be applied. One can for instance derive

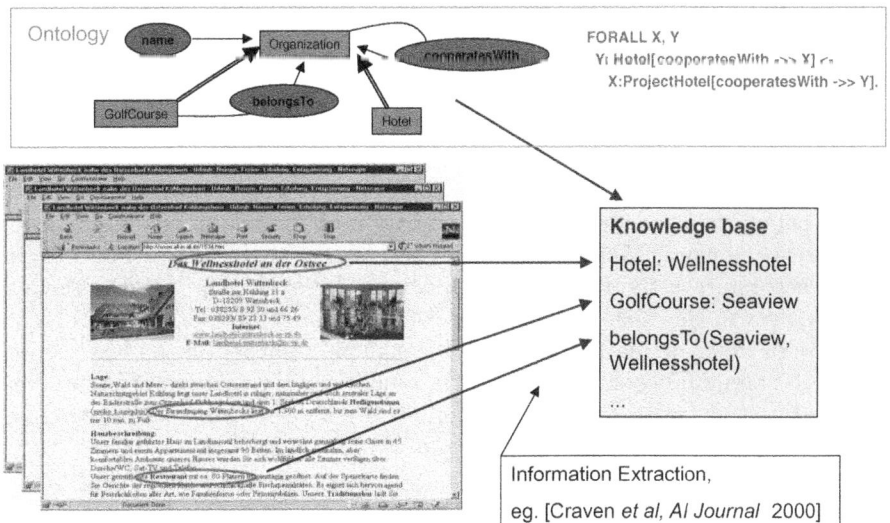

Fig. 3. Step 2: Mining the web for filling the ontology.

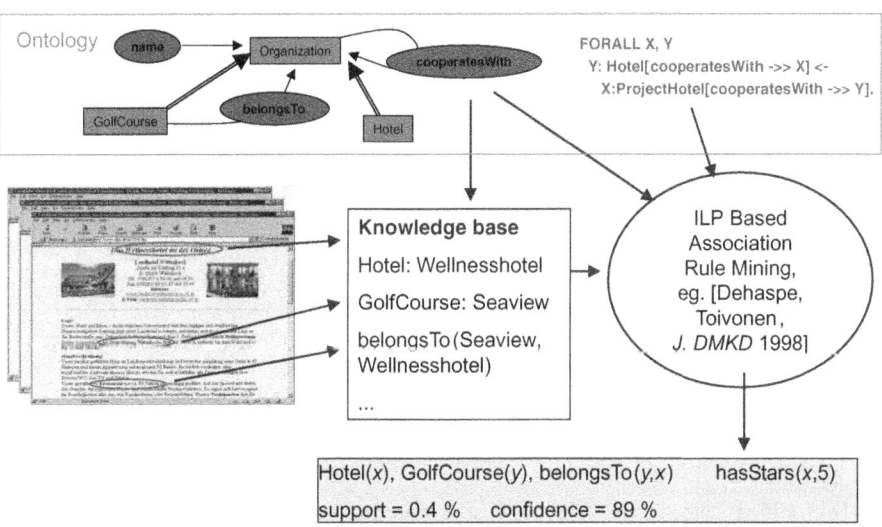

Fig. 4. Step 3: Using the ontology for mining again.

relational association rules, as described in detail in [13] (see Figure 4). Another possibility is to conceptually cluster the instances, e. g. using [45].

In the example shown in Figure 4, a combination of knowledge about instances like the Wellnesshotel and its SeaView golf course, with other knowledge derived from the Web pages' texts, produces the rule that hotels with golf courses often have 5 stars. More precisely, this holds for 89 % of hotels with golf courses, and 0.4 % of all hotels in the knowledge base are five star hotels owning a golf course.

The results of the last step may lead to further modifications of the ontology and/or knowledge base. When new information is gained, it may be used as input to the first steps in the next turn of the ontology life cycle.

7 Conclusion

In this paper, we have studied the combination of the two fast-developing research areas Semantic Web and Web Mining. We discussed how Semantic Web Mining can improve the results of Web Mining by exploiting the new semantic structures in the web; and how the construction of the Semantic Web can make use of Web Mining techniques. The example provided in the last section shows the potential benefits of further research in this integration attempt. The research questions arising from this interplay are likely to stimulate further research both in the Semantic Web as also in Web Mining.

References

1. B. Berendt. Using site semantics to analyze, visualize and support navigation. *Data Mining and Knowledge Discovery*, 6:37–59, 2002.
2. B. Berendt and M. Spiliopoulou. Analysing navigation behaviour in web sites integrating multiple information systems. *The VLDB Journal*, 9(1):56–75, 2000.
3. S. Chakrabarti. Data mining for hypertext: A tutorial survey. *SIGKDD Explorations*, 1:1–11, 2000.
4. S. Chakrabarti, B. Dom, D. Gibson, J. Kleinberg, P. Raghavan, and S. Rajagopalan. Automatic resource compilation by analyzing hyperlink structure and associated text. In *Proceedings of the 7th World-wide web conference (WWW7),30(1-7)*, pages 65–74, 1998.
5. S. Chakrabarti, M. van den Berg, and B. Dom. Focused crawling: A new approach to topic-specific web resource discovery. In *Proceedings of the 8th World-wide web conference (WWW8),31(11-16)*, pages 1623–1640, Toronto, May 1999.
6. Hans Chalupsky. Ontomorph: A translation system for symbolic knowledge. In *Principles of Knowledge Representation and Reasoning: Proceedings of the Seventh International Conference (KR2000)*, pages 471–482, 2000.
7. G. Chang, M.J. Healey, J.A.M. McHugh, and J.T.L. Wang. *Mining the World Wide Web. An Information Search Approach.* Boston: Kluwer Academic Publishers, 2001.
8. E.H. Chi, P. Pirolli, and J. Pitkow. The scent of a site: a system for analyzing and predicting information scent, usage, and usability of a web site. In *Proceedings of the ACM CHI 2000 Conference on Human Factors in Computing Systems*, pages 161–168, Amsterdam: ACM Press., 2000.
9. Richard Cole and Gerd Stumme. Cem - a conceptual email manager. In Bernhard Ganter and Guy W. Mineau, editors, *Proc. ICCS 2000*, volume 1867 of *LNAI*, pages 438–452. Springer, 2000.
10. R. Cooley. *Web Usage Mining: Discovery and Application of Interesting Patterns from Web Data.* PhD thesis, University of Minnesota, Faculty of the Graduate School, 2000.
11. R. Cooley, B. Mobasher, and J. Srivastava. Data preparation for mining world wide web browsing patterns. *Journal of Knowledge and Information Systems*, 1(1):5–32, 1999.

12. M. Craven, D. DiPasquo, D. Freitag, A. McCallum, T. Mitchell, K. Nigam, and S. Slattery. Learning to construct knowledge bases from the world wide web. *Artificial Intelligence*, 118(1-2):69–113, 2000.
13. L. Dehaspe and H. Toivonen. Discovery of frequent datalog patterns. *Data Mining and Knowledge Discovery*, 3(1):7–36, 1999.
14. Saso Dzeroski and Nada Lavrac, editors. *Relational Data Mining*. Springer, 2001.
15. M. Fernández, D. Florescu, A. Levi, and D. Sucin. Declarative specification of web sites with strudel. *The VLDB Journal*, 9:38–55, 2000.
16. B. Ganter. Attribute exploration with background knowledge. *TCS*, 217(2):215–233, 1999.
17. B. Ganter and G. Stumme. Creation and merging of ontology top-levels. In *Proc. ECAI02*. submitted, 2002.
18. B. Ganter and R. Wille. *Formal Concept Analysis: Mathematical Foundations*. Springer, Berlin – Heidelberg, 1999.
19. D. Hand, H. Mannila, and P. Smyth. *Principles of Data Mining*. Cambridge, MA: MIT Press, 2001.
20. Siegfried Handschuh and Steffen Staab. Authoring and annotation of web pages in CREAM. In *Proc. Of WWW11*. to appear, 2002.
21. Jerry Hobbs, Douglas Appelt, John Bear, David Israel, Megumi Kameyama, Mark Stickel, and Mabry Tyson. Fastus: A cascaded finite-state transducer for extracting information from natural-language text. In E. Roche and Y. Schabes, editors, *Finite State Devices for Natural Language Processing*. MIT Press, Cambridge MA, 1996.
22. A. Hotho, A. Maedche, and S. Staab. Ontology-based text clustering. In *Proceedings of the IJCAI-2001 Workshop "Text Learning: Beyond Supervision", August, Seattle, USA*, 2001.
23. A. Hotho, A. Maedche, S. Staab, and R. Studer. SEAL-II — the soft spot between richly structured and unstructured knowledge. *Journal of Universal Computer Science (J.UCS)*, 7(7):566–590, 2001.
24. E.H. Hovy. Combining and standardizing large-scale, practical ontologies for machine translation and other uses. In *Proc. 1st Intl. Conf. on Language Resources and Evaluation (LREC)*, Granada, 1998.
25. H. Kato, T. Nakayama, and Y. Yamane. Navigation analysis tool based on the correlation between contents distribution and access patterns. In *Working Notes of the Workshop on Web Mining for E-Commerce - Challenges and Opportunities (WebKDD 2000) at the 6th ACM SIGKDD International Conference on Knowledge Discovery and Data Mining*, pages 95–104, Boston, MA, 2000.
26. Michael Kifer, Georg Lausen, and James Wu. Logical foundations of object-oriented and frame-based languages. *Journal of the ACM*, 42:741–843, 1995.
27. Jon M. Kleinberg. Authoritative sources in a hyperlinked environment. *Journal of the ACM*, 46(5):604–632, 1999.
28. W. Lin, S.A. Alvarez, and C. Ruiz. Efficient adaptive-support association rule mining for recommender systems. *Data Mining and Knowledge Discovery*, 6:83–105, 2002.
29. A. Maedche. *Ontology Learning for the Semantic Web*. Kluwer, 2002.
30. A. Maedche, M. Ehrig, S. Handschuh, L. Stojanovic, and R. Volz. Ontology-focused crawling of documents and relational metadata. In *Proceedings of the Eleventh International World Wide Web Conference WWW-2002*, Hawaii, 2002.
31. A. Maedche and S. Staab. Discovering conceptual relations from text. In *ECAI-2000 - European Conference on Artificial Intelligence. Proceedings of the 13th European Conference on Artificial Intelligence*, pages 321–325. IOS Press, Amsterdam, 2000.

32. A. Maedche and S. Staab. Ontology learning for the semantic web. *IEEE Intelligent Systems*, 16(2):72 –79, 2001.
33. D. McGuinness, R. Fikes, J. Rice, and S. Wilder. An environment for merging and testing large ontologies. In *In the Proceedings of the Seventh International Conference on Principles of Knowledge Representation and Reasoning (KR2000)*, pages 483–493, Breckenridge, Colorado, USA, 2000.
34. B. Mobasher, R. Cooley, and J. Srivastava. Automatic personalization based on web usage mining. *Communications of the ACM*, 43(8):142–151, 2000.
35. B. Mobasher, H. Dai, T. Luo, Y. Sun, and J. Zhu. Integrating web usage and content mining for more effective personalization. In *Proceedings of the International Conference on E-Commerce and Web Technologies (ECWeb2000)*, pages 165–176, Greenwich, UK, 2000.
36. N. Noy and M. Musen. Prompt: Algorithm and tool for automated ontology merging and alignment. In *Proceedings of the Seventeenth National Conference on Artificial Intelligence (AAAI-2000)*, pages 450–455, Austin, Texas, 2000.
37. D. Oberle. *Semantic Community Web Portals - Personalization, Studienarbeit.* Universität Karlsruhe, 2000.
38. L. Page, S. Brin, R. Motwani, and T. Winograd. The pagerank citation ranking: Bringing order to the web. In *Proceedings of the 7th International World Wide Web Conference*, pages 161–172, Brisbane, Australia, 1998.
39. S. Parent, B. Mobasher, and S. Lytinen. An adaptive agent for web exploration based of concept hierarchies. In *Proceedings of the 9th International Conference on Human Computer Interaction*, New Orleans, LA, 2001.
40. Ramana Rao Peter Pirolli, James Pitkow. Silk from a sow's ear: Extracting usable structures from the web. In *Proc. ACM Conf. Human Factors in Computing Systems, CHI*, pages 118 – 125, New York, NY, 1996. ACM Press.
41. Tobias Scheffer and Stefan Wrobel. A sequential sampling algorithm for a general class of utility criteria. In *Knowledge Discovery and Data Mining*, pages 330–334, 2000.
42. M. Spiliopoulou and C. Pohle. Data mining for measuring and improving the success of web sites. *Data Mining and Knowledge Discovery*, 5:85–14, 2001.
43. J. Srivastava, R. Cooley, M. Deshpande, and P.-N. Tan. Web usage mining: discovery and application of usage patterns from web data. *SIGKDD Explorations*, 1(2):12–23, 2000.
44. G. Stumme and A. Maedche. FCA–Merge: Bottom-Up Merging of Ontologies. In *IJCAI-2001 – Proceedings of the 17th International Joint Conference on Artificial Intelligence, Seattle, USA, August, 1-6, 2001*, pages 225–234, San Francisco, 2001. Morgen Kaufmann.
45. G. Stumme, R. Taouil, Y. Bastide, N. Pasqier, and L. Lakhal. Computing iceberg concept lattices with titanic. *J. on Knowledge and Data Engineering (in print)*, 2002.
46. Gerd Stumme. Using ontologies and formal concept analysis for organizing business knowledge. In *Proc. Referenzmodellierung 2001 (in print)*, 2002.
47. A.B. Williams and C Tsatsoulis. An instance-based approach for identifying candidate ontology relations within a multi-agent system. In *Proceedings of the First Workshop on Ontology Learning OL'2000*, Berlin, Germany, 2000. Fourteenth European Conference on Artificial Intelligence.

Bringing Together
Semantic Web and Web Services

Joachim Peer

Institute for Media and Communications Management
University of St. Gallen
Blumenbergplatz 9, 9000 St. Gallen, Switzerland
joachim.peer@unisg.ch

Abstract. There are two major ongoing efforts to advance the World
Wide Web. On one side there is the Semantic Web research, on the
other side is the Web Service research. Both activities aim to make content on the web accessible and usable not only for humans but also
for machines in order to create a foundation for intelligent automated
services and business processes. These two efforts are highly complementary, and there is work in progress towards a unification of them. This
paper contributes to this process of unification by presenting a method
of connecting Web Services descriptions with Semantic Web ontologies.

1 Introduction

The World Wide Web is built for human use rather than for use by machines. At
the moment we can identify two efforts being undertaken to make information
on the web better accessible to machines. One of the efforts is the Web Service
initiative, the other effort is the Semantic Web research.

It is the objective of both of these efforts to create a "next generation web",
which provides new means for machines to use information on the web. While the
Web Service effort is primary focused on syntactical standardisation of data exchange and service publishing, the Semantic Web effort is focused on expressing
explicit semantics on the web.

This paper shows that the Semantic Web and Web Services are different
but complementary approaches which can be combined to enhance the current
web. Furthermore this paper will demonstrate that the convergence of these
two efforts can be achieved with technology already available today. As a first
step to validate this assumption the paper will present a concept of semantic
annotations of WSDL documents.

This paper is structured as follows: Section 2 presents the existing background
for this paper by describing the two approaches to provide a "next generation
web" as well as the needs for their combination and the gap existing between
them. Section 3 describes an approach to bridge this gap and illustrates it by
an example. The paper concludes with a summary of findings and an outlook of
activities to implement the suggested solution.

I. Horrocks and J. Hendler (Eds.): ISWC 2002, LNCS 2342, pp. 279–291, 2002.

2   Foundations

2.1   Web Services

Web Services are self contained, self described modular applications, which can be published, found and used on the web [12]. The infrastructural basis of the Web Services concept is formed by a small set of XML based standards.

Web services are important cornerstones of emerging architectures and application frameworks like Microsoft.NET, IBM Dynamic eBusiness and Sun ONE. Even eCommerce architectures like eSpeak or ebXML have been adapted to fit into the Web Service infrastructure. These and many other ongoing activities indicate the industrial backing of the Web Service efforts. The development of Web Service related efforts is coordinated by the World Wide Web consortium and by industrial consortia like the Web Service Interoperability Group.

The original motivation behind these activities is to enhance interoperability between heterogeneous information systems. Interoperability is primarily needed by two majors areas of application: on the one hand it is needed for enterprise application integration (EAI) in order to connect separated systems quickly and at low costs; on the other hand, interoperability is needed by business to business (B2B) integration, to reduce costs and enhance flexibility of cooperation.

The current Web Service architecture is built around a small set of de facto standards for message transfer, Web Service description and Web Service discovery:

Web Service Standards. The standard for the exchange of messages between Web Services is called Simple Object Access Protocol (SOAP) [22]. The SOAP specification defines an XML schema for a container which holds messages to be transported; it also defines a set of encoding rules and a convention for the representation of remote procedure calls (RPC) and responses.

The concept behind SOAP is not new. Many of its ideas are derived from RPC-related techniques like DCOM, CORBA or RMI. The key benefit of SOAP is its platform independence which its predecessors could not provide. SOAP is neither bound to Windows, nor to Java nor to some implementations of Object Request Brokers. This makes SOAP the preferred communication protocol in the world of Web Services.

The current standard of the description of Web Services is the Web Service Description Language (WSDL) [23] which is currently under review at the World Wide Web consortium. The syntax of WSDL is defined in XML Schema. If SOAP is to be compared with RPC related techniques such as CORBA or RMI, WSDL has to be compared with Interface Definition Languages (IDL). The technical requirements and details needed when accessing a Web Service are described by a WSDL document. A WSDL document describes the location of a web service, its available operations and their associated messages and data types as well as the format of their result values.

This paper will use some elements of the WSDL terminology; therefore the most important elements of WSDL documents will be described briefly: The

XML Schema types of message parameters may be defined using a `<types>` element. A `<message>` element is needed to compose such data types into messages. Messages need to be grouped into operations, which may define an `<input>`, an `<output>` and a `<fault>` message. Depending on the presence or absence of input- and output messages, operations may be defined as one-way messages, request/response messages, solicit/response messages or notifications. Operations are grouped within a specific `<portType>` element. All WSDL elements described so far allow the definition of web service signatures in an abstract and portable manner. To make these abstract operations available via a defined method of transport, `<binding>` elements are used which declare message formats and protocol details for operations and messages of a particular portType. An individual endpoint address of a binding is defined by a `<port>` element, which in turn may be referenced by a `<service>` element. WSDL documents can incorporate information from other WSDL documents using an `<import>` element. This allows modularization of WSDL descriptions and stimulates the reuse of common abstract messages, operations and data types. This way WSDL enables the standardization of abstract Web Service descriptions.

In order to help potential users to discover Web Services for particular tasks, infrastructures like "Yellow Pages" are needed. Various different architectures are proposed for this kind of service. The most important concept is the registry-based UDDI (Universal Description, Discovery and Integration) framework, which enables the registration of businesses and services using various kinds of taxonomies (e.g. UNSPSC, SIC, NAICS). Web Services that are not enlisted in registries may be published on Web Pages using Web Service Inspection Language [9] documents, which may be processed by search engines.

Limitations of Web Services. The Web Service standards described above are technical conventions which allow parties to easily exchange information in a standardized manner. These standards solve many problems on the technical level but the semantics of Web Services and Web Service descriptions as a whole are not addressed by them. The following fragment of a Web Service description illustrates this fact:

```
<message name="getTemperatureRequest">
  <part name="zipcode" type="xsd:string"/>
</message>
<message name="getTemperatureResponse">
  <part name="temperature" type="xsd:float"/>
</message>
<portType name="TemperatureServicePortType">
  <operation name="getTemperature" >
    <input message="tns:getTemperatureRequest"
           name="getTemperatureRequest"/>
    <output message="tns:getTemperatureResponse"
           name="getTemperatureResponse"/>
  </operation>
</portType>
```

An agent capable of WSDL can process this data structure and is able to interpret that the service offers messages called `getTemperatureRequest` and `getTemperatureResponse`. It can also interpret that these messages are used by a request/response operation called `getTemperature`. Furthermore it can determine the name and XML Schema types of the parameters `zipcode` and `temperature`. But it will not be able to figure out the actual meaning of these operations, e.g. that the service described will take Zone Improvement Plan (ZIP)-code of a North American city and will return the temperature of the air in that city expressed in units of Fahrenheit.

An agent is only able to interpret and process such information correctly if its internal model of the domain is in some way connected to the hidden semantics of the WSDL description. This kind of connection can be achieved if both the internal model of the agents and the description of the web service are related to a shared conceptualization.

A simple kind of a shared conceptualization is a domain-specific *standard*, which assigns a certain semantic meaning to a specific syntactical structure. The modularization of WSDL allows to define such standards; e.g. domain specific port types (and its supporting operations, messages and data types) may be multilaterally declared as a standard an may be incorporated into individual web service descriptions using WSDL `<import>` statements and can be bound to a specific protocol and physical address using `<binding>` and `<port>` elements.

As a result, agents programmed against that domain-specific standard descriptions can interact with every Web Service compliant to that standard; the agents' internal model is connected to the semantic meaning represented by the standard. This kind of connection is typically established by a developer who interprets the standard and incorporates its meaning into the agent she/he is implementing.

The benefits of this concept are the simple means for implementation and the predictable behaviour of automatic agents. The disadvantages of this concept can be described as follows: agents programmed against a specific set of Web Service interfaces can only solve a very restricted set of problems using a very restricted set of problem solving methods; they are basically static and inflexible.

If the semantics of such standards would be described explicitly in a machine interpretable manner, agents could gather information about purpose and usage of services at runtime and would be able to behave in a more flexible manner. This problem area is the object of investigations undertaken by Semantic Web research.

2.2   Semantic Web

The Semantic Web can be defined as "an extension of the current web in which information is given well-defined meaning, better enabling computers and people to work in cooperation" [1].

The core concept of the Semantic Web is the representation of data in a machine interpretable way. The basic means for this purpose is provided by the Ressource Description Framework (RDF) [18]. RDF allows the representation of data as triples of subjects, predicates and their values, thus providing a basic and widely applicable binary propositional language.

To build more complex models, a Frame-like technique [15] is needed to separate the universe of discourse in classes, properties and their instanciations thus providing stronger modelling capabilites. These are provided by the RDF Schema standard [19].

The use of RDF and RDF Schema enables the construction of semantic nets [17] which can describe all kinds of resources. However, the problem with semantic nets is that they tend to lead to very complex graphs with sub-optimal reasoning behaviour.

A proposed solution to this problem is to restrict the expressiveness of semantic nets. This topic is well studied by the research field of Description Logics. Description logics restrict semantic nets to adhere to a controlled set of epistemological constructors ("primitives") which may be used as building blocks defining complex structures (ontologies[1]).

The set of constructors supported by a Description Logics system determines its reasoning behaviour. These relationships are well studied not only in theory but also in concrete systems like FaCT [8] or CLASSIC [2].

Efforts to leverage the benefits of Description Logics to the Semantic Web have led to the creation of the ontology language DAML+OIL. The syntax and some basic semantics of DAML+OIL are defined using RDF Schema. The precise semantics of its constructors are defined by axiomatic semantics expressed in first order logics [3] as well as by model theoretic semantics [7].

Applying Semantic Web Technology to Web Services. Adding semantic information to syntactical Web Service definitions can help an automatic agent to better interpret the purpose and usage of Web Services, thus leading to a higher level of flexibility. However, this assumption is based on two premises (a) that the referenced ontologies are built in a way that supports automatic reasoning and (b) that the agent is able to relate the concepts provided in the ontology to concepts of its internal model of the world.

As it has been discussed above, premise (a) can be fulfilled by using Description Logics based ontology formalisms like DAML+OIL. However, premise (b) can only be satisfied if the elements used in the referenced ontology are derived from concepts, which are common to all parties involved. This calls for standardised top level ontologies and agreements of the semantics expressed by that ontologies.

A DAML+OIL based framework providing such well defined ontologies for semantic markup of Web Services is DAML-S [12,14], which is currently under development and available as version 0.6. DAML-S aims to provide a set of ontological constructs which enables agents to automatically discover, evaluate and invoke Web Services, potentially as a part of an overall task (workflow). Addi-

---

[1] This paper uses the definition provided by Gruber [6], who defines an ontology as a "formalization of a conceptualization".

tional capabilities like monitoring of Web Services are supposed to be supported by future versions of DAML-S.

DAML-S consists of a couple of top-level ontologies containing constructs to describe various aspects of services needed to express its aim and usage. They are expressed by a "ServiceProfile", a "ServiceModel" and a "ServiceGrounding".

A ServiceProfile contains information needed to get a high level overview of the purpose of a service, its general input and output, its requirements (preconditions like membership or financial liquidity) and the effects of its execution. Moreover a ServiceProfile may provide non-functional aspects of the service like guaranteed levels of quality and it can also provide some information about the service provider. This kind of data is needed by an agent to quickly determine the applicability of a particular service for a particular task.

A ServiceModel provides a more detailed description of the operations provided by the Web Service. It allows the description of a Web Service in terms of a set of processes and the input, output, preconditions and effects of each of the processes. The process structure may be built in a recursive way, i.e. services may consist of a set of sub-services. ServiceModels may also contain statements about the runtime behaviour and interaction patterns of processes by defining workflow constructs like conditional switches, loops or parallel executions.

This kind of modelling enables both the fine-grained description of Web Services on the lower level of operations and message-parameters as well as the description of a Web Service and its behaviour as a whole.

The Remaining Gap. In contrast to the ServiceProfile and ServiceModel the proposed ontology for a ServiceGrounding does not exist yet. Therefore it is currently not possible to exploit the benefits of the semantic description of Web Services. This paper provides an approach that can provide that missing link for the domain of Web Services.

3   Proposed Solution

This paper proposes a method to bridge the gap between the semantic descriptions of Web Services (i.e. DAML-S ServiceProfiles and ServiceModels) on the one side and the technical descriptions (i.e. WSDL documents) on the other side.

The motivation behind our approach is as follows: all the technical aspects of Web Service usage are already described in WSDL documents. Instead of modelling all of that information in a meta data language, we propose to use the data in the WSDL document directly. The bridge between WSDL descriptions an Semantic Web ontologies is defined within the WSDL document.

To bridge between the structural WSDL definition and its intended meaning, we need to map two kinds of structural data to its semantics:

- Message Parts, and indirectly their respective data types
- Operations

In order to map structural data types to their semantics, a flexible data mapping mechanism is required. Such a mechanism can be found in the Meaning Definition Language (MDL) [24]:

3.1 Meaning Definition Language

MDL is an XML based language which allows to explicitly define how the structures of an XML data type conveys meanings. The meanings referenced may be contained in ontologies expressed by languages like DAML+OIL.

Basically, MDL defines the semantic information carried by nodes of an XML Schema definition. Nodes are referenced using XPATH [21] expressions. The meta model of the MDL is based on a triple of objects, properties and associations. This meta model leads to a widely applicable way of mapping structure to meaning (i.e. classes, properties and associations defined in DAML+OIL ontologies): To define how an XML Schema definition represents an instance of a *class*, the XPATH of at least one node type needs to be provided; to define how a schema represents a *property*, the XPATHs of at least two node types need to be provided; to define how a schema represents an *association*, the XPATHs of at least three nodes types need to be provided [24].

XML documents are hiding information not only inside their structure, but also inside the actual values of related elements and attributes. For instance, a certain XML element with XPATH "/school/pupil" may be assigned to a class "mature-student" or to a class "young-student" in dependence of a related attribute "age". To handle these and much more complicated cases, MDL provides several ways to incorporate conditions, using XPATH-compliant syntax. The listing below illustrates this technique, demonstrating how to define the meaning of elements of an XML Schema by mapping them to ontology elements like "mature-student" and "young-student":

```
<element context = '/school/pupil>
 <me:object class= 'mature-student' >
  <me:when objectToLeftValue = '@age'
           test = '>' rightValue = '30'/>
  <me:inclusion>
    <me:condition assoc="attends"
    obj1="mature-student" obj2="school" />
  </me:inclusion>
 </me:object>
 <me:object class= 'young-student' >
  <me:when objectToLeftValue = '@age'
           test = '<=' rightValue = '30'/>
  <me:inclusion>
   <me:condition assoc="attends"
    obj1="young-student" obj2="school" />
  </me:inclusion>
 </me:object>
</element>
```

A very useful property of MDL mappings is their bi-directionality: a valid MDL mapping between the elements of an XML Schema type and the elements of an ontology contains sufficient information to transform ontological data to its respective XML representation as well as to extract the meaning of a given XML document.

This feature is of great importance for the overall concept of the integration of Web Services with the Semantic Web. An agent capable of processing DAML+OIL may use MDL to transform data from a DAML+OIL repository into the XML grammar required by the service it wants to interact with. In case of a service response, the agent may use MDL to automatically generate DAML+OIL representations from the XML-based service-output.

3.2   Hook-Ups

The actual application of data mappings is performed by links defined inside the WSDL document. We will call these links "Hook-Ups". Hook-Ups must not violate the structural integrity of a WSDL file, because SOAP containers, development environments and common Web Service applications dealing with WSDL documents would be unable to process such documents. Therefore we use an annotation method as used by systems like SHOE [11] or Ontobroker's HTMLA [4] and use an extension mechanism provided by the hosting data format. In the case of WSDL, which is based on XML, we can use the extensions mechanism provided by XML namespaces [20].

Hook-Ups for Message Parts and Data Types. For combining message parts with their respective meaning we propose to use a namespace-qualified Hook-Up "semantic:schema-adjunct" which refers to an external MDL definition (called "adjunct" in MDL jargon). Alternatively, the MDL definition may be part of the XML schema definition inside the <types> element of the WSDL document. The standardized XML Schema element <appinfo> could be used for this purpose. However, this option has the disadvantage of ignoring that the meaning of an XML Schema type may change with the context (e.g. message type) it is associated with. Therefore this paper proposes to define the reference to a schema-adjunct always in correspondence to the message it is used in (as it will be shown in Fig.1 below).

Hook-Ups for Operations. Semantic Hook-Ups for message-parts as described above already provide an important part of the semantics of an operation. However, this is not a sufficient description yet. We also need to map the semantics of an operation as a whole to its respective meaningful pendant in a (DAML-S) ontology.

For this reason this paper proposes to provide a WSDL <operation> element with a Hook-Up by introducing an attribute <operation> in the newly created namespace.

3.3   An Example

We will now illustrate this technique by annotating the WSDL code fragment already introduced in Sect. 2.1. The semantic annotations adhere to the namespace prefix semantic.

In this example we define the meaning of the operation "getTemperature" by adding a Hook-Up <semantic:operation> referring to the DAML+OIL construct which defines the meaning of the operation (in this case, this meaning is provided by the DAML+OIL class http://another.org/agentTasks2344.daml# MeasuringTemperature).

Message parts contained in this operation are linked to their meaningful pendants, a DAML-S process-input "zip_code" and a DAML-S process-output "temperature".

```
<?xml version="1.0" encoding="UTF-8"?> <!DOCTYPE uridef[
  <!ENTITY ont1 ''http://some.org/classificationschemate.daml">
  <!ENTITY ont2 ''http://some.other.org/nature.daml">
  <!ENTITY ont3 ''http://another.org/agentTasks2344.daml">
  <!ENTITY adj ''http://another.org/adjunct '''>
]> <definitions name="DemoTemperatureService"
 targetNamespace="http://weatherstation.org/temperature"
 xmlns:tns="http://weatherservice.com/temperature"
 xmlns:rdf ="http://www.w3.org/1999/02/22-rdf-syntax-ns#"
 xmlns:daml="http://www.daml.org/2001/03/daml+oil#"
 xmlns:semantic="http://some.org/spec/"
 xmlns="http://schemas.xmlsoap.org/wsdl/"

  <message name="getTemperatureRequest">
    <part name="zipcode" type="xsd:string"
     semantic:type="&ont1;#ZipCode"
        semantic:schema-adjunct="&adj;_zipcode.mdl"/>
  </message>
  <message name="getTemperatureResponse">
    <part name="return"
     semantic:type="&ont2;#CelsiusTemperature"
     semantic:schema-adjunct="&adj;_temperature.mdl"/>
  </message>
  <portType name="DemoTemperatureServicePortType">
    <operation name="getTemperature"
      semantic:operation="&ont3;#MeasuringTemperature" >
        <input message="tns:getTemperatureRequest"/>
        <output message="tns:getTemperatureResponse"/>
      </operation>
  </portType>
  <-- rest of the WSDL document (binding, service - element) -->
</definitions>
```

A graphical representation of this semantic annotation is shown in Fig. 1:

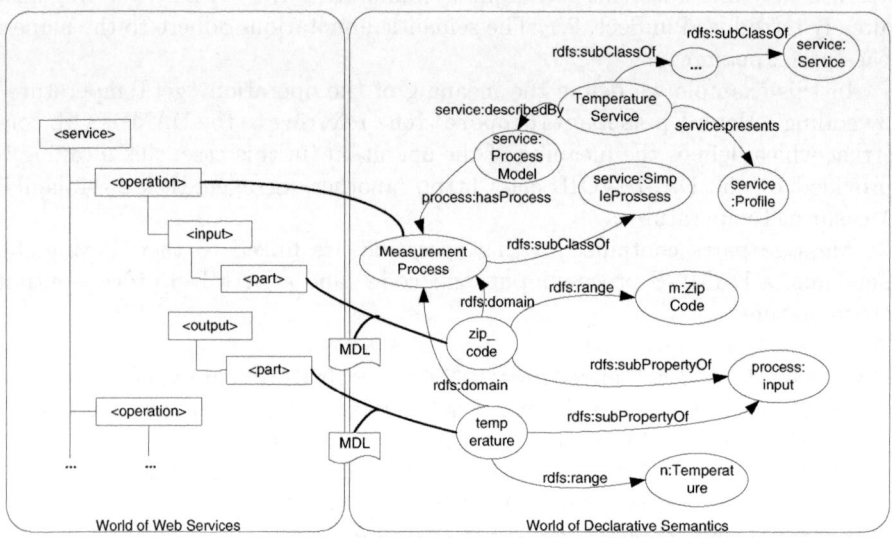

Fig. 1. Linking a WSDL document to its meaning

The annotated WSDL description may be referenced by a t-Model entry of a UDDI registry and it may be used by agents which are not capable of drawing logical inferences, thus providing necessary backward compatibility to existing solutions.

The DAML-S descriptions the WSDL annotations refer to may be stored at any other place on the web and may be found and processed by (Semantic) Web Crawlers and made accessible for search engines like ASCS (e.g. Agent Semantic Communication Service [10]). Such search engines or similar tools for semantic reasoning may be used to query DAML-S descriptions to find the Web-Services (and their WSDL descriptions) which fit the needs for a particular process or task.

If the search was successful and an URL of an annotated WSDL description of the matching service or services was found, then the agent can use the annotated WSDL document to gather the technical details needed for calling the services' operations and to transform DAML+OIL instances to XML elements used by the Web Service. The XML based result values returned by the Web Service may then be transformed back into DAML+OIL-instances, and may used for further processing by the agent, eventually triggering additional service calls.

4   Related Work

The idea of combining Semantic Web techniques with the concept of Web Services was presented in several publications, with different focus. A very influential work is DAML-S [13,14], which establishes a framework for reasoning over web service meta data. The relationships between WSDL and DAML-S were also briefly discussed in [13], where the authors state that WSDL differs from DAML-S, because DAML-S covers all aspects of service descriptions, whereas WSDL is primarily focussing on service grounding. The present paper is based on this finding and suggests a way how agents capable of DAML-S can interact with WSDL-based service groundings.

A proposal with some similarities to the ideas described in the present paper can be found in [16]. This paper demonstrates how WSDL descriptions can be expressed using RDF, thus providing a bridge between Semantic Web and Web Services. The concept presented in [16] has the advantage that all elements of (RDF encoded) WSDL descriptions are identified by an URI, thus allowing other RDF documents to assert statements about them. This way the semantic Hook-Ups could be defined completely outside the WSDL document. However, the disadvantage of such a method is that RDF encoded WSDL documents can not be considered as valid WSDL. This requires to maintain both an XML encoded and an RDF encoded version of the WSDL document and to keep both in sync.

5   Summary and Outlook

Semantic Web research and the Web Service initiative are different but complementary approaches to enable automatic agents accessing information on the web in a better way than on the classical human-centric World Wide Web.

Furthermore this paper argues that the convergence of these two efforts can be achieved with technology available today. As a first step to validate this assumption the paper presented a concept of semantic annotations of WSDL which link the structural elements of WSDL documents to semantics contained in DAML-S models. This concept contributes to the improvement of the current usage of Web Service technology.

However, the assumptions presented by this paper are not tested yet. The next step will be to build a prototype which actually demonstrates the concepts presented in this paper in order to test this approach. The challenge of this project lies in combining existing technologies such as WSDL-, UDDI- and SOAP-APIs, XML schema validators, MDL interpreters, RDF parsers and DAML+OIL engines.

Acknowledgements

The author would like to thank Izabella Mierzejewska, Markus Greunz and Rolf Grütter for their valuable inputs and support.

References

1. Berners-Lee, T.; Hendler, J.; Lassile, O.: The Semantic Web. *Scientific American*, Vol. 5/01, 2001.
   (http://www.scientificamerican.com/2001/0501issue/0501berners-lee.html)
2. Borgida, A.; Brachman, R.J.; McGuinness D.L; Alperin Resnick, L.: CLASSIC: A Structural Data Model for Objects. in *Proceedings of the 1989 ACM SIGMOD International Conference on Management of Data* , pp 59-67, 1989.
3. Fikes, R.; McGuinness, D.: An Axiomatic Semantics for RDF, RDF Schema, and DAML+OIL. Stanford University, 2001.
   (http://www.daml.org/2001/03/axiomatic-semantics.html)
4. Fensel, D.: Ontologies: A Silver Bullet for Knowledge Management and Electronic Commerce. Springer Verlag, 2001.
5. Festa, P.: Wanted: Web Service Standards. Online Magazine Article, 2001.
   (http://zdnet.com.com/2100-1104-835247.html)
6. Gruber, T.R.: A Translation Approach to Portable Ontology Specifications. Technical Report, Stanford University, 1997.
7. van Harmelen, F.; Patel-Schneider, P.; Horrocks, I.: A Model Theoretic Semantics for DAML+OIL. 2001. (http://www.daml.org/2001/03/model-theoretic-semantics.html)
8. Horrocks, I.: The FaCT system. In H. de Swart (editor), Automate Reasoning with Analytic Tableaux and Related Methods: *International Conference Tableaux'98*, number 1397 in Lecture Notes in Artificial Intelligence, pp 307-312, Springer-Verlag, 1998. (http:/www.cs.man.ac.uk/~horrocks/Publications/download/1998/t98-paper.ps.gz)
9. International Business Machines Corporation: Web Services Inspection Language (WS-Inspection) 1.0. Specification, 2001. (http://www-106.ibm.com/developerworks/webservices/library/ws-wsilspec.html?dwzone=webservices)
10. Lee, J.; Pease, A.; Barbee; C.: Experimenting with ASCS Semantic Search. Project Report, 2002. (http://reliant.teknowledge.com/DAML/DAML.ps)
11. Luke, S.; Spector, L.; Rager, D.: Ontology-Based Knowledge Discovery on the World Wid Web. In: *Proceedings of the Workshop on Internet-based Information Systems at the AAAI-96*, Portland, Oregon, USA, August 4-8, 1996.
12. Martin, J.: Web Services: The Next Big Thing. XML Journal 2, 2001.
    (http://www.sys-con.com/xml/archivesbad.cfm)
13. Martin, D.; Burstein, M.; Ankolenkar, A.; Paolucci, M.; Payne, T.; Sycara, K; Lassila, O.; McIlraith, S.; Son, T.C; Zeng, H.; Hobbs, J.; Narayanan, S; McDermott, D.: DAML-S: Semantic Markup for Web Services. White paper, 2001.
    (http://www.daml.org/services/daml-s/2001/10/daml-s.pdf)
14. McIlraith, S.A.; Son, T.C.; Zeng, H.: Semantic web services. *IEEEIntelligent Systems*, 16(2), March/April, 2001.
15. Minsky, M.: A Framework for Representing Knowledge. MIT-AI Laboratory Memo 306, June, 1974. (http://web.media.mit.edu/ minsky/papers/Frames/frames.html)
16. Ogbuji, U.: Supercharging WSDL with RDF - Managing structured Web Service metadata. IBM developerWorks article, 2000.
17. Quillian, M.R.: Semantic memory. In: Minsky, M(editor), *Semantic Information Processing*. M.I.T. Press, 1968.
18. World Wide Web Consortium: Resource Description Framework (RDF) Model and Syntax Specification. Specification, 1999. (http://www.w3.org/TR/1999/REC-rdf-syntax-19990222/)

19. World Wide Web Consortium: Resource Description Framework (RDF) Schema Specification 1.0. Specification, 1999. (http://www.w3.org/TR/2000/CR-rdf-schema-20000327)
20. World Wide Web Consortium: Namespaces in XML. Spezification, 1999. (http://www.w3.org/TR/1999/REC-xml-names-19990114)
21. World Wide Web Consortium: XML Path Language (XPath) Version 1.0. Spezification, 1999. (http://www.w3.org/TR/xpath)
22. World Wide Web Consortium: SOAP Version 1.2 Part 0: Primer. 2001 (http://www.w3.org/TR/soap12-part0/)
23. World Wide Web Consortium: Web Services Description Language (WSDL) 1.1. 2001 (http://www.w3.org/TR/wsdl)
24. Worden, R.: A Meaning Definition Language. White paper, 2001. (http://www.charteris.com/mdl/MDLWhitePaper.pdf)

Global vs. Community Metadata Standards: Empowering Users for Knowledge Exchange

Marek Hatala and Griff Richards

Technical University of British Columbia
2400 Surrey Place
10153 King George Highway
Surrey, BC V3T 2W1, Canada
{hatala, richards}@techbc.ca

Abstract. The idea of knowledge sharing has strong roots in the education process. With the current development of the technology and moving learning material into the web environment it acquired a new dimension. Learning objects are the chunks of knowledge shared by e-learning community. Organizations and individuals are building repositories of learning objects and annotate them with metadata to describe their educational values and standardization efforts are on the way to provide a franca lingua for the educators. In this paper we describe the peer-to-peer infrastructure for sharing learning object we are building in Canada. The POOL projects builds on the three types of nodes: SPLASH is an freely downloadable application which allows individuals to create metadata and maintain their collection of learning objects, PONDs are bigger repositories of learning objects connected to the peer-to-peer network and POOL centrals increase the speed and breadth of the searches in the peer-to-peer network. The POOL project uses CanCore - a subset of the IMS metadata protocol - to describe learning objects. In the second part of the paper we discuss the future direction of this initiative based on the maturing learning objects community and lessons learned in the deployment of POOL network. We argue that the standardization effort, although very important, currently provides solutions that are too complex. We see the communities where the knowledge is shared to be the main force in the creation of the metadata standards which would support the growth of semantic web. The implications of moving the responsibility for schemas and metadata creation on communities poses new requirements on interoperability and tools. We describe those requirements and we outline approach we are developing to address them.

1 e-Learning, Learning Objects, and Metadata Standards

With a growing number of organizations moving their training and education programs into the web environment, there is an increasing demand for high-quality, reusable components – learning objects (LOs). This demand comes from the realization that the development of learning objects is resource intensive and time consuming. The learning object is a definable, reusable chunk of digital content and process elements used for learning and instruction [1].

I. Horrocks and J. Hendler (Eds.): ISWC 2002, LNCS 2342, pp. 292–306, 2002.
© Springer-Verlag Berlin Heidelberg 2002

With the huge uptake of web technology in education and training has generated a flurry of un coordinated activity developing digital learning objects – images, animations, computer applets or textual content which could be used in the processes of education and training. Centralized digital learning object repositories evolved as a means of collecting and cataloguing these assets with hopes of reducing the redundancy of development and enabling others to build on the aggregated ideas and designs, and in many cases to preserve the elements, and protect the rights of ownership and usage.

1.1 Learning Object Metadata

It was immediately recognized that standards are important for interoperability between learning and business systems. Several standards for describing metadata have been developed through collaboration between the private and public sectors. The IEEE Learning Object Metadata [2] defines a set of metadata elements that can be used to describe learning resources. The IMS Global Learning Consortium has identified a minimum set of IEEE metadata elements called IMS Core [3]. The IMS metadata consist of over 80 elements describing different aspects of learning objects.

However, the business and educational communities have been slow to adopt the full IMS standard mainly due to the high number of the fields and vagueness with which the values for these fields have been defined. Too much information results in too much time spent cataloging that no one will bother. On the other hand, too little information in the tagging will result in too many false positive results. The alternate standard, the Dublin Core [4] protocol identifies only 15 fields.

The Canadian Core Learning Resource Metadata Protocol (CanCore) [5] has been defined to specifically address these problems. CanCore was developed in Phase I of the POOL project (described below) by the collaboration of Canadian researchers searching for a level of sufficient specificity to enable the efficient search of learning objects. CanCore is a concerted effort to identify a sufficient number of fields (36) to be useful for educators, without overburdening the indexing process. CanCore has sufficient flexibility in its protocol that not all fields need be completed, thus developers can ignore many fields that may be inappropriate for their purposes. CanCore is fully compliant with the IMS metatagging specification. As IMS matures, additional development will be required of CanCore. CanCore elements are organized into 9 groups describing different characteristics of the learning object. Table 1 provides a description of these groups, more detail information can be found on the CanCore website [5] and concrete examples of the metadata CanCore records are on [16].

Having a standard metadata protocol is of little use unless it is maintained and widely used. Only if a critical mass of educational users standardizes their cataloging with CanCore can the POOL repository protocols search and locate learning objects with efficiency. CanCore must also be embedded in repository systems – this has been promoted by a general agreement in Phase I among Canarie Learning Program projects [6] to use the CanCore protocol. To support CanCore adoption, the documentation, indexing guidelines, training and support is provided to educators by the CanCore team.

Table 1 CanCore elements

General	Groups information describing learning object as a whole. *Active elements:* Identifier, Title, Catalogentry.Catalog, Catalogentry.Entry, Learning Object Language, Description, Coverage
Lifecycle	History and current state of resource. *Active elements:* Version, Contribute.Role, Contribute.Entity, Contribute.Date
Metametadata	Features of the description rather than the resource. *Active elements:* Identifier , Catalogentry.Catalog, Catalogentry.Entry, Contribute.Role, Contribute.Entity, Contribute.Date, Metadata Scheme, Metadata Language
Technical	Technical features of the learning object. *Active elements:* Format, Size, Location, Other Platform Requirements, Duration
Educational	Educational or pedagogic features of the learning object. *Active elements:* Learning Resource Type, Intended End User Role, Context, Typical Age Range, User's Language
Rights	Conditions of use of the resource. *Active elements:* Cost, Copyright and Other Restrictions, Description
Relation	Features of the resource in relationship to other learning objects. *Active elements:* Kind, Resource.Identifier, Resource.Catalogentry
Classification	Description of a characteristic of the resource by entries in classifications. *Active elements:* Purpose, Taxonpath.Source, Taxonpath.Taxon.Entry, Keyword

1.2 Centralized vs Decentralized Learning Object Repositories

Centralized digital repositories evolved as a means of sharing resources for collecting, cataloguing and storing objects of a defined community. In addition to centralized control, a centralized repository offers advantages in rapid indexing and object retrieval. Unfortunately, a single centralized repository is unlikely to be of sufficient size to accommodate all of the web-based learning objects that have or will be created.

Secondly, there can be workflow disadvantages to the centralized repository as the objects are stored away from their point of origin and away from their point of use. Users have to be connected to the web for even the simplest operation, and off-line creation or modifications of learning objects are not captured until the object and its metadata are re-loaded. We believe the optimal storage sites for learning objects are *close to the creator and close to the user*. Further, as workstation storage increases, it becomes feasible for each learner to amass a personal collection of the learning objects which have influenced their intellectual growth, and to be annotated for future reference and review, much in the manner that study notes enabled classroom learners to keep track of significant content and conceptualizations.

Recent developments in peer-to-peer web technology have made it possible for individuals to amass local collections of entertainment content. Although Napster and Gnutella may have been lacking support for rights management, the peer-to-peer model demonstrated that a global community can benefit from decentralized storage of content on the users' own hard drives. For learning objects this means that individual instructors, if provided with the standard metadata and communication protocol, can develop and store their materials so that others may directly search and access their public materials, or become aware of semi-public materials which the individual may wish to negotiate consideration for use. Individuals may also store private materials that are under development, or are not intended for mass consumption.

Two projects exploiting peer-to-peer technology for learning objects are currently under development. Edutella [17] is a prototype peer-to-peer network which builds in a structured query service to help locate learning objects, an annotation service to allow users to comment on learning objects, and a mediation service to join metadata from different sources. In comparison, the POOL project which is the focus of this paper concentrates on the heterogeneous infrastructure and end-user tools utilizing CanCore standard to connect individual and organizational repositories.

2   POOL: Distributed Infrastructure Based on Standard Metadata

The Portal for Online Objects in Learning (POOL) Project [7] is a consortium of several educational, private and public sector organizations to develop an infrastructure for learning object repositories. It is one of several projects currently funded in part by Canarie's E-Learning Program – Canadian initiatives to build a national infrastructure for collections of high quality learning objects and related business models [6]. The Phase I of the POOL project ended in June 2001 with two major outcomes: the CanCore protocol and the POOL centralized repository prototype. The lessons learned from the evaluation of the prototype helped us to formulate requirements for the Phase II of the project which ends in September 2002. In this section we describe the redesigned POOL infrastructure – a hierarchical network of nodes communicating via peer-to-peer protocol using CanCore as a core metadata exchange schema.

2.1   POOL Architecture

Learning objects are developed mostly by individuals either for their individual purposes or for their organization's needs. Typically, the learning object evolves during its lifetime as it is getting feedback from its intended usage or is redeployed in new instructional contexts. This evolution is possible through a persistent stewardship that exists throughout the object's lifetime. This stewardship may frequently change as interest in using the object shifts from one person or community to another.

To support the evolutionary nature of learning objects we designed POOL as a network of individual peers communicating together using the POOL protocol (Fig. 1). Three types of peers participate in the network: SPLASH, POND, and POOL Central. The names evolved from the original POOL acronym from Phase I for the centralized repository model. It is our hope that the names of nodes represent their relative size, purpose and persistence level, all linked together by the 'water' analogy.

SPLASH is a desktop client communicating with other peers via the peer-to-peer POOL protocol. It provides the metadata creation tools, a limited storage capacity for metadata records and searching capability for the POOL network. SPLASH is developed using open source code, and distributed freely in the belief that thousands of small repositories held by learners and instructors will create a wide acceptance and use of both learning object technology and the CanCore protocol.

The wide distribution of SPLASH will not obviate the existence of community repositories. There is a role to be played for established collections of mature, accepted learning objects with common themes or purpose that can be stored in a selective gallery of learning objects. Indeed, an advantage of the SPLASH is that such galleries or PONDS can be set up with ease. Within the project we have tested the concept by incorporating several community repositories to create PONDs – repositories that are accessible using the POOL protocol and searchable using the CanCore metadata standard. A POND may be simply a larger, community implementation of SPLASH, or it may involve building an interface to a third party repository system. The ability to include such proprietary systems is expected to be an advantage over a single centralized pool, and will hopefully enable organizations already committed to a particular repository technology to contribute their content to the larger POOL movement. POND typically comes with a robust database support and a suite of tools for managing the learning objects workflow. These features are essential for organizations with intensive production of learning objects.

POOL Central is a specialized peer connected to the network and a high speed Internet. The purpose of the POOL Central is to replicate the queries through the other POOL Central peers over the broadband connection and enhancing the reach of the network. POOL Central does not necessarily have a storage capacity, although caching of records might be possible.

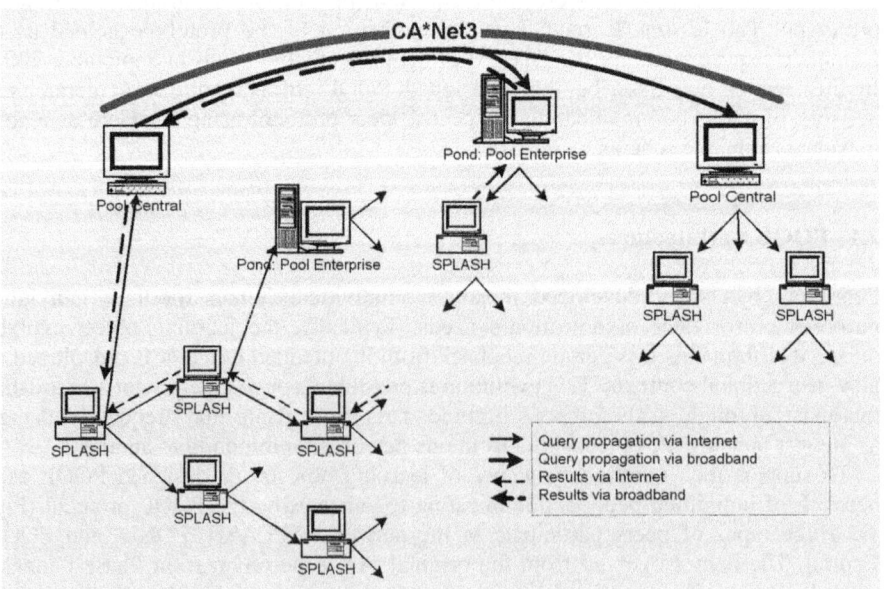

Fig. 1. POOL network architecture

Table 2. POOL network nodes functionality

	SPLASH	POND	POOL Central
Create/edit metadata record	+++	+	
View metadata records	+++	+	
Search for metadata records locally	++	+++	+
Search for metadata in the POOL network	++	++	+++
Respond to the search request from another peer	++	+++	+
Propagate search query and return collected results	++	+	+++
Robust database support	+	+++	
Management and workflow tools		+++	

+ supported ++ main functionality +++specialized

Also, within the proposed hybrid architecture we can see a role to be played by specialized nodes. An example of such a node is the LORI (Learning Object Review Instrument), which can be embedded in SPLASH, and link reviewers to specialized nodes for learning object collaborative assessment (LOCA). A prototype of this is currently being incorporated into the POOL network [8]. The appeal of specialized nodes is that they enable any user or interest group to add intrinsic value to the network without the need for centralized planning, resources or control.

Table 2 illustrates how the network functionality is spread over the network nodes.

2.2 POOL Protocol and Metadata Exchange

The POOL networking component builds on JXTA [9], the publicly available peer-to-peer platform from Sun Microsystems Inc. JXTA provides basic protocols for peer discovery, sending messages, obtaining information, routing and group membership. These protocols are low-level protocols and it is up to the developers to implement the content part of the messages being exchanged. Although POOL does not build on the JXTA Search [10] application it builds on its Query Routing Protocol that specifies message types, message formats, and message routing rules that must be supported. The POOL protocol expands the JXTA Search protocol by building in more control for distributed searches (Section 2.5) and provides for flexibility in metadata schemas used for queries and responses.

Fig. 2 shows a template for the query request. The query parameters specify both format of the query and response as well as parameters of the distributed search. The query space defines the metadata schema which is used to specify the query (with current possible values representing CanCore and IMS). The query-format attribute specifies the binding for the schema specified in the query space. Currently we have implemented formats are native XML-based SPLASH format, we plan to provide generic binding for XML, RDF, and specific binding to the Edutella set of query languages. [17]. The same applies to the response space and response format fields. Being able to specify formats and spaces for queries and responses separately gives us an ability to work with the metadata in different formats. The reasons for having this ability are outlined in the Section 3.2.

Returning results in the pre-specified format requires translation of the records from the "native" format in which they are stored in the repository to the specified format for transmission. We are using XSLT technology to transform between different schemas. Of course, such transformations may cause some loss of information when a direct mapping between schema elements does not exist.

2.3 Modeling Metadata

As might be deduced from the previous section in the design of the SPLASH, we are considering an option of handling of more than one format of the metadata represented by different schemas and exchanged using different formats. In SPLASH we model metadata at the element levels with the full information about the type of data the metadata element can hold (e.g. free text value, defined vocabulary, etc.) and how it is rendered on the entry form and search form screens. Table 3 shows examples of two metadata elements. The meaning of most of the attributes is self-explanatory; the cardinality attributes specify how many copies of the same element appear in the form, HasOtherOption specifies whether an extra text field for new values should be displayed, Expandable specifies whether a newly defined values should be automatically added to the existing vocabulary. Full details are available in [11]. In SPLASH we provide a tool for definition of new elements.

The metadata schema is defined as a collection of the elements. Even standard schemas such as CanCore or IMS are defined in this way. This enables us to treat each schema as a real core and create a community tailored schemas around this core.

The third component of our metadata creation tool is the users' ability to control how many elements from the particular schema are displayed in the forms and views. The user has an ability to define profiles using the profile editor. A set of default profiles is shipped with the SPLASH reflecting various roles the user can take in the

```
<request xmlns="http://www.edusplash.net"
    query-space=[(required)unique URL id for query space]

    query-format={XML|RDF|SPLASH|EDUTELLA}"
    response-space=[unique URL ids for response space]
    response-format={XML|RDF|SPLASH|EDUTELLA}
    query-uuid=[globally unique id of this query]
    query-lifetime=[number of milliseconds this query is valid]
    max-depth=[maximum number of peers to hop]
    max-fanout=[maximum number of peers to forward the query to]
    max-hits-per-provider=[return only n results from each peer]
    max-results=[maximum number of collected results peer sends back
in one flush]
    flush-after-providers=[flush the output stream to the client
after receiving responses from n peers]
    flush-after-ms=[flush the output stream to the client after this
time]
>
    [query specification (arbitrary valid XML)]

</request>
```

Fig. 2. Query specification in POOL protocol

Table 3. Representation of *Title* and *Intended User Role* elements

Attributes	Title	Intended User Role
ElementKey	general.title	educational.intendedenduserrole
PrintName	Title	Intended User
Tooltip	Learning objects name.	Normal user of the learning object, most dominant first.
SubmitStyle	TEXT	COMBO
QueryStyle	TEXT	COMBO
MaxSubmitCardinality	1	4
MaxQueryCardinality	1	2
HasOtherOption	False	False
Expandable	False	False
ElementValues	[]	[teacher, author, learner, manager]
NewValues	[]	[]
Mandatory	True	False
SubElements	[]	[]
ParentKey	General	Educational
AllowTextSearch	True	False
AllowVocabSearch	False	True

metadata creation process, e.g. educator, learner, editor, media developer, license specialist, etc. Two types of profiles are supported. First type preferred mainly by the professionals familiar with the metadata reflects semantic groupings of element as it is defined in the standards. For example, CanCore groups element into 9 groups as shown in Table 1 above. Second type of profiles is preferred mainly by the naïve users and organizes element into levels of relative importance or detail. The elements in the first level are those considered to be mandatory for the minimal valid record and those are the only ones displayed in the new form. The second level contains the more specific but still common elements; third and subsequent levels contain more specific but less used elements. The second and subsequent levels are hidden to reduce the mental load of the user and the user has to explicitly choose to display them.

Finally, the fourth feature of the metadata creation support in SPLASH is directed toward users creating high volumes of metadata. In such cases, the values in many fields as creator, educational level, etc., are the same and records differ only in some content specific fields. To speed up the metadata creation process the user can store any (partial) record as a template and later on can use this template as a starting point for metadata creation process. The template editor is provided to support the template management.

2.4 Discovering Peers

POOL is designed as a network of independent peers that are both the providers and consumers of learning objects. Discovery and communication with the other peers is the key to the sharing of learning objects.

The JXTA platform provides the basic discovery functionality including a mechanism for crossing firewalls. An interesting feature we take full benefit from is

JXTA's concept of rendezvous nodes. The rendezvous node is a specialized node that collects the list of other peers and provides this list to peers to speed up the discovery process. We have developed our POOL Central node as a rendezvous node positioned on the high speed Internet (40GB Ca*NET3).

In addition to the peer discovery we provide users with the utility to store information about the favorite peers (e.g. based on the previously obtained results) and organize them into the groups. The user can direct queries directly to selected peers or groups of peers.

2.5   Distributed Search

The search in the POOL network is a combination of the distributed peer-to-peer search and a deep search similar to the one in the JXTA Search application. The peer-to-peer search provides for the breath of the search by broadcasting the query to the neighbor peers in the network. There are several parameters controlling the scope of the search which are shown in Fig. 2. The deep part of the search occurs when the query reaches the POND built on top of an existing repository. In such case the local specific search algorithm is invoked and the results are passed back to the POOL network.

When the search request is received by each individual SPLASH peer a local search is invoked. Local search results are combined with the results received from the peers the query was forwarded to. The growing chain of results is eventually passed back to the originating node. The local search is a combination of four different approaches:

Text search for the text fields. The metadata record contains several fields which enable the creator of the record to enter a free text. Examples of this type of the field might be *general.title* or *general.description* elements. To search for the records with the specific values stored in these fields is possible using a full-text search.

Text search in the vocabularies. Some fields in the schema can be filled only with values selected from the predefined vocabularies. For example, the *educational.intendedenduser* element can only have values from the vocabulary *[Teacher, Author, Learner, Manager]*. In the most cases, these values are proper natural language words and therefore they should be searchable by the full text search.

Value-matching search in the vocabularies. This type of search applies to the fields with values selected from vocabularies. In this case the user specifies exact values for specific elements the record should satisfy.

Taxonomy-based search in the hierarchical vocabularies. This is a third type of the search applicable that applies to the fields with values selected from vocabularies. Some vocabularies can have values organized in the taxonomy. For example, the *general.mediatype* element has vocabulary consisting of values *[Text, Text.Correspondence, Text.Correspondence.Discussion, Text.Correspondence.email, etc.]*. The taxonomy-based search uses this information to find relevant records. For example, when searching for the record with the value *Text.Correspondence*, the record marked with *Text.Correspondence.Discussion* should be retrieved as it represents a more specific value of *Text.Correspondence*. Currently we use simple string parsing algorithm relying on the 'dot-notation' which we plan to replace it with the full ontology search.

The results from each type of search are ranked and multiplied with the coefficient representing the relative importance of the search type. Results from four types of searches are combined and a cumulative rank value is computed for each record. Because the number of results returned from each peer is limited, only the specified number of the best results is returned from each peer. The cumulative rank value is used again when merging local results with those coming from the network.

2.6 Implementation and Deployment

Although we have finished most of the technical development we are still working on the improving the technical solutions. Our main focus now is on deploying the solution by supporting a creation of the community repositories both by connecting existing repositories into the POOL network as well as working with the repository solution providers to make their products pluggable into the network.

SPLASH. The beta version of the SPLASH desktop application is available for the public download free of charge as of February 2002. The version available implements all the functionality listed in the Table 2, it includes a tagging engine enabling the user to create metadata records using CanCore and search engine searching through POOL network. SPLASH is designed with nearly all components designed to be customizable by the user which makes it easy to tailor it for the individual user needs or for other metadata schemas. We anticipate a number of revision cycles during the spring of 2002 to incorporate feedback from our beta testers.

Technically, SPLASH is a Java application running on the user's desktop computer. It uses mySQL as a database engine (bundled with the installation), which is replaceable by another SQL database. Fig. 3 shows a snapshot of the SPLASH search page.

PONDS. We have implemented and deployed so far three PONDS to test different ways how to build or incorporate large repositories going beyond desktop level. The repository at the Center for Curriculum, Transfer and technology in BC has evolved from the SPLASH by dedicating one SPLASH application to play a role of the common repository for the community. Individual community members run they own SPLASH but have a choice of storing the metadata records either at the centralized repository or locally.

The same mechanism has been used for the Canadian Learning Objects Metadata Repository (CanLOM). CanLOM has been built on top of the existing TeleCampus [12] database of over 50,000 learning objects which uses slightly different metadata schema. In the CanLOM case, the repository was a pre-existing system where we built a wrapper to connect it to the POOL network. The wrapper is a networking module from SPLASH connected to the TeleCampus system that is built on Oracle database and ColdFusion. CanLOM functions as a specialized node to expedite search of "published" learning objects. It also implements a registry protocol for the learning objects enabling the user to register the learning object in the CanLOM.

In the third case, we have connected the CAREO [13] repository that uses Web services. In this case, we have implemented a simple component translating between the POOL protocol and Web services.

POOL CENTRALs. The purpose of the POOL Central is to provide the network with the specialized nodes which function as reflectors broadcasting queries into the 'distant' areas on the network. Their efficiency depends on the speed of the connection between them. In Canada, most of the inter-university traffic is routed via Canarie's Ca*Net3 broadband connection, so once a SPLASH node communicates with a peer located on a university network, POOL Central is automatically invoked. So far we have placed POOL Central nodes into four provinces: Calgary in Alberta, Montreal in Quebec, Fredericton in New Brunswick and Vancouver in British Columbia.

3   Lessons Learned

The deployment of the infrastructure of such scale as POOL has a potential for a big impact on the education communities and the business active in this area. The benefit of a publicity accompanying big projects is that the potential users are more serious about considering new opportunities and willing to invest more effort in participation in such initiatives. For developers this brings an enormous opportunity to discuss the users' real needs and identifying their challenges in adopting new technology.

3.1   Communities Mature

The technology and its public acceptance are evolving so rapidly that even during a project as short as POOL the requirements of the communities are growing. On the one side the developers are getting satisfaction from the acceptance of their technology but at the same time the new requirements are arising even before the

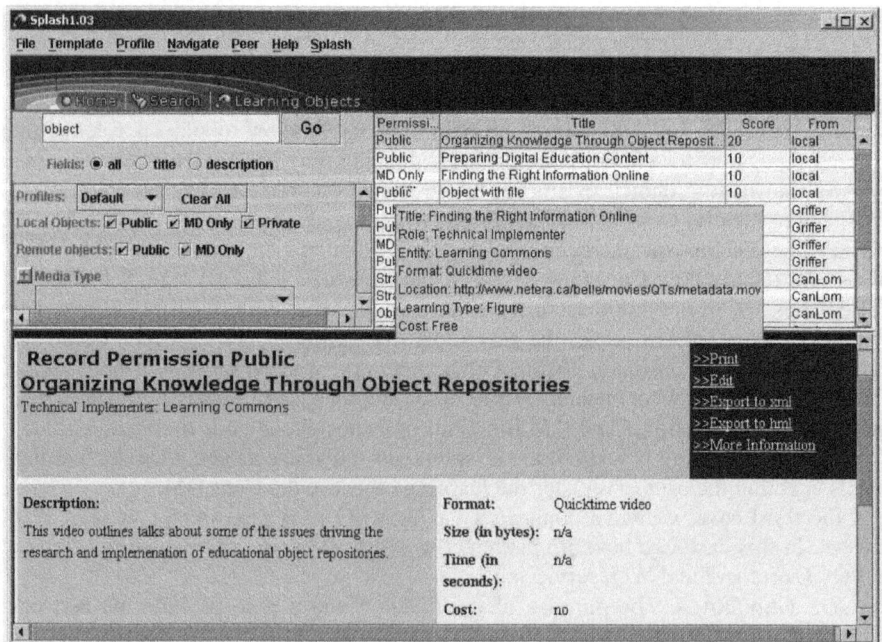

Fig. 3. SPLASH Search page (will provide new snapshot in final version)

system is completely deployed. The idea of metatagged resources brings new ways in which communities share knowledge and it is being cordially accepted Individual communities are starting to articulate their requirements to support their needs.

Working with the real users and communities always helps to sharpen the research ideas and keep them focused. In this section we would like to generalize our findings from the deployment of the POOL system and formulate a new set of requirements for the metadata sharing system supporting diverse communities.

3.2 Too Much Metadata

The role of metadata was to help solve the problems of search and discovery of learning objects. Ideally, each record could be tagged with catalogue information about its title, content, the intended audience, and other information about cost, availability, authorship, rights management, language of availability, revision history, relationship with other objects, etcetera. These metatag elements then become the targets for a sophisticated search as described in Section 2.5 The more precise the metadata, the more precise the search results. The quest for the management of learning objects became a two-pronged infrastructure-building program (of which POOL project became a part). Part one being the creation of repositories that facilitate common searching, and part two, the creation of international standards for the metadata that described the objects housed within. Corporate and national players are invited by the IMS Global Learning Consortium Inc. to identify their interests by paying $100,000 USD for a seat at the discussion table at a on-going series of globe-trotting workshops to discuss the precisely on what kind of information needs to be kept in each field of the IMS record. Right now the number of fields available to index an IMS learning object sits above 80, and we are graced with the prospects that the cost of providing this metadata can in some cases be greater than the original cost of creating the object itself. Although SCORM [14] based its metadata scheme on IMS, the marketplace pragmatically regards SCORM as a *de facto* standard because the US Department of Defense has instituted a clear and pragmatic policy of only buying instructional materials that are SCORM compliant.

The problem lies with the extent to which metadata should be conducted, and who should do the metadata tagging. It is not a question of if we should do metatagging, but a simple application of the law of diminishing returns – to what extent is metatagging really required. How many field are really necessary to describe a learning object to a useful level, and how much of the effort becomes counterproductive – a logistical barrier that has the unfortunate result in actually reducing the ability and interest of the educational community to participate.

Adding to this complexity is Doctorow's [18] observations about "metacrap", the foibles of human-generated metadata. As if deceit, stupidity, ignorance and sloth in metatagging efforts were not problematic enough, Doctorow points out that the schemas themselves are open to subjective interpretation and can be skewed by false metrics. However, he does not totally throw out metadata, but instead refines his quest for "observational metadata", the kind more likely to be automatically generated by a community of users than the originators of the object.

Fortunately, it is in the service of community interests that metadata is created. Moreover educational communities are starting to look at the technology and how they could benefit from it. It is interesting to look at the kind of metadata already in use in some collaborative learning object collections. For example, The Slice of Life (http://medlib.med.utah.edu/kw/sol/sss) is a consortium of health educators who have been pooling their pathology slides and other medical images since the early 1990's. As the medium of preference moved to digital images, the Slice converted many of their videodisc images to digital media. What has not changed however is the nature of the Slice of Life database, which continues to follow a rather idiosyncratic mix of community and contributors' information, and much of it adhering to Medline, a standardized labeling common to the medical field. A similar situation can be found in the Australian AVIRE collection of architectural objects – here an example of prime consideration is the fenestration of the buildings, hardly an IMS field. Truly, these examples show that there is a need for two levels of meta-data – some generic perhaps following the global standard of IMS, while the other specific to the needs of the specific community of practice.

The dilemma of this two-tiered requirement poses a whole set of new requirements on the tools supporting knowledge sharing at the community level and at the same time enabling global exchange.

Thus, the question of metadata is not in dispute, the question is which combination of global and local fields is required to generally search for relevant objects, allow for observational metadata creation in addition to that produced by object originator, and which should be retained at the community level to select specific items once the general collection has been discovered.

4   Potential Solution and Future Goals

To summarize the previous section, the amount and type of meta-data is best decided by the local user community in consideration of the global requirements. Rather than specifying and encouraging more work on standardized global metadata systems, it may be more appropriate to take stock of a simple schema as CanCore, deeming mandatory a handful of the fields as a global standard, and then encouraging the adoption of the remaining fields from the standard and definition of community based metadata for local operations.

Although the solution looks simple, it has an unprecedented consequences on the infrastructure, protocols and tools. We will address consequently different aspects of proposed scenario and imply the requirement for the tools supporting them.

Locally defined metadata schemas. The benefit of metadata is obvious when there is a community striving for getting a formalized understanding of different aspects of the (learning) objects. To enable the communities to define their own metadata the tools should support seamless process of creation, advertisement, and adoption of new schemas. In the process of creation of new schema not only the collection of metadata elements has to be compiled but also a mapping of new schema to the desired other standards has to be created. All this has to be supported by the tools in the way enabling the local developers without metadata expertise to achieve this task. In our experience in the most communities of practice some people volunteer to play the role of local 'gurus' and adopt and learn the tools for the benefit of community [15]. Once the new schema is defined the infrastructure has to support automatic sharing of this schema with the tools used by the community members. CanCore may be of use in this regard if it is used as a basis to define application profiles for specific collections of learning objects.

Global exchange with community schemas. The sharing culture within communities rarely limits its scope to the community itself. The solutions allowing for the global exchange are preferred over the closed ones. There are two ways of how to support the sharing beyond the ones community boundaries. First, the globally agreed minimum set of the elements provides a necessary nucleus. Secondly, if there is a greater need for the exchange between several communities and the mapping exists between local parts of the community schemas then the search and exchange mechanism should support the automatic translation between schemas using this mapping.

Observational metadata. The simplest example in POOL will be the construction of a review mechanism to enable consumers to flesh out metadata with new context and evaluative annotations. Nesbit [8] is working closely with POOL to integrate learning object review instrument with SPLASH.

Flexible tools. To summarize the requirements implied by the above functionality the tools should support defining new metadata elements and schemas, mapping between schemas, and they should update themselves automatically reflecting newly defined and upgraded schemas. Of course, tools by themselves will not solve the ontological problems associated with the creation and agreement of metadata requirements for any given community as the quest for collaborative meaning and shared understanding challenges most human conversations.

Supportive infrastructure. The infrastructure should provide the services to enable the communities to define themselves (including the definition and sharing of the community schemas), to define their relation with other communities and support the global exchange between the communities. For example, a community would define its schema, incorporating a handful of mandatory fields, and customizing those fields required to support the community functions. The resultant schema would then be advertised on the community repository, and the name and location of this schema would be incorporated into the metadata. Upon discovery of the object, the search tool could read in the community schema and enable a broader search within that community's repository. Although this simplistic solution might work well at the schema level, the solution at the ontological level are more complex and require more work. These issues are at the heart of the semantic web construction

Alternative interfaces. Tim Bray (www.antarcti.ca) has suggested non-textual methods for simplifying the task of metadata, is to create visual sorting bins through which simple drag and drop classification might be possible. Either explicit or implicit relationships derived from the sorting process would automatically fill in the metadata – this strategy may succeed by reducing the choices available, and also enable metatagging by association.

In POOL we were aware of the several of these requirements and we have incorporated some of these features into the SPLASH. Although SPLASH already supports a creation of new schema we are still working on the mapping issues. Another major task we are working on is the infrastructure support for the schema exchange and exchange between communities.

Acknowledgements

POOL is partly-funded under the Canarie Inc. Learning Program, and is a consortium involving The NewMedia Innovation Centre (NewMIC), TeleLearning Network of Centres of Excellence, New Bunswick Distance Education Network, The Electronic Text Centre at University of New Brunswick, the Technical University of British Columbia, TelesTraining Inc, BC's Centre for Curriculum, Transfer and Technology, and the Open Learning Agency. The development team at TechBC also includes Dr. Tom Calvert, Gordon Yip, April Ng, Timmy Eap, Nolan Boulanger and Jason Toal. A special acknowledgement is given to the nurturing community of the Technical University of British Columbia which has been recently subsumed by Simon Fraser University.

References

1. Porter, D.: Object Lessons for the Web: Implications for Instructional Development. In: Farrell G. (ed.): The Commonwealth of Learning (COL): The Changing Faces of Virtual Education (2001) 47{70.
2. IEEE Information Technology - Learning Technology - Learning Objects Metadata (P1484.12), Learning Object Metadata Working Draft (WD5), http://ltsc.ieee.org/doc/wg12/LOM WD6 3a.pdf
3. IMS Learning Resource Meta-data Information Model Version 1.2 - Final Speci_cation, http://www.imsproject.org/metadata/imsmdv1p2p1/imsmd infov1p2p1.html
4. Dublin Core Metadata Initiative, http://purl.org/dc
5. CanCore, http://www.cancore.org
6. Learning Program, Canarie Inc., http://www.canarie.ca/funding/learning/backgrounders(99).html
7. POOL Project, http://www.newmic.com/pool/
8. Vargo, J., Nesbit, J. C., Belfer, K., Archambault, A.: Learning object evaluation: Computer mediated collaboration and inter-rater reliability. Int. Conf. on Computers and Advanced Technology in Education (CATE), Cancun, Mexico (2002)
9. Project JXTA, http://www.jxta.org
10. JXTA Search, http://search.jxta.org
11. EduSplash, http://www.edusplash.net
12. TeleCampus, http://www.telecampus.com
13. CAREO, http://www.careo.org
14. Sharable Content Object Reference Model (SCORM), http://www.adlnet.org/
15. Mulholland P., Zdrahal Z., Domingue J., Hatala M., Bernardi, M.: A Methodological Approach to Supporting Organizational Learning. International Journal of Human-Computer Studies 55(3) (September 2001) 337{367
16. CanCore Examples, http://www.imsproject.org/metadata/mdv1p2p2/samples/cancore/cancore_ex1.xml, cancore_ex2.xml
17. Nejdl, W., Wolf, B., Qu, C., Decker, S., Sintek, M. Ambjorn Naeve, A., Nilsson, M., Palmer, M., Risch, T.: EDUTELLA: A P2P Networking Infrastructure Based on RDF, Edutella White Paper, http://edutella.jxta.org/reports/edutella-whitepaper.pdf
18. Doctorow, C.: Metacrap: Putting the torch to seven straw-men of the meta-utopia, Version 1.3, August 2001, http://www.well.com/~doctorow/metacrap.htm

Taking the RDF Model Theory Out for a Spin

Ora Lassila

Nokia Research Center*, 5 Wayside Road, Burlington MA 01803, USA

Abstract. Entailment, as defined by RDF's model-theoretical semantics, is a basic requirement for processing RDF, and represents the kind
of "semantic interoperability" that RDF-based systems have been anticipated to have to realize the vision of the "Semantic Web". In this paper
we give some results in our investigation of a practical implementation
of the entailment rules, based on the graph-walking query mechanism of
the WILBUR RDF toolkit.

1 Introduction

Resource Description Framework (RDF), the World Wide Web Consortium's
metadata framework [13], has emerged as a basic building block for the so-called
"Semantic Web" [3]. Semantic interoperability of systems processing RDF is
largely anticipated to emerge because of the implied polymorphism of shared
types and relations as defined using the ontological vocabulary of RDF [4]. Most
RDF-based software toolkits, however, merely concentrate on producing sets of
triples from XML serializations of RDF graphs, and leave the inferential part to
the application programmer. The recently published model-theoretical semantics
for RDF [10] formalizes the notion of inference in RDF, and provides a basis for
computing deductive closures of RDF graphs. Since it can be argued that this is
actually a basic requirement for interoperability of RDF-based systems, support
for this should be readily available to application programmers. Not only would
this ease the task of writing RDF-savvy software, but it would improve the
level of interoperability between these systems. Without this minimal support
for inference, RDF is largely relegated to mere structured data interchange, and
its utility will be seriously jeopardized.

In this paper we will investigate the computational aspects of deductive closures of RDF graphs, and pursue an implementation based on WILBUR [12,18],
Nokia Research Center's open source RDF toolkit. We will implement a "true
RDF processor" by viewing RDF graphs through a node-centric "slot access
function" A, defined as

$$value \in A(frame, slot) \iff \langle frame, value \rangle \in IEXT(I(slot)) \qquad (1)$$

where $I(x)$ is the RDFS-interpretation of a particular graph, and $IEXT(y)$ is
a binary relational extension of a property – i.e., the set of pairs which identify
the arguments for which the property is true – as defined in [10].

---

* Research described in this paper was supported in part by Nokia Research Center,
Nokia Mobile Phones and Nokia Venture Partners.

I. Horrocks and J. Hendler (Eds.): ISWC 2002, LNCS 2342, pp. 307–317, 2002.

The basic WILBUR frame API [18] provides a simple lookup implementation for A (we will call it A_{lookup}) where entailment is not considered. If D is the current database of triples $\langle s, p, o \rangle$, then A_{lookup} is basically defined as

$$value \in A_{lookup}(frame, slot) \iff \langle frame, slot, value \rangle \in D \qquad (2)$$

We will demonstrate one approach to implementing A, given an implementation of A_{lookup} and other query/update facilities for D.

2   Entailment and "RDFS-Closures"

The RDF Model Theory [10] defines entailment via the generation of a deductive closure from an RDF graph. The closure is a graph consisting of every triple $\langle s, p, o \rangle$ that satisfies $\langle s, o \rangle \in IEXT(I(p))$. Computing this so-called "RDFS-closure" consists of two steps:

1. Addition of a set of new (static) triples to the RDF graph in question. These triples effectively define classes and properties (and their domains and ranges) in the basic RDF ontological vocabulary. An XML-encoded RDF file producing these triples is given as an example in Appendix A.
2. Recursive application of forward-chaining rules to generate all legal triples entailed by the graph in question. These rules could be characterized as follows:
   - *Type Rules* assign default ("root") types for resources (rules **rdf1**, **rdfs4a** and **rdfs4b** in [10]).
   - *Subclass Rules* generate the transitive closures of *subclass* → *class* and *instance* → *class* links (rules **rdfs7**, **rdfs8** and **rdfs9**).
   - *Subproperty Rules* are used to generate the transitive closures resulting from *subproperty* → *property* links. They also propagate property values up the subproperty chain (rules **rdfs5** and **rdfs6**).
   - *Domain/Range Rules* infer resource types from *domain* and *range* assignments (rules **rdfs2** and **rdfs3**).

The rules are highly redundant, and their brute-force, exhaustive, iterative application of is not a realistic way of computing the closure. For example, given a graph with only one triple, the rules in step 2 would generate 17 new triples (in addition to the 19 "static" triples added in step 1), but would also result in 493 attempts to add a redundant triple (i.e., one that was already in the database). Forward-chaining rule-based techniques – such as RETE [8] – could be used to make this processing more efficient, but another issue is that the application of the rules may result in the addition of a large number of new triples in the database (and that most of these generated results may never be needed). It is therefore interesting to investigate whether some balance could be found between computing the closure in advance vs. defining the access function A in such a manner that it can dynamically (i.e., on-demand) generate correct results.

3   Graph Queries

WILBUR exposes RDF graphs through a node-centric (i.e., "frame system") API. As part of this API, the slot access function A_{lookup} supports a query language which allows complex access paths – expressed as regular expressions of *slot names* (i.e., RDF properties) – to be used in place of atomic slot names. The query language is an extension of the query mechanism of the BEEF frame system [11] which, in turn, is an efficient implementation of a simplification of the CRL/SRL path language [9]. It resembles query languages constructed for semi-structured and graph-based data (e.g., [1,6,14,5]).

Path expressions can take the following forms (expressed here in pseudo-syntax instead of the native s-expression syntax of WILBUR):

1. **Sequence** (*concatenation* in [14]):
   $seq(e_1, \ldots, e_n)$ matches a sequence of n steps in the graph, consisting of subexpressions $e_1, \ldots, e_n$.
2. **Disjunction** (*alternation*):
   $or(e_1, \ldots, e_n)$ matches any one of n subexpressions $e_1, \ldots, e_n$. The subexpressions are matched in the order they are specified.
3. **Repetition** (*closure*):
   $rep(e)$ matches the transitive closure of subexpression e; $rep^+(e)$ is equivalent to $seq(e, rep(e))$.
4. **Inverse**:
   Satisfaction of $inv(e)$ requires the path defined by the subexpression e to be matched in reverse direction – this is similar to the *inversion* operator of GraphLog [5].
5. **Value**:
   $val(e)$ causes the value e to be generated in the matching process, ignoring any actual slot accesses. It is useful in specifying *default values*, typically using the idiom $or(path, val(default))$.[1]
6. **Wildcards**:
   The query language supports wildcard "atoms" matching either *any* arc label or just RDF *container membership* properties.

Given a "root" node (i.e., a search start point) and a query expression, WILBUR provides functions for retrieving the first reachable node, retrieving all reachable nodes (function A_{lookup}), and determining whether a path exists between two specified nodes.

WILBUR transforms query expressions into optimized deterministic finite state automata [2, section 3.9] and uses these to effectively "walk" the underlying RDF graphs (which are stored as RDF triples in in-core databases with hashed indices). During traversal, graph nodes are marked with DFA states as in [14, section 5] except that we do not have to restrict ourselves to simple paths (by marking the nodes with *all* applicable states WILBUR is able to find the correct answer to [14, example 8]).

---

[1] The current implementation cannot satisfy queries of type $inv(val(e))$.

4   Implementing Closure Generation

We implement closure generation primarily by using graph-walking techniques. Our approach is based on the following of basic assumptions:

1. Generally, we are willing delay the computation of the closure (even at the expense of the time eventually spent in the computation) and to trade memory consumption for time spent in computation.
2. The computational burden is split in two: some of the work is undertaken during every insert into D (i.e., whenever new triples are asserted), and some during every access of A.
3. Some features of RDF are more prevalent than others in "typical" data; we will base the design of the system on this perceived distribution of prevalence:
   - subclassing is common,
   - subproperty definitions are used but sparsely,
   - subproperties of rdf:subPropertyOf are rare.
4. Retractions from D are not considered (so far).

With regard to the dynamic computation of closures, our approach is based on the WILBUR query language and rewriting access path expressions when accessing the underlying graph. The definition of the slot access function A now takes the form

$$A(frame, path) = A_{lookup}(frame, path') \qquad (3)$$

where $path'$ is the path expression $path$ suitably rewritten. We will express the algorithm as a set of rewrite patterns of the form $path \rightarrow path'$.

We will first demonstrate a partial solution: it implements only the *type* and *subclass* rules discussed in section 2. We will then extend this solution to a complete one by adding support for the *subproperty* rules.

4.1   Partial Solution

For the two core relations rdf:type and rdfs:subClassOf the rewritten paths (referring to equation 3) are, correspondingly:

$$\mathrm{rdf : type} \rightarrow or(seq(\mathrm{rdf : type}, rep(\mathrm{rdfs : subClassOf})), \qquad (4)$$
$$val(\mathrm{rdfs : Resource}))$$

$$\mathrm{rdfs : subClassOf} \rightarrow or(rep(\mathrm{rdfs : subClassOf}), \qquad (5)$$
$$val(\mathrm{rdfs : Resource}))$$

where rewrite pattern 4 says that in order to find all values of rdf:type of an instance, you first traverse the atomic rdf:type link once, and then the atomic rdfs:subClassOf link an arbitrary number of times (including zero). Accessing all values of this relation computes the transitive closure of rdfs:subClassOf, starting from the designated classes of the instance being queried. Similarily, rewrite pattern 5 accesses the transitive closure of rdfs:subClassOf. Note that the effects of pattern 5 are built into pattern 4 so that these rules do not need to be applied recursively. The disjunctions in both expressions ensure that if the exhaustive search (i.e., transitive closure computation) fails, a default value is generated.

Apart from `rdf:type` and `rdfs:subClassOf`, other atomic slot names (RDF properties) are unaffected by the rewrite process, since there is no semantic theory for them. Complex path expressions are rewritten by traversing them recursively, rewriting subexpressions.

Since the WILBUR implementation of a "triple database" always loads a basic "RDF schema" into every newly created database, step 1 of the closure generation process (in section 2) is implemented by defining the static triples in this schema (see Appendix A).

Please note that the approach we have taken only makes sense for certain types of triple database implementations. In a relational database implementation – given that queries for finding transitive closures cannot be expressed in relational calculus (see, for example, [14]) – it might make more sense to populate the database with additional triples. In an "in-core" implementation like WILBUR, stepping through the graph has relatively low cost, and therefore the dynamic approach makes sense, particularly when combined with the potential memory savings.

4.2   Complete Solution

We can extend the partial solution to provide support for the *subproperty* rules. Referring to equation 3, we rewrite access paths as follows: each atomic relation r is rewritten as

$$r \rightarrow or(r_1, \ldots, r_n) \tag{6}$$
$$\text{where } r_i \in A_{lookup}(r, rep(inv(or(p_1, \ldots, p_m))))$$

and where $p_1, \ldots, p_m$ are the relation `rdfs:subPropertyOf` and all of its defined subproperties. Please note that this rewriting also applies to all of the atoms of the results of applying the rewrite patterns 4 and 5. When all values of A are computed the ordering of r_i does not need to be considered. An implementation might, though, apply some specificity ordering to the values based on the graph distance of r_i to r (note that $r_1 = r$).

The set of subproperties of `rdfs:subPropertyOf`, $P = \{p_i\}$, is cached. Each insert into D where the triple is of the form $\langle s, p_i, p_j \rangle$ where $p_i \in P \vee p_j \in P$ invalidates and recomputes the cache. The recomputation is effected as follows: assume P_{old} is the current value of the cache, and P_{new} is the recomputed value of the cache; then

$$P_{new} = A_{lookup}(\text{rdfs}:\text{subPropertyOf}, inv(rep(or(p_1, \ldots, p_n)))) \tag{7}$$
$$\text{where } \forall i \in [1, n], p_i \in P_{old}$$

In addition to caching subproperty information of `rdfs:subPropertyOf`, the implementation offers other opportunities for caching results. Not only could more of the subproperty information be cached (that is, information about subproperties of *all* relations, not just `rdfs:subPropertyOf`), but other results computed by A could be cached as well.

4.3   About Domain/Range Rules

The *domain* and *range* constraints of RDF Schema were originally introduced to allow RDF data to be validated (e.g., by a metadata editor). The *domain/range rules* of the Model Theory make it impossible to use RDF Schema for this purpose since they effectively treat *domain* and *range* generatively and not restrictively – and these are the *only* validation constraints of the language. We believe these rules should not be part of the Model Theory in the first place.

If one did want to implement the *domain/range rules* using the access path rewriting technique, one would have to add additional triples to the database during insertions. For example, if for every triple $\langle s, p, o \rangle$ inserted into D one would insert the triples $\langle o, \mathtt{rr}, p \rangle$ and $\langle s, \mathtt{dr}, p \rangle$ into D, one could rephrase the rewrite pattern 4 as follows:

$$\mathtt{rdf : type} \rightarrow or(seq(\mathtt{rdf : type}, rep(\mathtt{rdfs : subClassOf})), \qquad (8)$$
$$seq(\mathtt{rr}, rep(or(p_1, \ldots, p_m))), \mathtt{rdfs : range}),$$
$$seq(\mathtt{dr}, rep(or(p_1, \ldots, p_m))), \mathtt{rdfs : domain})$$
$$val(\mathtt{rdfs : Resource}))$$

where $p_1, \ldots, p_m$ are the relation `rdfs:subPropertyOf` and all of its subproperties. This approach, however, would lead to an expansion of D and would thus work against the goals for this implementation in general.

4.4   Implementation Summary

The following table summarizes how our approach implements the rules of the Model Theory:

Rule	Implementation
rdf1	during insertions to D
rdfs2	*not implemented* (see section 4.3)
rdfs3	*not implemented* (see section 4.3)
rdfs4a	rewrite pattern 4 (default clause)
rdfs4b	rewrite pattern 4 (default clause)
rdfs5	rewrite pattern 6
rdfs6	rewrite pattern 6 + caching during insertions to D
rdfs7	rewrite pattern 5 (default clause)
rdfs8	rewrite pattern 5
rdfs9	rewrite pattern 4

5   Future Work

The complexity of path queries has been studied extensively (for example [16,17,14] just to name a few). Even though the general problems tend to be NP-complete [14], several restricted variations of the problem have lower complexity. Most of the graph processing required for our solution is reduced to the computation of transitive closures which can be accomplished in polynomial time [17]. Our future plans include not only analyzing the complexity of the current solution but also comparing it with others, such as generative forward-chaining rule-based approaches – e.g., CWM [19] – and backward-chaining theorem proving approaches – e.g., Euler [20] as well as SiLRI and TRIPLE [7,15].

Additional future work on this system will include dealing with retractions from D (for practical completeness – this will affect how rules **rdf1** and **rdfs6** are implemented), getting statistical data to back up the assumptions made of the distribution of various RDF features in "real-world" RDF data, and extending the underlying WILBUR system to deal with certain types of queries that include the pattern $inv(val(r))$.

6   Conclusions

"Semantic interoperability" of RDF-based systems has long been anticipated to materialize because of the polymorphism of shared types and relations as defined by the RDF Schema specification, but most RDF-based software packages merely concentrate on producing sets of triples from XML serializations of RDF graphs and leave the inferential part to the application programmer. The model theory for RDF formalizes this notion of inference in RDF. We have argued that the inferential mechanism is a basic minimum requirement for interoperability of RDF-based systems, and support for this should be readily available for application programmers. Not providing this support may compromise the interoperability between RDF-based systems.

The "true RDF processor" presented in this paper provides a "slot access function" which effectively allows the underlying graph to be viewed *as if* its RDFS-closure had been generated. RDF-based applications, if written using a toolkit like this, would not have to worry about the inferential implications specified by the standard, and would thus enable true interoperability with other similar systems.

Acknowledgements

The author would like to thank the following individuals for help in the preparation of this article: Mark Adler, Jos de Roo, Pat Hayes, Marcia Lassila, Deborah McGuinness, Esko Nuutila, Louis Theran and the anonymous reviewers of the ISWC program committee. The research work described in this paper was supported in part by Nokia Research Center, Nokia Mobile Phones and Nokia Venture Partners.

References

1. S. Abiteboul, D. Quass, J. McHugh, J. Widom, and J. L. Wiener. The Lorel query language for semistructured data. *International Journal on Digital Libraries*, 1(1):68–88, 1997.
2. A. V. Aho, R. Sethi, and J. D. Ullman. *Compilers: Principles, Techniques and Tools*. Addison-Wesley, 1986.
3. T. Berners-Lee, J. Hendler, and O. Lassila. The Semantic Web. *Scientific American*, 284(5):34–43, May 2001.
4. D. Brickley and R.V.Guha. Resource Description Framework (RDF) Schema Specification 1.0. W3C Candidate Recommendation, March 2000.
5. M. P. Consens and A. O. Mendelzon. GraphLog: a visual formalism for real life recursion. In *Proceedings of the Ninth ACM SIGACT-SIGMOD-SIGART Symposium on Principles of Database Systems*. ACM Press, 1990.
6. I. F. Cruz, A. O. Mendelzon, and P. T. Wood. A graphical query language supporting recursion. In *Proceedings of the ACM SIGMOD Annual Conference on Management of Data*, pages 323–330, 1987.
7. S. Decker, D. Brickley, J. Saarela, and J. Angele. A query and inference service for RDF. In *W3C Query Languages Workshop (QL'98)*, December 1998.
8. C. L. Forgy. A fast algorithm for the many pattern/many object pattern match problem. *Artificial Intelligence*, 19(1):17–37, September 1982.
9. M. S. Fox. Knowledge representation for decision support. In Methlie and Sprague, editors, *Knowledge Representation for Decision Support Systems*. Elsevier, 1985.
10. P. Hayes. RDF Model Theory. W3C Working Draft, February 2002.
11. J. Hynynen and O. Lassila. On the Use of Object-Oriented Paradigm in a Distributed Problem Solver. *AI Communications*, 2(3):142–151, 1989.
12. O. Lassila. Enabling Semantic Web Programming by Integrating RDF and Common Lisp. In *Proceedings of the First Semantic Web Working Symposium*. Stanford University, 2001.
13. O. Lassila and R. R. Swick. Resource Description Framework (RDF) Model and Syntax Specification. W3C Recommendation, February 1999.
14. A. O. Mendelzon and P. T. Wood. Finding regular simple paths in graph databases. *SIAM Journal on Computing*, 24(6):1235–1258, December 1995.
15. M. Sintek and S. Decker. TRIPLE—A Query, Inference, and Transformation Language for the Semantic Web. Accepted to ISWC 2002.
16. R. E. Tarjan. Fast algorithms for solving path problems. *Journal of the ACM*, 28(3):594–614, 1981.
17. M. Yannakakis. Graph-theoretic methods in database theory. In *Proceedings of the Ninth ACM SIGACT-SIGMOD-SIGART Symposium on Principles of Database Systems*, pages 230–242, 1990.
18. http://purl.org/net/wilbur/.
19. http://www.w3.org/2000/10/swap/doc/cwm.html.
20. http://www.agfa.com/w3c/euler/.

A   Basic RDF and RDFS Schema

This RDF document provides the initial (static) triples required by the RDFS closure generation algorithm (see [10, section 6]).

```
<?xml version="1.0"?>

<!DOCTYPE uridef [
  <!ENTITY rdf ''http://www.w3.org/1999/02/22-rdf-syntax-ns#">
  <!ENTITY rdfs ''http://www.w3.org/2000/01/rdf-schema#">
]>

<rdf:RDF xmlns:rdf="&rdf;" xmlns:rdfs="&rdfs;">

  <rdfs:Class rdf:about="&rdfs;Resource"/>
  <rdfs:Class rdf:about="&rdf;Property"/>
  <rdfs:Class rdf:about="&rdfs;Class"/>

  <rdf:Property rdf:about="&rdf;type">
    <rdfs:domain rdf:resource="&rdfs;Resource"/>
    <rdfs:range rdf:resource="&rdfs;Class"/>
  </rdf:Property>

  <rdf:Property rdf:about="&rdfs;subClassOf">
    <rdfs:range rdf:resource="&rdfs;Class"/>
    <rdfs:domain rdf:resource="&rdfs;Class"/>
  </rdf:Property>

  <rdf:Property rdf:about="&rdfs;subPropertyOf">
    <rdfs:range rdf:resource="&rdf;Property"/>
    <rdfs:domain rdf:resource="&rdf;Property"/>
  </rdf:Property>

  <rdf:Property rdf:about="&rdfs;range">
    <rdfs:range rdf:resource="&rdfs;Class"/>
    <rdfs:domain rdf:resource="&rdf;Property"/>
  </rdf:Property>

  <rdf:Property rdf:about="&rdfs;domain">
    <rdfs:range rdf:resource="&rdfs;Class"/>
    <rdfs:domain rdf:resource="&rdf;Property"/>
  </rdf:Property>

  <rdfs:Class rdf:about="&rdfs;Literal"/>

</rdf:RDF>
```

B Slot Access Example

Assume a simple example with instances, classes, subclasses and a subproperty for rdf:type, as defined by the following RDF document:

```
<?xml version="1.0"?>

<!DOCTYPE uridef [
  <!ENTITY rdf ''http://www.w3.org/1999/02/22-rdf-syntax-ns#'>
  <!ENTITY rdfs ''http://www.w3.org/2000/01/rdf-schema#'>
  <!ENTITY x ''http://www.lassila.org/schemata/Example#'>
]>

<rdf:RDF xmlns:rdf="&rdf;" xmlns:rdfs="&rdfs;" xmlns:x="&x;">

  <rdfs:Property rdf:about="&x;type">
    <rdfs:subPropertyOf rdf:resource="&rdf;type"/>
  </rdfs:Property>

  <rdfs:Class rdf:about="&x;A">
    <rdfs:subClassOf>
      <rdfs:Class rdf:about="&x;B"/>
    </rdfs:subClassOf>
  </rdfs:Class>

  <rdf:Description rdf:about="&x;foo">
    <x:type rdf:resource="&x;A"/>
  </rdf:Description>

</rdf:RDF>
```

When the above document is loaded into WILBUR's database it will produce the following 6 triples:

$$1 : \langle x : \text{type}, \text{rdf} : \text{type}, \text{rdfs} : \text{Property}\rangle$$
$$2 : \langle x : \text{type}, \text{rdfs} : \text{subPropertyOf}, \text{rdf} : \text{type}\rangle$$
$$3 : \langle x : A, \text{rdf} : \text{type}, \text{rdfs} : \text{Class}\rangle$$
$$4 : \langle x : A, \text{rdfs} : \text{subClassOf}, x : B\rangle$$
$$5 : \langle x : B, \text{rdf} : \text{type}, \text{rdfs} : \text{Class}\rangle$$
$$6 : \langle x : \text{foo}, \text{rdf} : \text{type}, x : A\rangle$$

Then, calling the new access function $A(x : \text{foo}, \text{rdf} : \text{type})$ will yield the result $\{x : A, x : B, \text{rdfs} : \text{Resource}\}$. The execution of the function call will result in the following lower-level calls:

$$1 : \begin{cases} A_{lookup}(\text{rdf} : \text{type}, inv(\text{rdfs} : \text{subPropertyOf})) \to \{x : \text{type}\} \\ A_{lookup}(x : \text{type}, inv(\text{rdfs} : \text{subPropertyOf})) \to \{\} \\ A_{lookup}(\text{rdfs} : \text{subClassOf}, inv(\text{rdfs} : \text{subPropertyOf})) \to \{\} \end{cases}$$

$$2: \begin{cases} A_{lookup}(\mathtt{x : foo, rdf : type}) \rightarrow \{\} \\ A_{lookup}(\mathtt{x : foo, x : typo}) \quad \rangle \; \{\mathtt{x : \Lambda}\} \\ A_{lookup}(\mathtt{x : A, rdfs : subClassOf}) \rightarrow \{\mathtt{x : B}\} \\ A_{lookup}(\mathtt{x : B, rdfs : subClassOf}) \rightarrow \{\} \\ A_{lookup}(\mathtt{x : B}, val(\mathtt{rdfs : Resource})) \rightarrow \{\mathtt{rdfs : Resource}\} \end{cases}$$

Step 1 represents the rewriting step for rdf:type: the accesses to A_{lookup} are the result of the addition of triple 2 above having invalidated the sub-subproperty cache (subsequent similar calls would be able to rely on the cached information). Step 2 represents the traversal of the rewritten path.

Concurrent Execution Semantics of DAML-S with Subtypes

Anupriya Ankolekar[1], Frank Huch[2], and Katia Sycara[1]

[1] Carnegie Mellon University, Pittsburgh PA 15213, USA
[2] Christian-Albrechts-University of Kiel, 24118 Kiel, Germany

Abstract. The DARPA Agent Markup Language ontology for Services (DAML-S) enables the description of Web-based services, such that they can be discovered, accessed and composed dynamically by intelligent software agents and other Web services, thereby facilitating the coordination between distributed, heterogeneous systems on the Web. We propose a formalised syntax and an initial reference semantics for DAML-S, which incorporates subtype polymorphism. The semantics we describe is derived from the semantics for Erlang and Concurrent Haskell. We contrast our semantics with an alternate semantics proposed for DAML-S, based on the situation calculus and Petri nets.

Keywords: Agents, Services, Languages and Infrastructure, Ontologies.

1   Introduction

The DARPA Agent Markup Language Services ontology (DAML-S) is being developed for the specification of Web services, such that they can be dynamically discovered, invoked and composed with the help of existing Web services. DAML-S, defined through DAML+OIL [4], an ontology definition language with additional semantic inferencing capabilities, provides a number of constructs or DAML+OIL classes to describe the properties and capabilities of Web services. DAML-S will be used by Web service providers to markup their offerings, by service requester agents to describe the desired services, as well as by planning agents to compose complex new services from existing simpler services.

Other approaches to the specification of Web services from the industry include UDDI, WSDL, WSFL and XLANG, which address different aspects of Web service description. UDDI (Universal Description, Discovery and Integration) [17], for instance, is primarily a repository technology and concerns itself with the storage and retrieval of Web service descriptions. WSDL (Web Services Description Language) [3] describes a Web service in terms how the interaction with it takes place: the messages it understands; the ports on which it can receive and send messages. WSFL (Web Services Flow Language) [11] and XLANG [16] describe how services can be composed together, and the behaviour/interaction protocol of a Web service. DAML-S is unique in that, due to its foundations in DAML+OIL, it provides markup that can be semantically meaningful for intelligent agents.

I. Horrocks and J. Hendler (Eds.): ISWC 2002, LNCS 2342, pp. 318–332, 2002.

An informal description of the semantics of DAML-S[1] has been given in [1]. An interleaving, strict operational semantics for DAML-S is presented in [2]. In this paper, we extend the type system for DAML-S with subclass polymorphism, which captures the subsumption-based component of DAML inferencing. Subclass polymorphism stems from object-oriented programming, where if an object expects a value of class τ, it can also accept values of any subclass τ' of τ. Similarly, an agent that accepts an input of class C_1 and recognises that C_1 is a subclass of C_2, can also accept instances of C_2, as inputs.

The next section, Section 2, presents the DAML-S ontologies and the process model of a service. A core subset of DAML-S, referred to as *DAML-S Core*, is modelled in [2], such that every service defined in DAML-S can be transformed into a functionally equivalent service definition in DAML-S Core, stripped of additional attributes that aid in service discovery or any quality-of-service parameters. The following sections 3 and 4 discuss some of the issues involved in developing a formal model for DAML-S and present the syntax and semantics of DAML-S Core. In the following Section 5, we extend the type system of DAML-S Core with subclass. Subclasses in DAML-S with the help of type constraints. Finally, in Section 6, we compare our approach to the definition of the semantics of DAML-S with another approach using situation calculus and Petri nets [14].

2   The DAML-S Ontology

The DAML-S ontology consists of three parts: a *service profile*, a *process model* and a *service grounding*. The service profile of a particular Web service would enable a service-requesting agent to determine whether the service meets its requirements. The profile is essentially a summary of the service, specifying the input expected, the output returned, the precondition to and the effect of its successful execution. The process model of a service describes the internal structure of the service in terms of its subprocesses and their execution flow. It provides a detailed specification of how another agent can interact with the service. Each process within the process model could itself be a service, in which case, the enclosing service is referred to as a *complex* or *composite* service, built up from simpler, atomic services. The service grounding describes how the service can be accessed, in particular which communication protocols the service understands, which ports can receive which messages and so forth.

In this paper, we will only be considering the service process model, since it primarily determines the semantics of the service's execution. The formalisation proposed here will however form the basis for an execution model. The inputs, outputs and effects of a process can be instances of any class in DAML+OIL. The preconditions are instances of class Condition. There are a number of additional constructs to specify the control flow within a process model: Sequence, Split, Split+Join, If-Then-Else, Repeat-While, Repeat-Until. The execution of a service requires communication, i.e. interaction between the participants in a

---

[1] DAML-S is currently under development and the language described here is the DAML-S Draft Release 0.5 (May 2001).

service transaction. The DAML-S grounding uses WSDL service descriptions to specify the communication between participants of a service transaction. Since modelling the communication within a service transaction is essential to describing the execution semantics of a service described in DAML-S, we will define a set of what we consider to be basic communication primitives, for example, for the sending and receiving of messages. These have close counterparts in WSDL.

In the next section, we first map DAML-S Core constructs onto a formal syntax, based on a core concurrent functional language. We then define a semantics for the DAML-S Core constructs in terms of the formal functional syntax.

3   Modelling DAML-S Core

The DAML-S class Process and its subclasses, representing services/agents[2], are modelled as functions. DAML-S agents essentially take in inputs and return outputs, exhibiting function-like behaviour. A Web document, for example, is an agent which has no input and as output, merely some HTML content. The input to a Process is not restricted and could be a Process itself, resulting in a *'higher-order'* agent, offering meta-level functionality. A simple example of a higher-order service is an agent that, when given a task and an environment of existing services, locates a service to perform the task, invokes the service and returns the result. The functionality of the agent thus depends on the set of services in the world that it takes as input.

Furthermore, agents can be composed together. This composition itself represents an agent with its own inputs and outputs. The composition could be sequential, dependent on a conditional or defined as a loop. The composition could also be concurrent, where the agents can interact with each other, representing relatively complex, distributed applications, such as chat systems.

DAML-S classes are defined through DAML+OIL, an ontology definition language. DAML+OIL, owing to its foundations in RDF Schema, provides a typing mechanism for Web resources [4], such as Web pages, people, document types and abstract concepts. The difference between a DAML+OIL class and a class in a typical object-oriented programming language is that DAML+OIL classes are meant primarily for data modelling and contain no methods. We model classes in DAML-S as type expressions and subclasses as subtypes with the help of type constraints, presented in Section 5. At this stage, we do not model the relations and properties between the classes in an ontology. More formally,

Definition 1 (Type Expressions). *A type expression $\tau \in \mathcal{T}$ is either a type variable $\alpha \in \mathcal{V}$ or the application, $(T\tau_1 \cdots \tau_n)$, of an n-ary type constructor $T \in \mathcal{F}$ to the type expressions $\tau_1, \ldots, \tau_n$.*

---

[2] Services have a description and an execution component and therefore, can be considered as active processes or agents. In the following, we do not distinguish between agents and services. Note the agents described here are simply processes and do not necessarily display any complex, autonomous behaviours.

Type constructors in $\mathcal{F}$ are determined by DAML-S Core classes, such as List, Book and Process. In addition to these, DAML-S Core has a predefined functional type constructor $\rightarrow$, for which, following convention, we will use the infix notation. All type constructors bind to the right, i.e. $\tau_1 \rightarrow \tau_2 \rightarrow \tau_3$ is read as $(\tau_1 \rightarrow (\tau_2 - > \tau_3))$.

DAML-S agents can be polymorphic with respect to their input and output. An example of a polymorphic agent is one which simply returns its input of arbitrary type, as output. Polymorphic types are type expressions containing type variables. The expression a $\rightarrow$ b, for instance, is a polymorphic type with type variables a and b, which can be instantiated with concrete types. The substitution [a/integer, b/boolean] applied to a $\rightarrow$ b results in the type integer $\rightarrow$ boolean. Identical type variables in a type expression indicate identical types. For the formalisation of polymorphism, we use *type schemas*, in which all free type variables are bound: $\forall \alpha_1, \ldots, \alpha_n.\tau$, where τ is a type and $\alpha_1, \ldots, \alpha_n$ are the generic variables in τ.

Although DAML-S Core agents can be functionally simple, they derive much of their useful behaviour from their ability to execute concurrently and interact with one another. The communication an agent is engaged in is a side-effect of its functional execution. Communication side-effects can be incorporated into the functional description of agents with the help of the IO monad. Monads were introduced from category theory to describe programming language computations, actions with side-effects, as opposed to purely functional evaluations. The IO monad, introduced in Concurrent Haskell [9], describes actions with communication side-effects.

The IO monad is essentially a triple, consisting of a unary type constructor IO and two functions, return and (>>=). A value of type IO a is an I/O action, that, when performed, can engage in some communication before resulting in a value of type a. The application return v represents an agent that performs no IO and simply returns the value v. The function (>>=) represents the sequential composition of two agents. Thus, action1 >>= action2 represents an agent that first performs action1 and then action2. Consider the type of (>>=): $\forall a,b.IO$ a $\rightarrow$ (a $\rightarrow$ IO b) $\rightarrow$ IO b. First, an action of type IO a is performed. The result of this becomes input for the second action of type a $\rightarrow$ IO b. The subsequent execution of this action results in a final value of type IO b. The expression on the right-hand side of (>>=) must necessarily be a unary function that takes an argument of type a and returns an action of type IO b.

Although the communication an agent is engaged in can be expressed with the IO monad, we still need to describe the means through which communication between multiple agents takes place. We model communication between agents with *ports* [8], a buffer in which messages can be inserted at one end and retrieved sequentially at the other. In contrast to the *channel* mechanism of Concurrent Haskell, only one agent can read from a port, although several agents can write to it. The agent that can read from a port is considered to own the port. Since we need to be able to type messages that are passed through ports, each agent is modelled as having multiple ports of several different types. This conceptualisation of ports is also close to the UNIX port concept and is therefore a natural model for communication between distributed Web applications. Agents and services are modelled as communicating asynchronously. Due to the unreliable nature of the Web, distributed applications for the Web are often designed to communicate asynchronously. The initial proposal for the DAML-S grounding, based on WSDL, also defines communication between services in terms of ports and messages. As we shall see, however, our notion of ports is related to the WSDL ports, but they are different abstractions.

Definition 2 (DAML-S Core Expressions). *Let Var^τ denote the set of variables of type τ. The set of DAML-S Core expressions over Σ, $Exp(\Sigma)$, is defined in Table 1. The set of expressions of type τ is denoted by $Exp(\Sigma)^\tau$.*

In Table 1, the base constructs which represent a composition of agents are cond, >>= (which is a binary service representing the sequential execution of its subprocesses), spawn and choice. Other constructs such as Split+Join can be defined in terms of these and we do not model them further.

Definition 3 (DAML-S Core Agents). *Let $x_i \in Var^{\tau_i}, x_i$ pairwise different and $e \in Exp(\Sigma)^\tau$. A DAML-S service definition then has the following form*

$$s\ x_1 \cdots x_n := e$$

$s \in S$ is said to have type $\tau_1 \to \cdots \to \tau_n \to \tau$. S denotes the set of services.

In the definition of $Exp(\Sigma)$ in Table 1, we use partial application and the curried form of function application. For a function that takes two arguments, we use the curried type $\tau_1 \to \tau_2 \to \tau_3$ instead of $(\tau_1, \tau_2) \to \tau_3$.

Port references are constructed with a unary type constructor Port $\in \mathcal{F}$. A send operation takes as argument a destination port and a message and sends the message to the port, resulting in an I/O action that returns no value. Similarly, a receive operation takes as argument a port on which it is expecting a message and returns the first message received on the port. It thus performs an I/O action and returns a message. To be well-typed, the type of the message and the port must match. The spawn operation takes an expression, an I/O action, as argument and spawns a new agent to evaluate the expression, which may not contain any free variables. The choice operation takes two I/O actions as arguments, makes a non-deterministic choice between the two and returns it as the result. For the application of choice to be well-typed, both its arguments must have the same type, since either one of them could be returned as the result.

4   Semantics of DAML-S

A formal semantics for DAML+OIL has been defined denotationally [18] and axiomatically [6]. Although the DAML-S ontology is defined in terms of DAML+OIL and therefore inherits its semantics, they are clearly inappropriate

Table 1. DAML-S Core Expressions

Σ	$\Sigma \subseteq Exp(\Sigma)$
var	$Var^\tau \subseteq Exp(\Sigma)^\tau$
abs	$\backslash x \;\texttt{->}\; e \in Exp(\Sigma)^{\tau_1 \to \tau_2}$ for $x \in Var^{\tau_1}$, $e \in Exp(\Sigma)^{\tau_2}$
appl	$(e_1\ e_2) \in Exp(\Sigma)^{\tau_2}$ for $e_1 \in Exp(\Sigma)^{\tau_1 \to \tau_2}$, $e_2 \in Exp(\Sigma)^{\tau_1}$
cond	$\texttt{cond}\ e\ e_1\ e_2 \in Exp(\Sigma)^{\texttt{IO}\ \tau}$ for $e \in Exp(\Sigma)^{\texttt{boolean}}$, $e_1, e_2 \in Exp(\Sigma)^{\texttt{IO}\ \tau}$
return	$\texttt{return}\ e \in Exp(\Sigma)^{\texttt{IO}\ \tau}$ for $e \in Exp(\Sigma)^{\tau}$
seq	$e_1\ \texttt{>>=}\ e_2 \in Exp(\Sigma)^{\texttt{IO}\ \tau_2}$ for $e_1 \in Exp(\Sigma)^{\texttt{IO}\ \tau_1}$, $e_2 \in Exp(\Sigma)^{\tau_1 \to \texttt{IO}\ \tau_2}$
send	$e_1\,\texttt{!}\,e_2 \in Exp(\Sigma)^{\texttt{IO}\ ()}$ for $e_1 \in Exp(\Sigma)^{\texttt{Port}\ \tau}$, $e_2 \in Exp(\Sigma)^{\tau}$
rec	$e\texttt{?} \in Exp(\Sigma)^{\texttt{IO}\ \tau}$ for $e \in Exp(\Sigma)^{\texttt{Port}\ \tau}$
port	$\texttt{newPort}\tau \in Exp(\Sigma)^{\texttt{IO Port}\ \tau}$ for $\tau \in \mathcal{T}$
spawn	$\texttt{spawn}\ e \in Exp(\Sigma)^{\texttt{IO}\ ()}$ for $e \in Exp(\Sigma)^{\texttt{IO}\ \tau}$
choice	$\texttt{choice}\ e_1\ e_2 \in Exp(\Sigma)^{\texttt{IO}\ \tau}$ for $e_1, e_2 \in Exp(\Sigma)^{\texttt{IO}\ \tau}$
serv	$s\ e_1 \cdots e_n \in Exp(\Sigma)^{\tau}$ for $e_i \in Exp(\Sigma)^{\tau_i}$, $s \in \mathcal{S}^{\tau_1 \to \cdots \to \tau_n \to \tau}$

for a definition of the operational meaning of DAML-S constructs. Describing the operational semantics of concurrent and distributed systems such as the DAML-S environment is often far simpler and more natural than describing the denotational semantics. Distributed systems tend to be non-terminating and non-deterministic, making it difficult to describe them simply on the basis of their input-output behaviour. Defining differing semantics for DAML+OIL and DAML-S does not constitute a problem. The operational semantics of DAML-S is layered on top of the denotational semantics of DAML+OIL, with the type system mediating between the two.

In this section, we describe a formal operational semantics for Core DAML-S. Our semantics is based on the operational semantics for Erlang [7] and Concurrent Haskell [9] programs, inspired by the structural operational semantics of CCS [12] and the π-calculus [13].

In a Σ-Interpretation $\mathcal{A} = (A, \alpha)$, A is a $\mathcal{T}$-sorted set of concrete values and α an interpretation function that maps each symbol in Ω, the set of all constructors defined through DAML+OIL, to a function over A. In particular, A includes functional values, i.e. functions.

Definition 4 (State). *A state of execution within DAML-S Core is defined as a finite set of agents: State* $:= \mathcal{P}_{fin}(Agent)$

An agent *is a pair* (e, φ)*, where* $e \in Exp(\Sigma)$ *is the DAML-S Core expression being evaluated and* φ *is a partial function, mapping port references onto actual*

Table 2. Semantics of DAML-S Core - I

$$(\text{FUNC}) \frac{\phi \in \Omega}{\Pi, (E[\phi v_1 \cdots v_n], \varphi) \longrightarrow \Pi, (E[\phi_{\mathfrak{A}} v_1 \cdots v_n], \varphi)}$$

$$(\text{APPL}) \frac{\text{free}(u) \cap \text{bound}(e) = \emptyset}{\Pi, (E[(\backslash x \ \text{->} \ e) \ u)], \varphi) \longrightarrow \Pi, (E[e[x/u]], \varphi)}$$

$$(\text{CONV}) \frac{y \text{ is a fresh free variable}}{\Pi, (E[\backslash x \ \text{->} \ e], \varphi) \longrightarrow \Pi, (E[\backslash y \ \text{->} \ e[x/y]], \varphi)}$$

$$(\text{SERV}) \frac{s x_1 \cdots x_n := e \in \mathcal{S}}{\Pi, (E[s v_1 \cdots v_n], \varphi) \longrightarrow \Pi, (E[e'[x_1/v_1, \ldots, x_n/v_n]], \varphi)}$$

ports:

$$Agent := Exp(\Sigma) \times \{\varphi \mid \varphi : \texttt{PortRef} \longrightarrow \texttt{Port}_\tau^{\mathfrak{A}}\}$$

for all τ, where $\texttt{Port}_\tau^{\mathfrak{A}} := (A^\tau)^*$ *and* $\texttt{PortRef}$ *is an infinite set of globally known unique port references, disjoint with A. Since no two agents can have a common port, the domains of their port functions φ are also disjoint.*

Definition 5 (Evaluation Context). *The set of evaluation contexts $\mathcal{EC}$ [5] for DAML-S Core is defined by the context-free grammar*

$$E := [\,] \mid \phi(v_1, \ldots, v_i, E, e_{i+2}, e_n) \mid (E \ e) \mid (v \ E) \mid E \texttt{>>=} e$$

for $v \in A$, $e, e_1, e_2 \in Exp(\Sigma)$, $\phi \in \Omega \cup \mathcal{S} \backslash \{\texttt{spawn}, \texttt{choice}\}$.

Definition 6 (Operational Semantics). *The operational semantics of DAML-S is $\longrightarrow \subset$ State $\times$ State is defined in Tables 2 and 3. For $(s, s') \in \longrightarrow$, we write $s \longrightarrow s'$, denoting that state s can transition into state s'.*

The application of a defined service is essentially the same as the application rule, except that the arguments to s must be evaluated to values, before they can be substituted into e. In a [SEQ], if the left-hand side of >>= returns a value v, then v is fed as argument to the expression e on the right-hand side. That is, the output of the left-hand side of >>= is input to e

Evaluating **spawn** e results in a new parallel agent being created, which evaluates e and has no ports, thus φ is empty. Creating a new port with port descriptor p involves extending the domain of φ with p and setting its initial value to be the empty word ϵ. The port descriptor p is returned to the creating agent. The evaluation of a receive expression $p?$ retrieves and returns the first value of p. The port descriptor mapping φ is modified to reflect the fact that the first message of p has been extracted. Similarly, the evaluation of a send expression, $p!v$,

Table 3. Semantics of DAML-S Core - II

$$\text{(SEQ)} \ \frac{\overline{}}{\Pi, (E[\texttt{return } v \texttt{ >>= } e], \varphi) \longrightarrow \Pi, (E[(e\ v)], \varphi)}$$

$$\text{(SPAWN)} \ \frac{\overline{}}{\Pi, (E[\texttt{spawn } e], \varphi) \longrightarrow \Pi, (E[\texttt{return } ()], \varphi), (e, \emptyset)}$$

$$\text{(PORT)} \ \frac{p \text{ new } \texttt{PortRef} \qquad \varphi'(x) = \begin{cases} \epsilon & \text{if } x = p; \\ \varphi(x) & \text{otherwise.} \end{cases}}{\Pi, (E[\texttt{newPort } \tau], \varphi) \longrightarrow \Pi, (E[\texttt{return } p], \varphi')}$$

$$\text{(REC)} \ \frac{p \in Dom(\varphi) \quad \varphi(p) = v \cdot w \quad \varphi'(x) = \begin{cases} w & \text{if } x = p; \\ \varphi(x) & \text{otherwise.} \end{cases}}{\Pi, (E[p?], \varphi) \longrightarrow \Pi, (E[\texttt{return } v], \varphi')}$$

$$\text{(SEND)} \ \frac{p \in Dom(\varphi_2) \quad \varphi_2(p) = w \quad \varphi_2'(x) = \begin{cases} w \cdot v & \text{if } x = p; \\ \varphi_2(x) & \text{otherwise.} \end{cases}}{\Pi, (E[p!\texttt{v}], \varphi_1), (e, \varphi_2) \longrightarrow \Pi, (E[\texttt{return } ()], \varphi_1), (e, \varphi_2')}$$

$$\text{(COND-TRUE)} \ \frac{\overline{}}{\Pi, (E[\texttt{cond True } e_1\ e_2], \varphi) \longrightarrow \Pi, (E[e_1], \varphi)}$$

$$\text{(CHOICE-LEFT)} \ \frac{\Pi, (E[e_1], \varphi) \longrightarrow \Pi', (E[e_1'], \varphi')}{\Pi, (E[\texttt{choice } e_1\ e_2], \varphi) \longrightarrow \Pi', (E[e_1'], \varphi')}$$

results in v being appended to the word at p. Since port descriptors are globally unique, there will only be one such p in the system.

The rules for (COND-FALSE) and (CHOICE-RIGHT) are similar to the rules for (COND-TRUE) and (CHOICE-LEFT) given in Table 3. If the condition b evaluates to `True`, then the second argument e_1 is evaluated next, else if the condition b evaluates to `False`, the third argument e_2 is evaluated next. For a choice expression $e_1 + e_2$, if the expression on the left e_1 can be evaluated, then it is evaluated. Similarly, the right-hand side e_2 is evaluated, if it can be evaluated. However, the choice of which one is evaluated is made non-deterministically.

5   Subclass Polymorphism in DAML-S

Due to its roots in DAML+OIL, a distinguishing characteristic of DAML-S is that it enables some measure of semantic inferencing to be made by an agent. DAML+OIL enables many kinds of inferencing. Here, we model subsumption-based semantic inferencing as subtype polymorphism. Our type system is similar to that of ObjectCurry [15]. In the case of ObjectCurry, subtype polymorphism was present only for objects and messages. In our case, it can occur during any service invocation. Additionally, subtype polymorphism is not restricted to classes, it can also occur over functional types. Furthermore, DAML-S Core supports multiple inheritance, which is not present in ObjectCurry.

Subtypes in DAML-S are expressed with the help of constraints on type expressions. Type schemas are thus extended to *constrained type schemas* of the form $\forall \alpha_1, \ldots, \alpha_n.\tau | C$, where $\forall \alpha_1, \ldots, \alpha_n.\tau$ is a type schema and C is a set of subtype constraints. A subtype constraint 'τ_1 is a subtype of τ_2' is written as $\tau_1 \lhd \tau_2$. Instead of $\tau | \emptyset$ we also write τ. For example, the class $\forall a.a \ |\{a \lhd \texttt{Book}\}$ is a constrained type schema, representing a subtype of Book. An instantiation of a constrained type schema yields a generic instance.

A *generic instance* of a type schema $\forall \alpha_1, \ldots, \alpha_n.\tau | C$ is a constrained type $\tau' | C'$, if a substitution σ exists, such that $\sigma \tau | \sigma C = \tau' | C'$ where $\sigma(\alpha_i) = \tau_i$ for all $i = 1, \ldots, n$ and $\sigma(\beta) = \beta$ for all $\beta \notin \{\alpha_1, \ldots, \alpha_n\}$.

Thus, the type AudioBook $|\{\texttt{AudioBook} \lhd \texttt{Book}\}$ is a generic instance of the constrained type schema $\forall a.a \ |\{a \lhd \texttt{Book}\}$. To be well-typed, an expression must be well-formed according to the rules in Table 1 and furthermore, it should satisfy the type constraints on its stated type. Whether the type constraints in a type expression are satisfied depends on whether the types in the constraints do in fact possess the required subtype relationships. This can be verified by checking the constraints against the class definitions in the specification and the ontologies it references.

Definition 7 (Direct Subclass and subclass hierarchy). *The* direct sub-class *relation $\mathcal{H}_S$ for a service specification S is defined as follows: $(C_1, C_2) \in \mathcal{H}_S$ if and only if there exists an ontology referenced by specification S, where class C_1 is a* subClassOf *class C_2.[3] A subclass hierarchy $\mathcal{H}^*$ induced by a direct sub-class relation $\mathcal{H}$ is formed by taking its reflexive and transitive closure. The base DAML+OIL ontology defines a top* Thing *class and a bottom* Nothing *class.*

Definition 8 (Satisfiability of Subtype Constraints). *A substitution σ satisfies a subtype constraint $\tau_1 \lhd \tau_2$ with respect to a subclass hierarchy $\mathcal{H}^*$ if $(\sigma \tau_1, \sigma \tau_2) \in \mathcal{H}^*$. We notate this as $\sigma \models_{\mathcal{H}^*} \tau_1 \lhd \tau_2$.[4]*

The subclass hierarchy $\mathcal{H}^*$ is defined over classes. However, subtype constraints can also involve functional type expressions and expressions involving the type constructors Port and IO. Such constraints can be broken down into simpler constraints involving solely classes, using the transformation described in Table 4. If a port can accept values of type τ_1, it can also accept values of

---

[3] In the following, we omit the subscript S and simply write $\mathcal{H}$ instead of $\mathcal{H}_S$, since we will usually be referring to a single specification S.

[4] A substitution σ satisfies a set of subtype constraints C, if, for all $c \in C$: $\sigma \models_{\mathcal{H}^*} c$. Notation: $\sigma \models_{\mathcal{H}^*} C$. A set of subtype constraints is *satisfiable* with respect to a subclass hierarchy $\mathcal{H}^*$, if there exists a substitution σ such that $\sigma \models_{\mathcal{H}^*} C$. Notation: $\models_{\mathcal{H}^*} C$.

Table 4. Simplifying Constraints with Type Constructors

[Port]	$\dfrac{\{\texttt{Port }\ \tau_1 \lhd \texttt{Port }\ \tau_2\} \cup C}{\{\tau_2 \lhd \tau_1\} \cup C}$	if $(\tau_2 \lhd \tau_1) \notin C$
[IO]	$\dfrac{\{\texttt{IO }\ \tau_1 \lhd \texttt{IO }\ \tau_2\} \cup C}{\{\tau_1 \lhd \tau_2\} \cup C}$	if $(\tau_1 \lhd \tau_2) \notin C$
[→]	$\dfrac{\{\tau_1 \to \tau_2 \lhd \tau_3 \to \tau_4\} \cup C}{\{\tau_3 \lhd \tau_1, \tau_2 \lhd \tau_4\} \cup C}$	if $(\tau_3 \lhd \tau_1), (\tau_2 \lhd \tau_4) \notin C$

any subtype τ_2 of τ_1 and thus also has type $\texttt{Port }\ \tau_2$. Thus, a constraint of the form $\texttt{Port }\ \tau_1 \lhd \texttt{Port }\ \tau_2$ can be simplified to the constraint $\tau_2 \lhd \tau_1$. Similarly, an I/O action of type $\texttt{IO }\ \tau_1$ also returns a value of any supertype τ_2 of τ_1 and thus also has type $\texttt{IO }\ \tau_2$. A function that accepts arguments of type τ_1 can also accept arguments of any subtype τ_3 of τ_1. A function that returns values of type τ_2 also returns values of any supertype τ_4 of τ_2. Thus, any function that has type $\tau_1 \to \tau_2$ also has type $\tau_3 \to \tau_4$. This relationship holds even if the type variables are themselves substituted with functional type expressions.

The satisfiability of the simpler constraints obtained through this transformation can then be checked against the subclass hierarchy $\mathcal{H}^*$. The initial typing environment used for typing DAML-S Core expressions will be denoted by $\Gamma_\mathcal{D}$. Most DAML-S Core constructors can be considered to be pre-defined higher-order agents and to simplify the typing rules, we will consider them as such. $\Gamma_\mathcal{D}$ can then be extended with their constrained type schemata, as summarised in Table 5.

Table 5. The DAML-S Core Type Environment $\Gamma_\mathcal{D}$

cond:	$\forall$a,b,c.IO boolean $\to$ a $\to$ b $\to$ c
return:	$\forall$a.a $\to$ IO a
>>=:	$\forall$a,b,c.IO a $\to$ (b $\to$ IO c) $\to$ IO c
!:	$\forall$a,b.Port a $\to$ b $\to$ IO ()
?:	$\forall$a.Port a $\to$ IO a
newPort:	$\forall$a.IO (Port a)
spawn:	$\forall$a.IO a $\to$ IO (IO a)
choice:	$\forall$a,b,c.IO a $\to$ IO b $\to$ IO c

Table 6. Typing DAML-S expressions

[Axiom]	$\dfrac{}{\Gamma, \mathcal{H}^* \vdash x : \tau \vert C}$ if $\tau \vert C$ is a generic instance of $\Gamma(x)$
[Abstraction]	$\dfrac{\Gamma[x/\tau \vert C], \mathcal{H}^* \vdash e : \tau' \vert C'}{\Gamma, \mathcal{H}^* \vdash \lambda x.e : \tau \to \tau' \vert C'}$
[Application]	$\dfrac{\Gamma, \mathcal{H}^* \vdash e_1 : \tau_1 \to \tau_2 \vert C_1 \quad \Gamma, \mathcal{H}^* \vdash e_2 : \tau_1' \vert C_2}{\Gamma, \mathcal{H}^* \vdash e_1 e_2 : \tau_2 \vert C_1 \cup C_2 \cup \{\tau_1' \lhd \tau_1\}}$

Definition 9 (Well-typedness of Service Definitions). *A service definition* $s \; x_1 \cdots x_n := e$ *is considered to be* well-typed *with respect to a type environment* Γ *and a subclass hierarchy* $\mathcal{H}^*$, *if the following conditions are fulfilled:*

- $\Gamma(s) = \forall \alpha_1, \ldots, \alpha_m . \tau \vert C$
- $\Gamma, \mathcal{H}^* \vdash \lambda e_1 \ldots \lambda e_m . e : \tau \vert C$ *can be derived from the typing rules in Table 6.*
- $\models_{\mathcal{H}^*} C$

Thus, for a service definition to be well-typed, the type derived for e must match the constrained type schema of s in the type environment. Furthermore, the constraints C on the type for e must be satisfiable with respect to the class hierarchy $\mathcal{H}^*$.

The typing rules [Axiom], [Abstraction] and [Application] are quite standard. Note that the constraint set C' in [Abstraction] does not need to be extended with the constraints in C. If the expression e already contains x in an application, then the constraints C' already contain the constraints C, that is $C \subseteq C'$. If the expression e does not contain x, then the type of x and its constraints are immaterial. In [Application], the type constraints on $(e_1 e_2)$ are the union of the constraints on e_1 and e_2. The requirement that τ_1' must be a subtype of τ_1 is captured through the additional constraint $\tau_1' \lhd \tau_1$.

5.1 Type Inference for DAML-S

We present an algorithm for determining the type of a expression in DAML-S, assuming the expression does not contain polymorphic data structures. Our algorithm extends the algorithm described in [10] and [15] with the verification of constraint satisfaction for type expressions with multiple inheritance. The algorithm $\mathcal{E}$, presented in Table 7, determines the type expression of an expression in DAML-S. First, a type environment Γ and an inheritance hierarchy $\mathcal{H}^*$ need to be constructed. We let the initial type environment be $\Gamma_{\mathcal{D}}$. Given an ontology, a corresponding inheritance hierarchy $\mathcal{H}^*$ can be easily constructed. With the definition of the inheritance hierarchy and the type environment, the function

Table 7. Type Inference Algorithm for DAML-S

$\mathcal{E}[\![x]\!](\Gamma, \mathcal{H}^*) = (\emptyset, \tau | C)$
    if $\tau | C$ is a generic instance of $\Gamma(x)$

$\mathcal{E}[\![\lambda x.e]\!](\Gamma, \mathcal{H}^*) = (\sigma, (\sigma \alpha) \rightarrow \tau | \sigma C)$
    if there exists a substitution σ and α a fresh variable, such that
    $(\sigma, \tau | C) = \mathcal{E}[\![e]\!](\Gamma[x/\alpha], \mathcal{H}^*)$

$\mathcal{E}[\![(e_1 e_2)]\!](\Gamma, \mathcal{H}^*) = (\sigma \circ \sigma_2 \circ \sigma_1, \sigma \beta | \sigma C)$
    if there exist substitutions $\sigma, \sigma_1, \sigma_2$ and fresh variables α, β, such that
    $(\sigma_1, \tau_1 | C_1) = \mathcal{E}[\![e_1]\!](\Gamma, \mathcal{H}^*)$
    $(\sigma_2, \tau_2 | C_2) = \mathcal{E}[\![e_2]\!](\sigma_1 \Gamma, \mathcal{H}^*)$
    $\sigma = mgu(\tau_1, \alpha \rightarrow \beta)$
    $C = \sigma_2 C_1 \cup C_2 \cup \{\tau_2 \lhd \alpha\}$

$\mathcal{E}$ can now be used to determine the constrained types of the defined service descriptions.

The function $\mathcal{E}$ determines the type of an expression e with respect to a type environment Γ and an inheritance hierarchy $\mathcal{H}^*$ as a pair, consisting of a substitution σ and a constrained type expression $\tau | C$. If e is a variable, then $\mathcal{E}$ simply looks up its type in the type environment Γ and returns an empty substitution.

If e is an abstraction of the form $\lambda x.e'$, we first assign the variable x a fresh type variable α and determine the inferred type of e' under the type environment Γ and the inheritance hierarchy $\mathcal{H}^*$. The type of the abstraction is then $(\sigma \alpha) \rightarrow \tau$ under the constraints σC, where $\tau | C$ is the type inferred for e' with the substitution σ. Finally, if the type of an application $(e_1 e_2)$ is to be determined, we first determine the inferred types of e_1 and e_2 individually. The inferred type of c_1 is then unified with a functional type $\alpha \rightarrow \beta$. The constraints of the inferred type of $(e_1 e_2)$ is the union of the inferred types of e_1 and e_2 and a constraint that the inferred type of e_2 is a subtype of the argument type expected by e_1.

The application of $\mathcal{E}$ can result in type expressions with subtype constraints, which must also be satisfiable. An algorithm to test the satisfiability of such a set of subtype constraints is presented in [15].

6   Related Work

Web services are modelled as processes in a distributed system in DAML-S. Although the Web does introduce new concepts such as service advertisements, service brokering, auctions and so on, these exist over the distributed model. XLANG also takes the process-oriented approach and models Web services through a process calculus. WSFL, in contrast, uses a workflow approach, which is well-suited to define the composition of processes, but is less so for the precise specification of processes themselves.

An alternative semantics for the process model has been proposed by Narayanan et al. [14], which uses the situation calculus to model a subset of DAML-S, essentially processes and their inputs, outputs, preconditions and effects. Axioms in the situation calculus are mapped onto Petri net representations, which are then used to describe the semantics of the DAML-S control constructs.

The situation calculus describes a state or situation in the world in terms of propositions, which can be true or false in that state. Actions are described in terms of the their preconditions and effects on the state: which propositions must hold for the action to take place and which propositions hold true after the action has taken place. In the case of multi-agent systems, however, every agent will have its own set of propositions, its own view on the world. Not only does this place a significant burden on the system designer to define the comprehensive set of relevant propositions and axioms, it is also not clear how the differing world views of the agents will be reconciled when they interact. How much does each agent need to know about the knowledge of the other agent? Or even about the world, to be able to perform an action?

An additional issue arises with respect to the composition of agents. Although, one can represent and reason about the sequences of actions a single agent can perform with the help of planning systems, the composition of agents is a slightly different matter. For instance, when performing two actions a_1 and a_2 in sequence, the agent's knowledge about the world after completing the first action a_1 is the same as the agent's knowledge before beginning the second action a_2. On the other hand, if the actions are performed by two separate agents, the knowledge of the first agent after performing a_1 cannot be guaranteed to be the same as the knowledge of the second agent about to perform a_2.

The Petri net semantics and the semantics described in this paper are equivalent in most respects, but there are a couple of minor differences. The choice agent described in this paper chooses a single agent for execution from among a set S of agents, whereas in the Petri net semantics, it is defined as choosing a subset of agents for concurrent execution. In our semantics, this alternate definition can be easily modelled as a choice between all the subsets of S that are to be concurrently executed. Since S contains a finite number of elements, the choice agent also has a finite number of arguments. The Petri net semantics of the Concurrent class also does not explicitly model the possibility of interaction between the concurrently running agents. Similarly, we do not describe the Unordered class explicitly because it is equivalent to the Concurrent class.

Within our approach, the inputs, outputs, preconditions and effects of a composite agent can be determined relatively easily from those of its component sub-agents. Furthermore, the semantics we describe explicitly describes subclass polymorphism and it is close to an execution model, since the grounding maps easily onto our semantics.

7   Conclusions

We have presented a formal syntax and semantics for the Web services specification language DAML-S, which can form a basis for the future DAML-S
execution model. A formal semantics facilitates the construction of automatic
tools to assist in the specification of Web services. Techniques to automatically
verify properties of Web service specifications can also be explored with the
foundation of a formal semantics. We extended the DAML-S formalisation with
subtype polymorphism, which captures certain aspects of DAML inferencing, in
particular subsumption. Since DAML-S is still evolving, the semantics needs to
be constantly updated to keep up with current specifications of the language.
Additionally, as DAML-S grows to incorporate service transactions and service
brokering, these notions can be formalised on top of the formal framework presented here.

This work was partially supported by DARPA/AFRL Contract No. F30602-00-2-
0592.

References

1. A. Ankolekar, M. Burstein, J. Hobbs, O. Lassila, D. Martin, S. McIlraith,
   S. Narayanan, M. Paolucci, T. Payne, K. Sycara, and H. Zeng. DAML-S: Semantic markup for Web services. In *Proceedings of the International Semantic
   Web Working Symposium (SWWS)*, pages 411–430, 2001.
2. A. Ankolekar, F. Huch, and K. Sycara. Concurrent semantics for the web services
   specification language DAML-S. In *Proceedings of the Fifth International Conference on Coordination Models and Languages*, volume 2315 of *Springer Lecture
   Notes in Computer Science*. Springer Verlag, April 2002.
3. E. Christensen, F. Curbera, G. Meredith, and S. Weerawarana. Web services
   description language (WSDL) 1.1, 2001.
4. D. Connolly, F. van Harmelen, I. Horrocks, D. L. McGuinness, P. F. Patel-
   Schneider, and L. A. Stein. DAML+OIL (march 2001) reference description.
   http://www.w3.org/TR/daml+oil-reference.
5. M. Felleisen, D. P. Friedman, E. E. Kohlbecker, and B. Duba. A syntactic theory
   of sequential control. *Theoretical Computer Science*, 52(3):205–237, 1987.
6. R. Fikes and D. McGuinness. An axiomatic semantics for RDF, RDF-S, and
   DAML+OIL, W3C note 12.
7. F. Huch. Verification of Erlang programs using abstract interpretation and model
   checking. In *Proceedings of the ACM SIGPLAN International Conference on Functional Programming (ICFP '99)*, volume 34-9 of *ACM SIGPLAN Notices*, pages
   261–272. ACM Press, September 1999. Proceedings of the ACM SIGPLAN International Conference on Functional Programming (ICFP '99).
8. F. Huch and U. Norbisrath. Distributed programming in Haskell with ports. *Lecture Notes in Computer Science*, 2011, 2000.
9. S. P. Jones, A. Gordon, and S. Finne. Concurrent Haskell. In *Conference Record
   of POPL '96: The 23rd ACM SIGPLAN-SIGACT Symposium on Principles of
   Programming Languages*, pages 295–308, St. Petersburg Beach, Florida, 1996.

10. S. Kaes. Type inference in the presence of overloading, subtyping and recursive types. In *Proceedings of the Conference on Lisp and Functional programming*, pages 193–204. ACM Press, 1992.
11. F. Leymann. Web services flow language (WSFL) 1.0.
12. R. Milner. *Communication and Concurrency*. Prentice Hall, 1989.
13. R. Milner. The polyadic π-calculus: A tutorial. Technical report, University of Edinburgh, 1991.
14. S. Narayanan and S. McIllraith. Simulation, verification, and automated composition of web services. In *Proceedings of the Eleventh International World Wide Web Conference (WWW2002)*, 2002.
15. P. Niederau. Objectorientierte erweiterungen einer deklarativen programmiersprache. Master's thesis, RWTH Aachen, August 2000.
16. S. Thatte. XLANG: Web services for business process design, 2001.
17. UDDI. The UDDI technical white paper. http://www.uddi.org/, 2000.
18. F. van Harmelen, P. F. Patel-Schneider, and I. Horrocks. A model-theoretic semantics for DAML+OIL.
   http://www.daml.org/2001/03/model-theoretic-semantics.html.

Semantic Matching of Web Services Capabilities

Massimo Paolucci[1], Takahiro Kawamura[1,2],
Terry R. Payne[1], and Katia Sycara[1]

[1] Carnegie Mellon University
Pittsburgh, PA, USA
{paolucci, takahiro, terryp, katia}@cs.cmu.edu
[2] Research & Development Center, Toshiba Corp.
1, Komukai Toshiba-cho, Saiwai-ku,
Kawasaki 212-8582, Japan
takahiro@isl.rdc.toshiba.co.jp

Abstract. The Web is moving from being a collection of pages toward a collection of services that interoperate through the Internet. The first step toward this interoperation is the location of other services that can help toward the solution of a problem. In this paper we claim that location of web services should be based on the semantic match between a declarative description of the service being sought, and a description of the service being offered. Furthermore, we claim that this match is outside the representation capabilities of registries such as UDDI and languages such as WSDL.
We propose a solution based on DAML-S, a DAML-based language for service description, and we show how service capabilities are presented in the Profile section of a DAML-S description and how a semantic match between advertisements and requests is performed.

1 Introduction

Web services provide a new model of the Web in which sites exchange dynamic information on demand. This change is especially important for the e-business community, because it provides an opportunity to conduct business faster and more efficiently. Indeed, the opportunity to manage supply chains dynamically to achieve the greatest advantage on the market is expected to create great value added and increase productivity. On the other hand, automatic management of supply chain opens new challenges: first, web services should locate other services that provide a solution to their problems, second, services should interoperate to compose complex services.

In this paper we concentrate on the first problem: the location of web services on the basis of the capabilities that they provide. The solution of this problem requires a language to express the capabilities of services, and the specification of a matching algorithm between service advertisements and service requests that recognizes when a request matches an advertisement. We adopt DAML-S as service description language because it provides a semantically based view of of web services which spans from the abstract description of the capabilities of

I. Horrocks and J. Hendler (Eds.): ISWC 2002, LNCS 2342, pp. 333–347, 2002.

the service to the specification of the service interaction protocol, to the actual messages that it exchanges with other web services.

DAML-S ability to describe the semantics of web services is in stark contrast with emerging XML [14] based standards related with web services. Standards such as SOAP [15] and WSDL [3] are designed to provide descriptions of message transport mechanisms, and for describing the interface used by each service. However, neither SOAP nor WSDL are of any help for the automatic location of web services on the basis of their capabilities. Another emerging XML based standard is UDDI [13]; it provides a registry of businesses and web services. UDDI describes businesses by their physical attributes such as name, address and the services that they provide. In addition, UDDI descriptions are augmented by a set of attributes, called TModels, which describe additional features such as the classification of services within taxonomies such as NAICS [2]. Because UDDI does not represent service capabilities, it is of no help to search for services on the basis of what they provide.

A limitation shared by the XML based standards described above is their lack of an explicit semantics: two identical XML descriptions may mean very different things depending on the context of their use. This proves to be a major limitation for capability matching: in fact, one crucial aspect of capability matching is that it can be done only at the semantic level. This is the case because the requester does not know what services are provided at any given time, otherwise it could contact the providers directly without need to search them; furthermore, advertisers and requesters have very different perspectives and different knowledge about the same service. The major problem with capability matching is that it is unrealistic to expect advertisements and requests to be equivalent, or even that exists a service that fulfills exactly the needs of the requester. For example, a service may advertise as a financial news provider, while a requester may need a service that reports stock quotes. The task of the matching engine is to use its knowledge of the World and its semantic understanding of the advertisement and request to recognize their degree of mismatch and retrieve the advertisements of services that more closely match the request.

DAML-S supports our need for semantic representation of services through its tight connection with DAML+OIL [4]. DAML+OIL supports subsumption reasoning on taxonomies of concepts. Furthermore, DAML+OIL allows the definition of relations between concepts so that, for instance, it is possible to express statements like X is part of Y or more generally that a relation R exists between X and Y. The main limitation of DAML+OIL is its lack of a definition of well formed formulae and an associated theorem prover. While these limitations affect the expressivity of advertisements and requests, the language and the reasoning that it supports are rich enough to allow the description of a wide range of services and to allow matches between these descriptions.

In the rest of the paper, we describe DAML-S profiles to some detail; we will then discuss a matching algorithm between advertisements and requests described in DAML-S that recognizes various degrees of matching. We will then conclude by showing how DAML-S and an implemented version of the matching algorithm are used to provide capability matching to the UDDI registry.

2   DAML-S Profiles

The objective of a Service Profiles is to describe the functionalities that a Web Service wants to provide to the community. Web Services may have many functionalities, but not all of them have to be advertised. For example, a book-selling service may provide two different functionalities: the first one is to allow other services to browse its data base to find books of interest; the second one is to allow them to buy the books they found. The book-seller has the choice of advertising just the book-buying service or both the browsing functionality and the buying functionality. In the latter case the service makes public that it can provide browsing services, implicitly allowing other services to browse its data base without buying a book. In contrast, by advertising only the book-selling functionality, but not the browsing, the service hides the browsing functionality from requesters that do not intend to buy. The decision as to which functionalities to advertise determines how the service will be used: a requester that intends to browse but not to buy would select a service that advertises both buying and browsing capabilities, but not one that advertises buying only.

Figure 1 shows the upper ontology for Service Profiles, an example of Service Profile used to advertise a service is shown in figure 7. The figure is logically divided in three parts: the bottom consists of the definition of *Actor*: it records information about the provider of the service. The middle part describes the *Functional Attributes* such as Quality Rating, that is the rating assigned to the service, to Geographic Radius, that specifies whether there are geographic constraints to the service. Such constraints are used to prevent that a request for Chinese food issued in Pittsburgh is served by a restaurant in Shanghai.

The top part of the figure represents the *Functional Description* of the service [12,11]. It describes the capabilities of the service in terms of inputs, outputs, preconditions and effects. An input is what is required by a service in order to produce a desired output. For example, the inputs of a book buying service are the title and the author of the desired book. The output is a confirmation that the order has been received and successfully processed. The preconditions represent conditions in the World that should be true for the successful execution of the service. In the book buying example a precondition would be a valid credit card. The execution of the service may result in actions in the World, these conditions are described as the effects of the agent. In the buying of a book example, the credit card is charged and the book changes property.

Service Profiles describe service requests as well as services provided. A request consists of a description of an hypothetical service that performs a task needed by the requester. For instance, a requester that needs the latest quotes from the stock market may compile a profile of an hypothetical financial news service. Requests are sent to registries of web services that match them against

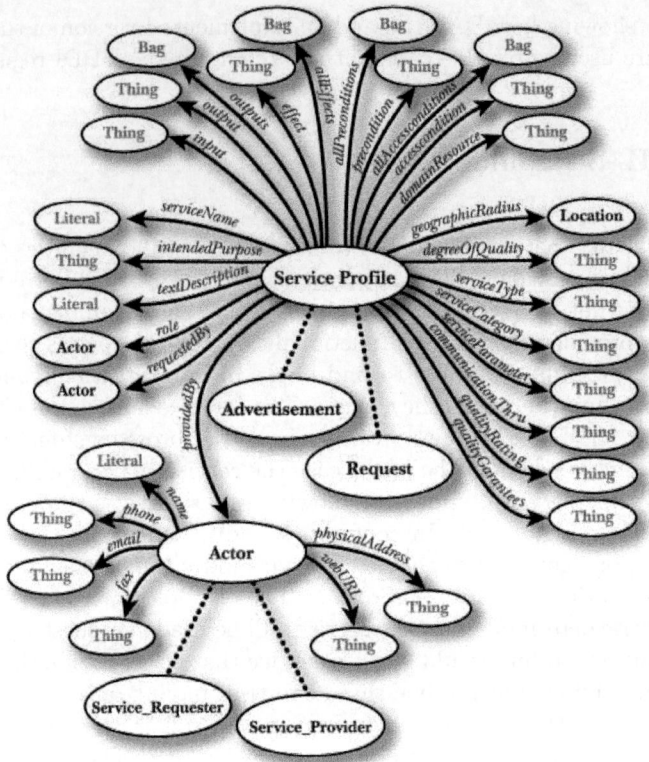

Fig. 1. Upper Ontology of Service Profiles

the profiles advertised by other services to identify which services provide the best match. An example of request is shown in figure 8.

3   Matching Engine

We envision a Web wide infrastructure for web services supported by a set of registries that function as directories. These registries record advertisements of services that come on line, and support search of services that provide a set of requested functionalities. In this section we describe an algorithm for matching service advertisements and service requests.

An advertisement matches a request, when the advertisement, describes a service that is *sufficiently similar* to the service requested. Of course, the problem of this definition is to specify what "sufficiently similar" means. In its strongest interpretation, an advertisement and a request are "sufficiently similar" when they describe exactly the same service. This definition is too restrictive, because advertisers and requesters have no prior agreement on how a service is represented; furthermore, they have very different objectives. A restrictive criteria on matching is therefore bound to fail to recognize similarities between advertisements and requests.

To accommodate a softer definition of "sufficiently similar" we need to allow matching engines to perform *flexible* matches, i.e. matches that recognize the degree of similarity between advertisements and requests. Service requesters should also be allowed to decide the degree of flexibility that they grant to the system. If they concede little flexibility, they reduce the likelihood of finding services that match their requirements, i.e. they minimize the false positives, while increasing the false negatives. On the other hand, by increasing the flexibility of match, they achieve the opposite effect: they reduce the false negatives at the expense of an increase of false positives.

An additional problem related with performing flexible matches is that the Matching Engine is open to exploitation from advertisements and requests that are too generic in the attempt to maximize the likelihood of matching. For instance, a service may advertise itself as a provider of everything, rather than to be honest and precise with what it does. Similarly, a the requester may ask for any service, rather than specifying exactly what it expects. The matching engine can reduce the efficacy of these exploitations by ranking advertisements on the basis of the degree of match with the request.

In a nutshell, we expect the matching engine to satisfy the following desiderata:

- The matching engine should support flexible semantic matching between advertisements and requests on the basis of the ontologies available to the services and the matching engine.
- Despite the flexibility of match, the matching engine should minimize false positives and false negatives. Furthermore, the requesting service should have some control on the amount of matching flexibility it allows to the system.
- The matching engine should encourage advertisers and requesters to be honest with their descriptions at the cost of paying the price of either not be matched, or being matched inappropriately.
- The matching process should be efficient: it should not burden the requester with excessive delays that would prevent its effectiveness..

The algorithm we propose strives to satisfy all four desiderata. Semantic matching is based on DAML ontologies: advertisements and requests refer to DAML concepts and the associated semantic. By using DAML, the matching process can perform inferences on the subsumption hierarchy leading to the recognition of semantic matches despite their syntactic differences and difference in modeling abstractions between advertisements and requests.

The use of DAML also supports accuracy: no matching is recognized when the relation between the advertisement and the request does not derive from the DAML ontologies used by the registry. Furthermore, the semantic of DAML-S descriptions allows us to define a ranking function which distinguishes multiple degrees of matching.

Finally, the matching process is necessarily a complex mechanism that may lead to costly computations. In order to increase efficiency, the algorithm described here adopts a set of strategies that rapidly prune advertisements that are guaranteed not to match the request, thus improving the efficiency of the overall matching engine while maintaining its precision.

3.1   Matching Algorithm

The main rational behind our algorithm is that an advertisement matches a request when the service provided by the advertiser can be of some use for the requester. Specifically, an advertisement matches a request when all the outputs of the request are matched by the outputs of the advertisement, and all the inputs of the advertisement are matched by the inputs of the request. This criteria guarantees that the matched service satisfies the needs of the requester, and that the requester provides to the matched service all the inputs that it needs to operate correctly.

In this section we discuss the matching algorithm in some detail. We will first present the main loop in which a request is matched against all the advertisements recorded by the registry; then we will discuss the rules for matching each advertisement with the request; we will then show how the degree of match is computed and how the results of the match are sorted. We will conclude the section with an example and a discussion of how the matching algorithm proposed satisfies the desiderata listed above.

The main control loop of the matching algorithm is shown in figure 2. Requests are matched against all the advertisements stored by the registry. Whenever a match between the request and any of the advertisements is found, it is recorded and scored to find the matches with the highest degree.

```
match(request) {
    recordMatch= empty list
    forall adv in advertisements do {
       if match(request, adv) then
          recordMatch.append(request, adv) }
    return sort(recordMatch);}
```

Fig. 2. Main control loop

A match between an advertisement and a request consists of the match of all the outputs of the request against the outputs of the advertisement; and all the inputs of the advertisement against the inputs of the request. The algorithm for output matching is described in detail in figure 3: a match is recognized if and only if for each output of the request, there is a matching output in the advertisement. The degree of success depends on the degree of match detected. If one of the request's output is not matched by any of the advertisement's output the match fails. The matching between inputs is computed following the same algorithm, but with the order of the request and the advertisement reversed:

whereas the request's outputs are matched against the advertisement's outputs, the advertisement's inputs are matched against the request's inputs.

```
outputMatch(outputsRequest, outputsAdvertisement) {
    globalDegreeMatch= Exact
    forall outR in outputsRequest do {
        find outA in outputsAdvertisement such that
            degreeMatch= maxDegreeMatch(outR,outA)
            if (degreeMatch=fail) return fail
            if (degreeMatch<globalDegreeMatch)
                globalDegreeMatch= degreeMatch
    return sort(recordMatch);}}
```

Fig. 3. Algorithm for output matching

The degree of match between two outputs or two inputs depends by the relation between the concepts associated with those inputs and outputs. For instance, consider how a request whose output is specified as vehicle matches the advertisement of a car selling service whose outputs are car and price. Given the ontology fragment shown in figure 5, the matching engine would match vehicle with car instead of matching it with price, because car is subsumed by vehicle, while no subsumption relation is found between vehicle and price.

```
degreeOfMatch(outR,outA):
    if outA=outR then return exact
    if outR subclassOf outA then return exact
    if outA subsumes outR then return plugIn
    if outR subsumes outA then return subsumes
    otherwise fail
```

Fig. 4. Rules for the degree of match assignment

The degree of match is determined by the minimal distance[1] between concepts in the taxonomy tree. We differentiate between four degrees of matching according to the rule displayed in figure 4, where outR corresponds to one output of the request and outA corresponds to one output of the advertisement[2]. The rational for the degree assignment is described below.

exact If outR=outA then outR and outA are equivalent, which we label as exact. The second clause is a bit more complicated; if outR subclassOf outA then

---

[1] DAML+OIL supports multiple inheritance, therefore there may be more than one path between two nodes. We optimistically always select the shortest.

[2] The degree of match of inputs is assigned in the same way, but the arguments reversed: degreeOfMatch(inA,inR)

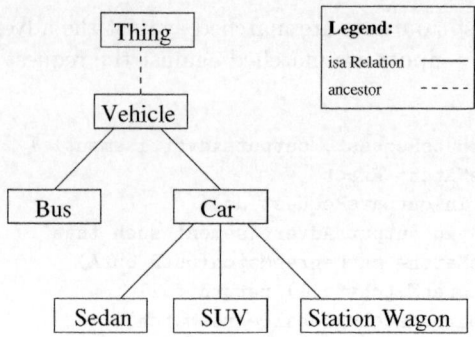

Fig. 5. A fragment of the Vehicle Ontology

the result is still `exact` under the assumption that by advertising `outA` the provider commits to provide outputs consistent with every immediate subtype of `outA`. This is like to say that, given the ontology fragment in figure 5, the provider, by advertising `car`, commits to provide `sedan`, `station wagon` and `SUV`. If instead it provides only `station wagon`, than a better strategy would be to restrict its advertisement to the latter.

plug in If `outA` subsumes `outR`[3] than `outA` is a set that includes `outR`, or, in other words, `outA` could *be plugged* in place of `outR` [16]. For example, the a service that provides (any type of ...) `vehicles` could be of use for another service that expects `station wagons`. This rule acknowledges that there is a weaker relation between `outR` and `outA` in this case, than in the exact case above: we can expect that a service that advertises an output of vehicle provides some type of cars, but we cannot expect that it provides every type of SUV.

subsumes If `outR` subsumes `outA`, then the provider does not completely fulfill the request. The requester may use the provider to achieve its goals, but it likely needs to modify its plan or perform other requests to complete its task.

fail Failure occurs when no subsumption relation between advertisement and request is identified.

Degrees of match are organized along a discrete scale in which exact matches are of course preferable to any another; plugIn matches are the next best level because the output returned can probably be used instead of what the requester expects. Subsumes is the third best level since the requirements of the requester are only partially satisfied: the advertised service can provide only some specific cases of what the requester desires. Fail is the lower level and it represents an unacceptable result.

The last piece of the algorithm to discuss is the scoring system used to sort the resulting matches. The rules used to sort are shown in figure 6. The

---

[3] subclassOf in DAML also defines a subsumption relation, therefore the exact match defined above is also based on the subsumption relation. The rules for *plug in* matching apply when the concepts are not the same and no subclassOf relation holds.

rationale behind them is that the requester expects first and foremost that the provider achieves the output requested at the highest degree. This is reflected in our rules by establishing that the main sorting criteria is to select the match with the highest score in the outputs. Input matching is used only as secondary score to break ties between equally scoring outputs: the requester may solve any mismatch between the information that it has available and the expectations of the provider with additional problem solving or by querying the registry to find additional providers.

```
sortRule(match1,match2) {
    if match1.output > match2.output then match1 > match2
    if match1.output = match2.output
        & match1.input > match2.input then match1 > match2
    if match1.output = match2.output
        & match1.input = match2.input then match1 = match2
```

Fig. 6. Rules for the degree of match assignment

3.2   An Example: Looking for Cars

In this section we show a simple example of how a request for service is matched with service advertisements. The service advertised is a car selling service which given a price reports which car can be bought for that price. A strip down version of the advertisement for the service is shown in figure 7: it shows that the inputs expected by the service are restricted to instances of the concept *Price* as defined in the *Concepts* ontology, while the outputs the service generates are instance of the concept *Car* as defined in the ontology *Vehicle* shown in figure 5.

A request for service is expressed in the same format of the advertisement; a possible request is expressed in figure 8. The request shows that the service sought sells sedans, specifically, it should accepts as inputs to instances of *Price* and it generates as outputs instances of *Sedan.*

The match between the advertisement and the request requires the matching between their inputs and outputs restrictions respectively. For ease of example, both inputs are restricted to the same concept, therefore they match exactly. The algorithm for output matching is shown in figure 3 and 4; it recognizes that *Car* and *Sedan* are an exact match because Car is a superclass of Sedan in the Vehicle ontology displayed in figure 5. As a result the advertisement and the request match exactly because of the exact match of both their inputs and outputs. As a consequence, the Car service advertised is reported to the requester.

The example shows a case of an advertisement and request that look superficially different but match exactly nevertheless using ontological information. More relaxed matches would result if the advertising service produces more general outputs, such as *Vehicle* instead of *Car.* The latter case would result in a

```
<profile:Profile rdf:ID="CarSellingService">
  <profile:serviceName>CarSellingService</profile:serviceName>
  <profile:providedBy> ... </profile:providedBy>
  <input>
    <profile:ParameterDescription rdf:ID="Price_Input">
      <profile:parameterName>Price</profile:parameterName>
      <profile:restrictedTo rdf:resource="Concets.daml#Price"\>
    </profile:ParameterDescription>
  </input>
  <output>
    <profile:ParameterDescription rdf:ID="Car_Output">
      <profile:parameterName>Car</profile:parameterName>
      <profile:restrictedTo rdf:resource="Vehcle.daml#Car"\>
    </profile:ParameterDescription>
  </output>
</profile:Profile>
```

Fig. 7. Advertisement of a car selling service

```
<profile:Profile rdf:ID="RequestSedanSellingService">
  <input>
    <profile:ParameterDescription rdf:ID="Price_Input">
      <profile:parameterName>Price</profile:parameterName>
      <profile:restrictedTo rdf:resource="Concets.daml#Price"/>
    </profile:ParameterDescription>
  </input>
  <output>
    <profile:ParameterDescription rdf:ID="Sedan_Output">
      <profile:parameterName>Sedan</profile:parameterName>
      <profile:restrictedTo rdf:resource="file:data/Vehcle.daml#Sedan"/>
    </profile:ParameterDescription>
  </output>
```

Fig. 8. Advertisement of car selling service

lower degree of matching: *plugIn* instead of *exact* because the output of the advertisement subsumes the output of the request. A failure would instead result if the outputs of the advertisement are instances of *Bus* because no subsumption relation is recognized between the outputs of the advertisement and the outputs of the request.

3.3 Satisfaction of Desiderata

The matching algorithm supports a flexible semantic match between advertisements and requests. The only thing that matters during matching is whether the matching engine can draw an inference between inputs and outputs of the advertisements and requests on the basis of the ontologies available to the registry. Furthermore, the result of the match is not a hard true or false, but it depends on the degree of similarity between the concepts in the match.

Despite this flexibility, the matching engine still rejects advertisements that do not match the requests, and accepts, but with a low score, matches that may be unsatisfactory for the requester. The requester can specify which types of match it wishes the matching engine to perform by constraining the minimal acceptable degree of match. Also, the amount of search required may be constrained by forcing the matching engine to restrict the search within a close subset of concepts in the ontology. The last desiderata: that the matching process be efficient is currently under testing.

4   Application to UDDI

Universal Description Discovery and Integration (hereafter UDDI)[13] is an industrial initiative whose goal is to create an Internet wide registry of web services. UDDI allows businesses to register their contact points, and the web services that they provide. UDDI supports the registration of attributes of services via a construct called *TModel*. A TModel is a form of meta data that provides a reference system for information about services. For instance services can specify that they are based on the WSDL specification by referring to a publicly known WSDL TModel. In general TModels have two functions: the first is to tag the type of service advertised and whether some specific conventions on the use of the UDDI registry have been applied. The second is to provide abstract keys to be associated with a service specific value. For example, a service may specify its category using the North American Industry Classification System (hereafter NAICS) [2] published by the US Census.

UDDI provides poor search facilities: it allows only a keyword based search of businesses, services and TModels on the bases of their names. In addition services can be searched by their type specification through TModels. For instance, it is possible to search for all the services that adhere to the WSDL representation or that have a some value associated with a TModel. Since search in UDDI is restricted to keyword matching, no form of inference or flexible match between keywords can be performed.

We implemented a matching engine that can be used to augment UDDI registries[4] with an additional semantic layer that performs a capability based matching. The matching engine that we implemented is based on the algorithm described above and it takes advantage of DAML ontologies published on the web. The result of this work is that services that advertise using DAML-S are also advertised with the UDDI registry, and therefore they can be found and retrieved by using UDDI keyword search. In addition, they can also be found through our capability matching engine.

The architecture of the combined DAML-S/UDDI Matchmaker is described in figure 9. The Matchmaker receives messages from outside through the *Communication Module*; upon recognizing that a message is an advertisement, the Communication Module sends it to the *DAML-S/UDDI Translator* that constructs a UDDI service description using information about the service provider,

---

[4] We are currently using the IBM test site.

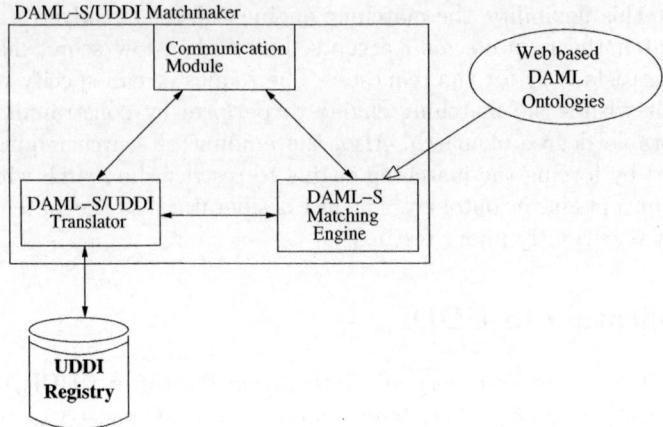

Fig. 9. The architecture of the DAML-S/UDDI Matchmaker

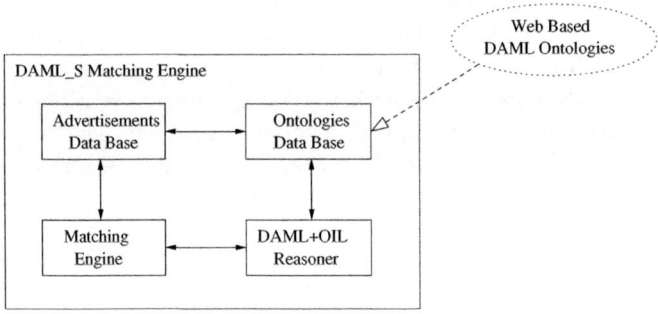

Fig. 10. The architecture of the DAML-S Matching Engine

and the service name. The result of the registration with UDDI is a reference ID of the service. This ID combined with the capability description of the advertisement are sent to the DAML-S Matching Engine that stores the advertisement for capability matching. Requests follow the opposite direction: the Communicator Module sends them to the DAML-S Matchmaker that performs the capability matching. The result of the matching is the advertisement of the providers selected and a reference to the UDDI service record. The combination of UDDI records and advertisements is then send to the requester.

The actual DAML-S based matching engine architecture is displayed in figure 10. Upon receiving a request, the *Matching Engine* component selects the advertisements from the *AdvertisementDB* that are relevant for the current request. Then it uses the *DAML+OIL Reasoner* to compute the level of match. In turn the DAML+OIL Reasoner uses the *OntologyDB* to as data to use to compute the matching process. The AdvertisementDB also takes advantage of the *OntologiesDB* to index advertisements for fast retrieval at matching time.

This system show the limits of UDDI and the value added by DAML-S and its support for functional descriptions and matching upon functional descriptions of services. In its current form UDDI does not provide any support for finding services on the basis of what tasks they perform. It is impossible ask UDDI for a "car selling service" because UDDI because such a request cannot even be expressed. By adding an additional layer for service capability matching and by using DAML-S as service capability language we allow services to select each other on the bases of what they do and ultimately to interoperate and solve problems autonomously minimizing human intervention.

5   Discussion

DAML-S and its Service Profile take up the challenge of representing the functionalities of web services. This paper contributes to this challenge by describing a matching engine that allows matching of advertisements and requests on the bases of the capabilities that they describe. This is a major improvement on current technology that allows only location of services based on keyword matching. Indeed we show how the matching engine can be used to improve the functionalities of existing web service repositories such as UDDI.

The Service Profile is an evolution of the work on representation of agents in open Multi-Agents Systems (hereafter MAS) and specifically of LARKS [12]. DAML-S as well as LARKS represents services on the bases of their inputs and outputs. The major difference between DAML-S and LARKS is that DAML-S relies on DAML and its ontologies, while LARKS allowed for their incremental creation by associating needed concepts directly with the advertisements and requests. The two systems rely on similar matching algorithms. LARKS identifies a set of filters that progressively restrict the number of advertisements that are candidates for a match. The filtering mechanism allows services to strike the most advantageous trade off between the precision of matching and the time required for a match: the higher the precision, the longer the time the matchmaker needs before delivering an answer. The matching engine described in this paper is based on the more restrictive of the LARKS filters that performs logic and ontological inferences between advertisements and requests. While, the filters adopted by LARKS cannot be efficiently ported into DAML-S, we suggest similar filters that achieve the same results.

The Multi-Agent community has addressed the problem of capability based matching in an open MAS suggesting a number of solutions. The OAA [6] represents agents by their "solvables": a representation of the queries the agent replies to. The problem with OAA solvables is that any agent should know at request time what solvables the provider replies to, but the solvables are not known until the provider is selected. Ultimately this impasse can be solved only by abstracting from the solvables to the information that is exchanged. Infosleuth [9] associates an ontological concept with each type of services that agents perform, then at matching time, it selects only those services that perform the desired function. In practice InfoSleuth uses an extensive representation of functionalities (one concept for each possible type of services), while DAML-S use an intensive representation in which services are implicitly defined by the transformation that they produce. More recently DReggie [8] defined an ontology based on DAML+OIL to describe mobile devices and then use a matching engine to locate devices on the bases of their features. Unfortunately, publicly available descriptions of the system are still sketchy.

Software Reuse Systems also need to index software components appropriately for efficient and precise retrieval. Still, work on software reuse differs sharply from our attempt to represent and match web services principally because software reuse requires programmers, rather than automatic services, to construct a request for a software component to search; furthermore, our aim with DAML-S as a whole, is automatic interaction between services, while work in software reuse requires programmers to program the interaction between different software components. Because of this difference, techniques like the faceted classification [10] are of no use to help automatic queries since they represent features of the providers rather than the goals it achieves. Techniques such as analogical software reuse [7] share a representation of components that is based on goals achieved by the software, roles, conditions. To this extent their approach is similar to ours, but it requires a complex compilation of a case to match against. Zaremsky and Wing [16] describe a specification language and matching mechanism for software components that bear many similarities with the Matching Algorithm described here. As in our work they allow for multiple degrees of matching. We depart from their work because we match on the semantics associated with inputs and outputs, while they consider only type information. Of all the reuse models UPML [5] shares the greater similarities with our representation by representing inputs, outputs, preconditions and effects of tasks. Nonetheless, UPML still requires programmers in the loop.

Despite superficial similarities with Case Based Reasoning Systems (CBR), and specifically CBR supported planning [1], the work described here is very different. The goal of Case Base Reasoning Systems is to retrieve a previously learned case and to adapt it to the problem solving case that they are facing. To this extent they have a fix retrieval function while here is flexible retrieval mechanism is used. Furthermore, when a profile is retrieved by the repository it is not applied as a case, rather the requesting service and the provider interact following a script described by the DAML-S Process model.

The result of the research effort shows that web services can indeed find each other automatically and interoperate autonomously without the need of hardcoded interactions. Our matching algorithm provides a way for automatic dynamic discovery, selection and interoperation of web services, which is a crucial feature in the web of the future in which services dynamically reconfigure their supply chain to better match changes in the market.

References

1. Jim Blythe and Manuela Veloso. Analogical replay for efficient conditional planning. In *Proceedings of the 14th National Conference on Artificial Intelligence (AAAI-97)*, pages 668–673. AAAI Press / MIT Press, 1997.
2. US Census Bureau. North american industry classification system (naics). http://www.census.gov/epcd/www/naics.html, 1997.
3. Erik Christensen, Francisco Curbera, Greg Meredith, and Sanjiva Weerawarana. Web Services Description Language (WSDL) 1.1. http://www.w3.org/TR/2001/NOTE-wsdl-20010315, 2001.
4. DAML Joint Committee. Daml+oil (march 2001) language. http://www.daml.org/2001/03/daml+oil-index.html, 2001.
5. Dieter Fensel, V. Richard Benjamins, Enrico Motta, and Bob J. Wielinga. UPML: A framework for knowledge system reuse. In *IJCAI*, pages 16–23, 1999.
6. David Martin, Adam Cheyer, and Douglas Moran. The Open Agent Architecture: A Framework for Building Distributed Software Systems. *Applied Artificial Intelligence*, 13(1-2):92–128, 1999.
7. P. Massonet and A. van Lamsweerde. Analogical reuse of requirements frameworks. In *Proc. of the 3rd IEEE Int. Symp. on Requirements Engineering (RE'97)*, pages 26–39, 1997.
8. Yun Peng and Nenad Ivezic. Semantic resolution inf multi-agent systems. In *Proc.of Goddard/JPl Workshop On Radical Agent Concepts*, 2002.
9. Brad Perry, Malcolm Taylor, and Amy Unruh. Information aggregation and agent interaction patterns in infosleuth. In *cia99*. ACM Press, 1999.
10. Ruben Prieto-Diaz. Implementing Faceted Classification for Software Reuse. *Communications of ACM*, 134:88–97, 1991.
11. Katia Sycara and Mattheus Klusch. Brokering and matchmaking for coordination of agent societies: A survey. In Omicini et al, editor, *Coordination of Internet Agents*. Springer, 2001.
12. Katia Sycara, Mattheus Klusch, Seth Widoff, and Janguo Lu. Dynamic service matchmaking among agents in open information environments. *ACM SIGMOD Record (Special Issue on Semantic Interoperability in Global Information Systems)*, 28(1):47–53, 1999.
13. UDDI. The UDDI Technical White Paper. http://www.uddi.org/, 2000.
14. W3C. Extensible markup language (xml) 1.0 (second edition). http://www.w3.org/TR/2000/REC-xml-20001006, 2000.
15. W3C. Soap version 1.2, w3c working draft 17 december 2001. http://www.w3.org/TR/2001/WD-soap12-part0-20011217/, 2001.
16. Amy Moormann Zaremski and Jeannette M. Wing. Specification matching software components. *ACM Transactions on Software Engineering and Methodology*, 1997.

DAML-S: Web Service Description for the Semantic Web

DAML-S Coalition: Anupriya Ankolekar[2], Mark Burstein[1], Jerry R. Hobbs[4], Ora Lassila[3], David Martin[4], Drew McDermott[6], Sheila A. McIlraith[5], Srini Narayanan[4], Massimo Paolucci[2], Terry Payne[2], and Katia Sycara[2]

[1] BBN Technologies
[2] Carnegie Mellon University
[3] Nokia Research Center
[4] SRI International
[5] Stanford University
[6] Yale University

Abstract. In this paper we present DAML-S, a DAML+OIL ontology for describing the properties and capabilities of Web Services. Web Services – Web-accessible programs and devices – are garnering a great deal of interest from industry, and standards are emerging for low-level descriptions of Web Services. DAML-S complements this effort by providing Web Service descriptions at the application layer, describing *what* a service can do, and not just *how* it does it. In this paper we describe three aspects of our ontology: the service profile, the process model, and the service grounding. The paper focuses on the grounding, which connects our ontology with low-level XML-based descriptions of Web Services.

1 Services on the Semantic Web

The Semantic Web [2] is rapidly becoming a reality through the development of Semantic Web markup languages such as DAML+OIL [9]. These markup languages enable the creation of arbitrary domain ontologies that support the unambiguous description of Web content. Web Services [15] – Web-accessible programs and devices – are among the most important resources on the Web, not only to provide information to a user, but to enable a user to effect change in the world. Web Services are garnering a great deal of interest from industry, and standards are being developed for low-level descriptions of Web Services. Languages such as WSDL (Web Service Description Language) provide a communication level description of the messages and protocols used by a Web Service. To complement this effort, our interest is in developing semantic markup that will sit at the application level above WSDL, and describe *what* is being sent across the wires and *why*, not just *how* it is being sent.

We are developing a DAML+OIL ontology for Web Services, called DAML-S [5], with the objective of making Web Services computer-interpretable and hence enabling the following tasks [15]: **discovery**, i.e. locating Web Services (typically through a registry service) that provide a particular service and that adhere to

I. Horrocks and J. Hendler (Eds.): ISWC 2002, LNCS 2342, pp. 348–363, 2002.

specified constraints; **invocation** or activation and execution of an identified service by an agent or other service; **interoperation**, i.e. breaking down interoperability barriers through semantics, and the automatic insertion of *message parameter translations* between clients and services [10,13,22]; **composition** of new services through automatic selection, composition and interoperation of existing services [15,14]; **verification** of service properties [19]; and **execution monitoring**, i.e. tracking the execution of complex or composite tasks performed by a service or a set of services, thus identifying failure cases, or providing explanations of different execution traces. To make use of a Web Service, a software agent needs a computer-interpretable description of the service, and the means by which it is accessed. This paper describes a collaborative effort by BBN Technologies, Carnegie Mellon University, Nokia, Stanford University, SRI International, and Yale University, to define the DAML-S Web Services ontology. An earlier version of the DAML-S specification is described in [5]; an updated version of DAML-S is presented at http://www.daml.org/services/daml-s/2001/10/. In this paper we briefly summarize and update this specification, and discuss the important problem of the *grounding*, i.e. how to translate what is being sent in a message to or from a service into how it is to be sent. In particular, we present the linking of DAML-S to the Web Services Description Language (WSDL). DAML-S complements WSDL, by providing an abstract or application level description lacking in WSDL.

2 An Upper Ontology for Services

In DAML+OIL, abstract categories of entities, events, etc. are defined in terms of *classes* and *properties*. DAML-S defines a set of classes and properties, specific to the description of services, within DAML+OIL. The class SERVICE is at the top of the DAML-S ontology. Service properties at this level are very general. The upper ontology for services is silent as to what the particular subclasses of SERVICE should be, or even the conceptual basis for structuring this taxonomy, but it is expected that the taxonomy will be structured according to functional and domain differences and market needs. For example, one might imagine a broad subclass, B2C-TRANSACTION, which would encompass services for purchasing items from retail Web sites, tracking purchase status, establishing and maintaining accounts with the sites, and so on.

The ontology of services provides two essential types of knowledge about a service, characterized by the questions:

- *What does the service require of agents, and provide for them?* This is provided by the *profile*, a class that describes the capabilities and parameters of the service. We say that the class SERVICE *presents* a SERVICEPROFILE.
- *How does it work?* The answer to this question is given in the *model*, a class that describes the workflow and possible execution paths of the service. Thus, the class SERVICE is *describedBy* a SERVICEMODEL

The SERVICEPROFILE provides information about a service that can be used by an agent to determine if the service meets its rough needs, and if it satisfies constraints such as security, locality, affordability, quality-requirements, etc. In contrast, the SERVICEMODEL enables an agent to: (1) perform a more in-depth analysis of whether the service meets its needs; (2) compose service descriptions from multiple services to perform a specific task; (3) coordinate the activities of different agents; and (4) monitor the execution of the service. Generally speaking, the SERVICEPROFILE provides the information needed for an agent to discover a service, whereas the SERVICEMODEL provides enough information for an agent to make use of a service. In the following sections we discuss the service profile and the service model in greater detail, and introduce the *service grounding*, which describes how agents can communicate with and thus invoke the service.

3   Service Profile

A service profile provides a high-level description of a service and its provider [23,24]; it is used to request or advertise services with discovery services and capability registries. Service profiles consist of three types of information: a *description* of the service and the service provider; the *functional behavior* of the service; and several *functional attributes* tailored for automated service selection.

The profile includes a high-level *description* about the service and it's provenance, which typically would be presented to users when browsing a service registry (see Table 1). The class *Actor* is also defined to describe entities (e.g. humans or organizations) that provide or request Web Services. Two specific classes are derived from the *Actor* class; the *Service-Requester* class and *Service-Provider* class, to represent the requester and provider of the service respectively. Properties of *Actor* include `physicalAddress`, `WebURL`, `name`, `phone`, `email`, and `fax`. *Functional attributes* specify additional information about the service, such as what guarantees of response time or accuracy it provides, the cost of the service, or the classification of the service in some registry such as the NAICS [3].

Implicitly, service profiles specify the intended purpose of the service, because they specify only those *functional behaviors* that are publicly provided. A book-selling service may involve two different functionalities: it allows clients to browse its site to find books of interest, and it allows them to buy the books they find. The book-seller has the choice of advertising just the book-buying service or may also advertise browsing functionality. In the latter case the service publicizes the fact that agents may browse without buying a book. In contrast, by advertising only the book-selling functionality, the service discourages browsing by requesting agents that do not intend to buy.

While service providers define advertisements for their services using the service profile, service requesters also use the profile to specify their needs and expectations For instance, a provider might advertise a service that provides quotes for a given ticker symbol, whereas a requester may look for a service that reports current market prices and stock quotes. Services advertise their profiles with Internet wide *discovery services*, such as Middle Agents [21] and other registries (e.g. UDDI [25]), which then match *service requests* against the advertised

Table 1. Description Properties and Functional Attributes.

Description Properties

serviceName	The name of the service.
intendedPurpose	A high-level description of what constitutes (typical) successful execution of a service.
textDescription	A brief, human readable description of the service, summarizing what the service offers or what capabilities are being requested.
role	An abstract link to *Actors* involved in the service execution.
requestedBy	A sub-property of role referring to the service requester.
providedBy	A sub-property of role referring to the service provider.

Functional Attributes

geographicRadius	Geographic scope of the service, either at the global scale (e.g. e-commerce) or at a regional scale (e.g. pizza delivery).
degreeOfQuality	Quality qualifications, such as providing the cheapest or fastest possible service.
serviceParameter	An expandable list of properties that characterize the execution of a service, such as averageResponseTime or invocationCost.
communicationThru	High-level summary of how a service may communicate, e.g. what communication language is used (e.g., KQML, SOAP).
serviceType	Broad classification of the service that might be described by an ontology of service types, such as B2B, B2C etc.
serviceCategory	Categories defined within some service category ontology. Such categories may include *Products*, *Information Services* etc.
qualityGuarantees	Guarantees that the service promises to deliver, e.g. guaranteeing to provide a response within 3 minutes, etc.
qualityRating	Industry-based ratings, such as the "Dun and Bradstreet Rating" for businesses.

profiles, and identify which services provide the best match[1]. Service requests are constructed as partial service profile descriptions, which can then be matched to the profiles of advertised services stored in the registries using DAML+OIL subsumption relations. Advertisements and requests can differ sharply, in level of detail and in the level of abstraction of the terms used. Matches are generally recognized whenever the service advertised is subsumed by (is a particular case of) the service description requested.

The service representation of DAML-S is much richer than the representation provided by emerging standards such as UDDI or WSDL. UDDI's description of a service does not include any capability description, limiting itself to the name, a pointer to the provider of the service and a port where to access the service. In addition, UDDI allows services to refer to "TModels" that are used to link a service to technical specifications or to classification schemes. Therefore, it is possible to ask UDDI for all the services that have a WSDL scheme, but not for all the services that provide a requested functionality. The WSDL

---

[1] Despite repeated reference to UDDI, DAML-S, like research in Multi-Agent Systems (e.g., [6,21,26]), may be used with a variety of different registries and protocols.

specification defines and formats query interactions with a service, but does not provide a model for the semantics of such exchanges. DAML-S service profiles have similarities with service description languages emerging in the Multi-Agent interaction community such as LARKS and OAA [12,24]. Those languages, like DAML-S, focus on the representation of what the service does rather than where to find the service. DAML-S improves on those service locating models by taking advantage of DAML+OIL ontologies and its inferential capabilities that greatly enhance the possibility for locating relevant services.

4   Modeling Services as Processes

Web Services are Web-accessible programs or devices. Their operation is described in terms of a process model, which details both the control structure and data flow structure of the service, i.e., the possible steps (typically initiated by messages sent by the client) required to execute a service. The process model comprises subclasses and properties of the PROCESSMODEL class.

The two chief components of the process model are the *Process Ontology* which describes a service in terms of its inputs, outputs, preconditions, effects, and, where appropriate, its component subprocesses; and the *Process Control Ontology* which describes each process in terms of its state, including initial activation, execution, and completion. A version of the Process Ontology is released in the current version of DAML-S and can be used to support automated Web Service invocation, composition and interoperation. The Process Control Ontology, which is useful for automated execution monitoring, has not yet been released. We have also defined an ontology of *resources*, and a simple ontology of *time*; they will be described in other publications.

We expect our process ontology to serve as the basis for specifying a wide array of services. In developing the ontology, we drew from a variety of sources, including work in AI on planning languages [8], work in programming languages and distributed systems [16,17], emerging standards in process modeling and workflow technology such as the NIST's Process Specification Language (PSL) [20] and the Workflow Management Coalition effort[2], work on modeling verb semantics and event structure [18], work in AI on modeling complex actions [11], work in agent communication languages [7,12] and Multi-Agent infrastructure[23], and finally previous work on action-inspired Web Service markup [15].

The primary kind of entity in the Process Ontology is, unsurprisingly, a *process*. The basic PROCESS class has several associated properties. A process can have any number of inputs, representing the information that is, under some conditions, required for the execution of the process. It can have any number of outputs, the information that the process provides, conditionally, after its execution. Besides inputs and outputs, another important type of parameter specifies the participants in a process. There can also be any number of preconditions, which must all hold in order for the process to be invoked. Finally, the process

---

[2] http://www.aiim.org/wfmc

can have any number of effects, which are the side effects in the world that result from execution of the program. Outputs and effects can have conditions asso ciated with them. The range of each of these properties, at the upper ontology level, is THING; that is, left totally unrestricted. For most service applications, more specific range restrictions will be used, together with cardinality restrictions. We anticipate that in many cases the range of properties will be subclasses of the class of well-formed formulae in a logical language whose ontology we can define in DAML+OIL.

In DAML-S, we distinguish between *atomic*, *simple*, and *composite* processes:

1. *Atomic* processes are directly invokable (by exchanging messages with the service), have no subprocesses, and execute in a single step, from the perspective of the service requester. (That is, the requester sends a single message, and receives back a single message, in making use of the service.) Atomic processes must provide a grounding that enables a service requester to construct an invocation message and interpret a response message.

2. *Simple* processes, on the other hand, are not directly invokable and are not associated with a grounding. Like atomic processes, they *can* be conceived as having single-step executions. Simple processes are used as elements of abstract processes; a simple process may be used either to provide a view of (a specialized way of using) some atomic process, or a simplified representation of some composite process (for purposes of planning and reasoning). In the former case, the simple process is *realizedBy* the atomic process; in the latter case, the simple process *expands* to the composite process.

3. *Composite* processes are decomposable into other (non-composite or composite) processes. Their decompositions are specified using control constructs such as SEQUENCE and IF-THEN-ELSE (Table 2). Decompositions show, among other things, the control structure associated with a composition of processes and the input-output dataflow of the composition.

A COMPOSITEPROCESS must have a *composedOf* property by which the control structure of the composite is indicated, using a CONTROLCONSTRUCT. Each control construct, in turn, is associated with an additional property called *components* to indicate the ordering and conditional execution of the subprocesses (or control constructs) of which it is composed. For instance, the control construct, SEQUENCE, has a *components* property that ranges over a PROCESSCOMPONENTLIST (a list whose items are restricted to be PROCESSCOMPONENTs, which are either processes or control constructs). In the process upper ontology, we have included a minimal set of control constructs that can be specialized to describe a variety of Web Services.

A process can often be viewed at different levels of granularity, either as a primitive, undecomposable process (the "black box" view) or as a composite process (the "glass box" view). When a composite process is viewed as a black box, a simple process can be used to represent this. In this case, the relationship between the simple and composite is represented using the *expand* property, and its inverse, the *collapse* property.

Table 2. Process Constructs

Construct	Description
Sequence	Execute a list of processes in a sequential order
Concurrent	Execute elements of a bag of processes concurrently
Split	Invoke elements of a bag of processes
Split+Join	Invoke elements of a bag of processes and synchronize
Unordered	Execute all processes in a bag in any order
Choice	Choose between alternatives and execute one
If-Then-Else	If specified condition holds, execute "Then", else execute "Else".
Repeat-Until	Iterate execution of a bag of processes *until a condition holds.*
Repeat-While	Iterate execution of a bag of processes *while a condition holds*

The DAML-S ontology provides a set of distinguished classes and properties for describing the content and capabilities of Web Services. The DAML+OIL language in which it is specified has a well-defined semantics; however the expressive power of DAML+OIL is not sufficient to restrict DAML-S to all and only the intended interpretations. Recently, we have developed proposals for both an model-theoretic and an execution semantics for DAML-S descriptions. [19,1]. One approach provides a model-theoretic semantics by describing the intended interpretation of DAML-S in a more expressive first-order logic language [19]. To provide an operational semantics, the representation is then translated into a distributed operational semantics based on High-Level Petri Nets. This allowed us to determine the complexity of important decision procedures (such as reachability and deadlock) for various subsets of the DAML-S process language. In our other approach [1], we use a functional core language to describe DAML-S constructs. A (concurrent) interleaving strict operational semantics for DAML-S is defined, which provides a formal basis for the DAML-S execution model. Together, these proposals allow us to translate DAML-S specifications into an executable process model that can be used for simulation, verification, and composition of DAML-S-described services.

5   Grounding a Service to a Concrete Realization

The grounding of a service specifies the details of how to access the service – details having mainly to do with protocol and message formats, serialization, transport, and addressing. A grounding can be thought of as a *mapping* from an *abstract* to a *concrete* specification of those service description elements that are required for interacting with the service; for our purposes, the inputs and outputs of atomic processes. Note that in DAML-S, both the *ServiceProfile* and the *ServiceModel* are conceived as abstract representations; only the *ServiceGrounding* deals with the concrete level of specification.

In DAML-S, the abstract content of a message is specified, implicitly, by the input or output properties of an atomic process. Thus, atomic processes, in addition to specifying the primitive processes from which larger processes are composed, can also be thought of as the communication primitives of an (abstract) process specification.

Concrete messages, however, *are* specified explicitly in a grounding. The central function of a DAML-S grounding is to show how the (abstract) inputs and outputs of an atomic process are to be realized concretely as messages, which carry those inputs and outputs in some specific transmittable format. Industry is a long way towards adopting a concrete message specification. As such, in crafting our DAML-S grounding mechanism, we use Web Services Description Language (WSDL), a particular specification language proposal that is representative of efforts in this area and that has strong industry backing.

WSDL "is an XML format for describing network services as a set of endpoints operating on messages containing either document-oriented or procedure-oriented information. The operations and messages are described abstractly, and then bound to a concrete network protocol and message format to define an endpoint. Related concrete endpoints are combined into abstract endpoints (services). WSDL is extensible to allow description of endpoints and their messages regardless of what message formats or network protocols are used to communicate" [4].

The DAML-S concept of grounding is generally consistent with WSDL's concept of *binding*. Indeed, by using the extensibility elements already provided by WSDL, along with one new extensibility element proposed here, it is an easy matter to ground a DAML-S atomic process. In this section, we show how this may be done, relying on the WSDL 1.1 specification.

5.1   Relationships between DAML-S and WSDL

The approach described here allows a service developer who is going to provide service descriptions for use by potential clients to take advantage of the complementary strengths of these two specification languages. On the one hand (the abstract side of a service specification), the developer benefits by making use of DAML-S' process model, and the expressiveness of DAML+OIL's class typing mechanisms, relative to what XML Schema provides. On the other hand (the concrete side), the developer benefits from the opportunity to reuse the extensive work done in WSDL (and related languages such as SOAP), and software support for message exchanges based on these declarations, as defined to date for various protocols and transport mechanisms.

We emphasize that a DAML-S/WSDL grounding involves a *complementary* use of the two languages, in a way that is in accord with the intentions of the authors of WSDL. Both languages are required for the full specification of a grounding. This is because the two languages do not cover the same conceptual space. As indicated by figure 1, the two languages *do* overlap in the area of providing for the specification of what WSDL calls "abstract types", which in turn are used to characterize the inputs and outputs of services. WSDL, by default, specifies abstract types using XML Schema, whereas DAML-S allows for

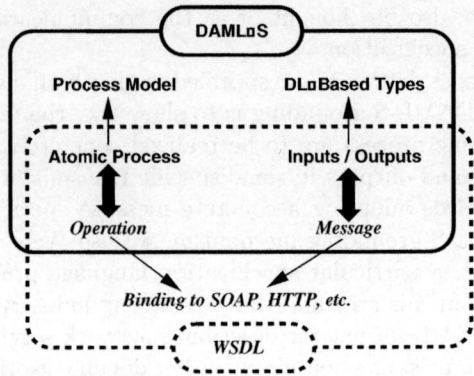

Fig. 1. Mapping between DAML-S and WSDL

the definition of abstract types as (description logic-based) DAML+OIL classes[3]. However, WSDL/XSD is unable to express the semantics of a DAML+OIL class. Similarly, DAML-S has no means, as currently defined, to express the binding information that WSDL captures. Thus, it is natural that a DAML-S/WSDL grounding uses DAML+OIL classes as the abstract types of message parts declared in WSDL, and then relies on WSDL binding constructs to specify the formatting of the messages[4].

A DAML-S/WSDL grounding is based upon the following three correspondences between DAML-S and WSDL. Figure 1 shows the first two of these.

1. A DAML-S atomic process corresponds to a WSDL *operation*. Different types of operations are related to DAML-S processes as follows:
   - An atomic process with both inputs and outputs corresponds to a WSDL *request-response* operation.
   - An atomic process with inputs, but no outputs, corresponds to a WSDL *one-way* operation.
   - An atomic process with outputs, but no inputs, corresponds to a WSDL *notification* operation.
   - A composite process with both outputs and inputs, and with the sending of outputs specified as coming before the reception of inputs, corresponds to WSDL's *solicit-response* operation[5].

---

[3] XML Schema primitives can also be used to define DAML+OIL properties.

[4] The DAML+OIL classes can either be defined within the WSDL *types* section, or defined in a separate document and referred to from within the WSDL description. In the remainder of this exposition, we describe only the latter approach.

[5] Since a composite process has no grounding, this construct would be grounded indirectly by means of its relationship to a simple process (by the *collapse* property), and hence to an atomic process (by the *realizedBy* property), as mentioned in Section 4. We are considering whether to create a new kind of atomic process in DAML-S, which corresponds directly to the solicit-response operation.

2. The set of inputs and the set of outputs of a DAML-S atomic process each corresponds to WSDL's concept of *message*. More precisely, DAML S inputs correspond to the parts of an input message of a WSDL operation, and DAML-S outputs correspond to the parts of an output message of a WSDL operation.

   Note that WSDL allows (at most) one input, and (at most) one output message to be associated with an operation. This is in accord with a decision made independently, in DAML-S, that a grounding must map all inputs to (at most) a single message, and similarly for outputs.

3. The types (DAML+OIL classes) of the inputs and outputs of a DAML-S atomic process correspond to WSDL's extensible notion of *abstract type* (and, as such, may be used in WSDL specifications of message parts).

The job of a DAML-S/WSDL grounding is first, to define, in WSDL, the messages and operations by which an atomic process may be accessed, and then, to specify correspondences (1) and (2). Although it is not logically necessary to do so, we believe it will be useful to specify these correspondences both in WSDL and in DAML-S. Thus, as indicated in the following, we allow for constructs in both languages for this purpose.

5.2   Grounding DAML-S Services with WSDL and SOAP

Because DAML-S is an XML-based language, and its atomic process declarations and input/output types already fit nicely with WSDL, it is easy to extend existing WSDL bindings for use with DAML-S, such as the SOAP binding. In this subsection, we indicate briefly how an arbitrary atomic process, specified in DAML-S, can be given a grounding using WSDL and SOAP, with the assumption of HTTP as the chosen transport mechanism.

Grounding DAML-S with WSDL and SOAP involves the construction of a WSDL service description with all the usual parts (*message, operation, port type, binding*, and *service* constructs), except that the *types* element can normally be omitted. DAML-S extensions are introduced as follows:

1. In each *part* of the WSDL *message* definition, the *daml-property* attribute is used to indicate the fully-qualified name of the DAML-S input or output property, to which this part of the message corresponds. From the property name, the appropriate DAML range class – the class of object which this message part will contain – can easily be obtained.

2. In each WSDL *operation* element, the *daml-s-process* attribute is used to indicate the name of the DAML-S atomic process, to which the operation corresponds.

3. Within the WSDL *binding* element, the *encodingStyle* attribute is given a value such as
   "http://www.daml.org/2001/03/daml+oil.daml", to indicate that the message parts will be serialized in the normal way for class instances of the given types, for the specified version of DAML.

Having completed the WSDL service description, a WSDLGROUNDING object is constructed (in the DAML-S specification), which refers to specific elements within the WSDL specification, using the following properties:

- *wsdlReference*: A URI that indicates the version of WSDL in use.
- *otherReferences*: A list of URIs indicating other relevant standards employed by the WSDL code (e.g., SOAP, HTTP, MIME).
- *wsdlDocuments*: A list of the URIs of the WSDL document(s) that give the grounding.
- *wsdlOperation*: The URI of the WSDL operation corresponding to the given atomic process.
- *wsdlInputMessage*: An object containing the URI of the WSDL message definition that carries the inputs of the given atomic process, and a list of mapping pairs, which indicate the correspondence between particular DAML-S input properties and particular WSDL message parts.
- *wsdlOutputMessage*: Similar to *wsdlInputMessage*, but for outputs.

6   A Short Walk through DAML-S

In this final section, we walk through a small DAML-S example[6]. Here we restrict ourselves to illustrating some aspects of the process model and how they relate to the service grounding. Our walk-through utilizes the example of a fictitious book-buying service, CongoBuy. This service is actually a collection of smaller Congo programs (e.g., LocateBook, PutInCart, etc.), each Web-accessible and composed together to form the CongoBuy program.

For a complete specification of DAML-S, please refer to the DAML-S reference document[7]. DAML-S comprises several ontologies in the DAML+OIL (March 2001) markup language. Throughout this example, we will refer to the profile ontology[8] and the process ontology[9]. These ontologies define classes and properties that form the foundation of a service description. To describe a particular service, we specialize these classes and properties by creating subclasses and subproperties specific to the service.

Step 1: Describe Individual Programs.
The first step in marking up a Web Service is to describe the individual programs that comprise the service. It is the process model that provides a declarative description of a program's properties. The process model conceives each program as either an atomic process, simple or composite process. A non-decomposable Web-accessible program is described as an atomic process. An atomic process is characterized by its ability to be executed by a single (e.g., http) call, that returns a response.

An example of an atomic process is the LocateBook program that takes as input the name of a book and returns a description of the book and its price, if

---

[6] A more detailed example can be found at http://www.daml.org/services.

[7] http://www.daml.org/services/daml-s/2001/10/daml-s.html

[8] http://www.daml.org/services/daml-s/2001/10/Profile.daml

[9] http://www.daml.org/services/daml-s/2001/10/Process.daml

the book is in Congo's catalogue. The simplest way to proclaim LocateBook an atomic process is using the subClassOf construct as follows.

```
<daml:Class rdf:ID="LocateBook">
  <rdfs:subClassOf rdf:resource="&process;#AtomicProcess"/>
</daml:Class>
```

Associated with each process is a set of properties. Using a program or function metaphor, a process has parameters to which it is associated. Two types of parameters are the DAML-S properties input and (conditional) output, which are defined in the process ontology.

An example of an input for LocateBook might be the name of the book. We proclaim this using the subPropertyOf construct.

```
<rdf:Property rdf:ID="bookName">
  <rdfs:subPropertyOf rdf:resource="&process;#input"/>
  <rdfs:domain rdf:resource="#LocateBook"/>
  <rdfs:range rdf:resource="&xsd;#string"/>
</rdf:Property>
```

Inputs can be mandatory or optional. In contrast, outputs are generally conditional. For example, when you search for a book in the Congo catalogue, the output may be a detailed description of the book, if Congo carries it, or it may be a "Sorry we don't carry." message. Such outputs are characterized as conditional outputs. To describe a conditional output, the range of output is a class called ConditionalOutput, which is a subclass of Thing. ConditionalOutput in turn has two properties: the condition coCondition, and the output coOutput. An unconditional output has a zero cardinality restriction on its condition. An example of a conditional output is bookDescription, which is an output conditional upon the book being in the Congo catalogue. If the book is not in Congo's catalogues, then the output is a message to this effect[10].

As above, we can proclaim the conditional outputs of LocateBook by specializing our process ontology using subClassOf and subPropertyOf. Rather than provide the markup here, we illustrate the relations in Figure 2.

The designation of inputs and outputs enables the programs/services that we are describing in DAML-S to be used for automated Web Service invocation. In order to enable the programs/services to be used for automated service composition, we must additionally describe the side-effects of the programs, if any exist. To this end, me must describe the precondition and (conditional) effect properties of our program. They are described analogously to inputs and outputs.

Step 2: Describe the Grounding for Each Atomic Process.
Here, we relate LocateBook to its grounding, LocateBookGrounding. Since LocateBook is a class, we need to say: "Every instance (i.e., invocation, or use) of this class has an instance of the hasGrounding property, with value LocateBookGrounding." The hasGrounding property is defined in Process.daml.

---

[10] For many nontrivial applications, the range of the output will be restricted to subclasses of logical well-formed formulae.

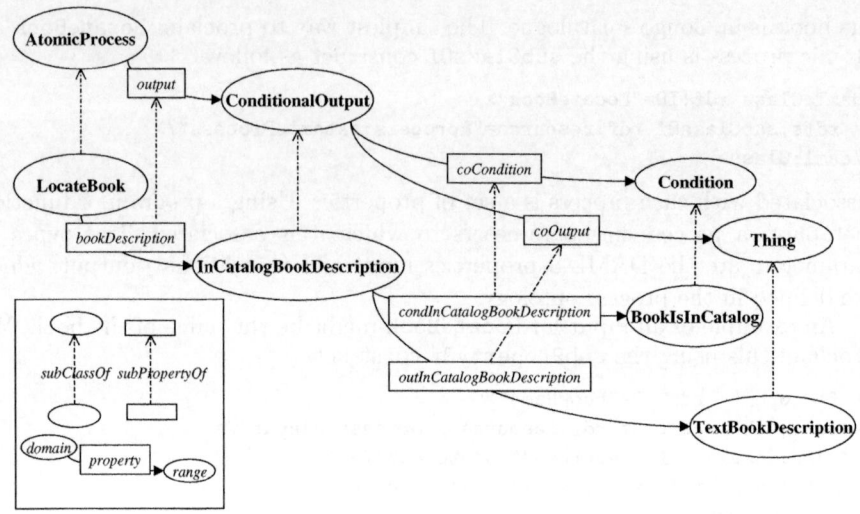

Fig. 2. A Conditional Ouput for LocateBook in DAML-S

```
<daml:Class rdf:about="LocateBook">
  <daml:sameClassAs>
    <daml:Restriction daml:cardinality="1">
      <daml:onProperty rdf:resource="#hasGrounding"/>
      <daml:hasValue rdf:resource="#LocateBookGrounding"/>
    </daml:Restriction>
  </daml:sameClassAs>
</daml:Class>
```

The following is an example of a DAML-S Grounding Instance. The "example.com" URIs (...#FindBook, ...#LocateBookInput, etc.) refer to constructs in the corresponding WSDL document (not shown here).

```
<grounding:WsdlGrounding rdf:ID="LocateBookGrounding">
  <grounding:wsdlReference
      rdf:resource="http://www.w3.org/TR/2001/NOTE-wsdl-20010315">
  <grounding:otherReferences rdf:parseType="daml:collection">
    ''http://www.w3.org/TR/2001/NOTE-wsdl-20010315"
    ''http://schemas.xmlsoap.org/wsdl/soap/"
    ''http://schemas.xmlsoap.org/soap/http/"
  </grounding:otherReferences>
  <grounding:wsdlDocuments rdf:parseType="daml:collection">
    ''http://example.com/congo/congobuy.wsdl"
  </grounding:wsdlDocuments>
  <grounding:wsdlOperation
      rdf:resource="http://example.com//locatebook.wsdl#FindBook"/>
  <grounding:wsdlInputMessage
      rdf:resource="http://example.com/locatebook.wsdl#LocateBookInput"/>
  <grounding:wsdlInputMessageParts rdf:parseType="daml:collection">
```

```
  <grounding:wsdlMessageMap>
    <grounding:damlsParameter rdf:resource=#BookName>
    <grounding:wsdlMessagePart
    rdf:resource="http://example.com//locatebook.wsdl#BookName">
  </grounding:wsdlMessageMap>
  ... other message map elements ...
</grounding:wsdlInputMessageParts>
<grounding:wsdlOutputMessage
    rdf:resource="http://example.com/locatebook.wsdl#LocateBookOutput"/>
<grounding:wsdlOutputMessageParts rdf:parseType="daml:collection">
  ... similar to wsdlInputMessageParts ...
</grounding:wsdlOutputMessageParts>
<grounding:WsdlGrounding>
```

Space precludes inclusion of steps 3, 4, and 5 of our walk-through. Step 3 is to describe compositions of the atomic processes. For example, we might describe the composite process CongoBuyBook which is a composition of LocateBook, PutInCart, etc. Step 4 is an optional step, in which we can describe a simple process for our service. Last, but certainly not least is the profile description, which we perform in Step 5. The profile description provides a declarative advertisement for the service. It is partially populated by the process model, if one exists, and this is why it is the last step of our service description.

7   Conclusion

In this paper we have presented DAML-S, an upper ontology for describing Web Services, written in DAML+OIL. Three aspects of DAML-S were presented: the service profile, the process model, and the service grounding (with focus on the last one). Service grounding is critical to the successful deployment of DAML-S, since it provides the connection between our Semantic Web approach and the emerging industry standards for Web Service description (e.g. WSDL), demonstrating that DAML-S is complementary to the mainstream industry efforts.

Acknowledgments

This work has profited from discussions with a number of people, most notably including Jim Hendler. The research was funded by the Defense Advanced Research Projects Agency as part of the DARPA Agent Markup Language (DAML) program under Air Force Research Laboratory contract F30602-00-C-0168 to SRI International, F30602-00-2-0579-P00001 to Stanford University, and F30601-00-2-0592 to Carnegie Mellon University. Additional funding was provided by Nokia Research Center and Nokia Mobile Phones.

References

1. A. Ankolekar, F. Huch and K. Sycara. Concurrent Semantics for the Web Services Specification Language Daml-S. In *Proc. of the Coordination 2002 Conf.*, 2002.
2. T. Berners-Lee, J. Hendler, and O. Lassila. The Semantic Web. *Scientific American*, 284(5):34–43, 2001.
3. U. C. Bureau. North american industry classification system (naics). http://www.census.gov/epcd/www/naics.html, 1997.
4. E. Christensen, F. Curbera, G. Meredith, and S. Weerawarana. Web Services Description Language (WSDL) 1.1. http://www.w3.org/TR/2001/NOTE-wsdl-20010315, 2001.
5. DAML-S Coalition: A. Ankolekar, M. Burstein, J. Hobbs, O. Lassila, D. Martin, S. McIlraith, S. Narayanan, M. Paolucci, T. Payne, K. Sycara, and H. Zeng. DAML-S: Semantic markup for Web services. In *Proc SWWS*, pages 411–430, 2001.
6. K. Decker, K. Sycara, and M. Williamson. Middle-agents for the internet. In *IJCAI97*, 1997.
7. T. Finin, Y. Labrou, and J. Mayfield. KQML as an agent communication language. In J. Bradshaw, editor, *Software Agents*. MIT Press, Cambridge, 1997.
8. M. Ghallab et. al. PDDL-the planning domain definition language v. 2. Tech Report,CVC TR-98-003/DCS TR-1165, Yale University, 1998.
9. J. Hendler and D. L. McGuinness. Darpa Agent Markup Language. *IEEE Intelligent Systems*, 15(6):72–73, 2001.
10. O. Lassila. Serendipitous Interoperability. In E. Hyvönen, editor, *The Semantic Web – Proc. the Kick-Off Seminar in Finland*, To appear, 2002.
11. H. Levesque, R. Reiter, Y. Lesperance, F. Lin, and R. Scherl. GOLOG: A Logic programming language for dynamic domains. *Journal of Logic Programming*, 31(1-3):59–84, April-June 1997.
12. D. Martin, A. Cheyer, and D. Moran. The Open Agent Architecture: A Framework for Building Distributed Software Systems. *Applied Artificial Intelligence*, 13(1-2):92–128, 1999.
13. D. McDermott, M. Burstein, and D. Smith. Overcoming ontology mismatches in transactions with self-describing agents. In *Proc. SWWS*, pages 285–302, 2001.
14. S. McIlraith and T. C. Son. Adapting Golog for composition of Semantic Web services. In *Proc. KR2002*. To appear, 2002.
15. S. McIlraith, T. C. Son, and H. Zeng. Semantic Web services. *IEEE Intelligent Systems*, 16(2):46–53, 2001.
16. J. Meseguer. Conditional Rewriting Logic as a Unified Model of Concurrency. *Theoretical Computer Science*, 96(1):73–155, 1992.
17. R. Milner. Communicating with Mobile Agents: The pi-Calculus. Cambridge University Press, Cambridge, 1999.
18. S. Narayanan. Reasoning about actions in narrative understanding. In *Proc. IJCAI'1999*, pages 350–357. 1999.
19. S. Narayanan and S. McIlraith. Simulation, verification, and automated composition of Web Services. In *Proc.WWW2002*, To appear 2002.
20. C. Schlenoff, M. Gruninger, F. Tissot, J. Valois, J. Lubell, and J. Lee. The Process Specification Language (PSL): Overview and version 1.0 specification. NISTIR 6459, National Institute of Standards and Technology, Gaithersburg, MD., 2000.
21. M. Paolucci, T. Kawmura, T. Payne and K. Sycara. Semantic Matching of Web Services Capabilities. In *First Int. Semantic Web Conf.*, To appear 2002.

22. T, Payne, R. Singh and K. Sycara. Browsing Schedules - An Agent-based approach to navigating the Semantic Web In *First Int. Semantic Wob Conf*, To appear 2002.
23. K. Sycara and M. Klusch. Brokering and matchmaking for coordination of agent societies: A survey. In *Coordination of Internet Agents*, 2001.
24. K. Sycara, M. Klusch, S. Widoff, and J. Lu. Dynamic service matchmaking among agents in open information environments. *Journal ACM SIGMOD Record*, 28(1):47–53, 1999.
25. UDDI. The UDDI Technical White Paper. http://www.uddi.org/, 2000.
26. H.-C. Wong and K. Sycara. A taxonomy of middle-agents for the internet. In *ICMAS'2000*, 2000.

TRIPLE—A Query, Inference, and Transformation Language for the Semantic Web[*]

Michael Sintek[1,2] and Stefan Decker[2]

[1] DFKI GmbH Kaiserslautern
[2] Stanford University Database Group

Abstract. This paper presents TRIPLE, a layered and modular rule language for the Semantic Web [1]. TRIPLE is based on Horn logic and borrows many basic features from F-Logic [11] but is especially designed for querying and transforming RDF models [20].

TRIPLE can be viewed as a successor of SiLRI (Simple Logic-based RDF Interpreter [5]). One of the most important differences to F-Logic and SiLRI is that TRIPLE does not have a fixed semantics for object-oriented features like classes and inheritance. Its layered architecture allows such features to be easily defined for object-oriented and other data models like UML, Topic Maps, or RDF Schema [19]. Description logics extensions of RDF (Schema) like OIL [17] and DAML+OIL [3] that cannot be fully handled by Horn logic are provided as modules that interact with a description logic classifier, e.g. FaCT [9], resulting in a hybrid rule language. This paper sketches syntax and semantics of TRIPLE.

Keywords: Metadata, Knowledge Representation and Reasoning, RDF, DAML, F-Logic

1 Introduction

On the Semantic Web many different communities are publishing their formal data, and it is unlikely that established data models for representing this data will disappear. Examples of already established data models include UML, TopicMaps, RDF Schema, Entity Relationship Models, DAML+OIL, and more, highly specialized data models. Integrating data based on these different data models has proven to be an error-prone and expensive task: different storage and query engines have to be combined into one program, and data has to be translated constantly from one representation to another. A first step to improve this situation is the use of RDF as a common representation formalism for all data involved.[1] This, however, does not solve the problem entirely. Although many query languages and inference engines for RDF exist (e.g., SiLRI [5], RQL

---

[*] This work was supported by the German Ministry for Education and Research, bmb+f (Grant: 01 IW 901, Project FRODO: A Framework for Distributed Organizational Memories) and the DARPA DAML Program, Project OntoAgents.

[1] See http://www-db.stanford.edu/~melnik/rdf/uml/ for a representation of UML in RDF and [12] for a representation of TopicMaps in RDF.

I. Horrocks and J. Hendler (Eds.): ISWC 2002, LNCS 2342, pp. 364–378, 2002.

[10], SQUISH[2]), none of them is capable of representing multiple semantics as required by the different heterogeneous data models. E.g., when querying UML data the `Generalization` relation should be treated as a transitive relationship, as well as `rdfs:subClassOf` in RDF Schema. None of the cited query languages has the ability to query different data models with different kinds of semantics. Although some of them (RQL and SiLRI) have a built-in semantics for RDF Schema, this does not generalize to other data models.

To remedy the situation we propose TRIPLE, a rule language, aiming to support applications in need of RDF reasoning and transformation under several different semantics. The core language is based on Horn logic which is syntactically extended to support RDF primitives like namespaces, resources, and statements (triples, which gave TRIPLE its name). This core language can be compiled into Horn logic programs and enacted by Prolog systems like XSB [18].

Inference systems for data models like RDF Schema can be implemented directly in TRIPLE if expressible in Horn logic or may be provided as modules interacting with external reasoning components, if not implementable with Horn logic (e.g., for Description Logic based languages like DAML+OIL).

TRIPLE provides a (human readable) ASCII-syntax as well as an RDF-based syntax.

In this section we introduce TRIPLE. Section 2 presents the layered architecture of TRIPLE, Section 3 introduces its RDF-based syntax (for the subset $TRIPLE_0$), and Section 4 gives a semantic characterization. Section 5 finally concludes the paper.

The reader is supposed to be familiar with RDF and RDF Schema.

1.1   Features of TRIPLE

In the following, the main features of TRIPLE (i.e., those extending Horn logic) are informally described. Note that not all the features are available in $TRIPLE_0$ (cf. Section 2).

Namespaces and Resources TRIPLE has special support for namespaces and resource identifiers. Namespaces are declared via clause-like constructs of the form *nsabbrev := namespace.*, e.g.

$$rdf := "http://www.w3.org/1999/02/22-rdf-syntax-ns\#".$$

Resources are written as *nsabbrev:name*, where *nsabbrev* is a namespace abbreviation and *name* is the local name of the resource.

Resource abbreviations can be introduced analogously to namespace abbreviations, e.g.

$$isa := rdfs:subClassOf.$$

---

[2] See http://ilrt.org/discovery/2000/10/swsql/

Statements and Molecules An RDF statement (triple) is—inspired by F-Logic object syntax—written as

$$subject[predicate \rightarrow object]$$

Several statements with the same subject can be abbreviated as "molecules":

$$stefan[hasAge \rightarrow 33; isMarried \rightarrow yes; \ldots]$$

RDF statements (and molecules) can be nested, eg.:

$$stefan[marriedTo \rightarrow birgit[hasAge \rightarrow 32]]$$

Models RDF models, i.e., sets of statements, are made explicit in TRIPLE ("first class citizens").[3] Statements, molecules, and also Horn atoms that are true in a specific model are written as *atom@model* (similar to Flora-2 module syntax), where *atom* is a statement, molecule, or Horn atom and *model* is a model specification (i.e., a resource denoting a model), e.g.

$$michael[hasAge \rightarrow 34]@factsAboutDFKI$$

TRIPLE also allows Skolem functions as model specifications. Skolem functions can be used to transform one model (or several models) into a new one when used in rules (e.g., for ontology mapping/integration):

$$O[P \rightarrow Q]@sf(m1, X, Y) \longleftarrow \ldots$$

If all (or many) statements/molecules or Horn atoms in a formula (see Section 3) are from one model, the following abbreviation can be used: *formula@model*. All statements/molecules and Horn atoms in *formula* without an explicit model specification are implicitly suffixed with @*model*.

Instead of constants, variables, and Skolem functions also boolean combinations can be used, eg.: $(model_1 \cap model_2)$ specifying the intersection of two models, $(model_1 \cup model_2)$ specifying the union of two models, and $(model_1 \setminus model_2)$ specifying the set-difference of two models.

Reified Statements Reified statements are written as $<statement>$ and can be used inside other statements, allowing "modal" statements like

$$stefan[believes \rightarrow <Ora[isAuthorOf \rightarrow homepage]>]$$

Path Expressions For navigation purposes, path expressions have proven to be very useful in object oriented languages. TRIPLE allows the usage of path expressions instead of subject, predicate, or object definitions (and at all other places where terms are allowed). Path expressions are dot-delimited sequences of resources, e.g.:

$$stefan.spouse.mother$$

denotes Stefan's mother in law.

---

[3] Note that the notion of *model* in RDF does not coincide with its use in (mathematical) logics.

Logical Formulae TRIPLE uses the usual set of connectives and quantifiers for building formulae from statements/molecules and Horn atoms, i.e., $\wedge$, $\vee$, $\neg$, $\forall$, $\exists$, etc.[4] All variables must be introduced via quantifiers, therefore marking them is not necessary (i.e., TRIPLE does not require variables to start with an uppercase letter as in Prolog).

Clauses and Blocks A TRIPLE clause is either a fact or a rule. Rule heads may only contain conjunctions of molecules and Horn atoms and must not contain (explicitly or implicitly) any disjunctive or negated expressions.

To assert that a set of clauses is true in a specific model, a model block is used:

$$@model \; \{clauses\}$$

or, in case the model specification is parameterized:

$$\forall \; Mdl \;\; @model(Mdl) \; \{clauses\}$$

1.2   Example: Dublin Core Metadata

The Dublin Core Metadata Initiative [4] defines a set of elements for marking up documents with metadata like title, creator, date, subject, etc. An encoding of Dublin Core metadata in RDF is straightforward. The example in Figure 1 adds some simple metadata to a document and defines a (Horn) rule that searches for documents with a specified subject.[5]

2   The TRIPLE Layered Architecture

As already mentioned, TRIPLE is a layered rule language. Two different kinds of layers are supported:

- syntactical extensions of Horn logic to support basic RDF constructs like resources and statements
- modules for semantic extensions of RDF like RDF Schema, OIL, and DAML+OIL, implemented either directly in TRIPLE or via interaction with external reasoning components

TRIPLE is the extension of Horn logic as described in Section 1.1. $TRIPLE_0$ is the subset of TRIPLE without quantifiers and negation (and has already been implemented on top of XSB, see http://www.dfki.uni-kl.de/frodo/triple/), $TRIPLE_0^-$ is the subset without quantifiers, but with negation. $TRIPLE_0$ and

---

[4] For TRIPLE programs in plain ASCII syntax, the symbols AND, OR, NOT, FORALL, EXISTS, <-, ->, etc. are used; cf. the example in Section 2.1.

[5] Note that symbols in TRIPLE can be enclosed in single or double quotes; if a symbol does not contain special characters and starts with a letter, no quotes are needed. Thus, TRIPLE, 'TRIPLE', and "TRIPLE" all denote the same symbol.

```
rdf := "http://www.w3.org/1999/02/22-rdf-syntax-ns#".
dc := "http://purl.org/dc/elements/1.0/".
dfki := "http://www.dfki.de/".

@dfki:documents {

    dfki:d_01_01[
        dc:title → "TRIPLE";
        dc:creator → "Michael Sintek";
        dc:creator → "Stefan Decker";
        dc:subject → RDF;
        dc:subject → triples; ... ].

    ∀ S, D  search(S, D)  ⟵
        D[dc:subject → S].
}
```

Fig. 1. Example: Dublin Core Metadata

TRIPLE_0^- mainly exist to simplify the implementation of the higher layers. For TRIPLE_0, a representation in RDF exists which is explained in Section 3.

The following two sections describe the modular extensions for RDF Schema and DAML+OIL, called TRIPLE/RDFS and TRIPLE/DAML+OIL.

2.1   TRIPLE/**RDFS**

This section shows how rules axiomatizing (part of the) semantics of RDF Schema are implemented in TRIPLE. The rules can be used together with a Horn logic based inference engine like XSB to derive additional knowledge from an RDF Schema specification.

Figure 2 show the RDF Schema module in plain ASCII notation.

The first lines define namespaces (for RDF and RDF Schema) and abbreviations (for type, subPropertyOf and subClassOf).

The rules are enclosed by a model specification block:

$\forall$ *Mdl* @rdfschema(*Mdl*) {...}

The Skolem function rdfschema(*Mdl*) is the model identifier of all facts derived by the rules enclosed by the model specification block. The parameter *Mdl* denotes the RDF Schema specification. The model rdfschema(*Mdl*) contains all statements from the model *Mdl* plus everything derived additionally by the rules. The rule

$\forall$ *O, P, V* $O[P \rightarrow V]$ ⟵
        $O[P \rightarrow V]$@*Mdl*.

specifies that every triple contained in the model *Mdl* is also element of the model with the identifier rdfschema(*Mdl*). The next rule defines the inheritance of values from sub properties to super properties. The remaining rules define the

```
rdf := 'http://www.w3.org/1999/02/22-rdf-syntax-ns#'.
rdfs := 'http://www.w3.org/2000/01/rdf-schema#'.
type := rdf:type.
subPropertyOf := rdfs:subPropertyOf.
subClassOf := rdfs:subClassOf.
FORALL Mdl @rdfschema(Mdl) {
  transitive(subPropertyOf).
  transitive(subClassOf).
  FORALL O,P,V   O[P->V] <-
      O[P->V]@Mdl.
  FORALL O,P,V   O[P->V] <-
    EXISTS S   S[subPropertyOf->P] AND O[S->V].
  FORALL O,P,V   O[P->V] <-
    transitive(P) AND
    EXISTS W   (O[P->W] AND W[P->V]).
  FORALL O,T   O[type->T] <-
    EXISTS S   (S[subClassOf->T] AND O[type->S]).
}
```

Fig. 2. RDF Schema in TRIPLE

semantics of transitive properties (subPropertyOf and subClassOf) and of the type property.

In Figure 3, a simple RDF Schema for motor vehicles is given: the root class is xyz:MotorVehicle, which has the direct subclasses xyz:PassengerVehicle, xyz:Truck, and xyz:Van. xyz:MiniVan is defined as a common subclass of xyz:Van and xyz:PassengerVehicle.

The following query searches for all direct and indirect subclasses of xyz:MotorVehicle, using the RDF Schema definition for rdfs:subClassOf as defined in the rdfschema(Mdl) model.

```
FORALL C <- C[rdfs:subClassOf->xyz:MotorVehicle]@rdfschema(cars).
```

```
@cars {
   xyz := ``http://www.w3.org/2000/03/example/vehicles#".
   xyz:MotorVehicle[rdfs:subClassOf -> rdfs:Resource].
   xyz:PassengerVehicle[rdfs:subClassOf -> xyz:MotorVehicle].
   xyz:Truck[rdfs:subClassOf -> xyz:MotorVehicle].
   xyz:Van[rdfs:subClassOf -> xyz:MotorVehicle].
   xyz:MiniVan[
     rdfs:subClassOf -> xyz:Van;
     rdfs:subClassOf -> xyz:PassengerVehicle].
}
```

Fig. 3. RDF Schema Example

This is achieved by passing the ontology (cars) as a parameter to the RDF Schema rules, whereas the query

```
FORALL C <- C[rdfs:subClassOf->xyz:MotorVehicle]@cars.
```

results in just the direct subclasses of xyz:MotorVehicle.

2.2   TRIPLE/DAML+OIL

DAML+OIL [3] (and also OIL [17]) are description logics extensions of RDF Schema that cannot be mapped to Horn logic directly. For this reason, a model daml_oil(Mdl) is provided that accesses a description logics classifier (e.g., FaCT) to realize the semantics of DAML+OIL. Access to the daml_oil(Mdl) model is restricted to premises in rules; facts and rule heads must not contain any references to it.

The resulting rule language is a hybrid rule language amalgamating Horn rules and description logics similar to Carin [13]. The main difference is that Carin's primary goal is to remain complete and correct. This is achieved by restricting the Horn part to function-free, recursive rules and by either restricting the description logics part by removing the constructors $\forall R.C$ and $(\leq n\,R)$ or by further restricting the Horn rules to be *role-safe* (i.e., by restricting the way in which variables can appear in role atoms in the rules, similar to safety conditions on Datalog KBs).

In TRIPLE/DAML+OIL, neither the Horn rules nor the description logics part are restricted in any way, resulting in an incomplete language. But since Prolog implementations for Horn logic are already incomplete, this does not make things worse. The resulting language is, on the other hand, quite powerful and meets the pragmatic requirements of a rule and transformation language for the semantic web.

In the DAML+OIL example in Figure 4, Herbivore and Carnivore are (incorrectly) defined to be disjoint, therefore the class Omnivore is unsatisfiable which will be revealed by the query unsatisfiable(animals:Omnivore) @ check(animals:ontology).

3   TRIPLE$_0$ in RDF

In this section, we describe how to represent TRIPLE$_0$ in RDF. Appendix A contains the RDF Schema definition for TRIPLE$_0$.

Representing a rule language like TRIPLE in RDF (or XML) allows rules to be distributed on the Web, e.g. between communicating agents, which is the primary goal of the RuleML initiative [2].

A possible scenario could be similar to that of mobile agents, e.g.: a customer intending to purchase some goods formulates his interests/preferences etc. as a set of TRIPLE rules and facts, sends them (encoded in RDF) to some vendors who enact them on their local knowledge bases (after transformation into their own rule languages), and then send the results back to the buyer.

```
daml := 'http://www.daml.org/.../daml+oil#'.
animals := 'http://www.example.org/animals#'.
@animals:ontology {
  animals:Animal[rdf:type -> daml:Class].
  animals:Herbivore[rdf:type -> daml:Class;
    daml:subClassOf -> animals:Animal].
  animals:Carnivore[rdf:type -> daml:Class;
    rdfs:subClassOf -> animals:Animal;
    daml:disjointWith -> animals:Herbivore].
  animals:Omnivore[rdf:type -> daml:Class;
    rdfs:subClassOf -> animals:Herbivore;
    rdfs:subClassOf -> animals:Carnivore].
}
FORALL Ont    @check(Ont) {
  FORALL C    unsatisfiable(C) <-
    C[daml:subClassOf ->
      daml:Nothing]@daml_oil(Ont).
}
```

Fig. 4. Animals Example for TRIPLE/DAML+OIL

Namespace for TRIPLE *in RDF* In the following, 'triple' denotes the TRIPLE namespace (something like 'http://www.semanticweb.org/2001/06/30/triple#').

Abbreviations Abbreviations for namespaces and resources are not necessary: we simply use the XML namespace and entity declarations.

Triples, Molecules, Path Expressions a[b → c] becomes an instance of triple:Triple which is a subclass of rdf:Statement·

```
<triple:Triple>
  <triple:subject rdf:resource="#a"/>
  <triple:predicate rdf:resource="#b"/>
  <triple:object rdf:resource="#c"/>
</triple:Triple>
```

There is no need for an RDF representation of molecules like a[b → c; p → q;...] since they are equivalent to the conjunction of single Triples. The same holds for path expressions (which can be split into separate Triples).

Associated Models, Model Expressions Every Triple can have an *associated* model: a[b → c]@m becomes

```
<triple:Triple>
  <triple:subject rdf:resource="#a"/>
  <triple:predicate rdf:resource="#b"/>
```

$$A : N \longrightarrow \text{resource}(A, N) \tag{1}$$
$$O[P \to V] \longrightarrow \text{statement}(O, P, V) \tag{2}$$
$$S@M \longrightarrow \text{true}(S, M) \quad \text{for statements (and atoms) } S \tag{3}$$
$$<S> \longrightarrow S \quad \text{for statements } S \tag{4}$$
$$O[P_1 \to V_1; P_2 \to V_2; \ldots]@M \longrightarrow O[P_1 \to V_1]@M \ \wedge \tag{5}$$
$$O[P_2 \to V_2]@M \ \wedge \ \ldots$$
$$\text{true}(S, M_1 \cap M_2) \longrightarrow \text{true}(S, M_1) \ \wedge \ \text{true}(S, M_2) \tag{6}$$
$$\text{true}(S, M_1 \backslash M_2) \longrightarrow \text{true}(S, M_1) \ \wedge \ \neg \ \text{true}(S, M_2) \tag{7}$$
$$X := Y. \ S(X) \longrightarrow \forall \ X \ \ (X = Y \ \wedge \ S(X)) \tag{8}$$
$$\text{for clause sequences } S(X)$$

Fig. 5. The RDF-specific Rewrite Rules

```
<triple:object rdf:resource="#c"/>
<triple:model rdf:resource="#m"/>
</triple:Triple>
```

Note that triple:model is a property that may be used on all formulas and clauses, not only on Triples (see the section on @-Expressions below). Any term can be used as a model; complex model expressions can be built with triple:ModelUnion, triple:ModelIntersection etc., e.g.:

```
<triple:ModelUnion>
<triple:firstModel rdf:resource="#m"/>
<triple:secondModel rdf:resource="#n"/>
</triple:ModelUnion>
```

Furthermore, a triple model may be denoted by a Skolem function to allow parameterized models (triple:SkolemModel).

Terms triple:Term comprises rdfs:Literal, triple:Variable, triple:Structure, triple:Resource, triple:ReifiedTriple, triple:Model etc.

Atoms and Formulas We have two sorts of Atoms: triple:Triple and triple:HornAtom, where HornAtoms are the normal Horn atoms like p(a,X).

Since we do not support Lloyd-Topor transformations in TRIPLE$_0$, Atom and And/Or formulas are the only formulas.

Clauses A triple:Clause simply consists of a head (with range triple:Atom) and a body (with range triple:Formula), both of which may be empty to form facts and queries. It may also have an associated model (see below).

@-Expressions All forms of @-expressions are mapped to usages of the triple:model property, even for the { } enclosed blocks, e.g.

```
@someModel {
  clause1.
  clause2.
}
```

becomes

```
<triple:Clause rdf:ID"clause1">
  <triple:model rdf:resource="#someModel"/>
</triple:Clause>

<triple:Clause rdf:ID"clause2">
  <triple:model rdf:resource="#someModel"/>
</triple:Clause>
```

4   Semantic Characterization of TRIPLE

This section provides a first indirect semantic characterization of TRIPLE by defining a mapping to Horn Logic. This allows TRIPLE to be implemented on top of XSB (i.e., Prolog with tabled resolution), analogously to the F-Logic Flora [15].

Figure 5 shows the rewrite rules for mapping RDF-specific features like resources and statements. All other mappings are well-known (Lloyd-Topor transformations for handling of quantifier [14]) or straightforward (see the SiLRI system [5]). Example:

p:jdow[p:lastname $\rightarrow$ doe]@$m1$. $\longrightarrow$

```
true(statement(resource(p, jdow), resource(p, lastname), doe), m1)
```

In a future document, a model-theoretic semantics based on minimal Herbrand models and fixpoint operators will be provided. Compared to the Model Theory proposal to RDF [8] we did not yet consider anonymous resources. This is subject of further investigation.

5   Conclusion

In this paper, we presented TRIPLE, a novel query and transformation language for RDF. Its core is a syntactical extension of Horn logic similar to F-Logic, but specialized for the requirements on the semantic web by making web resources, (RDF) models, and statements first class citizens.

Its main purpose is to query web resources in a declarative way, e.g. for intelligent information retrieval based on background knowledge like ontologies and search heuristics. For early approaches in this area, refer to, e.g., [7,6,16].

TRIPLE's layered architecture allows extensions of RDF to be implemented as extension modules (via parameterized models). Simple object-oriented extensions like RDF Schema can be directly implemented with the extended Horn logic features of TRIPLE, other extensions like DAML+OIL are realized via interaction with external reasoning components like a description logics classifier.

TRIPLE's model concept (esp. the parameterized models) enables the transformation of models, thus enabling knowledge base and ontology mapping/integration tasks which are needed in distributed settings as the semantic web (see, e.g., [21]).

Since models are first class citizens in TRIPLE, modal functionalities as needed in agent communication are also provided (e.g., agent A "believes" statements in model M, which has been received from agent B, to be true).

TRIPLE is currently being developed by the authors. An implementation of TRIPLE based on XSB is available at: http://triple.semanticweb.org. In this version, all RDF data and TRIPLE rules are compiled into a single PROLOG program, therefore restricting the size of the knowledge base to what the underlying PROLOG system (i.e., XSB) can handle.

Future versions will allow querying distributed RDF data without compiling remote data to the local (PROLOG) knowledge base.

References

1. Tim Berners-Lee. *Weaving the Web: The Original Design and Ultimate Destiny of the World Wide Web by Its Inventor.* Harper San Francisco, September 1999.
2. Harold Boley, Said Tabet, and Gerd Wagner. Design Rationale of RuleML: A Markup Language for Semantic Web Rules. In *International Semantic Web Working Symposium (SWWS)*, 2001.
3. DAML Joint Committee. DAML+OIL, 2001. URL: http://www.daml.org/2001/03/daml+oil-index.html.
4. DCMI. Dublin Core Metadata Initiative, 2001. URL: http://purl.org/dc/.
5. Stefan Decker, Dan Brickley, Janne Saarela, and Jürgen Angele. A query and inference service for RDF. In *QL'98 — The Query Languages Workshop*, Boston, USA, 1998. WorldWideWeb Consortium (W3C).
6. Stefan Decker, Michael Erdmann, Dieter Fensel, and Rudi Studer. Ontobroker: Ontology Based Access to Distributed and Semi-Structured Information. In R. Meersman et al., editor, *Semantic Issues in Multimedia Systems.* Kluwer Academic Publisher, 1999.
7. Dieter Fensel, Stefan Decker, Michael Erdmann, and Rudi Studer. Ontobroker: The Very High Idea. In *Proc. 11th Int. Florida AI Research Symposium (FLAIRS-98)*, May 1998.
8. Patrick Hayes. RDF model theory (W3C working draft). Technical report, W3C, 2002.
9. Ian Horrocks. The FaCT System, 2001. URL: http://www.cs.man.ac.uk/~horrocks/FaCT/.
10. G. Karvounarakis, V. Christophides, D. Plexousakis, and S. Alexaki. Querying CommunityWeb portals, 2001.
11. M. Kifer, G. Lausen, and J. Wu. Logical foundations of object-oriented and frame-based languages. *Journal of the ACM*, 42:741–843, July 1995.
12. Martin S. Lacher and Stefan Decker. RDF, Topic Maps, and the Semantic Web. *Markup Languages: Theory and Practice*, 2002. Accepted for publication.

13. Alon Y. Levy and Marie-Christine Rousset. CARIN: A Representation Language Combining Horn Rules and Description Logics. In *12th European Conference on Artificial Intelligence*, 1996.
14. J.W. Lloyd and R.W. Topor. Making Prolog more Expressive. *Journal of Logic Programming*, 3:225–240, 1984.
15. B. Ludäscher, Guizhen Yang, and Michael Kifer. FLORA: The secret of object-oriented logic programming. Technical report, SUNY at Stony Brook, 1999.
16. Sean Luke, Lee Spector, David Rager, and Jim Hendler. Ontology-based Web Agents. In *Proceedings of First International Conference on Autonomous Agents (AA-97)*, 1997.
17. OIL. Ontology Inference Layer, 2001. URL: http://www.ontoknowledge.org/oil/.
18. SUNY. The XSB Programming System. Dept. of Computer Science, SUNY at Stony Brook, 2000. URL: http://www.cs.sunysb.edu/~sbprolog/xsb-page.html.
19. W3C. Resource Description Framework (RDF) Schema Specification 1.0, 2001. URL: http://www.w3.org/TR/2000/CR-rdf-schema-20000327/.
20. W3C. Semantic Web Activity: Resource Description Framework (RDF), 2001. URL: http://www.w3.org/RDF/.
21. Gio Wiederhold, editor. *Intelligent Integration of Information*. Kluwer Academic Publishers, July 1996.

A   RDF Schema for TRIPLE$_0$

```
<?xml version='1.0' encoding='ISO-8859-1'?>
<!DOCTYPE rdf:RDF [
 <!ENTITY rdf 'http://www.w3.org/1999/02/22-rdf-syntax-ns#'>
 <!ENTITY rdfs 'http://www.w3.org/2000/01/rdf-schema#'>
 <!ENTITY triple 'http://www.semanticweb.org/2001/06/30/triple#'> ]>
<rdf:RDF xmlns:rdf="&rdf;"  xmlns:rdfs="&rdfs;"
 xmlns:triple="&triple;"  xmlns="&triple;">

<rdfs:Class rdf:ID="Triple">
  <rdfs:subClassOf rdf:resource="&rdf;Statement"/>
  <rdfs:subClassOf rdf:resource="&triple;Atom"/>
</rdfs:Class>

<rdf:Property rdf:ID="subject">
  <rdfs:subPropertyOf rdf:resource="&rdf;subject"/>
  <rdfs:domain rdf:resource="&triple;Triple"/>
  <rdfs:range rdf:resource="&triple;Term"/>
</rdf:Property>

<rdf:Property rdf:ID="predicate">
  <rdfs:subPropertyOf rdf:resource="&rdf;predicate"/>
  <rdfs:domain rdf:resource="&triple;Triple"/>
  <rdfs:range rdf:resource="&triple;Term"/>
</rdf:Property>
```

```
<rdf:Property rdf:ID="object">
  <rdfs:subPropertyOf rdf:resource="&rdf;object"/>
  <rdfs:domain rdf:resource="&triple;Triple"/>
  <rdfs:range rdf:resource="&triple;Term"/>
</rdf:Property>

...

<rdfs:Class rdf:ID="Term"/>

<rdfs:Class rdf:ID="Variable">
  <rdfs:subClassOf rdf:resource="&triple;Term"/>
</rdfs:Class>

<Description rdf:about="&rdfs;Literal">
  <rdfs:subClassOf rdf:resource="&triple;Term"/>
</Description>

<rdfs:Class rdf:ID="Resource">
  <rdfs:subClassOf rdf:resource="&triple;Term"/>
</rdfs:Class>

<rdfs:Class rdf:ID="ReifiedTriple">
  <rdfs:subClassOf rdf:resource="&triple;Term"/>
</rdfs:Class>

<rdf:Property rdf:ID="triple">
  <rdfs:domain rdf:resource="&triple;ReifiedTriple"/>
  <rdfs:range rdf:resource="&triple;Triple"/>
</rdf:Property>

<rdfs:Class rdf:ID="Structure">
  <rdfs:subClassOf rdf:resource="&triple;Term"/>
</rdfs:Class>

<rdf:Property rdf:ID="functor">
  <rdfs:domain rdf:resource="&triple;Structure"/>
  <rdfs:range rdf:resource="&rdfs;Literal"/>
</rdf:Property>

<rdf:Property rdf:ID="args">
  <rdfs:domain rdf:resource="&triple;Structure"/>
  <rdfs:range rdf:resource="&triple;TermSeq"/>
</rdf:Property>

<rdfs:Class rdf:ID="TermSeq">
  <rdfs:subClassOf rdf:resource="&rdf;Seq"/>
</rdfs:Class>
```

```
<rdfs:Class rdf:ID="Formula"/>

<rdf:Property rdf:ID="model">
  <rdfs:domain rdf:resource="&triple;Clause"/>
  <rdfs:domain rdf:resource="&triple;Formula"/>
  <rdfs:range rdf:resource="&triple;Term"/>
</rdf:Property>

<rdfs:Class rdf:ID="BinaryFormula">
  <rdfs:subClassOf rdf:resource="&triple;Formula"/>
</rdfs:Class>

<rdf:Property rdf:ID="firstFormula">
  <rdfs:domain rdf:resource="&triple;BinaryFormula"/>
  <rdfs:range rdf:resource="&triple;Formula"/>
</rdf:Property>

<rdf:Property rdf:ID="secondFormula">
  <rdfs:domain rdf:resource="&triple;BinaryFormula"/>
  <rdfs:range rdf:resource="&triple;Formula"/>
</rdf:Property>

<rdfs:Class rdf:ID="And">
  <rdfs:subClassOf rdf:resource="&triple;BinaryFormula"/>
</rdfs:Class>

<rdfs:Class rdf:ID="Or">
  <rdfs:subClassOf rdf:resource="&triple;BinaryFormula"/>
</rdfs:Class>

<rdfs:Class rdf:ID="UnaryFormula">
  <rdfs:subClassOf rdf:resource="&triple;Formula"/>
</rdfs:Class>

<rdf:Property rdf:ID="formula">
  <rdfs:domain rdf:resource="&triple;UnaryFormula"/>
  <rdfs:range rdf:resource="&triple;Formula"/>
</rdf:Property>

<rdfs:Class rdf:ID="Atom">
  <rdfs:subClassOf rdf:resource="&triple;Formula"/>
</rdfs:Class>

<rdfs:Class rdf:ID="HornAtom">
  <rdfs:subClassOf rdf:resource="&triple;Atom"/>
</rdfs:Class>

<rdf:Property rdf:ID="predicateSymbol">
  <rdfs:domain rdf:resource="&triple;HornAtom"/>
  <rdfs:range rdf:resource="&rdfs;Literal"/>
```

```
</rdf:Property>

<rdf:Property rdf:about="#args">
  <rdfs:domain rdf:resource="&triple;HornAtom"/>
</rdf:Property>

<rdfs:Class rdf:ID="Clause"/>

<rdf:Property rdf:ID="head">
  <rdfs:domain rdf:resource="&triple;Clause"/>
  <rdfs:range rdf:resource="&triple;Atom"/>
</rdf:Property>

<rdf:Property rdf:ID="body">
  <rdfs:domain rdf:resource="&triple;Clause"/>
  <rdfs:range rdf:resource="&triple;Formula"/>
</rdf:Property>

</rdf:RDF>
```

A Data Integration Framework
for e-Commerce Product Classification

S. Bergamaschi [1], F. Guerra, and M. Vincini

Dipartimento di Ingegneria dell'Informazione
Università di Modena e Reggio Emilia
Via Vignolese 905 – Modena
{bergamaschi.sonia, guerra.francesco, vincini.maurizio}@unimo.it

Abstract. A marketplace is the place in which the demand and supply of
buyers and vendors participating in a business process may meet. Therefore,
electronic marketplaces are virtual communities in which buyers may meet
proposals of several suppliers and make the best choice. In the electronic
commerce world, the comparison between different products is blocked due
to the lack of standards (on the contrary, the proliferation of standards)
describing and classifying them. Therefore, the need for B2B and B2C
marketplaces is to reclassify products and goods according to different
standardization models. This paper aims to face this problem by suggesting
the use of a semi-automatic methodology, supported by a tool (SI-
Designer), to define the mapping among different e-commerce product
classification standards. This methodology was developed for the MOMIS
system within the Intelligent Integration of Information research area. We
describe our extension to the methodology that makes it applyable in
general to product classification standard, by selecting a fragment of
ECCMA/UNSPSC and ecl@ss standard.

1 Introduction

The large amount of Internet sites, which have grown in the few last years, has
increased the availability of information on the web, even if, due mainly to its
structure, this information is less and less machine-readable and machine-
understandable. Nevertheless, in the context of electronic commerce, many
companies, organizations, and customers are exploiting the opportunities offered by
Internet-based solutions and many more are expected to follow. Companies have been
putting their databases and product catalogues on the web. Consequently, customers
and suppliers have increased the amount of available information, but also the "noise"
generated from these information sources has increased. This situation has allowed a
third party, called the *marketplace*, to assume a key role in electronic commerce.

A marketplace is the place in which the demand and supply of buyers and vendors
participating in a business process may meet. Therefore, marketplaces are virtual
communities in which buyers may meet proposals of several suppliers and make the
best choice. Then, marketplaces seem to be an interesting solution for e-commerce

---

[1] CSITE-CNR viale Risorgimento 2, 40136 Bologna, Italy

I. Horrocks and J. Hendler (Eds.): ISWC 2002, LNCS 2342, pp. 379–393, 2002.
© Springer-Verlag Berlin Heidelberg 2002

actors, because they show products, distributed by different vendors, but that may be compared since they have similar classification and they represent comparable products. In the e-commerce world, the comparison between different products is blocked due to the lack of standards describing and classifying them. Numerous proposals of classification standards have resulted in each supplier describing his own product in his own way (cf. [11], [18]).

Considering B2B e-commerce marketplaces, an economic transaction is further given difficult by the buyers' need to use only a standard to classify and describe products provided by different vendors, so as to assure an easy integration with its ERP system. Hence, the marketplace has to provide an environment using which to mediate among different standards used by the different participant to the transaction. In this way, each actor of the business process may exchange information using his own format. Therefore, the need, for B2B and B2C marketplaces, is to reclassify products and goods according to different standardization models.

This paper aims to face this problem by suggesting the use of a semi-automatic methodology to define the mapping among different e-commerce product classification standards. The methodology was developed for the MOMIS system ([4], [5], [6]) within the Intelligent Integration of Information research area. MOMIS (Mediator envirOnment for Multiple Information Systems) is a mediator-based system aiming to extract and integrate information from heterogeneous data sources, such as relational, object, semistructured sources (XML). Starting from source descriptions, the system generates an integrated global virtual schema of all data sources that is expressed in XML. MOMIS creates a global virtual schema by using different techniques, and by creating a common thesaurus of intra- and inter-schema relationships, which defines an ontology of the terms used to represent the information provided by the different sources. The common thesaurus contains intra-schema relationships extracted by using inference techniques, inter-schema relationships obtained using the lexical WordNet system (www.cogsci.princeton.edu/wn) (which identifies the affinities between inter-schema concepts on the basis of their lexicon meaning) and inter-schema relationships explicitly given by the integration designer. In addition, MOMIS enriches the thesaurus using the Artemis system [10], which evaluates structural affinities among inter-schema concepts and ODB-Tools Engine [2], a tool based on Description Logics which performs checking consistency and subsumption computation. As an example of our integration methodology, we show how it is possible to define a mapping between a fragment of the ECCMA/UNSPSC and a fragment of the ecl@ss standard. With respect to previous works on MOMIS, we introduce a wrapper for semistructured data able to map XML/XML-Schema/RDF file into the common languages of MOMIS; a new method to create a mapping between XML/RDF sources and an XML representation of this mapping.

The paper is organized as follows. Section 2 introduces the two chosen e-commerce code product standards, namely ecl@ss and ECCMA/UNSPSC; section 3 describes our methodology and the results of the mapping process, section 4 presents related work and, finally, section 5 gives some concluding remarks.

2 Product Classification Systems and e-Commerce

Coding products and services according to standardized classification systems are useful for speeding up commerce among companies. In addition, the development of e-commerce solution has rapidly increased the requirement of machine-readable product names that assist marketing and sales functions to find customers and provide better customer and distribution channel services.

By inserting the codes in various electronic trade documents and media such as product catalogs, Web sites, purchase orders, invoices, inventory/sales advices, and others, computer applications throughout an extended supply chain (seller, buyer, distributor, independent sales representative, end user) can process transaction data automatically and can perform management, analysis and decision functions in time-critical and labor-efficient ways that would not be possible without the codes. A useful product classification scheme should be hierarchical, so that individual commodities represent unique instances of larger classes and families. Hierarchical organization allows a given company to focus on a level of specificity that best suits its purposes and situation. In addition to maintain a hierarchical taxonomy, a classification scheme must be constantly revised (to add new products and modify existing structures to adapt to changing market offers), it must be responsive to industry (because delays hurt business), and code assignments to products and services must be impartial (to prevent unfairly promoting one company's products at the expense of others) [15]. Within the different standard classification systems proposed, the most used into U.S. is the United Nation Standard Products and Services Code System (UNSPSC), a hierarchical classification with five levels. The levels allow users to search products more precisely (because searches will be confined to logical categories and eliminate irrelevant hits) and it allows managers to perform expenditure analysis on categories that are relevant to the company's situation. Each level contains a two-character numerical value and a textual description as follows:

XX **Segment**	The logical aggregation of families for analytical purposes
XX **Family**	A commonly recognized group of inter-related commodity categories
XX **Class**	A group of commodities sharing a common use or function
XX **Commodity**	A group of substitutable products or services
XX **Business Function**	The function performed by an organization in support of the commodity

In the e-commerce area, the ECCMA (*Electronic Commerce Code Management Association*) (www.ucec.org), has proposed an initiative to enhance the UNSPSC with local attributes to describe the bottom level. The current version consists of more than 16.000 terms.

Another standardization code, used by the statistical agencies of the United States, is the North American Industry Classification System as the industry classification system (NAICS) (www.ntis.gov/product/naics.htm). Finally, an important european initiative that built a new classification scheme from scratch is ecl@ss (www.eclass.de). Ecl@ss is a standard for information exchange and is characterized by a 4-level hierarchical classification system with a key-word register of 12,000 words. Ecl@ss maps market structure for industrial buyers and supports engineers at development, planning and maintenance. Through the access either via the hierarchy or over the key words both the expert as well as the occasional user can navigate in the classification. A unique feature of ecl@ss is the integration of attribute lists for the description of material and service specifications.

The previously mentioned product classification systems are only three of the many proposed and used in B2B marketplaces, where industrial standard are emerging to define the overall interchange process (RosettaNet, ebXML, OAGIS, BizTalk, xCBL, cXML, ...). Each of these proposals defines a protocol for the communication and the data description structure (often described in XML) in order to realize an e-commerce orchestration framework: by using different protocols a reconciliation of product information must be defined.

3   Reconciliation of Different Standards

In this paper, we propose an information reconciliation methodology, implemented within the MOMIS system, for the product mapping and reclassification among different code classification systems. The methodology is shown over a fragment of ECCMA/UNSPSC and ecl@ss standard but is easy scalable to the whole code system and can be used, without loss of generality, over any other hierarchical product classification system.

Our methodology uses MOMIS in order to obtain a mapping between elements of the different schemas that correspond semantically to each other. MOMIS is a system designed to provide a global virtual schema of a set of sources to be integrated. We show that the use of MOMIS at the metadata level, i.e. the schemas involved in the integration process describing the two chosen e-commerce standards, is effective to perform the mapping process between the two chosen standards in a semi-automatic way. In [7] it is provided a largely orthogonal classification of the algorithms used by match systems. On the basis of these criteria, our approach may be described as follows:

- *Schema derived*: our algorithm considers schema-level information. We are considering how to apply extensional knowledge in the process.
- *Matching granularity*: the match can be performed for combinations of objects, such as complex schema sub-graph. By setting specific parameters, we have the control of the dimension of sub-graph matched.
- *Language derived*: Our matcher uses a linguistic-based approach by interacting with a lexical database system (WordNet).
- *Auxiliary information based*: Our approach exploits further information given by the user input.

3.1. Overview of the MOMIS System

MOMIS (see Fig. 1) follows a "semantic approach" to information integration based on the conceptual schema, or metadata, of the information sources, and on the mediator architecture [25]. In the MOMIS system, each data source provides a schema and a global virtual schema of all the sources is obtained in a semiautomatical way. The global schema has a set of *mapping descriptions* that specify the semantic mapping between the global schema and the sources schema.

The system architecture is composed of functional elements that communicate using the CORBA standard. A data model, ODM_{I3}, and a language, ODL_{I3} are used to describe source schemas. ODL_{I3} and ODM_{I3} have been defined as subset of the corresponding ones in ODMG, augmented by primitives to perform integration. ODL_{I3} is a source-independent language and it is used to describe heterogeneous schemas of data sources. In particular, ODL_{I3} includes the following *terminological relationships*:

- SYN (synonym of) is a relationship defined between two terms t_i and t_j where $t_i \neq t_j$ that are synonyms in every involved source.
- BT (broader terms) is a relationship defined between two terms t_i and t_j where t_i has a broader more general meaning then t_j. The opposite of BT is NT (narrower terms)
- RT (related term) is a relationship defined between two terms t_i and t_j that are generally used together in the same context in the considered sources.

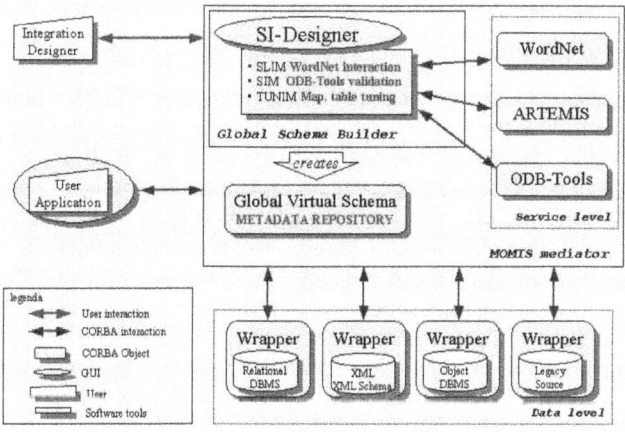

Fig. 1. The MOMIS Architecture

To interact with a specific local source, MOMIS uses a *Wrapper*, which has to be placed over each source. The wrapper translates metadata descriptions of a source into the common ODL_{I3} representation. The core of the MOMIS system is the *Mediator*. The Global Virtual Schema (GSB) module processes and integrates descriptions received from wrappers to derive the global shared schema by interacting with different service modules, namely ODB-Tools, an integrate environment for reasoning on object oriented database based on Description Logics [2], WordNet lexical database that supports the mediator in building lexicon-derived relationships, and ARTEMIS tool that performs the clustering operation [10].

3.2. Wrapping of Source Schemas

To manage the information heterogeneity, a mediator system typically encapsulates each source by a wrapper, which logically converts the underlying data structure to the common data model. In this way, the wrapper architecture and interfaces are crucial for managing the diversity of data sources [24]. In particular, during the MOMIS integration process, the wrapper translates the schema of a source into the common data model of the mediator. For a conventional structured information source (e.g. relational databases, object oriented databases), schema description is always available and can be directly translated into the common data model. For semistructured information sources (e.g., Web data sources), a schema description is in general not directly available at the sources, in fact, a basic characteristic of semistructured data is that they are "self-describing", hence the information associated with the schema is specified within data [8]. According to the different proposed models [8] [22], MOMIS represents semistructured information sources as rooted, labeled graphs with the data (e.g., an image or text) as nodes and labels on edges. A semistructured object can be viewed as a triple of the form <id, label, value>, where id is the object identifier, label is a string describing what the object represents, and value is the value, that can be atomic or complex. The atomic value can be integer, real, ... while the complex value is a set of semistructured objects, that is, a set of pairs (id, label). A complex object can be thought as the parent of all the objects that form its value (children objects). An object can have one or more parents. In semistructured data models, labels are descriptive as much as possible. Generally, the same label is assigned to all objects describing the same concept in a source. To represent the schema of a semistructured source S, we introduce the notion of object pattern. All objects so of S are partitioned into disjoint sets, such that all objects belonging to the same set have the same label. An object pattern is then extracted from each set to represent all the objects in the set. Then, an object pattern is representative of all different objects that describe the same concept in a semistructured source. According to our data model (ODM$_{I3}$), we developed a wrapper to manage XML and RDF(S) files. The wrapper aims to map the data model of an XML file into the corresponding object pattern model.

The Extensible Markup Language (XML) is a W3C recommendation and it arises as a language to describe information sources by using a universal format. One of the main goals of this standard is to exchange files across the Internet. An XML file may be thought as self-describing like a semistructured data source. The main analogies may be summarized as follows:

- *object pattern* attribute → XML tag
- *object pattern* → DTD element
- atomic value of an *object pattern* attribute →   PCDATA value

By using this mapping, the XML data model allows to describe semistructured information sources according to our data model. The XML wrapper parses the DTD associated to each well-formed XML file and generates a translation from an XML statement into an ODL$_{I3}$ statement. This mapping implies some critical aspects due to the lack of semantics of XML w.r.t. ODL$_{I3}$. In particular, the most relevant are: the order in which attributes are described in the DTD, the translation of the concept of attribute from XML language into ODL$_{I3}$ language, the poor type system provided by XML and the weak semantics of intra-schema references. In this last case, to avoid loss of information during the translation process, the designer may be asked to supply further information by a graphical interface. XML Schema, a recent W3C standard, allows to express more semantics on structures and datatypes, by using a XML-based language. Our wrapper is able to integrate XML-Schema sources generating a more significant translation in ODL_{I3}.

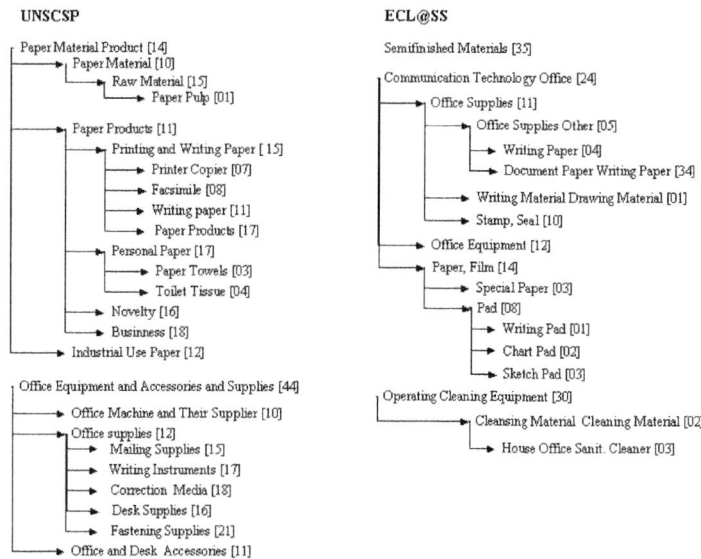

UNSCSP

- Paper Material Product [14]
  - Paper Material [10]
    - Raw Material [15]
      - Paper Pulp [01]
- Paper Products [11]
  - Printing and Writing Paper [15]
    - Printer Copier [07]
    - Facsimile [08]
    - Writing paper [11]
    - Paper Products [17]
  - Personal Paper [17]
    - Paper Towels [03]
    - Toilet Tissue [04]
  - Novelty [16]
  - Business [18]
  - Industrial Use Paper [12]
- Office Equipment and Accessories and Supplies [44]
  - Office Machine and Their Supplier [10]
  - Office supplies [12]
    - Mailing Supplies [15]
    - Writing Instruments [17]
    - Correction Media [18]
    - Desk Supplies [16]
    - Fastening Supplies [21]
  - Office and Desk Accessories [11]

ECL@SS

- Semifinished Materials [35]
- Communication Technology Office [24]
  - Office Supplies [11]
    - Office Supplies Other [05]
      - Writing Paper [04]
      - Document Paper Writing Paper [34]
    - Writing Material Drawing Material [01]
    - Stamp, Seal [10]
  - Office Equipment [12]
  - Paper, Film [14]
    - Special Paper [03]
    - Pad [08]
      - Writing Pad [01]
      - Chart Pad [02]
      - Sketch Pad [03]
- Operating Cleaning Equipment [30]
  - Cleansing Material Cleaning Material [02]
    - House Office Sanit. Cleaner [03]

Fig. 2. The ECCMA/UNSPSC and ecl@ss writing paper fragment

The Resource Description Framework (RDF) is a foundation for processing metadata; it aims at providing a method to describe metadata in a manner, which guarantees the interoperability among different sources on the web. RDF model and syntax may be expressed in XML. In this way, a standard model to represent knowledge and a standard language to describe this knowledge are provided for applications on the web. An RDF-Schema is given in order to interpret and manage the statements contained in a RDF data model. RDF Schema defines a *schema specification language* that may be used to model the specific domain of knowledge. The XML wrapper has been extended in order to manage the knowledge generated from the RDF description of the sources that use XML language to express their own information. In particular, the wrapper translates *RDFS classes* into *object pattern*, *RDF properties* into *object pattern attribute*, the *RDFS subClassOf property* into a *parent-child relationship* and the *RDFS seeAlso property* into a *part-of relationship*.

3.3. The MOMIS Integration Process

In order to create a global virtual schema of involved sources, MOMIS generates a common thesaurus of terminological intensional and extensional relationships describing intra and inter-schema knowledge about classes and attributes of the source schemas. On the basis of the common thesaurus contents, MOMIS evaluates affinity between intra and inter-sources classes and groups similar classes together in clusters using hierarchical clustering techniques. A *global class*, that becomes representative of all the classes belonging to the cluster, is defined for each cluster. The global view for the involved source data consists of all the global classes. The MOMIS methodology is supported by a graphical tool, the Source Integration Designer, SI-Designer in short.

Let us apply the MOMIS methodology to a fragment of the two standard targets. Both the sources represent an extract of classification standard related to the domain of writing paper (Fig. 2). Since ecl@ss contains a standard set of attributes only at the last level and ECCMA/UNSPSC is not descriptive on the attribute level (even if it will be published the EGAS schema containing the attribute level), in the following we take into account only the category names. We assume that these standard schemas have been provided using XML-based files.

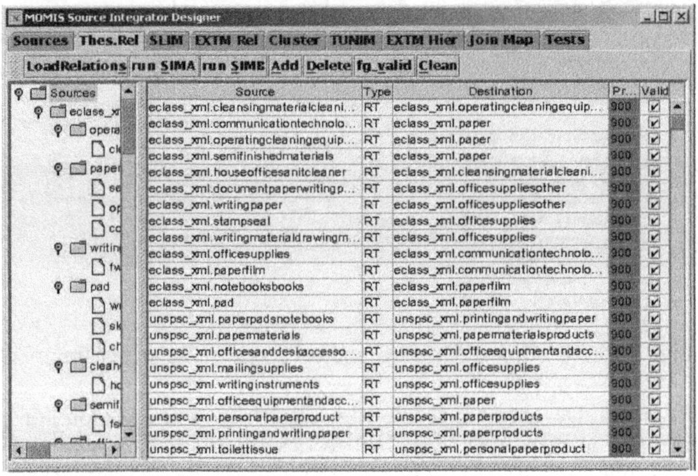

Fig. 3. A part of the intra-schema derived relationships

Building the Common Thesaurus

An important feature of semantic integration is the availability of a shared ontology providing a reference vocabulary on which to base the identification of heterogeneity and the subsequent resolution for conflicts. To achieve this goal we build a common thesaurus that expresses inter-schema knowledge in the form of terminological knowledge (such as SYN, BT, NT and RT) between classes and attribute names by exploiting WordNet-supplied ontology and Description Logics supplied by ODB-Tool. The common thesaurus is built through an incremental process during which relationships are added in the following order: schema-derived relationships (not modifiable by the designer), lexicon-derived relationships, designer-supplied relationships and inferred relationships. Using the SI-Designer tool, the designer is assisted during all the integration process and can refine lexicon-derived explicitly supplied relationships at each step of the integration process.

Schema-derived relationships. MOMIS extracts intensional relations from schemas structure knowledge, by analyzing each ODL_{I3} schema separately. In particular, MOMIS extracts each intra-schema RT relationships from the specification of foreign keys in relational source schema and from part-of relationship in hierarchical sources (i.e. XML files representation). When a foreign key is also a primary key both in the original and in the referenced relation, MOMIS extracts a BT-NT relationship. BT-NT relationships are also generated from the inheritance relationships in object-oriented schema and from ID-IDREF couples in XML file. Remember that in this latter case the designer, interacting with SI-Designer, has to identify each couple ID-IDREF. Fig. 3 shows some of the relationships extracted from the ecl@ss and ECCMA/UNSPSC writing paper fragments. For example, we observe:

```
<eclass_xml.semifinishedmaterials rt eclass_xml.paper>
<eclass_xml.notebooksbooks rt eclass_xml.paperfilm>
<unspsc_xml.personalpaperproduct rt unspsc_xml.paperproducts>
<unspsc_xml.mailingsupplies rt unspsc_xml.officesupplies>
```

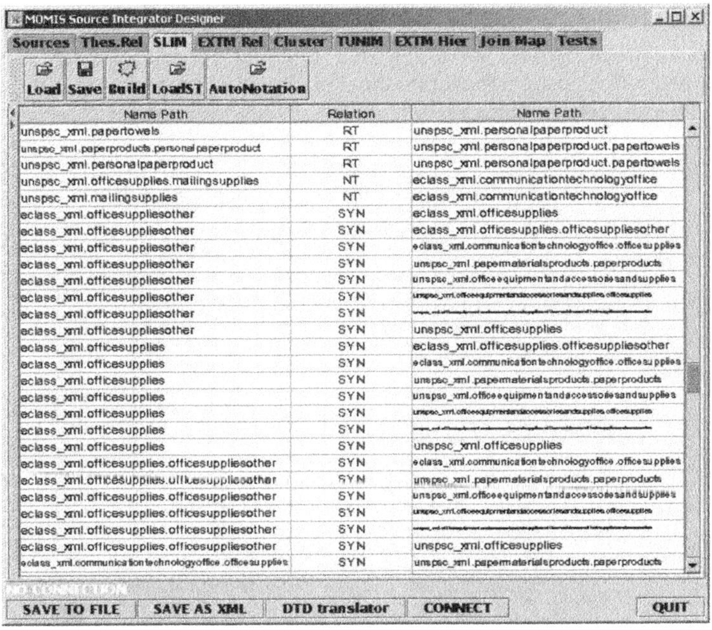

Fig. 4. A part of the lexicon-derived relationships

Lexicon-derived relationships. MOMIS extracts the lexical relationships by analyzing different source schemas, according to the WordNet (www.cogsci.princeton.edu/wn) ontology. WordNet's starting point for lexical semantics comes from a conventional association between the forms of the words – that is, the way in which words are pronounced or written – and the concept or meaning they express. These associations, which are of the many-to-many kind, give rise to several properties, including synonymy, polysemy and so forth. Synonymy is the property of a concept or meaning that can be expressed with two or more words (a synonym group is called a *synset*). Only one synset exists for each concept or meaning. In contrast to synonymy, polysemy denotes the property of a single word that has two or more meanings. For each element composing the schemas of the involved sources, the user has to choose the associated word. This choice consists of choosing both a base form and a meaning. Our system tries to automatically suggest a base form. Starting from the base form and the meanings associated to each sources' element, the system inserts into the common thesaurus the lexicon-derived relationships obtained by exploiting the names properties stored in WordNet. Fig. 4 shows some of the generated relationships. In particular, we have:

```
<eclass_xml.officeSupplies SYN unspsc_xml.officeSupplies >
<eclass_xml.pad  SYN unspsc_xml.notebooksBooks>
<unspsc_xml.paperProducts unspsc NT  eclass_xml.writingPaper>
<eclass_xml.paper RT unspsc_xml.officesupplies>
```

Designer-supplied relationships. The designer may supply further relationships to capture specific domain knowledge about the source schemas. For example in the ECCMA/UNSPSC the element *mailing supplies* may be considered as a more general concept of the element *stamp* in the ecl@ss standard. This relationship may be defined as follows:

```
<unspsc_xml.mailingSupplies BT eclass_xml.stamp>
```

This is a critical operation because new relationships are added to the common thesaurus and will be used to generate the global view. This means that if the designer supplies incorrect relationships the integration process can produce a wrong result.

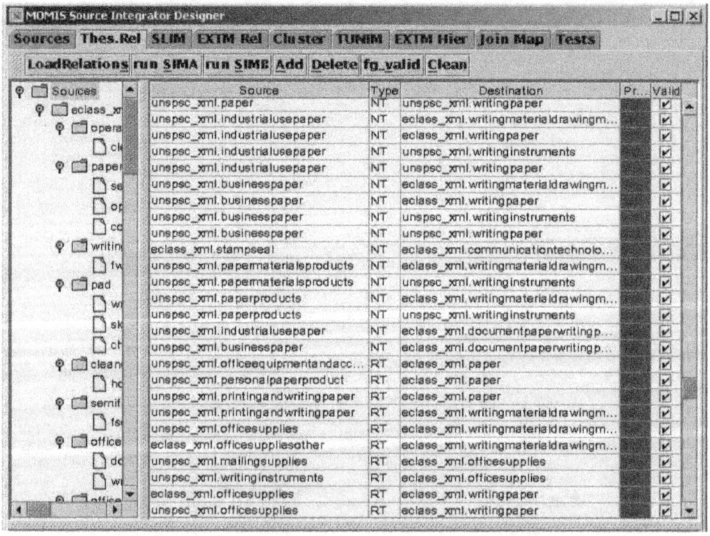

Fig. 5. A part of the new inferred relationships

Checking consistency and inferring new relationships. In this step, MOMIS performs reasoning about the common thesaurus relationships by exploiting the subsumption and inheritance computation, reasoning techniques of Description Logics performed by ODB-Tool [2]. Fig. 5 shows some of these relationships:

```
<unspsc_xml.industrialusepaper NT eclass_xml.writingpaper>
<unspsc_xml.businesspaper  NT eclass_xml.writingmaterialdrawingmaterial>
<unspsc_xml.toilettissue RT eclass_xml.houseofficesanitcleaner>
```

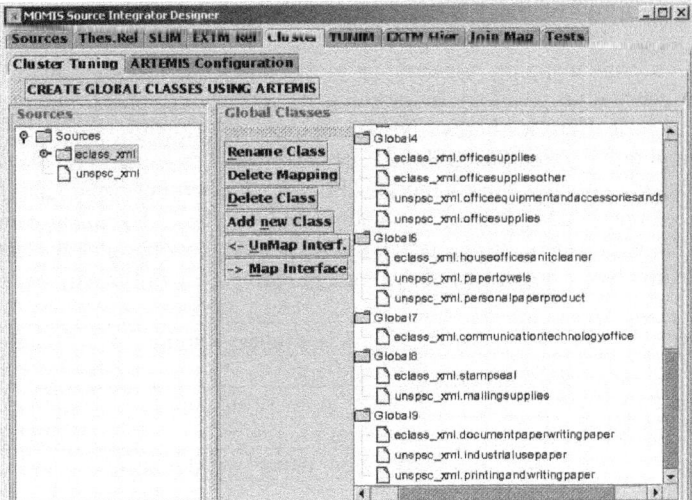

Fig. 6. The generated cluster

Clustering ODL$_{I3}$ Classes

To integrate the ODL$_{I3}$ classes of the different sources into a global ODL$_{I3}$ classes, we employ hierarchical clustering techniques based on the concept of affinity. In this way, we identify ODL$_{I3}$ classes that describe the same or semantically related information in different source schemas and give a measure of the level of matching of their structure. This activity is performed by ARTEMIS [10], evaluating a set of affinity coefficients (numerical values in the range [0,1]) for all possible pairs of ODL$_{I3}$ classes on the basis of the relationships of the common thesaurus. Affinity coefficients determine the degree of semantic relationship between two classes based on their names (name affinity coefficient) and on their attribute refined by the data type validation (structural affinity coefficient). A comprehensive affinity value, called global affinity coefficient, is the linear combination of the name and structural affinity coefficients. The output of the clustering procedure is an affinity tree, where the classes themselves are the leaves and intermediate nodes.

Global Virtual Schema Generation

The latter phase of integration methodology consists in the generation of a global virtual schema composed of ODL$_{I3}$ global classes derived from the clusters. This is a synthesis activity performed interactively with the designer. Synthesis of clusters of ODL$_{I3}$ classes requires taking into account semantic heterogeneity, which has to be treated properly to come up with an integrated and uniform representation at the global level. Let Cl$_i$ be a selected cluster in the affinity tree and gc$_i$ the global ODLI3 class to be defined for Cl$_i$. First, we associate with gc$_i$ all classes belonging to Cl$_i$ and a set of global attributes corresponding to the union of the attributes of these classes. The attributes having a valid terminological relationship are unified into a unique global attribute in gc$_i$. The attribute unification process is performed automatically for what concerns names according to the following rules: for attributes that have a SYN relationship, only one term is selected as the name for the corresponding global attribute in gc$_i$; for attributes that have a BT/NT relationship, a name which is a broader term for all of them is selected and assigned to the corresponding global attribute in gc_i. Furthermore, ODLI3 provides the designer with the syntax and semantics to define mapping rules among global and local attributes and to refine the unification process proposed by the system. As in our example, we considered only product categories (no attributes), we concentrate our attention on the global/local classes mapping. For example, global cluster "Global9", re-defined by the designer as "Writing paper", contains the categories "Printing and writing paper" and "Industrial use paper" of the ECCMA/UNSPSC standard and the class "Document paper, writing paper" of the ecl@ss one. In the following table, we show the global class "Writing Paper", the involved categories and the corresponding code of the native standards.

Sources	Class (Category) name	Code
Mediator Shared Level	Writing Paper	Writing Paper
ECCMA/UNSPSC	Printing and writing paper	14111500
ECCMA/UNSPSC	Industrial use paper	14120000
ecl@ss	Document paper, writing paper	24113400

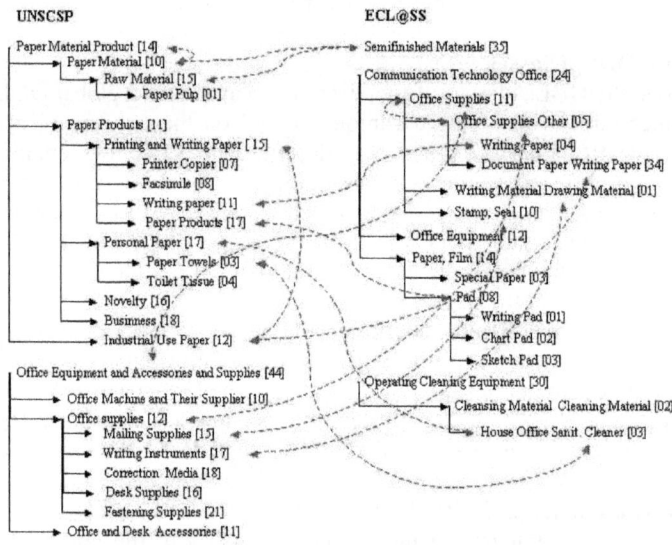

Fig. 7. The obtained mapping

The mapping between concepts of the two standards is graphically shown in Fig. 7, with dashed lines. The system produces the whole global shared schema in an XML-like format, where, for each global class the mapping into the local sources' classes is described. In particular, the MOMIS output for the obtained mapping is an XML file according to this trivial DTD:

```
<!ELEMENT cluster (interface)>
<!ATTLIST cluster name CDATA #IMPLIED>
<!ELEMENT interface EMPTY>
<!ATTLIST interface name CDATA #REQUIRED>
<!ATTLIST interface code CDATA #REQUIRED>
```

For example, we show how "Writing Paper" cluster is exported using our formalism:

```
<cluster name="Writing Paper">
<interface name="eclass_xml.documentpaperwritingpaper" code="24113400"/>
<interface name="unspsc_xml.industrialusepaper" code="14120000" />
<interface name="unspsc_xml.printingandwritingpaper" code="14111500"/>
</cluster>
```

By considering the mapping among the clusters of the global virtual schema and the local product code, it is possible to compare two different standard categories or to consider as a unique entity all the elements contained in the cluster. In this paper, we have exemplified our mapping approach by referring to a fragment of standard classification related to the paper domain. Nevertheless, due to the scalability of MOMIS methodology, the process may easily extended to map every term between the two considered standards. The approach may be further extended in order to obtain mapping among other product classification standards.

4 Related Work

The integration of information has become the main prerequisite for a scalable business process in B2B e-commerce area. The problem to be overcome is related both to the structural and applicative heterogeneity, as well as to the lack of a common ontology, that causes semantic differences among information sources. "Virtual Catalogs" synthesize this approach, as are defined as instruments for the dynamic retrieval of information from multiple catalogs which have been created with the goal to present product data in a unified virtual manner, without directly storing information of the single catalogs [17]. The most popular, the Tsimmis project[21], follows a structural approach and uses a self-describing model to represent heterogeneous data sources. The Garlic project [16] builds a wrapper-based architecture to describe the local source data using an OO language, while the Sims project [1] proposes to create a global schema definition by exploiting the use of description logics. Another approach based on Description Logics is taken in the OBSERVER system to support semantic interoperation and formulation of rich queries over distributed information repositories where different vocabularies are used [20]. Here the idea is that each repository has its own ontology. Inter-ontology relationships are specified in a declarative way (using Description Logics) in an inter-ontology manager module to handle vocabulary heterogeneities between ontologies of different information repositories for query processing. In this respect, our approach tries to extract as much information as possible from source descriptions and from WordNet and we show how this information can be used for integration purposes.

The analysis, discovery, and representation of inter-schema properties are another critical aspect of the integration process and research proposals have appeared on this topic. In DIKE system [23], semi-automatic techniques for discovering synonyms, homonyms and object inclusion relationships from database schemas are described and an algorithm for integrating and abstracting database schemas is proposed. More specific contributes concerning the product integration of information in B2B is provided by Fensel et al. [12]. Their first proposal apply XSL-T [13] technology to B2B document interchange, by defining specific XSL-T rules that directly translate each XML element or attribute of one catalog into XML element of another ones. These rules try to carry out the complete transformation process in one shot, so the different aspects of integration, like syntax heterogeneity, structural and granularity level of representation mismatches are encapsulated into the rules. For this reason any re-use of such rules is practically impossible. To overcome this problem, the same authors developed a multi-layer framework [19], where three layers (syntax layer, object layer and ontology layer) are proposed for information modeling on the Web. The integration is performed by using only the syntax and the object layer through the translation of the XML catalog (syntax layer) into its normalized RDF data model (object layer), the transformation between a pair of RDF data models of different catalogs and the translation from the data model back into XML target catalogs [14]. In our approach the syntax layer represents the wrapper level, while the object layer and ontology layer correspond to the global virtual schema; in addition, we propose a semi-automatic methodology for the creation of the common ontology.

5   Conclusions

In this paper, we proposed a methodology to define the mapping among different e-commerce product classification standards. We have exemplified the methodology by showing how it is possible to create a mapping between a fragment of the ECCMA/UNSPSC and a fragment of the ecl@ss standard, but the process may be successfully applied to other product classification standards. The obtained XML mapping file may be inserted within an electronic marketplace in order to define automatic rules to manage products classified using the ECCMA/UNSPSC and ecl@ss standards. These rules may generate automatic data translation to give to the marketplace seller a unique code representing the same product that is classified by the vendors in different manners. In this way, by given a common manner to describe goods involved in the e-commerce process, the marketplace really becomes the place in which sellers and vendor may interact without any change in their data management system. In the future, we are going to investigate this idea by using the obtained XML mapping file within the MOMIS Query Manager [3] that permits optimized query processing in distributed information system.

References

[1] Ambite J. L., Knoblock C. A., *Flexible and scalable cost-based query planning in mediators: A transformational approach*, Artificial Intelligence 118(1-2), (2000).
[2] Beneventano D., Bergamaschi S., Sartori C., Vincini M., *ODB-Tools: A Description Logics Based Tool For Schema Validation and Semantic Query Optimization in Object Oriented Databases*, Proc. of Int. Conf. on Data Engineering (ICDE-97), Birmingam UK 1997.
[3] Beneventano D.,   Bergamaschi S., Guerra F., Vincini M., *Exploiting extensional knowledge for query reformulation and object fusion in a data integration system*, Proc. of the Convegno Nazionale Sistemi di Basi di Dati Evolute (SEBD2001), Venezia, June, 2001.
[4] Beneventano D., Bergamaschi S., Castano S., Corni A., Guidetti R., Malvezzi G., Melchiori M., Vincini M., *Information Integration: the MOMIS Project Demonstration*, Proceedings of 26th Int.Conf.on Very Large Data Bases (VLDB2000), 000, Cairo, Egypt.

[5] Bergamaschi S., Castano S., Beneventano D., Vincini M., *Semantic Integration of Heterogeneous Information Sources*, Special Issue on Intelligent Information Integration, Data & Knowledge Engineering, Vol. 36, Num. 1, 215-249, Elsevier Science B.V. 2001.

[6] Benetti I., Beneventano D., Bergamaschi S., Guerra F., Vincini M., *An Information Integration Framework for e-commerce*, IEEE Intelligent Systems, (Jan/Feb 2002).

[7] Bernstein P.A., Rahm E., *A survey of approaches to automatic schema matching*, VLDB Journal 10(4): 334-350 (2001).

[8] Buneman P., *Semistructured Data*, Proceedings of Symposium on Principles of Database systems (PODS97), Tucson, Arizona, (1997), 117-121.

[10] Castano S, De Antonellis V., De Capitani Di Vimercati S, *Global Viewing of Heterogeneous Data Sources*, IEEE Transactions TKDE 13(2): 277-297 (2001).

[11] Fensel D., *Ontologies: Silver Bullet for Knowledge Management and Electronic Commerce*, Springer-Verlang, Berlin(2001).

[12] Fensel D., Ding Y., Schulten E., Omelayenko B., Botquin G., Brown M., Flett A., *Product Data Integration in B2B E-commerce*, IEEE Intelligent System, 16(4), 2001.

[13] Omelayenko B., Fensel D., *Ontologies: An Analysis of Integration Problems of XML-Based Catalogues for B2B E-commerce*, In Proc. of the 9th IFIP 2.6 Working Conference on Database (DS-9), April 2001.

[14] Omelayenko B., Fensel D., *Ontologies: A Two-Layered Integration Approach for Product Information in B2B E-commerce*, Second Int. Conference on Electronic Commerce and Web Technologies, EC-Web 2001 Munich, Germany, September 4-6, 2001.

[15] Granada Research, *Why Coding and Classifying Products is Critical to Success in Electronic Commerce*, White paper, 2002. www.un-spsc.net.

[16] Haas L. M., Miller R. J., Niswonger B., Roth M. T., Schwarz P. M., Wimmers E. L., *Transforming Heterogeneous Data with Database Middleware: Beyond Integration*, IEEE Data Engineering Bulletin, 22(1):31-36 (1999).

[17] Hull R., *Managing Semantic Heterogeneity in Databases: A Theoretical Perspective*, ACM Symp. on Principles of Database Systems, pp. 51-61, 1997.

[18] Li H., *XML and Industrial Standards for Electronic Commerce*, Knowledge and Information Systems, 2 (2000), 487-497.

[19] Melnik S., Decker S., *A Layered Approach to Information Modeling and Interoperability on the Web*, in ECDL 2000 Workshop on the Semantic Web.

[20] Mena E., Illarramendi A., Kashyap V., Sheth A. P., *OBSERVER: An Approach for Query Processing in Global Information Systems Based on Interoperation Across Pre-Existing Ontologies*, Distributed and Parallel Databases 8(2): 223-271 (2000), Kluwer.

[21] Garcia-Molina H., Quass D., Rajaraman A., Sagiv Y., Ullman J., Vassalos V., Widom J., *The TSIMMIS approach to mediation: Data models and Languages*, in Journal of Intelligent Information Systems, JIIS(8)(2): 117-132 (1997).

[22] Papakonstantinou Y, Garcia-Molina H., Widom J., *Object Exchange Across Heterogeneous Information Sources*, Proc. of Int. Conf. on Data Sources, Taiwan (1995)

[23] Rosaci D., Terracina G., Ursino D., *A Semi-automatic Technique for Constructing a Global Representation of Information Sources Having Different Formats and Structure*, Proc. of 12th Int. Conf. Database and Expert Systems Applications (DEXA 2001), 2001.

[24] Roth M. T., Schwarz P. M., *Don't Scrap It, Wrap It! A Wrapper Architecture for Legacy Data Sources*, Proceedings of 26th Int. Conf. on Very Large Data Bases, 266-275, 1997.

[25] Wiederhold G., Genesereth M. R., *The Conceptual Basis for Mediation Services*, IEEE Expert 12(5): 38-47 (1997).

Nonmonotonic Rule Systems
on Top of Ontology Layers

Grigoris Antoniou

Dept. of Computer Science, University of Bremen, Germany
ga@tzi.de

Abstract. The development of the Semantic Web proceeds in layers. Currently the most advanced layer that has reached maturity is the ontology layer, in the from of the DAML+OIL language which corresponds to a rich description logic. The next step will be the the realization of logical rule systems on top of the ontology layer.

Computationally simple nonmonotonic rule systems show promise to play an important role in electronic commerce on the Semantic Web. In this paper we outline how nonmonotonic rule systems in the form of defeasible reasoning, can be built on top of description logics.

1 Motivation and Overview

The Semantic Web initiative [17] promises to improve dramatically the World Wide Web, and in doing so, to have significant impact on the way information is exchanged and business is conducted. The main idea is to use *machine processable* data and knowledge.

The development of the semantic web proceeds in layers, each layer being on top of lower layers. At present, the highest layer that has reached sufficient maturity is the *ontology layer* in the form of the DAML+OIL language [4]. DAML+OIL was designed to be sufficiently rich to be useful in applications, while being simple enough to allow for efficient reasoning support. In fact, it corresponds to an expressive *description logic*. Stated another way, the realization of the ontology layer could draw benefits from extensive previous work on description logics [3,12,11], both with regard to clear semantics and efficient reasoning support.

The next step in the development of the semantic web core will be the realization of the *logic* and *proof layers*. These layers will be built on top of ontology languages, and will offer enhanced representation and reasoning capabilities. A key ingredient of these layers will be *rules*, which look likely to become an action focus of the W3C. *Monotonic rule systems* are well known and widely in use. Seen as a subset of predicate logic (Horn logic), they are orthogonal to description logics: none is proper subset of the other. The realization of a monotonic rule layer on top of the ontology layer can draw on work on hybrid reasoning, combining description logics with Horn logic, or at least Datalog [12,6,7].

But there exist other kinds of rule systems that are *nonmonotonic*. Such systems are important in practice because they can deal with inconsistencies in a

I. Horrocks and J. Hendler (Eds.): ISWC 2002, LNCS 2342, pp. 394–398, 2002.
© Springer-Verlag Berlin Heidelberg 2002

declarative way, and because they model naturally phenomena like exceptions and priorities. In the past few years, such systems have attracted significant attention in the nonmonotonic reasoning community, e.g. courteous logic programs [9] and defeasible logics [14,1]. Their use in various application domains has been advocated, including the modelling of regulations and business rules [10], modelling of contracts [10], legal reasoning [15] and agent negotiations [8]. In fact, defeasible reasoning (in the form of courteous logic programs [9]) provides the foundation for IBM's Business Rules Markup Language and for current W3C activities on rules. Therefore defeasible reasoning is arguably one of the most successful subarea in nonmonotonic reasoning as far as applications and integration to mainstream IT is concerned.

One important advantage of such systems is their focus on implementability and their low computational complexity [13]. So seen, it makes sense to study the integration of description logics with defeasible reasoning, since both share a focus on efficiency. The integration of nonmonotonic rule systems with description logic based ontologies can serve two purposes: (1) Enhanced reasoning capabilities may be used to express richer ontological knowledge. For example, defeasible ontologies can be built, an idea that appears reasonable in the legal domain. (2) Rule- based systems define ontology-based applications using vocabulary defined in description logic. This idea is compatible with significant work on hybrid reasoning, e.g. [12].

In this paper we concentrate on the second approach, and we will study defeasible reasoning [14] running on top of description logics. Our task is more complex than the integration of Horn rules with description logics because of the following observation: both Horn logic and description logics are subsets of predicate logic. Therefore *semantically* there is no difficulty at all, and the focus of work on hybrid reasoning has been on efficient algorithms and limits of computability. However nonmonotonic rules are not a subset of predicate logic, and we need to define the semantics of such a combination, too. On the other hand, because nonmonotonic rules with variables are interpreted as schemas, their integration with description logics does not have difficulties encountered in other works on hybrid reasoning with regard to instantiation [6].

The situation gets more complicated if concept and role predicates are allowed in the heads of rules as well. We intend to study such tighter integration in the future. Also we have not addressed issues of language design. In this sense, this paper reports on ongoing work. However the preliminary results are still significant, because they show for the first time how, in principle, a defeasible logic and inference layer can be realised on top of the ontology layer.

2   Knowledge Bases

A *knowledge base* $K = (T, F, R, >)$ consists of

- A terminology T, defined in a description logic.
- A set F of facts. Each fact has the form $p(a_1, \ldots, a_m)$, where p is a predicate, and $a_1, \ldots, a_m$ are constants. F is the disjoint union of a set F_T of facts

with a concept or role predicate, and a remainder F_O. Predicates that are not concept and role predicates are called *ordinary*.

- A set R of rules

$$L_1, \ldots, L_n \Rightarrow L$$

such that all L and L_i are literals $p(a_1, \ldots, a_m)$ or $\neg p(a_1, \ldots, a_m)$, with constants $a_1, \ldots, a_m$ and a concept, role or ordinary predicate p. Additionally, the predicate of L must be an ordinary predicate. $\{L_1, \ldots, L_n\}$ is the set of *antecedents* of the rule r, denoted $A(r)$. And L is called the *head* (or *consequent*) of r, denoted $C(r)$.
- an acyclic relation $>$ on R.

Now we make a number of remarks.

1. Rules with variables are interpreted as schemas: they represent the set of their ground instances. This interpretation is standard in many nonmonotonic reasoning approaches, among others in default logic [16] and defeasible logics [14].
2. The logical language does not have function symbols, thus the Herbrand universe is finite.
3. Concept and role predicates are not allowed to occur in facts, or the heads of rules. This design decision follows the idea that rules may not be used to derive ontological knowledge. All knowledge about concepts and roles is provided by the description logic component. The same idea was followed by other work on hybrid reasoning involving description logic and monotonic rules, e.g. [12]. The motivation for such an approach, and its relevance to the semantic web initiative, were outlined in the introduction.
4. Defeasible logic usually offers strict rules, and sometimes defeaters, in addition. We have omitted defeaters here, because they can be simulated by other means [1]. And we have decided to omit strict rules, because typically they include taxonomical, or other kinds of certain knowledge. We assume that such knowledge will be included in the ontology, and treated by the description logic. Instead we have allowed a set of facts about ordinary predicates. If need be, strict rules can be easily added to our logical system.

Given a set R of rules, $R[L]$ denotes the set of rules in R with head L. In the following $\sim L$ denotes the complement of L, that is, $\sim L$ is $\neg L$ if L is an atomic formula, and $\sim L$ is L' if L is $\neg L$.

3   Defeasible Reasoning Using Terminological Knowledge

Given a rule r

$$L_1, \ldots, L_n \Rightarrow L$$

suppose $\{L_1, \ldots, L_n\}$ is partitioned into $\{L^{(1)}, \ldots, L^{(k)}\}$ and $\{L^{(k+1)}, \ldots, L^{(n)}\}$, such that the predicates of $\{L^{(1)}, \ldots, L^{(k)}\}$ are ordinary, and the predicates of $\{L^{(k+1)}, \ldots, L^{(n)}\}$ are concept or role predicates. Further suppose that $T \cup F \models L^{(j)}$ for all $j \in \{k+1, \ldots, n\}$. Then the rule

$$L^{(1)} \dots, L^{(k)} \Rightarrow L$$

is called the *reduct* of r; otherwise the reduct is undefined. For a set R of rules, $Red(R)$ collects the reducts of all rules in R.

Now we briefly outline the proof theory. A *conclusion* of a defeasible theory D is a signed tagged literal. Here we use only one tag, ∂, which denotes defeasible provability. Also we use the signs $+$ and $-$. A conclusion $+\partial L$ means that the literal L is defeasibly provable in D. And $-\partial q$ means that we have proved that q is not defeasibly provable in D.

A *derivation* (or *proof*) P is a finite sequence of signed tagged literals. $P(1..i)$ denotes the first i elements of this sequence. Now we proceed to give the inference conditions for $+\partial$ and $-\partial$. Let L be a literal with an ordinary predicate (Here we define ∂L only for such literals. A simple extension would be to derive $+\partial L$ iff $T \cup F \models L$, where the predicate of L is a concept or role predicate).

$+\partial$: If $P(i+1) = +\partial L$ then either
  (1) $L \in F$ or
  (2) (2.1) $\exists r \in Red(R)[L] \; \forall L' \in A(r) : +\partial L' \in P(1..i)$
       (2.2) $\sim L \notin F$ and
       (2.3) $\forall s \in Red(R)[\sim L]$ either
             (2.3.1) $\exists L' \in A(s) : -\partial L' \in P(1..i)$ or
             (2.3.2) $\exists t \in Red(R)[L] \forall L' \in A(t)$
                     $+\partial L' \in P(1..i)$ and $t > s$.

Let us illustrate this definition. To show that L is provable defeasibly we have two choices: (1) We show that L is a fact; or (2) we need to argue using rules. In particular, we require that there must be a rule reduct with head L which can be applied (2.1). But now we need to consider possible "counterattacks", that is, reasoning chains in support of $\sim L$. To be more specific: to prove L using rule reducts we must show that $\sim L$ is not a fact (2.2). Also (2.3) we must consider the set of all rule reducts which are not known to be inapplicable and which have head $\sim L$. Essentially each such rule s attacks the conclusion L. For L to be provable, each such rule s must have been established as non-applicable (2.3.1). Altenratively there must be a rule reduct with head L stronger than the attacking rule (2.3.2).

The inference condition $-\partial$ is the so-called strong negation of $+$ (de Morgan is applied, and $+$ and $-$ are interchanged).

Implementation will involve interleaving of description logic reasoners and defeasible reasoners. Derivability of antecedents with concept or role predicates will be checked by a description logic reasoner, the remainder is treated as specified in the inference conditions above.

Example 1. Imagine an online store which has organised its stock according to an ontology. Among others, the ontology contains the information $physicsBook \sqsubseteq scientificBook \sqsubseteq book$. The pricing policy of the store is written in defeasible logic, and might include the following information (scientific books get a special 5% discount).

$r_1 : \Rightarrow \neg discount(X, Y, Z)$
$r_2 : \ scientificBook(X) \Rightarrow X, Y, 5\%)$

(where X denotes an article and Y a customer). The item with id 93215 is stored in the corporate data base as a physics book:

$physicsBook(93215)$

Putting all this information together, we can derive $+\partial discount(93215, Y, 5\%)$.

References

1. G. Antoniou, D. Billington, G. Governatori and M.J. Maher. Representation Results for Defeasible Logic. *ACM Transactions on Computational Logic* 2,2 (2001): 255–287.
2. F. Baader and B. Hollunder. A terminological knowledge representation system with complete inference algorithm. In *Proc. Workshop on Processing Declarative Knowledge*, LNAI, Springer 1991, 67–86.
3. M. Buchheit, F. Donini and A. Schaerf. Decidable Reasoning in terminological knowledge representation systems. *Journal of Artificial Intelligence Research* 1 (1993): 109–138.
4. D. Connolly et al. *DAML+OIL (March 2001) Reference Description.* http://www.w3.org/TR/daml+oil-reference.
5. F. Donini, M. Lenzerini, D. Nardi and A. Schaerf. Reasoning in Description Logics. In G.Brewka (ed): *Principles of Knowledge Representation and Reasoning*, Studies in Logic, Language and Information, CLSI Publications 1996, 193–238.
6. F. Donini, M. Lenzerini, D. Nardi and A. Schaerf. A hybrid system with datalog and concept languages. In E. Ardizzone, S. Gaglio, F. Sorbello (eds): *Trends in Artificial Intelligence*, LNAI 549, Springer 1991, 88–97.
7. A. Frisch (ed). *Workshop Notes of the AAAI Fall Symposium on Principles of Hybrid Reasoning.* AAAI Press 1991.
8. G. Governatori, A. ter Hofstede and P. Oaks. Defeasible Logic for Automated Negotiation. *Proc. Collecter'2000.*
9. B. Grosof. Prioritized conflict handling for logic programs. In *Proc. International Logic Programming Symposium*, MIT Press 1997, 197–211.
10. B. Grosof, Y. Lambrou and H. Chan. A Declarative Approach to Business Rules in Contracts: Courteous Logic Programs in XML. In *Proc. 1st ACM Conference on Electronic Commerce*, ACM 1999.
11. I. Horrocks and U. Sattler. Ontology reasoning in the SHOQ(D) description logic. In *Proc. of the 17th Int. Joint Conf. on Artificial Intelligence (IJCAI-01)*, Morgan Kaufmann 2001, 199–204.
12. A. Levy and M-C. Rousset. CARIN: A Representation Language Combining Horn rules and Description Logics. *Artificial Intelligence* 104(1-2), 1998, 165–209.
13. M.J. Maher. Propositional Defeasible Logic has Linear Complexity. *Theory and Practice of Logic Programming*, 1,6 (2001): 691–711.
14. D. Nute. Defeasible Logic. In D.M. Gabbay, C.J. Hogger and J.A. Robinson (eds): *Handbook of Logic in Artificial Intelligence and Logic Programming Vol. 3*, Oxford University Press 1994, 353–395.
15. H. Prakken. *Logical Tools for Modelling Legal Argument: A Study of Defeasible Reasoning in Law.* Kluwer Academic Publishers 1997 .
16. R. Reiter. A Logic for Default Reasoning. *Artificial Intelligence* 13(1980): 81–132.
17. www.w3.org/2001/sw/

An RDF NetAPI

Andy Seaborne

Hewlett-Packard Laboratories, Bristol
andy_seaborne@hp.com

Abstract. This paper describes some initial work on a NetAPI for accessing and updating RDF data over the web. The NetAPI includes actions for conditional extraction or update of RDF data, actions for model upload and download and also the ability to enquire about the capabilities of a hosting server. An initial experimental system is described which partially implements these ideas within the Jena toolkit.

1 The Need for a NetAPI for RDF

Part of fulfilling the vision of the Semantic Web is the exchange of RDF[1] data between computer systems. The web enables the reuse of resources so that people, and now systems, can obtain, combine and process information from other systems without explicit producer-consumer relationships being set up.

One precursor for the Semantic Web to achieve critical mass will be a common framework for accessing RDF data, one sufficiently common that the majority of applications will use it, the majority of publication host systems support it and only specialized applications will choose to develop their own protocols.

Given a common protocol, the network effect of bringing in more and more semantic applications can start. Application developers can concentrate on the application, and not on the plumbing. Tool builders (server and client side) do not need to support multiple protocols, and can target client-side or server-side environments. Publishers can know that many systems and applications can access their RDF information.

In this paper, we argue for the use of "conditional GET" and "partial PUT" as the central operations for accessing RDF datasources. In the outline framework, we incorporate existing actions of HTTP [2], such as HTTP GET and PUT, as the simplest level but, as the semantic web grows, and as large metadata repositories appear, the paradigm shifts to one that is more like database access than web page download.

We have built a small experimental system that demonstrates part of the NetAPI. We do not propose specific protocols here and this is not the only attempt to create remote interaction with RDF data. We are investigating what it would take to create mass deployment on the current web infrastructure.

I. Horrocks and J. Hendler (Eds.): ISWC 2002, LNCS 2342, pp. 399–403, 2002.

2 Design Challenges

One challenge is to balance simplicity of implementation, leading to widespread deployment, with adequate functionality. We want a simple, widely used infrastructure.

In any complex system, there is often a gap between the requirements of the application and the capabilities of the general infrastructure that is properly met by domain-specific sub-systems. These domain specific systems appear as "applications" to the infrastructure and as "infrastructure" to the end applications.

Another challenge in the design of a NetAPI for RDF-based systems is to provide a useful protocol that separates the evolution of client and server software in a community that is pulled from diverse research and industrial domains so the protocol should be simple and domain independent.

We envisage further protocols, both on top of the common access framework proposed here and also more specialized protocols for specific uses where the common access framework is insufficient. A basis for a general system will rarely meet the needs of all possible domains directly.

We also want to utilize as much of the common web infrastructure for the access of RDF data, using existing protocols and existing server systems. This decreases the barriers to deployment.

3 Outline Framework

We limit the discussion here to operations on single models, viewed as collections of RDF statements. Applications will also want to merge data sources, issue queries across several data sources or (consistently) update multiple sources. This should be considered for possible later addition: the focus here is to identify a simple set of clearly defined operations, which will boost the adoption of the semantic web.

There are 3 categories of operations, which have been identified:

- Operations on the RDF data itself (query, update)
- Transfer of complete sets of RDF data as RDF models.
- Operations relating to the hosting server, such as enquiring about its capabilities and the range of operations on particular RDF stores.

We do not see the basic operations of RDF data as a fetch but one that is conditioned to select a subset of the data available. For this we need selection languages – we do not anticipate that one language will meet a sufficiently wide set of needs at the moment so we make the selection language a parameter of the operation. In future, we hope that a single language emerges with sufficient coverage that both RDF data providers and RDF data consumers can expect to find support for it in all toolkits.

Server Capabilities

The execution model is one where there are client-initiated actions. Some of the operations have optional parameters so client-side toolkits and applications may need to enquire about the capabilities offered by a host server and about the legal operations and parameters on each of the data sources hosted at that server. This reduces to the server needing to provide information about its capabilities, both overall and with regard to specific RDF data sources.

Model Operations

Operations that fetch or store whole RDF models are the simplest level of operation for an RDF data source and these naturally map to the HTTP operations GET and PUT. These are already supported by existing web servers, where the data source is an RDF document. Simple extension to retrieving the metadata about a web object, instead of the object itself, based on, say, the MIME type is also natural.

Abstractly, the operations are:

- GET(model, format)
- PUT(model, format)

These operations give a sea of RDF models with client systems loading RDF data and performing the extraction and merging of data at the client. These may or may not map directly to the HTTP verbs PUT and GET.

Such whole model operations are not suitable where the quantity of RDF information is large, yet the actual information required by the client is small (for example: data about a publication from a digital library). Nor does it provide for the update of data source, only complete replacement.

For these operations, we need operations acting on client-defined sets of RDF statements, not the whole model (which is a set defined by the server).

Triple operations

In order to operate on specific data sources we propose operations:

- GET-TRIPLES(model, language, condition, format)
- UPDATE-TRIPLES(model, data-to-delete, data-to-add)

These are not proposed as new verbs for HTTP.

The language parameter means that we can have a variety of languages for extraction of data from RDF sources: we anticipate that this will usually be a query language and there are advantages in providing a common mechanism where possible. However, we recognize that a single language cannot meet the needs of, say, query and of inferencing rules systems at this stage.

The choice of a "delete-add" operation allows for consistent bulk update of a data source. The deletions are performed before the additions.

The "format" parameter allows variable in the output format even for the same query language (examples: returning bound variables or the RDF subgraph that matched the query: providing XML or N-triple for update).

4   An Experiment: An RDF Server

The experimental system implements the operations of GET-TRIPLES and UPDATE-TRIPLES.

Protocol Style

We seek a simple, fixed, set of operations that can be widely implemented, enabling client and server toolkits to evolve independently (see[8] for a discussion of protocol styles).

At the same time, we wish to reuse the existing deployed web infrastructure. To maximize this, we currently build on top of HTTP POST, partly in the style of SOAP[9], but, unlike SOAP, we restrict the operations strictly to those outlined in this paper. The protocol uses RDF model transfer as the message format; we do not suggest that this represents the best choice for a production protocol – it is an outbreak of "next-bench" syndrome.

Protocols and Query Language

The protocol consists of a number of layers (from lowest to highest in the stack):
1.   A model exchange layer
2.   A request-response layer
3.   A query layer for conditional GET

Each operation is encoded as a single RDF model to give SOAP-like operation, with higher levels on the stack attaching their protocol information via properties to the message URI. Both body and header information are contained in the same RDF model. The request-response layer simply matches responses to the request that caused them.

Conditional Selection Language

The conditional selection language is RDQL, an implementation of SquishQL[3] for the Jena toolkit[7]. SquishQL is an SQL-like query language that matches a graph pattern to a data source; filter functions can restrict the values of variables. RDQL returns both bound variables and the triples that caused the binding. SquishQL has been variously implemented [4,5,6].

The query request contains an RDQL query, complete with URI to specify the data source. The response contains the variable bindings in an RDF data structure, and the triples that cause the binding are associated with the particular binding using reification. The return format is N-Triple because there are usually shared bNodes.

Client Interface

The client-side implements remote query operations and remote update for the Jena toolkit. The same Java interface is provided for remote query as for query of local models by implementing the same interface. The URI of the data source in included in the query itself as usual. The client creates a remote query engine that takes the URL as the location of the remote server.

The client processes the results through an iterator in the same programming paradigm as for local queries. The only difference is the creation of the query execution object; a remote query engine takes a location URL.

Server

The server implementation is a conventional servlet in a servlet-container web server, with HTTP POST, and the reply to the POST, used as the transport for model exchange. Both GET-TRIPLES and UPDATE-TRIPLES are supported.

The server is configured with a set of RDF models, each with its own URI (not tied to the host server), the location within the host of the data for the model and the URL of the servlet. This separation of the name of the data source (the model URI) from the location of the action (the URL where the operations are performed) allows systems administrators control over the location of models on the host systems and hides information such as filenames and JDBC connection URLs. RDF data sources can be relocated on the server without change to the client code.

Review

This experimental system is not finished. The use of the query and batch update paradigms for processing information is well suited to the network environment where operations are coarser grained and higher latency than API calls directly on a model implementation. The application writer sees the conventional query result processing paradigm that masks the network details and see explicit "batch and execute" for update.

One difference is that the client application can not fully mix the query calls with Jena API calls as is possible when the local model is available. This is because only a partial copy of the RDF data is available at the client as a model.

Next Steps

We plan to use the experimental RDF server in the construction of RDF driven applications, to test the protocol structure, the client programming paradigm and the server-side issues in managing RDF data.

References

1. Ora Lassila, Ralph R. Swick (editors), "Resource Description Framework (RDF) Model and Syntax Specification", 22 February 1999.
2. RFC2616, "Hypertext Transfer Protocol -- HTTP/1.1"
3. L. Miller, A. Seaborne, A. Reggiori, "Three Implementations of SquishQL, a Simple RDF Query Language", submitted to ISWC2002.
4. A. Seaborne, RDQL – RDF Data Query Language. RDQL grammar: http://www.hpl.hp.com/semweb/rdql-grammar.html
5. L. Miller, "Inkling: RDF query using SquishQL", web page: http://swordfish.rdfweb.org/rdfquery/
6. A. Reggiori, D. W. van Gulik, RDFStore, http://rdfstore.sourceforge.net
7. The Jena toolkit: HPLabs Semantic Web activity, http://hpl.hp.com/semweb/
8. R.T. Fielding, "Architectural Styles and the Design of Network-based Software Architectures". Doctoral dissertation, University of California, Irvine, 2000.
9. M. Gudgin, M. Hadley, J. Moreau, H.F. Nielsen (editors), "SOAP Version 1.2" (working draft), http://www.w3.org/TR/2001/WD-soap12-part1-20011217/

A Mini-experiment in Semantic Annotation

Guus Schreiber, Inger I. Blok, Daan Carlier, Wouter P.C. van Gent,
Jair Hokstam, and Uri Roos

University of Amsterdam, Social Science Informatics
Roetersstraat 15, NL 1018 WB Amsterdam, The Netherlands
schreiber@swi.psy.uva.nl
http://www.swi.psy.uva.nl

Abstract. This paper describes a mini-experiment in using a tool for semantic annotation to index photographs of Windsor chairs, a type of antique furniture. The annotation tool makes use of an ontology based on art standards. We report on the experiences of subjects using the tool. The results suggest that a certain level of domain expertise is needed for semantic annotations, but also that an annotation tool has a clear added value for indexers.

1 Introduction

The semantic web requires semantic annotations of resources. The majority of the semantic-web research is at the moment targeted at languages (e.g., RDF(S), DAML+OIL) and architectures for the specification of semantic annotations. In our view however, there is a also a real need to explore the issues related to the use of these techniques in applications.

We report on a small study in which subjects were asked to annotate objects with the help of an ontology. As subject domain we chose photographs of antique furniture, in particular Windsor chairs. In general, annotation and search for large sets of art-object images is becoming an important issue, as musea start making their collections available through the web. Within the art domain large knowledge corpora have been developed, such as the Art and Architecture Thesaurus [1], which makes semantic annotation in principle feasible. Another characteristic of the art-image domain is the manual indexing is standard practice. Musea routinely employ people to do this.

Not much is known yet about the semantic annotation process. The goal of this study is to get data about the following questions:

- What is the required level of domain expertise to be able to make useful semantic annotations?
- Can an ontology be presented in a way that is understandable to the indexers?
- What kind of tool support is useful for semantic annotation?

In Sec. 2 we briefly describe the semantic-annotation tool we used for this study and the ontologies which serve as the basis for the annotations. Sec. 3 describes the setup of the annotation study. In Sec. 4 we describe the results of the study. Finally, we discuss some issues arising from the study and speculate on the potential value of the semantic annotation for improving the search process.

I. Horrocks and J. Hendler (Eds.): ISWC 2002, LNCS 2342, pp. 404–408, 2002.

2   Ontologies and Annotation Tool

For this study we used an ontology-based annotation tool that was previously developed to annotate photographs of apes [2]. In a nutshell, the tool reads in a set of ontologies that provide:

- a object-description template, i.e. a structured set of object properties, and
- subsumption hierarchies of concepts which act as potential property values for the object-description template.

The annotation tool assumes the ontologies are represented in RDF Schema. From the ontologies the tool automatically generates an annotation interface. The internal structure of the object-description template (e.g., grouping of properties) is represented in the tool interface through a tab structure (for an example, see the tabs in Fig. 1).

The ontologies for antique furniture we used in this study are described in more detail in a previous publication [3]. The basis of the object-description template is formed by the Visual Resource Association (VRA) Core Categories. VRA version 3.0 [4] defines 17 "data elements" for describing visual resources (with a bias towards the art domain). The VRA data elements are defined as a specialization of Dublin Core. In addition to the VRA data elements the description template contains eight data elements resulting from the European GRASP project. This project developed an ontology for describing and retrieving stolen art objects.

The data elements (i.e. properties of an antique-furniture object) were grouped into four sets:

1. *General features* such as the main type and the title of the object
2. *Production-related descriptors* such as creator ("maker"), style/period, technique, culture
3. *Physical descriptors* such as measurements, color
4. *Administrative descriptors* such as collection ID, rights, current location

In addition, we used the Art and Architecture Thesaurus (AAT) [1] as an ontology of concepts for describing art objects. Where possible, the value set of object-description properties is linked to relevant subhierarchies of AAT. For example, the property style/period is linked to three parts of the AAT hierarchy in which the approbate style and period concepts can be found. For a detailed discussion of the underlying ontologies, of the RDF Schema representation and of the ontology mapping, the reader is referred to the aforementioned publication [3]. For this study we made one amendment: we restricted the main type of the art object to "Windsor chair". AAT contains a hierarchy of Windsor chair types (in total 18 classes).

A snapshot of the annotation tool is shown in Fig. 1. The tab with "production-related descriptors" is shown, which contains six properties. The properties labeled with a "magnifier" icon (style/period, material and culture) are linked to hierarchies of AAT concepts.

3   Annotation Study Setup

Subjects. For this study we asked two "experts" and two "non-experts" to annotate the photographs. The experts were art historians working for a major auction house in

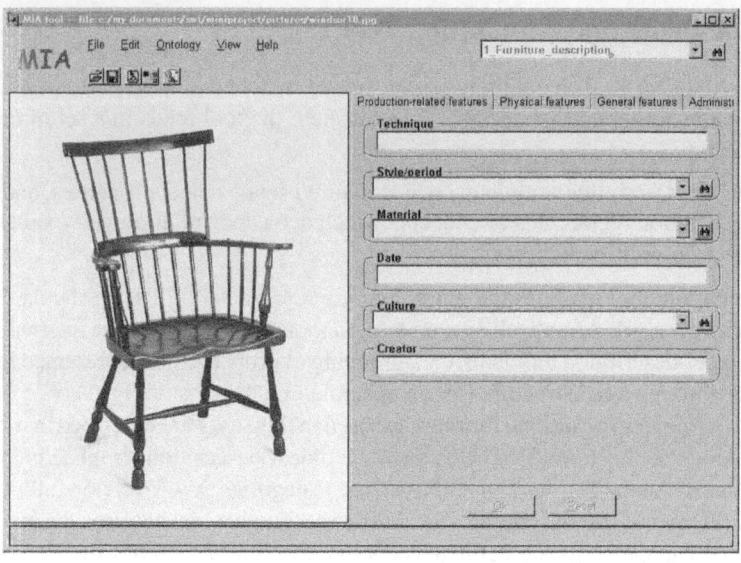

Fig. 1. Snapshot of the annotation tool for Windsor chairs. A the right, the tab for "production-related descriptors" is displayed

Amsterdam. It should be noted that they were not experts on Windsor chairs, although they had some basic knowledge about it. The non-experts were information-science students.

Data collection. Data collection consisted of four steps:

1. The subjects were asked to fill in a questionnaire containing in total eight questions about motivation, knowledge about the domain and computer/internet skills.
2. The non-expert subjects were given some background material on Windsor chairs and were asked to study this for 15 minutes. During the actual annotations they were allowed to consult this material. All subjects received a short oral instruction on the use of the annotation tool plus a one-page written instruction.
3. All subjects were presented with eight photographs of Windsor chairs and were asked to create an annotation for the image with the help of the tool. The first three photo's were used as a training set. The following process data were collected while the subjects annotated the second set of five photographs:
    (a) Time required per annotation object.
    (b) Remarks made by the subjects during annotation.
    (c) Resulting annotations (stored by the tool).
4. After annotating the photographs the subjects were asked to fill in a questionnaire about their experiences.

4   Results

Motivation, background knowledge and computer skills. The two experts were interested in Windsor chairs. They had some basic knowledge of Windsor chairs, but were not experts in this particular subfield. The non-experts had had no prior interest in antique furniture. Both had heard about "Rococo chairs", one about Windsor chairs, but they did not know exactly the meaning of these terms. All subjects worked with computers and internet browsers on a daily basis.

Annotation process. Table 1 lists the respective times required by the subjects to annotate the photographs. The annotation time decreases for successive images, which suggests a learning effect. The experts use considerably more time for annotations than the non-experts (34 and 30 minutes versus 15 and 21 minutes). During the annotation process, the

Table 1. Time in minutes required by the subjects for annotating five photographs of Windsor chairs (P1-P5), plus the average and total time per subject

Subject/ time	P1	P2	P3	P4	P5	Average time	Total time
Expert 1	10	6	5	7	6	6.8	34
Expert 2	8	9	5	4	4	6.0	30
Non-expert 1	4	3	3	3	2	3.0	15
Non-expert 2	6	5	4	3	3	4.2	21

experts said they found "the hierarchy" to be large and easy to understand. They made some remarks about the naming or ordering of properties, e.g. "First title and then type is more logical for us"and "Source is a bad name for origin". Some features of the photo were difficult to establish, given the available information. One expert said: "We could use such a tool. There is nothing like this yet." The non-experts mainly made remarks about the functionality of the tool ("how can/should I ....") and about the meaning of terms.

A review of the resulting annotations made clear that (as expected) the annotations by the experts are more detailed. They fill in more slot values of the object-description template and the slot values themselves are more specific (i.e., at a lower level of the AAT hierarchy).

In the post questionnaire, all subjects agreed with the statement "this is a comfortable annotation tool", and with the statement "the structure of the hierarchies is easy to understand". Two experts and one non-expert agreed with the statement "the photo properties form a logical set"; one non-expert disagreed. The two experts disagreed with the statement "it is difficult to make annotation errors in this way"; one non-expert agreed and the other was unsure. All subjects disagreed with the statement "most people would annotate the object in the same way as I did" and with the statement "One does not need much background knowledge to annotate such photographs".

5   Discussion

This small study does not warrant any strong conclusions. Some remarks can be made, however, on the questions raised in the introduction.

We were pleasantly surprised with the detailed comments made by the experts. They had no detailed knowledge about particular subject of Windsor chairs and seemed to use the ontology as a kind of on-line knowledge base. They clearly liked working with the tool and spent much time on the annotations. Such an annotation device surely is of potential value to them. The non-experts probably did not have enough domain knowledge to do the annotation job, but were not dissatisfied with the tool.

All subjects said that they expected other people might create different annotations. The damaging effect of this is probably less than in a pure keyword approach, due to the fact that some non-defined properties can be inferred. Also, if an indexer, e.g. due to lack of domain knowledge, annotates an object one level higher in the hierarchy, this only reduces the value of the annotation in a limited manner.

The subjects did not have many problems in understanding the hierarchy. The ontology structure makes clear which AAT concepts can be used for particular object features, which is likely to have helped here. The user interface of the tool can be improved, though. In the current tool, the interface is generated automatically from the ontology. This leads to non-logical ordering of tabs and of properties on a tab (see the remarks by the experts). It would have been better to introduce an explicit ontology-interface mapping into the tool, similar to the mechanisms in Protègè-2000 [5].

To get some (speculative) ideas about the added value of the semantic annotations for search purposes, we looked at a website for antique furniture, AntiqueArts.com, with in total 50K images. For general categories such as "chair" and "Windsor chair" retrieval is good (precision and recall > 0.8). However, for queries like "wooden chair" and "British chair", recall of the search engine drops to almost zero. Semantic annotation would have enabled inferences to improve this drastically.

Acknowledgments. This first author was supported by the ICES-KIS project "Multimedia Information Analysis" funded by the Dutch government.

References

1. Peterson, T.: Introduction to the Art and Architecture Thesaurus. Oxford University Press (1994) See also: http://shiva.pub.getty.edu.
2. Schreiber, A.T., Dubbeldam, B., Wielemaker, J., Wielinga, B.J.: Ontology-based photo annotation. IEEE Intelligent Systems **16** (2001) 66–74
3. Wielinga, B.J., Schreiber, A.T., Wielemaker, J., Sandberg, J.A.C.: From thesaurus to ontology. In Gil, Y., Musen, M., Shavlik, J., eds.: Proceedings 1st International Conference on Knowledge Capture, Victoria, Canada, New York, ACM Press (2001) 194–201
4. Committee, V.R.A.S.: VRA core categories, version 3.0. Technical report, Visual Resources Association (2000) URL: http://www.gsd.harvard.edu/ staffaw3/vra/vracore3.htm.
5. Grosso, W.E., Eriksson, H., Fergerson, R.W., Gennari, J.H., Tu, S.W., Musen, M.A.: Knowledge modeling at the millennium: The design and evolution of Protégé-2000. In: 12th Banff Workshop on Knowledge Acquisition, Modeling, and Management. Banff, Alberta. (1999)

SWAD-Europe:
Semantic Web Advanced Development in Europe
A Position Paper

D.Brickley[1], S.Buswell[2], B.M.Matthews[3], L.Miller[4], D. Reynolds[5],
and M.D.Wilson[3]

[1] World-Wide Web Consortium, INRIA, France
[2] Stilo Ltd., UK
[3] CLRC Rutherford Appleton Laboratory, UK
[4] ILRT, University of Bristol, UK
[5] Hewlett-Packard Laboratories, UK

Abstract. For the Web to reach its full potential, it must evolve into a Semantic Web, providing a universally accessible platform that allows data to be shared and processed by automated tools as well as by people. The 'Semantic Web' is a recent initiative of the World Wide Web Consortium (W3C), with the goal of extending the current Web to facilitate Web automation, universally accessible content, and the 'Web of Trust'. However, if the semantic web is going to be adopted and assimilated a clear migration path from present technologies to new ones is required. The SWAD-Europe project aims to support the W3C's Semantic Web initiative in Europe, providing targeted research, demonstrations and outreach to ensure Semantic Web technologies move into the mainstream of networked computing. The project aims to support the development and deployment of W3C Semantic Web specifications through implementation, research and testing activities.

1 Introduction

Tim Berners-Lee has provided a roadmap for developing the Semantic Web [TBL98] with a "pyramid of technologies", with XML at the base, through RDF, RDF Schemas, ontologies, queries and rules, logic and proof to arrive, with Digital signatures, at the Web Of Trust. This scheme has inspired a large amount of activity at various levels of the pyramid, including RDF [RDF] and RDF Schema [RDFS], the DAML+OIL initiative and a variety of other approaches which come under the W3C's Semantic Web Activity Domain. This work has been taken up in some practical applications, notably CC/PP for customising content to different devices, P3P for privacy preferences [P3P], and RSS [RSS] for site syndication. However, this ambitious body of work is in danger of passing the average web developer by. So far, the work undertaken has concentrated on solving the important technical questions underlying the semantic web, with not enough effort on providing complete and readily comprehensible tools and examples for the practical user. If semantic web technologies are going to be adopted as a normal and natural part of the next

I. Horrocks and J. Hendler (Eds.): ISWC 2002, LNCS 2342, pp. 409–413, 2002.

generation of the web, then an effort has to be made to provide such accessible material. A new European project, SWAD-Europe, seeks to fill this gap.

2   A Scenario-Led Perspective

As longstanding participants in the Semantic Web, XML and Web developer communities, the project team are familiar with a number of *'frequently asked questions'* that arise when considering Semantic Web technology. These come from technical, consumer, content creator and business perspectives, but a common theme recurs: *technology integration.*

"Which standard should I use?"

"How do use RDF with XML Schemas? "

"...or Web Services with Web Ontologies? ...MathML with RDF-rules?"

Such questions are often themselves a means to an end. The goal is typically not to integrate two different W3C data formats, but to complete some more specific task. Technology-oriented questions often mask an application-oriented need.

We often hear questions such as:

"I am re-engineering our Intranet and want a standards-based way of exchanging (amongst other things) 'organisational chart' information about departments and groups. The XML Schema Specification seems relevant, since we keep much of this data in relational databases, and tools exist to export data using XML Schema. Everybody recommends the use of XML, but there seem to be so many different ways of using it. The XML specification provides DTDs; there is also now an XML Namespaces specification, and a number of alternative XML Schema languages."

"Added to this, articles I read about the Semantic Web suggest I should be using an 'Ontology language' (instead?), based on RDF Schema and(/or) DAML+OIL. Since the information we are trying to represent is an organisational chart, we are also considering the use of SVG to create, exchange and edit this information. It is not clear which, if any, of these technologies are most appropriate to use, nor what the relationship between them is."

From the concerns of managers and technologists, content creators and policy makers, we note this same need. Web technology, and now Semantic Web technology in particular, presents a daunting array of tools, specifications and techniques. The full range of relevant technology, while in principle extremely powerful, also risks stifling or delaying innovation through providing *too much* to choose from.

3   The SWAD Project

While exaggerated here for effect, these concerns are real, current and addressable. To answer this, we need a combination of advanced technology development and a programme of documentation, demonstration, education and outreach.

Semantic Web Advanced Development for Europe (SWAD-Europe) aims to play a key role in the evolution of the Semantic Web, through education and outreach to developers, organisations and content creators; through Open Source implementation and testing, and through pre-consensus technology development to drive and inform the creation of new Semantic Web standards.

The overarching aim of the project is thus to provide, through all appropriate means, a body of answers to questions that have to date gone unanswered, and to foster grassroots communities within which such concerns are addressed. It is more important to offer clear answers to these questions than it is for us to write software or complex technical reports. The technical research and advanced development activities are a means to an end: facilitating wide-scale Semantic Web deployment. The project will therefore remain responsive to external developments (such as the appearance of unanticipated third-party work, software libraries etc.), refining the technical focus of the research to track the current state of the art, and to respond to the concerns of stakeholder communities.

The period 2002-2004 will see the first wave of mainstream Semantic Web applications. SWAD-Europe's role will be to ensure that the critical technology components required for widespread Semantic Web adoption are readily accessible to European industry, consumers, and developers. This involves finding and maintaining a balance between "in-house" Open Source tool development, community building, outreach and evangelism, combined with more technologically advanced research and analysis to support and field-test Semantic Web standards.

Goals of SWAD-Europe

- To implement scenario-led examples showing the integration of multiple Semantic Web technologies drawing practical use cases from industry, consumer, and developer perspectives.
- To develop a Semantic Web technology integration strategy that emphasises the utility of XML languages (such as SVG, HTML, MathML, XLink) as complementary rather than competing components of the Web.
- To ensure that the European developers, citizens and content creators are kept aware of Semantic Web technology for supporting universal accessibility, device independence and internationalisation.
- To ensure that European Community is kept aware of international best practice, and that best practice within Europe is recognised internationally.
- To undertake targeted research and development in support of these objectives, and in collaboration with the wider European developer community, W3C Member organisations, and related Open Source initiatives.

The SWAD-Europe project is designed to further the evolution of the Semantic Web through a combination of targeted research and community outreach, taking a set of use-case driven scenarios and illustrating how Semantic Web technologies relate to the practical needs of European consumers, business and content producers.

The most innovative aspect of this project lies in the combination of strategies that will be focussed on the problem. By ensuring that our research and development work is driven by scenario-led case studies, SWAD-Europe will provide the European community with a 'big picture' understanding of the Semantic Web, as well as with detailed knowledge of the tools and techniques that make it practically deployable.

4   Practical Steps towards the Semantic Web in Europe

The project will concentrate on the following areas.

Semantic Web Services.   Several aspects of the project address the need for convergence between the Semantic Web and Web Service perspectives. This is addressed at three levels: through demonstrating specific worked examples of Semantic Web Services such as those relating to Annotations and to Trust; through exploring options for technical convergence between RDF and Web Service specifications (e.g. W3C RDF and SOAP serialisation syntaxes); and through showing new functionality gained by the application of a Semantic Web approach to the creation, discovery and exploitation of Web Services.

XML / Semantic Web Integration. The project seeks to show significant progress towards the integration of Semantic Web technology (specifically RDF and Web Ontology languages) with the broader family of XML specifications. This includes the creation of strategies that allow knowledge represented diagrammatically (in SVG) to be made accessible to RDF tools and to non-visual user environments such as speech browsers and mobile phones. Similarly, combining MathML with RDF logic will progress the integration of mathematical information into the Semantic Web. Considering the amount of information currently represented in diagrams (e.g. PowerPoint) and spreadsheets (e.g. Excel), advances in these two content areas alone could expose vast amounts of structured information to Semantic Web tools.

APIs and Query Languages. The SWAD-Europe work on API and Query language convergence is intended to combine advances in technical knowledge with the rationalisation and documentation of deployed best practice. If the Semantic Web is to provide a stable platform for advanced information services, it is important to seek consensus amongst developers and application creators on basic functionality for query and data access. While this work will necessitate a certain amount of technical innovation, the emphasis here is on consolidating and stabilising the interface conventions that have emerged over the last 2-3 years amongst RDF developers.

Trust. SWAD-Europe includes research work focussed on issues of trust management for the Semantic Web. Building on earlier RDF-based work at W3C/MIT and elsewhere, this will include an analysis of the *Capabilities* and *Proof Carrying Authentication* approaches to trust, to digitally signed Semantic Web content, and to the creation of '*Web of Trust*' applications. The related work on annotations provides a practical, consumer-oriented test-bed for exploring the deployment of this technology.

Annotations and information quality. The developer community has for many years been exploring a variety of strategies for building Annotation systems for Web content. Recent RDF-based Annotation systems have shown the potential offered by Semantic Web technology in this area. The technical innovation targeted by SWAD-Europe is, again, centred around convergence, integration and scalability. Web Annotation systems will only realise their true potential when there is a large body of data accessible for applications to use. We therefore focus our efforts on the identification of common ground amongst current annotation systems, and on demonstrating systems that combine the best aspects of each. This is complemented by the workpackage on scalability, which addresses a need apparent from existing Annotations systems, the storage and query of large bodies of RDF data. Annotations also provide one of the project's application scenario areas, and as such will be the subject of documentation in the Education and Outreach work, and be the basis of worked examples for the work on queries, the API, trust and scalability.

Scalability. Scalability is a common concern amongst Web developers exploring Semantic Web technology. The project will identify and document a number of strategies and techniques for storing and querying large repositories of RDF data. This technical research will also seek to progress the state of the art in this area, through the exploration of schema-aware data storage and indexing systems.

Thesaurus management. Thesaurus and classification systems are a critical technology for the Semantic Web. They provide a bridge between traditional digital library applications and more complex Ontology-based Semantic Web systems. The need for classification and semantic-tagging was one of the prime motivations for the creation of RDF. As with Annotations, there is a significant body of knowledge in the Semantic Web developer community (and the project team) relating to the use of RDF with Thesaurus systems. Rather than seek a 'great leap forward' in the underlying approach, the innovation goal here is to innovate through consolidation. SWAD-Europe will provide a stable, well-documented approach to RDF Thesaurus deployment that will allow application developers and content producers to integrate established traditional digital library systems with other Semantic Web tools. The importance of multilingual thesauri in a European context motivates the focus on developing a language-tagged multilingual thesaurus system in this workpackage. Particularly in the context on non-linguistic content (e.g. Multimedia, especially digital images), the use of a multilingual thesaurus can provide a very cost-effective means to re-purpose content to new audiences across national and linguistic boundaries.

References

[TBL98] Berners-Lee (1998) *Semantic Web Road map*
         http://www.w3.org/DesignIssues/Semantic.html
 [RDF] Lassila O & Swick R (1999) *Resource Description Framework (RDF) Model and Syntax.* http://www.w3.org/RDF/Group/WD-rdf-syntax/
[RDFS] Guha L. & Brickley D. (2000). Resource Description Framework (RDF) Schema Specification   1.0   W3C   Candidate   Recommendation   27   March   2000 http://www.w3.org/TR/rdf-schema
 [RSS] RDF Site Summary (RSS) 1.0
         http://groups.yahoo.com/group/rss-dev/files/specification.html
 [P3P] Brian McBride, Rigo Wenning, Lorrie Cranor, *An RDF Schema for P3P* W3C Note 25 January 2002. http://www.w3.org/TR/p3p-rdfschema/

Preemptive Reification

Steven R. Newcomb

Coolheads Consulting
1527 Northaven Drive
Allen, Texas 75002 USA
srn@coolheads.com
http://www.coolheads.com

Abstract. It is useful to express the location of a node in a semantic graph in terms of a sequence of knowledge-bearing arcs that lead to the node from a node that is used as a point of reference. If the arcs on which such "graph-based addressing expressions" depend disappear, the expressions become invalid.

When an arc is reified as a node, the reified arc may or may not be removed. If it is not removed, the semantic graph may exhibit unnecessary complexity, ambiguity, and lack of parsimony. Alternatively, if the original arc is removed, the value of dependent graph-based addressing expressions may be lost.

For systems intended to support collaborative knowledge aggregation, such as the Semantic Web, one way to resolve this dilemma is to disallow "lazy" reification, and, in effect, preemptively reify everything that may, at any future time, require reification. Preemptively reified nodes can be "virtual" until they are actually needed, thus effectively maintaining parsimony.

The Reference Model of the Topic Maps paradigm, now under development in the ISO, shows how the need for "lazy" reification can be avoided by means of a fixed set of arc types and rules used to represent fully elaborated assertions.

1 Introduction

A demonstration of a certain critical difference between Topic Maps and RDF was Michael Sperberg-McQueen's wrap-up keynote at the Extreme Markup Languages Conference (www.extrememarkup.com) in August, 2001.

Sperberg-McQueen used colored ribbons to represent arcs, and several volunteers to represent nodes. He began by using a blue ribbon to represent the statement that "Tom buttered the bread".

```
Tom -------> the bread
       (blue
       ribbon)
```

"Now," Sperberg-McQueen said, "what if I want to say that Tom buttered the bread with a knife, on Friday? In order to attach the knife to this statement,

I. Horrocks and J. Hendler (Eds.): ISWC 2002, LNCS 2342, pp. 414–418, 2002.

I need a node for the knife, a node for 'on Friday', and I also need a node to represent the buttering itself. (There must be some sort of a 'buttering event' going on here.)"

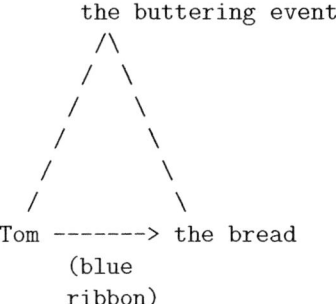

```
          the buttering event
               /\
              /  \
             /    \
            /      \
           /        \
          /          \
        Tom ------->  the bread
            (blue
            ribbon)
```

Now, with the buttering event in existence, it was possible to use a ribbon to connect it to the knife, and yet another ribbon to connect it to "on Friday".

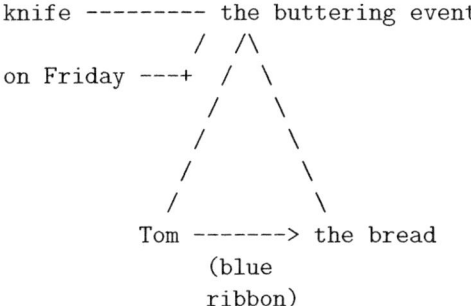

```
knife --------- the buttering event
                 / /\
on Friday ---+  /  \
               /    \
              /      \
             /        \
            /          \
          Tom ------->  the bread
              (blue
              ribbon)
```

Once "the buttering event" existed as a distinct node, it was no trouble at all to say anything about that event. However, *before* there was a buttering event, there was no way to say anything about it.

Once the "buttering event" existed, there was no further need for the original blue ribbon connecting Tom to the bread. In the interests of parsimony and the avoidance of ambiguity, the blue ribbon should disappear:

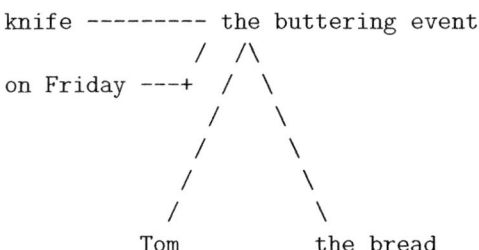

```
knife --------- the buttering event
                 / /\
on Friday ---+  /  \
               /    \
              /      \
             /        \
            /          \
          Tom          the bread
```

In Topic Maps, unlike RDF, there is no way to say "Tom buttered the bread" without creating an explicit "buttering event" – a "buttering association" between Tom and the bread. Instead of making a direct connection between Tom and the bread, the Topic Maps paradigm requires the creation of a "buttering event" node. In other words, what in RDF might have been an arc that might later be reified as a node only if and when necessary ("lazy reification"), in a Topic Map is "preemptively reified."

The advantage of preemptive reification is that we can always say something new about anything that already exists, without having to choose between the two evils of creating redundant connections, on the one hand, or invalidating existing lore about how things are connected together, on the other. If someone wants to say something about Tom's buttering of the bread, there is guaranteed to be something to which those remarks can be attached.

2   The Depth of Preemptive Reification

If we accept the idea of forbidding lazy reification, and demanding some degree of preemptive reification, we must also accept that there is some level of recursion below which reification – or rather "reification *in situ*[1]" – is forbidden.

Is it advisable, or even practical, to forbid *in situ* reification at a specific level of recursion? The Topic Maps Reference Model answers this question affirmatively. It uses the yardstick of "substantiveness with respect to the semantics of the assertion" to justify its decisions as to the level at which further *in situ* reification is forbidden. This doctrine of substantiveness is intuitively satisfactory when it is applied in such a way that, for each remaining "unreifiable" arc, there is no reason to talk about it other than to discuss the Reference Model itself. In other words, in the Topic Maps Reference Model, *in situ* reification does not occur when its only conceivable purpose would be to allow assertions to be made about the subterranean mechanics of the graphic representation of an assertion.

Before the various components of an assertion can be discussed, it's necessary to introduce a few of the basic concepts of Topic Maps.

At the Reference Model level, a topic map consists of nodes that reify **subjects** ("subjects of conversation" – specific semantics, ideas, concepts, etc.), and arcs. There are exactly four arc types.[2] Some subjects are **assertions**. An assertion is reified by a node that serves as certain specific ends of a specific set of arc types. Assertions are strongly-typed relationships between subjects; the

---

[1] In Topic Maps, literally anything – any subject of any kind, without exception – can be reified as a node. Even an arc that is non-reifiable according to the Topic Maps Reference Model is reifiable. The kind of reification that is forbidden by the Topic Maps Reference Model, below a certain "floor" level, is a specialized kind of reification, *in situ* reification, in which the reifying node literally replaces what would otherwise be an arc in exactly the same place (*"in situ"*) in the graph. In other words, an *in situ* reifying node will always necessarily be encountered in the course of traversing the path described by the arc that has been replaced by a node and two new arcs.

[2] Since the "arcs" used to describe the Reference Model are all bidirectional, eight distinct arc types are required in order to describe the Reference Model in RDF terms.

subjects related by an assertion are called "**role players**" in the assertion. Each played **role** is also a subject. An assertion can optionally be an instance of an **assertion pattern**, which is, like everything else in Topic Maps, a subject. For each role defined by an assertion pattern, there can optionally be a set of **role player constraints**. In addition, an assertion has one or more **scope**s, each of which is a set of subjects; each scope is a subject. (Scopes are used as a kind of shorthand, to qualify the semantics of an assertion with a level of specificity that would be burdensome to handle by means of traditional subtyping.)

In a topic map, there is a one-to-one correspondence between subjects and nodes; every node is the surrogate for exactly one unique subject. At the usual, application-defined level at which "statements" are made in RDF, "assertions" are made in Topic Maps. However, because of preemptive reification, scoping, the more detailed nature of assertions, and the fact that assertions are n-ary and n-directional, Topic Maps "assertions" are not exactly the same as RDF "statements". Several RDF statements are required in order to represent a single Topic Maps assertion. The translation of an RDF statement into a Topic Maps assertion is an up-translation.

2.1   Assertions and Role Players

It is beyond the scope of this position paper to survey the Topic Maps Reference Model,[3] but a description of one aspect of it should be sufficient to illustrate how the yardstick of "substantiveness with respect to the semantics of the assertion" can be used to determine where the "floor" of reification is.

The following elaboration of Sperberg-McQueen's example shows the two roles involved in a "buttering event": the "butterer" role and the "buttered" role.

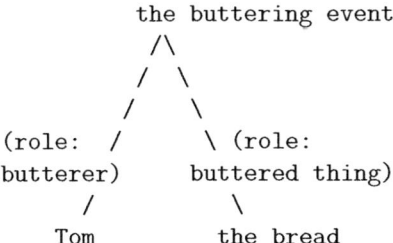

We may wish to make assertions about all of the following substantive aspects of the buttering event:

– The buttering event assertion (node A in the diagram below),
– the role of "butterer" in any buttering event assertion (node R1), and the role of "buttered thing" (R2),
– Tom himself (X1) and the bread itself (X2), and

---

[3] ...and, in any case, the Topic Maps Reference Model is a work in progress.

– the fact that Tom plays the butterer role in this assertion (C1),[4] and the fact that the bread plays the buttered role (C2).

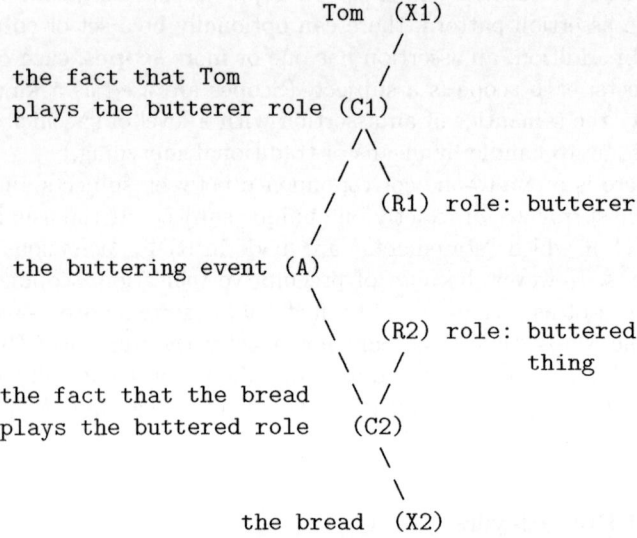

```
                        Tom   (X1)
                         /
                        /
 the fact that Tom     /
 plays the butterer role (C1)
                       /\
                      /  \
                     /    (R1)  role: butterer
                    /
 the buttering event (A)
                     \
                      \    (R2)  role: buttered
                       \  /            thing
 the fact that the bread  \ /
 plays the buttered role   (C2)
                            \
                             \
                 the bread   (X2)
```

None of the remaining arcs can conceivably be interesting *from the perspective of the substance of the buttering event assertion*. It is hard to imagine why anyone who is more interested in the buttering event than in the underlying mechanics of assertions in topic maps would ever want to make assertions about:

arc A-C1 The aspect of this assertion that the aspect of this assertion that Tom plays the butterer role is one of the casting aspects of this assertion.

arc C1-X1 The aspect of this assertion that it is Tom who plays the butterer role in the aspect of this assertion that Tom plays the butterer role.

arc C1-R1 The aspect of this assertion that it is the "butterer" role that is the role aspect of the aspect of this assertion that Tom plays the butterer role.

3   Parsimony

The Semantic Web's ability to protect the value of investments made in graph-based addressing expressions may be critically important, but so is parsimony. Fortunately, if there are no explicit assertions about them, it won't be necessary for Topic Maps systems to physically instantiate every preemptively reified node, as long as such systems behave in the same way that they would have behaved if such nodes actually existed. The important thing is to agree that these preemptively reified nodes *virtually* exist, even when nobody has yet made assertions about them.

---

[4] The letter *C* here is a mnemonic for the idea of *casting*, a metaphor drawn from the jargon of theatrical productions. A *C* node always represents the fact that a specific role player has been cast in a specific role in a specific assertion.

Four Steps Towards the Widespread Adoption of a Semantic Web

Brian McBride

Hewlett Packard Laboratories, Filton Road, Bristol, BS12 6QZ

Abstract. This paper suggests four steps towards the realization of a semantic web. Promotion of the idea should be based on practical application. There is need for the immediate development of practical demonstration applications. Simplicity and tolerance of error should be prime targets of research and development. An Open Source project to develop and populate a framework of tools and applications should be started.

1 Introduction

The profile of the semantic web has increased over the past year. Higher visibility attracts both supporters and critics. Expectations have been set by articles such as that in the Scientific American[1]. Failure to deliver that vision or replace it with something similarly attractive will lead to a perception of failure. This paper describes four steps that might be taken to facilitate delivery of a semantic web. It is not suggested that these are sufficient, or even necessary. It is suggested that they are helpful.

2 Promote Practical Applications

Google classified last year's SWWS workshop under Computers> Artificial Intelligence . This year it is Science > Math > Logic and Foundations. Semanticweb.org is classified as Computers> Artificial Intelligence> Knowledge Representation. The perception that the semantic web is concerned with artificial intelligence is not helpful to its widespread adoption in the IT industry.

This perception is understandable. The semantic web is often presented as the technology that will achieve marvelous things, exemplified perhaps by a scene from "Star Cops", a 1980's television program:

> The workaholic hero Nathan is suspended from duty and decides to take a holiday. He calls across the room to his PDA and instructs it to get him two tickets for the Milan opera. A short time later the PDA replies that Nathan is booked on the next shuttle back to earth, on a fast train to Milan and into his favourite hotel for three nights. He has to two tickets to La Traviata on Saturday night.

Much of the excitement and motivational power of such scenarios come from the handling of speech, natural language processing, general purpose problem solving,

I. Horrocks and J. Hendler (Eds.): ISWC 2002, LNCS 2342, pp. 419–422, 2002.
© Springer-Verlag Berlin Heidelberg 2002

scheduling, common sense reasoning and other features commonly associated with intelligence. These are not what the semantic web is about.

The semantic web is about creating an infrastructure in which information, from a variety of sources, can be integrated on demand to achieve some task. The semantic web provides mechanisms that enable access to and integration of information. Data is not the same thing as information. Data becomes information when it can be understood. Data with associated metadata to describe its meaning, becomes information that can be processed by a computer.

An intelligent agent will find access to such an infrastructure useful in accomplishing its goals. Until such agents are available however, this infrastructure will be very useful to everyday implementers of information systems using conventional programming techniques. Information integration is a key problem for many IT managers. Technology that will ease that problem is valuable.

Consider a simple example, a servlet, to display the members of a mailing list. The servlet first sends a query to the mailing list server, and receives in response an RDF graph that lists each member of the mailing list and their email address. It then sends the graph to an LDAP server with a request to add any information it has about any resources in the graph. The LDAP server, knowing that an email address uniquely identifies a person, can fill in the names, locations, URL's of home pages, link to the corporate organization chart etc and return the augmented graph to the servlet, which transforms it into a pleasant human readable representation. All it took to get the information was two simple RDF queries to the (appropriately augmented) servers.

The integration of information is possible because there is a standard syntax for the exchange of information, a global naming scheme that the systems share, a shared means of describing the characteristics of information (email address is a unique property) and a schema so that the servlet developer knows how to turn the information received into a presentable form. This ability to integrate disparate information sources is a clear commercial justification for the development of a semantic web.

3 Develop Applications Now

The specification of RDF, possibly the bottom layer of the semantic web, has been available since 1999. There are widespread applications that use it; Mozilla; RedHat's Update Agent, RSS and others. What is disappointing, indeed worrying, about these applications, is they do not demonstrate the advantages claimed for the semantic web, or at least not the advantages claimed by this author.

The first web, had not only freely available tools which folks could use to learn and experiment, it also had many examples of cool things to do, demonstrating its use and usefulness. These examples, as well as encouraging others to copy them, also stimulated innovation in the use of the technology. Innovation in the use of the web has been far greater than in its underlying technology. HTML and HTTP have not changed that much from their original form, but a considerable fraction of the planet has set about doing something original with them. Much of this innovation was in content, but it did lead also to demand for improvements in the technology.

The semantic web community should now be doing the same. Enough of the technology is available to create applications that demonstrate its value. Developing such applications will persuade the skeptical, stimulate innovation and speak most clearly of the value the semantic web can bring.

4   Simple and Tolerant of Error

HTML is simple, and was even simpler when the web was young. Web browsers are tolerant of error. They will try to do something sensible with whatever HTML they encounter. As a result, users in the early days of the web could learn to create web pages by cribbing from existing pages; it was easy to guess what the various bits of markup meant. The tolerance of the browsers ensured that it didn't matter much if the author of the content made some mistakes, there was a good chance the browser would do something acceptable with it. Inexpert users were able to be successful quickly, and thrilled with that success, were motivated to learn more and develop more sophisticated content.

Some argue that this tolerance was a mistake; that it caused many problems that were hard to resolve. But those who argue this are usually computer scientists for whom it probably did cause many problems that were hard to resolve. Users on the other hand don't complain that they did not get enough error messages. The simpler and more tolerant of error a system is, the more rapid and more widespread its adoption is likely to be.

This author recently wrote an RDF schema for a W3C specification. This simple task turned out to be harder than expected, even for someone with a good understanding of RDF and RDF schema. The lesson to be learned is that good schemas are hard to write; even for experts; even when the underlying data model is already done.

Unless we are willing to accept that schemas will only be written by a select few, well trained and expert in the art, an acceptance that contradicts the essence of the principles of the web and immediately places limits on its rate of growth, we have to accept that flawed information models will be prevalent in the semantic web. Models will use literals where they should use resources, will use instances where they should use classes, will confuse numbers and numerals and contain many other flaws.

Delivering a semantic web requires the technology be simple to reduce the possibility of error, and tolerant where there is error.

5   Open Source

The web has always been blessed by the availability of free, high quality software. The Mosaic browser, the CERN server, the Netscape browser/html editor, Internet Explorer, the Apache server and Mozilla have all meant that it was easy and inexpensive for individuals and organizations to first experiment and then to create production quality content and services. Cost was not a barrier to adoption by providers or users.

Commercial organizations like to dominate an infrastructure. The economic power this realizes has been apparent for over a century. Dominance of an infrastructure by a single organization can lead to the stifling of innovation. What would the web be like if its evolution had been controlled by a single corporation?

The Open Source community is enjoying some success in resisting the commercial domination of infrastructure. Where OS/2 failed to challenge the dominance of the Windows operating system, linux is succeeding. Apache is the most common web server on the internet. This should not be surprising. Open Source has a philosophy that combines collaboration and excellence. It is well suited to the development of infrastructure where it is in the best interests of all to cooperate and avoid dominance by a few commercial interests.

The semantic web community, though growing, is small. It cannot afford to use its limited development resources in wasteful duplication. How many RDF parsers does the world really need? There have been early experiments in the design of the lower layers of the technology. Enough has been learned to suggest that we have reached the time to create and populate an open source framework of tools for the semantic web. This "Apache" for the Semantic Web could be an independent organization, or could be born within the Apache organization itself as a peer of projects like Jakarta. Such an initiative would benefit all. The cost barrier to adoption of semantic web technology would be reduced facilitating early experiment and innovation in application development. The research community would also benefit, having a framework of tools to facilitate their research and into which to deliver the fruits of their labours. All can feel secure that no commercial organization can hope to attain a position of control of the infrastructure.

6   Conclusion

If a semantic web is to be successful and achieve wide adoption, its supporters should:
- emphasize practical applications
- software must be simple and tolerant of error
- develop applications now
- Develop a common open source infrastructure of high quality References

References

[1] Berners-Lee, T., Hendler, J., Lassila, O., : The Semantic Web. Scientific American, (2001)

Three Implementations of SquishQL,
a Simple RDF Query Language

Libby Miller[1], Andy Seaborne[2], and Alberto Reggiori[3]

[1] ILRT, Bristol University, UK
libby.miller@bristol.ac.uk
[2] Hewlett-Packard Laboratories, Bristol, UK
andy_seaborne@hp.com
[3] Web Weaving Internet Engineering, Arnhem, The Netherlands
areggiori@webweaving.org

Abstract. RDF provides a basic way to represent data for the Semantic Web. We have been experimenting with the query paradigm for working with RDF data in semantic web applications. Query of RDF data provides a declarative access mechanism that is suitable for application usage and remote access. We describe work on a conceptual model for querying RDF data that refines ideas first presented in at the W3C workshop on Query Languages [14] and the design of one possible syntax, derived from [7], that is suitable for application programmers. Further, we present experience gained in three implementations of the query language.

Introduction

An SQL-ish query language for RDF provides consistent, human-understandable, access to repositories of semantic data, whether stored files or large databases, enabling application programmers to create semantic web applications quickly. SquishQL syntax and model is designed to reflect RDF's graph syntax, and uses SQL-like constructs so that application developers can pick it up as quickly as possible.

As application programmers ourselves, working with RDF, we have implemented query software because we needed it to use RDF effectively. RDF APIs provide a high degree of control at a fine level of granularity that supports a range of programming paradigms; query is one such paradigm which is coarser-grained and useful when there is large amounts of data with semi-regular structure. The query paradigm makes for more intuitive access with a shorter learning curve, as well as making access possible in situations where there is a high operation overhead, for example, over remote access protocols such as SOAP.

The query paradigm is also suitable for scripting environments, enabling the creation of RDF-driven applications quickly and easily. Reduced "time-to-deploy" is an important issue in enabling the semantic web.

In this paper, we describe the conceptual framework for the query language: this is closely tied to the RDF graph, providing a base level of query of RDF data. We relate this work to other systems, then describe a syntax for our query language suitable for application programmers. We describe our experience with three different

I. Horrocks and J. Hendler (Eds.): ISWC 2002, LNCS 2342, pp. 423–435, 2002.
© Springer-Verlag Berlin Heidelberg 2002

implementations and note experiments in providing inference support without modifying the query language itself.

A Query Framework for RDF

The RDF Model and Syntax specification [15], which has been formalized in the proposed model theory for RDF [16], makes the graph the primary syntax for RDF. This graph is a partially labeled, directed graph where the node labels are URIs or literals, and the arc labels are URIs. No two nodes can have the same label; there cannot be two arcs with the same label between the same pair of nodes. Not all nodes need be labeled giving rise to bNodes (anonymous nodes) which have no URI label. The N-Triples syntax [22] records such a graph as a list of its edges.

In [14], a query model for RDF is proposed in which the query is an RDF model, where any resource, property or literal can be replaced by a variable.

The result is a pair: a subgraph of the target knowledge base that matches the query and a table of sets of legal values for the variables. In addition, the paper notes that RDF schema constructs such as *subClassOf* and *subPropertyOf* provide some specific inferencing. Their query proposal is to provide a query parameter which specifies whether the query is on the underlying RDF graph or the deductive closure of the graph, thought of as a knowledge base.

Such a query model provides a baseline query model for the semantic web – the query language works against the RDF model without any higher-level constructs in the language for inference or interpretation. While an RDF model implementation may itself provide additional features, this approach to query works by assuming any feature (such as inferencing) manifests itself as an RDF graph that can be accessed by some graph API.

The SquishQL Model of Query

The RDF Working Group has defined a graph syntax as the primary representation of the conceptual model for RDF. Concrete syntaxes in XML and N-Triples are defined. We see that the query form proposed in [14] is a fixed-sized graph pattern over the syntax of the RDF graph where the pattern is formed from variables for nodes (labeled or unlabeled), arcs or literals. This matching does not depend on the graph interpretation. SquishQL adds to this baseline query model, introducing filter functions over the variables, which restrict the values that the variables can take. These filter functions do not change the expressive power of the graph pattern.

The pattern language is formed from:
- Triple patterns, which describe one edge of the graph, allowing either a variable or an explicit value for each of subject, predicate and object. In the syntax below, variables are indicated by '?': the most general pattern is (?x, ?y, ?z) which matches any triple.
- Graph patterns, which describe the graph shape, expressed as a collection of triple patterns. In the syntax below, there is a list of triple patterns which are interpreted

as the conjunction of the triple patterns. This list is an edge-list of the graph pattern.

This results in quite a weak pattern language but it does ensure that in a result all variables are bound (there is no disjunction). The language does not express transitivity or other forms of unknown length paths in the graph.

The filter functions are Boolean expressions over the values of URIs or literals.

We return all the possible ways the graph pattern and filter functions can be matched against the graph. Because the language does not have disjunction or repetition, we only need to return the values for the variables, and not the particular subgraph that caused each possible match, because substitution of the values for the variables into the original query is sufficient to identify the particular sub graph (set of edges) that caused a particular match.

Variables and bNodes
A variable in a query is not the same as a bNode (an unlabeled "blank" node in an RDF graph). Although bNodes are treated as existentially bound variables in the proposed model theory for RDF there are some differences from the variables in edge patterns:
1. The set of variables in a query is distinct from the set of bNodes in the data graph.
2. Query variables match nodes; hence can match resource URIs or literals or graph bNodes.
3. Query variables can label arcs, hence can match property URIs.

RDF as N-Triples
If we think of the RDF model as a table of triples in N-Triples form, then the subgraph pattern becomes a list of triples, except with the possibility of variables. Then, both triple patterns and Boolean expressions are constraints on the results of a query. Each of the constraints must be true, either because a triple pattern becomes a triple to be found in the RDF graph, or because a Boolean expression evaluates to true.

Other Systems

There are a number of other query languages of RDF available, some of which have been in use for several years. One of the earliest was rdfDB [7] and this is the basis for SquishQL syntax. It is a simple graph-matching query language designed for use in the rdfDB database system. It differs slightly syntactically from SquishQL and also does not contain the constraints on the variables used by SquishQL. It returns results as a table.

Algae [6] is another early query language for RDF. It uses an S-expression syntax to do graph matching. It is used to power the W3C's Annotea annotations system [12], and other software at the W3C. It is written in Perl, and can be used with an SQL database. It returns a set of triples in support of each result. One of our implementations (RDQL/Jena) does retain the triples used to bind variables and the application can access this information.

RQL [9,8] is a combined RDF store and query system. It also provides a schema validating parser and has a syntax targeted at RDFS[17] applications. It can perform similar queries to SquishQL, with the added power of support for transitive closure on RDFS subclass and subproperty. This is also the query language used by Sesame [10].

The EDUTELLA system [11] provides a hierarchy of query languages: the lowest level, RDF-QEL-1 provides a graph pattern language, expressed as an RDF model.

Other systems with similar query languages include RDFQL [20] and one described in [13]. RDFQL combines a rules language with query; the underlying database system interprets the rules. The language in [13] has syntactic support for regular expression path expressions.

SquishQL - A Textual Language

In this section, we describe a syntax that has been implemented in at least three systems [1,2,3]. The syntax described below is just one possible syntax for the abstract query model outlined. We have chosen to define a syntax for the application developer (a person). Other syntactic forms, more suited to production by tools, such as RDF or XML, will also be needed; see [23] for an experiment in a RuleML syntax.

In SquishQL, there are two classes of constraints; patterns and filter expressions. Patterns are generative (they create bindings) and the filters are restrictive (they remove possibilities). SquishQL separates these into the WHERE clause (generative) and the AND clause (restrictive).

Some query systems have followed the tradition of having predicate first. We have chosen instead to mimic N-Triples syntax and specify triple patterns as subject-predicate-object.

```
SELECT ?title
FROM http://example.com/xmleurope/presentations.rdf
WHERE
    (?doc, <dc:title>, ?title) ,
    (?doc, <rdf:type>, <foaf:Document>)
USING
  dc   FOR <http://purl.org/dc/elements/1.1/>,
  foaf FOR <http://xmlns.com/foaf/0.1/>,
  rdf  FOR <http://www.w3.org/1999/02/22-rdf-syntax-ns#>
```

Fig. 1. Query: Find me the titles of documents in
http://example.com/xmleurope/presentations.rdf

In SQL, a database is a closed world; the FROM clause identifies the tables in the database; the WHERE clause identifies constraints and can be extended with AND. By analogy, the web is the database and the FROM clause identifies the RDF models. Variables are introduced with a leading '?' and URIs are quoted with <> [19]; unquoted URIs can be used where there is no ambiguity.

SELECT Clause
>   Identifies the variables to be returned to the application. If not all the
>   variables are needed by the application, then specifying the required results
>   can reduce the amount of memory needed for the results set as well as
>   providing information to a query optimizer.

FROM Clause
>   The FROM clause specifies the model by URI.

WHERE Clause
>   Specifies the graph pattern as the conjunction of the list of triple patterns.

AND Clause
>   Specifies the Boolean expressions over values of URIs and literals, including
>   arithmetic comparisons, and boolean expressions, including disjunction and
>   negation.

USING Clause
>   A way to shorten the length of URIs. As SquishQL is likely to be written by
>   people, this mechanism helps make for an easier to understand syntax. This
>   is not a namespace mechanism; instead, it is simply an abbreviation
>   mechanism for long URIs by defining a string prefix.

The RDF specification defined the form of containers and of reification. There is no
explicit syntax for these in SquishQL. As shown in the examples, this does not affect
retrieving data from containers, but the query can become cumbersome. Similarly,
with reification, the lack of syntactic support can make expressing some queries
awkward.

```
SELECT ?y
WHERE (<http://somewhere.com/aBag>, ?x, ?y)
AND ! ( ?x eq <rsyn:type> && ?y eq <rsyn:Bag>)
USING
  rsyn FOR http://www.w3.org/1999/02/22-rdf-syntax-ns#
```

Fig. 2. Extract the contents of a bag

Query Evaluation Issues

A number of issues arise in defining the evaluation of a query:
1. Treatment of anonymous nodes, which are scoped to the document containing the
   syntactic RDF.
2. Expression evaluation in the absence of formal datatyping in RDF.

Anonymous Nodes
In general, it is not possible to write SquishQL syntax queries that contain bNodes as
values in triple patterns because they have no syntactic representation. Some systems
manifest bNodes as automatically generated URIs and could have queries with
bNodes. In RDQL/Jena, it is possible to construct queries through a programmatic
API, not just via a parser, so bNodes, as Jena resources, can be included. This has an

impact on remote operation where queries are passed to a server for execution – this requires a serialisable form.

Data Types and Filter Evaluation
RDF does not define a type system for literals. However, to provide a range of operators for Boolean filters, we have to decide on the type for a literal. This is currently done by attempting to parse the literal during query execution as the type required by the expression (number, string etc).

Inkling

Inkling [1,5] is a Java™ implementation of SquishQL created to be API and database-independent for testing the usefulness of SquishQL for comparatively small-scale projects. The aim was to have a query engine that could be used with almost any RDF database implementation written in Java, and which could be used for experimenting with the SquishQL query language.

API and Database Independence
Inkling can query most Java RDF database implementations and most Java RDF APIs, whether the implementations are in memory or use some form of persistent storage. For Inkling to be able to talk to an RDF database or service, that service just has to implement an extremely basic interface consisting of a single method. This method is a three-place search method:

```
queryDatabase(subject, predicate, object)
```

where any argument can be null, which was the lowest common denominator of methods supported by the APIs examined (Jena [4] and Stanford RDF [18] API).

This provides a generic interface to database storage. This mechanism allows the storage subsystem to make decisions about access to stored triples. Different database layouts can make different tradeoffs between efficient indexing structures and increased storage costs. There are some problems with the simplicity of the interface, for example, if there are optimizations the database can perform for certain kinds of queries such as reification, bags and sequences, then this per-triple interface won't be useful.

This is the simplest means for accessing the database. Where optimizations are possible, for example if the underlying database supports a similar query language, efficiencies can be made by passing the entire query to the underlying database.

JDBC Interfaces
Inkling uses the JDBC interfaces to make SquishQL queries. This enables the implementation to be fairly independent of the database to be searched, and also means that Java programmers will be familiar with the means of accessing the queries.

Example

One way we have used Inkling is as an access mechanism for a testbed of information about people, RDFWeb (http://rdfweb.org). The test data consists of files containing information about people, the people they know, images of them, and information about documents they have created, rather like homepages. The files are created by many different people, and may contain arbitrary information from any vocabulary. Much of the data is in the experimental 'foaf' (friend of a friend) vocabulary, which is continually expanding as people see the need for other characteristics.

Inkling enables the information to be harvested from the web, so that the database can be rebuilt at the frequency desired. Then the information can be pulled out of the database as it is required. RDFWeb displays a person-centric view of the data, where queries pull out information about a particular person within a server-side JSP page.

```
SELECT ?name, ?mbox
WHERE
   (?libby, <foaf:mbox>,
            <mailto:libby.miller@bristol.ac.uk>) ,
   (?libby, <foaf:knows>, ?someone) ,
   (?someone, <foaf:mbox>, ?mbox) ,
   (?someone, <foaf:name>, ?name)
USING foaf for <http://xmlns.com/foaf/0.1/>
```

Fig. 3. Query: Get names and email addresses of the people that the person with email address libby.miller@bristol.ac.uk knows.

This works well if all the people in the database have both mailboxes and names associated with them, but will fail if the data is inconsistent, which it may be, since this is a distributed database with many authors. There is no way of saying that a subquery is optional in SquishQL: a safer course may be to query for the email addresses of people known, and then query for their names.

```
SELECT ?title, ?description, ?name
WHERE
  (?libby, <foaf:mbox>,
            <mailto:libby.miller@bristol.ac.uk>) ,
  (?paper, <dc:contributor>, ?libby),
  (?paper, <dc:title>, ?title) ,
  (?paper, <dc:description>, ?description) ,
  (?paper, <dc:contributor>, ?someone) ,
  (?someone, <foaf:name>, ?name)
USING foaf for <http://xmlns.com/foaf/0.1/> ,
      dc   for <http://purl.org/dc/1.1/>
```

Fig. 4. Query: Get me the titles and descriptions of papers that Libby has written, and the names of anyone who wrote the paper with her.

This query will pull out anything to which the person with email address libby.miller@bristol.ac.uk is a contributor where there is at least one other contributor with an email address - although this could be libby.miller@bristol.ac.uk. Where there is more than one contributor, the result set will be repetitious: it will pull out the title and description again for each contributor. Similarly, if a contributor has more than one name in the database it will pull out the title and description again for that. Finally, if libby has done a paper on her own, and is therefore listed as the dc:creator rather than the dc:contributor then this query will not get that information. There is no way of writing 'or' of graph patterns in SquishQL, for reasons of simplicity and tractability. Instead one would have to make two queries to access this information.

These types of queries can be made using one or more RDF files from an in-memory database, or from an SQL backed database. Because of the flexibility of query it is a simple matter to alter the information shown: if a great deal of data about, say, eye colour, is made available, then it is simple to add an additional query into the Java Server page.

RDQL

RDQL[2] is an implementation of SquishQL for the Jena RDF toolkit[4]. Jena is a collection of RDF tools written in Java that includes:
- A Java API
- ARP: An RDF parser
- RDQL: A query system
- Support classes for DAML+OIL ontologies
- Persistent storage based on BerkeleyDB.
- Persistent storage based on various relational databases.

Jena and RDQL
RDQL allows queries to be made on RDF models from Java on any Jena model so the query system is independent of the storage implementation and of the RDF syntax. RDQL can be mixed with Jena API calls because a query returns the underlying Jena objects that satisfy the query so the Resources, Properties or Literals retrieved can be used for model update or other API calls. Combining programming paradigms can be useful; for example, this has been used in calculating RDF Schema closures, where each rule condition is a query and each additional statement is added though the Jena API.

Execution
In order to reduce the amount of working memory needed by a query, the execution of a query is carried out in parallel with the application consuming the results. In the simple query engine currently supplied in the Jena toolkit, there are three threads, one is used for matching triple patterns against the model in a depth-first traversal, one is used for filter evaluation and one is the application thread that issued the query and is processing the results. The bounded buffers between the threads control the query execution so that the query execution engine is limited in how far ahead of the application processing. The amount of working memory needed is independent of the size of the data in the model, but not the query. If the application does not process results fast enough, the query system will pause when buffers become full.

Implementation in Jena

The triple pattern matcher uses a similar scheme to Inkling. the main Jena operation used takes a description of the triples used, in the form of fixing the Resources, Properties or Literals or leaving that item unconstrained. All the current implementations of a Jena model provide indexes by Subject, Predicate or Object so access is efficient.

However, the filter expressions used to restrict the values are not passed down to the underlying storage. RDF does not define type information so general stores hold only strings and RDQL interprets whether a value is, say, an integer, based on whether it can interpret it as such when filtering a result generated by the triple matcher.

An Inferencing Store for Jena

An experimental inferencing store based on Prolog has been developed. This inferencing system has been used for queries of RDFS [17] data. The properties *subClassOf* and *subPropertyOf* are made to behave transitively and the property type *rdf:type* returns inferred types of resources as well as the declared types. Like RQL, we have chosen to redefine the standard properties *subClassOf* and *subPropertyOf*: although this is done as part of the model, not as part of the query language. An alternative design would be to create new properties for the transitive relationships, *anySubClassOF*, *anySubPropertyOf*, leaving the original properties for access to the original data.

```
SELECT ?x
WHERE (<http://somewhere/resource>, <rdf:type>, ?x)
USING
   rdf FOR <http://www.w3.org/1999/02/22-rdf-syntax-ns#>
```

Fig. 5. Query: return all the types for the resource

RDFStore

RDFStore [3] implements the SquishQL language to query RDF repositories directly from Perl. The toolkit consists of a Perl API, a streaming SiRPAC parser and a generic hashed data storage custom designed for the RDF model. The storage subsystem allows transparently storage and retrieval of RDF nodes, arcs and labels, either from an in-memory structure, from the local disk or from a very fast and scaleable remote storage [24]. The latter is a fast networked TCP/IP based transactional storage library that uses multiple single key hash based BerkeleyDB files together with an optimized network routing daemon with a single thread/process per database. The data indexing model is general enough to retrieve RDF subgraphs and properties using free-text and statement-group sensible matching. Each literal value gets indexed in its full Unicode [25] form and in-memory data structures or objects can also be serialised on disk. The API supports bNodes (blank Nodes or anonymous-resources) but the storage internally does treat them like any other resource. Being in Perl, an untyped language, the toolkit at the moment does not treat typed literals in any special way; all query filtering operations on the values are processed using pure Perl regular expressions and eval constructs.

Running RDF Queries with RDFStore

The API implements the Stanford RDF API [18] and supports the basic three-place search method (or triple matching) which is the atomic query construct available; each result set consists of an RDF model which can be further queried, serialized or enumerated in its component statements. A much more property-centric programming interface to an RDF repository is provided via the RDQL driver; by running an SQL-like query on an actual storage it is possible to access the single nodes, arcs and labels as resources or literals. Such a query paradigm being much more consistent and human-understandable, has proved to be very practical and flexible compared to other similar approaches. Once the query has been carried out, the result set is actually being stored into a Perl hash data structure and further processed with common programming constructs.

Query Processing and Execution

The query processing and execution is performed on the client side and the approach is fundamentally different from other similar techniques such as rdfdb [7] where the query parsing, processing and execution is done entirely on the server side. Having it running on the client makes the DBMS server back-end much more generic and lightweight; then by using some kind of compression of data indexes both storage and network traffic can be reduced.

RDFStore contains a hand-written top-down LL(1) parser for the RDQL syntax with extensions to the basic pattern language to run free-text selection of RDF graph elements. When a query is processed, it gets parsed into an in-memory structure that is then used to run the actual query on the back-end database; the RDQL query internally is implemented as a join of a series of basic three-place searches on the RDF graph. Then the constraints are applied and the actual results returned to the user. RDFStore contains a module to make basic RDF Schema inferencing on triples but the RDQL sub-system is not using it yet. By using free-text words present into literal values it is possible to select the nodes matching a query criteria in a much more selective way.

```
SELECT ?link
FROM <http://xmlhack.com/rss10.php>
WHERE
   (?item, <rdf:type>, <rss:item>),
   (?item, <rss:title>, %"Apache"%),
   (?item, <rss:link>, ?link)
USING
   rdf for <http://www.w3.org/1999/02/22-rdf-syntax-ns#>,
   rss for <http://purl.org/rss/1.0/>
```

Fig. 6. Query involving free-text matching in an RDFStore query.

Such an extension is similar to the SQL LIKE operator present in most of out-of-the-shelf database solutions today; this kind of filtering can also be applied to the restrictive part (constraints) of the query by using the LIKE operator directly with Perl regular-expressions. The following returns the same result of the example above in less efficient way:

```
SELECT ?link
FROM <http://xmlhack.com/rss10.php>
WHERE
   (?item, <rdf:type>, <rss:item>),
   (?item, <rss:title>, ?title),
   (?item, <rss:link>, ?link)
AND ?title LIKE '/Apache/i'
USING
   rdf for <http://www.w3.org/1999/02/22-rdf-syntax-ns#>,
   rss for <http://purl.org/rss/1.0/>
```

Real-World Example of RDQL

For the ETB project [26] we successfully used the RDQL syntax to query fully RDF DC/DCQ metadata records classified accordingly to a multilingual thesaurus in 8 languages. An ETB metadata record is describing an educational resource having a specific target audience, rights management and quality selection criteria; each single record describes a Web resource, which can reside on several distributed servers having several different multilingual translations of it. Each record description is put in the statement group of a specific indexing term of the multilingual thesaurus and associated with a Collection Level Description (CLD) [27].

```
SELECT ?title_value, ?title_language,
       ?subject_value,?subject_language,
       ?description_value, ?description_language,
       ?language, ?identifier
WHERE (?x, <dc:title>, ?tt),
       (?tt, <rdf:value>, ?title_value),
       (?tt, <dc:language>, ?ttl),
       (?ttl, <dcq:RFC1766>, ?title_language),
       (?x, <dc:subject>, ?ss1),
       (?ss1, <etbthes:ETBT>, ?ss2),
       (?ss2, <rdf:value>, ?subject_value),
       (?ss2, <dc:language>, ?ss3),
       (?ss3, <dcq:RFC1766>, ?subject_language),
       (?x, <dc:description>, ?dd),
       (?dd, <rdf:value>, ?description_value),
       (?dd, <dc:language>, ?ddl),
       (?ddl, <dcq:RFC1766>, ?description_language),
       (?x, <dc:identifier>, ?identifier),
       (?x, <dc:language>, ?lll),
       (?lll, <dcq:RFC1766>, ?language)
USING
   rdf for <http://www.w3.org/1999/02/22-rdf-syntax-ns#>,
   rdfs for <http://www.w3.org/2000/01/rdf-schema#>,
   dc for <http://purl.org/dc/elements/1.1/>,
   dcq for <http://purl.org/dc/terms/>,
   dct for <http://purl.org/dc/dcmitype/>,
   etb for <http://eun.org/etb/elements/>,
   etbthes for <http://eun.org/etb/thesaurus/elements/>
```

Fig. 7. Example query from the ETB system.

The example below is in practice very simple compared to other full-blown Boolean SQL statements we need to run in the advanced search of the production system. Such an advanced feature has been implemented using a hybrid solution using RDQL, simple triple-matching and basic programming data structures; the result has shown quite a good scalability but we are investigating the real implications and aspect of running full queries with disjunction and negation.

Conclusions

We have described a refined framework for the querying of RDF data. We developed this to meet our needs in writing RDF applications. The query framework follows the RDF graph syntax very closely and provides for extraction of RDF data (URIs, literals, bNodes) from a data source.

The syntax we present is modeled after SQL. It is targeted at the application developer. Other syntaxes would be appropriate for different communities.

We have implemented SquishQL in three systems. The first, Inkling, stores RDF data in relational databases or in external XML files. The second implementation, RDQL, is part of the Jena RDF toolkit and combines query with manipulation of the RDF graph at a fine-grained level through the Jena RDF API. The third, in RDFStore, is close coupling of RDF and Perl data access styles.

We have shown the utility of this simple approach to query of RDF data in a number of applications as well as other applications developed by the RDF developer community.

References

1. L. Miller, "Inkling: RDF query using SquishQL", web page: http://swordfish.rdfweb.org/rdfquery/
2. A. Seaborne, RDQL – RDF Data Query Language, part of the Jena RDF Toolkit, HPLabs Semantic Web activity, http://hpl.hp.com/semweb/, RDQL grammar: http://www.hpl.hp.com/semweb/rdql-grammar.html
3. A. Reggiori, D. W. van Gulik, RDFStore, http://rdfstore.sourceforge.net
4. B. McBride, "Jena: Implementing the RDF Model and Syntax Specification", in: Steffen Staab et al (eds.): "Proceedings of the Second International Workshop on the Semantic Web - SemWeb'2001", May 2001 http://www.hpl.hp.co.uk/people/bwm/papers/20001221-paper/
5. D. Brickley, L. Miller, "RDF, SQL and the Semantic Web - a case study", http://ilrt.org/discovery/2000/10/swsql/
6. E. Prud'hommeaux, Algae in "RDF Database Library", http://www.w3.org/2001/Talks/0505-perl-RDF-lib/slide5-0.html
7. R.V.Guha, "rdfDB : An RDF Database", web page: http://guha.com/rdfdb/
8. G. Karvounarakis, V. Christophides, D. Plexousakis, S Alexaki, "Querying Community Web Portals", SIGMOD2000, http://www.ics.forth.gr/proj/isst/RDF/RQL/rql.html
9. Greg Karvounarakis, "The RDF Query Language (RQL)"

10. Sesame, see http://sesame.aidministrator.nl/, part of the OntoKnowledge project, http://www.ontoknowledge.org/
11. W. Nejdl, B. Wolf, C. Qu, S. Decker, M. Sintek, A. Naeve, M. Nilsson, M. Palmér, T. Risch, "EDUTELLA: A P2P Networking Infrastructure Based on RDF", http://edutella.jxta.org/reports/edutella-whitepaper.pdf
12. J. Kahan , M Koivunen, E. Prud'Hommeaux, R R. Swick "Annotea: An Open RDF Infrastructure for Shared Web Annotations", http://www10.org/cdrom/papers/488/
13. D. Allsopp, P. Beautement, J. Carson, M Kirton "Toward Semantic Interoperability in Agent-Based Coalition Command Systems", Proceedings of the First International Semantic Web Workshop, July 30-31, 2001, http://www.semanticweb.org/SWWS/program/full/paper10.pdf
14. R.V. Guha, Ora Lassila, Eric Miller, Dan Brickley, Enabling Inference, W3C Query Language meeting, Boston, December 3-4, 1998.
15. Ora Lassila, Ralph R. Swick (editors), "Resource Description Framework (RDF) Model and Syntax Specification", 22 February 1999.
16. P. Hayes (editor), "RDF Model Theory" (work in progress) http://www.w3.org/TR/rdf-mt/
17. Dan Brickley, R.V. Guha (editors), "Resource Description Framework (RDF) Schema Specification 1.0", 27 March 2000 (W3C Candidate Recommendation).
18. Sergey Melnik, "Stanford RDF API", web page: http://www-db.stanford.edu/~melnik/rdf/api.html
19. T. Berners-Lee, R. Fielding, L. Mastiner, "Uniform Resource Identifiers (URI): Generic Syntax", RFC2396
20. Intellidimension Inc. "RDFQL" http://www.intellidimension.com/RDFGateway/Docs/rdfqlgettingstarted.asp
21. J. De Roo, Euler proof mechanism, http://www.agfa.com/w3c/euler/
22. N-Triples syntax in W3C Working Draft "RDF Test Cases" http://www.w3.org/TR/rdf-testcases/#ntriples
23. G. Chappell, RuleML combined with RDF query model: http://209.198.94.130/ruleml/query.asp
24. Dirk Willem-van Gulik, "The DB engine", August 1999, http://rdfstore.sourceforge.net/dbms.html
25. The Unicode Consortium, "The Unicode Standard Version 3.0", ISBN 0-201-61633-5
26. European Schoolnet (EUN) European Treasury Browser (ETB) project, http://etb.eun.org
27. Andy Powell, "Collection Description – Study, Recommendation, Specification", 3 September 1999, http://www.ukoln.ac.uk/metadata/rslp/proposal/

ClaiMaker:
Weaving a Semantic Web of Research Papers

Gangmin Li, Victoria Uren, Enrico Motta,
Simon Buckingham Shum, and John Domingue

Knowledge Media Institute, The Open University, Milton Keynes, MK7 6AA, UK
{g.li, v.s.uren, e.motta,
s.buckingham.shum, j.b.domingue}@open.ac.uk
http://kmi.open.ac.uk/projects/scholonto/

Abstract. The usability of research papers on the Web would be enhanced by a system that explicitly modelled the rhetorical relations between claims in related papers. We describe ClaiMaker, a system for modelling readers' interpretations of the core content of papers. ClaiMaker provides tools to build a Semantic Web representation of the claims in research papers using an ontology of relations. We demonstrate how the system can be used to make inter-document queries.

1 Introducing ScholOnto

The Web has facilitated access to many scholarly documents by making available copies of papers, technical reports etc. in digital libraries and on individuals' home pages. Reasonable keyword access is provided by Web search engines. Access via citations is available using tools such as Research Index (Citeseer) [1], and research to extend this approach to eprint servers is ongoing [2]. However, there are few tools to track debate and analyse ideas in a domain. The Semantic Web [3] approach of augmenting Web documents with machine understandable information offers a potential means of addressing this need.

The Scholarly Ontologies (ScholOnto) project [4, 5] takes this approach. We are developing an ontology-based *Claims Server* to augment existing papers, by modelling authors' and readers' interpretations of them. This produces a *claim space* above digital libraries; effectively, a semantic web of inter-linked concepts. The system enables researchers to make claims concerning their view of a document's contributions and its relationship to the literature. These claims may support or contest existing claims; in contrast to most Semantic Web applications ScholOnto does not require consensus.

The semantic structure of the claim space provides a basis for making queries based on the interpretation of research papers, rather than just keywords or citations. In this paper, we consider one example of an apparently simple question, which requires interpretation of multiple documents in a more specific way than is possible from plain citations: *"Are there any arguments against the intellectual framework on which this paper builds?"*. We will show how building a semantic network of claims over a distributed document collection can start to answer such questions.

I. Horrocks and J. Hendler (Eds.): ISWC 2002, LNCS 2342, pp. 436–441, 2002.

2 Ontology of Rhetorical Relations

We take the position that, although *what* authors are discussing in a domain will, by the nature of research, be in flux, *how* the discourse is conducted will be stable. Consequently, the conceptual glue of ScholOnto, the links between ideas, is reified using an ontology of rhetorical relations [6]. A claim triple is the assertion that a particular relationship holds between two ideas. The relations in the ontology act as attributes in triples, in which object and value are each one of concept, set or data. Concepts are stored as short pieces of free text, and sets are collections of related concepts gathered under a free text name. A typical data object is a set of metadata giving the reference of a document in a digital library.

Claims were modelled in a range of research domains, including computer supported collaborative work, text categorization, and literary criticism. Relations common to several domains were identified. We found we could classify these into groups with similar rhetorical implications: Supports/Challenges, Problem Related, Taxonomic, Causality, Similarity, and General. Each relation belongs to one group. We also found that some relations occurred in pairs of opposites, e.g. *proves* and *refutes*, where one has positive and the other negative implications. We call this property "polarity". For example, *refutes* has negative polarity; it implies *dis*proof. Referring to our question, *refutes* would be an *"argument against"*.

```
:SchProperty rdfs:subClassOf :Property .              :polarity rdf:type :StructuringProperty .
:StructuringProperty rdfs:subClassOf :SchProperty .   :polarity rdfs:domain :SchProperty .
:RhetProperty rdfs:subClassOf :SchProperty .          :polarity rdfs:range :PolarityType .
:SupportsChallenges rdfs:subClassOf :RhetProperty .
                                                      :refutes rdf:type :SupportsChallenges .
:PolarityType rdf:subClassOf :Resource .              :refutes :polarity :negativePolarity .
:negativePolarity rdf:type :PolarityType .            :proves rdf:type :SupportsChallenges .
:positivePolarity rdf:type :PolarityType .            :proves :polarity :positivePolarity .
```

Fig. 1. Parts of an RDFS specification for the ScholOnto ontology (in Notation3 for clarity http://www.w3.org/DesignIssues/Notation3)

By defining relations in terms of type and polarity we can reason with them at a higher level of granularity than individual relations; it is not just the claims made using the *refutes* relation that represent *"arguments against"* something, but any claims made using links that have negative polarity. Furthermore, the same ontology of relations can be employed by research communities which speak different "dialects", or even different languages, simply by changing the labels of the relations, without changing the underlying functionality of ScholOnto.

To illustrate claim triples, we will take a paper entitled "Evaluation of decision forests on text categorization" [7]. The claims of this paper include the following:

[Decision Forest Classifier] (uses/applies/is enabled by) [Decision tree learning]

This uses one of the General relations *uses/applies/is enabled by* to assert that the *Decision Forest classifier* studied in the paper uses a well known method, *Decision tree learning*. The latter concept was introduced in a different document, so this link has a contextual role: it locates the paper near similar claims.

[Decision Forest classifier improves on C4.5 and kNN](is inconsistent with) [SVM and kNN outperform other classifiers]
This claim uses the negative, Supports/Challenges relation *is inconsistent with* to link
one of the experimental results of this paper to a result in a third paper. In addition to
its contextual role, locating the claim near other comparisons of classifiers, this claim
has a rhetorical role: it contrasts pieces of evidence that make contradictory
assertions.

3   The ClaiMaker System

ClaiMaker is implemented as a client/server system (Fig. 2). The Claim Server
interprets users' requests, and accesses the database and/or file server to retrieve the
results. It may invoke the inference engine, based on the relation ontology, if it is
necessary.

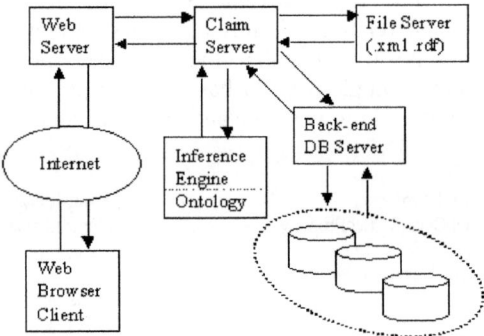

Fig. 2. Architecture of the ClaiMaker Claim Server

ClaimMaker has a form-based interface to help ourselves and early uptake users build
a claim space, which describes a collection of electronic documents. The operations it
performs include: adding or importing metadata for new documents; creating new
concepts, sets and links associated with a document; and browsing and querying the
database about objects on the server to discover interesting facts, and potential trends.
The interface leads the user through ScholOnto tasks stepwise. For example, Figure 3
shows a user selecting concepts to include in a set about reminding.

ID	IPOwner	Creator	Article	Concept name	Select
644	Victoria	Victoria	2464	Reminding and Memory	☐
645	Victoria	Victoria	8707	Reminding is a crucial aspect of human memory	☑
647	Victoria	Victoria	8707	Events can remind you of events in the same domain	☐
648	Victoria	Victoria	8707	Events can remind you of events in different domains	☐
652	Victoria	Victoria	8707	Understanding means being reminded of the closest previously experienced phenomenon.	☐
663	Victoria	Victoria	8707	Reminding can show how memory is organized	☑
664	Victoria	Victoria	8707	Reminding tells us about learning and generalization	☑

Selection is done

Fig. 3. Selecting concepts to construct a set

In Figure 4 the user is making a claim using this set, which they have named "Importance of Reminding" and the relation *is consistent with*. The next step will be to click the button *Search concept/set* which will call a screen where they can make keyword searches of other users' concepts and sets, and select one to link to.

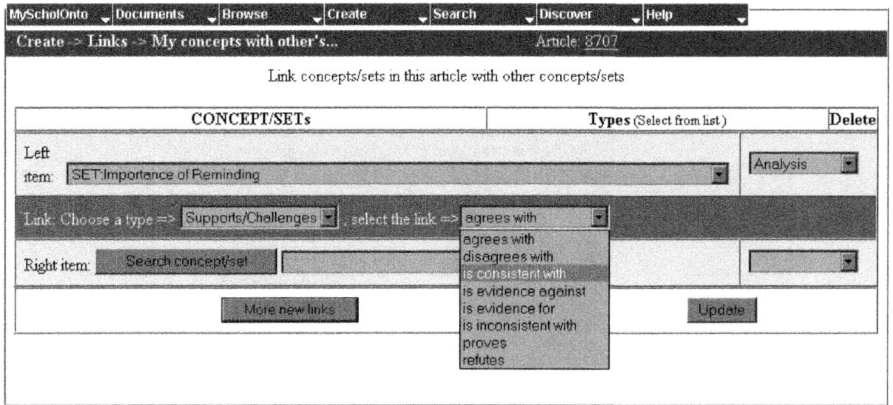

Fig. 4. Creating a claim using the ClaiMaker system

4   Providing Semantic Discovery Services

We will now return to our example query to demonstrate how expressing the claims made by documents using the ontology of relations gives added value over retrieval of documents based on keywords. The question as asked, *"Are there any arguments against the intellectual framework on which this paper builds?"*, has three components. It is looking for *"arguments against"*, defined as negative relations of any type. It refers specifically to a *"paper"*, and it is easy to find the set of concepts belonging to a document. It also refers to the *"intellectual framework"*. This is an ambiguous requirement that must be constrained if it is to be modelled. For the experimental function described here, we used a pragmatic definition: *the intellectual framework of a set of concepts is the extended set of concepts that are linked to/from the concepts in the original set by a positive relation.* Clearly, this is a gross simplification of the notion of *"intellectual framework"*, but it makes the problem tractable. For a given paper the discovery function does the following:
1. Finds the concepts associated with that paper
2. Extend the set of concepts by adding linked concepts from other papers
3. Returns any arguments against the concepts in the extended set
Typical results are presented below (Fig. 5). Note the two numbers to the right of the claim that *disagrees with* one of the related issues in the query. The first, 8621, is a hyperlink to the metadata of the paper that provides the backing for the claim, which includes a URL to the paper itself. The second, 2, is a link to the personal details of the reader who made the claim; this allows the user, or, potentially, a discovery agent working on behalf of the user, to make a judgement about the credentials of a claim; can it be trusted?

Term based information retrieval handles documents as isolated entities defined by the words in them. Citations in a document are noncommittal about authors' intentions in referring to other work; we cannot even tell if a paper is referenced because the authors support its position or because they are diametrically opposed to it. This simple example of a search for arguments against a position demonstrates how the ontology of relations can make the connections between ideas in different documents explicit, allowing better kinds of query.

The key issues you are concerned with:	
445	Decision Forest classifier
446	Decision Forest classifier improves on C4.5 and kNN

The related issues you may be concerned with:	
515	Instance based learning
511	Decision tree learning
277	decision trees and naive Bayes perform well for text categorization

The following claims disagree ...		
1	[Optimised rules outperform Naive Bayes and decision trees] «disagrees with» [decision trees and naive Bayes perform well for text categorization]	8621 2

Fig. 5. Arguments that contrast with the concepts in the paper by Chen & Ho [7]

5   Summary & Future Work

The ontology we have implemented in ScholOnto permits us to represent researchers' claims about their work as a claim space over Web documents. This opens up opportunities for answering more interesting questions about scholarly discourse.

We are now developing more discovery services. These will be of two types. We will start by developing specific functions of the sort discussed here. These will tackle common tasks, like finding the arguments against a position, or assessing the impact of an idea. Novice users will be able to use these to learn about the sorts of query possible in ScholOnto. In addition, we plan to develop a structural query system, exploiting the inference engine. This system will be aimed at expert users.

Data visualisation will become increasingly important. We need visualisations for browsing that illustrate the claim space at different levels of granularity. A visual input system is required also. When making a list of claims it is easy to lose track of the shape of the argument that is being made, and how it relates to other parts of the network. Users need to be able to see the connections between their claims as they create them. We are also investigating ways to extract claims from papers semi-automatically, and to suggest semantic links, as a way of easing the claim acquisition bottleneck.

The Claims Server implementation described here provides a controllable, centralised environment in which we can test our ideas. However, an agent approach [8] offers some exciting alternatives. One is a distributed ScholOnto in which authors' interpretations of their own papers are published alongside the originals. These could be perused by discovery agents. Another is a more personalised model in which a user's agent might crawl the Web, harvesting interesting claims as they are published, and depositing them in a private knowledge base. They could then be annotated and extended, without the social constraints imposed by making claims about other researchers' work in public. Such private spaces could be shared by the members of a research group as a discussion forum.

References

1. Bollacker,K.D., Lawrence, S., Giles, C.L.: CiteSeer: an autonomous web agent for automatic retrieval and identification of interesting publications. Proc. 2nd Int. Conf. on Autonomous Agents, Minneapolis, MN (1998) 116-123
2. Hitchcock, S., Carr, L. Jiao, Z., Bergmark, D., Hall, W., Lagoze, C., Harnad, S.: Developing services for open eprint archives: globalisation, integration and the impact of links. In: Proc. 5th ACM Conf. on Digital Libraries, San Antonio, TX. (2000) 143-151
3. Berners-Lee, T., Hendler, J., Lassila, O.: The Semantic Web, Scientific American, May (2001) 34-43
4. Motta, E., Buckingham Shum, S., Domingue, J.: Ontology-Driven Document Enrichment: Principles, Tools and Applications. Int. J. Human-Computer Studies., 52, (2000) 1071-1109
5. Buckingham Shum, S., Motta, E., Domingue, J.: ScholOnto: An Ontology-Based Digital Library Server for Research Documents and Discourse. Int. J. Digit. Libr., 3, (2000) 237-248
6. Buckingham Shum, S., Uren, V., Li, G., Domingue, J., Motta, E., Mancini, C.: Designing Representational Coherence into an Infrastructure for Collective Sensemaking. In: 2nd Int. Workshop on Infrastructures for Distributed Collective Practices, San Diego CA (2002)
7. Chen, H. & Ho, T.K.: Evaluation of decision forests on text categorization. In: Proc. 7th SPIE Conference on Document Recognition and Retrieval (2000) 191-199
8. Hendler, J.: Agents and the Semantic Web. IEEE Intelligent Systems, 16(2) (2001) 30-37

Business and Enterprise Ontology Management with SymOntoX[1]

Michele Missikoff and Francesco Taglino

LEKS, IASI-CNR,
Viale Manzoni 30 – 00185 Rome, Italy
{missikoff, taglino}@iasi.rm.cnr.it

Abstract. Ontologies are emerging as a key solution for knowledge sharing in co-operative business environment. From the technology point of view, the growth of Internet use has favoured the development of environments devoted to collaborative and distributed work, allowing different communities to increase flexibility and effectiveness in their work. From the representation point of view, an ontology management system represents a powerful tool to create common and shareable knowledge repositories. The goal of this work is to present SymOntoX, a web-based ontology management system. It is an open source environment supporting collaborative and distributed ontology construction and maintenance.

1 Introduction

SymOntoX (<u>Sym</u>bolic <u>Onto</u>logy manager <u>X</u>ML-savvy), is a software prototype for the management of domain ontologies. It has been developed by LEKS (Laboratory for Enterprise Knowledge and Systems), at IASI-CNR.

An ontology [1] [2] entails some sort of world view with respect to a given domain. It gathers a set of concepts (concerning entities, attributes, processes, etc.), together with their definitions and inter-relationships, obtained by an abstraction process (a conceptualisation [3] that starts from the observation of a given domain).

Therefore, an ontology [4] is a representation of a shared conceptualisation of a domain. Such a shared conceptualisation is necessary for establishing effective communication among actors (human or not) that operate in the domain.

An Ontology may have different degrees of formality and may be constructed using different techniques, but, necessarily, it includes a vocabulary of terms with their meaning (definitions) and their relationships. In this perspective, an ontology can be seen as a domain vocabulary containing a set of precise definitions, or axioms, that
- provide the meaning of the terms,
- enable a consistent interpretation of the terms defined in the vocabulary.

---

[1] This work has been partially supported by the European project IST-2000-29329 (Harmonise).

I. Horrocks and J. Hendler (Eds.): ISWC 2002, LNCS 2342, pp. 442–447, 2002.
© Springer-Verlag Berlin Heidelberg 2002

SymOntoX has been conceived for business and enterprise ontology management. Therefore, it offers a few native meta-concepts, such as Business Process, Object, and Actor that help the enterprise experts to better categorise the identified concepts, supporting the demanding ontology building task. In this perspective, its knowledge model is more focused than existing systems, such as Protegé 2000 [5], OntoEdit [6], KSL Ontology Server [7].

Below, in Section 2 the main lines of SymOntoX representation method are represented. The functionalities, and the architecture of SymOntoX are briefly illustrated in Section 3 and 4, respectively. The conclusion reports a brief account of current experimental activities.

2   The Ontology Representation: The OPAL Methodology

In SymOntoX, domain concepts and relations are modelled according to OPAL (Object, Process, and Actor modelling Language) [8], a methodology for ontology representation developed by LEKS, at IASI-CNR, within the Harmonise European project for semantic interoperability in the tourism domain [9].

According to OPAL, concepts are organised by means of three primary modelling ideas: Actor, Processes, and Object. More precisely, we have:

Actor – any relevant entity of the domain that is able to activate or perform a process (e.g, Tourist, Travel Agency);
Object – a passive entity on which a process operates (e.g., Hotel, Flight);
Process – an activity aimed at the satisfaction of a goal (e.g., Making_a_reservation).

Besides the above primary modelling ideas, OPAL proposes the following complementary modelling ideas:
Goal – is a desired state of the affairs that an actor seeks to reach. (e.g., Go_vacation);
State – is a characteristic pattern of values that instance variables of an entity can assume. (e.g., Flight_full);
Rule – is an expression that is aimed at restraining the possible values of an instance of a concept (constraint rule) or that allow to derive new information (production rule). (e.g., "Ticket purchase 30 days before departure");
Information Component - a cluster of information pertaining to the information structure of an Actor or an Object (e.g., Flight_info, Hotel_address);
Information Element - atomic information element that is part of an Information Component (e.g., Flight_price, Nr_of_rooms);
Elementary Action - activity that represents a process component that is not further decomposable (e.g., Cancel_reservation).

The above modelling ideas are necessary for defining (unary) concepts. According to OPAL, concepts are linked together by means of a number of ontological relations, that can be seen as vertical or horizontal.
Vertical relations are: *Broader* (B), that, given a concept, relates its more general concepts; *PartOf* (Pa), and *InstaceOf* (with an evident meaning).

Horizontal relations are: *Similarity* (S), that gathers the similar concepts (with an associated similarity degree); *Predication* (Pr), that link *Information Components* and *Elements* to the current concept, and the (generic) *Relatedness* (R), to link the other related concepts.

More synthetically, in OPAL, a core (i.e., without a reference to instances and with a simplified view, without goal/state/event references) definition of a concept c, is represented by the following 8-tuple:

$$c = (n, k, d, B, Pa, S, Pr, R),$$

where: n is the label of the concept; k is the kind, i.e., one of the modelling ideas of OPAL (Actor, Process, …); d is the description, explaining the meaning of the concept, generally in natural language. Then we have the set of concept labels B, Pa, S, Pr, R related to c as reported above.

Ontological relations play a key role since they allow concepts to be inter-linked according to their semantics. The set of concepts, together with their links, forms a semantic network [1].

In table 1 we provide an example of a concept structured according to OPAL.

Table 1. The Hotel concept in OPAL (simplified)

Hotel	
Def: A building where travellers can pay lodging and meals and other services	*XML tag*: <Hotel> *Kind: Object*

Broader: Accommodation
 Similar: Guest_Farm [0.8]
          Bed&Breakfast [0.8]
 Predication: Hotel_Address,
          Hotel_Category
	PartOf: Receptivity system
	 Related-object: Restaurant
	 Related-actors: H_Reservation_Service
	 Related-processes: Hotel_Reserving
	          Hotel_Room_Purchasing,

(all reported terms, except in the row below the concept label, correspond to concepts in the ontology)	

3 SymOntoX functionalities

SymOntoX is able to manage several ontologies (like a DBMS for databases). Since ist linguistic component is largely independent from the conceptual structures, it seamlessly manages multilingual implementations. Its architecture is organized in three tiers: a front-end, with a Graphical User Interface (GUI); a back-end where concepts are stored and managed; a central layer where the management logic resides.

3.1 The SymOntoX Front-End

SymOntoX supports three kinds of users: **User,** with only reading rights; **SuperUser** who has read and write capabilities (the latter subject to validation); **Ontology Master** who has the full responsibility on the ontology contents and has the task to validate the concepts proposed by the SuperUsers.

The GUI is adaptive, that is, the windows and the enabled functionalities depend on the user access rights. The SymOntoX user interface has several windows, for different functions (create, view, edit, …). There is a primary window that presents two main panels. The left panel presents the list of all the concepts in the ontology; the right panel is dedicated to the management of a single concept. The aspect of the right panel changes depending on what the user is doing (essentially, editing or viewing). The operational prototype can be accessed at http://www.symontos.org.

3.2 The SymOntoX Back-End

SymOntoX provides the standard functionalities for the management of a knowledge base: inserting, modifying and deleting concepts. Furthermore it provides a set of additional functions:

Querying capabilities, that allows one to retrieve concepts that satisfy a given search expression. The search criteria can be expressed by using a guided form.

Multimedia examples management, that allows multimedia documents to be attached to a concept, to foster an intuitive representation of concepts. It is possible to attach texts, images, videos, and VRML files.

References annotation module, that allows information sources useful for the definition of a concept to be referenced. This module provides hyper-linking functions to reach referenced electronic documents and web-sites.

The subsystem aimed at the automatic validation of an ontology, that resides in the middle tier, is currently under development.

4 Architecture and Implementation Issues

SymOntoX has been conceived to be a service available on Internet. It is mainly based on XML technology [10], to guarantee maximal flexibility, interoperability and platform-independence. Furthermore it has been developed as a client-server architecture and, in particular, as a three tier architecture (Fig. 1).

The first tier concerns the client-side that represents the GUI (Graphical User Interface). The SymOntoX client is a web browser. Portability, platform-independence and light weight of HTML, allow SymOntoX to be executed from any remote workstation.

The second tier concerns the server-side that encloses both the manager of the communication with the clients and the SymOntoX application logic. The communication between client and server is performed through HTTP the most common Inter-

net communication protocol. Data (in XML format) are retrieved from the database
and transformed into a HTML page by using XSLT[11] and Java. Applying different
style sheets, the produced HTML page changes depending on the user role. Then the
HTML page is sent to the client.

The third tier is the storage subsystem back-end. SymOntoX is built on an XML-
based DBMS (in this first implementation we decided to use Excelon [12], a commercial database system, but we are investigating other free-software solutions). At
the database level, there are, for each ontology

- a database containing the concept (ontology content),
- a database containing the instances (of the above concepts),
- a log database containing the history of the activity performed by the users.

Furthermore there is a database devoted to the administration, containing the information about the existing ontologies and the registered users.

The interaction between the application server and the storage subsystem is performed through a set of Java APIs that enable the communication with the Excelon
databases and XQuery [13] as data retrieval language.

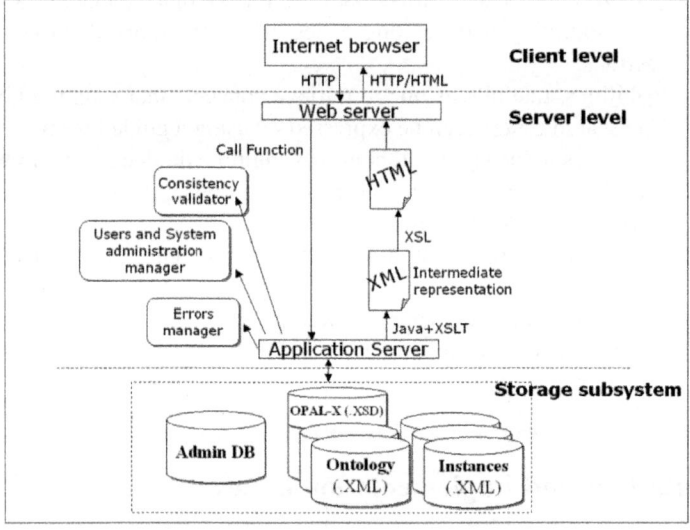

Fig. 1. SymOntoX architecture

5 Experimental Activities and Conclusions

SymOntoX in his preliminary form (called SymOntos) is currently used by a few
concrete projects. Among others, worth mentioning *OntoPrivacy*, supporting the
research activities of the organisation for the protection of personal information; *Business and Enterprise Ontology* (BEO), that represents the core of an ontology-based
platform for Business Games; *Ontotour*, an ontology on the tourism domain.

Ontotour is currently the most advanced activity, taking place within the European project Harmonise, an FP5-IST project aiming at building an interoperability platform for SME operating in the tourism domain [9]. More than 1000 ontologies entries have been already entered in Ontotour, and the number is constantly growing.

Till now the response of the communities that are using SymOntos is very positive. Nevertheless, since SymOntoX represents a significant evolution towards the XML-technology, we expect to further improve its characteristics, expecially in the direction of flexibility and openness. In particular in the near future, a set API (Application Programming Interfaces) will be published, in order to allow external systems to directly interact with SymOntoX. These API will be based on SOAP [14], a simple and lightweight XML protocol for exchanging structured and typed information.

References

1. Genesereth, M. R., Nilsson, N. J.: Logical Foundations of Artificial Intelligence. Morgan Kaufmann Publisher Inc (1987).
2. Uschold, M., Gruninger, M.: Ontologies: Principles, Methods and Applications, The Knowledge Engineering Review, V.11, N.2, (1996).
3. Gruber, T. R.: Towards Principles for the Design of Ontologies Used for Knowledge Sharing, Technical Report KSL 93-04, Knowledge Systems Laboratory, Stanford University (1993). http://ksl-web.stanford.edu/knowledge-sharing/papers/#onto-design.
4. Gruber T. R.: A translation approach to portable ontologies. Knowledge Acquisition 5(2), (1993), pp. 199-220. http://ksl-web.stanford.edu/knowledge-sharing/papers/#ontolingua.
5. http://protege.stanford.edu/.
6. http://ontoserver.aifb.uni-karlsruhe.de/ontoedit/.
7. http://www.ksl.stanford.edu/software/ontolingua/
8. Missikoff, M., Navigli, R., Velardi, P.: The Usable Ontology: An Environment for Building and Assessing a Domain Ontology. 1st International Semantic Web Conference (ISWC2002).
9. Missikoff, M., Callegari, G.: Preliminary Architectural Specification. Technical report within the Harmonise European project IST-2000-29329.
10. http://www.w3c.org
11. http://www.w3.org/Style/XSL/
12. http://www.exceloncorp.com
13. http://www.w3.org/XML/Query
14. Scriber, K., Stiver, M.C.: Understanding SOAP: The Authoritative Solution. Paperback (2000).

Is Participation in the Semantic Web Too Difficult?

Stefan Haustein and Jörg Pleumann

University of Dortmund, Computer Science VIII / X,
Baroper Str. 301, D-44221 Dortmund, Germany,
{stefan.haustein, joerg.pleumann}@udo.edu

Abstract. As long as there is not a sufficient base of RDF-annotated pages, the benefits of participating in the Semantic Web are barely visible. This is true in particular for content providers like individuals or small institutions. These potential participants can't afford the additional work necessary for the Semantic Web, yet they're needed for the Semantic Web to reach the critical mass that will make it a success. This paper discusses problems that may prevent small content providers from participating in the Semantic Web, as well as a possible way to lower the barrier for entry using tools like our own Information Layer system.

1   Introduction

Roughly a decade ago, a handful of more or less technically interested people started participating in the collaborative effort of creating something later to be called the World Wide Web. Among others, there were two significant reasons for the success of the project: Participation was simple, and the results of the work were immediately visible to the creator.

As an example, in order to build a basic web presence for a university department, it was sufficient to place a few HTML files in a directory structure and then start an HTTP daemon delivering the content on request of a client. Since HTML was easily understood, pages could be generated without the assistance of specialised tools – at least by people who were familiar with SGML, TeX or other structured text formats. Since an HTML user agent could also be used to display files residing in the intranet or even on the local harddisk, WWW technologies were – as a side effect – also used as a means of discussion or personal documentation, which resulted in quick and wide-spread adoption of the whole idea.

Now, ten years from then and with the World Wide Web truly deserving its name, we are at a point that is similar to some extent: The emergence of the Semantic Web. Theoretically, this more formal and machine-readable add-on to the existing web could undergo an evolution quite similar to its predecessor. One would just need to annotate existing HTML pages with the desired RDF code, RDF being, again, a language that is easily understood and quickly written down. However, there are some problems in this approach that might turn out to be an obstacle for the success of the Semantic Web.

The biggest problem is redundancy: Adding RDF annotations to HTML pages generates redundant information, since parts of the content have to be duplicated in a machine-readable manner. The usual problem of maintaining consistency between the two versions arises, and it gets even worse once the RDF information is moved into a separate

I. Horrocks and J. Hendler (Eds.): ISWC 2002, LNCS 2342, pp. 448–453, 2002.

file. As a result, there is a significant amount of additional work necessary for participating in the Semantic Web, but there is no immediate benefit for the participant. RDF information is primarily meant to be consumed by computer programs – other people's computer programs, to be accurate –, and it is usually not useful for the original provider of the content. Thus, the Semantic Web relies on the "network effect" even more than the original Web did: It becomes useful only when a large enough number of participants exists. Unfortunately, given this currently limited usability, it is hard especially for individuals and small institutions to take the initial migration step t o the Semantic Web: The barrier for entry is too high.

2   Tools to Lower the Barrier

One way to lower the barrier might be tool support. Programs like Protégé [1], Onto-Broker [2] or Ontology Builder [3] ease ontology and RDF(S) data management. They could be seen as the Semantic Web equivalent to HTML editors, and they help to solve the language issue. The redundancy issue, however, persists as long as one still wants a plain HTML version of the pages, viewable with a regular browser. The latter is, of course, a requirement for a smooth transition from the traditional Web to the semantic one.

To get rid of the dilemma caused by the redundant information, it seems to be a promising solution to hold the "semantically-relevant" information in a fine-grained storage, say, a relational database, and generate HTML as well as RDF output on-the-fly by using templates for both targets. This approach is somewhat similar to the blend of database and XML-generating front-end that is quite common these days (e.g. Cold Fusion[4], PHP, Enhydra etc.). It would also allow to address additional targets, say, WML or different HTML versions, without additional effort.

However, if we start modelling the tables for, say, a university department's Web presence, another problem becomes obvious: Assume we need at least tables for persons, their research topics, projects, and publications. Since most of the associations between these tables are n:n and thus require separate association tables in a relational database, the example results in quite a lot of tables (10, to be accurate), each of which potentially contains only a very small subset of all the possible instances at run-time.

In this case, the benefit for the content provider, that is, the dynamic generation of RDF, HTML or WML from a single set of data, obviously does not outweigh the extra effort inherent in maintaining all these tables. The barrier for entry to the Semantic Web is still too high.

3   Design Goals for a Semantic Web Server

So what are the requirements for an easy-to-use Semantic Web "server" aimed at our target audience of individuals and small institutions? This section discusses a set of design goals for a tool that may allow small content providers to easily participate in the Semantic Web.

Build on existing knowledge: First it should solve the language issue. Users having a
  background in AI may be expected to be familiar description logics. For mainstream

acceptance, though, building on a recognised standard for conceptual modelling might be the better alternative. We have chosen to adopt the ideas of [5] here, who propose UML as a language for ontology modelling. Most students of computer science or related engineering disciplines can be assumed to be familiar with UML and modelling tools like Together or Rational Rose.

Avoid redundancy: Second, the server should reduce the workload posed on the administrator. In particular, the redundancy between RDF code and HTML needs to be avoided. Instead, there should be a simple way to dynamically generate HTML and RDF pages from a common fact base. While it is relatively easy to provide a generic mapping from a fact base to HTML pages, this mapping needs to be sufficiently configurable to match the user's preferences or a given corporate design.

Provide additional benefits: Third, the Semantic Web server should provide "added value" that helps in lowering the entry barrier for the planned target audience of individuals and small institutions. In conjunction with an integrated storage and user management, for example, it can provide significant advantages over usual content management systems, such as HyperWave[1], Zope[2] or OpenCMS[3] These systems, which are widely used for managing a set of HTML pages, usually have a fixed set of metadata for annotating the pages. Here, ontology-based Semantic Web solutions would provide much more flexibility.

Immediate gain needs to outweigh extra cost: Finally, while the initial migration step will generate some extra effort, the system needs to ensure that this cost is outweighed by the gain for the content provider. This gain should not count too much on the network effect of the Semantic Web, because this effect might take some time to really pay off. Instead, the gain has to be immediately visible to the content provider.

4   The Information Layer System

In order to prove that the ideas of storing content in a fine-grained database and generating output on-the-fly actually works and provides significant advantages even without counting the "network effect" of the Semantic Web, we have chosen to modify our own "Information Layer" [6] system with respect to the design goals listed above. The reasons for building on our own system instead of modifying, for example, Protégé were mostly of pragmatic nature: It provided a solid basis, an d we know it well enough to make adoptions in a predictable time frame.

The Information Layer system was originally conceived as an integrated information platform for software agents and human users, and its design took into account the data redundancy issue that turns out to be an obstacle for the Semantic Web now. The system stores data in a simple object-oriented XML format the structure of which is determined by an ontology, and it features an XML-based template mechanism that is suitable for generating HTML output as well as more "formal" output consumable by software a gents. Obviously, when information is already machine-readable for agents, it is not a

---

[1] http://www.hyperwave.com

[2] http://www.zope.org

[3] http://www.opencms.org

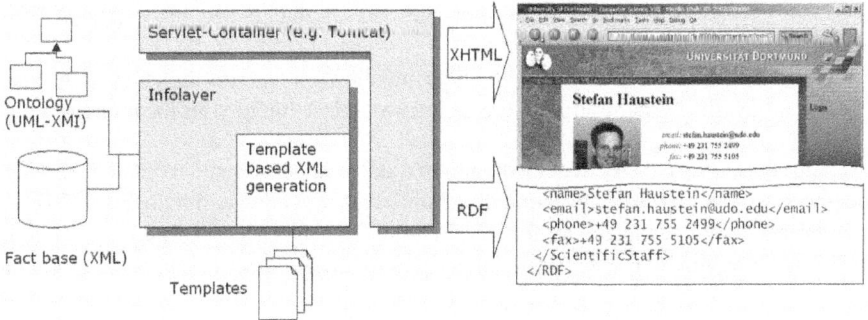

Fig. 1. Architecture of the Information Layer system

big leap to bring this information to the Semantic Web – we simply made use of the template mechanism to add the ability to output RDF data as well.

The architecture of the system, which is depicted in figure 1, consists of these main components or ideas:

- The Information Layer runs as a Java servlet. It makes use of the ontology, the fact base and the templates to generate its output.
- The ontology is described in UML, following the the argument raised in section 3. It can be read into the system from an XMI file, which allows to utilize an existing CASE tool for ontology modelling. No extra RDFS editor is necessary.
- A subset of the Object Constraint Language (OCL) [7] is used as a query language in the system. While other languages would have been possible (and actually have been used in the system before), the OCL suits the UML-based approach to ontology modelling very well.
- The system generates a user interface of HTML pages for browsing the fact base and viewing individual entries on-the-fly. It also generates form-based HTML pages to modify the fact base, so that, again, no additional tool is needed to modify the facts stored in the system. The HTML forms take into account all the rules imposed by the ontology, so that, for example, an 1:n relation will always have the proper cardinalities at both ends.
- There is an option to upload arbitrary files (PDF, MPG, ...). While this feature might look a bit odd at the first sight, it is a typical feature of content management systems and we incorporated it as an example of the added value mentioned in section 3. Of course, the content of the uploaded files is opaque to the system, which is kind of controversial to the idea of providing fine grained information in RDF-format. Yet, the system supports the addition of detailed meta-information.

The installation of an Information Layer based system is rather straightforward and includes the following steps:

1. Build a simple base ontology with the UML tool of your choice, or just use the sample ontology available from the InfoLayer homepage as a starting point.

2. Install Apache/Tomcat or any other Web server that is capable of running Java servlets.
3. Copy the Information Layer servlet files into the Web services directory of the server and adjust the configuration in the `servlet.xml` file to your local environment.

After these steps, the system is already in a state that allows you to add content using the generic Web interface. This content is immediately available to both the HTML and, with proper templates installed, the RDF world. The right side of figure 1 shows how staff data belonging to the university department scenario mentioned before might look like.

To improve the InfoLayer installation further, the following two steps might be performed in an arbitrary order or even in an iterated manner until a point is reached where the system perfectly suits the needs of the user:

– The ontology can be extended, either by adding new classes or by insertings new attributes or relationships into existing classes.
– The default look and feel of the system can be customized to match, for example, a corporate Web design by using HTML templates.

Please note that the temporal frame of the latter two steps is not fixed. One can, in the university department scenario, start with managing publications only, and add other concepts like projects, topics, persons or courses later. This, together with the fact that the InfoLayer servlet integrates well with an already existing Web presence, ensures a smooth migration from the traditional Web to the semantic one.

5   Experiences with the System

The InfoLayer system has been in development for several years now. The most up-to-date version is currently being used as a prototypical Web presence for MuSofT, a Germany-wide project that develops multimedia teaching material for software engineering education. The goal of this web presence is to manage and distribute the learning objects contributed by the various project partners. To allow efficient retrieval of material, LOM[4]-conforming metadata is provided using the system's ontology capabilities. Since the whole HTML user interface is dynamically generated from the ontology and the fact base, the initial extra work to get the system running has already paid off: Changes to the fact base, which occur whenever a learning object is added, changed or removed, are immediately visible to both the human and the machine-readable worlds. Even changes to the metadata, that is, to the ontology itself, can be made easily without having to modify the rest of the system afterwards. This application also makes use of the content management ability provided by the file upload feature.

Another project that utilizes the Information Layer in its current form is a database for Java-enabled small devices like cell phones and personal digital assistants[5]. Here, the ontology descibes the devices, their capabilities, vendors, available protocols and

---

[4] http://ltsc.ieee.org/wg12/index.html
[5] http://www.kobjects.org/devicedb

known bugs. Again, changes to the fact base are quite frequent, but do not require the duplicated effort of updating a human and a machine-readable version, which makes the website very easy to maintain.

Previous versions of the Information Layer system are still in use for MLnet teaching information server[6] and in other internal projects. For more details about the information layer software and it current applications, please refer to the homepage at `http://infolayer.org`.

6   Conclusion and Outlook

The Semantic Web is a great vision. However, for a broad adoption, simple tools that allow participation without a background in AI are still rare. Protégé and similar tools seem to aim in this direction. We would like to contribute our own Information Layer system. While other tools focus on the ontology building process, we mainly tried to address simplicity. This way we hope to improve availability of structured information suitable for the Semantic Web. We did not put a focus on advanced features like full DAML+OIL support, nor do not have a priority here in the future.

References

1. Stanford University: Using Protégé-2000 to Edit RDF. (2000)
   http://protege.stanford.edu/protege-rdf/protege-rdf.html.
2. Decker, S., Erdmann, M., Fensel, D., Studer, R.: Ontobroker: Ontology based access to distributed and semi-structured information. In Meersman, R., other, eds.: Semantic Issues in Multimedia Systems, Kluwer Academic Publisher, Boston, 1999. Kluwer Academic Publisher, Boston (1999)
3. Das, A., Wu, W., McGuinness, D.L.: Industrial strength ontology management. In: International Semantic Web Working Symposium (SWWS), California, USA, Stanford University (2001) 17–37
4. Brooks-Bilson, R.: Programming ColdFusion. O'Reilly (2001)
5. Cranefield, S., Purvis, M.: Uml as an ontology modelling language. In: Proceedings of the Workshop on Intelligent Information Integration, 16th International Joint Conference on Artificial Intelligence (IJCAI-99. (1999)
6. Haustein, S.: Utilising an ontology based repository to connect web miners and application agents. In: Proceedings of the ECML/PKDD Workshop on Semantic Web Mining. (2001) to appear, accepted for publication.
7. Object Management Group: OMG Unified Modeling Language Specification, version 1.3. http://www.omg.org/technology/documents/formal/unified_modeling_language.htm (2000)

---

[6] http://kiew.cs.uni-dortmund.de:8001/

Consistency Checking
of Semantic Web Ontologies

Kenneth Baclawski[1], Mieczyslaw M. Kokar[2],
Richard Waldinger[4], and Paul A. Kogut[3]

[1] College of Computer Science, Northeastern University
[2] Department of Electrical and Computer Engineering, Northeastern University
[3] Lockheed Martin Management and Data Systems
[4] SRI International

Abstract. Ensuring that ontologies are consistent is an important part
of ontology development and testing. This is especially important when
autonomous software agents are to use ontologies in their reasoning. Reasoning with inconsistent ontologies may lead to erroneous conclusions.
In this paper we introduce the ConsVISor tool for consistency checking
of ontologies. This tool is a consistency checker for formal ontologies,
including both traditional data modeling languages and the more recent
ontology languages. ConsVISor checks consistency by verifying axioms.
ConsVISor is part of the UBOT toolkit that uses a variety of techniques
such as theorem proving and logic programming. Some examples of the
use of these tools are given.

1 Introduction to ConsVISor

Formal ontologies are fundamental for the Semantic Web. They are especially
important for autonomous software agents for which a shared ontology is necessary for meaningful communication. However, because autonomous software
agents perform their reasoning and come to conclusions without human supervision, it is essential that the shared ontology be consistent. If an ontology is
inconsistent, then any conclusion may be deduced.

The ConsVISor tool is a consistency checker for formal ontologies. ConsVISor
can check consistency for a variety of languages. It currently supports class
diagrams specified in the Unified Modeling Language (UML) [1], and formal
ontologies specified in RDF [11] and DAML+OIL [3]. ConsVISor is part of the
UBOT toolkit [14]. In addition to UML, RDF and DAML+OIL, the UBOT
toolkit can be used to check the consistency of logical theories specified using
the Knowledge Interchange Format (KIF) [5].

The architecture of ConsVISor is shown in Figure 1. The ontology file is first
translated from the input ontology language to the language required by a logic
programming engine. The translation step incorporates some of the semantics of
DAML. For example, if two names are explicitly stated to represent equivalent resources (by using a property such as daml:equivalentTo or daml:sameClassAs,

I. Horrocks and J. Hendler (Eds.): ISWC 2002, LNCS 2342, pp. 454–459, 2002.

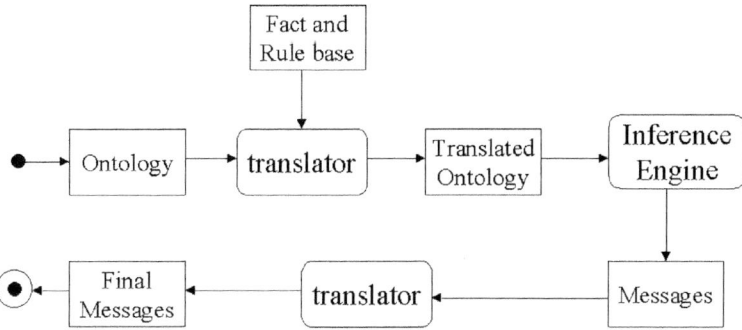

Fig. 1. ConsVISor Architecture

then the names are mapped to the same internal name. A background framework (fact and rule base) is combined with the translated ontology and also used by the logic programming engine. The output of the logic programming engine is translated back to a form compatible with the input ontology language and presented to the user.

The ConsVISor tool currently uses Prolog as its logic programming engine, but we are in the process of adding support for other engines such as Jess [7]. ConsVISor not only checks all of the axioms of the ontology, but it also checks for situations that might be mistakes even though they are not inconsistencies. Such cases are less severe than inconsistencies and can be suppressed if requested. For example, suppose that an ontology developer inadvertently misspelled a class name at one place in an ontology. This is both syntactically correct and semantically consistent because one can infer that the misspelled name is a class by the fact that it has been used as a class. Yet it is clearly a mistake, and finding such situations is of great practical benefit. Another example of a typical mistake in ontology development is given in Section 3 below.

If no error messages or warnings are printed by ConsVISor, then the ontology is consistent. However, an ontology might be consistent even though ConsVISor prints warnings. For example, ConsVISor does not support paramodulation. In particular, this means that ConsVISor is implicitly assuming that if two resources have different names and are not explicitly specified to be the same, then they are distinct resources. In other words, if s and t are resources that are mapped to distinct names by the translation step (see Figure 1), then ConsVISor adds the axiom $not(s = t)$. More generally, ConsVISor uses "negation as failure" rather than logical negation. The limitations of ConsVISor are a consequence of its use of Prolog, whose logical limitations are well known. In addition, ConsVISor cannot check the consistency of the logical system within which it resides (i.e., KIF, RDF, RDFS and DAML+OIL). To deal with these limitations, one can make use of another component of UBOT. Section 4 gives an example of the use of the SNARK theorem prover to find a logical inconsistency in the axioms for RDF.

If there is an inconsistency, then there is a good chance that SNARK can find it. Unlike the error messages and warnings produced by ConsVISor, these are true inconsistencies, not just possible mistakes. Since SNARK need not terminate, it either finds an inconsistency or it gives up when it runs out of time or space.

In Section 5 we conclude the paper and discuss some of the future work we have planned for ConsVISor and UBOT.

2   Related Work

There are a number of other systems for consistency checking. The OilEd [10] ontology editor that is intended for small-scale ontology development and consistency checking. It is not a complete ontology development environment. OilEd uses FaCT for its consistency checking. FaCT [6] is description logic classifier that can also be used for modal logic satisfiability testing. It can check the consistency of a DAML+OIL ontology, but it cannot check DAML+OIL itself. Furthermore, one can use FaCT only if one imposes some additional limitations on a DAML+OIL ontology that go beyond those of DAML+OIL itself. For example, one cannot have a cardinality restriction on a transitive property. Finally, FaCT only checks consistency, it does not issue warnings that indicate possible mistakes that are not inconsistencies in themselves.

JTP is a theorem prover written in Java [4]. JTP accepts KIF axioms, but it doesn't support paramodulation and only accepts axioms in Horn clause form. Since the DAML+OIL axioms contain equalities, equivalences and other non-Horn structures, it is not compatible with DAML+OIL.

Chimæra is a software system that supports users in creating and maintaining distributed ontologies on the web [2]. Two major functions it supports are merging multiple ontologies together and diagnosing individual or multiple ontologies. It supports users in such tasks as loading knowledge bases in differing formats, reorganizing taxonomies, resolving name conflicts, browsing ontologies, editing terms, etc. While the Chimæra system is an effective tool for ontology integration, its diagnostic suite is currently limited and not connected to a full theorem prover [9].

3   The Expression/Operation Ontology

In this section we give some an example of an inconsistent ontology that can arise in ontology development, and the results of running ConsVISor on it. The example is an ontology for expressions consisting of binary or higher operators that can be combined recursively. For example, $(x+y+5)*(z+3)*(a+b)$ would be such an expression. This includes operators such as addition and multiplication. In the first diagram, the notion of Expression is introduced with two exclusive subtypes, Elementary and Operation. An elementary expression has no further substructure. It would include constants and variables. This ontology is shown in Figure 2 using UML. An association, called *operands* between Expression and

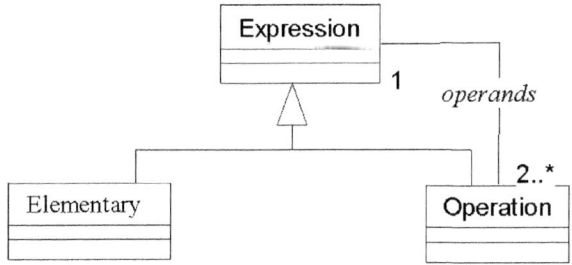

Fig. 2. Expression/Operation Ontology

Operation specifies that an operation is a subexpression that combines operands that are either elementary expressions or other operations.

The Expression/Operation ontology is not obviously inconsistent. The cardinality restrictions of the association between Operation and Expression specify that there are at least twice as many instances of Operation as there are instances of Expression. However, Operation is a subtype of Expression, so every instance of Operation is also an instance of Expression. Using the symbol # to mean *the number of instances*, we have shown that:

$$\#\text{Expression} \geq \#\text{Operation} \geq 2\#\text{Expression}$$

which implies that the Operation class (as well as the Expression class) is either empty or has an infinite number of elements.

The problem with this ontology is that the cardinality restrictions are in the wrong order. Reversing cardinality restrictions is a common mistake in data modeling languages. The ConsVISor tool will, in this case, warn the user that some of the classes cannot be instantiated.

4   Functional Property Example

The example in this section considers a logical theory that cannot be checked by the ConsVISor approach, and it illustrates the role of theorem proving in consistency checking. The theorem prover in the UBOT toolkit is SNARK [12,13]. The principal inference rules used by SNARK are resolution and paramodulation. Some distinctive features of SNARK are its support for special unification algorithms, sorts, nonclausal formulas, answer construction for program synthesis, procedural attachment, and extensibility by Lisp code.

The example is an axiom written in KIF as follows:

```
(<=> (Type ?fp FunctionalProperty)
     (and (Type ?fp Property)
        (=> (and (PropertyValue ?fp ?s ?v1)
                 (PropertyValue ?fp ?s ?v2))
            (= ?v1 ?v2))))
```

All of the variables in this axiom are implicitly universally quantified. This axiom was, at one time, one of the axioms in the RDF ontology language. The axiom attempts to formalize the concept of a functional property, i.e., a property that takes exactly one value on every element of its domain, much as a mathematical function (or more precisely a partial function) does. It should exclude properties that are sometimes multi-valued.

The SNARK theorem prover very quickly found an inconsistency due to this axiom. The problem is that the axiom, as originally formulated, allows one to deduce that *every* property is functional. As a result, if a property is multi-valued, then one can deduce that some of its values must be equivalent. For example, the rdf:type property is heavily used by RDF and is highly multi-valued. For example, rdf:Bag is both of type rdfs:Class and rdf:Resource which implies that rdfs:Class is the same as rdf:Resource. Here is the output produced by SNARK at the conclusion of its refutation of consistency:

```
(Row 604 (= Class Resource) (resolve 407 406))
(Row 637 false (rewrite (paramodulate 70 604) 394))
```

The problem with the axiom above is that the variables ?s, ?v1 and ?v2 should not be quantified using a global universal quantification. Their quantification must be scoped as follows:

```
(<=> (Type ?fp FunctionalProperty)
     (and (Type ?fp Property)
          (forall (?s ?v1 ?v2)
             (=> (and (PropertyValue ?fp ?s ?v1)
                      (PropertyValue ?fp ?s ?v2))
                 (= ?v1 ?v2)))))
```

SNARK also uncovered an inconsistency in the axioms for KIF, which served as a basis for the DAML axioms and which had been published since 1998 [5]. But probably the most far-reaching discovery SNARK made was that the axioms for the DAML cardinality restrictions were too weak to imply their intended consequences.

For example, in the Structured Walk-Through [15], a cardinality restriction was used to define a class (say OneFather) of elements with precisely one father. While it was possible to prove that an element of OneFather had at least one father, SNARK was unable to prove, because of the error in the axioms, that it could not have two fathers. As a result of SNARK's critique, the error was corrected in the revised axioms, which do imply the intended consequences.

5   Conclusions and Future Work

We have introduced the ConsVISor consistency checking tool that can be used to verify consistency of formal ontologies. A demonstration version is now available [8]. We are in the process of introducing new features to ConsVISor. One area of special concern is the problem of building more complex ontologies by merging smaller ontologies. The smaller ontologies are distinct but overlap one another. When two ontologies are combined, it is necessary to specify how to mediate between concepts that are similar, but not entirely the same, in the ontologies. Inconsistencies are a common occurrence due to the differing assumptions and commitments made in the two ontologies, and ConsVISor can help to identify such problems and to correct them.

References

1. G. Booch, J. Rumbaugh, and I. Jacobsen. *UML Notation Guide, Version 1.1*, September 1997.
2. Chimæra. Web site. www.ksl.Stanford.edu/software/chimaera.
3. DAML. DARPA Agent Markup Language Web Site, 2001. www.daml.org.
4. G. Frank. Hybrid reasoning architecture general purpose first-order logic theorem prover suite of special-purpose reasoners. www.ksl.stanford.edu/software/JTP.
5. M. Genesereth. Knowledge Interchange Format draft proposed American National Standard (dpANS) NCITS.T2/98-004, 1998. Available at logic.stanford.edu/kif/dpans.html.
6. I. Horrocks. FaCT: Fast Classification of Terminologies Web Site. www.cs.man.ac.uk/~horrocks/FaCT.
7. Jess. Java expert system shell. herzberg.ca.sandia.gov/jess.
8. M. Kokar, J. Letkowski, K. Baclawski, and J. Smith. The ConsVISor consistency checking tool, March 2001. Available at vis.home.mindspring.com/consvisor.html.
9. D. McGuinness, R. Fikes, J. Rice, and S. Wilder. An environment for merging and testing large ontologies. In *Proceedings of the Seventh International Conference on Principles of Knowledge Representation and Reasoning (KR2000)*, Breckenridge, Colorado, USA, April 12–15 2000.
10. OilEd. Ontology editor for DAML+OIL. oiled.man.ac.uk.
11. RDF. Resource description framework (RDF) model and syntax specification, Feburary 1999. www.w3.org/TR/REC rdf-syntax.
12. SNARK. SRI's new automated reasoning kit. www.ai.sri.com/~stickel/snark.html.
13. M. E. Stickel, R. J. Waldinger, and V. K. Chaudhri. A Guide to SNARK. www.ai.sri.com/snark/tutorial/tutorial.html.
14. UML Based Ontology Toolset. Web Site, 2001. ubot.lockheedmartin.com.
15. F. Harmelen van, P. Patel-Schneider, I. Horrocks, D. Connolly, L. Stein, and D. McGuinness, editors. *Annotated DAML+OIL Ontology Markup*. DARPA Agent Markup Language, March 2001. www.daml.org/2001/03/daml+oil-walkthru.html.

WebTheme™: Understanding Web Information through Visual Analytics

Mark A. Whiting and Nick Cramer

Pacific Northwest National Laboratory, PO Box 999, Richland, WA 99352 USA
{Mark.A.Whiting, Nick.Cramer}@pnl.gov

Abstract. WebTheme combines the power of software agent-based information retrieval with visual analytics to provide users with a new tool for understanding web information. WebTheme allows users to both quickly comprehend large collections of information from the Web and drill down into interesting portions of a collection. Software agents work for users to perform controlled harvesting of web material of interest. Visualization and analysis tools allow exploration of the resulting document space. Information spaces are organized and presented according to their topical context. Tools that display how documents were collected by the agents, where they were gathered, and how they are linked further enhance users' understanding of information and its context. WebTheme is a significant tool in the pursuit of the Semantic Web. In particular, it supports enhanced user insight into semantics of large, pre-structured or ad-hoc, web information collections.

1 Introduction

Information workers from many domains are discovering the Web as a convenient repository for both casually and formally published information. The Web is now often the primary reference for many information collection activities. Web information grows rapidly, changes frequently, and can be well-advertised and apparent to users or inconspicuous and hidden within the depths of a Web site. For an information user, it is often difficult to develop an overall understanding of a site or discover the most interesting nuggets of information without extensive and time-consuming manual processing.

WebTheme provides an alternative to manual browsing or searching via general search engines to help users understand large collections of Web pages. WebTheme uses both abstract display formats and visual interaction tools to facilitate user understanding. Expressive visualizations engage peoples' perceptual abilities to grasp structure and discern patterns and relationships within information collections. Analytic tools allow both quick, high level investigation to understand document sets as a whole, but also more detailed, specific investigations.

WebTheme is a harvester and a visual analytic tool. Given a URL, a list of URLs, or a query string, WebTheme launches parallel software agents to collect web pages. Pages are processed by text analysis software, clustering and visualization projection

I. Horrocks and J. Hendler (Eds.): ISWC 2002, LNCS 2342, pp. 460–468, 2002.

software, and then made available to to the user for analysis. Specifics about the tool and examples on its use are presented in the following sections.

2 Background

WebTheme is one component of Pacific Northwest National Laboratory's (PNNL) information analytics product offering. The foundation of this product line is the Spatial Paradigm for Information Retrieval and Exploration (SPIRE) system [1], that provides innovative visual tools and approaches to analyzing large sets of textual information. Other components of that product line include tranSPIRE, a tool for translingual visualization, and Topic Islands, a tool that identifies natural transition points at various levels of detail within large individual documents. WebTheme extends the capabilities of the SPIRE software to use the web in two ways – first, to harvest and analyze web information, and second, to deliver this capability and information over the web via a browser. WebTheme was created as an internal research and development project by the Pacific Northwest National Laboratory (PNNL). Subsequent sponsorship from the NASA Goddard Space Flight Center advanced WebTheme from proof-of-concept to the current prototype version. WebTheme is currently deployed at several government installations and the system is now being rolled out at our laboratory as a common desktop tool for our information workers.

3 WebTheme Overview

WebTheme is a tool that allows web information workers to see and interact with information in an uncommon – visual – manner. Web information semantics are better understood for both large document collections and for individual documents within a collection. WebTheme visualizations allow a user to grasp what a document collection describes and represents much more quickly than does text browsing or viewing search engine query results. The visualizations also allow documents to be seen in context within a collection, that is, identifying how they relate to the other documents.

WebTheme consist of two primary components:

- a *web harvester*, which collects web information from both shallow and deep web sources, and

- *visualizations* and a set of *visual analytics tools*, that allow users to see and analyze the harvest results.

3.1 Web Harvester

Users may specify Web-based retrieval in two ways[1]. First, an anchor URL may be specified, from which WebTheme agents will crawl down into the site to retrieve pages. Second, the user may specify a search engine query, to be sent to a general search engine or a site-specific search page. Documents resulting from that search will then be retrieved and processed. Users may set several other parameters to control retrieval agent behavior, such as:

1. Block harvesting of certain Web sites that are known to be of no interest.
2. Limit the search to a particular Internet domain.
3. Specify how many layers or levels of URL links to be followed from the initial target set.
4. Specify minimum and maximum numbers of pages to harvest.
5. Specify that the search should proceed for a specified period of time, rather than setting a target number of documents to be retrieved.
6. Set filters to eliminate certain kinds of unwanted items, including those in foreign languages.

In the case of the URL-based or search engine query, the harvester behaves as a specialized Web client, making contact with Web servers and then requesting and receiving Web documents. Harvesting agents are tasked in parallel from the WebTheme server. This significantly increases harvest speed, because each retrieval may involve delays from the remote servers. The harvesting process retrieves the documents in the initial list, searches those documents for HTML links, and continues by following links on retrieved documents to whatever depth the user requested. Harvesting continues until a user-specified number of documents are retrieved or a user-specified time period has elapsed.

3.2 Document Processing

The WebTheme text engine automatically produces a suitable knowledge base of themes (key words) that can be used to distinguish groups within the document collection under analysis. The system creates n-dimensional signature vectors characterizing each document with respect to those themes or topics. The document vectors are clustered and projected from n-space into 2-space, and the lower order projection is used to create the visual representations. The specifics of the signature vectors and visualization projection algorithms are beyond the scope of this paper. However, PNNL is doing extensive research into intelligent software agents that use document and concept signatures to performed enhanced information discovery. We anticipate using this research in conjunction with the use of DAML and other context and semantic enhancement approaches.

---

[1] A user may also specify a Z39.50 query for retrieval from a digital library, but this functions more like a database query and response than the other approaches.

3.2 Visualizations and Analytics Interface

WebTheme provides two visualizations of the analyzed information space. First, in a ThemeView™ visualization, themes of the document space are shown as a relief map of natural terrain, where taller peaks show dominant themes. This display is particularly good for helping users orient their understanding of the collection. It conveys the main themes in a collection and an overall sense of how they are related. Second, a Galaxy visualization shows the document space with individual web pages presented as stars in on a black space-like background.

We will introduce the visualizations and analytic tools using a practical web information analysis. In this example, we were interested in exploring associations between ontologies and software agents. We began in a typical fashion for most information workers – we entered a query into a general search engine. Unfortunately, merely entering the terms resulted in over 13,000 hits and scanning the resulting links and text quickly became tedious. When we processed this query through WebTheme, we first generated the ThemeView depiction in Figure 1.

From this ThemeView, we quickly see strong peaks related to multi (agents), learning, ontologies, and KQML, and we note these as potentially interesting topical areas to explore. Note that words appearing together as a peak label are not processed as a phrase; they are simply terms that are both strongly evident at that point in the collection, not necessarily in the same documents.

The Galaxy visualization for the same data set is shown in Figure 2. Each white dot in the visualization represents an individual

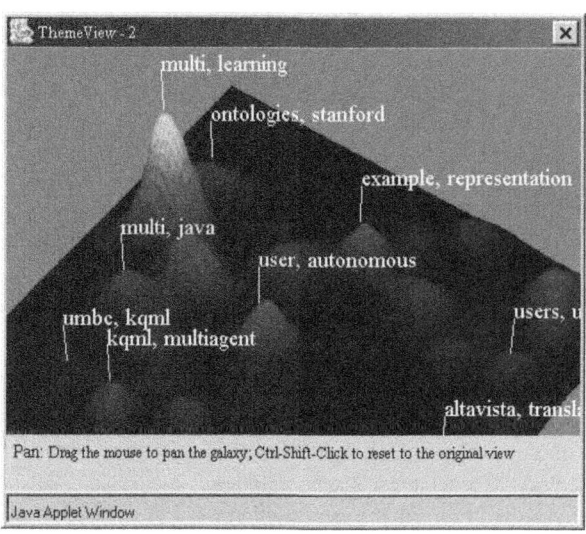

Fig. 1. ThemeView

Web page that was harvested. The distance between points indicates their thematic similarity. Thus, if points in the visualization are close together, then it is likely that the corresponding documents will contain thematically similar information. If they are far apart, the documents will probably be very different. The spatial layout of the points in the X-Y plane is not meaningful to users—only proximity.

The blue cloud-like areas are a 2-D presentation of the ThemeView peaks. These blue ThemeClouds, resembling nebulae, carry along the ThemeView peak labels to the Galaxy display. Labels are automatically shown for peaks, or locations of greatest density, to provide some orientation to the set when switching between a ThemeView and a Galaxy display.

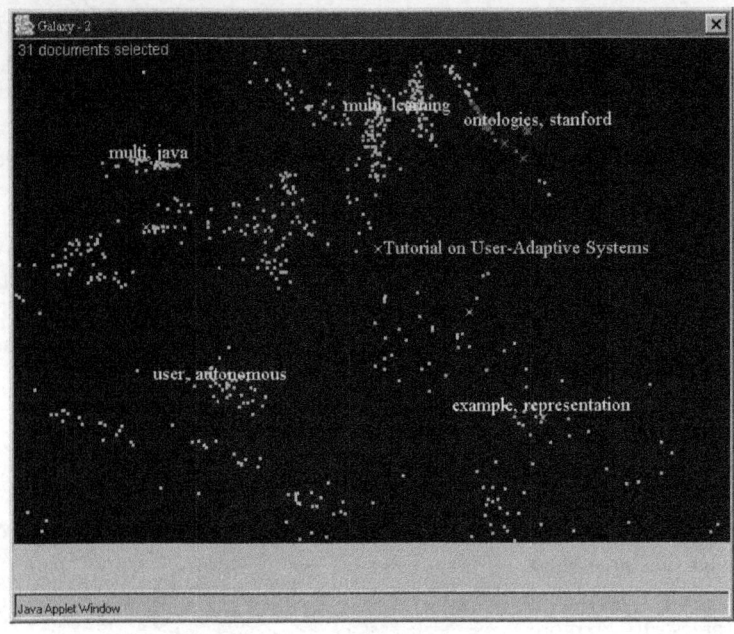

Fig. 2. Galaxy

We may further explore the set using the visual analytic tools. At the simplest level, document titles may be revealed individually or in groups. In Figure 2, one document label is turned on in light blue text color, "Tutorial on User-Adaptive Systems" toward the center of the display. This is one form of browsing this space. Groups of documents may also be selected and reviewed. Curious about the information contained around the ThemeCloud of "ontologies, Stanford", we can select a batch of these documents (selections are highlighted in green on the Galaxy display) and peruse them using the Document Viewer tool (Figure 3). The Document Viewer shows the

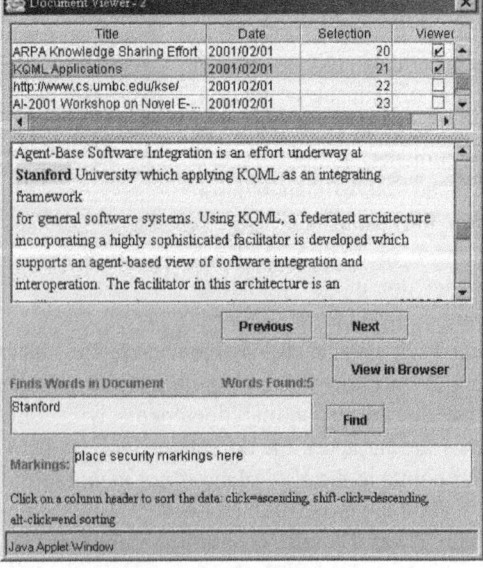

Fig 3. Document Viewer

list of all of the selected documents in the top panel, displays the text of the document in the middle, highlights words of interest that we would like to search for within documents, and allows us to view the original document in a web browser by clicking on the "View in Browser" button.

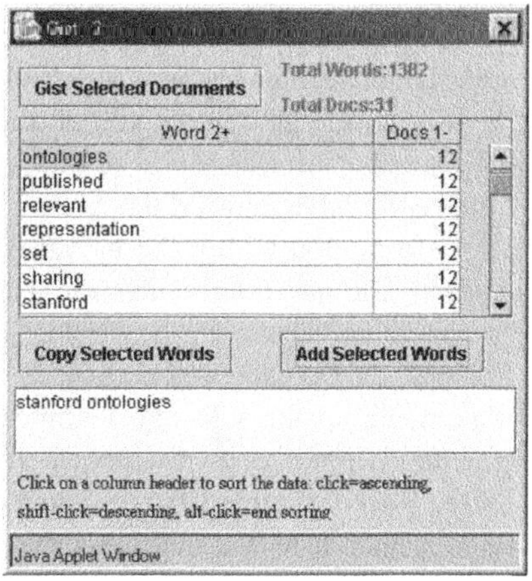

There are a couple of tools we can use to better understand the context of both individual and groups of documents. The Gisting Tool (Figure 4) lists frequently occurring terms in our selected documents, reporting the number of documents in that set which contain each word. The list is ordered from highest frequency to lowest. From our selected around the ontologies and

Fig. 4. Gist Tool

Stanford region, we find associated frequent terms such as "representation" and "sharing", possibly new context information for our examination.

A Probe Tool allows users to explore the thematic space of the information set, such that when a user clicks anywhere on the Galaxy with the Probe tool, a panel shows the list of themes associated with that position, whether or not a document is located in that exact spot.

At this point we may be interested in using information in ways not anticipated by the authors. To look at how the authors originally linked information, we use the Link tool (Figure 5) to see how documents in the harvested set are hyperlinked to one another. Clicking on a document with the link tool displays these links. Several documents may be displayed with their links at the same time, or the tool may display multiple levels of links. In Figure 5 these links are shown as yellow and green arrows. In our figure, we see links between a document discussing the Knowledge Sharing Effort and the web page for UMBC's KQML web. Using the link tool allows

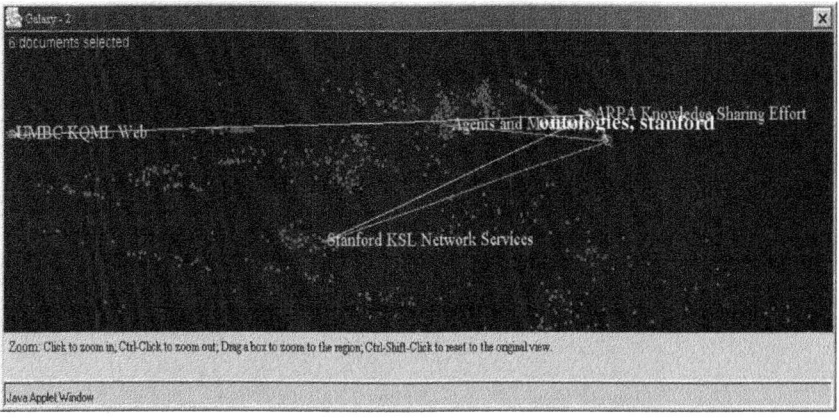

Fig. 5. Galaxy documents showing links

us to understand associations the web page authors found important to explicitly incorporate in their documents, overlaid on the automatically generated topical associations found by WebTheme. It provides us suggestions as to how we may want to use
the information and guide our continuing investigations, in this case, we may wish to
explore other information from both of these topical areas.

Once we have perused the overall information space, we may be interested in specific information within the harvested collection. WebTheme includes the capability
to search the harvested collection using two types of Query Tool searches: Words in
Document and Query-by-Example. The Query Tool window is shown in Figure 6.

Words in Document allows Boolean queries. If the Document Viewer is opened,
titles matching the selected documents appear in the top of the viewer. Users also
have the option to open documents in their Web browser.

Query-by-Example triggers a vector space search and selects the document that is
the best match to the query — the one that is closest in the n-dimensional vector
space to the query vector. A slider on the Query Tool window allows the user to vary
the number of documents selected. By manipulating the slider and thus changing
which dots are highlighted, the user can distinguish the location of documents that are
closest to the query in the vector space from those that are further away.

A Query History pane is provided on the right side of the Query Tool window. The
Query History is a line-by-line record of queries made during a search session. Each
line of the query history represents a single query. The first letter on the line signifies
the type of query, followed by a colon and the first few words of the query string. The
number of documents retrieved is shown in parentheses at the end of the line. The

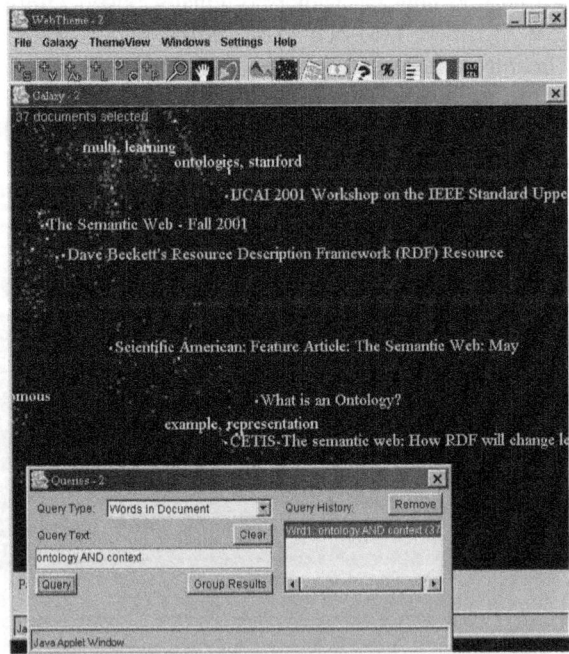

Fig. 6. Query Tool with selected document titles

most recently executed query will be highlighted in the Query History. In Figure 6, we see the results of a query on "ontology" and "context". The results are highlighted yellow dots on the Galaxy display. We have displayed titles of several of the identified documents (some discussing the Semantic Web).

There are several other tools in the WebTheme toolbox, including a Grouping tool that provides subsetting capabilities, a display that shows the cluster centroids and titles of the visualization, and a Twilight tool which provides an animation of how the harvesting agents collected the documents from the web. Twilight is particularly interesting in that it provides high level visual insight into how web site developers group related web pages as well as how they are discovered by the harvesting agents.

4 Related Work

Much attention is being paid to large scale web harvesting agents. HiWE [2] is a crawler developed by Garcia-Molina to extract content from the hidden web. This capability is invaluable for agents to make use of the Semantic Web. WebTheme seeks to associate this enhanced harvesting capability with the power of visualization. Several systems exploit the advantages of information visualization and information retrieval to various extents. Many visualization interfaces for information retrieval systems present ranked query-document similarity and clustering. VIBE [3] allows users to input query terms, which are associated with a portion of the visualization window, with document icons positioned to illustrate the relevance of documents to the selected terms. TileBars [4] developed at Xerox PARC allows the user to enter search terms as topics. After the system retrieves documents, a graphical, tiled bar is displayed next to the title of each document showing the relationship between the document and query terms. These tools are not presenting the same degree of analytical capability present in WebTheme. Other efforts have focused on creating navigational maps of Web site content. Mappucino allows visual mapping and exploration of web sites [5]. WebTheme can be used in a similar way, but is more focused on both the harvesting and analytical capabilities.

5 Current Status and Future Work

WebTheme is a functional prototype in use at PNNL and NASA. We are strongly encouraging its use as a common desktop system at PNNL to support information workers dealing with various aspects of information overload in their science and technology endeavors. WebTheme is of the class of tools that can help make the goals of the Semantic Web become reality. Combining the behind the scenes work of software agents with the power of information visualization and analytics allows users to truly engage with their information spaces and discover and mold those elements meaningful to their work.

WebTheme works with existing web page descriptions, primarily HTML and text. Enhancements to semantic understanding of web information that will be provided by

DAML and other Semantic Web efforts will enable WebTheme to be even more exciting to users. We are currently working to enhance WebTheme in two particular areas of interest to the Semantic Web community. First, we want to employ much more sophisticated agents to work for the WebTheme user. We are already able to interact with our agents' activities to a certain extent; we envision these agents becoming very able research assistants. We have active research projects in agents working with large document spaces and ontology development. As it stands, WebTheme is valuable to the Semantic Web community, particularly in the area of unintended use of information. WebTheme's ability to unveil implicit context via the text analysis and visualizations provides a complementary capability to the developers of semantic description technologies for web documents. WebTheme also provides a capability to help understand ad-hoc collections where no semantic description exists. This ability can enable automatic generation of semantic descriptions following the text analysis activities.

References

1. Battelle Memorial Institute. 2001. "SPIRE - Spatial Paradigm for Information Retrieval and Exploration" http://www.pnl.gov/infoviz/spire/spire.html .
2. Garcia-Molina, H., Raghavan, Sriram. "Crawling the Hidden Web." *Stanford Database Group Publication Server.* http://dbpubs.stanford.edu:8090/pub/2001-19. May 2001.
3. Olsen, K. A., Korfhage, R. R., Sochats, K.M., Spring, M. B, & Williams, J. G. Visualization of a document collection: The VIBE system. Information Processing and Management, 29, 1 (1993) 69-81
4. Hearst, M. A. TileBars: Visualization of Term Distribution Information in Full Text Information Access, in Proceedings of CHI '95 (Denver, Colorado, May 7-11, 1995) pp. 59-66.
5. IBM Alphaworks. 1999. "Mappucino". http://www.alphaworks.ibm.com/tech/mapuccino.

Browsing Schedules - An Agent-Based Approach to Navigating the Semantic Web

Terry R. Payne, Rahul Singh and Katia Sycara

Carnegie Mellon University
5000 Forbes Avenue
Pittsburgh, PA 15213
{terryp, kingtiny, katia}@cs.cmu.edu

Abstract. The Semantic Web promises to change the way agents navigate, harvest and utilize information on the internet. By providing a structured, distributed representation for expressing concepts and relationships defined by multiple ontologies, it is now possible for agents to *read* and *reason* about published knowledge, without the need for scrapers, information agents, and centralized ontologies. Agents can utilize this knowledge to seek and invoke other agents and web services, thus supporting navigation across the Semantic Web. We demonstrate how agents support enhanced navigation within a conference-schedule domain, and present three agent-based services: the *RETSINA Calendar Agent*, which reasons about schedules marked up on the Semantic Web; the *DMA2ICal Translation Agent* which provides translation services between schedules grounded in different ontologies, and a *Conference Agent* that invokes the Calendar Agent.

1 Introduction

The World Wide Web was originally designed as a distributed information space that seamlessly supported human navigation through related, linked documents. Although this medium was originally designed to do more than simply support human-to-human communication [2], an emphasis on presentation and physical design has resulted in a lack of structure at the content level, and rendered documents opaque to machine comprehension. The Semantic Web [2] goes beyond the World Wide Web by using a structured, logically connected representation to encode knowledge. It also provides sets of inference rules that can be used to reason over this knowledge. Since the Semantic Web supports the use of many different ontologies, one cannot assume that agents will understand all possible markup. However, translation services that convert markup from one ontology to another may be solicited by an agent when it encounters unknown concepts. By communicating and exchanging information, agents can present the user with a new agent-oriented approach to navigating the Semantic Web. This transition from using a homogeneous markup for layout on the Web to heterogeneous ontologies for semantic markup will allow agents to seamlessly interoperate, and provide easier, faster, and more flexible access to relevant data.

I. Horrocks and J. Hendler (Eds.): ISWC 2002, LNCS 2342, pp. 469–473, 2002.

In this paper, we describe agents and services that share information about conference schedules, and thus provide functionality to the user beyond that available with current web browsers. Section 2 describes the *Retsina Calendar Agent* which provides browsing functionality for Semantic Web schedules. This agent can be invoked remotely from the *Conference Agent* when the user indicates that they would like to browse events pertaining to a specific topic. However, if the ontologies used by the schedule are unknown to the *Calendar Agent*, it contacts a service discovery mechanism to locate a domain-specific markup translation service, such as the *DMA2ICal* service. This process is discussed before concluding the paper in Section 3.

2   RCal - RETSINA Calendar Agent

The *RETSINA Calendar Agent (RCal)* is a distributed meeting scheduling agent that can navigate Semantic Web content to gather and reason about calendar events and contact details. It works synergistically with a commercial Personal Information Manager (PIM) to contrast and store schedules such as conference programs, or recurring appointments with existing events within the user's calendar. Published Semantic Web events that are stored can be monitored by the agent, and updated if necessary. In addition, notifications can be associated with events and sent via email or via another agent to a mobile device to remind the user when each talk is about to start.

RCal understands several different ontologies that may be used to generate schedule markup. The schedules and events themselves are described using the Hybrid RDF Calendar Ontology (iCal)[1]. User resources and contact details are described using the Friend-of-a-Friend ontology (*http://xmlns.com/foaf/0.1/*), whereas the Dublin Core ontology (*http://dublincore.org*) is used to provide meta-data about the schedule.

Schedules found on the Semantic Web can be browsed via the *Schedule Browser* (Fig. 1), and compared with existing appointments to identify conflicting events. The browser lists the events, times, location and attendees of each event. The user can then select all, or a subset of the events and import them into the PIM for perusal at a later date. Notifications can also be associated with the imported events to remind the user of impending meetings. The contact details of the people attending the meetings can also be imported into the user's contact list. As the URI referring to each event is stored with the information about the event, *RCal* can periodically check to see if the event has changed, and thus notify the user of the change. In addition, further information can be explored, such as visiting relevant web pages, or invoking services that provide driving instructions or local restaurant recommendations.

The ability to refer to resources defined in different ontologies facilitates the navigation of information not directly related to a schedule. For example, when listing the events within the Semantic Web schedule, *RCal* locates the *Name* property of an <ical:ATTENDEE> resource to list the name of each meeting

---

[1] See *http://ilrt.org/discovery/2001/06/schemas/ical-full/hybrid.rdf*

Fig. 1. Browsing schedules & invoking context-based services/agents.

attendee. Other information may be defined by this resource, such as email or webpage properties, that could facilitate additional browsing or offer additional services (e.g. the user right-clicks the concept *"Katia Sycara"* in Fig. 1). These properties can also be used to query service providers (i.e. other agents) via a discovery infrastructure such as a DAML-S Matchmaker [1,5]. This form of serendipitous service discovery attempts to find services that might be of use to the user. For example, if the location of an event is selected, such as the *Hyatt Regency Hotel* in Fig. 1, then the properties of the location resource will be examined. A request for service will be constructed containing details about the location's address or latitude and longitude, and submitted to a Matchmaker. Advertised service descriptions that match the service request are then returned and offered to the user as additional services. In the *Hyatt* example in Fig. 1, *RCal* discovers the existence of the *RetsinaRestaurantAgent*, and presents this via a drop-down menu option.

2.1   Agent-Based Browsing - Invoking the RCal Schedule Browser

As agents reason about Semantic Web markup, they will encounter concepts unrelated to their domain of expertise. By identifying these concepts, and searching for other local agents that provide browsing capabilities, an agent can share the responsibility for browsing this data. This mechanism can be demonstrated by using *RCal's* schedule browser via a *Conference Agent*, which was designed for browsing conference information marked up on the Semantic Web. This agent organizes the presentation of annotated conference details, such as location, date, hotels, etc, and publishes this content as HTML with additional controls to invoke other Semantic Web agents. A user who is browsing a conference site can select the subject areas of interest and browse a schedule containing only presentations on the selected subject areas. The *Conference Agent* locates the user's *Calendar Agent* by querying a service registry for agents that: (1) supports schedule browsing; (2) belong to the current user; and (2) are capable of providing browsing facilities on the same display as that used by the *Conference Agent*. Once an agent is found, a KQML-based browse request is sent to this agent (i.e. *RCal*) containing resource references to events corresponding to the subject areas of interest. The *RCal* schedule browser then appears on the user's display, listing the subset of events. By tasking the *Conference Agent* in this way, users do not need to visually inspect all the individual events, but can utilize *RCal* to rapidly compare events of interest with others stored in the user's calendar.

2.2   DMA2ICal - Agenda Markup Translation Service

Whilst *RCal* can provide browsing and download functionality for schedules marked up using the iCal ontology, it is unable to understand markup using other ontologies, such as that used by *ITTalks* or the DAML Markup Agenda (DMA) Ontology. To comprehend this markup, an agent would need additional rules (e.g. articulation rules [4]) or the use of translation services. *RCal* overcomes this by locating and soliciting the help of translation services that convert markup from one ontology to another. These services are located using a discovery service based upon the DAML Services Ontology (DAML-S) [1], which describes a service in terms of its capabilities (through an advertised *Service-Profile*), how the service works (though a *Service-Model*) and how it can be invoked (though a *Service-Grounding*).

The *DMA2ICal* agent is a simple domain-specific translation service that translates agendas that are marked up using the DMA ontology[2] into markup using the iCal ontology. It was designed not only to translate markup between two ontologies, but to demonstrate how such services could be dynamically located and tasked when unknown markup is detected. When this service is made available on the Semantic Web, it advertises its capabilities with a service registry, such as the DAML-S Matchmaker [5]. When *RCal* detects an unknown concept within the markup (for example, the <dma:Meeting> resource defined in Fig. 2), it constructs a DAML-S request for the service based on this concept. This request simply consists of the unknown concept, and a desired <ical:VCALENDAR> concept. This is then submitted to the DAML-S Matchmaker, which performs a semantic capability match between the request and advertised Service Profiles, before returning a list of possible matching services, including the profile for the *DMA2ICal* translation service. *RCal* then selects and invokes one of these returned services by sending it the URI of the unknown concept. The service then constructs new markup using the iCal ontology, and returns this markup to *RCal* which then presents the schedule to the user. This is the same mechanism used by *RCal* to discover browsing and other services when the user selects concepts from the schedule browser (Fig. 1).

3   Discussion

This paper demonstrates how service discovery and information sharing can allow agent communities to locate and present relevant services to a user, based on the information that is being browsed. Although several different ontologies may be used to markup content, translation services can transform unknown

---

[2] See *http://www.daml.org/2001/10/agenda/*

```
<dma:Meeting rdf:ID="TAC01">                              <ical:VCALENDAR ID="TAC01">
  <dma:name>Trading Agent Competition 2001 Workshop</dma:name>    <dc:title>Trading Agent Competition 2001 Workshop</dc:title>
  <dma:location resource="#HRTampa" />                   <ical:VEVENT-PROP resource="http://www.tac.org/2001event.rdf#PainInNEC"/>
  <dma:day>                                              <ical:VEVENT-PROP>
    <dma:Day>                                              <ical:VEVENT ID="RetsinaTrading">
      <dma:start>2001-10-14T13:45:00</dma:start>            <ical:DTSTART>
      <items rdf:parseType="daml:collection">                 <ical:DATE-TIME><value>20011014T134500</value></ical:DATE-TIME>
        <dma:Talk resource="http://www.tac.org/2001event.rdf#PainInNEC"/>    </ical:DTSTART>
        <dma:Talk ID="RetsinaTrading">                      <!-- end not included in this example -->
          <dma:title>Presentation: Retsina</dma:title>      <ical:LOCATION resource="#HRTampa" />
          <dma:speaker resource="http://www.daml.ri.cmu.edu/people.rdf#ks" />    <ical:ATTENDEE resource="http://www.daml.ri.cmu.edu/people.rdf#ks" />
          <dma:duration>PT15M</dma:duration>                <ical:DESCRIPTION>Presentation: Retsina</ical:DESCRIPTION>
        </dma:Talk>                                       </ical:VEVENT>
```

Fig. 2. Translating markup from DMA to ICal.

markup into that which can be understood by the agent. *RCal* makes use of a serendipitous search to look for services that may be of use to the user, based on selected resources. However, in a service rich environment, many irrelevant services may be presented to the user. Thus, work is currently underway to develop profiles of the user's interest, and to infer context (such as locating restaurants in favor of hardware stores when examining the location of a conference site). The *ITTalks* Agent system [6] is an existing web-based system that provides automated, intelligent notification of information technology seminars. Profiles of user preferences, annotated in DAML+OIL [3], are used to suggest those seminars that might be of interest to the user. These examples demonstrate how, by combining the semantics now available through the Semantic Web, communities of agents can interoperate and work synergistically to provide better access to information and functionality than was previously available on the WWW.

Acknowledgments

The research was funded by the Defense Advanced Research Projects Agency as part of the DARPA Agent Markup Language (DAML) program under Air Force Research Laboratory contract F30601-00-2-0592 to Carnegie Mellon University.

References

1. A. Ankolekar et. al. DAML-S: Semantic markup for web services. In *Int. Semantic Web Working Symposium*, pages 411–430, 2001.
2. T. Berners-Lee, J. Hendler, and O. Lassila. The Semantic Web. *Scientific American*, 284(5):34–43, 2001.
3. J. Hendler and D. L. McGuinness. Darpa agent markup language. *IEEE Intelligent Systems*, 15(6):72–73, 2001.
4. P. Mitra, G. Wiederhold, and S. Decker. A scalable framework for the interoperation of information sources. In *Semantic Web Working Symposium*, pages 317–329, 2001.
5. M. Paolucci, T. Kawamura, T. Payne, and K. Sycara. Semantic Matching of Web Services Capabilities. In *First International Semantic Web Conference*, 2002.
6. R.Scott Cost et. al. ITTalks: A case student in how the semantic web helps. In *Int. Semantic Web Working Symposium*, pages 477–494, 2001.

Author Index

Lecture Notes in Computer Science

For information about Vols. 1–2269
please contact your bookseller or Springer-Verlag

Vol. 2305: D. Le Métayer (Ed.), Programming Languages and Systems. Proceedings, 2002. XII, 331 pages. 2002.

Vol. 2306: R.-D. Kutsche, H. Weber (Eds.), Fundamental Approaches to Software Engineering. Proceedings, 2002. XIII, 341 pages. 2002.

Vol. 2307: C. Zhang, S. Zhang, Association Rule Mining. XII, 238 pages. 2002. (Subseries LNAI).

Vol. 2308: I.P. Vlahavas, C.D. Spyropoulos (Eds.), Methods and Applications of Artificial Intelligence. Proceedings, 2002. XIV, 514 pages. 2002. (Subseries LNAI).

Vol. 2309: A. Armando (Ed.), Frontiers of Combining Systems. Proceedings, 2002. VIII, 255 pages. 2002. (Subseries LNAI).

Vol. 2310: P. Collet, C. Fonlupt, J.-K. Hao, E. Lutton, M. Schoenauer (Eds.), Artificial Evolution. Proceedings, 2001. XI, 375 pages. 2002.

Vol. 2311: D. Bustard, W. Liu, R. Sterritt (Eds.), Soft-Ware 2002: Computing in an Imperfect World. Proceedings, 2002. XI, 359 pages. 2002.

Vol. 2312: T. Arts, M. Mohnen (Eds.), Implementation of Functional Languages. Proceedings, 2001. VII, 187 pages. 2002.

Vol. 2313: C.A. Coello Coello, A. de Albornoz, L.E. Sucar, O.Cairó Battistutti (Eds.), MICAI 2002: Advances in Artificial Intelligence. Proceedings, 2002. XIII, 548 pages. 2002. (Subseries LNAI).

Vol. 2314: S.-K. Chang, Z. Chen, S.-Y. Lee (Eds.), Recent Advances in Visual Information Systems. Proceedings, 2002. XI, 323 pages. 2002.

Vol. 2315: F. Arhab, C. Talcott (Eds.), Coordination Models and Languages. Proceedings, 2002. XI, 406 pages. 2002.

Vol. 2316: J. Domingo-Ferrer (Ed.), Inference Control in Statistical Databases. VIII, 231 pages. 2002.

Vol. 2317: M. Hegarty, B. Meyer, N. Hari Narayanan (Eds.), Diagrammatic Representation and Inference. Proceedings, 2002. XIV, 362 pages. 2002. (Subseries LNAI).

Vol. 2318: D. Bošnački, S. Leue (Eds.), Model Checking Software. Proceedings, 2002. X, 259 pages. 2002.

Vol. 2319: C. Gacek (Ed.), Software Reuse: Methods, Techniques, and Tools. Proceedings, 2002. XI, 353 pages. 2002.

Vol.2320: T. Sander (Ed.), Security and Privacy in Digital Rights Management. Proceedings, 2001. X, 245 pages. 2002.

Vol. 2322: V. Mařík, O. Stěpánková, H. Krautwurmová, M. Luck (Eds.), Multi-Agent Systems and Applications II. Proceedings, 2001. XII, 377 pages. 2002. (Subseries LNAI).

Vol. 2323: À. Frohner (Ed.), Object-Oriented Technology. Proceedings, 2001. IX, 225 pages. 2002.

Vol. 2324: T. Field, P.G. Harrison, J. Bradley, U. Harder (Eds.), Computer Performance Evaluation. Proceedings, 2002. XI, 349 pages. 2002.

Vol 2326: D. Grigoras, A. Nicolau, B. Toursel, B. Folliot (Eds.), Advanced Environments, Tools, and Applications for Cluster Computing. Proceedings, 2001. XIII, 321 pages. 2002.

Vol. 2327: H.P. Zima, K. Joe, M. Sato, Y. Seo, M. Shimasaki (Eds.), High Performance Computing. Proceedings, 2002. XV, 564 pages. 2002.

Vol. 2329: P.M.A. Sloot, C.J.K. Tan, J.J. Dongarra, A.G. Hoekstra (Eds.), Computational Science – ICCS 2002. Proceedings, Part I. XLI, 1095 pages. 2002.

Vol. 2330: P.M.A. Sloot, C.J.K. Tan, J.J. Dongarra, A.G. Hoekstra (Eds.), Computational Science – ICCS 2002. Proceedings, Part II. XLI, 1115 pages. 2002.

Vol. 2331: P.M.A. Sloot, C.J.K. Tan, J.J. Dongarra, A.G. Hoekstra (Eds.), Computational Science – ICCS 2002. Proceedings, Part III. XLI, 1227 pages. 2002.

Vol. 2332: L. Knudsen (Ed.), Advances in Cryptology – EUROCRYPT 2002. Proceedings, 2002. XII, 547 pages. 2002.

Vol. 2334: G. Carle, M. Zitterbart (Eds.), Protocols for High Speed Networks. Proceedings, 2002. X, 267 pages. 2002.

Vol. 2335: M. Butler, L. Petre, K. Sere (Eds.), Integrated Formal Methods. Proceedings, 2002. X, 401 pages. 2002.

Vol. 2336: M.-S. Chen, P.S. Yu, B. Liu (Eds.), Advances in Knowledge Discovery and Data Mining. Proceedings, 2002. XIII, 568 pages. 2002. (Subseries LNAI).

Vol. 2337: W.J. Cook, A.S. Schulz (Eds.), Integer Programming and Combinatorial Optimization. Proceedings, 2002. XI, 487 pages. 2002.

Vol. 2338: R. Cohen, B. Spencer (Eds.), Advances in Artificial Intelligence. Proceedings, 2002. X, 197 pages. 2002. (Subseries LNAI).

Vol. 2342: I. Horrocks, J. Hendler (Eds.), The Semantic Web – ISCW 2002. Proceedings, 2002. XVI, 476 pages. 2002.

Vol. 2345: E. Gregori, M. Conti, A.T. Campbell, G. Omidyar, M. Zukerman (Eds.), NETWORKING 2002. Proceedings, 2002. XXVI, 1256 pages. 2002.

Vol. 2347: P. De Bra, P. Brusilovsky, R. Conejo (Eds.), Adaptive Hypermedia and Adaptive Web-Based Systems. Proceedings, 2002. XV, 615 pages. 2002.

Vol. 2348: A. Banks Pidduck, J. Mylopoulos, C.C. Woo, M. Tamer Ozsu (Eds.), Advanced Information Systems Engineering. Proceedings, 2002. XIV, 799 pages. 2002.

Vol. 2349: J. Kontio, R. Conradi (Eds.), Software Quality – ECSQ 2002. Proceedings, 2002. XIV, 363 pages. 2002.

Vol. 2350: A. Heyden, G. Sparr, M. Nielsen, P. Johansen (Eds.), Computer Vision – ECCV 2002. Proceedings, Part I. XXVIII, 817 pages. 2002.

Vol. 2351: A. Heyden, G. Sparr, M. Nielsen, P. Johansen (Eds.), Computer Vision – ECCV 2002. Proceedings, Part II. XXVIII, 903 pages. 2002.

Vol. 2352: A. Heyden, G. Sparr, M. Nielsen, P. Johansen (Eds.), Computer Vision – ECCV 2002. Proceedings, Part III. XXVIII, 919 pages. 2002.

Vol. 2353: A. Heyden, G. Sparr, M. Nielsen, P. Johansen (Eds.), Computer Vision – ECCV 2002. Proceedings, Part IV. XXVIII, 841 pages. 2002.

Vol. 2359: M. Tistarelli, J. Bigun, A.K. Jain (Eds.), Biometric Authentication. Proceedings, 2002. XII, 373 pages. 2002.